The Judgment of Sense

IDEAS IN CONTEXT

Edited by Richard Rorty, J. B. Schneewind, Quentin Skinner, and Wolf Lepenies

The books in this series will discuss the emergence of intellectual traditions and of related new disciplines. The procedures, aims, and vocabularies that were generated will be set in the context of the alternatives available within the contemporary frameworks of ideas and institutions. Through detailed studies of the evolution of such traditions, and their modification by different audiences, it is hoped that a new picture will form of the development of ideas in their concrete contexts. By this means, artificial distinctions among the history of philosophy, of the various sciences, of society and politics, and of literature may be seen to dissolve.

This series is published with the support of the Exxon Education Foundation.

The Judgment of Sense

Renaissance Naturalism and the Rise of Aesthetics

DAVID SUMMERS

University of Virginia

CAMBRIDGE
UNIVERSITY PRESS

Published by the Press Syndicate of the University of Cambridge
The Pitt Building, Trumpington Street, Cambridge CB2 1RP
40 West 20th Street, New York, NY 10011-4211, USA
10 Stamford Road, Oakleigh, Melbourne 3166, Australia

First published 1987
First paperback edition 1990
Reprinted 1994

Printed in the United States of America

Library of Congress Cataloging-in-Publication Data is available

British Library Cataloging-in-Publication applied for

ISBN 0-521-38631-4 paperback

For my father and my mother
John and Ellen Harris Summers

So many sunlit days

Contents

Figures

Preface

These studies continue to develop themes stated in my *Michelangelo and the Language of Art,* and grew out of research done while finishing that book at the Institute for Advanced Study in Princeton during the academic year 1978–9. A grant from the National Endowment for the Humanities supported my research, and I am once again indebted to Irving Lavin for the chance to have worked in such ideal circumstances. Most of the writing of the book was done during the last year of my appointment to the Center for Advanced Studies at the University of Virginia. I am grateful to Frederick Hartt and to W. Dexter Whitehead, the Director of the Center, for that opportunity. I am also grateful to my colleagues in the Department of Art at the University of Virginia, Keith Moxey and Paul Barolsky, not least for their patience in listening to arguments far from their own concerns, and certainly for their criticisms, tips, and help in reading certain texts. Daniel T. Devereux of the Department of Philosophy at the university assisted my interpretation of Aristotle, and is answerable only for what is soundest about it. Richard Rorty was generous with his time and with valuable criticisms. Carl Nordenfalk kept me abreast of his own work on the iconography of the five senses. Martin Kemp, a reader for the Cambridge University Press who chose not to be anonymous, made a number of shrewd and careful observations I have tried to incorporate. I am therefore indebted to him for more than his scholarship, to which I shall often refer.

Members of a graduate seminar given in the fall of 1983 at the University of Virginia listened to these arguments in various forms and contributed to their clarity. In general, this project has been enriched over the years by conversations with my students Bernadine Barnes, Claire Farago, and Dwight Shurko. Joy Thornton explored ideas related to those examined here in her dissertation on Renaissance color theory submitted to the Department of Fine Arts at the University of Pittsburgh in 1979. This is cited below in Chapter 8 and listed in the Bibliography.

As always, nothing could have gone at all as well as it has without the constant support, informed criticism, and good sense of my wife, Nancy.

Citations of Plato and Aristotle are included in the text according to their standard editions and English translations. For other classical authors I have used Loeb Classical Library editions when possible, sometimes adjusting the translations in the direction of a more literal reading, and I have bracketed key terms and phrases in the texts as I present them. Translations are of course always interpretations, and I have both taken advantage of the interpretations of others and tried to make my own interpretations as available for the scrutiny of the reader as possible. Translations of Renaissance art literature are mine, unless noted.

I am happy for the opportunity to publish this work in the Ideas in Context series not only because I believe with its editors that distinctions among intellectual disciplines are artificial, but also because I believe the removal of these distinctions points toward a more complete art history, one in which the relation of thinking to making can be more realistically described. I consider this book first of all to be an essay in what would formerly have been called the theory of style, an attempt to explain the appearance of works of art in their most general characteristics, in this case, to explain the advent and development of the characteristics that define late Medieval and Renaissance naturalism. I have tried to write – or contribute to the writing of – a history of definite relations, not animated by the spirits and forces that seem to be necessary to give cogency to isolated histories, but rather shaped by human choices and acts made in the face of the consequences of previous human choices and acts. The attempt to place the history of art in relation to the significance art has had, and the further attempt to plot some of the major affiliations, associations, and implications of this significance, will be seen to lead into unfamiliar art historical and intellectual historical terrain at the same time that it points more clearly to broader Renaissance contexts. The most important thing, however, is not the familiarity or usefulness or correctness of the ideas we shall consider; it is rather the question of the adequacy of the demonstration of the intimate and intricate interconnection of thinking, communicating, and making within a tradition.

D.S.

Charlottesville, Virginia

Abbreviations

AB	*Art Bulletin*
BScr	P. Barocchi, ed., *Scritti d'arte del cinquecento*, 3 vols., Milan–Naples, 1971–76
BT	P. Barocchi, ed., *Trattati d'arte del cinquecento fra manierismo e controriforma*, 3 vols., Bari, 1960
BVM	P. Barocchi, ed., G. Vasari, *La Vita di Michelangelo nelle redazioni del 1550 e de 1568*, 5 vols., Milan–Naples, 1962
CCSL	*Corpus Christianorum. Series latina*
DHI	*Dictionary of the History of Ideas*
GBA	*Gazette des Beaux-Arts*
JHI	*Journal of the History of Ideas*
JWCI	*Journal of the Warburg and Courtauld Institutes*
MLA	D. Summers, *Michelangelo and the Language of Art*, Princeton, N.J., 1981
MPG	J. P. Migne, ed., *Patrologiae cursus completus . . . series graeca*, 161 vols., Paris, 1857–1903
MPL	J. P. Migne, ed., *Patrologiae cursus completus . . . series latina*, 221 vols., Paris, 1844–96
VBB	G. Vasari, *Le vite de' più eccellenti pittori, scultori, ed architettori nelle redazioni del 1550 e 1568*, ed. P. Barocchi and R. Bettarini, Florence, 1966–
VM	G. Vasari, *Le vite de' più eccellenti pittori scultori ed architettori*, 8 vols., ed. G. Milanesi, Florence, 1906

Introduction

Plato and Aristotle

In the foreword to the first edition of his *Idea,* published in 1924, Erwin Panofsky acknowledged a debt to a lecture by Ernst Cassirer, "The Idea of the Beautiful in Plato's Dialogues," and modestly described his own book as the tracing of the history of the same theme. Panofsky's history is considerably more complex than his characterization would indicate. It begins with the Platonic condemnation of imitative art but for the most part plots the history of the Aristotelian idea of the mental conception governing artistic activity as it moves toward or away from transcendental ideas, thus toward or away from the beautiful and the true. The richness and cautiousness of Panofsky's study notwithstanding, the influence of the book has been very largely consistent with its simply stated aim: to trace the history of the Platonic idea of the beautiful.

Our reading of Panofsky's *Idea* is reinforced by the coincidence of its arguments with a general historical scheme of the development of Western art. As classical art developed and declined in antiquity, to be forgotten, misused, and transformed in the Christian Middle Ages, then to reemerge in the Italian Renaissance, so the intellectual counterpart of classical art, a version of the Platonic *idea,* waxed, waned, recrudesced in late medieval and early Renaissance naturalism, bloomed fully in the High Renaissance, and, having put aside the perturbation of Mannerism, was finally reestablished in the theory of academic classicism.

Whatever Panofsky's intentions in writing it may have been, his *Idea,* its reading shaped by the assumption that there was a single "Renaissance mind," has helped to establish Neoplatonism as the philosophical language of Renaissance art, in the terms of which it is properly apprehended critically, and in terms of which its essential intentions must be supposed to have been set. This view has also been supplemented by the argument that the pervasive tradition of allegory is a fundamentally Platonic tradition.[1]

In the chapters that follow, I shall argue that however great the importance of the Platonic idea of beauty (or beauty of the idea) may have been in the Renaissance, other traditions of meaning shaped the discussion of the art of the period at its deepest levels, at the level of its naturalism, of its composition and expressiveness, and of the articulation of the judgments concomitant to its actual execution. If we regard allegory and idealization of both forms and relations of forms as Platonic (as many do), then these Platonic characteristics were realized in deep accommodation with characteristics stating the necessity of the determination of particular works by individual judgment and point of view. The language justifying such opinionative judgment was predominantly Aristotelian.

According to Plato's famous allegory of the cave, we live our lives in the face of a flickering shadowplay, cast by marionettes at our backs, dancing before fires we cannot see. Only the philosopher can turn his gaze from this shadowplay and be led slowly away from it, out of the cave and into the bright light of the real world, by which his eyes are at first dazzled. For Plato the shadows on the wall are the phantasms of the everyday world, the marionettes are the "real" forms we apprehend only by means of these phantasms, and the light of day is the clarity and self-evidence of the intelligible, which we "see" only with great difficulty.

For Aristotle matters are quite different; humankind finds itself from the outset in the light of the physical world, in which it is always active and to which it is adequately fitted. This fit begins at the very basis of the apprehension of the world, at the level of sensation. The relation between intellect and the world that begins at the level of sense is at once as close and as absolutely different as the relation between convex and concave, between a seal and its impression in wax, to use Aristotle's own metaphor. For Aristotle the human soul does not "unforget" its heavenly origins; rather, it is the potential to apprehend and know everything it can apprehend and know. Aristotle's is a much more active, practical conception of the human soul, and, as a foundation of one of the twin pillars at the beginning of Western thought, has been a conception with the deepest and broadest consequences. We shall examine some of these consequences, and, to make a long story into one simple statement, argue that the development of art based on point of view at the dawn of the modern period was deeply bound up with the Aristotelian notion that the human soul, from sensation upward, is suited to its world, and with the further notion that the beautiful itself is conformity to human sense before it is evidence of transcendental value.

[1] E. Panofsky, *Idea: A Concept in Art Theory,* tr. J. S. Peake, Columbia, S.C., 1968, p. ix; on allegory, E. H. Gombrich, "*Icones symbolicae:* Philosophies of Symbolism and their Bearing on Art," in *Symbolic Images: Studies in the Art of the Renaissance,* II, London, 1972, pp. 123–195. This was first published as "*Icones symbolicae:* The Visual Image in Neo-Platonic Thought," *JWCI,* 11, 1948, pp. 163–192.

Naturalism and point of view

It will be useful at this point to define naturalism in the way I am going to use the term. "Naturalism" refers to art – the paradigm is really the art of painting as opposed to sculpture or architecture – the elements of which are presumed to coincide with the elements of optical experience. "Naturalism" and "realism" are sometimes used interchangeably, but it is necessary to distinguish carefully between them. "Realism" is at base a category of subject matter, and refers to art having a concrete historical reference or an apparent concrete historical reference. Nineteenth-century realist painting, whatever its difference from photography, is like photography in that realistic themes are presented in a naturalistic way, which is to say that real, or purportedly real, things are shown to us as if they were the physical – and finally optical – events that any subject necessarily is in an unaltered photograph. That such a union of realism and naturalism is not necessary is shown by modern expressionism, such as that of E. L. Kirchner, which may set real subject matter against antinaturalistic drawing and color. It might be noted too that by such a definition utterly fantastic art may be as naturalistic as ostensibly more realistic art.In his *Saint John on Patmos* (Fig. 1), Hieronymus Bosch represents the "historical" Saint John just as he represents the strange creature next to him, with the same description of texture, the same sparkling light. In fact, the formulation of naturalistic painting might be said to have opened up the whole rich vein of verisimilitudinous fantasy characteristic of so much Renaissance art, Northern and Italian alike.[2]

The term "naturalism" must also be distinguished from the term "imitation," which is a broader category, referring to art that makes artificial analogues to things. Imitated forms may refer to natural forms but do not necessarily reduce them to their optical elements. A marching army might be shown as a frieze of undifferentiated soldiers, and the simple repetition of the forms of the soldiers themselves made to stand for the army's movement without any further concessions to the description of the appearance of an army on the march. In these terms, naturalism is a kind of imitation, but a kind of imitation in which the artificial analogue is a virtual relationship of light, dark, and color determined at least in principle by optics, by the physical geometry of sight. This at once rephrases and clarifies our definition of naturalism.

[2] The category of naturalism is deeper than the distinction between description and narration, to which S. Alpers (*The Art of Describing: Dutch Art in the Seventeenth Century*, Chicago, 1983, p. xvii and passim) has related Northern and Italian Renaissance art respectively. Fundamental visual differences between Northern and Italian painting are admirably set forth by E. H. Gombrich, "Light, Form and Texture in Fifteenth-Century Painting North and South of the Alps," *The Heritage of Apelles: Studies in the Art of the Renaissance*, Ithaca, N.Y., 1976, pp. 19–35, the distinction being that between painting that uses light to define three-dimensional volumes (Italian) and painting that uses light to describe reflective surfaces, i.e., textures (Northern). Although the Northern Renaissance tradition has no literature corresponding to that of the Italian Renaissance, it must be supposed that many of the ideas we shall examine bore in some way upon the making of images in the North, even if the results were characteristically different.

Fig. 1. Hieronymus Bosch, *Saint John on Patmos,* 1504–5, oil on panel. Staatliche Museen Preussischer Kulturbesitz.

E. H. Gombrich has pointed out in several places the uniquely central role played by the convention of modelling in Western painting.[3] Modelling is the systematic gradation of either hue or value within a contour that makes it appear that the contour bounds a form "in" light, and therefore in space. If a circle on a piece of paper, in other words, is gradually darkened from one side to the other, it will become a virtual sphere, and the area surrounding it will become a virtual space.

A circle might be a two-dimensional sign for a sphere, as, when we draw a stick figure, a circle stands for the head. When we add modelling to the circle, and it becomes a virtual sphere, it necessarily becomes implicitly and explicitly *optical*. It becomes explicitly optical in that it is defined in terms of light and dark, which are elements of vision; and it becomes implicitly optical in that its very definition as a sphere not only points to a surrounding space but also indicates a source of light and implies spatial relation both to this source of light and to the sphere itself. In the simple example we are considering, a circle gradually and evenly "shaded" from side to side, a light source to one side of the plane of the paper and the perpendicularity of my gaze to that light are both implied.[4] We are very much accustomed to this convention, so much so that it is hard for us not to take it for granted, and it is difficult for us to regard it as merely optional, and peculiar to a single tradition. But if modelling entails what I have said it does, then it is perhaps less difficult to understand why it developed in Greek painting in fairly close proximity to the beginnings of the science of optics and why both modelling and optics have been so fundamental and so interdependent in the history of Western art.

When we model a circle it immediately becomes not just a possible sign for sphericity but its contour falls back into virtual space to become the farthest visible edge of a sphere in light. The crucial means by which this transformation in the significance of line is effected is, of course, light or, more exactly, gradation of light–dark contrast. The first element of the optical, then, is virtual light, which is visible in painting as light–dark contrast. The language of optics, which treats the physical relation between sight and its object, is also set in terms of

[3] E. H. Gombrich, *The Heritage of Apelles*, p. 16.

[4] If I draw a circle on a piece of paper, I assume and enforce for any viewer a normative perpendicular and axial relationship to the circle. The evident assumption of this relation is practically universal in images, a most significant exception being perspective drawing, in which *virtual* forms of things are placed obliquely to the surface (and, at the same time, more or less parallel to the line of sight); this, however, is done by making the viewer's gaze perpendicular to the format as a whole (the "picture plane") so that the whole scene in effect becomes the image. In any case, when our imaginary circle becomes a sphere through modelling, the normative relation holds and the implicit light source "in" the drawing is necessarily perpendicular to the viewer's gaze. Thus modelling transforms the normative relation of viewer and image into a relation of viewer and object, or virtual object, and also implies a source of light and relation of the viewer to that source. Source of light having become an issue, it may become the object of development and variation. Not only may the source be placed, say, higher and lower, it may be placed outside the virtual space altogether (or in the space of the viewer) by being made to reflect on painted surfaces. See again Gombrich, "Light, Form and Texture."

light. In his *De pictura,* the first Renaissance treatise on painting, Alberti speaks of the "rays" of vision that, whether they pass from eye to object or object to eye, behave with the same economy and regularity. In a sense, then, the development of optics may be seen as the development of what was implicit and potential in the simple convention of modelling; and what optics – and finally painter's perspective – accomplished was the simultaneous generalization of a whole pictorial field presumed to be an optical field in which objects are seen, a generalization achieved by the precise definition of the spatial relation of the viewer–artist to that field. This happened, as we are all aware, in the early fifteenth century when Filippo Brunelleschi made the demonstrations that initiated the tradition of painter's perspective, that is, *perspectiva* (the Latin term for optics) accommodated to the needs of the art of painting. One of the primary purposes of these chapters will be to explore some of the dimensions of this development.

The completion of the system of naturalism by the invention of perspective thus made the viewer's point of view integral to the basic visual structure of painting. As the language we use still recognizes, and as Panofsky stressed in his "Perspective as Symbolic Form," the definition of point of view raised a paradox: that the "objective" world is only visible from the standpoint of a subject, that we may only see how things "really are" from a point of view.[5]

One of the themes uniting the chapters to come will be that the definition of point of view entailed more than simply the precise location of viewer–artist in relation to represented forms, that point of view may be said to have emerged on more than one level, and that this development is evident in the deepest formal elements distinguishing Renaissance art.

Let us very much extend our simple example of a sphere in light to a consideration of Leonardo da Vinci's splendid Burlington House cartoon (Fig. 2). Here are all the same elements: the contours within which light is gradually modulated to dark to create virtual forms; the axial address of these forms to the viewer; a consistent source of light, this time high above the figures to our right, above the corner of the painting into which Saint Anne points. But the play of light and dark cannot be explained simply by the geometric regularity of light from a source falling over three-dimensional forms. Saint John the Baptist casts a deep shadow, but the Virgin does not, and in general the relations of light and dark are wonderfully resolved and harmonious. In Renaissance terms light and dark are *composed;* that is to say, they have been given a pleasing artificial order.[6] There were of course principles for the realization of such order – unity, variety, and counterposition, for example – but finally such relations were not simply applications of rules; rather, they were solutions that had to be found in each instance. Leonardo's image is not simply an image of what putatively strikes the eye; it is also a unique order of optical elements (the colors set in the deeper framework

[5] E. Panofsky, *La prospettiva come "forma simbolica" e altri scritti,* Milan, 1966.

[6] On composition, see M. Baxandall, *Giotto and the Orators: Humanist Observers of Painting in Italy and the Discovery of Pictorial Composition,* Oxford, 1971.

Fig. 2. Leonardo da Vinci, *Virgin and Child with Saint Anne* (the Burlington House cartoon), ca. 1500–8, charcoal on brown paper heightened with white. National Gallery, London.

of light and dark contrasts would have been similarly adjusted to one another, and to the framework itself, much as contours are adjusted to the description of the turning of optically defined surfaces).

All of these unique relationships are *aesthetic* in a very simple but important way. They are aesthetic in that they are determined by sense, by the *judgment* of sense. Beginning with what were presumed to be optical elements, the "right" relation among these elements was found in the case of *this* painting, not by consulting the laws of optics or the study of light and shadow to which Leonardo was so devoted, but, going beyond such knowledge, by doing what seemed best to the eye. In fact, these "right" relations could be found in no other way.

Although Leonardo's figures are uniformly three-dimensionally clear and cogent, he did not use perspective to establish a virtual space for his figures. Nonetheless, the appearance of his figures is still emphatically determined by point of view, but point of view at a metaphorical level. The *aesthetic* determination of relationships, which may seem incidental to the optical structure of naturalism, or merely trivial, is really a new possibility concomitant with naturalism, a possibility that, as the tradition initiated in the Renaissance unfolded into the modern period, would finally transform and overthrow naturalism itself. The sensibility that finds these highly characteristic aesthetic relationships is inevitably Leonardo's. His image not only shows us what might fall under vision, but what has fallen under his "vision," and it has not only the character of what it shows but the "character" of a work of Leonardo's as well. The deeper, metaphorical notion of point of view thus points to *maniera,* to *aria,* to personal style.

We are accustomed to thinking of all art as "aesthetic," and we usually think of this term as having a more complex definition than I have just given it. When we speak of the "aesthetics" of a period we usually mean two things. We may refer either to what writers said about the beautiful or about art in general, or we may refer to certain visual characteristics of the art of the period, to what amounts to its "vision" or "sensibility." We might say, for example, that High Renaissance art is harmonious and immediately extend this judgment to say that the High Renaissance "vision" was a harmonious one. When we make such an extension from the sensed character and quality of a work of art to the "sensibility" or "vision" that stands behind its making, we have actually made some very problematical inferences. We have assumed that the work of art is an adequate reflection of the sensibilities immediate to its making and that it is adequate specifically in that our apprehension of the work is symmetrical to the sensibilities that produced it, that its characteristics express the circumstances of its origin. When we do art history, we may be content simply to evoke or enumerate the qualities of the works with which we are concerned, to write a history of works that is in fact understood to be a history of the sensibilities behind the works. Or we might try to bring our two meanings of "aesthetics" together by relating visual characteristics to what writers of the period said about the beautiful or about art in general. In this way our reaction to the characteristics of High Renaissance art gives onto another corroborating expression of the "Renaissance mind." In whatever way we might set out to interpret the work, however, we begin from our aesthetic apprehension of it, and, in large part to avoid the complexities conjured up in our minds by the word "aesthetic," I wish to stick to its simplest etymological meaning and to examine the historical point at which it began to be thought that art *is* aesthetic and that inferences of the kind we make from a certain kind of visual experience can be made. Such a consensus emerged in the late Middle Ages and the Renaissance. This is not to say, of course, that earlier art is not aesthetic in the simple sense that artists adjusted the elements of their art to one another in a way pleasing to sight; but it *is* to say that it was in the late Middle Ages and the Renaissance that art became explicitly visual, psychological, and aesthetic, with consequences we are still gathering. And it was artists like Leonardo da Vinci, the inventors of the painting corresponding to such a view, who first adapted the language of psychology to the discussion of what art is and what artists do. This book is about the beginnings of the adaptation of psychological language to the discussion of art and about the first attempts to formulate properly aesthetic language in association with the rise of naturalism itself.

From the foregoing argument a general conclusion may be drawn: that the emergence of naturalism should not be understood as the inevitable consequence of progress in the arts, nor as a stage in an inevitable formal sequence, but as a complex set of pictorial inventions arising from meaning and immediately both amplifying and transforming meaning. In order to ask why art changes at the depth of the emergence of naturalism, and why these deep changes persist and are extended, it is necessary to ask what naturalism might have meant. In fact, what we call naturalism meant many things in the late Middle Ages and the early Renaissance. The exploration of these meanings will not only "contextualize" the development of naturalism in many ways, it will also show how the visual arts, far from simply illustrating meaning or being "influenced" by ideas, became a uniquely powerful cultural force. And it will help us to understand the ways in which this art is the art of the early modern period.

Representation

At the beginning of the third book of his treatise on painting, Leon Battista Alberti wrote that "the task of the painter is this: to describe with lines and tint with colors, on whatever panel or wall is given him, visible surfaces similar to any body whatever, such that, at a certain distance, and at a certain central position, these surfaces seem to be in relief, and like the surfaces of real bodies. The end of painting is to render grace and goodwill and praise to the artist much more than riches. And these will come to painters when their painting will hold the eye and the mind of whoever looks at them." Alberti then moves to a discussion of patronage. The painter should be a "good man learned in good letters" in order to appeal to the rich, who are often better at judging character than at judging art. The painter must know the liberal arts, especially geometry, as was demanded by Pamphilos, who according to Pliny instructed noble youths in painting. The painter should also keep the company of poets and orators, who have "many ornaments in common with the painter," are knowledgeable of many things, and may greatly assist in beautifully composing the *istoria,* "of which every praise consists in invention," which has such force that "a beautiful invention is pleasing per se, alone, even without painting." One delights, for example, in Lucian's description of the *Calumny* of Apelles, which Alberti repeats. "This *istoria* pleases as it is recited; think how great would have been the grace and pleasure in seeing it painted by the hand of Apelles."[7]

In passing from perspective and composition – which had occupied the first two books of his treatise – to invention, Alberti moved from what he regarded as a potentially universal audience for painting to a possibly more limited one. The appearance of relief and the devices of composition hold the eye of anyone who looks at a painting; but the *Calumny* of Apelles, however delightful it might be, necessarily addresses a smaller, learned audience. Even if everyone can see that some event has been depicted, only some can tell what it might be, and it is these for whom the pure undepicted "invention" is pleasing. Other subject matter – most religious subject matter, for example – would have had a practical universality comparable to the understood universality of the naturalistic means of representation themselves. A *Descent from the Cross* or a *Crucifixion* would have been evident to everyone as what it was, at the same time that relief seized the eye by presenting the theme as a physical event and composition seized the eye with its delightful artifice.

Alberti's argument thus implies a simple but important distinction between "form" and "content": that the first is more universal than the second. This is to say nothing more than that Alberti thought painting should be what all Renaissance painting in fact is, namely, naturalistic, regardless of subject matter. And if there were ways of bridging the gap between form and content – by the manipulation of composition according to a decorum of subject matter, for example – it is still the case that a Renaissance painting always shows us an apparent physical event before it tells us what the event is, and on the firm basis of this simple observation we may make the distinction between subject matter and the means of representation.

The idea of the unity of form and content very much favors content; that is, if a work of art is successful, and such a unity is achieved, the means of representation become the vehicle of content. If this is so, then the history of art becomes the history of content, and the means of representation become the clay of art history. In this book I will proceed from the rejection of this assumption and deal with the question of the history of the significance of the means of

[7] L. B. Alberti, *Della pittura,* in *Opere volgari,* ed. C. Grayson, Bari, 1973, III, p. 92.

representation as such. Although it may seem necessary in any given work to explain how the means of representation are adapted to content, it is in my view simply not possible to pass from such a characterization to the explanation of why the means of representation themselves change. Even if form and content change together – even if, for example, themes become more historical and narrative at the same time that they become more naturalistic, this is not necessarily to be explained by the subordination of form to content. Such reciprocity might also be explained by the adaptation of content to form. But it is perhaps best to abandon this polarity altogether and to look instead for ways in which form and content are continuous with one another.

If we think of style as having to do with the "formal" aspects of art, then style and meaning must be considered to be distinguishable from one another in important respects. That is simply to say that we may talk about the history of a theme and the history of the means of representation separately, even if in individual works there is an undeniable expressive interdependence of a theme and its presentation. But the separability of form and content in such analyses need not imply radical and substantial difference between them. Instead of supposing such difference it would seem preferable to think of them as different, more or less deep kinds of significant elements with different rates of change, so that what we call "form" simply becomes the most inclusive mode of content. In the case we are considering, naturalism, or the formal means of light–dark contrast upon which naturalism is based, form, as the most inclusive category of significance, would change most slowly as the condition for the representation of other meaning. And in such a case, this formal basis would be sensitive to – and a major modality for the articulation and exploration of – kinds of meaning related to its own range of meaning. The relation between the invention of such formal devices and psychology, say, or optics, was close in the Renaissance and, because practical equivalences of form and meaning are involved, it is difficult to say which in general may have been prior. That is to say, naturalism opened up a realm of significance to which both painting and psychology were deeply and essentially relevant. Such a formulation, of course, means that naturalism in any given instance is culturally specific. What might be called Chinese naturalism, painting also based on light–dark contrast, must be supposed to have developed in intimate relation with kinds of significance different from those that shaped the appearances of its Western counterpart, just as the characteristic use of the elements of naturalism distinguish it at once from its Western counterpart.

The investigations that follow are guided by this hypothesis: that the characteristics of naturalism as the precondition for Renaissance painting regardless of subject matter were themselves both significant and value-laden, and that the development of these characteristics in their specific historical forms (Western naturalism really resembles no other naturalism) are only explainable in terms of those meanings and values.

When we try to explain deep stylistic change, we must not only describe what takes place, and offer reasons for it, we must also explain why changes compel more or less universal assent. The assumption that styles move toward naturalism of course obviates such explanations, stringing out over time Aristotle's dictum that by nature we delight in imitation; if we delight in imitation of appearances, we also delight in progressive improvements in the imitation of appearance. These arguments instead urge the conclusion that the development of naturalism in the late Middle Ages was part of a vast, uneven, but relentless transformation in attitude toward the world, which became visible in terms of the meaning of naturalism, just as the development of naturalism concentrated and transformed these meanings, giving them new and potent cultural forms, pointing toward unforeseen consequences. It is for this reason that naturalism is deeply implicated in the rise of science, the rise of the individual, even the rise of the modern state.

It should be insisted that naturalism does not simply illustrate the ideas that articulated its significance or even stated the intentions behind its working out and use. The ideas we shall consider, with their myriad historical affiliations, meanings of both connotation and use, led to the threshold of invention, beyond which they passed into another realm of historical efficacy. At the same time, to continue the metaphor, the integral relation of the exterior and interior joined at this threshold must be kept in mind. That is, the independence of the world of form from the world of language cannot be taken to mean that word and form are unrelated; on the contrary, it is assumed – and, I hope, demonstrated – that the historical specificity of one is inextricably related to the historical specificity of the other. In the language we shall examine we shall find not only an explanation of the origins of naturalism, we shall also find the archaic language of modern aesthetics, the two confounded in much the same way that literal and metaphorical point of view are mutually implicative.

Remarks on procedures

The chapters that follow trace the history of different facets of what I shall call the particular intellect, made up of the "inner senses," which, although they were variously listed, included the fantasy, common sense, the faculties of estimation and cogitation, and memory. These postsensory and prerational faculties of the human soul were postulated in a long tradition to account for our judgments and actions based on the intuitive grasp of the presence and character of objects and individuals, circumstances and situations. Although there are distinguished and thorough histories of the ideas of fantasy and memory, others of these postsensory faculties have been much less studied. The common sense, a faculty to which we shall pay much attention, has been relatively little examined previously. A moment's thought tells us that common sense has been one of the most influential notions in Western intellectual discourse over a very long period, and the continuing importance of the idea is still evident in the unconscious ease with which we appeal to its modern descendant "common sense" as a standard in argument of all kinds. In this book I have been able to point only in the directions I think study of this idea in modern times might take and have concentrated on its earlier history, hoping that these later directions will be studied by others. To say that the idea of common sense has not been thoroughly studied is only to suggest the oblivion into which the faculties of estimation and cogitation have fallen. Owing to the deficient state of historical definition of the faculties of the particular intellect, then, it has been necessary to write fairly extensive accounts of certain ideas, accounts that in some cases may seem to dwarf the discussions that make up the guiding themes of these chapters, the explanation of a fundamental part of the language of Renaissance art. There is no way to avoid this imbalance.

It will be noticed that many more texts have been cited than are necessary to define a term under investigation. I have done this for several reasons. I have tried to give enough examples to make it clear how ideas are systematically related to one another and to establish the range of a term's connotations at any given time while attempting to plot and characterize its changes in meaning. Many examples make it possible to understand how a term *might* have been used and to understand something of the resonance of any actual use, the richness of its connections, and the boundaries within which it might be interpreted. The texts cited also provide some notion of the pervasiveness of what are now utterly unfamiliar ideas, and some sense – however abstract and inadequate – of the unconscious seriousness with which these ideas were used in real situations. Simply to define a term is to imply that it has a fixed meaning, whereas it is more accurate to say that terms cover a wide range of effective meaning that only becomes fully evident in the contexts in which they are used. The many examples of terms are thus also meant partly to give a sense of their transformation by adaptation. Insistence on the functional dimension of terms binds ideas more closely to contexts of human use and points to their integration with choice and action. At the same time, the meaning of terms cannot be reduced to the significance of situations in which they are used. If terms were never, strictly speaking, used in the same way twice, it is still centrally important that the same terms were used. The continuity of terms itself is deeply conservative, which is to say that something like the agreement on the meaning of terms that makes communication possible is, in its historical dimension, a conservative principle essential to the fabric of a tradition. At the same time, it is a conservative principle taking part in a process of continual transformation.

The uses to which ideas are put, and the emphasis on some possible meanings rather than others demanded by these uses, thus have as much to do with their histories as any "evolution" they might be thought to undergo. At the same time, ideas also change internally, by criticism, or by systematic adjustment to the criticism of related ideas, as we shall see in many cases.

These investigations proceed by tracing single terms and historically connected equivalents in other languages through time. The condition "historically connected" is added because the assumed equivalence of terms in historically unrelated languages imposes the further assumption of the adequate translatability of all languages; thus, Latin *imaginatio* is related historically to Greek *phantasia* and is specifiably relatable to it in a way that neither term may be assumed to have an equivalent in an unrelated language like Nahuatl, even if there is a Nahuatl term that "might best be translated" as "fantasy" or "imagination" (our own late cognate forms of the Greek and Latin terms.) To make such a translation without the closest possible attention to the contextual relations of terms is to do one of two things: either it is to impose Western psychology over the Aztecs (not only because "imagination" or "fantasy" has many meanings, associations, values, and uses for us, but also because psychology itself is a Western endeavor, and has a strong predisposition to find certain entities and relations among these entities); or it is to assume that there is a universal psychology that is merely differently named in various languages. In practice these two difficulties are one, because the "psychology" we assume to be universal is really our own, or a generalization of our own.

These examples lead to an important general conclusion: that members of any culture do not have simple reflective access to their mental activity, but that reflection concerning this activity is interdependent with the language used to articulate it, and therefore culturally shaped. If this is so, then statements *about* mental activity become much more centrally important than they are if it is assumed that the human mind has always and everywhere been the same, regardless of what has been said or written about it.

In this book I trace the history of a part of the Western tradition of psychological speculation and its relation to the language of art. Some of this psychological language is no longer meaningful or at first even intelligible. The *vis cogitativa* is as mysterious to us as the superego or id might have been to a thirteenth-century reader. The activity of "cogitation," which is now a general, almost meaningless, and slightly ironic term for concentrated thinking, was for many centuries a centrally important human power, corresponding more closely to our "imagination" than to Renaissance terms more obviously related to imagination. Cogitation was, moreover, a power linked to a network of other meanings no longer current – hence at least in part its expiration. This is not to say, of course, that, if we do not "cogitate" as our ancestors did, we cannot be made to understand what was meant by the term *cogitatio*. This may be accomplished by explaining the place of *cogitatio* in the system to which it belonged and by examining its purported functions, by comparing it to modern psychological ideas or to mental activities that are no longer properly psychological but that have settled into the relatively unconscious usage of everyday language.

If psychological language is not simply given but is culturally specific, then such questions as the origin, original meaning, use, continuity, transformation, and diffusion of language imply the historical concreteness of transformations of meaning. One of the corollaries of this notion might be called the *principle of specialization,* which simply means that in most cases the discussion of a subject will take place in the available language of that subject. This happens in "most" cases because novelty is always possible, because other traditions may be more or less available (which would mean that there was a choice among languages, and would not contradict the principle), and because in rare instances fundamental reconsiderations of things do take place. But usually existing ideas are adapted to new uses, or partly new ones, and new formulations are adjustments of old ones.

Turning to the matter at hand, a Renaissance artist interested in discussing his aims in psychological terms did not simply have recourse to the reality of his own mind; rather, he had the possibility of access to a varied and culturally definite language *about* the reality of his own mind. The historical emergence of the articulation of art in such terms is significant in itself, indicating both a reorientation of the preceding language of art and a magnification of the significance of art, its definition as a new mode of thought and investigation. When art is implicitly and explicitly defined as a model of vision and, more broadly, of perception, then it comes into intimate historical contact with the culturally specific significance of the visual and of perception. Leonardo da Vinci's invention of *chiaroscuro* composition is probably unthinkable without Aristotle's definition of vision as discriminating colors as intermediates between the extremes of light and dark. But if this definition provided a conceptual armature for the invention, it also made painting subject to the theory of vision as well as a means by which that theory could be revised. More generally, it brought painting squarely into line with questions of the rhetoric of the visual, of the uses to which images should be put.

The adaptation of language to the purposes of art is by no means a simple question of the astrological metaphor of "influence." If Aristotle's theory of vision shaped Leonardo's invention at its base, this theory began to lead another historical life after the invention had been formulated. Leonardo's solution could not have been completely defined by Aristotle's theory in the nature of the matter; but it is necessary to appreciate the ways in which it was defined by this theory and the ways in which it was not in order to understand both the long tradition of expressive possibilities and the problems opened up by this single constructive device of *chiaroscuro.* Vasari tells us that the High Renaissance painter Albertinelli was a restless, carnal man who became so disgusted with the *sofisticherie* and intellectual puzzles of painting that he abandoned the art for a time and opened an inn instead. He was, in short, hardly the sort of person to have known about the then scientific background of *chiaroscuro* composition. But when he painted he still struggled and invented within the limits of Leonardesque tonal painting, trying to make paintings in which there was at once the strong relief of deep shadow and the *dolcezza* of pure bright color.[8] Again, there is no reason to believe that Caravaggio or Rembrandt knew anything about Aristotle's theory of vision. Still, they practiced an art stating at least implicitly that the basis of vision is light–dark contrast, and this presupposition was evident in their painting, which could be justified or criticized in those terms (although not only in those terms.) Ultimately, painting as value contrast provided the schema according to which the "visual field" of the painting could be said to be color contrast rather than value contrast, and painting could be put on a different – but still optical – basis.

If the principle of specialization is sound, then it follows that it is necessary to look for meanings and contexts in the appropriate language before the use of a certain term. If Leonardo used the term *senso comune,* or common sense, it might at first be supposed that he used it much as we might. But context and further examples make it clear that he meant something by it that we do not, and that in fact for him the term had quite another range of meaning. Scholarship informs us that his remarks are more nearly consistent with Aristotle's idea of common

[8] VM, IV, pp. 222–223. On the conflict of hue and value in Italian Renaissance painting, J. Shearman, "Leonardo's Color and Chiaroscuro," *Zeitschrift für Kunstgeschichte,* 24, 1962, pp. 13–47; and C. Dempsey, *Annibale Carracci and the Beginnings of Baroque Style,* Florence, 1977. See also K. Weil Garris Posner, *Leonardo and Central Italian Art,* 1515–1550, New York, 1974. Black is characterized as a deprivation or failure of sight in several Aristotelian texts (see D. E. Hahm, "Early Hellenistic Theories of Vision and the Perception of Colour," in *Studies in Perception: Interrelations in the History of Philosophy and Science,* ed. P. K. Machamer and R. G. Turnbull, Columbus, Ohio, 1978, pp. 82–83, n. 61 for citations), and darkness is often linked with distance (see my " 'Contrapposto': Style and Meaning in Renaissance Art," *AB,* 59, 1977, p. 348, n. 66). P. Marshall, "Two Scholastic Discussions of the Perception of Depth by Shading," *JWCI,* 44, 1981, pp. 170–175, suggests that explanations of the illusion of three dimensions given to shapes by modelling provided by Nicole Oresme and another anonymous writer might have resulted from the reinvention of explanations like those found in classical sources to account for the vestiges of classical relief to be seen in medieval painting. Marshall also notes that a cogent discussion of modelling does not appear in the literature of painting before Cennino Cennini (after 1390). But see Francesco della Lana's commentary on Dante's *Paradiso,* XXIV, 25–27, in J. von Schlosser, *La letteratura artistica,* Florence, 1964, p. 91. "The painter, when he wishes to paint folds [*pieghe*], ought to have a color less bright [*vivo*] than that of the cloth, that is, darker, and then folds will appear; inasmuch as in every fold the air is darker than at the surface; moreover if the color of the fold should exceed the cloth in brightness, then the cloth would appear to fold in and the brighter color would appear to be surface." This last argument means that in general the darker color is always seen to be more distant, which is the Aristotelian principle. If Francesco della Lana's commentary explains Dante's words correctly, then this simple scheme may be pushed back toward the years of the appearance of *rilievo* in Tuscan painting. The formula continues to be repeated in close conjunction to painting. Toward the middle of the Quattrocento, Giovanni da Fontana, a humanist close to Jacopo Bellini, wrote that the "art of painting teaches that the near should be painted with bright colors, the far with dark, and the middling with mixed" in the context of a discussion of optics. See G. Mariani Canova, "Riflessioni su Jacopo Bellini e sul libro dei Disegni del Louvre," *Arte veneta,* 26, 1972, pp. 22–23. In the middle of the sixteenth century, Giorgio Vasari, in his technical introduction to the art of painting (VM, I, p. 180) still refers to what "we see in life, that those parts that present themselves nearer the eye have more light, and the others, failing to sight, also lose light and color." Sight weakens with distance and this weakening is proportionate to dark and loss of color.

sense. But it is not clear that Aristotle himself had ever adequately formulated this idea, and, even if he had, Leonardo did not simply read Aristotle's *De anima* and *Parva naturalia.* Aristotle's writings came down to the Renaissance sheathed in a long tradition of commentary and interpretation. If Leonardo read Aristotle, he read him in Latin with a Latin commentator, and it is more likely that in many instances he read someone who had read Aristotle – Avicenna, Roger Bacon, Bartholomaeus Anglicus, even Dante – or talked with those who had. His discussion of common sense – and therefore of perception in general – is close to Avicenna, but it is also closer to much more contemporary transformations of Aristotle's idea, to the interpretation of Biagio Pelacani da Parma, and to the tradition that fused common sense with optics, perhaps closest to him in Lorenzo Ghiberti. The whole tradition, in short, was not simply a transmission of Aristotle's ideas, it was rather a continual interpretation of them; moreover, it was a tradition more or less available all at once, and Leonardo might have had access to this tradition of interpretation at many points, however directly or indirectly. The context of choice was thus complex, bounded not merely by the originative ideas of Aristotle – which still demand interpretation – but by the intervening history of interpretation, adaptation, and transformation of these ideas.

One group of related terms we shall be following includes all those that might be translated as "art." The meaning of art has, of course, changed very much between the period under discussion and the present, and the continuity of these terms provides a relatively fixed standard against which parts of this change may be plotted. It is important not only that the meaning of art has changed but also that the meaning of what was always called "art" was always changing. The simple continuity of terms indicates the continuity of a tradition, and the transformation of the meaning of those terms indicates the transformation of that tradition. I have tried to avoid modern notions of "fine art," or of art as imitation or expression, in favor of a broader and more premodern definition of art as all useful human skills and as the products and results of these skills. One way in which the thesis of this book might be stated would be to say that an essential part of the development of the modern notion of art was the rise to prominence of faculties that, as subrational and opinionative, were associated with art in this inclusive sense of the term. I believe that the traditional language about art in a broad sense helped shape the Renaissance and hence the modern notion of art; the very ancient idea that the mechanical arts fill us with wonder and are inherently deceptive, for example, stands behind the Renaissance understanding of painting as illusive, fictive and poetic, and this understanding in turn provided the boundaries within which invention and personal style, or modern notions of imitation or expression, could develop.

In the following arguments much attention will be given to commentaries on texts. In tracing the history of ideas it is at least as important to determine what was thought to have been meant by an author as it is to determine what was meant, and commentaries as immediate interpretations and adaptations provide access both to the effective meaning of a text and to the patterns and purposes of its transformation.

The arguments of Leonardo and Lorenzo Ghiberti about perception point to philosophers and theologians, by whom such matters were given their major and authoritative statements at a time in which there were no "psychologists" at all. In general, it must be supposed that vernacular language reinforced and enriched the discussion we shall be following, as in fact the language of everyday affairs is not simply grammar and syntax put to practical use but is an endlessly fruitful source of invention, of wit, proverb, and metaphor. The vernacular notion of *senno,* which more or less corresponds to a modern phrase like "good, common sense," might surface after centuries of nontechnical use as an important critical concept. We are told by one of the authors we shall consider, Francesco Bocchi, who wrote in the third quarter of the Cinquecento, that Donatello conceived his *St. George* with *molto senno,* that Michelangelo studied anatomy with *senno profondo,* that Jacopo Pontormo had painted his controversial (and destroyed) frescoes in the church of San Lorenzo with *poco senno.*[9] Here the term combines meanings of *giudizio* and *ingegno,* but replaces these standard and ubiquitous terms with one of an altogether different reach and resonance. Again, the constant and powerful tradition of the Vulgate must have given some of the ideas we shall examine pointed meanings less obvious to us now. *Cogitatio* figured especially prominently in moral speculation, and the term must have rung very differently in the ears of people for whom God's acknowledgment that "the imagination of man's heart is evil from his youth" (Genesis 8:20) ran "sensus enim et cogitatio humani cordis in malum prona sunt ab adolescentia sua."

[9] BT, III, pp. 162, 189, 185.

In the late medieval *Bestiario toscano* (*Il Bestiario toscano secondo la lezione dei codici di Parigi e di Roma,* ed. M. S. Garver and K. McKenzie, Rome, 1912, p. 17), we are told that there are two paths to knowledge, *senno* and *scientia,* very roughly corresponding to sense and intellect. The argument is based on the assumption of a fit between nature and human nature. God made nature true, and also made that which belongs to nature true; and the union of these two truths is *senno naturale.* C. S. Lewis (*Studies in Words,* Cambridge, 1967, pp. 133–164) offers interesting reflections on the history of the word "sense" and related words ("sentence," "sensibility," and "sensible"). He traces two meanings of "sense," what he calls "ordinary intelligence" or "gumption" and "perception by sight, hearing, taste, smell or touch," which he calls *aesthesis.* Lewis argues that the first meaning is certainly prior to the second, that is, that what in the course of his discussion he calls "gumption or judgment" is prior to the meaning of sense as perception and not vice versa, as is often assumed from the standpoint of modern sensationalism. "Sense" thus merges with "mind" in its immediate, intuitive, and judgmental relations to things and only later gets associated with the "senses," understood as the immediate agents of intuition and judgment.

In his *Truth and Method* (New York, 1975, pp. 19–39), H.-G. Gadamer offers sections on *sensus communis* and related ideas such as tact, judgment, and taste. Gadamer is centrally interested in circumstantial and opinionative judgments immediate to action and stresses the rhetorical and communal nature of common sense, which is like prudence in being "directed toward concrete situations" and in being able to "grasp the 'circumstances' in their infinite variety." In such terms the kind of judgment common sense typifies is crucial to the existential and practical dimension of the understanding Gadamer seeks as an alternative to scientific knowledge, and is the cutting edge of "hermeneutical consciousness." Gadamer indicates the importance of G. B. Vico in the history he sketches, "whose appeal to the *sensus communis* belongs . . . in a wider context that goes right back to antiquity and the continued effect of which into the present day" he calls the subject of his book.

For the most part, however, the adaptations of psychological terms by Renaissance writers on art strayed little from what was to be found in Scholastic writers. This is not to say that Leonardo or Ghiberti simply repeated Scholastic ideas; it is rather to say that they took up existing language for discussing what they wished to treat when formulating their own thoughts, which bore about the same relation to previous formulations that painter's perspective bore to earlier optics. To suppose they did otherwise is again to suppose that they had recourse to language corresponding to a "natural" psychology. There is no reason to believe that such an access is articulatable if it is even possible.

However important commentaries, encyclopedias, and various "popularizations" may be to such an enterprise as this, it is also necessary to consider major writers because not to do so obscures the cogency and reach of traditions of ideas. A pronouncement on the nature and use of images may be widely available in an encyclopedist, but it possesses a different magnitude of authority and is subject to a different kind of analysis in its original formulation by Saint Bonaventure.[10] Although it seems more closely to contextualize ideas to consider them near the level of their implementation, it is also essential not to lose sight of their origin, because from their point of origin they may have taken on many forms that, however various they may be, are related to the one under scrutiny. Throughout, it has been necessary to consider ideas both as they develop internally, that is, as they are subject to criticism as ideas, and as they change in response to their myriad adaptations.

When we read the third commentary of the Florentine sculptor Lorenzo Ghiberti, we may be at several removes from Avicenna, even if Ghiberti cites his work or quotes it. Still, Avicenna explains Ghiberti's words, and provides access to a more general framework in which they are meaningful. It might be possible to find a historically closer connection – we might, for example, find Ghiberti's copy of Avicenna's *Canon,* or find out the name of its lender – but such a discovery would not go very far toward explaining what Ghiberti made of Avicenna or why, and that is finally what interests us. We are saved from the most difficult – and the most important – tasks of historical reconstruction and interpretation

[10] See M. Baxandall, *Painting and Experience in Fifteenth Century Italy,* Oxford, 1972, p. 41, citing the *Catholicon* of John of Genoa, whose source in Bonaventure is *Commentaria in Quatuor Libros Sententiarum Magistri Petri Lombardi,* III, dist. IX, art. 1, quaest. II, conclusio (*Opera omnia,* Florence, 1887, III, p. 203), a text cited by E. Panofsky, *Early Netherlandish Painting,* New York, 1971, I, p. 141. In justification of his position on images, Bonaventure cites Horace *Ars poetica.* 180, here in the translation of D. A. Russell and M. Winterbottom, *Ancient Literary Criticism,* Oxford, 1972, p. 284: "What comes in through the ear is less effective in stirring the mind than what is put before our faithful eyes and told by the spectator to himself." The notion of the precedence of sight over hearing as the sense to which one most effectively appeals in teaching is repeated by other Scholastic writers and should be considered a part of the justification of naturalism in religious images on a very broad scale; see G. Scavizzi, "La teologia cattolica e le immagini durante il XVI secolo," *Storia dell'arte,* 21, 1974, pp. 174–213. Another writer cited by Baxandall, Fra Michele da Carcano, also followed Bonaventure closely and recognized that his first principle repeated the traditional principle of Gregory the Great, that images are the books of the illiterate. For the opposing view that hearing is the chief sense through which we learn, see C. Nordenfalk, "The Five Senses in Late Medieval and Renaissance Art," *JWCI,* 48, 1985, pp. 1–22.

by the assumption that we already know the language of artists (the forms of their art) and that we already know the relation between this art and communicable intention (none).

These studies raise questions about historical periodization. Although it may be possible to characterize a period, that is, to describe its distinguishing features, it obviously is not possible to explain whatever happens within a period only by reference to the period itself. In some ways the Renaissance is distinct from the Middle Ages, but in other ways it is deeply continuous with the Middle Ages. Both the Middle Ages and the Renaissance may be discussed as distinct periods, but both are deeply related in many ways to classical antiquity. There are also basic continuities among these periods – the rhetorical tradition, for example – which, while they persist, are also transformed. Both the language of art and psychological language were more or less continuously developing traditions from antiquity through the Renaissance, that is, through the periods of our major concern.

Periodization has also skewed one of the great continuities between the Middle Ages and the Renaissance, the thought of Aristotle. Aristotle, whose philosophy is one of the crowning achievements of classical antiquity, has suffered the strange fate of having become a medieval author in Renaissance and modern perspective. Perhaps the modern world looks on Aristotle so unkindly because so many of its own intellectual foundations owe to the lineal criticism of his works. The influence of his philosophy, not only in the Middle Ages, but also through the Renaissance, however, was deep, broad and constant. This is especially so of the issues we shall treat, issues for the discussion of which he and his commentators provided a supple and complex language of analysis and investigation.[11]

If ideas were passed along over many centuries, why did they only shape historical events at a certain time? This question is often asked, and it betrays a kind of *Zeitgeist* thinking, an assumption that at any time all parts of a section taken through the flow of history are somehow unified, that because both art and ideas express "the spirit of the age" they are deeply reflective of one another. A major burden of this enterprise is to demonstrate that such a view is false, and that it must falsify our view of how both art and ideas work in history. It may or may not be possible to characterize the choices made at any time as in some way typical of that time. But it is not possible to simplify the context of choice itself. The idea that everything that occurs at a given time somehow expresses a transcendent unity also conceals the connections between choice and its precedent conditions. Leonardo could state his views about painting partly because systematic

[11] The study of Renaissance Aristotelianism is greatly aided by *The Cambridge History of Later Medieval Philosophy: From the Rediscovery of Aristotle to the Disintegration of Scholasticism, 1100–1600*, ed. N. Kretzmann, A. Kenny, and J. Pinborg, Cambridge, 1982. And see C. B. Schmitt, *A Critical Survey and Bibliography of Studies on Renaissance Aristotelianism, 1958–1969*, Padua, 1971; and the same author's *Aristotle and the Renaissance*, Cambridge, Mass., 1983. See also F. E. Cranz, "The Renaissance Reading of the *De anima*," *Platon et Aristote à la Renaissance*, Paris, 1976, pp. 259–276.

clarifications or minute adjustments of Aristotle's ideas were made centuries before by writers who could never have dreamed that anyone would use these ideas as he did.

The problem of judgment

In a short article published in 1961, Robert Klein argued that the modern notion of taste, which we understand to be associated with both the making and appreciation of works of art, replaced the earlier Renaissance notion of *giudizio*. Klein's arguments might be said more to have established the terms of a long discussion than to have demonstrated a development through that discussion, since Filarete wrote in interesting ways about *gusto* in the fifteenth century, as did Luca Pacioli at the beginning of the sixteenth, and *giudizio* was clearly still a functioning art-critical term in the seventeenth century. Klein also acknowledged that many Renaissance usages of *giudizio* slipped through the net of his analysis. Still, with the appropriate qualifications, he felt confident in stating that in the course of the development he was tracing "the intellectual faculty of judgment, as a metaphor for artistic understanding, is ousted by the most immediately sensual, the most irrevocably subjective of the five senses."[12]

Klein's article was based on a fairly limited number of texts from writers of the fifteenth to the seventeenth centuries, and, concerned as he was with clarifying the Renaissance meaning of the terms under examination, he gave little attention to the complex history of the idea of judgment before the Renaissance. He did note that "for the Renaissance, judgment was not a purely intellectual act" but belonged instead to a "domain intermediate between the mind and the senses. It related the sensible particular to the intelligible universal, or, inversely, the universal to the particular." Klein also related judgment to the instinctive "estimations" of animals on the one hand and on the other stressed the antinomous, proto-Kantian nature of judgment as involving immediate reaction to things perceived, and wrote that this reaction may be rationalized "in the sense that reasons may be found for it."

More recently, it has been asserted that the usages of the term "judgment" in the texts examined by Klein "directly derive from Aristotle's *Nicomachean Ethics*, VI, ix–xi." If this is correct, and if Klein's sample of texts is representative, then it follows that all Renaissance discussion of artistic judgment must somehow fall within the domain of Aristotle's practical intellectual virtue of prudence (*phronesis*), defined as the virtue that "allows the artist to adapt the particular case to the universal principle and vice versa."[13] There are a number of difficulties with this

[12] R. Klein, "Judgment and Taste in Cinquecento Art Theory," *Form and Meaning: Essays on the Renaissance and Modern Art*, Princeton, 1981, pp. 161–169. On Filarete, G. Tonelli, "Taste in the History of Aesthetics from the Renaissance to 1779," *DHI*, IV, p. 354; and L. Pacioli, *Divina proportione*, ed. C. Winterberg, Vienna, 1899, p. 35.

[13] C. Dempsey, *Annibale Carracci*, pp. 69, 71, 97 n. 138.

view. First of all, prudence is a virtue of the practical intellect, the concerns of which were usually thought to be ethical and political. Although art, which Aristotle repeatedly compared to the activity of the practical intellect, was discussed in terms of prudence in antiquity, the Middle Ages, and the Renaissance, it is by no means certain that this was meant to refer in most cases to the virtue of the practical intellect. Moreover, as we shall see, Aristotle's own discussion of prudence had a complex historical life, becoming prominent in Scholastic writers after centuries of the dominance of other definitions that continued to be current after its reintroduction.

The most serious difficulty with such a view of judgment is much simpler than any of those just raised; because the judgment associated with the practical intellectual virtue of prudence was very far from the only kind of judgment discussed by Renaissance writers on art. There was a long tradition of speculation concerning prerational sensate judgment upon which Renaissance writers drew, a tradition to which Klein in fact pointed in several of his essays, but which he did not systematically explore. As we shall see, this same tradition contributed substantially to modern aesthetics when it was finally defined as such by Alexander Baumgarten. In order to begin our investigations, we shall briefly consider the meaning of the word "judgment."

The term "judgment" is used very frequently in writing of all kinds, and it is most often used as if its meaning were already understood. We have just considered the example of the judgment of a particular act in light of a universal principle. But this is obviously not the only meaning of the term. In everyday use "judgment" means evaluation or discrimination, and in logic the term has a much broader and more precise meaning, referring to the linking of any subject and predicate.[14] In the texts we shall consider, the term "judgment" is closer to the first, ordinary meaning of evaluation or discrimination, with the more specific meaning of evaluation or discrimination according to the nature of the faculty of apprehension involved.

Let us begin with a modern translation of Aristotle's *De anima* (426b–c), in which we read the following statement: "Now each sense . . . judges the specific differences of its own sensible object. . . . Sight pronounces upon white and black, taste upon sweet and bitter, and so with the rest." A medieval Latin translation of this text reads as follows: "unusquisque sensuum . . . *iudicat* differentias sensibilis sibi subiecti, v. g. visus album et nigrum, et gustus dulce et amarum, et sic de aliis."[15] Such terminology is usual in commentaries on the *De anima* and in the vast literature stemming at one or another remove from the work.

The Greek term translated by *iudicare* is *krinein,* meaning to distinguish, dis-

[14] E. D. Hirsch, Jr., *Validity in Interpretation,* New Haven, Conn., 1967, p. 143.

[15] Throughout I have used Aristotle, *De anima,* ed. and tr. R. D. Hicks, New York, 1970; for the Latin translation, *Averrois Cordubensis commentarium magnum in Aristotelis de anima libros,* ed. F. S. Crawford, Cambridge, 1953, p. 348.

criminate, or separate. The Latin cognate of *krinein* is *cernere,* which means to separate, divide, to see distinctly, to select, choose, or decide, hence our "discern." The substantive corresponding to *krinein* is *krisis,* from forms of which we take the English *critic* and *criterion.* When Robert Grosseteste translated the *Nicomachean Ethics, iudicium* was always used to translate *krisis,* with one exception. *Iudicare* was always used to translate *krinein.*[16]

Two points may be drawn from these examples. First, *iudicium* may refer to a broad range of kinds of right discriminations, from the operations of sense to moral decision; and second, as this simple conclusion implies, judgment is more general than any specific application of judgment. It always means to discern or distinguish in relation to a mean or standard. This in itself is an important distinction. A mean might be defined as a point in a continuum between two extremes, a standard as something above any actual thing, relative to which the truth or validity of an actual thing may be determined. The relation between means and standards is, of course, a difficult question in its own right. In principle, means are relative to real states of affairs in a way standards are not, but the matter is seldom so simple, as we shall have ample opportunity to see in what follows. We may consider the example of what Aristotle called the practical syllogism.[17] The universal premise may be regarded as relative to past experience (we have found that in such conditions it is best to do this) or as absolute (because this is so, all men should do this in such conditions). If the standard is absolute, then it must be innate or transcendent (or both), sanctioned by human nature or by reason, revelation, or the higher interests of some group. In one case the premise is amendable by experience; in the other, it is not. These are, of course, familiar paradoxes, and for our purposes it is sufficient to say that judgment cuts across them.

If Plato was most interested in standards (in the sense in which we have just discussed them), Aristotle, with whose writings we shall be mostly concerned, was also interested in means. At many points Aristotle preserved a strong Platonic distinction between thought and sense, which he associated with rest and motion respectively (*De anima* 434a16ff). This distinction between thought and sense of course raised questions about how the two interact, a question never satisfactorily resolved, and a perennial bone of contention through the tradition we shall follow.

[16] *Ethica Nicomachea,* in *The Basic Works of Aristotle,* ed. R. McKeon, New York, 1941; and *Ethica Nicomachea. Translatio Roberti Grosseteste Lincolniensis, Aristoteles Latinus,* 26, 1–3, fasc. 3, ed. R. A. Gauthier, Leiden, 1972, p. 265.

[17] We shall encounter the practical syllogism from time to time, and it has not always been interpreted as it is presented here for the sake of the argument. M. C. Nussbaum (*Aristotle's "De motu animalium,"* Princeton, N.J., 1978, pp. 165–220) argues that Aristotle used the practical-theoretical parallel not to construct a deductive science of ethics but to elucidate certain notions involved in the explanation of action. The major and minor premises are the desire for a goal and a belief that certain behavior is necessary to that goal. The conclusion is not verbal but is rather the action itself. And A. R. Mele, "The Practical Syllogism and Deliberation in Aristotle's Causal Theory of Action," *New Scholasticism,* 55, 1981, pp. 281–316.

In Aristotle's own psychology, as we shall see, imagination is the literally crucial point at which sense and reason meet. The imagination is passive to sensation from below, to dreams and hallucinations from within, to the mental forms and diagrams of the arts and sciences, or notions of right behavior from above. Sensation yields inner images, thought proceeds from these inner images and must return to them in order to act. Thought and reason thus confront and overlap in the imagination. But Aristotle also writes about thought as a transition between sense and reason, or motion and rest, an ascent by abstraction in which the sensate becomes more like the rational. This notion of continuity leads us back to the subject of judgment. In its ability to make distinctions, the human soul is one nature, from the level of sensation upward. The activity of the soul might, in fact, be regarded as a succession of judgments. The animal soul is not only the faculty of originating local movement but is also the "capacity to judge, which is the function of thought and perception" (*De anima* 432a15). Imagination, sensation and mind are each a *kritikon,* a faculty of judgment (*De motu animalium* 700b20). The "capacity to judge, which is the function of thought and perception," is common to both thought and perception and it is consequently difficult to classify the sensitive as either irrational or rational (*De anima* 432a30). Sense discriminates light from dark, near from far, pleasure from pain; higher faculties discriminate right from wrong, true from false. Cumulative judgments produce a standard, a judgment against which future judgments may be made, and this, as we are told at the beginning of the *Metaphysics,* is the origin of art and science.[18]

The psychology of Aristotle never departed from the principle that we do in fact inevitably make discriminations, and that more than simply discriminating, we act as if our discriminations are true, or we treat things and states of affairs as if they were adequately grasped in our everyday affairs. Again, such judgments occur from the level of sensation upward. "Why," Aristotle asks in the *Metaphysics* (1008b14ff),

> does a man walk to Megara and not stay at home, when he thinks he ought to be walking there? Why does he not walk early some morning into a well or over a precipice, if one

[18] See J. H. Randall, *Aristotle,* New York, 1960, p. 80. "The power to respond with discrimination to the object of desire is the power to know. Knowing takes place on two levels, that of sensing, and, in the case of animals that possess the power of *nous,* that of the operation of *nous* . . . . Aristotle groups the two powers together under the common heading *to kritikon,* the power of selective response . . . in his analysis of these two powers and their operation, he attempts throughout to deal with "nousing" on the analogy of the more accessible process of sensing." S. van den Bergh, "Perception and Knowledge According to Aristotle," *Islamic Philosophy and the Classical Tradition. Essays Presented by His Friends and Pupils to Richard Walzer on His Seventieth Birthday,* ed. S. M. Stern, A. Hourani, and V. Brown, Oxford–Columbia, S.C., 1972, pp. 27–33, calls Aristotle "very little consistent" on the point that perception is not knowledge, since he argues that the senses judge, especially sight. D. W. Hamlyn, "Aristotle's Account of *aisthesis* in the *De anima,*" *Classical Quarterly,* 53, 1959, p. 67, writes that "the faculty of sense perception is that faculty by means of which we are able to characterize or identify things as a result of the use of our senses. It is reasonable, therefore, to connect perception with judging, as Aristotle does; although it is incorrect to identify it with judging, as he also does."

happens to be in his way? Why do we observe him guarding against this, evidently because he does not think that falling is alike good and not good? Evidently, then, he judges one thing to be better and another worse. And if this is so, he must also judge one thing to be a man and another to be not-a-man, one thing to be sweet and another to be not-sweet. For he does not aim at and judge all things alike, when, thinking it desirable to drink water or to see a man, he proceeds to aim at those things; yet he *ought,* if the same thing were alike a man and not-a-man. But as was said, there is no one who does not obviously avoid some things and not others. Therefore, as it seems, all men make unqualified judgments, if not about all things, still about what is better and worse.

Aristotle completes his arguments by calling the results of such judgment opinion in contrast to knowledge, and calls one who lives according to opinion in need of healing in comparison to one who knows. But his preference for the philosophical as higher should not be allowed to obscure the importance of pre-philosophical apprehension (or judgment) in his scheme. This realm of "opinion" will emerge as the realm of the powers – of sensation, perception, imagination, and memory – making up the particular intellect, which will be one of our principal themes.

Consistently with such ideas, Aristotle often draws analogies between intellectual activity and sensation, and does so in most important instances. Sensation (*De anima* 431a8ff.) is *analogous* to simple assertion or simple apprehension by thought, and when the sensible thing is pleasant or painful, the pursuit or avoidance of it by the soul is a *sort* of affirmation or negation. In fact, to feel pleasure or pain is precisely "to function with the sensitive mean, acting upon good or evil as such." But it is not simply that sensation is analogous in its judgments to reason, it is also the case that judgments of practical reason (speculative reason cannot act) are somehow analogous to judgments of sense. So (*De sensu* 441b23) "the activity of sense perception in general is analogous, not to the process of acquiring knowledge, but to that of exercising knowledge already acquired"; or as Aristotle observes in the *Nicomachean Ethics* (1109b20), the right mean in ethical behavior "is not easy to determine by reasoning, any more than anything else that is perceived by the senses; such things depend on particular facts, and the decision rests with perception."

These antinomies, between sense and reason, between the continuity and discontinuity of the activities of the human soul, far from vitiating Aristotle's psychology seem only to have deepened its authority, rooting it in the deeper mystery, from which these antinomies finally arise, of how and why the mind knows the world at all. Aristotle's doctrine of the human soul thus posed perennial problems for resolution, resolutions made by successive emphasis now upon sense, more usually upon reason, by one thinker or another. But throughout the tradition he initiated there persisted the possibility that, as Aquinas wrote, sense, too, is a kind of reason, and it is with the history of this possible understanding, and its flowering and reflowering in the Italian Renaissance, that we shall be mostly concerned.

For Aristotle, real things are unions of form and matter, and mind somehow apprehends the forms of things, which are thinkable. As Aristotle's psychology was adapted over the centuries to Platonism, his symmetry between matter and form yielded to a decided imbalance in favor of the latter. That is, form, as the thinkable, was associated with mind, and what we apprehend was thus progressively spiritualized as matter withered into the merely necessary hypothesis of pure potentiality. In such schemes, judgment survived as proof of the activity of the soul at all levels, in contrast at all levels to the passivity of matter. We may consider the representative and influential example of Boethius. Beginning from the principle that nothing is known according to its own force, but rather according to the faculty by which it is known, Boethius proceeds through a series of progressively higher kinds of "vision." Sight and touch "intuit" and "comprehend" respectively (*intueor* meaning to look or gaze upon, *comprehendere,* to grasp). The same man is seen (*contueor,* also looked at, considered attentively) by sense, imagination, reason, and intelligence. Sense judges (*iudicat*) the figure of a man in the subject matter that constitutes him, and imagination judges his shape. Reason weighs (*perpendit*) and considers the universal species, and intelligence "sees that simple form with the clear gaze of the mind" (*illam simplicem formam pura mentis acie contuetur*).

Boethius argued further that the higher faculties may judge the lower, but not vice versa. Sense cannot transcend its relation to matter, imagination cannot see the universal species of reason, and reason cannot grasp the simple forms of the intelligence. But intelligence, having conceived its forms, and "as it were looking downwards," judges (*diiudicat*) everything below, comprehending it in its peculiar fashion. It knows (*cognoscit*) the universality of reason, the figure of imagination, and the material of sense "formally," without using reason, imagination, or sense. Imagination, although it depends on the senses in seeing and forming figures, may in the absence of sense represent sensible things, not "by a sensible but by an imaginary power of judging" [*non sensibili sed imaginaria iudicandi*]. Here judgment is the distinctive act of imagination, its own transformation of sensation, that is, its own transformation of matter judged by sense. Such distinction must be respected, and Boethius concludes that "all judgment is the act of him who judges." The point of this argument is not simply that reason judges all but that every faculty of the soul judges in its own way. The question, then, is not one of normative judgment but of *kinds* of judgment.[19]

Other writers insisted on the activity of sensation, arguing that sense is not alteration but rather the awareness of sensation.[20] For Augustine perception was

[19] Boethius, *The Consolation of Philosophy, with the English Translation of "I. T." (1609),* ed. H. F. Stewart, Cambridge, Mass.–London, 1962, pp. 388–391. See also *Avicenna Latinus: Liber de Anima seu Sextus de Naturalibus,* IV–V, ed. S. van Riet, Louvain–Leiden, 1968, V, 1, p. 79. "Ergo est in homine iudicans sensibilis et iudicans imaginativa et iudicans aestimativa et iudicans contemplativa et iudicans activa."

[20] Nemesius of Emesa, *De natura hominis. Traduction de Burgundio de Pise,* ed. G. Verbeke and J. R. Moncho, Leiden, 1975, V, p. 72.

passive on the part of the body, active on the part of the soul.[21] Late medieval writers also called the activity of the faculties of the soul "judgment." In sensation, Saint Bonaventure wrote, "the reception of the species depends upon the body, but judgment [*iudicium*] depends upon the sensible virtue." That is, we must see with our material eyes, but it is the power of the soul to see that works through this material organ, and that in its activity is said to judge.[22] For Bonaventure the body undergoes the action of external objects, but the soul immediately reacts, and this reaction is judgment. And this judgment *is* sensible knowledge.[23]

In many late classical, early Christian, and late medieval writers, then, Aristotle's relatively materialist definition of sensation, represented by his metaphor of wax impressed by a signet ring, was replaced by a definition of sensation as existing for some interior vision or series of visions, a conception to which the idea of judgment was readily adapted. This understanding of judgment was to have a long life.

The "senses" with which we shall be concerned are both what were called the "external" and "internal" senses. The internal senses were all faculties of the soul thought to deal with mental images. Imagination (or fantasy), the power to call up "before the mind's eye" what was not actually present, was essential to the operations of all these faculties, which were called "senses" because they dealt with particulars. These particulars were, of course, the "forms" of particulars at the first level of abstraction from external sense. They were not, however, sufficiently abstracted to be the "universals" subject to the activities of intellect. The internal senses performed judgments, which were acts of distinction, comparison, association, and combination. These judgments and operations were literally prerational, although the syllogism, as the paradigmatic operation of reason, and therefore the paradigm of right thinking, seems to have provided the dominant model in attempts to characterize the peculiar structure and cogency of fantasy, memory, recollection, or quick-wittedness. By implication these operations were deficient kinds of reason. As we shall see, however, by the time of the Renaissance these lower faculties of the soul had come to occupy an unprecedented position of importance, and their relation to reason – even their distinctness from it – was very much in question.

The most comprehensive definition of the internal senses – and of the discriminatory powers of the human soul in general – was provided by Averroes in his notion of the *vis cogitativa,* which he called the particular reason or intellect. Referring to Averroes, Aquinas observed that reference is sometimes made to two kinds of reason. There is a lower reason (the *vis cogitativa*), which is a power of the *sensitive* soul, the sum of human internal sense, the activity of which he describes as the bringing together and comparing of individual forms. Higher

[21] *De genesi ad litteram,* XII.16.33 (MPL, 34, col. 467).
[22] Bonaventure, *Opera omnia,* II, pp. 221, 623.
[23] E. Gilson, *History of Christian Philosophy in the Middle Ages,* New York, 1955, p. 335.

reason, reason properly so-called, performs analogous operations with universal forms.[24] It must be emphasized that the relation between the activities of higher and lower reason was considered to be one of analogy, not of similarity, and the discursive operations of particular reason (as they were called), although consistent in their own right, were not thought to be like the inferences of universal reason. These discursive operations of postsensory faculties, which involve or presuppose one or another kind of discrimination, are, taken together, the judgment of sense. By far the most attention has been given to problems of the definition of universal reason. This book will examine instead the less visible but persistent tradition of the particular reason and will attempt to plot the historical fortunes of this idea into the early modern period.

More than a millennium before Averroes and Aquinas wrote, Seneca argued, as we shall see in Chapter 11, that philosophers did not invent the arts, but rather that they were simply invented by those who concerned themselves with such necessary things. The arts – weaving, farming, and baking are examples Seneca discusses, corresponding to some of what would be called the mechanical arts in the Middle Ages – were devised by reason but not by *right* reason. In fact, the arts tended to be associated with lower reason in a long tradition. In the late Middle Ages and the Renaissance this long tradition can be seen to have changed. It is not simply that the arts had come to be discussed in terms of higher reason (although that also occurred), but that the faculties associated with lower reason had come to enjoy a new prominence and stature. This state of affairs gave new authority to both art and artists, and at the same time art and artists played an indispensable role in the definition of behavior and institutions based on these newly important faculties. Consequently, as we follow the history and transformation of the particular intellect we shall also be following the history and transformation of some of the deepest themes of the Western language of art.

Artistic principles in the age of humanism

Although this book is mostly about the language of Renaissance art and its formation in the periods preceding the Renaissance, I have occasionally moved forward to consider authors of the seventeenth and eighteenth centuries. I have done this either to try to indicate what I think became of the ideas under discussion as they moved into modern times, or, more centrally to my purposes, to pursue the thesis that these ideas shaped the foundations of modern aesthetics, which began as a definite field of philosophical investigation in the eighteenth century. It should be said right away that these studies are not intended to deny that the notion of taste became much more visible in post-Renaissance debate about art, nor are they meant to erase distinctions between the Renaissance and the eighteenth

[24] J. Peghaire, *Intellectus et Ratio selon S. Thomas d'Aquin*, Paris, 1936, p. 15.

century. Rather, these arguments are meant to demonstrate that eighteenth-century aesthetic ideas did not simply spring up as historical necessity demanded but were instead adaptations, transformations, and magnifications of ideas whose histories may be followed to the very Pythagorean roots of the Western tradition. And, as might be expected, development of these ideas into modern form began in the late Middle Ages and the Renaissance, when the development of optical naturalism began to press the issue of point of view, understood in all its dimensions.

The assumption of such historical continuity has important implications for art-historical interpretation. We may consider Rudolf Wittkower's *Architectural Principles in the Age of Humanism,* first published in 1962. This book, which has very much shaped the way we think about Renaissance art in general, and therefore shaped the way we "picture" the Renaissance altogether, linked the architectural theory of the period with the principles of harmonic proportion. Again, one would not want to deny the central importance of these principles to Renaissance art. At the same time, however, it must not be imagined that their importance is essential in such a way as to exclude other ideas as "Renaissance."

In the last chapter of his book, Wittkower considers the "break-away from the laws of harmonic proportion," a rupture pointing at once to the modern age and to the gulf that separates us from the Renaissance. As an example of this break, Wittkower cites the words of the late seventeenth century architect Guarino Guarini, who wrote that "to satisfy the eye one must take away from or add to measures, since an object appears one way when beneath eye level, another when at a great height, one way in an enclosed space, otherwise in the open."[25] Wittkower called these words "radical," as indeed they stand in opposition to what he regarded as the basic principles of Renaissance architecture. Although proportion did cease to be normative as it had been in the Renaissance in later centuries, these "radical" words are very nearly exactly the words of the ancient Roman architect Vitruvius, as we shall see at note 13 in Chapter 2. Nor were these words simply the invention of a solitary Roman architect working in the age of Augustus. On the contrary, they belonged to the much broader tradition I shall try to indicate in its main outlines, a tradition that, far from being dormant

[25] R. Wittkower, *Architectural Principles in the Age of Humanism,* New York, 1971, p. 150. Art historical debate of Wittkower's thesis has turned around correspondence or noncorrespondence of measurements of actual buildings to systems of proportion. See most recently C. Wilkinson, "Juan de Herrera's Design for the Facade of the Basilica of the Escorial," *AB*, 67, 1985, pp. 229–242. If the arguments set forth in this book are correct, then proportion would have more to do with the process of design than with its evidence in the result. The point was to make a beautiful building, and toward that end the architect could adjust proportions without being "free to handle proportion without the firm basis of science," as Wittkower feared (p. 138). In other words, just because the final building does not conform to a scheme of proportion does not mean that proportion was not important to its conception. Wittkower (pp. 140–141) recognized that Palladio also advocated reliance on individual judgment and experience, which he regarded as a "typically North Italian Aristotelian accretion to the Platonic substance with which the foregoing pages were concerned."

in the Renaissance, was as intimately related to the theory – and practice – of Renaissance art as were the ratios of harmonic proportion.

A Renaissance work of art is not just the application of principles, it is also an intricate and unique adjustment of the forms set down in accordance with those principles. Leonardo may have prescribed that painting should be made of contrasts and modulations of light and dark, as his Burlington House cartoon is (see again Fig. 2), but it was also necessary to find just those relations of light and dark pleasing to the eye in that instance. Leonardo sought such rightness as avidly as he sought the principles of physical nature, and the evidence of such visual order – in our simple sense of the term, such *aesthetic* order – is one of the deep distinguishing marks of Renaissance art and the tradition it began, which is not yet at its end. The emergence of such aesthetically determined relations was coterminous with the emergence of personal style and the problems of taste and judgment style involves. Renaissance artists possessed the language to discuss these issues. As Giorgio Vasari wrote in his theoretical introduction to the art of sculpture, "one may use no better measure than the judgment of the eye; which, even if a thing may be most well measured, and the eye remain offended by it, it will for this reason not cease to censure it."[26] Some of the deepest characteristics of Italian Renaissance art might thus be viewed as consequences of the endlessly fruitful irreconcilability of definable principles and sensate judgment.

When Vitruvius recommended the adjustment of ratios, he was distinguishing between "paper" architecture and real architecture, architecture in the actual circumstances of its being seen. For Vitruvius the ingenuity and judgment necessary to make such adjustments were essential to good architecture and were symptomatic of the gifts distinguishing the good architect. They were innate talents, honed by experience, brought to bear in practice, in the realization of works. Although these faculties were tied to the particularity of individual natures and events, they were not themselves without definition or effective structure. Moreover, the discriminations of "inner sense" were integral to the making of things, to the finding of new solutions that, like Vitruvius's temple necessarily realized at a point in space, time, and light, were inevitably particular.

Perhaps the most instructive lesson to be taken from the prehistory of modern aesthetic language is the relation of the earlier language to the more general problem of the particular. The kinds of judgments made about works of art in their fashioning were like ethical judgments in that both of them were finally "right" or "good" only in the face of an actual state of affairs; and the kinds of judgments about works of art already made – "taste" – involved the faculties necessary to make the judgments about actual states of affairs that made "right" action – even the application of "true principles" – possible at all. The separation of ethics and aesthetics has long since been effected, although in terms other than

[26] VM, I, p. 151.

those under examination here. Still, it is perhaps useful to look back to a long discussion in which the demarcation was not so sharp, not to revive an old confusion but to consider those modes of apprehension and judgment between sensation and reason – the stubbornly opposed poles of most argument – for which the particular was given, and an absolute value.

1

The primacy of sight

Sight as heuretic

Plato's distrust of sense is well known, as are his reservations about the art of painting, which, as he usually represented the matter, simply imitates things seen. But at the end of the *Timaeus* (47a–c), Plato also praised sight as the most exalted of the senses, in words of which we shall hear many echoes in what follows. "Vision is the cause of the greatest benefit to us, inasmuch as none of the accounts now given concerning the universe would ever have been given if men had not seen the stars or the sun or the heavens." Not only does the clearest knowledge of the natural world proceed from the sense of sight, but, over and above this, the sustaining principles of order and harmony are also most evident through it. Through sight not only knowledge but wisdom may thus be attained, or at least approached, "rectifying the revolutions within our head, which were distorted at our birth, by learning the harmonies and revolutions of the universe, and thereby making the part that thinks like unto the object of thought" (90d).

Plato's ambivalent attitude toward painting (and therefore toward sense) was remarked by Panofsky,[1] who observed that although disapproval is certainly Plato's dominant attitude toward it, he also occasionally spoke of painting in more positive terms. So in the *Republic* (VI.501), he compared the state fashioned by philosophers to "the fairest painting," made by looking now "at justice, beauty, sobriety and the like as they are in the nature of things," now at what they wished to realize by the constitution of their state, "deriving their judgment from that likeness of humanity which Homer too called, when it appeared in men, the image and likeness of God." Painting could in some sense look to the ideal, to that by virtue of which some are seen to be more beautiful – or godlike – than others, and in some way cause this to appear. Insofar as it could do this, painting was, in the term used by Panofsky, "heuretic." It both invents and discovers, and by

[1] *Idea*, p. 3. On Plato and the arts, see most recently E. Keuls, *Plato and Greek Painting*, Leiden, 1978.

doing so reveals true knowledge. Nor is this "finding" a mere expression of inner vision. The imagined painters "would erase one touch or stroke and paint another until in the measure of the possible they had made the character of men pleasing and dear to God as may be."[2] The painter and the philosopher-statesman fashion a perfect man within the measure of the possible.

Plato's words imply that the painter is able through a continual series of adjustments to realize a beauty like the beauty that distinguishes some human beings from others. His two statements may be reconciled by saying that insofar as it merely reflects, and merely serves to transcribe, appearances, painting is of no value; but insofar as it helps to uncover and to realize the higher, painting is worthy, a means by which the eye may be not simply an organ of sense but a privileged organ of sense, an indispensable tool for the understanding and realization of more than we can know by simple or lesser sensation. Painting may thus be a source of knowledge and even of wisdom, magnifying the power of sight itself. It is heuretic not only in that it may have access to the ideal, but in the actual process of realizing the ideal, and finding the visual relations that give its figures the splendor and inevitability of the godlike.

With this in mind, we may proceed to the second major text on the primacy of sight, the opening lines of Aristotle's *Metaphysics* (980a). Aristotle justified his famous assertion that all men by nature desire to know by referring to our delight in sense, and especially in sight. "For not only with a view to action, but even when we are not going to do anything, we prefer seeing (one might say) to everything else. The reason is that this, most of all the senses, makes us know and brings to light many differences between things." Characteristically of each of them, Plato praised sight for its ability to apprehend what might be true; Aristotle, for its ability to make the greatest number of discriminations, although it must quickly be added that a belief in the heuretic function of sight is common to both of them.

These two texts reinforced each other in a long tradition, and the wear of some two millennia hardly shows in their repetition by the Renaissance Neoplatonist Leone Ebreo. The ideas bear the clear imprint of late antiquity and the Christian Middle Ages, but they are still substantially unchanged. According to Leone Ebreo, sight is the most spiritual of the external senses because it "sees things that are in the last circumference of the world" [that is, the fixed stars], and "comprehends all their species without passion whatsoever" [that is, without being materially modified in sensation]. The eye "knows [*conosce*] distances, colors, positions, movements, and everything of this world with many particular differences, as if the eye were a spy of the intellect and of all intelligible things."

[2] See *Timaeus* 28a, where in the account of the fashioning of the world it is argued that "the work of the creator, whenever he looks to the unchangeable and fashions the form and nature of his work after an unchangeable pattern, must necessarily be made fair and perfect." Throughout, unless otherwise noted, references are to *The Collected Dialogues of Plato Including the Letters*, ed. E. Hamilton and H. Cairns, Princeton, N.J., 1973.

Citing Aristotle, he argues that sight is chief among the senses because it is *il più conoscitivo,* and expands his reflection to the microcosmic/macrocosmic breadth suggested in Plato's original formulation. In the *piccolo mondo* of man, the corporeal eye is to the parts of the body as the intellect, of which the eye is *simulacro e seguace,* is to the virtues of the soul, just as the sun, in whose light sight is possible, is the image of the divine intellect.[3]

The transmission of Plato's pronouncements on sight to the Middle Ages owes to the partial translation of the *Timaeus,* with commentary, made by Chalcidius in the fourth century A.D. Plato, after stating the importance of sight for philosophical knowledge in the words with which we began, wrote that it provided many further blessings, which he did not name. It is clear that he did not value these blessings highly, nor did he wish to see them confused in any way with philosophy, saying that no true philosopher should lament the loss of the sight of them. Chalcidius conveyed this negative evaluation in his translation, but in his commentary gave it a rather different meaning. Even if lower than philosophy, the other "commodities" were still dependent on sight and derived their activity from the true order of the world and the soul that reflects it. "Neither navigation nor agriculture nor even the skill of painting and sculpture [*pingendi fingendique sollertia*] is able to produce its own work rightly without sight."[4] The arts, because sight is essential to them, are rooted in the heuretic nature of sight, which does not so much discover the reasons in nature as it is indispensable to the invention and making of things. To a degree, of course, the understanding of things insofar as they are visible and the fashioning of things that are visible are similar, merely two aspects of the relation of thought to its object. Perhaps Nicomachus of Gerasa meant to identify *zoographia* with sight understood in this way when he wrote that it "contributes to the menial arts toward a correctness of theory."[5] That is, drawing, which participates in the rationality of sight, or in the ability of sight to apprehend *ratio,* is useful in the right conduct of the arts. However that may be, by the time of William of Conches the "commodities" of Chalcidius were identified with the mechanical arts, which minister to the wants and needs of human life. Strengthening Plato's dismissal of them, William associated the lesser arts nourished by sight with blindness and darkness, placing them far from the true vision of philosophy.[6]

[3] Leone Ebreo, *Dialoghi d'amore,* ed. S. Caramella, Bari, 1929, p. 184. For the idea of the primacy of sight as "Aristotelian," see *The Cambridge History of Later Greek and Early Medieval Philosophy,* ed. A. H. Armstrong, Cambridge, 1967, p. 514.

[4] Chalcidius, *Timaeus a Calcidio translatus commentarioque instructus,* ed. J. Waszink, London, 1962, p. 44. Chalcidius may have seen this distinction as that made by Plato between arts concerned with the body and those concerned with the soul (*Gorgias* 464b, 465e, 450b–c), although here Plato's two arts are politics (soul) and medicine and gymnastics (body).

[5] Nicomachus of Gerasa, *Introduction to Arithmetic,* I.2.2–3, tr. M. L. D'Ooge, New York, 1926, p. 184. The ever popular Isidore of Seville (*Etymologiarum* XI. i.21–22), who gives a brief physical definition of sight, writes that it is called *visus* because it is quicker (*vivacior*) than the other senses, or swifter (*velocior*), and is more lively (*ampliusque vigeat*); its preeminence among the senses is shown in its proximity to the brain and by the fact that we say "*see* how it sounds, or tastes."

[6] William of Conches, *Glosae super Platonem,* ed. E. Jeauneau, Paris, 1965, p. 253.

When Hugh of St. Victor took up the question of the arts he considerably rearranged things. It is no longer simply the arts that are higher and lower, but human nature. Man is a "double substance," and one of his essential parts is immortal, the other is "fallen;" he is perfected by knowledge and virtue, through which we are similar to the divine. As for the arts themselves, Hugh, following a distinction made by Chalcidius himself, probably one of the distinctions at the root of his inclusion of the arts together with philosophy, states that there are three works: *opus Dei, opus naturae, opus artificis imitantis naturam.* The work of God is to create what previously was not, and the work of nature is to bring into actuality what was previously hidden (that is, what was only potential); and the characterization of the third work, human art, constructs in the arena provided by divine and natural art. Human art unites the scattered and divides the united (*opus artificis est disgregata coniungere vel coniuncta segregare*). What is united and divided is so only relative to human purpose; thus, the work of art is a transformation of the work of nature for human ends, and because it is for human ends it is "mechanical," *id est adulterinum.* Despite such language (which we shall examine in Chapter 11) Hugh does not mean to place human art outside the pale; by the simple fact of the transformation of natural material, human art shows great power. But human art does not work in conflict with nature; rather, it works in concert with her. Art imitates nature. A house with a pointed roof, like a mountain, withstands the storm; the inventor of clothing must have examined the bark of trees, the feathers of birds, and the scales of fish. From this the conclusion is drawn that man, alone of all creatures, is born naked and unarmed, so that, consulting nature, he may provide for himself with his powers of invention. In this way "arise painting, weaving, sculpture, casting and numberless other arts."[7] All of these arts, to return to Chalcidius, depend on sight, and in some sense are informed by the potential rationality of sight. Sight is at once related to reason and invention. These ideas were repeated through the Renaissance.

When Roger Bacon set out the justification for his attention to the science of optics (*perspectiva*), he also argued that we especially delight in our sense of sight, the objects of which, light and color, are the most beautiful things apprehended by sense, from which, in addition to beauty, utility and necessity also arise, by which he meant that sight is the chief means by which the mechanical arts tend to the needs of human life. Citing Aristotle, he writes that "only sight shows us the differences of things; by means of it we search out certain knowledge of everything that is in heaven and earth." Bacon also adds Aristotle's physical mathematics to the number of things to which sight is uniquely fitted. In addition to optics, we know astronomy and meteorology, and "the altitude of [stars, comets and rainbows] above the horizon, and magnitude, shape and multitude and everything about these things is certified by instruments that work in the manner

[7] Hugh of St. Victor, *Didascalicon. De studio legendi: A Critical Text,* ed. C. H. Buttimer, Washington, D.C., 1939, p. 17. See also my *MLA*, pp. 528–539.

of sight." In words that anticipate Leonardo da Vinci, Bacon argues that all that is to be truly learned from experience is learned through sight, "whence a blind man may find out by experience nothing that is worthy in this world." Bacon praised sight in its practical, certifying role, as an agent of the intellect.[8]

Albertus Magnus explained Aristotle's statement that the senses, and especially sight, are loved for themselves, saying that "only man delights in the use of sense, in things sensed in themselves and *per accidens,* in proper and common sensibles, on account of sensation itself, over and above any other delight arising from advantage or usefulness. We delight in our senses as the font from which all knowledge flows, and we delight in their conformity with the intellectual." Such disinterested delight in sense is the foundation of our desire to know. We "especially delight in sight," which is "more rapid" than the other senses, representing *sensata communia* and *sensata per accidens* (Aristotle's common and incidental sensibles, as we shall presently see in detail), all things that are seen, corruptible and incorruptible. Moreover, whatever is seen, is seen because of the action of light and the lighted, which are "the first forms of all corporeal things." Sight also makes more distinctions than any other sense. The common sensibles of magnitude and shape represent things to us most certainly, and sight in turn represents them to us in a better way than the other senses do, and makes us know them with certainty. Sight is consequently the sense by which we invent (or discover), as hearing is the sense by means of which we teach and learn.[9]

Uniting the theme of the dignity of sight with the equally ancient theme of human uprightness, Aquinas wrote that the human body is upright because human senses are meant not simply for obtaining necessary things, but for the purpose of knowledge. "Wherefore, whereas the other animals take delight in the objects of the senses only as ordered to food and sex, man takes pleasure in the beauty of sensible objects for its own sake." Animals face downward, "whereas man has his face erect, in order that by the senses, and chiefly by sight, which is more subtle and penetrates further into the differences of things, he may freely survey the sensible objects around him, both heavenly and earthly, so as to gather intelligible truth from all things."[10] And when he in his turn commented on the beginning of the *Metaphysics,* Aquinas wrote that "sight judges about sensible objects in a more certain and perfect way than the other senses do," arguing like Albertus Magnus that sight (and, to a lesser degree, touch) distinguishes the common sensibles, and therefore informs us best about the physical world.[11] To follow these Scholastic versions of the theme into the Renaissance, and to Florence,

[8] *Opus Maius,* 2 vols., (Parts I–VII, ed. J. H. Bridges, Oxford, 1897; Supplementum, London, 1900), V, 1, dist. 1, cap. 1.

[9] *Opera omnia,* ed. A. Borgnet, Paris, 1890–9, XVI, 1, p. 16.

[10] *Summa theologiae* I.XCI. 3 ad 3. Also D. C. Lindberg and N. H. Steneck, "The Sense of Vision and the Origins of Modern Science," in *Science, Medicine and Society in the Renaissance: Essays to Honor Walter Pagel,* ed. A. G. Debus, New York, 1972, pp. 29–45, quotes John of Jandun to the point that those senses are most *cognoscitivi,* the judgment (*iudicium*) of which extends to more *sensibilia* than the judgment of other senses.

[11] *Commentary on the Metaphysics of Aristotle,* ed. J. P. Rowan, Chicago, 1961, I, p. 8.

Saint Antoninus called sight most spiritual because it is not altered in sensation, at once the most perfect of the senses and the most common.[12]

In all the texts we have considered, visual apprehension is not knowledge but might rather be called the best potential knowledge, knowledge available only through sight. The "common" or "confused" knowledge we experience when we apprehend particulars (which we shall discuss at length in Chapter 9) is identified with *admiratio,* or wonder, which, still according to the opening pages of Aristotle's *Metaphysics,* is the beginning of philosophy. "It is owing to wonder," Aristotle wrote, "that men both now begin and at first began to philosophize . . . and a man who is puzzled and wonders thinks himself ignorant (whence even the lover of myth is in a sense a lover of wisdom, for myth is composed of wonders) . . . all men begin, as we said, by wondering that things are as they are, as they do about self-moving marionettes, or about the solstices or the incommensurability of the diagonal of a square with the side" (983a14ff.). Knowledge begins from the manifestness of particular things of which we do not know the causes, and our disinterested delight in sense is concentric with the disinterested delight we take in philosophy, which only begins when major practical problems have been solved. Consistently with these ideas, and representatively, Saint Antoninus argued that *admiratio* causes delight because it is a "certain desire of knowing; it occurs when we see the effect, but the causes surpass our understanding." The contemplation of the known is greater than inquiry after the unknown, but seeking is more delightful as it proceeds from greater desire. "Whence man delights most in those things that are newly invented or said."[13] Here an extremely important addition has been made; *admiratio* is caused by the *novitas* of human "creative" activity. *Admiratio* is thus not simply amazement or the ignorance of causes, but the prerational apprehension of particulars, which here presses for differentiation from potential knowledge. The implication is that we wonder at *novitas* for its own sake and therefore because of its very particularity, not just because the apprehension of the particular is the prelude to rational knowledge. In a remarkable text, Vincent of Beauvais, apparently enlarging upon Aristotle's inclusion of both myths and automatons together with the solstices as sources of wonder, compares nature and the products of human *ingenium* in point of *varietas,* which becomes at once an aesthetic principle and an explanation of *admiratio.* In the careful consideration of the smallest muscle, he writes, stupefaction of the mind is engendered, because, again, we see the effect, but the cause surpasses our understanding. We are moved by such experience, he says, to praise the Creator.[14] But we also marvel at the *varietas,* and we are moved by such experience, which sight best gives us, to understand causes.

To return to our immediate theme of the primacy of sight, and to bring it to the Renaïssance, a period the characteristic forms of which are intricately involved

[12] *Sancti Antonini Archiepiscopi Florentini ordinis praedicatorum Summa Theologica,* Verona, 1750, tit. II, cap. II, II (facs. Graz, 1959, vol. 1, col. 71E).

[13] Ibid., tit. VI, II (vol. I, col. 467); citing Aquinas *Summa theologiae* I.II.32.

[14] *Speculum naturale,* Douai, 1624 (facs. Graz, 1964), XXIX, cap. xi.

Fig. 3. Matteo de' Pasti, *Portrait Medal of Leon Battista Alberti,* ca. 1446–50. National Gallery of Art, Washington: Samuel H. Kress Collection.

with sight and with reflection upon sight, we may briefly consider the words of two figures whose ideas we shall examine in detail in what follows. Leon Battista Alberti, explaining his own emblem of the winged eye (Fig. 3), praises the eye as "more powerful than anything, swifter, more worthy; what more can I say? It is such as to be the first, chief, king, like a god of human parts. Why else did the ancients consider God as something akin to an eye, seeing all things and distinguishing each separate one."[15] The writings of Leonardo da Vinci may be regarded as the culmination of the ideas we are tracing, not because he repeated these ideas so enthusiastically, but because he translated them into a lifetime of pursuit of the *admiratio* engendered by seeing, and to the invention of pictorial schemata that were to be fundamental to painting for centuries. He praised sight in his treatise on painting in the following well-known words:

> Whoever loses vision loses the sight and beauty of the universe, and remains like one buried alive in a tomb in which he has only movement and life. Now, do you not see that the eye embraces the beauty of the whole world? It is master of astronomy, it makes cosmography, counsels and corrects all the human arts, moves men to different parts of this world, is the prince of mathematics; its sciences are most certain, it has measured the height and size of the stars, generated architecture, perspective and divine painting. O most excellent painting, above all other things created by God, what praises are there to express your nobility? What people, what tongues may fully express your true operation? The eye is the window of the human body through which it examines its way in the world and enjoys the beauty of the world. Because of this the soul is content in its human prison, and without sight this human prison is its torment; by means of the eye human industry has found fire, so that the eye itself reacquired that which darkness had previously taken

[15] R. Watkins, "L. B. Alberti's Emblem, the Winged Eye, and his name, Leo," *Mitteilungen des Kunsthistorischen Institutes in Florenz,* 9, 1960, pp. 256–257.

away. The eye has ornamented nature with agriculture, and delightful gardens. But what need is there to extend myself in such heights and lengths of discourse? What has not been done by the eye? It moves men from east to west, has found navigation; it surpasses nature because things made by nature are finite, and the works that the eye commands of the hands are infinite, as the painter shows in his feignings of infinite forms of animals, herbs, plants and places.[16]

Sight and memory

The notion of the special dignity and priority of the sense of sight also entered the tradition at the very foundation of the art of rhetoric, and its formulation much preceded – and perhaps very much influenced – the representationalist psychology of Aristotle with which we shall be mostly concerned in what follows. The late sixth-early fifth-century poet Simonides – the one who is supposed to have said that painting was mute poetry, poetry a speaking painting[17] – was also the inventor of the art of memory. As Cicero tells the story,[18] Simonides was miraculously spared from the collapse of the roof over a banquet hall, and he identified the mangled remains of the victims by remembering where each had been sitting. (A comparable story of a royal banquet and prodigious visual memory is told by Pliny of the great painter Apelles.)[19] From his experience Simonides drew the conclusion that our mind is shaped first of all by what comes to it through sense, and that of all of our senses, the sense of sight is *acerrimus*. Things heard or thought are more powerfully apprehended if they are conveyed to the mind "with the recommendation of the eyes," so that things "far from the judgment of sight" have some form and are as if seen. The art of memory thus came to consist of visualizable places, in which mental images were formed and arranged, like a wax writing tablet with letters written on it. But what was imagined was not just a wax writing tablet, it was also a painting. In order to be remembered, things must be arranged clearly, at moderate distances, with the power to penetrate the mind, "on the system and method of a consummate painter distinguishing the positions of objects by modifying their shapes."

The principle of the memorability of the inner visual was extended beyond the art of memory proper to become one of the basic principles of rhetoric itself, that the first appeal of speech was to the inner eye of the beholder, and that

[16] Leonardo da Vinci, *Treatise on Painting* [*Codex Urbinas Latinus 1270*], ed. and tr. A. P. McMahon, Princeton, N.J., 1956, I, 34. See also J. Bialostocki, "The Eye and the Window: Realism and Symbolism of Light-Reflections in the Art of Albrecht Dürer and his Predecessors," *Festschrift für Gert von der Osten*, Cologne, 1970, pp. 159–176, and, on the eighteenth century with some review of earlier sources, H. von Einem, "Das Auge, der Edelste Sinn," *Wallraf-Richartz-Jahrbuch*, XXX, 1968, pp. 275–286.

[17] See R. W. Lee, *Ut Pictura poesis. The Humanistic Theory of Painting*, New York, 1967, p. 3 and passim.

[18] *De oratore* II.354–357 (2 vols., tr. E. W. Sutton and H. Rackham, Cambridge, Mass.–London, 1942).

[19] Pliny the Elder, *Natural History* XXXV.89.

conviction was achieved, or could be achieved, when the matter being argued stood as if real before the inner eye of the listener. And not only did the principle govern classical rhetoric, but it was taken up again in the late Middle Ages, now reinforced by the psychology of Aristotle, the writings of the pseudo-Dionysius, and the theology of the great Scholastics.[20] The tradition was sufficiently broad and long to have shaped the discussion of rhetoric, poetry, and painting through the Renaissance, and it is certainly the case that Alberti's rhetorical definition of pictorial composition – the first utterance of Renaissance art theory – made his *istoria* not only pleasing and convincing but memorable.[21]

Inner vision

Before leaving the theme of the dignity of sight we must also consider the endlessly elaborated notion of inner vision. Not only is sight reason-like, but reason is sight-like. We shall consider this idea in two major examples, but we shall find it continually intertwined with our subjects, and especially with the central theme of judgment.

Near the end of the sixth book of the *Republic* (507bff.), Socrates remarks that there are some beautiful things that can be seen, others that can be thought. Those that can be seen are seen with the sense of sight. "Have you observed . . . how much the greatest expenditure the creator of the senses has lavished on the faculty of seeing and being seen?" Seeing and being seen, vision and color, are distinguished from the activities of other senses because they are made possible by the noble medium of light. The source of light is the sun, and the eye is the most sunlike. For its part, the sun is not vision but, as the cause of vision, is beheld by vision. This relationship provides the basis for analogy between the world of things that can be seen and the world of things that can be thought. The idea of the good is the sun, and reason is like an inner eye that perceives the goodness of things. The mind that knows things in their intelligibility seems to know them in a kind of light that becomes dark as they enter the realm of coming to be and passing away, just as forms in the light of day become dim with darkness. At the same time, the idea of the good nourishes objects of knowledge as the sun nourishes the things of the world. The idea of the good "is sovereign over the intelligible order and region" and the sun is sovereign "over the world of the eyeball, not to say the skyball." That is, the sun dominates the whole world that the eye can see. In the visible world, images, shadows, and reflections are in the same relation to the objects of which they are images as opinion is to truth in the realm of the intelligible.

Saint Augustine also made sight the paradigm of mental vision.[22] This was

[20] F. Yates, *The Art of Memory*, Chicago, 1966, pp. 50–82.

[21] M. Baxandall, *Giotto and the Orators*.

[22] This discussion is based on *De Trinitate* XI (MPL, 42, col. 997–1012; and *The Trinity*, tr. S. McKenna, Washington, D.C., 1963.) On cogitation, see Chapter 10 of this book.

justifiable both on the basis of vicinity and analogy. That is, as the highest of the senses, sight is nearest to mind; and it is also most like mind. Augustine's psychology was built on a descending series of similitudes of the Trinity, each feebler than the one above it. In sight we can distinguish three things: the external object of vision, the act of sensation in the eye, and the attention (*intentio animi*) that fixes the eye on the object. The form is a likeness or image of an external thing; sensation and attention belong to the subject. The trinitarian structure of perception works in the following way: Sensation and the external object of sensation are substantially different from each other and are bound together by *intentio*, attention or will. Perception is thus always for someone. The temporality of individual existence is integral to it, and this temporality is in turn integral with will. Finally, we choose what we look at and are responsible for our choice.

The trinity of external vision is concentric with an immediately higher trinity of *cogitatio*, made up of memory, internal vision, and will, which directs attention to the *phantasia* in the memory. Both sense and imagination may lead us astray, and we must not live according to the trinity of the outward man. These trinities are not the image of God, but some "prideful and preposterous similitude," according to which the first parents were deceived when the serpent said, "You will be as gods." Still, memory and cogitation are higher; things we remember are spiritual before we remember them by an act of spirit. Memory is defined by sense, but imagination is not, because it can combine things at will. It is thus again more clearly related to will. Will, and ultimately *free* will, thus cuts through perception and imagination, linking them to the very nature of the soul. On this view real perception and imagination are not separable from questions of value and responsibility. We shall encounter these ideas of vision, metaphorical vision, and the integration of both with the will frequently throughout this book.

2

The fallacies of sight

Illusion and hierarchy

If according to Plato sight can perceive more that the mind can know than any of the other senses can, everything that sight perceives is not true. Plato also strongly associated the realm of sense with the irrational, an association from which sight was by no means exempt. His definition of the relation between reason and sense had the broadest and deepest influence, and largely on his authority it was assumed and believed that no wisdom, or even knowledge, was to be found in the realm of sense. Precisely because it showed us most about this realm, sight was most often deceived, since what it showed us was always fleeting and incomplete; and when catalogues of the deceptions of sense were drawn up, deceptions of sight always far outnumbered those of the other senses. I have therefore called this short section "The Fallacies of Sight."

In the famous tenth book of his *Republic* (596–7), Plato condemned the universality of the poet, painter, and sophist, arguing that their power to reproduce all things owes to the absolute superficiality of their art, their concern with mere appearances, with colors and surfaces. They do not imitate ideas, or even the copies of ideas in real forms, but rather the appearances of these copies. Since they convince through the imitation of surfaces and colors, the poets are "marvelous sophists"; and to illustrate his argument, Plato used an unforgettable example, the reflections of the surface of a constantly moving mirror, the quicksilver surface of which is a metaphor for the dazzling and dizzying passage of phenomena. Anyone may be universal, like the poet and painter, "if you should choose to take a mirror and carry it about everywhere. You will speedily produce the sun and all the things in the sky, and speedily the earth and yourself and the other animals and implements and plants and all the objects of which we just now spoke . . . the appearance of them, but not the reality and the truth."

A little later (602–3) Plato introduces the theme of the fallacies of sight. The imitator does not know good from bad, but imitates whatever "appears beautiful to the ignorant multitude." Such activity is "a form of play, not to be taken seriously," and results from the exercise of a lowly faculty of the soul.

> The same magnitude . . . viewed from near and from far does not appear equal . . . and the same things appear bent and straight to those who view them in water and out, or concave and convex, owing to similar errors of vision about colors, and there is obviously every confusion of this sort in our souls. And so scene painting in its exploitation of this weakness of our nature falls nothing short of witchcraft, and so do jugglery and many other such contrivances.

Plato evidently has in mind something like his distinction between phantastic and eikastic imitation. He rejects phantastic imitation, which only repeats the contradictions and confusions of sense experience and appeals to a "weakness of our nature," immediately contrasting it with the operations of a higher part of the soul that reasons and calculates, that measures, numbers, and weighs, the more certain judgments of which are always to be preferred to appearances. Plato in effect rejects the possibility of a science of optics (much less of painting), because optics and phantastic imitation must always be based on apparent magnitudes and therefore on contradictions.

Summarizing his argument, Plato returns to the social theme he has raised at the beginning, which he elaborates in a metaphor scornfully echoing the formula that imitation is twice removed from the truth. "Mimetic art, then, is an inferior thing cohabiting with an inferior and engendering inferior offspring." This association of the optical and phantastic (the latter meaning having to do with phantasms or sense impressions, although the issue of imagination is never far off) not only with the irrational but with the classless and "common" will reemerge from time to time in the coming chapters, and is in fact one of the deep themes we shall be following. In general it may be said that as the operations of sense, the lower faculties of the soul and all the arts that depended on them came to be regarded as structured and therefore "rational" in their own right, the consequences and implications of these changes were egalitarian, even if new justifications for social hierarchy of course continued to be devised.

The data of sense – and especially of sight – are thus phantasms, appearances of things in the light, in themselves without truth, even perhaps illusive and chimerical. In writers who held this view, pagan or Christian, images that might seem to us to reveal keen observation in painting or poetry were treated as "phantasms," as examples of the untrustworthiness of sense, and, either implicitly or explicitly, as evidence of the difficulty of obtaining any knowledge, wisdom, or salvation in this world. We may consider an example from Proclus's commentary on Plato's *Republic.* Proclus tells of a poet who wrote of the sun "rising" from a lake as proceeding according to his *phantasia.*[1] He meant by this that the poet

[1] Cited by M. W. Bundy, *The Theory of Imagination in Classical and Medieval Thought*, Urbana, Ill., 1927, p. 142.

had described just what he saw, what we might call an "impression," a phenomenon we associate with "pure vision," as in fact Proclus's words must inevitably remind a modern reader of Monet's *Impression: Sunrise.* To us, the "sun rising from the lake" is merely descriptive and involves no contradiction. But for Proclus such a description stood at odds with the real state of affairs, which was, as he understood it, that the sun orbited the world. For Proclus the description was clearly not "real" at all, but rather – as we still say – was only what the poet "seemed to see."

Writers on rhetoric urged the use of such *phantasia* for the purpose of setting the subject treated clearly before the eyes of the listener, which was one of the chief goals of the orator.[2] But this was nothing more than the positive presentation of what Plato condemned. As his comparison of painter, poet, and sophist makes clear, Plato was deeply distrustful of rhetorical art, and for precisely the reason that it dealt only with appearances, presenting glittering surfaces to fool the unwary, making the false seem true. And so he might have rejected such a pictorial device on two grounds: because it was an illusory, infinitely possible play around reality; and because, insofar as it inevitably stood apart from the truth, it was deeply related to fiction.

Illusion and knowledge

The issues involved are in fact momentous because the question of the value of sense data raises the further questions of whether or not sense is the sole source of knowledge and, beyond that, of how the intelligible is known through the sensible, the relation of the intelligible to the sensible, and the nature of the reality of the intelligible. The standard illustration used as an argument against the claim that we know only through the senses was a phantasm similar to the one we have just considered: the contention attributed to Epicurus that the sun is as it appears to be, little more than a foot in diameter.[3] This example spoke at once for the necessity of the intervention of higher powers of the soul in order for right judgments to be made, and at the same time, because such judgments were in fact made, demonstrated the existence of faculties of the soul higher than sense.

The mention or enumeration of the "fallacies" of sense (or sight) was a commonplace in ancient, medieval, and Renaissance literature, and always turned around this problem of the relation of sense to truth. If Plato and his followers resolved the dilemma in favor of reason, Lucretius (as a conspicuous exemplar of a much more limited tradition) resolved it in favor of sense, as did all materialists after him. Both used the same examples. In his *De rerum natura* (IV.426–32), Lucretius provides a long, careful analysis of illusions, among which is his famous account of perspective. "A colonnade may be of equal line from end to end and

[2] Quintilian *Institutio oratoria* 6.2.29–30; and Longinus *De sublimitate* 15.1.

[3] See, for example, Cicero, *De finibus* 1.30.

supported by columns of equal height throughout, yet when its whole length is surveyed from one end it seems gradually to contract into the point of a narrowing cone, completely joining roof to floor and right to left until it has gathered all into the points of the cone." Such appearances aside, Lucretius concluded that the senses are our best and only real guide.

> We do not admit that the eyes are in any way deluded. It is their function to see where light is, and where shadow. But whether one light is the same as another, and whether the shadow that was here is moving over there, or whether on the other hand what really happens is what I have just described – that is something to be discerned by the reasoning power of the mind. The nature of phenomena cannot be understood by the eyes. You must not hold them responsible for this fault of the mind. [IV.380ff.]

The eyes simply see what they see, and that is the foundation of our knowledge. The eye does not form opinions about what is seen, that instead is done by reason, and it is here that endless error arises. Even what we know to be false, we know because of what we are told by sense.

To other purposes, Seneca, accounting for the nonvisibility of the nature of rainbows, invoked the general principle that "nothing is more deceiving than our eyesight, both in what is distant and close at hand . . . an oar is covered with shallow water and gives the appearance of being broken. Fruits are much larger when seen through glass. The intervals of the columns of a portico join at a distance."[4]

The Skeptics turned the fallacies of sight to the purpose of discrediting all judgment concerning the nature of things. Because all phenomena are seen in a certain place, at a certain distance and position relative to us, they never appear as such but only as phantasms determined by these circumstances. Sextus Empiricus defined the fifth "trope" by means of which suspension of judgment regarding external reality is achieved in terms of the uncertainty arising from the concrete circumstances of real sensation.[5] "The same porch when viewed from one of its corners appears curtailed, but viewed from the middle symmetrical on all sides"; a ship at a distance seems small and stationary, but large and in motion when nearby. The same tower appears quadrangular when near at hand, round when seen at a distance. Change of location works similar paradoxical changes in things seen. A lamp is dim in sunlight, bright in the dark; an oar is bent in the water, straight when removed from it. And much as he argued that perception varies with the health and complexion of the perceiver, so he argued that the same sound is different in quality when played on one instrument or another. Like Vitruvius, he also used the example of the illusion of relief in painting.

[4] *Naturales questiones* I. 3, 9. On the fallacy of diminution, Plotinus, *Enneads* II.8.1–2; and A. Grabar, "Plotinus et les origines de l' esthétique médiévale, " *Cahiers archéologiques*, I, 1945, pp. 15–34.

[5] Sextus Empiricus, *Outlines of Pyrrhonism* I.118–123 (tr. R. G. Bury, Cambridge, Mass.–London, 1949).

"The same painting when laid flat appears smooth, but when inclined forward at a certain angle it seems to have recesses and prominences." (In another place, Sextus Empiricus argues that the senses do not tell us the same thing, so that to the eye a painting seems to have relief, but to touch it does not.)[6] The colors of the necks of doves also change as we change our position relative to them.

As we shall have several occasions to see, the Stoics believed that certain fantasies were distinguished from others by clarity and "perspicuity." The *phantasia kataleptike*, the grasped *phantasia*, was "comprehended" or "perceived," and this grasping provided a criterion. Like all criteria, this was vigorously attacked by the Skeptics who argued that the phantasm itself had to be sufficient, even though it was constantly changing and provided only probable knowledge, or opinion. They argued that it was not possible to affirm that one phantasm was more real than another, and that it was therefore necessary to withhold assent.

In Cicero's *Academica* this Stoic position is defended against the arguments of the Skeptics.[7] Proceeding from the Stoic definition of art as the result of "many perceptions of the mind," it is argued that the Skeptics make art impossible, and even make it impossible to tell the craftsman from the ignoramus by denying "perception." How is it possible to act at all if nothing can be distinguished as true? How is memory possible if it is only the memory of the false? And if memory is not possible, how are either philosophy or art possible? Neither those who practice the arts that "perceive things by the mind, such as the geometer or the harpist completing his rhythms, nor those who practice arts that do things by exertion may work unless they have perceived many things correctly."

The Skeptic reply to this argument is that the Stoics, although they claim to believe that the unwise may grasp many things, really argue that true knowledge is above "perception," which means that knowledge based on perception is not knowledge at all, so that it is they, and not the Skeptics, who undercut the arts, denying them the kind of probable knowledge appropriate to them. Still, Zeuxis, Phidias, and Polyclitus would be perfectly happy to know that they knew nothing if they also understood what the Skeptics know, that no one is indisputably wise anyway; and they might in addition be content with their own wisdom, the skill (*sollertia*) that works in the realm of the probable, of seeming rather than being, about which no more than opinions can be given.[8]

The Skeptic does not deny that we have sensations, or phantasms, only that we may certainly know more than sensation, or act in the certain knowledge that our inferences from sensation are more than probable. The inhabitants of Plato's cave cannot turn to see the real marionette show behind them, much less be led into the dazzling sunlight of the world of forms. They must content themselves to be "the quickest to make out the shadows as they pass, and best able to

[6] Ibid. I.91–92.
[7] Cicero, *Academica* II (Lucullus). vii. 22.
[8] Ibid. xlvii. 144.

remember their customary precedences, sequences, and coexistences" (*Republic* 516c–d). The Skeptic finally accepts only the flux of things, only the fallacies of sight; and these are only nothing if truth is possible. If truth is not possible, if there is no criterion, then the phantasms are absolute, and our ability to act in the face of them, however provisionally, is crucial. According to such a view the skill of the artist is a positive paradigm of the practical wisdom of the Skeptic, and to demand that art obey principles of which no one can be sure is to separate it from its own principles.

Yonder see that which now with the west wind rising looks purple, will look the same to our wise man, though at the same time he will not "assent" to the sensation, because even to ourselves it looked blue just now and tomorrow it will look grey, and because now where the sun lights it up it whitens and shimmers and is unlike the part immediately adjoining, so that even if you are able to explain why this occurs, you nevertheless cannot maintain that the appearance that was presented to your eyes was true.[9]

Tertullian, citing the authority of Heraclitus, Empedocles, and "Plato in the *Timaeus*," also condemned the irrationality of sense, and especially of sight, referring to the familiar examples: the stick that seems broken in the water when we know it is not, the square tower that appears round at a distance, the perfectly regular portico that seems to diminish at the end, the high heavens that seem joined to the sea at the horizon.[10]

With Tertullian the fallacies of sight at once returned to their fully negative Platonic significance and entered Christian literature; with Augustine their negative meaning was completed in the simple usage of the term "phantasm" as a synonym for mere illusion, a significance it long continued to have. The negative and decidedly moral significance of this term did not owe simply to Augustine. The Stoics distinguished between *phantasia* and *phantasma*, the first being an impression in sense conforming to a real object, the second a mental image, like a dream.[11] This formulation gave an extraordinary authority to sensation, which we shall have cause to consider again. But it also placed both dream and reality in the imagination, which, as it was for Aristotle, was central for the explanation of action. Thus, Epictetus could recommend that we question all the images that come before us, recognizing that they are phantasms, deciding which of them are within our control, and consistent with our nature, and which of them are not.[12] This placed the constant flow of images from within and without integral to our life and behavior at a distance from a consciousness that constantly subjected them to moral judgment, a conception that must have contributed to Augustine's.

[9] Ibid., xxxiii.105–106.

[10] Tertullian, *Liber De anima* xvii; MPL, vol. 2, col. 674.

[11] Diogenes Laertius, *Vitae philosophorum* vii.50.

[12] Epictetus, *Enchiridion* I.

Deception, optics, and judgment

Before leaving our brief review of the idea of the fallacies of sight in classical antiquity, it must be pointed out that this tradition had positive aspects as well. In the first place, as Tertullian himself pointed out, the fallacies of sight could be explained: the "broken stick" by refraction, the tower by the substance of intervening air, the diminution of the portico by the geometry of sight, the union of sea and sky by the weakening of sight with distance. This is nothing more than to say that the fallacies of sight stand at the phenomenal basis of the science of optics, which in its classical form might be defined as the systematic, usually geometric, explanation of what we "really" see. The phenomena of sight thus might involve (and originally were perhaps related to) physical – and, more specifically, optical – speculation.

But before transformation into the explanations of geometric optics, the phenomena of sight, that is, the immediate reflection of things as they are seen, also had value and these values were once again recognized in practice, in dealing with particular things. Vitruvius, an author of obvious importance to the literature of art, provides an exceedingly interesting discussion of these issues. The same building, he observes, appears differently when close at hand, otherwise when elevated, otherwise still when it is closed in, or standing in the open.[13] In these matters, he says, a great effort of *iudicium* is necessary. "For the effects of sight are not always true, and the mind is often fooled in making judgments based upon them." As an example of such falsehood he offers painting, in which projecting columns and moldings are to be seen, and figures standing forth like statues, when the panel is undoubtedly perfectly flat. He then compares the illusions of painting to one of the fallacies of sight with which we are by now familiar. "In a similar fashion, the oars of ships, although straight, seem to the eye to be broken when seen under water." This he explains by refraction, or by the difference in the medium through which the parts of the oar are seen. Finally, in words that suggest Alberti (although this is a common idea in such discussions, also to be found in Tertullian, Lucretius, and Boethius), he observes that whether rays go from the object to the eye, or from the eye to the object (as the physicists have it), vision induces false judgments; and since sight makes things that are right seem false, and may approve what is otherwise than it seems, it is necessary to adjust the proportions of buildings in order to achieve *eurhythmia*. This is done not by the application of *doctrina* (which would have determined the proportions in the first instance), but by *acumen ingenii*. It is necessary, in other words, not just to counteract, but to work with the fallacies of sight, and this was done by *ingenium*, the natural gift of the architect, and, given equal *doctrina*, was done well to the degree that this *ingenium* also possessed *acumen*. The architect, who in the nature of his art has to work with real bodies in real spaces, might apply

[13] *De architectura* VI. II.2.

his understanding of optics to such problems, but more importantly, he has to bring the building to a harmonious relation to its actually being seen. Such adjustment stands to the ratios of the building somewhat as ornament stands, and is doubly like ornament in that it demands *ingenium* in addition to *doctrina*, constitutes display of skill, and seeks *venustas*, governed both by decorum and the demand of the eye. All of this requires judgment immediate to sense, and in practice a kind of compromise is made between the implications of Platonism and Epicureanism. It is necessary to adjust the ratios in order that they seem to be right. Or, sense is the final judge of the *appearance* of *ratio*. Such judgment arises not only from the fallacious particularity of the building but from the particularity of the architect who solves the problem presented by its real appearance.

3

The harmony of the spheres

Cicero's sense of the beautiful

In his *De officiis,* Cicero, amending the opinions of the Stoic Panaetius on the components of moral choice, began his argument from the absolute basis of those dispositions given to human beings by nature. Every animal seeks its own preservation, and to this end avoids the injurious and labors to provide itself with the necessities of life. All animals seek to reproduce and care for their offspring. Human beings share these characteristics, but are different from other animals in that, whereas other animals are moved by sense alone and therefore live almost entirely in the present, men, because they possess reason, discern causes and consequences, and are able to compare past and present and anticipate the future. The bond of language among men is an exercise of reason, related to family and public life.

The highest human activity is the search after truth. Having put aside the necessary cares of life, we find our highest happiness in seeing, hearing, and understanding hidden and wonderful things. Both nature and reason make man the only animal that senses order, propriety, and moderation. These are seen at once – *aspectu videantur* – and so man is the only animal that senses (*sentit*) beauty, loveliness, and harmony of parts (*pulchritudo, venustas, convenientia partium*).[1]

In later chapters we shall treat in detail Cicero's idea that we sense the beautiful. But in this short section we shall be concerned with the implications that Cicero draws from this human "sense of beauty." Nature and reason, he argues, "transfer" the "similitude" of what we gain from sense from a lower to a higher sphere, "from the eyes to the mind". We assimilate ourselves to that in which our senses delight, and this assimilation is reformative. Thus by our contemplation of beauty, loveliness, and harmony our thoughts and finally our deeds are informed by beauty, constancy, and order.

[1] *De officiis* I.IV.

This argument descends from the argument – or vision – at the end of Plato's *Timaeus,* where the eyes are turned to the spheres of heaven, there to find the curative wisdom that will unite the earthbound mind with itself, and with its true object.[2] But here we are interested in Cicero's argument as an example of an even deeper habit of thought, which might be called the assumption of the heuretic value of the aesthetic, the assumption that aesthetic experience tells us more than itself, that it indicates something like itself, but higher. In Chapter 1 we examined the idea that the *admiratio* felt in the face of the particular was the prelude to more or less general knowledge about it. Now we shall consider the assumption that the apprehension of such characteristics as order and harmony also give on to higher understanding, that the experience of the beautiful is in some way access to the good and the true. This assumption may be primarily responsible for the great and enduring significance that what we now call aesthetic experience has been felt to have in Western culture. At the same time, it must also be seen to be responsible for much of the confusion surrounding the word "aesthetic."

Although the sense of the beautiful is possible only for a rational animal, it is important to stress that the apprehension of the beautiful, the lovely, and the harmonious is not an apprehension of reason. We sense these qualities at once; we intuit them about particulars, and in some way we know them because of a conformity with our simplest human nature. From this intuition, which is inseparable (still in Cicero's view) from human sensation, the inference may be made that the cause, not just of sensing something but of our *delighting* in sensing it, is in conformity with it, that is, that what delights sense, over and above being merely truly sensed, is also truly sensed as beautiful. On such a view, the apprehension of the beautiful is as absolute as sensation, and is a solid basis for building away from sensation, like abstraction. Thus delight in sound became the laws of musical harmony, which in turn became a hypothesis about the structure of the universe itself.

It is sufficient for our present purposes simply to have raised the issue of the heuretic value of the aesthetic, and we can here follow only one of its implications, which is of central concern to us. If we think from the particular to the general, from events to "laws" and "rules," then the second level of reflective aesthetic experience may come to be regarded as the "true" experience, as the "laws of harmony" may come to mean "music"; but when this occurs the origin of these laws is forgotten, which is, of course, to relinquish the possibility of finding new "laws" by cutting all generalization away from its vital source in sense.

[2] Vitruvius, *De architectura,* II.1.2. describes how men were brought from a savage to a civilized state, first by the discovery of fire. Language followed, then assemblies, which needed to be housed. They found themselves by nature different from other animals in two respects: They did not walk with their heads to the ground, but rather upright, facing the stars; and they easily did what they wished with their hands and fingers. Perhaps the most often repeated version of this theme is Ovid, *Metamorphoses* I.85–86.

Pythagoras

We shall now consider the example of perhaps the greatest and most momentous of these "transferences" of aesthetic experience: Pythagoras's discovery of the basic laws of harmony. The legend of the discovery of these laws was told in variant forms by many ancient authors and repeated by writers of the Middle Ages.[3] Here we shall examine the version given in Macrobius's *Commentary on the Dream of Scipio.*[4] This account begins with a consideration of the harmony of the spheres. This harmony is explained as the consequence of the movement of the spheres, which generate sound, which in turn "comes to the ears as something sweet and melodious or dissonant and harsh. An agreeable concord results when the percussion is in keeping with certain musical relations, but a grating discord results from a random blow, lacking proportionate intervals."

Macrobius wrote as if Pythagoras actually heard the music of the spheres and, knowing that the heavens, the great regulators of earthly time, were pervaded by reason, assumed that *ratio* and harmony must be related. Pythagoras then "ascertained with his eyes and hands what he had been searching for in his mind." He noticed in the beating of hammers on an anvil that harmonies were always produced when two hammers struck together, and, after varying the conditions, determined that this happened because of the proportions between the weights of the hammers. Pythagoras thus determined that there was a relation between a quality of sound – harmony – and quantity, and in his subsequent investigations with stringed instruments established that there was a relation between fundamental harmonies and simple ratios of whole numbers. This established the base of Greek music and, by the kind of "transference" to which Cicero referred, provided the basis for cosmology that Pythagoras sought.

Once the science of music had been defined, or once harmony had come to mean its mathematical explanation, it was easy to forget that its laws were in fact rooted in sense, and in the judgment of sense that the harmonies were first of all heard. But it was because of the origin of rule in sense that Aristoxenus could argue that the ear is the final judge of harmony, even if all the intervals determined by the ear are not reducible to the simple ratios of Pythagorean music.[5] Pythagoras's discovery was truly epochal because it seemed to establish the heuretic relationship between the experience of the beautiful, the rational, and the frame of the world at large. At the same time, the reasons of sense became the basis for systems the development of which cut harmony away from its simple aesthetic origin. Although music as a metaphor had developments in Western thought that other arts did not, the story of its origin is little different from Cicero's

[3] See G. E. R. Lloyd, *Magic, Reason and Experience: Studies in the Origins and Development of Greek Science,* Cambridge, 1979, p. 144, for a list and comparison of the various classical accounts.

[4] II,I; ed. W. H. Stahl, New York, 1952, pp. 185–187.

[5] See Boethius *De musica* V.IV; MPL, vol. 63, col. 1288; on Aristoxenus, see also P. De Lacy, "Plato and the Method of the Arts," *The Classical Tradition: Literary and Historical Studies in Honor of Harry Caplan,* Ithaca, N.Y., 1966, p. 127.

account of the origin of the art of rhetoric, according to which those sounds that most pleased the ear were noted and preserved, so that sense and experience became the mother of the art.[6] And whatever developments the art may have undergone consequent to its definition, the practising orator – like the practicing musician or architect – neglected its basis in sense, and in the judgment of sense, at grave risk.

[6] *Orator* xlviii.160–161; li.173; liii.177–178; lvi.184–187.

4

The harmony of the senses

The pleasure of sense

In Plato's *Hippias major* (297e–298a), the proposition is put forward that "beauty is the pleasant which comes through the senses of hearing and sight." Examples of things affording such pleasure are "beautiful human beings, decorative work, pictures, plastic art, beautiful sounds, music, discourses and tales of imagination." Socrates immediately raises objections; although he is willing to concede it might be permissible to say that laws and actions are beautiful under such a definition, it is no easy matter to say why it is that only pleasures of sight and hearing are beautiful, and why pleasures of food, drink (taste and smell), and sexual intercourse (touch) are not. It is nonetheless agreed that we – and ordinary language – recognize a distinction between pleasures of sight and hearing and those of the other senses, which cannot be called beautiful. The argument is also made that the beautiful cannot be beautiful just because it comes through sight, otherwise the beautiful could not be apprehended through hearing, and that beauty must therefore consist in some quality shared in common by objects appealing to both senses.

Croce wrote a brief essay on the "theory of aesthetic senses" in which he jumped from the *Hippias major* to the eighteenth century.[1] But in fact there is a long tradition linking Plato to the eighteenth century, and what is remarkable is how little the terms of discussion changed in over two millennia. To begin with Aristotle, he used Plato's proposition as an example of the ambiguous use of "and" and "or" (*Topics* 146a). But if he used the argument to another purpose, it is probably fair to say that Aristotle's treatment of these basic aesthetic issues stayed within the bounds defined in the *Hippias major;* and the psychological

[1] *Aesthetic as Science of Expression and General Linguistic*, tr. D. Ainslie, New York, 1962, pp. 460–463. See Augustine *De ordine* ii.32; and *De libero arbitrio voluntatis* ii.7,16–19, and ii.14, 38; and Thomas Aquinas *Summa theologiae* I–II.27. 1 ad 3; and I.1.5.4: "Pulchrum autem respicit vim cognoscitivam, pulchra enim dicuntur, quae visa placent."

framework in which he set his discussion was new and, as we shall see, vastly influential. We shall now examine it in detail.

Aristotle defined a sense (*aisthesis*) (*De anima* 424a15–20) as "that which is receptive of sensible forms apart from their matter, as wax receives the imprint of the signet-ring apart from the iron or gold of which it is made." He also argued that individual senses apprehend what each is fitted to apprehend, sight the visible, touch the tangible, hearing the audible. The qualities appropriate to each of the senses he called "special" sensibles, as opposed to "common" and "incidental" sensibles, which we shall consider later.

In themselves, Aristotle stresses (*Metaphysics* 982a10ff.), the senses cannot give wisdom; but they do give authoritative knowledge of particulars, *that* fire is hot, but not why it is hot. "Sense perception is common to all; it is easy, whereas wisdom is difficult and farthest from sensation."

Consistently with their nature, the senses seek conditions in which a mean exists, although they may be said also to apprehend opposites or extremes, so that sight may be said to apprehend the invisible, or taste the tasteless, and sight may also be said to apprehend the overbrilliant (*De anima* 422a20ff., 424a10ff.). Their rejection or avoidance of situations in which a mean does not exist is a judgment. Any eye, even the eye of an animal, avoids extremes of light and dark. But explaining the judgment of sense, Aristotle also used several simple examples of art that caters to sense as a mean. Pure sensibles, the "shrill, the sweet or salt," are pleasing when they fall within the proportionate range between extremes; but usually we are pleased by mixture (that is, by a *relation* of things causing sensation), and prefer harmony to high or low pitch alone; because "the due proportion constitutes the sense, while objects in excess give pain or cause destruction" (*De anima* 425a27, 426b7).

Aristotle gives only hints of the structure of sense beyond its discrimination of opposites. He does note, however, that the sense of taste, the highest form of the most "sensitive" sense of touch, makes discriminations that can be compared to those of color made by sight, and he remarks that there are "about" seven basic flavors, just as there are seven colors, which would further imply that flavors might be artfully combined just like colors or sounds, which last provided the basic metaphor for the whole discussion. Also in the *Topics* (106ff.), Aristotle examined with some care the problems surrounding the language of the judgment of the senses, that "sharp" and "dull," "heavy" and "light," mean different things when applied to objects of different senses, that "color" means something different for color and sound, and that opposition has a different significance for extremes (e.g., light and dark) and means between them.[2]

[2] On the mean and the structure of sensation, see T. J. Tracy, *Physiological Theory and the Doctrine of the Mean in Plato and Aristotle,* Chicago, 1969, pp. 197–222 and passim. For similar remarks on the language of the judgment of sense, see Sextus Empiricus, tr. R. G. Bury, *Against the Musicians,* 39ff.

In the *De sensu et sensato* (443b), Aristotle remarks that only man is sensible of agreeable and disagreeable odors, noting that animals do not shun the disagreeable, only the positively noxious, which harms them or taints their food (445a). Only man enjoys the fragrance of flowers (444a31–33). Little is made in the *De sensu* of this principle, which is, however, fundamentally important because it implies that there is, or can be, a qualitative difference between human and animal sensation. The idea was, however, given a somewhat fuller development in the *Nicomachean Ethics.* In his consideration of the virtue of temperance (1117b23), Aristotle remarks that we do not call those who delight in objects of vision, such as colors and shapes and painting, temperate or self-indulgent even though they are concerned with sensation and even though there may be a proper and excessive degree of such delight. He explains this by saying that only man takes pleasure in sense. Other animals do so only "incidentally." That is, dogs do not delight in smelling hares, rather they delight in eating them, and their pleasure in the smell of a hare is in anticipation of that end. Such "disinterested" human experience is, moreover, associated with the judgment of sense as such. The glutton is intemperate because he literally eats indiscriminately. He only *feels* his food, and touch (here opposed to taste) is the most common and beastly of the senses. He who eats in order to enjoy the pleasures of "higher" touch (or taste) is presumably like the lover of paintings, and is not intemperate in his enjoyment. Rather than simply taking pleasure in the touch of food, he discriminates flavors, thus taking delight in the function of his own sense of taste *as a mean.* For taste is the judgment of flavors (*Gustus enim, est iudicium saporem,* according to the translation of Grosseteste).[3]

These arguments imply that the qualitative difference between human and animal sense is that human sense is the immediate object of reflection. A human world may be built on this foundation.

Perhaps the fullest account of reflective sensation in Aristotle's writings is to be found at the beginning of the *Metaphysics,* where the ascent from sensation to intellect is described. Here, however, as we have seen, reflection upon sensation is presented as the source of knowledge, and this compiicates the matter. Our natural delight in knowledge is evident in our love of our senses, "for even apart from their usefulness they are loved for themselves." Here Aristotle has laid the base for the argument that follows, saying that we are aware of our senses as such, that is, that we are reflectively aware of sensation as defined by the senses. The same applies to the highest of the senses, to sight. "For not only with a view to action, but even when we are *not going to do anything,* we prefer seeing to everything else" (my emphasis). He praises sight, as we have seen, because it makes many distinctions and "makes us know." Two things may be concluded from this, that we may delight in the discriminations made by sight *and* that these discriminations are heuretic in a high degree.

[3] Grosseteste, *Nicomachean Ethics* 1117b23.

Aristotle separated the arts into those pursued for the sake of utility, those pursued for recreation and pleasure, and those pursued for neither (*Metaphysics* 981b12ff.). He imagined a compact history corresponding to his distinction between experience and art. At first those were admired and "thought wise and superior to the rest" who invented useful arts. But as time went by there appeared arts whose knowledge did not aim at utility, and precisely because their arts did not arise from the exigencies of life, the inventors of these "were naturally regarded as wiser." Finally, there emerged arts that were neither essentially useful nor pleasant, and this occurred together with leisure. It was because the priests of Egypt were allowed to be at leisure that mathematics was discovered there.

The "arts of recreation" (or which "give pleasure") in this scheme occupy a middle position. They are higher than the useful arts precisely because they are not useful, but although they are not useful, they are not concerned with unchanging principles. Some light may be thrown on the nature of these arts once again by an argument set out in Book VII of the *Nicomachean Ethics*. Aristotle is considering objections to the idea that pleasure is a good. Pleasures arise when we are exercising some faculty; it is the "activity of the natural state." Thus, the pleasure of sense (to use our example) consists in conformity to the structure (not, as he insists, in the process) of sensation. It is clear that Aristotle does not regard the pleasure of sense as a very high kind of pleasure, and that such pleasure should in most circumstances be superseded by other satisfactions, fulfillments of other aspects of human nature. But in principle his argument is consistent through the whole scale of pleasures; pleasure arises from the perfection of, or accommodation to, nature. This position allows him to answer the objection of those who say that there is no art of pleasure, and that every good is the product of some art. Pleasure, he says, is not the product of art because there is no art of any activity, but "only of the corresponding faculty," and he adds that the arts of the perfumer and cook are arts of pleasure.[4]

By this argument, an art that addresses itself to sense would not simply be the ability to do something, but the ability to do something in conformity with the faculties relevant to it, and a definition of these faculties would, of course, be of fundamental importance for the conduct of art; one cooks differently in the belief that the sense of taste is a mean. The art of cooking (to continue that simple example) would conform to the sense of taste, and experience, or even theory, might dictate what should be done in order to bring this conformity about, at the same time that, in any instance of the practice of the art of cooking, the judgment of sense would be paramount. That is, food prepared according to the precepts of the art of cooking might not taste good, a fact that no appeal to the principles of the art itself could change.

[4] When Aquinas (*Opera omnia*, XLVII, Rome, 1969, p. 429) commented on this passage, he followed Grosseteste's translation in writing that "pigmentaria ars et pulmentaria videtur ordinari ad delectationem, tamen non sunt ipsius delectationis factivae, sed delectabilium" (that is, they do not make delight in themselves, but rather make the delightful).

In Book X of the *Nicomachean Ethics,* in which he considers the question of the highest good, Aristotle distinguishes pleasure from change by comparing it to sight. Just as vision is whole and complete at each moment, so is pleasure. He then continues this analogy, stating the principle that "a sense which is in good condition acts perfectly in relation to the most beautiful of objects." This provides the basis for a definition of pleasure as a kind of proportion between any faculty and its objects. Although the highest of such proportions is that between the intellect and its object, there are also pleasures of sense. "That pleasure is produced in respect to each sense is plain; for we speak of sights and sounds as pleasant." (When Aquinas explained this, he wrote that "we experience *visiones* to be delightful, say of beautiful forms, and also *auditiones,* say of sweet melodies.")[5]

Aristotle consistently divided pleasures into those of thought and those of perception, and although he ranked these pleasures ("sight is superior to touch in purity, and hearing and smell to taste; the pleasures, therefore, are similarly superior, and those of thought superior to these" [1176a1ff.]), he also recognized that pleasures differ in kind, according to the various faculties, and that so do the pleasures that complete them. Aquinas understood this to mean that we delight in things evidently perfect after their kind. In nature we delight in the sharp-sensed animal or the fruitful tree. In artificial things we take one kind of delight in the "perfection of paintings, which are clearly distinguished by delightful colors," and another in the perfection of images, when they "represent well those things of which they are images." The perfection of a house consists in its being a sturdy shelter; that of a vessel, in its being of a good capacity.[6] All these perfections are apprehended as such because of their correspondence to the appropriate faculties of the human soul, whether those faculties are sensory or intellectual. And it must be stressed that all of these delights are to be kept separate among themselves. Aquinas in fact did not stray far from Aristotle when he wrote that we could delight in color in itself as appealing to sight, or in "representation"; representation appeals to our delight in imitation, which in turn is grounded in our desire to know. This also explains our fascination with novelty, and the extinction of that fascination by familiarity.[7] The generic differences of pleasures are also beneficial to the objects of those pleasures, and to those who engage in the practices producing those objects. So, Aristotle says, "those who are fond of music or of building, and so on, make progress in their proper function by enjoying it." As Aquinas observed, the mind is much detained by that in which it is delighted.[8]

With all this in mind we might hazard a look at the famous passage in the *Nicomachean Ethics* (1106b8ff.) in which Aristotle mentions the importance of the mean in art. When he raises the subject, he has just argued, using the example

[5] Ibid., p. 569.
[6] Ibid., p. 572.
[7] Ibid., p. 570, commenting on 1175a6ff.
[8] Ibid., p. 572.

of an athletic trainer, that the mean is not arithmetical and that it is not "in the object but relatively to us." Art is thus concerned, like virtue, with qualitative relations of neither too much nor too little, relations that may be mathematical only incidentally.[9] Aristotle argued, however, that works of art and acts of virtue are different in that in the first, goodness consists in the "character" of the object, and in the second, in the agent (1105a25ff.). Thus the good character of the work is determined by qualitative relations of neither too much nor too little. In a parallel argument a few paragraphs later (1109b) it is stated that the mean is said to be hard to find by reasoning because the necessity of finding it is always in the face of the particular, and the decision therefore "rests with perception." The work of art is also a particular, and it may be suggested that its character, or evident goodness, is the result of its conformity with sense as a mean. Finally, Aristotle states the principle that "every art does its work well by looking to the intermediate and judging its works by this standard (so that we often say of good works of art that it is not possible either to take away or add anything, implying that excess and defect destroy the goodness of works of art, while the mean preserves it . . .)." At least insofar as it is comparable to an act of virtue, then, a work of art is a particular, the relation of whose qualitative elements can only be determined by the judgment of the sense appropriate to the art.

For Aristotle, sight and hearing were higher senses than taste (and touch and smell) in the order of things. We apprehend many more things that we can know through these senses than through the other three, and the arts corresponding to them are properly mimetic. And because we apprehend so much through these senses, the kind of mimesis associated with each of them involves unique and complex issues. Whereas we only taste the tastable, we *see* much more than the visible, that is, actual vision is more than the discrimination among the special sensibles of sight. We also see individuals and relations of individuals, and if it is possible to think of sensation as such (as a *ratio* in a magnitude), it is no more possible actually to see without apprehending incidental and common sensibles than it is to hear without emotional response and comprehension.

If an understanding of the structure of sense might determine the way in which color and sound are constructed artificially, this understanding would not determine *what* is imitated, and it is with what is imitated that Aristotle was clearly most concerned. The question of imitation was moral and political, therefore also educational. It seems certain, for example, that music was one of his recreative arts. In the *Politics* (1339b15) it is presented as the "remedy to pain caused by toil," one of the sweetest consolations of mortals, which gladdens our hearts. The weariness resulting from the same hard lot that made the invention of the mechanical arts necessary, and their constant practice unavoidable, is soothed by

[9] A similar meaning may perhaps be found in Sextus Empiricus, tr. R. G. Bury, *Against the Musicians*, 2: "it is sometimes our habit to apply the same name in a loose sense to correctness in some performance. Thus we speak of a work as 'musical,' even though it be a piece of painting, and of the painter who achieved therein 'musical.' "

music and by the arts of pleasure generally. But there are higher and lower pleasures, thus higher and lower music, and the higher and lower must not be confused. The pleasures of art may be an illusion; because the attainment of virtue is accompanied by pleasure (as all fulfillment is accompanied by pleasure), and we imagine when we experience pleasure that we have reached our goal. It is very possible to mistake the means of recreation, which make further effort possible, for the end we seek. Aristotle recognized that music is not simply sensate, and that the artful manipulation of sound is not simply a "movement of sense" but is a transformation of the soul through the movement of sense. "Rhythm and melody supply imitations of anger and gentleness, and also of courage and temperance, and of all the qualities contrary to these, and of the other qualities of character, which hardly fall short of the actual affections . . . in listening to such strains our souls undergo a change." Aristotle in effect denies the possibility of "aesthetic distance" for music, painting, and sculpture. We cannot, he says, simply listen to music without being swayed by its mimetic values, an argument he illustrates with the example of sculpture. "The habit of feeling pleasure or pain at mere representations is not far removed from the same feeling about realities; for example, if one delights in the sight of a statue for its beauty only, it necessarily follows that the sight of the original [from which it was imitated] will be pleasant to him." That is, we cannot see an image without seeing that of which it is an image.

It is only for the senses of sight and hearing, or for the *arts* of sight and hearing, that such problems arise, as we have just seen. "The objects of no other sense, such as taste or touch, have any resemblance to moral qualities." The art of sight does not have the immediate force of music, but still painting provides access to similar apparent realities. "Figures and colors are not imitations, but signs, of moral habits, indications which the body gives of states of feeling. The connection of them with morals is slight, but insofar as there are any, young men should be taught to look, not at the works of Pauson, but at those of Polygnotus, or any painter or sculptor who expresses moral ideas" (*Politics* 1340a29ff.; *Poetics* 1448a5, 1450a26).

As for "disinterestedness," the young should study drawing not for any practical purposes (*Politics* 1338b) but to make them judges of the beauty of the human form and also in order to enable them to make correct judgments of the works of artists (1338a19). Because "there seems to be in us a sort of affinity to musical modes and rhythms, which makes some philosophers say that the soul is a tuning, others, that it possesses tuning" (*Politics* 1340b17ff.), the young should study music. But because melodies imitate character, and because some rhythms "have a character of rest, others of motion, and of these latter again, some have a more vulgar, others a nobler movement," it is desirable to pursue each study "only until they are able to feel delight in noble melodies and rhythms, and not merely in that common part of music in which every slave or child and even some animals find pleasure" (1341a10–16). Here, it may be noted the social distinction is not between music and the lack of it, but between high music and low, or between "virtuous" music and "natural" or "common" music.

Aristotle more than once based important arguments on the distinction between a painting as such and a painting as an image of something. Memory differs from delusion in that a memory, as an image of mind, refers to something, as a sensation also does, whereas a delusion is simply an image in the mind. He distinguishes imagination from opinion, saying that we can imagine without thinking that what we imagine is real, just as we can look at a picture of a frightening subject without being frightened. In the *Poetics* (1448b4ff.) he links this kind of distinction to our endless capacity for imitation, a capacity that again marks us off from other animals. It is natural to everyone to delight in imitation, even if the objects imitated are painful to see, even if they are the "lowest animals and dead bodies." We are fascinated by imitation as such, and he explains the pleasure of this fascination much as he explained our pleasure in reflective sight in the *Metaphysics,* by connecting it with our delight in knowing, in seeing that it is an image of someone or something. If we do not know what it is, then our pleasure will be in execution or coloring, which must be regarded as a more trivial pleasure. Imitation is natural to us (in fact, we are the most imitative animal), as is a sense of harmony and rhythm, and it is from this natural basis that poetry arises. In this parallel, resemblance of appearance and duplication of emotion seem to be compared, and at a simpler level of sense, harmony and rhythm are compared to execution and coloring.

It is clear that Aristotle either did not value very highly the kinds of imitation immediate to sight and hearing, or else he regarded them with distrust. Painters, who imitate by "colors and form," either by art or constant practice (*Poetics* 1447a16), could appeal in their paintings to the sense of sight, to our natural desire to imitate and thus to know, but they could only dimly suggest character. Tragedy, an imitation "not of persons but of action and life, or happiness and misery" (1450a16ff.), was the much higher art, showing not simply character but character in action, in circumstances, that is, in which character became actual. Plot is thus primary and character secondary, as, now using the metaphor of painting in a different way – a simple black and white drawing is more pleasurable than beautiful colors laid on at random (1450b1ff.). As for music, Aristotle regarded it as a powerful affective art, able to move us to vice or virtue and therefore open to the objections to be brought against rhetoric, that it was able, simply by appeal to sense, to change our minds and even our characters.

Still, Aristotle occupies an essential place in the history we are tracing because he defined the structure of sense and therefore specified the nature of the judgment of sense. Nor did Aristotle identify the aesthetic – that is to say, what is reflectively evident of sensation itself, which defines the activity, end, and pleasure of sense – with higher intuition, as Plato did, but agreed with Plato in associating its discriminations with the beginning of knowledge. Thus narrowly defined, the aesthetic is the realm of epicures, those who delight in arts that minister to sense;

it is a uniquely and essentially human activity, but insofar as it is defined only by relation to sense, painting is only little higher than cooking.

For Aristotle, sensation is the concomitant of locomotion, and all animals therefore possess sensation. The differences in sensation among animals are sometimes discussed quantitatively (dogs have more senses than worms), and the claim is made that human touch exceeds that of all other animals. But the difference may also be qualitative, that is, they may be said to owe to substantial differences between men and lower animals. The reasons for this ambivalence fall along the fundamental lines discussed in Chapter 3. If the intellect is simply added to sensation, then a dualism of sense and reason (or of the animal soul and intellective soul) is established; and if, on the other hand, human sense is different from animal sense, then sense may be supposed to be related in some way to the constitutively human intellective soul. Aristotle seems to have thought both ways; but he did recognize that animals do not make harmonies of colors and sounds and flavors.

Pleasures of imagination

It is appropriate at this point also to elaborate a bit on Aristotle's notion of imagination (*phantasia*), even though we have not yet discussed more than special sensation. As we shall see time and again, the importance Aristotle placed on imagination can hardly be overstressed, and the ability of the mind in some sense to form images is essential to his explanation of both thought and action. But precisely because imagination is so central it must be distinguished from any of the activities to which it is joined. "Imagination, in fact, is something different from both perception and thought, and is never found by itself apart from perception, any more than is belief apart from imagination" (427b14ff.). By "perception" (*aisthesis*), Aristotle must mean those movements initiated by sensation (429a1) which linger in the soul as memories and which are necessary for the explanation of what we imagine. He means that when we imagine we have experiences, just as when we believe that what we imagine is true or false. We may control our imaginations, unlike our perceptions, which is to say that we can call images to mind more or less at will. This ability is obviously related to memory and to the peculiarly human faculty of reminiscence. Not only may we recall things at will, but we may consider them as such, as phantasms, without believing them to be true or false. Thus, he argues, we may look at a painted image of something horrifying without being horrified by it. Just as that which is generated in the seat of the sentient soul by sensation – that is, memory – is "some such thing as a picture" (*De memoria et reminiscentia* 450a27), so we may simply regard that imagined picture of a remembered thing in our mind's eye.

There is also pleasure to be taken in imagination. Pleasure, Aristotle says (*Rhetoric* 1370a25ff.), "is the consciousness through the senses of a certain kind of emotion"; for its part, imagination "is a feeble sort of sensation, and there will always be in the mind of a man who remembers or expects something like an image or picture of what he remembers or expects. If this is so, it is clear that memory and expectation also, being accompanied by sensation [that is, by remembered phantasms] may be accompanied by pleasure." Aristotle provides examples. A lover enjoys doing things that "remind" him of his beloved because they may make him "actually present to the eye of the imagination. Indeed it is always the first sign of love, that besides enjoying someone's presence, we remember him when he is gone, and feel pain as well as pleasure, because he is there no longer." Similarly we take a certain pleasure in mourning for the departed. "There is grief, indeed, at this loss, but pleasure in remembering him and as it were seeing him before us in his deeds and in his life."[10]

A few paragraphs later (1371b4ff.) Aristotle observes that, "since learning and wondering are pleasant [because in learning "one is brought into one's natural condition"] it follows that such things as acts of imitation must be pleasant – for instance, painting, sculpture, poetry – and every product of skillful imitation; this latter, even if the object imitated is not itself pleasant; for it is not the object itself which here gives delight; the spectator draws inferences ('That is a so-and-so') and thus learns something fresh."

Human and animal sense

If Aristotle did not systematically define the difference between animal and human sense, he certainly defined the problem, and this simple distinction is fundamental to much of the discussion that follows. At the beginning of the *Poetics* (1448b7) he stated that we are by nature inclined to mimesis, harmony, and rhythm. In this he had the precedent of Plato, who wrote in the *Laws* (653e–654a) that animals have no perception of the order or disorder in the motions of their bodies or the sounds of their voices, "no sense of what we call rhythm or melody. But in our case, the gods . . . have likewise given us the pleasurable perception (*aisthesis*) of rhythm and harmony. Through this sense they stir us and become our choir leaders. They string us together on a thread of song and dance, and have named our choirs so after the delight they naturally afford." For Plato this "sense of rhythm and melody" was the foundation of distinctively human life and for that reason the foundation of education, and was to be shaped toward a life of virtuous action. As we have begun to see in Chapter 3, the idea of an innate sense of rhythm and harmony was of great importance for Cicero.

But it was in the more properly Aristotelian tradition that such ideas developed most fully. In al-Farabi's "Philosophy of Aristotle" the notion of disinterested perception is developed at considerable length, and even though this text does not seem to have been available in the West, it represents a developme)f the

[10] These arguments lead a long and significant life in the discussion of love; see *MLA*, p. 124; 491, n. 60.

ideas we are examining that in principle was always possible.[11] By nature, al-Farabi argued, we seek the soundness and the means to maintain the soundness of our body and senses. Our nature thus impels us to the practical sciences. Because we also desire to know the causes of things, we are also impelled to the speculative sciences. In this scheme the senses are associated with the practical sciences. But, he says, we may also use the senses to apprehend what is not useful or practical, "for instance, statues, elegant sceneries, objects delightful to hear and to smell, and objects pleasurable to touch – for nothing else besides having them as pleasurable objects of sense perception." "Pleasurable" he defines as the best apprehension of the best thing to be apprehended, a close variant of the Aristotelian definition of pleasure as a kind of fit between sense and the sensed. It is clear that al-Farabi does not consider such pleasures very high ones, or very far removed from animal pleasures, but it is still clear that he regarded them as distinctively human, and he extended the same principle of disinterested apprehension to higher powers of the soul. That is, we may delight in the harmony of certain things sensed to knowing and apprehending: "for instance, the myths, stories, histories of peoples, and histories of nations, that man narrates and to which he listens solely for the delight they give. . . . Likewise, looking at imitations and listening to imitative statements, listening to poems, and going over what one comprehends of the poems and the myths he recites or reads, are used by the man who delights in them and is comforted by them only for his pleasure in what he comprehends." The more certain such apprehensions are, the higher the pleasure.

Farther along in the development of the "inner senses" (which we shall examine in detail in the coming chapters), Avicenna noted in passing that the interior powers of man were different from those of animals owing to the presence of reason. He lists these faculties from those immediate to sense upward. Because of the uses he makes of compositions of sound, color, smell, and flavor, man has "hopes and desires" that other animals do not have.[12] (By this he must mean that human beings make music, painting, perfume and cooking that arise from

[11] *Alfarabi's Philosophy of Plato and Aristotle*, tr. M. Mahdi, New York, 1969, p. 73.

[12] *Avicenna Latinus*, (IV.3), pp. 35–36. Avicenna *Liber de anima* I.4, cited by M. Kemp, "From 'Mimesis' to 'Fantasia': The Quattrocento Vocabulary of Creation, Inspiration and Genius in the Visual Arts," *Viator*, 8, 1977, p. 356, n. 40, lists the actions of the soul as nutrition and generation (vegetative and animal), feeling, imagination and moving freely (animals), and actions that are proper to man, as perceiving intelligibles, discovering arts, meditating on creatures and discerning between the beautiful and the ugly. Avicenna did not explain this list, which is perhaps from al-Farabi; see *Avicenna's Commentary on the Poetics of Aristotle: A Critical Study with an Annotated Translation of the Text*, ed. I. M. Dahiyat, Leiden, 1974, p. 16–17. When he wrote that the soul "perceives intelligibles" he meant, of course, that the soul perceives the potentially intelligible, not the intelligible in itself; thus all possess intellect, but not all men realize their intellectual natures. Later (I.5) the discovery of the arts is associated with estimation and imagination, and the final coupling of "meditation upon creatures and the discernment of the beautiful and the ugly" may echo Aristotle's association of wonder, delight in sense, and the impulse to knowledge or Plato's argument (*Theatetus*, 185d) that beautiful and ugly are apprehended directly by the soul.

intentions and appetites not shared with other animals, as Averroes wrote that man is moved by song, which beasts are not.)[13] Avicenna does not say what interior faculty it is that accomplishes this composition, although it cannot differ much from common sense or fantasy. All of these arts, it may be noticed, correspond closely to the arts of sense as Aristotle occasionally discussed them. It may also be noted that there is once again no distinction between music and painting, perfumery and cooking, even though all respond to a uniquely human definition of sense. At the level of fantasy, man's "interior imaginative power" is useful for the sciences, perhaps meaning that the geometrician may imagine his proofs, or that, as he continues, fantasy is linked to memory (later he repeats Aristotle's claim that only human beings have reminiscence), which helps knowledge, makes experience possible, and assists in the consideration of singulars. These suggestions are not followed up. They appear in the course of a consideration of "estimation" and imply that there is a qualitative difference between animal and human estimation, as many later writers would argue. But this implication is not developed, and Avicenna remains interested in those "like animals" (he uses the example of small children) who mistake honey for dung because of their common color, that is, in those who are guided by common judgment immediate to sensation.

Plotinus combined our delight in *phantasia* as such (and not just in vision; *phantasia*, according to Aristotle, is so called from *phaos* because sight is the highest of the senses and it is not possible to see without light [*De anima* 429a3ff.]) with our delight in knowing. "Apart from all question of practical utility, objects of sense provide occasion for a knowing which brings pleasure: thus we ourselves take delight in looking upon sun, stars, sky and landscape for their own sake."[14]

Eurhythmia

J. J. Pollitt notes that a distinction may be observed in classical texts between two kinds of *eurhythmia*, one "actual and measurable," the other "optical."[15] This range of usage falls precisely along the lines suggested by the relation between art and sense as we have discussed it, and the two meanings of the word are actually continuous and complementary. Insofar as it is a real building, to be seen in certain circumstances (as opposed to an embodiment of a simple or symbolic

[13] Averroes, *Compendium de Sensu et Sensato*, in *Compendia Librorum Aristotelis qui Parva naturalia vocantur*, ed. A. Shields, Cambridge, Mass., 1942, p. 42. See also Averroes, *Epitome of the Parva naturalia*, ed. and tr. H. Blumberg, Cambridge, Mass., 1961, p. 20. The question of the superiority of human sense had a reverse in the arguments for the superiority of those of the animals, on which see A. O. Lovejoy and G. Boas, *Primitivism and Related Ideas in Antiquity*, Baltimore, 1935, pp. 389–420.

[14] Plotinus *Enneads* IV.4.23.

[15] J. J. Pollitt, *The Ancient View of Greek Art: Criticism, History, Terminology*, New Haven, Conn., 1974, p. 179.

function, or a necessary configuration owing to the demands of construction), a building must be "homologous to sight."[16] This homology may be codified, that is, it may be determined that certain proportions are pleasing to sense, just as it may be determined that certain proportions give rise to harmonies in music. The codifications necessarily become part of the art, and this in turn may allow the art to be related to other kinds of meaning. Music may be related to cosmology, for example, and such properly aesthetic proportion may complement – or even conflict with – the demands of measure (or descriptive proportion), or with the symbolism of proportion (that, for example, the orders of architecture must have characteristic ratios of height to width). But insofar as proportion is homologous to sight, that is, insofar as the rules of art arise from reflection on the pleasing, there is no contradiction between measurable and optical *eurhythmia.* The eurhythmic may simply be the well-shaped, like Vitruvius's *homo bene figuratus,* and it may be the definite proportions of such a pleasing appearance, *unless* in the actual circumstances of artistic construction it is not pleasing to the eye.

It must be insisted that the well-shaped *precedes* normative proportion; that is, it is the beautiful that we measure in order to duplicate the beautiful, and if the measures are repeated and the results are not pleasing, then the homology of sight and the seen has been denied, and appeals must be made to the more basic principle, that is, to the judgment of the eye itself. The major factor contributing to the disrelation between proportion and vision is the particularity of the real building and its relations. It is the nature of sight not only to apprehend proportion but, as a sense, to do so in individual instances. The homology between sight and object is thus always real, never abstract, and the rules of art insofar as they are determined by this homology must consequently be adjusted and adapted to circumstances *on the assumption* that vision itself is a kind of *ratio.* Of the texts expressing this idea, certainly the best known in the Renaissance was that of Vitruvius.[17]

Since, therefore, things which are in fact true appear to be false and some things which are affirmed by the eyes as being other than what they really are, there should be no doubt about the fact that subtractions or additions ought to be made according to the nature and necessity of the sites, but they should be made in such a way that nothing is wanting in the buildings. These changes are effected, however, by the spontaneous solutions of *ingenia* [*acuminibus ingeniorum*] and not simply by the application of learned rules. Therefore it is necessary first to establish a theoretical system for the relationship of parts, from which adjustment can be made without hesitant uncertainty; thereupon a unit of length for the site of the future work should be laid out, and once its length is determined, the

[16] Ibid., p. 170–171, s.v. *eurhythmia,* text 2, from Philo Mechanicus. Philo wrote that when the eye is deceived by the circumstances in which a building is seen, and its proportions do not appear right, it is necessary to proceed by trial and error, adding and subtracting, trying all possible means to find forms "suited to vision" with "the appearance of being well-shaped."

[17] *De architectura* VI.2.4–5. See again Pollitt's discussion of this text, p. 388, and J. von Schlosser, *La letteratura artistica,* pp. 69–71.

construction of the work should follow it while paying heed to appropriateness of proportion, so that the appearance of being well formed should be beyond doubt to all viewers.

According to the simplified Platonic view current in antiquity – and not without its adherents even today – there was an absolute difference between sense and reason, and a necessary antagonism between them. But, as we have seen, Aristotle placed a certain *ratio* at the very doorway of intellection, in the structure of sensation itself, and these ideas were evidently not without both roots and consequences. Sight continues to report the apparent size of the sun even when the intellect sense serves knows the measurable truth of the matter. For the painter or sculptor or architect, whose work made its initial appeal to the eye, the eye had to be pleased or the appeal to higher faculties simply was not made. The colossal sculptures whose objective proportions were modified in order to make them look true embodied an apparent truth discoverable by the eye, an apparent truth that, although it might hinder speculation, was indispensable to art insofar as it addressed sense. It is this division that Plato made in his distinction between eikastic and phantastic imitation, the imitation of the measurable and the true as opposed to the imitation of appearances. But again it is only in Plato's scheme that this opposition is truly antithetical. The possibility exists that when Greek sculptors were said to work – not like the Egyptians, who used a rigid and thoroughgoing canon, but rather according to the "phantasies of sight" – they did so because they considered the sense of sight itself to be a *ratio*.[18] A writer like Vitruvius represents a mean between these two extremes; he, too, recognizes, however, that in any actual building the judgment of sense is essential both to its making and to its being seen. It may be imagined that such ideas continued to nourish the crafts, in the simplest of which the eye finds right relations, even when Aristotle and the whole classical tradition had been all but forgotten. In the Italian Renaissance, which both inherited and developed these craft traditions, such ideas were rejoined to art, with the most brilliant consequences.

Augustine and Augustinians

If Aristotle could not accept the definition of the soul itself as a harmony (*De anima*, 407b25ff.), our susceptibility to music, as we have seen, led him to give some credence to those philosophers who believed it was so, perhaps because he

[18] E. Panofsky, *Meaning in the Visual Arts: Papers in and on Art History*, Garden City, N.Y., 1955, pp. 69–70. From such a standpoint, the remarks of Socrates set down by Xenophon are perhaps more interesting (*Memorabilia* III.X.1.) In conversation with the great painter Parrhasios, Socrates defines painting as a representation of visible objects, which is further characterized as a faithful copying with colors of hollows and ridges (that is, of the relief of three-dimensional forms), of light and darks (that is, modelling), and of textural differences (hard and soft, rough and smooth, the skin of the youthful and the old). The visible as the object of imitation, in short, is presented as a set of opposing qualities. Extremes might be used to describe (dark for night, for example, or wrinkled for the old), but a mean would delight sense, and could only be found by sense.

himself imputed harmony to the senses, the organs of the human soul. Because he understood harmony as a spatial magnitude (*De anima* 408a5ff.), it may be suggested that his comparison of sense to a lyre should be taken quite literally; that, because sense is a ratio in a magnitude (that is, all sensation is through a material organ) excess not only overwhelms the sense but destroys its ability to discriminate a range of sounds or tastes or colors. However that may be, later writers seem to have resisted the location of so much *ratio* in such immediacy to sense, in immediate relation to matter.

Augustine preserved the notion of the harmony of sense, justifying it in terms that must owe to Cicero at the same time that they owe to later Neoplatonism and bring the idea into accord with Christian theology. Augustine insisted that music is physical, that it therefore has its own numbers, and that when these numbers are consonant with those in sense, delight follows. Sense, which is somehow measure and proportion, is a kind of reason.[19] (The actual *hearing* of music, our ability to assemble a sequence of sounds as pleasing rhythm, demands common sense, as we shall presently see.) For Augustine, sight and hearing were the highest senses because they are capable of apprehending numbers, which the other senses are not.[20] Because all created things – even cockfights and worms – possess measure, beauty, and order,[21] they all invite us to the contemplation of the source of such qualities, which is God, and sight, like hearing, has access to the *ratio* that makes this "transference" possible. Augustine did not consider the experience of visual or aural beauty to be an end in itself; rather, he thought that the harmony of the numbers of beautiful things led to the contemplation of God. Music was thus subject to the judgments of the higher faculties able to comprehend harmony in itself. At the same time, it may not be forgotten that the first access to harmony is provided by the proportion between music and human sensation itself.[22]

The idea of sense as a harmony was given new force by the reintroduction of the philosophy of Aristotle, and it is in the Scholastics that we may begin once again to observe it in more nearly ancient form. When Aquinas wrote that "the senses are delighted by things duly proportioned, as analogous to themselves,"[23] he certainly referred to Aristotle's principle. Albertus Magnus also took up the Philosopher's idea, although he located the faculty of judgment in the common sense rather than in the special senses.[24]

[19] *De musica* vi.2.3, and vi.13.38; and *De vera religione* 39.72.

[20] *De ordine* ii.32; and *De libero arbitrio voluntatis* ii.17.16–19, ii.14.38.

[21] *De vera religione* 41.77.

[22] See E. J. Dehnert, "Music as Liberal in Augustine and Boethius," in *Arts libéraux et philosophie au Moyen Age,* Montreal–Paris, 1969, pp. 987–991.

[23] *Summa theologiae* I.5.4.

[24] *Opera omnia,* Westphalia, 1968, VI, pars I, p. 155 (*De anima,* lib. 2, tr. 4, cap. 6). In what will shortly become familiar language for us, Albertus writes that the particular senses are like rivers deriving from a common source, "and this *sensus communis* is a judgment [*iudicium*] about particular actions, which are particular things sensed." It is the means by which the *virtus sensitiva* reflects upon itself and judges [*iudicat*] concerning itself. Whereas the particular senses are passive, the common sense is active, judging and comparing, composing and dividing.

Bonaventure was able to embrace Aristotle's definition of sense because, as an Augustinian, he could immediately translate sensate judgment to a higher plane. He argued that if a thing is "convenient" to its mode of apprehension, then pleasure results. The "convenience" is a kind of proportion, and insofar as the sensation corresponds to the *ratio* of sense, that is, as long as the agent is not disproportionate to the recipient, then *suavitas* will result, "quia sensus tristatur in extremis et in mediis delectatur."[25]

After delight, sensation is subject to a higher judgment (*diiudicatio*). We do not, Bonaventure says, simply judge that this is white, which is a judgment of particular sense, or that it is beneficial or harmful, which (as he understood the matter) is a judgment of interior sense. Rather we seek after the reason of our delight. Following Augustine closely, he argues that the *ratio* of equality is the same in large or small, that is, it is the same without respect to dimension (or matter), it is not altered by movement, and it is in no sense physical. *Diiudicatio* thus leads us through the "vestiges" of divinity in pleasing sensation "into eternal truth by certain speculation."

Diiudicatio, it should be noted, is a judgment of a judgment, and it is finally the *ratio* of sense that is apparent to reason in the pleasure of sense. For our purposes it is sufficient to observe that these Augustinian ideas had the effect of identifying the reflective experience of the pleasure of sense with a higher intuition, and therefore gives an absolute, Platonic justification to the judgment of sense.

Imagination, reason, and will

Before turning to other facets of Aristotle's psychology, it will be useful to consider briefly what became of his idea that imagination played a central role in the explanation of human behavior. The idea had a long and deep life, not least because it implicated images – both mental and real ones – in questions of morality, questions that were both theoretical and practical, and that touched very fundamental pedagogical practices. It should, of course, be pointed out that the notion that images are unacceptable not simply because what they show is unacceptable in itself but because they corrupt the imagination – and therefore the will and behavior – is hardly extinct and, whether this is made explicit or not, points to assumptions about the relation of mental images and action like Aristotle's.

Origen provides an interesting and representative abbreviation of Aristotelian psychology in which *phantasia* is made crucial to motivation.[26] *Phantasia* here is identified with a kind of lower reason, like the later *estimatio* or even *cogitatio,* which is, however, finally subject to free will. All things with souls, Origen argues, move "from within themselves," and they move when an image – a *fantasia* in the translation of Rufinus – identified as a kind of desire or incitement

[25] Bonaventure, *Opera,* Venice, 1754, V, pp. 300–301.

[26] See *Origenes vier Bücher von den Prinzipien,* ed. H. Görgemanns and H. Karpp, Darmstadt, 1976, p. 464; and Origen, *On First Principles,* ed. H. de Lubac, New York, 1966, p. 160.

(*voluntas vel incitamentum*) impels them to ordered and composed movement. So the spider forms the *fantasia* of spinning a web and then does it. They are guided only by this sense in their work. Bees do the same, and so of animals generally. The rational animal behaves similarly on impulses integral with fantasy, but has in addition the power of reason, which is able to judge and discern (*iudicare et discernere*), approving some things and rejecting others. Reason is defined in a way somewhat comparable to prudence and is closely associated with the ability to distinguish good and evil, hence to lead a good or a bad life. Since rational nature itself includes the faculty of distinguishing between good and evil, we choose one or another when we judge, and thus lead a praiseworthy or a blameworthy life. Arguing in a Stoic fashion, Origen stated that we cannot utterly control what fantasies we will encounter, but we can control how we will judge them. Should he be accosted by the sight (that is, the phantasm) of a nude temptress, she is not the cause of his fall, but rather his rational choice, which is free.

It is important to remember how far from intellect and how close to what will be called internal sense *ratio* is in this discussion. Origen himself argued that all animals possess reason – which is evidently the power to discriminate, to do the "right" thing in a situation – but in different degrees, observing that the behavior of hunting dogs and war-horses is near reason. When he translated this argument, Rufinus considerably softened it, saying that such animals only seemed to be guided by "some rational sense," but that they were actually impelled by an instinct more complex than the instinct of other animals.

5

The common sense

Leonardo's *senso comune*

Not to forget our final purpose, which is the explication of the language basic to Renaissance art, it is perhaps best to raise the next question by beginning at the end with a number of remarks by Leonardo da Vinci. In one of his *paragone* arguments, Leonardo compares poetry unfavorably to painting. Whereas painting is born in the light of nature, poetry is born in the *occhio tenebroso* of the imagination. He describes the light-filled process of the real vision from which painting arises as follows: "the eye receives the species, or similitudes of objects and [the similitudes pass] from there to the *impressiva,* and from this *impressiva* to the common sense (*senso comune*), and there it is judged (*è giudicata*)." Leonardo means that configurations of light come to the eye and are impressed upon the seat of vision [one of the surfaces of the eye], whence it is delivered to the common sense, where it is subjected to "judgment."[1] Leonardo's account of visual perception, as we shall see, is a fairly close adaptation of Aristotle's arguments on the subject, arguments he could have had from a great number of sources, and which he most probably had from one of the many writers in whom Aristotle's psychology had been adapted to post-Galenic physiology. What interests us here is the term *senso comune.* As others have noted, this is the Aristotelian *sensus communis* (or *koine aisthesis*), and its activity is quite properly described by Leonardo as a kind of judgment. This echo of Aristotle might be put aside as a mere psychological archaism, were it not that the idea of the *senso comune* occupies an extraordinarily important place in Leonardo's deliberations. As Martin Kemp has shown, his early skull studies are earnest and elegant attempts to establish the location of the common sense according to its often repeated definition as the center of all the senses. The inscription in the middle left of one of these first anatomical studies (Fig. 4) reads as follows: "Where the line *am* intersects the line *cb* will

[1] I. A. Richter, *Paragone: A Comparison of the Arts by Leonardo da Vinci,* London, 1949, p. 20; see also *Treatise,* ed. McMahon, I, 23.

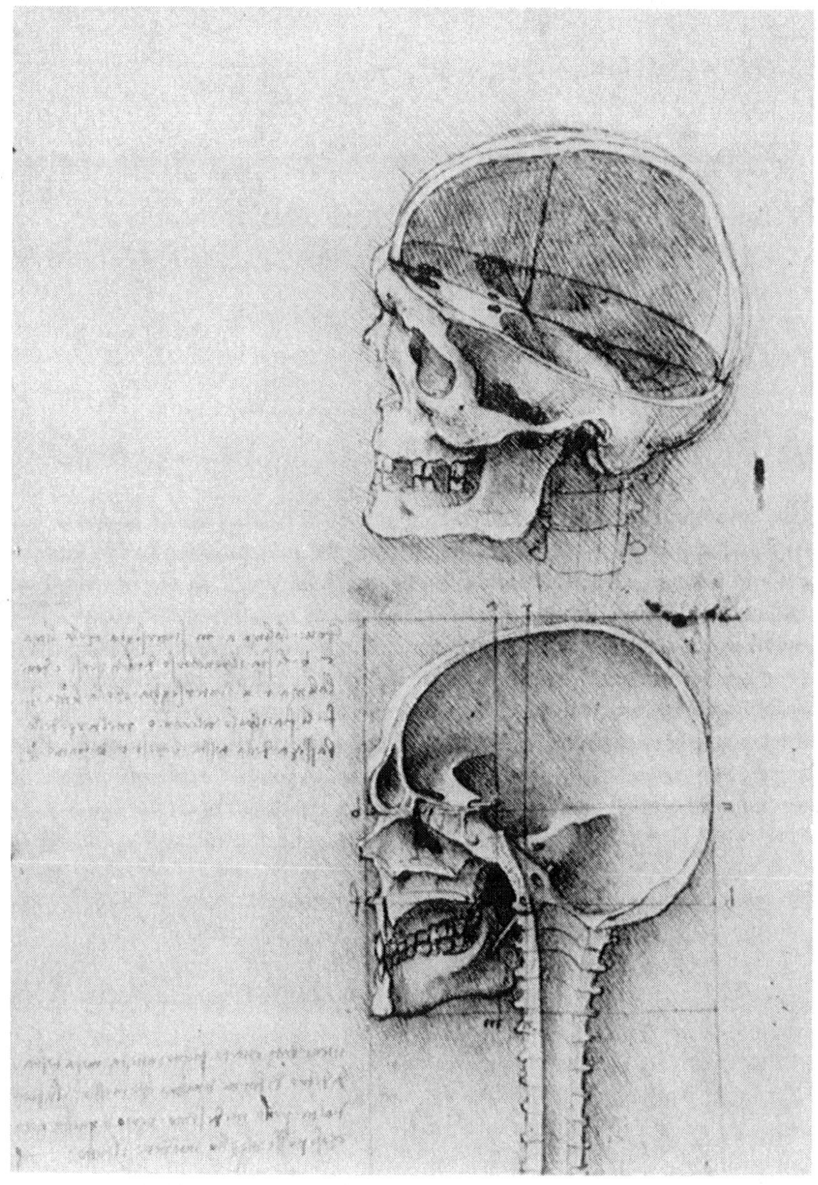

Fig. 4. Leonardo da Vinci, *Studies of Skulls,* 1489, pen and ink. Royal Library, Windsor Castle 19057 r.

be the confluence of all the senses and where the line *rn* intersects the line *hf* will be the pole of the cranium, at a third of the head, and *cb* will therefore be half."[2] Leonardo is not only seeking the geometric structure of the principle of human sense and judgment, he is also trying to reconcile this structure with the proportions of the head and, presumably, of the body in general. In another place, he entertains the idea that "this mind of ours, or common sense, which scientists claim resides in the middle of the head, maintains its spiritual extension for a great distance away from itself, and this is clearly seen in the fact that the lines of visual rays which terminate in the object immediately give to the seat of reason the character of the object they hit."[3] Again we are told that the *senso comune* is that which "judges" [*giudica*] the things given to it by the other senses.[4] But to this simple retelling of Aristotle other more impressive powers are also added. The common sense is "most rapid" in its operation and, as closest to the eye and to the seat of vision, is the prince of the other senses. Leonardo also relates the eye and painting directly to the common sense. "The eye, that is called the window of the soul, is the principal way whence the common sense may most copiously and magnificently consider the infinite works of nature."[5] Here Leonardo has understood the eye, not as an opening through which the soul itself is visible, the usual understanding of "the eye is the window of the soul," but rather as an Albertian perspective window, into which light comes and through which the common sense surveys the world. The common sense is the point from which one sees a Renaissance painting. This passage is at once a praise of sight as the most discriminating sense and an identification of common sense with sight, which apprehends all the common sensibles.

Leonardo did not fail to consider separately the judgmental powers of the common sense, in words that pertain both to sight and to the making of paintings based on the reasons of sight. We know from experience, he says, "that the eye apprehends ten different natures of objects, light and shadow, the first being the cause of the other nine, the second of their privation; the others are color and body, shape and position, distance and proximity, movement and quiet."[6] These are special sensibles of sight (light, dark and color) and common sensibles ap-

[2] See M. Kemp, " 'Il Concetto dell'anima' in Leonardo's Early Skull Studies," *JWCI*, 34, 1971, pp. 115–134; "Leonardo and the Visual Pyramid," *JWCI*, 40, 1977, pp. 128–149; and "From 'Mimesis' to 'Fantasia,' " pp. 347–398. For the earliest representations of the common sense, see C. Nordenfalk, "The Five Senses in Late Medieval and Renaissance Art," pp. 5–6.

[3] J. S. Ackerman, "Leonardo's Eye," *JWCI*, 41, 1978, p. 127. In the Codex Huyghens (E. Panofsky, *Codex Huyghens and Leonardo da Vinci's Art Theory*, London, 1940, p. 60) it is stated that "according to Plato" the eye is to the microcosm as the sun is to the macrocosm: "it discovers and attracts the images and appearances of the objects" and conveys them to the center of the soul, "rettrice del tutto," which is impressed by colors and recognizes forms, bodies, proportions, species, and individual things." The eye is thus identified with the *hegemonikon* (see this chapter, n. 21 below) with which Leonardo also identified the *senso comune* in texts such as this one. The eye is also very nearly identified with the particular intellect.

[4] *The Literary Works of Leonardo da Vinci*, ed. J. P. Richter, London, 1883, n. 836.

[5] *Treatise*, I, 30.

[6] See Chapter 8 n. 68, below.

prehensible through sight, all of which are described as subject to the judgment either of the eye or of the common sense immediate to it.

Still again, the great anatomist explains that the joints of the bones obey the nerves, the nerves the muscles, the muscles the tendons, and the tendons the common sense, and the common sense is the seat of the soul [*è sedia dell'anima*]. And throughout, the connection with judgment is never lost. The five senses, Leonardo continues, "are the ministers of the soul." "The soul seems to reside in the judgment [*parte juditiale*], and the judgment seems to be in the place where all the senses run together; this is called the common sense."[7] These ideas may easily be carried farther. In well-known arguments, Leonardo explained the Florentine proverb that every painter paints himself by saying that the same *giudizio* that governs images as the painter makes them also shaped the body of the painter himself.[8]

In one of his so-called *paragone* arguments, in which Leonardo tried to establish the superiority of painting over other arts – and incidentally gave a powerful impetus to the beginning of the modern critical tradition of distinguishing the arts – Leonardo appeals to the idea of the common sense to explain fundamental characteristics and values of the art of painting. In the *paragone* arguments Leonardo insisted upon the then newly explicit principle that paintings should be like what is visible as a whole, and the idea of the common sense enables him further to explain how a painting is not only a visual unity but an aesthetic unity. In this argument Leonardo compares painting favorably to music, unfavorably to poetry. The difference between painter and poet is the difference between whole and dismembered bodies. The painter shows us things all at once, the poet shows them only partially and sequentially, as if in music the parts of a harmony were to be sung one after the other. In words that – as we shall see – seem clearly to echo those of Alhazen on the perception of beauty, Leonardo uses the example of a lovely face, the "harmony" of the qualities of which is immediately and instantaneously evident. A painting should be like that, and should be comparable to music rather than poetry because of the simultaneity of its elements in harmony.

Music also makes sweet melodies composed of its various voices in its harmonic time. The poet is deprived of the discrimination [*discretione*] of these. Although poetry enters through the sense of hearing to the seat of judgment [*la sedia del giuditio*], just like music, the poet may not describe the harmony of music because he does not have the power to say different things in the same time, as the sweetness of the harmonic proportionality of painting, composed in the same time, is judged at the same time, so in common as in particular. In common with respect to the intention [*intento*] of the composition [*composto*],

[7] *Literary Works*, n. 838.

[8] See M. Kemp, " 'Ogni dipintore dipinge se': a Neoplatonic echo in Leonardo's Art Theory?" in *Cultural Aspects of the Italian Renaissance: Essays in Honour of Paul Oskar Kristeller*, Manchester, England, 1976, pp. 311–323. Professor Kemp would probably not wish to follow all the consequences drawn from Leonardo's text in the present argument. For Leonardo's *paragone* argument, see *Treatise* I.41. See also G. Manetti, *De dignitate et excellentia hominis*, ed. E. R. Leonard, Padua, 1975, p. 29.

in particular with respect to the components of which the whole is composed. Because of this the poet remains far behind the painter in the figuration of corporeal things, and behind music with respect to invisible things.

The *sedia del giuditio* is, of course, the common sense, which Leonardo writes of as having the power instantly to perceive harmonious relations among things present to sight and hearing. These harmonious relations must be higher than simple sensation and "spiritual," because he associates harmony in music with "invisible things." Painting is concerned not only with the visible but with what is apparent through the visible, that is, the activity of the human spirit, and the unity of painting should be like the harmony that appeals to the human spirit. The harmony of painting is not simply visual, and is judged by a higher sense capable of apprehending harmony both in sight and hearing. The common sense is thus a sense of harmony, an idea we shall encounter not only in the writings of Leonardo and his circle but also in the writings of Leon Battista Alberti. Leonardo distinguishes the common sense from memory (because it is not possible for it to judge harmonious relations among things heard over time) and he thinks that the common sense judges the composition both as a whole and in its parts. If this is so, then painting for Leonardo is absolutely dependent upon the faculty of the common sense, which judges particular things and the qualities of relations among them in the very act of perception. The apprehension of the common sense corresponds to the harmonious whole of the painting as Leonardo thought it should be.

Leonardo thus identified the *senso comune* with judgment and judgment with the soul, more specifically with the soul of the painter. We must now ask how this shadowy Aristotelian faculty came to occupy such a position of prominence in the thoughts and activities of a great artist. The answer to this question will occupy us through much of the rest of this book. In order to begin to answer it, we must continue our examination of Aristotle's doctrine of sensation and try to plot at least the outline of the tradition of this doctrine. And to do that, we must first go back even farther, to Plato.

Plato's *psyche*

In Book VII of the *Republic,* which begins with the allegory of the cave, Plato remarks that some of our perceptions do not provoke further thought because "the judgment of them by sensation" is adequate, while others encourage reflection because sensation reports nothing trustworthy (523b). By "untrustworthiness" Plato means something deeper and simpler than the fallacies of sight, such as things obscured by distance or illusionistic painting. The untrustworthiness arises from what he calls the "contradictoriness" of perception. He gives the example of three fingers held up together. Sight tells us that fingers are fingers regardless of their qualities or situation, and such recognition demands no further thought. Bigness or smallness, on the other hand, are relative as reported by sense, and because one thing may be big or small depending on its situation, thought is compelled to consider what it is that may be both. The many qualities of things are all relative, and the mind is driven by these differences in the same thing to think of both unity and duality. This argument is of very great importance, for by it Plato begins to explain the way in which the intelligible is gathered from the sensible.

"Adequate judgments of sensation" are evidently bare apprehensions of particular things. The implied "inadequate judgments of sensation" are not ne~essarily negative, or even inaccurate, but are "wrong" in the sense that explanation is required in order to account for what seems to be the case. The apple appears to be black because it is set against the light, the coin appears to be oval because it is seen at an angle. Any quality or circumstance could also be its opposite (the far could be near, the hot could be cold, the dark could be light), and this untrustworthiness stimulates thought to try to find uniformities in such flux. Plato called the relative judgments of sense "unseparated and confounded," a characterization that was to have a long philosophical life, as we shall see in Chapter 9. He meant that precisely insofar as it made relative judgments, sensation had the potentiality not just to provoke thought but to reveal the intelligible, which was unconfounded and distinct.

Sensation productive of thought serves a central purpose as the paradigm for the proper relation between all knowledge and the highest philosophical knowledge. Sensation itself, then, might be described as heuretic, to use our earlier term, and the arts and sciences, to take a higher example, may be similarly heuretic. Later in Book VII, when Plato retold the myth of the cave (532bff.) he spoke of eyes that, unaccustomed to looking at forms in daylight, looked instead at shadows and at "likenesses and reflections in water." Gradually such liberated eyes would not only adjust to sunlight but would look to the sun itself, not at reflections or phantasms of the sun on the earth, but to the sun in the heavens, whence to understand the turn of the seasons and the measures of time. So the mind turns from the sensible to the intelligible. Sensation is essential to such an ascent. The highest sense of sight is "framed" for astronomy, which is to say that only sight can see the heavens and "provoke" thought to consider the movements of the heavens. The philosopher, however, is not concerned just with the movements of the stars and planets, but with the eternal laws of geometry, mathematics, and harmony that may be seen as more general principles transcending the physical order of the heavens and their orderly change. At this most general level sight and hearing are related as astronomy and music can be shown to be related in their intelligible principles, both pointing beyond these principles to the last unity of the good, the beautiful, and the true. By means of such ascent from sensation the arts and sciences may "lead the best part of the soul up to the contemplation of what is best among realities, as in our parable the clearest organ of the body [the eye] was turned to the contemplation of what is brightest in the corporeal and visible region."

Plato was most interested in the "best part of the soul." This is even truer of later Platonists – up to the present day – and Plato's own concerns with sensation, or with the border of sensation and thought, are a less familiar aspect of his thought. Arguments like those just considered, however, are in essential respects ancestors of Aristotle, and in the *Theatetus* (184ff.), Plato raised and weighed much more carefully the question of the production of thought by sensation.

The *Theatetus* addresses the Protagorean argument that perception (*aisthesis*) is knowledge (*episteme*), an idea Socrates wishes to reject. He also rejects the metaphysical basis of this skepticism, the Heraclitean principle that all things change, arguing that if such were the case there would be no difference between perceiving and not perceiving. The dialogue then turns to the opposite Parmenidean position, according to which nothing changes, still keeping to the theme of sensation and knowledge.

Socrates begins by arguing that the eyes and ears are not what see and hear but rather that by *which* we see and hear. We do not simply contain separate senses, like so many soldiers in the Trojan horse, rather the senses are organs – this is the first such use of that word – of a single power, which might be called "a soul (*psyche*) or something else." All the senses, through which we perceive opposing qualities (light and dark by vision, for example) are parts of the body, and Socrates seems to wish to counterpose the physical senses against a higher psychic principle. We cannot perceive the objects of one sense through another, and thought about more than one sense at a time cannot be done through the senses themselves. At the same time, we believe that both sound and color exist (that is, at the same time that we apprehend them we also apprehend them as existing); that something we sense is different from something else we sense but is the same as itself; that both are two and each is one; that they are alike and unlike. How do we think these things? We cannot grasp what is common to the heard and the seen through hearing or sight, nor may we determine by means of them whether sight and sound are bitter. By things "common" to our sensations Socrates means things that are provocative of thought – being and not-being, difference, similarity and self-identity, number – that are evident in perception to "that part of us which perceives." "You are," Theatetus observes (185d), "evidently asking also through what bodily organs we perceive by our soul the odd and the even and everything else that is in the same category," concluding that there is no special organ like the other organs of sense; rather "the soul views by itself directly what all things have in common." To this list of things apprehended directly by the soul Socrates adds the beautiful and the ugly, the good and the bad. The soul sees these things in relation to one another, "reflecting within itself upon the past and present in relation to the future." The soul also perceives the hardness of the hard through touch; that is, it perceives the essential nature of the sensed, as well as the fact that the sensed things exist, and that they exist in opposition (hard and soft, light and dark). It also perceives the nature of this opposition and tries to judge all of this by comparison. The conclusion is reached that knowledge is not in sensations but in the process of reasoning about them, which demands reflection. Men and animals perceive from birth, but knowledge is acquired slowly and with difficulty, through education. Although the argument is not completed as it was in the *Republic,* there is no reason to believe that this analysis of the border between sensation and thought was not meant finally to establish the difference between the sensible and the intelligible, and, even though a definition of knowledge was not reached, that the argument did not once again provide a basis for intellectual ascent.

Aristotle's common sense

Plato's argument that the senses are "organs," instruments of use, raised the momentous question of just what the entity is that they might be supposed to serve. In the *Theatetus* the matter is left undecided, and Aristotle, identifying the "common sense" as something closely linked to sense itself, placed that which immediately reflects upon the data of the five senses at the base of the intellectual powers of the soul. At the same time, the very ambivalence of Plato's *psyche* points again to the fundamental ambivalence between sense and reason, to the difficulty if not the impossibility of saying where one left off and the other began. In Aristotle the idea that sensation taken as a whole is a kind of intuition was more forthrightly expanded. But already in Plato what immediately reflects upon sensation is associated with both intuition and opinion. This intuition amounts to what we shall call "common sensation," the simple universally accessible givenness of things (that a finger is a finger, a man a man), which possesses "confusedly" in its actual qualities and relations the possibility of higher thought, much as the idea of "form" implied not just visible shape but all that could be understood about a thing. Aristotle would stress that in some way the discriminations evident to the soul must arise both from the nature of sense itself and from the nature to which sensation was immediate.

Aristotle presents his perennially difficult notion of the common sense[9] as if it were a necessary consequence of his treatment of the five senses. This may be attributed to a choice or to a habit of presentation, reasoning from the parts to the whole and reversing analysis in construction. As the matter is set forth, it

[9] On the problem of common sensation, see J. I. Beare, *Greek Theories of Elementary Cognition from Alcmaeon to Aristotle,* Oxford, 1906; A. C. Lloyd, "Nosce teipsum and Conscientia," *Archiv für Geschichte der Philosophie,* 46, 1964, pp. 188–200; C. H. Kahn, "Sensation and Consciousness in Aristotle's Psychology," *Articles on Aristotle. 4. Psychology and Aesthetics,* ed. J. Barnes, M. Schofield, and R. Sorabji, New York, 1978, pp. 2–31; and D. Hamlyn, "Koine aisthesis," *The Monist,* 52, 1968, pp. 195–209. A. N. Foxe, *The Common Sense from Heraclitus to Peirce,* New York, 1962, treats the idea in an essentially unhistorical manner, its title notwithstanding, and lacks much useful scholarly apparatus. It is, however, thorough and thoughtful, and should be used by anyone interested in the long and complex history of this idea. See also S. A. Grave, in *The Encyclopedia of Philosophy,* New York, 1967, s.v. "Common sense," for a discussion of the idea in philosophy from the eighteenth century onward, with additional bibliography. See also L. Turco, *Dal sistema al senso comune. Studi sul newtonismo e gli illuministi brittanici,* Bologna, 1974.

seems that it was necessary to postulate a central unifying faculty because of the differences in the qualities apprehended by the various senses.

For Aristotle the attachment of knowledge to sensation was essential in a way that it was not for Plato. For Aristotle the soul (*psyche*) was an active principle, always intent and attentive. Although it was rational, the human soul for Aristotle was also "animal," grounded in the body and suited to its activities. Toward the realization of its ends, it possessed certain faculties. Why, Aristotle might have asked, do we possess the ability to imagine? How do we use this ability, and why is it necessary? How does it interact with movement and with the necessary activities of human life? Just as Democritus's argument that the act of vision takes place on the surface of the eye could not explain to Aristotle why any shiny object is not an eye – that is, could not explain the functional physiology of the eye – so on Plato's argument none of these faculties could be explained, and Aristotle, while maintaining the basic notion that the senses were organs of a higher, central principle, substantially modified the relation between sense and reason. Ultimately sensation was still "for" reason; but the nature toward which the senses converge is no longer reason itself, but rather a lower unity, a principle of unity in the material individual, dependent on the physiology of the individual as a base. It was to this lower unity that the common sense belonged, both as the origin of special sensation and as the more general principle of a considerable range of human activities inferior to reason. Within such a scheme all of Aristotle's various scattered remarks that have been associated with common sensation can be drawn together.

Aristotle called that in which the power to receive sensible forms resides "the primary sense organ" (424a24–25) and like the activity of the special senses, the activity of this primary sense organ was referred to as a kind of judgment. "Since we compare white and sweet [*et quia iudicamus etiam album et dulce* in the Latin Aristotle], and each of the sensibles with each, what in fact is it by means of which we perceive a difference between them?" (*De anima* 426b15ff). Arguing that like implies like, Aristotle concluded that what perceives these differences must itself be a sense; and in order to avoid an infinite regress of senses judging senses, he argued further that what judges all the special sensibles must be one. This faculty, although it was referred or alluded to fairly often in Aristotle's writings – especially his psychological writings – was never really defined as such, nor were its powers precisely defined. In *De somno et vigilia* (455a12), Aristotle referred to "some part which is common to all sense organs, one faculty of sense and one master sense organ." He called it the "ultimate point of arrival," and, initiating a long tradition of geometric metaphors (*De anima* 427a), described the common sense as a point which is one in itself, but two as it terminates either end of a line it divides (or one in itself and five as it forms the junction of the senses). This central faculty to which Aristotle related the individual senses stands to the data of the senses as the eye stands to sight. "The air impresses a certain quality on the pupil of the eye, and this in turn upon something else, and so also with the organ of hearing, while the last thing to be impressed is one and is a single mean, though with a plurality of distinct aspects" (431a15–20). The "something else" upon which the act of sight is impressed is one and is a "single mean," which, unlike the special senses, which were described in the same language, mediates in many ways. Aristotle (431a22–25 and 426b9–10) even seems to suggest it is the common sense that is responsible for the discrimination of objects of the same sense (for example, light and dark in sight), which would in turn suggest that the common sense was the principle of all sensory discrimination.

In order to perform its function, the common sense had to distinguish the qualities of the special senses, telling, to use Aristotle's example again, white from sweet. At the same time, the common sense also had to recognize that qualities are of one thing, as, to use another of Aristotle's examples, we know at once that gall is bitter and yellow (or that yellow and bitter is gall) (425a29ff.). We may be deceived in these matters, however, because when we see something yellow we may take it to be gall and therefore also to be bitter, or, to use an example used by later writers, we may mistake honey for gall. Error, in short, may be attributed to acts of analysis and composition of the common sense, which thus becomes the first – or most basic – source of error in Aristotle's psychology, special sensation being practically infallible. "Common sensation" was thus linked to the "fallacies" of the sense of sight. As we shall see, for later writers the activities of analysis and composition by the common sense had the status of low-level inferences. But as inferences they are quasi rational, and on this base later traditions of the common sense as a faculty of intuitive judgment was set.

From its central position the common sense was aware of sensation. "It is not with sight that the mind sees that it sees, but with some organ common to all sensoria" (*De somniis* 455a17). And from this notion of its awareness of sensation, the common sense has been connected with self-consciousness in general. In the *Nicomachean Ethics* (1170a28), Aristotle writes that "he who sees perceives that he sees, and he who hears, that he hears, and he who walks, that he walks, and in the case of all other activities similarly there is something which perceives that we are active, so that if we perceive, we perceive that we perceive, and if we think, that we think." He concludes from this that the perception that we perceive or think is the perception that we exist, because existence is perception or thinking, and this is good (because life itself is good and pleasant) and better still when one is good oneself.

Aristotle seems to have thought of the common sense as a kind of interior vision (it *sees* that we see) and it also "contains" images. For Aristotle the completed sensation in the common sense *is* sensation, and it is therefore in the common sense that the sensible world actually exists for us. As the unifier of special sensation, the common sense is closely related to the image-making faculty essential to Aristotle's explanation of both thought and action. The word *phantasia* referred both to sensation and to the remembered or transformed sensation of memory and imagination, showing once again the intimate relation of sight, common sense, and imagination. All of the common sensibles (movement, rest, shape, magnitude, number, and unity, in Aristotle's most comprehensive list of them [*De anima* 425a15]) were apprehended by sight (*De sensu* 437a8ff.) and were variously apprehended by the other senses.[10] Aristotle called the *phantasia* the *phantasia* because, he says (*De anima* 429a2–3), "sight is the principal sense," which presumably means that what we see is most like what is, at the same time that it is most like what we imagine. Consistently with such arguments, Aristotle also suggests that sight is more authoritative in perception than the other senses. Thus, a ball placed between crossed fingers feels like two, but sight intervenes to tell us the truth of the matter. Sight may thus correct mistaken inferences made by the common sense on the basis of the data of the lower senses, although it may still make errors of its own, as we shall see, errors corrected by optics and astronomy. (In a similar discussion, Juan Luis Vives argued that touch – the other candidate for the chief sense – may verify the falsity of the illusion of relief in painting).[11]

The "common sensibles" listed in the last paragraph were not sensed by the common sense, but rather by more than one sense. Magnitude, for example, is apprehended by both sight and touch. Aristotle is emphatic in denying that the common sense was like the five special senses (425a14ff.), arguing that if there were such a sixth sense, then the relation of, say, magnitude to red or sweet would be one of equality, which would be a fundamental confusion of categories. Common sensibles were thus apprehended *through* the special senses, especially sight and touch.

As models of relation, the common sensibles (movement, rest, shape, magnitude, number, and unity) coincide at many points with Aristotle's ten categories (*Topics*, 103b20ff.): substance, quantity, quality, relation, place, time, position, state, action, and passion. According to Averroes, as we shall see, these were apprehended by the *vis cogitativa,* that is, they were apprehended together with particulars, and the concentric relation between the common sense and the more embracing *vis cogitativa* suggests that the earlier idea was indeed the nucleus of the later one. In any case, their similarity eventually made it possible to understand the common sense as the particular intellect.

Relative to the physical objects of which they are qualities, the special sensibles are accidents, and the common sensibles – at least shape, magnitude, number,

[10] In *De sensu et sensato* (442b6), Aristotle also mentions rough and smooth, sharp and blunt.

[11] J. L. Vives, *Opera Omnia,* Valencia, 1782 (facs. London, 1964), III, p. 325: "magnam habent visus et tactus communionem, quasique amicitiam, ut alterius errores corrigat, in sensili utique ambobus communi, ut in pictura oculus sibi eminentias quasdam videtur conspicere, tactus vero accedens, qui est sensus in homine certissimus, errorem hunc eximit." This, of course, immediately calls to mind one of the central issues in the Renaissance *paragone* between painting and sculpture.

and unity – are substantial, or at least prior.[12] Medieval writers, as we shall see, connected the common sensibles with the physical, and regarded it as the way in which we apprehend the substantial characteristics of physical things. We may begin to understand this by considering Democritus's distinction between primary and secondary qualities. According to Democritus, secondary qualities (for example, color and sound) are to be referred to the perceiver, and primary qualities (for example, weight and density) to the object perceived.[13] Secondary qualities correspond to Aristotle's special sensibles, and it may be suggested that Aristotle meant to preserve the same distinction, but on different grounds. Democritus's primary qualities were conceived as a kind of touch. Although Aristotle defined all sensation as the result of a contiguous agent (*Physics* 245a), he rejected the notion that all sensation was reducible to touch because it could not be explained on such a theory why we have five senses. Aristotle's paradigm of sensation was vision, and his notion of the physical substrate was more "abstract" from matter, more solid geometric.

Aristotle argued that special sensibles always occur together with magnitudes, that, for example, a color is the color of a surface, and argued in general that we possess several senses (*De anima* 425b8) in order that we clearly apprehend the common sensibles. This is the deeper demand simply because the common sensibles are the physical characteristics of things. (It may also be noted that this formulation places the special senses in the right "instrumental" relation to common sense.) The apprehension of common sensibles is thus the particular apprehension of physical objects by physically specified existent consciousness.

As we have seen, Aristotle argued that error is relatively frequent in judgments concerning the common sensibles. What this means is that common sensibles

[12] I. Block, "Truth and Error in Aristotle's Theory of Sense Perception," *Philosophical Quarterly*, XI, 1961, pp. 1–9, compares the common sensibles to Locke's primary qualities. (See also, below, Chapter 9, n. 1.) Block argues that common sensibles may be in error because no organ is suited to apprehend them directly, as in the case of the special senses, citing *De sensu* 442b8, where it is argued that *because* the common sensibles are apprehended by more than one sense they are liable to error, relating this to Aristotle's teleological definition of normal sensation. And, it might be added, because we possess five senses *in order that* we may apprehend the common sensibles (*De anima* 425b8), Aristotle may simply have meant that we experience special sensibles immediately and common sensibles (magnitudes) mediately, and therefore approximately. S. R. L. Clark, *Aristotle's Man: Speculations upon Aristotelian Anthropology*, Oxford, 1975, pp. 79–83, points to *Posterior anlytics* 99b35, where it is asserted that "all animals have an inborn critical faculty called sense," and identifies this with the central or common sense, which is more or less complex in one or another kind of animal and, depending on the animal, may be associated with memory or thought. Clark also likens the distinction between common and proper sensibles to that between common and proper objects of the sciences (*Posterior analytics* 76a37ff.). He was probably not the first to do so, and it may be suggested that the tradition of this last discussion has a place in the early modern notion of primary and secondary qualities (which we shall encounter more than once in what follows) and of the association of the common sense with the mathematical and with "common notions." See Descartes, *Rules for the Direction of the Mind*, XII, where common sense is associated with *figura*, which is common to everything sensible.

[13] W. A. Hammond, *Aristotle's Psychology: A Treatise on the Principle of Life* (*De anima and Parva naturalia*), New York, 1902, p. 101, citing Theophrastus *De sensu* 63.

have a kind of conditional infallibility. That is, we really do see that someone is at a distance from us, just as we see that red is red, but we cannot say exactly how far from us he is; we really do see that he is approaching, or even approaching rapidly, but we cannot say just how quickly.

To say that we always apprehend a quality in a magnitude simply means that all sensation has a material cause; it is this material cause that all the senses apprehend, each in its own way (perhaps insofar as they are themselves material magnitudes), and it is this in turn that is the basis of the common in sensation. The unity of common sensation is not merely a necessary unification of scattered sense data, but is a unity corresponding to the material unity of things sensed. The identification of the common sensibles with physical substance casts a different light on the question of the erroneous judgments of common sense; because although these judgments may be by nature inexact, they are judgments about the measurable, and therefore admit of verification and demonstration. It is for this reason that, as we shall see, the history of the common sense is so clearly bound up with optics and astronomy. These "physical" mathematics (*Physics* 194a) reasoned from appearance to the reality of appearance by means of geometric demonstration.

We continually judge sizes, movements, and distances in the conduct of our affairs. We grasp the doorknob at the right moment "without thinking"; we run at once to the right spot to catch the ball; we step up each riser of the stairs. But however indispensable to our activities such responses may be, such judgments are not necessarily adequate to knowledge, and it is to the discrepancy between sensate judgment of a matter and rational judgment about it that Aristotle wishes to point. Sensate judgment, although richly adequate to our particular activities in the physical world, cannot give us scientific knowledge of the physical world. We may consider this large question with the example of the sense of sight, according to the judgments of which it is possible to think the oar to be broken in the water, or the sun to be a foot in diameter. In such cases optics and astronomy must come to our aid. Optics, in fact, might be described as the science of the common sense par excellence, and provides a clear example of the relation between the common sense and reason. We always perceive particular shapes and magnitudes under real circumstances and therefore in a certain sense perceive them "incorrectly," and optics tells us what we "really" see. A coin is "smaller" than it "is" because of its distance from us; it is an oval and not a circle because its diameter is not perpendicular to the line of sight. Only the intervention of reason may provide these clarifications. On the other hand, the very intervention of reason may also reveal the essential rationality of the act of vision.

In *De memoria et reminiscentia* (450a9–14), Aristotle seems to have added time to the common sensibles. Here we are told that the "primary capacity of sense" is responsible for perceiving time as well as the common sensibles, since the apprehension of motion and magnitude involves time. Aristotle's definition of time ("the number of motion") also involves two common sensibles, and time must therefore be apprehended through them. There is no reason, however, to conclude that time is not apprehended by the central faculty as an apprehension immediate to that of the common sensibles, much as the common sense apprehends common sensibles through the special senses, which transmit but do not judge them. In such a case, time would be higher than common sensibles, and it may be suggested that the "primary capacity of sense" referred to here should be understood not just as what apprehends the common sensibles, but rather as the "center" for which sensation occurs.

Before leaving the strictly apprehensive aspect of common sensation, we shall briefly consider the idea that the principle of basing art on conformity to sense may be extended from special to common sensation. Aristotle wrote that in order for a living creature – or "every whole made up of parts" – to be beautiful, it must not only be of orderly arrangement but must also be of a certain definite magnitude. It must neither be so small as to be imperceptible nor so large as not to be able to be seen all at once. (He gives the example of a creature a thousand miles long.) A beautiful whole must be of a size to be taken in by the eye, just as the plot of a drama must be of a size to be taken in by the memory (*Poetics* 1450b34ff.).

This mean in the common sensible of magnitude is addressed not just to the object (the drama) but to the object in relation to the physical limitations of sight; it produces pleasure in being proportional to sense, and this pleasure is the sensible foundation of the beauty of the object. It is made in conformity with sense, and sense delights in this conformity. Within this definition a certain properly expressive adjustment is possible, and, Aristotle argues, the drama is "grander" the larger it is without being too large. These principles did not apply simply to drama, and in the *Rhetoric* (1409a35), Aristotle defined the period as that which has a beginning and an end, "being at the same time not too big to be taken in at a glance." Such periods have the advantage not only of conforming to sense but also of being able to be made metric, number (or rhythm) being the easiest thing to remember.

Aristotle argued that there are two sources of local movement, appetite and mind, and that appetite is impossible without imagination. Any animal, including the human, may want food, and Aristotle presented this as a process in which the animal forms an image of what it lacks, an image that becomes the goal for its activity. We may not only want something, as animals do, but we may also want to do something, to go for a walk or build a house, for example. Such activity is "deliberative," and once again requires the imagination of a goal; but it also requires higher discrimination. It is not sufficient to tell the edible from the inedible; rather, one must also distinguish between better and worse, or greater and lesser, and to do this we must be able to make a unity out of several images (that is, to benefit from experience) in order to provide ourselves with a "single standard measure" for our conduct. The formation of such images is the result of the capacity to form them and of experience and education, the foundations for both art and virtue. Deliberative imagination not only involves an inward image to which our activity is directed, but also implies procedure toward that end. Thus, the good carpenter is also skilled and knows how to make what he imagines.

Aristotle is at pains to distinguish imagination from opinion. If we have an opinion, he argues, it must be about something, that is, on the premises of his psychology, it must be about a mental image, but it is not the same as a mental image. As we have seen, he argues that we may imagine something in the same way that one looks at a painting of a frightening subject without being frightened, whereas an opinion is about truth and falsehood. Aristotle associates opinion with deliberation and appetite with sensation, the first implying choice, the second not. Both, however, share the common ground of imagination; but whereas appetite is simply governed by imagination, opinion (and deliberation in general) is a kind of judgment, of which knowledge and prudence are also kinds (427b27), and has to do with the particular in relation to the universal. Above the bare alternative of truth and falsehood (opinion), the particular may also be judged in relation to knowledge, which is relatively at rest. This is the realm of the so-called practical syllogism; the first premise (or universal judgment) says that such and such a kind of man should do such and such, the second that this is an act of the kind meant, and that I am a person of the kind meant.

When Aristotle described the implementation of local movement by appetite, he wrote that the instrument is not psychical but bodily, so that the examination of it falls within the province of functions common to body and soul (*De anima* 433b19; and *De motu animalium* 703a23). It is the unmoved point relative to which the movement occurs (perhaps just as the imagined end of action is the unfixed point relative to which movement occurs in the preceding discussion), so that imagination and the *locus* of imagination are identified with the *arche* of movement, the center of the body.

Aristotle placed the common sense, or the "center" to which common sensation is properly related, in the heart. The common sense has been associated with Aristotle's principle (*De partibus animalium* 667b21–31) that "all animals possess a sensory soul with is actually one," cited as an explanation of the unity of the vascular system in the heart.[14] In the *De motu animalium* 703a13ff.), he argued that the origin of the *pneuma* – the metaphorical "air," the semiphysical substance by which the *arche* of sensation communicates with the body as a whole – must be in the heart because the principle or center of control is there. The common sense (or central sense) is thus passive in sensation, active in imagination; and in its passivity it presents images to the intellect and these images may be compared

[14] Kahn, "Sensation and Consciousness," p. 20. The center of sensation is perhaps related to Plato's *phronimos* (*Timaeus* 64b3–6); see F. Solmsen, "Greek Philosophy and the Discovery of the Nerves," *Museum helveticum*, 18, 1961, pp. 161–162.

to universals in the higher forms of rational judgment. At the same time, it is possible for the geometer to imagine his diagrams, or the carpenter the house he is going to build, and these conceptions arise from deliberation, so that to some degree imagination must be subject to mind just as it is subject to sense. At the same time, the faculty by means of which this occurs is corporeal, or semicorporeal, pneumatic, or, as later writers would say, spiritual.

Although the central sense was near-material, it was also peculiarly human, and in the *De partibus animalium* (686a32) it was associated with uprightness, the sign of human "godlike nature and essence," the end of which is to think and be wise. The appropriate mental activities are made possible by the uprightness and proportions of the adult human body, and were it otherwise the weight of the body would press down and its weight would impede the motions of the intellect and the general sense, apparently meaning that images from the common or general sense are necessary to thought. This at once distinguishes and relates the intellect and the central sense and subjects both to their material circumstances. Animals possess common sensation, after all, but not of the same kind or in the same degree, and this qualitative difference is rooted in the structure, even in the characteristic posture and movement, of the human body. For Aristotle all souls are higher than matter, higher, that is, than the four elements. At the same time, all souls are contiguous with matter and exist in union with matter. The contiguity of the human soul with matter is like the contiguity of heaven and earth, and he seems to associate the "divine" rational soul, separable from matter, with the quintessence, the element of the stars (*De generatione animalium* 736b–737a). This provides a physiological and a microcosmic basis for Plato's vision of the human soul in its uniquely upright body, its eyes turned toward the heavens as toward its own end and nature.

When the common sense is discussed in immediate relation to sensation, it seems abstract and "epistemological." But at other times Aristotle writes of it as if it were a faculty that fully apprehends particulars, and as if its "judgments" were actual modes of inference about particulars. In general, Aristotle seems to have thought that we apprehend three things by sensation (which should include common sensation). These are special sensibles, individuals, and common sensibles. As we have seen, the first of these is least liable to error (we see white); the second is more liable to error (this white thing may or may not be the son of Cleon); as is the third (his apparent size owing to this distance from us may in itself make identification difficult or impossible). Aristotle carefully distinguishes between the incidentally sensible (the son of Cleon) and the common sensible (the apparent state and circumstances of the son of Cleon). Again, he gives the example (431bff) of a beacon. When we see it, we say "that is a fire," but when we apprehend by the common sense that it is moving rather than still, then we recognize that this movement signifies the approach of the enemy. "But sometimes by means of the images or thoughts which are within the soul, just as if it were seeing, it calculates and deliberates what is to come by reference to what is present."[15]

In Book VI of the *Nicomachean Ethics*, Aristotle considers the difference between intellect and prudence. Young men, he observes, may be geometricians and mathematicians, but they are never prudent. This is because they have no experience, and prudence arises from experience (1142a10–15). Thus, "some who do not know, and especially those who have experience, are more practical than others who know" (1141b15ff). The intellect knows the universal, which in turn constitutes *scientia* (this and the following Latin terms are from Grosseteste's translation of the *Ethics*). Prudence is instead "concerned with the ultimate particular fact, since the thing to be done is of this nature." Aristotle here presents the soul as working between two extremes. On the one hand, the intellect knows intuitively – that is, without being able to demonstrate them – that certain things are true; and on the other hand, things are given to us by sense with what according to the symmetry of the argument is also a kind of intuition, but of particulars, and it is at this level that prudence operates. The ultimate particular fact is the object not of *scientia* but of sense [*sensus*]. The manifest state of affairs provided by sense is also provided in a certain way. It is "not the perception of qualities peculiar to one sense but a perception akin to that by which we perceive that the particular figure before us is a triangle . . . this is rather perception than practical wisdom [*prudentia*], though it is another kind of perception than that of qualities peculiar to each sense" (1142a20ff).

Commentators both medieval and modern have understood Aristotle to refer here to the common sense, which apprehends shape and completes sensation. Aquinas explained that this sense is not that by which we perceive color and sound, but an "interior sense" by which we perceive *imaginabilia*, just as in doing mathematics we must imagine some particular triangle corresponding to a single triangle in nature. "And to this sense, that is, interior sense, prudence very much pertains, by which particular reason is perfected to the right estimation of singular operable intentions, whence brute animals that have good natural estimation [or instinct] are said to participate in prudence."[16] When he summarized this argument in the *Summa theologiae*, Aquinas wrote that "prudence . . . does not consist in exterior sense, by which we know proper sensibles, but in interior sense, which is perfected by memory and experience, and expert in the ready

[15] Averroes, *Commentarium magnum . . . de anima* III, t.c. 33 (p. 476), discusses the *vis cogitativa* at length in explanation of this text. As we shall presently see, for Averroes the *vis cogitativa* was the particular intellect, and in making such a connection he again raised the common sense to a level of generality to which it was often raised in the centuries to follow. This generalization was not without a basis in Aristotle's own words, even if the idea was not systematically developed by him.

[16] Thomas Aquinas, *Sententia Libri Ethicorum* VI.7 (*Opera omnia*. Rome, 1882–1919, XLVII, 2, p. 359).

judgment of particulars [*ad prompte judicandum de particularibus expertis*]."[17] The constantly variable facts, which we know intuitively and absolutely, must be judged, and this judgment reaches into the nature of apprehension itself. Sense is a kind of intellect: *oportet habere sensum, hic autem est intellectus* (1143b5). Again, when Aquinas commented on this passage, he associated such "sense" with inner rather than outer sense. The knowledge of singulars demands not only exterior sense but also interior sense, which he calls "prudence, or the *vis cogitativa*, or *estimativa*, or *ratio particularis*. . . . This *sensus* is called *intellectus* with respect to singulars, and this in the third book of *De anima* the Philosopher calls the passive intellect, which is corruptible."[18]

The common sense, or the central faculty with which common sensation was associated, was essential to Aristotle's account of dreams (which he associated with the nutritive faculty, which "has no share in human excellence, since goodness and badness are least manifest in sleep" [*Nicomachean Ethics*, 1102b]). It is, in fact, in the short treatises on sleep and memory that this faculty is most fully explained. In these explanations it may be noted that the powers of the central faculty very considerably expand beyond the definition of the common sense as a unifier of special sensation, and the kinds of judgment associated with it become complex and various. As we consider these activities, it is important to remember

[17] *Summa Theologiae* 2–2.47.3. See H. A. Wolfson, "The Internal Senses in Latin, Arabic and Hebrew Philosophic Texts," *Studies in the History of Philosophy and Religion*, ed. I. Twersky and G. H. Williams, Cambridge, Mass., 1973, I, p. 303, citing J. A. Stewart, *Notes on the Nicomachean Ethics of Aristotle*, Oxford, 1892, II, p. 72. Stewart provides a major discussion of the common sense and concludes that the relation between the common sense and prudence is one of analogy. Aristotle was fond of the example of geometric demonstration. He wrote (*De memoria* 450a) that when we do geometry we imagine a triangle of a determinate magnitude, just as a triangle on a blackboard is necessarily of a determinate size, because it is singular and corporeal; that is, what is imagined is corporeal and stands for any triangle. In *Nicomachean Ethics* 1112b12ff., it is argued that we deliberate means but not ends, and again the example is one who analyzes a geometric construction, in which "what is last in order of analysis seems to be first in order of becoming." (This seems to recall *De anima* 433a15ff., where it is argued that practical imagination is essential to human action and that "that which is last in the process of thinking is the beginning of the action"; that is, we may imagine what to do as the result of deliberation, and this conception then guides our behavior). The process of deliberation is *like* the analysis of a geometric construction in that it always concerns the particular in relation to the universal, *and* it produces a solution that becomes the end toward which action is directed. And just as we do not deliberate about ends, so we do not deliberate about matters at hand. One can only make choices and "bring the moving principle back to himself" when he has *already* judged the things before him to be so and so. Particular facts cannot be subject to deliberation, "as whether this is bread, or has been baked as it should; for these are matters of perception." If we make the same kinds of judgments about particulars, we shall make them to infinity. This seems to me to be a variation of the present argument, and it also implies that perception affords an adequate grasp of particulars. Obviously there is a very considerable comprehension attributed to sense, and this comprehension is a kind of prudence in its own right, a tacit correct judgment preceding choice. Most modern writers on Aristotle seem to reject this more or less traditional reading, which makes what is apprehended a "particular." See A. Edel, *Aristotle and his Philosophy*, Chapel Hill, N.C., 1982, p. 291, for a summary of recent readings. Here, of course, we are concerned with traditional readings of the text.

[18] *Sententia libri Ethicorum* VI.9 (*Opera omnia*, Rome, 1882–1919, XLVII, 2, p. 367. We shall consider these ideas in more detail in Chapter 10 below.

that it is subrational faculties that are being dealt with. Or, to put it another way, it is in the activities of the central faculty of sensation that the relation between the rationality of sensation and reason itself once again becomes critical.

For Aristotle both sleep and dreams are affections of the central sense, and just as the world is first truly apprehended in this central sense, so the quasi apprehensions of dreams occur there, brought on by the various remnants of sensation borne to the heart from the organs of special sense. Similar results may be brought about by passions, so that lovers, cowards, and others in one or another pathological state think they see what they do not really see. "The cause of these occurrences is that the faculty in virtue of which the controlling sense judges is not identical with that in virtue of which presentations come before the mind" (*De somniis* 460b16). That is, the central sense "judges" what is given to it by sense, either immediately or mediately, through the inner disturbance of the central sense by fantasy, and makes its judgment on that basis. Aristotle illustrates his argument with an example also given in the *De anima*. The sun presents itself to us as being a foot in diameter, even if we know that it is not. That is to say, the judgment of reason does not alter the judgment of sense, which is thus an independent judgment, not to be confused with mere image formation. So the eye of a person in a boat believes the land to be moving because to the eye the sensation is the same whether boat or land is moving.

Aristotle characterized memory as "some such thing as a picture" (*De memoria et reminiscentia* 450a30), "impressed" by sensation in the part of the body which is the seat of the sentient soul. This metaphor of painting (which must be done "in" the common sense) provides the basis for a distinction between sensation, memory, dream, and delusion. We may, Aristotle argues, consider a painting on a panel as either a painting or a likeness, the distinction being that between a painted figure and an image of someone, of Coriscus. A real memory is a likeness that may be referred to something. A phantasm to which nothing may be referred is some sort of delusion.

It follows from this that when we remember Coriscus, whom we have not seen for a long time, we compare the phantasm of the present Coriscus with the impression made by our previous experience of him, and call the present Coriscus Coriscus. When we dream, however, we may call the phantasm Coriscus, and we may believe it to be him (even though Aristotle thought that we may know when we are asleep, although not always). This argument has the important implication of again placing the recognition of particulars in the common sense, or of making such recognition an activity of the "controlling and judging sensing faculty."

Syllogizing

In a passage in *De memoria et reminiscentia,* Aristotle set out an argument about the operation of recollection that must have been especially significant for later

Arab writers. Recollection is uniquely human; whereas animals have memory (that is, animals may have phantasms that are likenesses of phantasms), only human beings may recollect things. Memory is a function of the common sense, "the primary faculty of sense perception . . . that faculty whereby we perceive time" (451a15ff.). His definiton of recollection presupposes this apprehension of time, because recollection presupposes sequence. "As regular sequence of events is in accordance with nature, so, too, regular sequence is observed in the actualization of movements [in consciousness]" (452a28ff). Events happen in sequence, and it is our central sense that apprehends this. In order to recollect, we must be aware of the time relation of what is to be recollected. There is, Aristotle says, "something by which one distinguishes a greater and a smaller time," and, he continues, "it is reasonable to think that one does this in a way analogous to that in which one discerns spatial magnitudes." In a brief interruption of his almost complete silence on the subject of optics, Aristotle wrote that "it is not by the mind going out to things that we think of large distant objects (since we may also imagine them) rather we do this by a proportional mental movement" (450b10ff.). There are figures and movements in the mind that are proportional to the figures and movements of external things. "Now, as we may assume within a person something proportional to the forms [of distant magnitudes], so, too, we may doubtless assume also something else proportional to their distances." Aristotle then argues from the principle of the similarity of triangles that "when the movement [that is, the modification of sense] corresponding to the object and that corresponding to its time concur, then one actually remembers."[19] In other words, in remembering we infer relations in time much as we infer relations in space when we see. It is essential to establish the nature of this "inference." Aristotle does not mean that we actually calculate or measure magnitudes and distances with our eyes, rather he means that we judge them, as in fact we constantly make myriad judgments about our relations to things in time and space, judgments that are practically useful and may become conscious in various ways. I may wonder just how far it is from here to there, or just how long ago something happened. I may supplement this judgment by surveying or optics, but these activities are finally based upon the nature of common sensation, much in the same way that the harmonics of music are based upon the nature – and the judgment – of sense.

In the conclusions to this argument Aristotle returns to the question of the faculty that makes such judgments. In the first place, it is "corporeal," and recollection is "a searching for an image in a corporeal substrate." Its operation is affected by the moisture around the center of sense perception, and we know that it is corporeal because we feel discomfort when we cannot remember. Only human beings possess recollection, we are told, because it is "as it were," a mode

[19] On this troubled text, see Beare, *Greek Theories*, p. 321, n. 1, where another interpretation still turns around the principle of the similarity of triangles; and R. Sorabji, *Aristotle on Memory*. Providence, R.I., 1972, pp. 57, 18–21.

of inference. "He who endeavors to recollect *infers* that he formerly saw, or heard, or had some such experience, and the process is, *as it were,* a sort of investigation." And such investigation, he concludes, "belongs naturally to those animals alone which are also endowed with the faculty of deliberation."

Aristotle is talking about a sensate, corporeal function, uniquely human and quasi inferential in its activity. But it is important to stress again the status of the operations Aristotle is describing. We may recollect consciously and at will, and we do so according to the nature of recollection. Again, we may formulate an "art of memory," and this, too, must conform to the nature of recollection, which is not only sequential but works by association. One skilled in mnemonics "passes swiftly in thought from one point to another, e.g. from milk to white, from white to mist, and thence to moist, from which one remembers Autumn [the season of mists], if this be the season he is trying to recollect" (452a13). And an art of memory mirrors the nature of recollection, just as we may use colors at will, but, if we use them artfully, must use them in conformity with our apprehension of color.

Aristotle regarded the syllogism as the paradigm of all right thinking. Logic was, so to speak, the theory of right thinking, but in itself right thinking could be relatively unconscious. So "quick wittedness" (*Posterior analytics* 89b34) is "a faculty of hitting upon the middle term instantaneously." This is exemplified by a man who, seeing that the moon always has its bright side to the sun, inferred that it was lighted by the sun. The inference is correct, but it is "seen" at once, as the result of the possession of a faculty not universally possessed, or not possessed in the same degree, just as prudence (or practical judgment) may be defined (and may be defined as the application of the practical syllogism), but some people are innately prudent. As we have just seen, reminiscence proceeded by association, by a series of resemblances, the relations between which were characterized as syllogistic. Such an understanding of syllogism as unconscious right inference draws near to Aristotle's praise of the ability of poets to find metaphors; this is "the greatest thing by far," the one thing that cannot be learned from others; "it is also a sign of genius [*euphuia*], since a good metaphor implies an intuitive perception of the similarity in dissimilars" (*Poetics* 1459a). In *De memoria et reminiscentia* (449a5–10) the quick-witted and clever are described as distinguished by their powers of recollection as opposed to mere memory.

The *sensus communis* in the earlier Middle Ages

Aristotle's notion of the common sense had a complex career in later antiquity, a career too complex to be unravelled here. At the same time, it is necessary to gain some understanding of the transformations it underwent, because these transformations substantially determined the way in which the idea was understood in the Middle Ages and the Renaissance. Most Renaissance students of Aristotle – and certainly those with whom we shall be mostly concerned – did not simply construe his own words, or translations of them; rather, they read what he had written together with commentaries either at hand or in mind, or they read digests that smoothed together numbers of related ideas, or they gathered his meaning from contexts to which his ideas had been adapted for one or another purpose. So, at least in outline, Aristotle's original ideas must be considered in constant reference to their changes in both content and emphasis.

Aristotle's central principle of sensation became fused with the Stoic idea of the *hegemonikon,* which was defined as the highest part of the human soul. "It produces representation, assent, sensation and spontaneity, and they call it rational." According to this version, there are seven parts of the soul, the five senses plus a seminal principle (in the testicles) and voice (in the tongue). The *hegemonikon* communicated with its seven parts through the *pneuma,* and was compared to the sun in the center of the cosmos.[20] It was variously located in the head, following Plato and the physiologists, or in the heart, following Aristotle. For the Stoics the common sense became unambiguously the principle of self-awareness and self-identity[21] and, it may be noted, the comparison of the *hegemonikon* to the sun reinforces another materialist metaphor, the often repeated comparison attributed to Democritus of the soul to a spider, which both controls its web and is sensitive to whatever touches it.[22]

At the farthest remove from materialism, the Neoplatonist Plotinus wrote that all sensation must be for one and identified this unity with a "center of consciousness." "When sight and hearing gather their varying information, there must be some central unity to which they both report. How could there be any

[20] G. H. Clark, *Selections from Hellenistic Philosophy,* New York, 1940, p. 95. And H. von Staden, "The Stoic Theory of Perception and Its 'Platonic Critics,'" in *Studies in Perception,* ed. P. K. Machamer and R. G. Turnbull, Columbus, Ohio, 1978, pp. 96–136, with bibliography.

[21] See G. P. Klubertanz, *The Discursive Power: Sources and Doctrine of the Vis Cogitativa According to St. Thomas Aquinas,* St. Louis, 1952, p. 39, with references. The Stoic *hegemonikon* is both described and ridiculed in Plutarch "Against the Stoics on Common Conceptions" 1084A–C, in *Moralia,* tr. H. Cherniss, London, 1976, XIII, pt. II, pp. 854–857, with useful notes. "For it's pretty absurd of them to take the virtues and vices and all the skills and memories besides and mental images, moreover, and affections and impulses and acts of assent for bodies and say that they do not reside or subsist in any subject but to have left these things a single place no bigger than a point, the duct in the heart, into which they cramp the soul's ruling faculty." Similar ideas lived on not only in Leonardo's notes but in Descartes, who identified the pineal gland as the junction of body and spirit, and also called it the seat of the common sense. In the *Optics* (*Discourse on Method, Optics, Geometry and Meteorology,* tr. P. J. Olscamp, New York, 1965, p. 100), Descartes discusses judgments of vision and the common sense integrally, so that sight apprehends light, color, location, distance, size, and shape. Descartes seems to have drawn on the *centrum omnium sensuum* scheme when he fixed on the pineal gland, which, he wrote, is deep in the middle of the brain and is one, whereas the organs of sense are double, and their data in need of unification (*Passions of the Soul,* I, XXXI, and I,XXXII). See also *Philosophical Writings of Henry More,* ed. F. I. MacKinnon, New York, 1925, pp. 127–155. More considered the common sense both a sensorium and the principle of movement, much like the *hegemonikon.*

[22] F. Solmsen, "Greek Philosophy," pp. 161–162. This metaphor had a long life. Bartholomaeus Anglicus (*De proprietatibus rerum* 3.3 [Frankfurt, 1601 (facs. Frankfurt am Main, 1964), p. 47]) compared the soul to a spider, citing Chalcidius (Waszink ed., p. 233), who attributed the idea to Chrysippus. The argument is that the soul resides in the heart, and the senses are as messengers to it. What is conveyed to it it "judges, like a king." This is similar to Leonardo's version of the

statement of difference unless all sense impressions appeared before a common identity able to take the sum of all?" This "common identity" he compares, as the common sense was compared, to the center of a circle, struck by lines from its circumference.

Plotinus does not mention the common sensibles. He was at pains to separate the soul in general and the common sense in particular from magnitude, which pertained to matter, and was consequently more interested in the activity than in the passivity of sensation. He emphatically rejected Aristotle's seal-impression theory of sensation in favor of a notion of "sympathy," and related perception to quality rather than quantity. When he described sensation he wrote as follows. "Suppose the sense-object be such a unity as a face; all the points of observation must be brought together in one visual total, as is obvious since there could be no panorama of great expanses unless the detail were compressed to the capacity of the pupils." He means by this that just as the eye is a small unity that takes in a vast magnitude, so the center of consciousness is one thing that in bringing together the parts preserves the unity of the thing seen. And were this center itself a magnitude, then the parts would simply divide it, and thus themselves remain scattered and disunited.[23]

We also encounter in Plotinus the clear statement of a notion we shall encounter frequently in what follows, that the central sense is a mean between sense and reason. When Plotinus writes of the "faculty presiding over sensation and impulse . . . vested in the sensitive and representative soul," he describes it at once as "drawing upon the Reason-principle immediately above itself" and as in immediate contact with its inferior, the senses. He locates this faculty in the brain, arguing that there must be some linkage of reason and sense because "in perception there is some element of judging, in representation something intuitional." The reasoning faculty "is present where these experiences occur, present not as in a place but in the fact that what is there draws upon it."[24] He argues that there is a distinction in sensation between affections (which are passive) and judgments, the former belonging to the body, the latter to the soul.[25] Elsewhere, Plotinus

common sense, an identification that was perhaps inevitable given such common definitions as the following, based on Aristotle, from the *Compendii Theologicae veritatis* (II, XXXV): "omnes sensus unam habent originem, scilicet sensum communem, a quo velut a centro quasi lineae quaedam exeunt" (in Albertus Magnus, *Opera,* Paris, 1890, XXXIV, pp. 63–64); according to Macrobius (*In somnium scipionis* I.XIV.19), Asclepiades defined the soul as a harmonious functioning of the five senses (see Macrobius, *Commentary on the Dream of Scipio,* p. 146 for further references). Macrobius's definition is repeated by Bartholomaeus Anglicus *De proprietatibus rerum* 3.4, in a chapter on the definitions of the soul given by the physicists. The effect of this "physical" definition is to identify soul and the common or central sense. On the soul as a monarch judging the senses, see Gregory of Nyssa, *De opificio hominis* 10, 12, and 15, in the early Christian translation of Dionysius Exiguus (MPL, 67, col. 359–361, 370–371) followed by William of St. Thierry *De natura hominis et animae* II.3 (MPL, 180, col. 711C).

[23] *Enneads* IV.7.6.

[24] Ibid. IV.3.23.

[25] See H. J. Blumenthal, *Plotinus' Psychology: His Doctrines of the Embodied Soul,* The Hague, 1971, p. 70.

calls judgment "the foundation of perception."[26] All this suggests that there is, if not a continuity, a concentricity between reason and sense, even if sense is bound to the particular and liable to error and more certain judgments must be left to the higher faculties.[27] Although Plotinus was a Platonist in that he maintained the strictest antithesis between soul and matter, and believed that knowledge arose from the comparison of sensation and ideas, his incorporation of Aristotle's faculty psychology had the effect of unifying all mental activity as the activity of a single principle.

It has been argued on the basis of texts such as those we have just considered that Plotinus was the first to make the self the substratum of inner and outer experience, which stands in a relation of ownership to that experience. Various writers considered the question of the relation of sense and reason in the *arche* of sense or *hegemonikon,* a question Aristotle had left unresolved. Alexander of Aphrodisias, Aristotle's late second-, early third-century commentator, seems to have been close to his text in distinguishing perception from apperception and linking the latter with the common sense. Through this discussion run the problems of the relation of sense and reason, and of animal sense to human sense, with which we are familiar. The sixth-century commentator Simplicius shifted apperception from the common sense to reason, arguing that animals also have the common sense; but he evidently felt that this adjustment demanded a correlate adjustment in sensation and followed Iamblichus in arguing that human perception is in some sense rational, and that this *logike aisthesis* distinguishes men from animals. The participation of all the faculties of the soul in rationality made it a single subject that is the center of our experience. Philoponus attributed apperception to an "attentive faculty," attributing to Plutarch the idea that it is a function of the rational soul to know the acts of the senses, a function to be associated with its "least noble part," with *doxa,* or opinion. Plutarch is also said to agree with Alexander of Aphrodisias in relating apperception to the *sensus communis,* which would in turn identify the common sense with the "least noble part" of reason.[28]

Review of these arguments is sufficient to show that the common sense, reason, self, self-consciousness and individual soul may all entail one another. In Avicenna these ideas attained a formulation that at once simplified them and greatly magnified their historical potency. He identified the individual soul with the *ego* and, moreover, compared it to the common sense. Just as the *sensus communis* is a common bond among the special senses, so the ego is a common, transcendent bond among the faculties of the soul.[29] Nor must this necessarily be regarded

[26] *Enneads* IV.4.23.

[27] Ibid. I.1.9.

[28] *Avicenna's Psychology: An English Translation of 'Kitab al Najat,' Book II, Chapter VI with historico-philosophical notes and textual improvements on the Cairo edition,* ed. and tr. F. Rahman, London, 1952, pp. 14, 112–113.

[29] *De anima* V.7, with commentary and bibliography in G. Verbeke, "Le 'De anima" d'Avicenne. Une conception spiritualiste de l'homme," introduction to *Avicenna Latinus,* ed. S. van Riet, p. 38, referring to p. 158, sect. 94ff.

simply as an analogy. The *ego* or individual soul might be regarded as the whole greater than the sum of the internal senses, and although as we shall see Avicenna placed the common sense itself near sensation, his analogical common sense is close to the *arche* with which Aristotle associated common sensation, or with the *cogitativa,* the human *phantasia.* This higher notion of the common sense, together with Avicenna's remarks about vision and the common sense,[30] is very near Leonardo's understanding of the common sense, to which it may well have contributed.

In the earlier Latin tradition, Augustine, in his *De libero arbitrio,* had deliberated about sensation in a way that looks back to Aristotle and forward to Descartes. Beginning from the premise that we must know ourselves to exist because even if our existence is an illusion, we still are aware of having the illusion, he begins the examination of what he calls "interior sense," which is clearly related in some way to Aristotle's common sense.[31] This interior sense is closely identified with awareness of sensation in the simple sense of consciousness (we know that we are awake or asleep) and with the "instinct of self-preservation." It is aware ("judges") that the special senses perceive, and that they perceive things in common. Although it is higher than the special senses, as their moderator and judge (*iudex*), this awareness of consciousness is explicitly distinguished from reason. It is said to be shared with animals, and is defined in terms similar to those that would be used to define the instinctive *vis estimativa* of animals by later medieval writers. At the same time, the interior sense is the *ministerium rationis* and is thus a kind of mean between pure sense and reason, as the common sense and imagination were often said to be. By the interior sense we perceive everything we know, and through it distinctions knowable by reason are grasped.[32]

In his *De musica,* Augustine wrote of the *sensus communis* in terms that derive not so much from Aristotle as from Cicero, raising a theme with which we shall be much concerned in Chapter 7. Meters, he wrote, are apparent even to *semidocti* because they are judged not by the rules of science but rather by a natural and common sense (*naturali et communi sensu judicarent*). Like Cicero, Augustine spe-

[30] *De anima* III.8; ed. cit. p. 269.

[31] Augustine, *De libero arbitrio voluntatis,* II. 3–5; Wolfson, "Internal Senses," in *Studies in the History of Philosophy and Religion,* p. 252. See also Augustine *Confessions* I.20 and VII.17.

[32] Augustine, *De libero arbitrio voluntatis* II.3. In the *De quantitate animae* (XXXIII), Augustine wrote of *sensus* as the second degree of the soul, following *animatio* and preceding *ars.* The soul is extended in touch, by which it feels and discerns hot and cold, rough and smooth, hard and soft, light and heavy; it also judges (*diiudicat*) innumerable differences of flavor, odors, sounds and forms by tasting, smelling, hearing and seeing; it approves and seeks those things sensed that agree with the nature of its (the soul's) body; it rejects and flees those that are contrary. The soul as *sensus* embraces common sense and phantasy (although they are not named); so it withdraws from the (particular) senses in sleep, at once allowing the senses to "vacate" and "tumultuously and variously turning" the images of things taken from sense in dreams. The soul is delighted by ease of movement, and "orders the concord of members" without effort. It pursues sexual union and social bonds, nourishes, cares for, and protects offspring; it is connected to the things among which the body acts, and by which the body is sustained, by habit (*consuetudo*), and is separated from these only with difficulty, as from its own members. When through this *vis consuetudinis* the soul does not forget, and distinguishes similar things such that some become past, others present, it is called memory (see Ibid., XXXVIII). This soul is also shared with animals.

cifically universalizes the kind of judgment to which he means to refer by rooting it in the nature of human perception.[33] But he means more than to say that all men sense magnitude through hearing and that they also sense meter. Rather, he means that we all take delight in what conforms to our sensation, common as well as special, and that art may – or must – appeal to the nature of sense. Again the recognition by sense of its own conformity with artificial order is itself a kind of judgment.

Avicenna on the common sense

We have already seen that the early eleventh-century Arab philosopher Avicenna compared the common sense to the ego, establishing a pattern to be followed by his twelfth-century successor Averroes, as we shall see in Chapter 10. Avicenna was also the first to place the common sense proper among the "internal senses." He provided a seminal discussion of the common sense, and his words were repeated by medieval and Renaissance writers on many subjects.

Avicenna identified the common sense closely with the *phantasia* and placed it, as did most later writers on the subject, in the first concavity of the brain, where it receives all forms impressed upon it by the external senses.[34] It is in fact "what truly senses." Avicenna agreed with Aristotle in making the *sensus communis* the means of immediate awareness of sensation and of discrimination among special sensibles. He also examined the temporality of the common sense, its ability to judge the apprehension of a thing in the place where it is and was; this was a more complex kind of judgment that obviously involved the common sensibles. In order to describe the activities of the soul, it is necessary to posit more than a means of perception; it is also necessary to have a means of retention, a faculty Avicenna's translators called *imaginatio vel formans.* This functions as a kind of perceptual memory, retaining what is received in the common sense after the object has changed or disappeared, or after the attention has shifted. Avicenna compared the activity (or passivity) of common sense to that of water, which may receive *insculptiones et depictiones et omnino figuram,* but cannot retain them. He thus preserved a sense of *phantasia* close to its original Platonic meaning of an appearance, the first contact of sense with the world. To explain the difference between mere sense and the *sensus communis,* he used the examples of illusions, a falling drop of water that seems to be a line or a bar that seems to be a circle when twirled around rapidly. Sense alone cannot apprehend either line or circle because strictly speaking it only sees things in a moment in space. The common sense, on the other hand, like the viewer of a film, provides the interior analogue

[33] Augustine *De musica* IV.16.31. The earlier related ideas of Cicero will be considered in Chapter 7 of this volume.

[34] Avicenna, *Liber de Anima* I.V. For the incorporation of a similar argument about the common sense and its relation to the fallacies of sight in the context of an Augustinian discussion of falsehood and similitude, see Albertus Magnus, *Summa theologiae,* tr. VI, Q. 25, m. 4.

to the persistence in time of the object and, in comparing one fading phantasm to the next, assembles the illusion. Thus, error is not found in sense, which perceives the "real" instantaneous thing, nor in reason but in the common sense. In seeing the drop of water as a straight line, the common sense misjudges such categories as *situs, motus, figura,* and *magnitudo,* and thus again becomes the unwitting agent of deception. We must see and momentarily remember a falling drop of water in one place and then in another in order to "see" it as a straight line, and it is the common sense that blurs the truth of the matter.

Of all writers, Avicenna wrote most as if the common sense were an external sense, and especially as if it were the sense of sight, which simply reflects what it finds before it. At the same time, the participation of memory and imagination in perception in the examples we have just considered makes perception even at the lowest level a "spiritual" process. The treatise on the soul of John Blund provides an instructive example of the fusion of Avicenna's arguments with the widely held psychology of "spiritual vision" of Augustine (which we shall consider in the next chapter), with which Avicenna's arguments were generally compatible.[35] It must be stressed that other instances of this fusion need not be attributed to the influence of Blund's treatise, but are more likely explained simply by the possibilities available within the conceptual system we are considering. In any case, when he repeated Avicenna's argument about the falling raindrop, Blund described the sequence of impressions on the eye as drawn out in a line on the common sense in the anterior part of the brain; and the gaze of the mind (*acies animi* – this is the key Augustinian phrase, which Blund used often in the course of his arguments) finds the impression in the common sense to be linear and "therefore judges [*indicat*] the drop the image of which is that impression, also to be linear." In this case it is not simply the common sense that judges by the nature of its activity; rather, spiritual vision surveys the expressly physical image of the common sense and forms its judgment. The merging of the ideas of Avicenna and Augustine, which might have occurred at any time, made them mutually reinforcing, at once specifying Augustine's spiritual vision (here fantasy is specified as the image-making power of the common sense) and involving the internal sense in the significance of the activities of Augustine's *spiritus*.

The common sense and the particular intellect

The functions of Aristotle's central sense went far beyond that of unifying special sensation, although such unification, as the first apprehension of particulars, was essential to the operations about particulars associated with it. The central sense was linked to the *pneuma* and to the *hegemonikon,* and was thus intimately associated with fantasy in all its aspects, with time as the condition of things sensed, remembered, and imagined, and thus with prudence, and with memory and rem-

[35] Johannes Blund, *Tractatus de Anima,* ed. D. A. Callus and R. W. Hunt, London, 1970, p. 64.

iniscence. The central sense was corporeal, or immediate to the corporeal, and after Aristotle became closely identified with the physiology of the nervous system. With the discovery of the nervous system, the *arche* of sensation was moved from the heart to the head, establishing a physiological pattern followed by most (but not all) writers through the Renaissance.[36]

The term "the common sense" may thus refer not only to a faculty but also to a system of faculties, and we shall see that the term may expand and contract within these bounds. As we have seen, Leonardo da Vinci still understood this whole system, and for him the common sense immediately raised the subject of the *hegemonikon* or, as he called it, the "seat of the soul," which commands the anatomical mechanism of the body in response to the world flowing into it from the senses.

In its more general aspect, as the central sense, the common sense formed the core of what came to be called the "internal senses" by the Arabs and Western Latin writers of the Middle Ages.[37] The internal senses – the *sensus communis*, the *phantasia, estimativa, cogitativa,* and *memoria* – were called senses because they dealt with particulars (unlike the intellect, which dealt with universals), and, more than simply continuing by sheer weight of Aristotle's authority, were necessary to explain the real operations of the soul. The relation among the parts of the soul – sense, internal sense, and intellect – was complex and, far from being agreed upon, was constantly shifting and at issue. In real human activity, in the actual functioning of the human soul, of course, all these parts interacted as one. But it is crucial to understand that different faculties of the soul had different functions and activities that were not reducible to the activities of any other. These activities were judgments, and we are concerned with the faculties that were thought to make judgments about particulars. The farthest development of the idea of the inner senses is to be found in the *vis cogitativa* of Averroes. For Averroes, this summarizing sensate faculty was the "particular intellect," a term

[36] See F. Solmsen, "Greek Philosophy," pp. 151–167, 169–197. Strato regarded sensation, perception, emotion, and thought as aspects of a single consciousness (Plutarch *De libidine et aegritudine* 697b) in a central organ in the front part of the brain, communicating with the sense organs and parts of the body by *pneuma*. Sensations occur in this sensorium. This erased the distinction between rational and irrational faculties, making mind the concomitant of sensation and reason. The data of sense required attention in order to be registered (Plutarch *De sollertia animalium* 961a). These ideas were probably shaped by medical ideas of the kind discussed by Solmsen. See A. A. Long, "Psychological Ideas in Antiquity," *DHI*, IV, pp. 6–7.

[37] The basic article on the internal senses is H. A. Wolfson, "The Internal Senses," in *Studies in the History of Philosophy and Religion*, I, pp. 250–314 (originally in the *Harvard Theological Review*, 28, 1935, pp. 69–133); followed by "Isaac Israeli on the Internal Senses" (*Studies*, pp. 315–330); "Notes on Isaac Israeli's Internal Senses" (ibid., pp. 331–343); and "Maimonides on the Internal Senses" (ibid., pp. 344–370). See also G. P. Klubertanz, *The Discursive Power*, and E. R. Harvey, *The Inward Wits: Psychological Theory in the Middle Ages and the Renaissance*, London, 1975. Alexander of Aphrodisias, who identified sense in general with the judicative power of the soul (in contrast to the intellective, which treats universals), followed Aristotle in locating the common sense and the *hegemonikon* in the heart. See A. P. Fotinis, *The De Anima of Alexander of Aphrodisias: A Translation and Commentary*, Washington, D.C., 1979, pp. 135, 255–262.

I shall appropriate for the whole cluster of ideas that developed around Aristotle's central sense.

Avicenna on *ingenium*

Ingenium (and the Italian *ingegno*) means talent, the natural gift of a person, and is opposed to what may be learned from art and experience. In a long tradition spanning all the centuries with which we are concerned, the term *ingenium* was used to refer either to natural talent in general or to the results of the exercise of talent, to those characteristics of works attributable to the innate differences of one artist from others. In medieval authors *ingenium* acquired associations it had not had in classical writers, associations that would have made possible a whole dimension of meaning for the classical antithesis *ars et ingenium* that cannot have been intended in the texts in which the phrase was found. At the same time, it must be insisted that it is the same core idea of innate talent that is being successively elaborated and specified. Once again Avicenna provided an exemplary and influential discussion.

Avicenna called *recordatio* (which corresponds to Aristotle's reminiscence) an *ingenium revocandi*, found in no animal but man.[38] For Avicenna, *ingenium* seems to have been the point of contact between the material and agent intellect. It is associated with Aristotle's "faculty of quickly discovering middle terms" and is called *actus rationis*, by which Avicenna must have meant that *ingenium* immediately perceives what is right by a kind of illumination. At the same time, *ingenium* is also a principle of individual difference. Human beings are not the same in their aptitude for understanding; some find more middle terms and some find them more quickly.[39] These differences in "material intellect" owe to differences in *subtilitas*, and the subtlety in question is the subtlety of the corporeal substrate of intelligence, just as such differences accounted for individual differences in intelligence in Aristotle.[40] *Subtilitas* exists in degrees and achieves its highest form in the *intellectus sanctus*. The *phantasia* of the prophet who embodies this intellect is purely spiritual, and is immediately passive to the agent intellect. This is a Neoplatonic argument that again gives an absolute dimension to Aristotle's "syllogizing." It has the important result of putting all *ingenium* on a continuous scale running from mere cleverness to prophetic vision. To return to *recordatio*, or reminiscence, Avicenna must have meant, when he called it *ingenium* (or what was translated as *ingenium*), that the operations of reminiscence were not only a kind of inference but were also dependent on their corporeal substrate.

[38] *Liber de Anima* IV.3; ed. cit., pp. 14, 61.

[39] Ibid. 152. 0–5. Boethius called Aristotle's faculty *sollertia*, which he defined as "quaedam subtilitas" (MPL, vol. 64, col. 744). Grosseteste, *Commentarius in posteriorum analyticorum libros*. ed. P. Rossi, Florence, 1981, pp. 281, 286, calls it a *vis penetrativa* by which mental sight "penetrates" matters. The "subtlety" belongs to the power of this sight itself, which swiftly comprehends the caused from causes or causes from the caused. It is a *bonitas ingenii inveniendi*.

[40] Avicenna, *Liber de Anima* V.6; pp. 151, 84.

This explains why *ingenium* was sometimes included among the inner senses by medieval writers,[41] and it also explains why *ingenium* was so closely related to taste.

The art of *ingenium*

Aristotle gave only scattered attention to the question of prerational processes of thought. Still, his definition of them at all both established the boundaries for later investigations and for the interpretation of his own writings. The definition of reminiscence, for example, promised an art of memory, an art which reached a high state of development, especially in the Late Renaissance.

In general, the definition of the inner faculties, whether by conscious elaboration and critical commentary or by further analysis or accommodation of ideas to one or another purpose, gradually brought into view an art of *ingenium,* which earlier would have been regarded as a paradox. That is, by progressively specifying what *ingenium* was and did, it became possible to attempt to resolve the antithetical poles of *ars* and *ingenium,* to be taught quick-wittedness, thus to correct human nature by art. As this development occurred, the characterization of the processes of inner sense as syllogizing gave way to other alternative definitions of psychological activity.

Emmanuele Tesauro's *Cannocchiale aristotelico,* first published in 1654, may be taken as a culmination of the late Renaissance attempt to close the opposites of *ars* and *ingenium* in a circle. Beginning from the same Aristotelian texts we have examined in the preceding sections, Tesauro defined metaphor as the mother of all *argutezze:*[42] "it is *ingegnosissimo,* because *ingegno* consists in binding together the remote and separate notions of appropriate objects, and just this is the purpose of metaphor, and of no other figure."[43] When he defined *ingegno naturale* (a "marvelous gift of intellect"), he divided it into two kinds of instantaneous analytical insight. The first is *perspicacia,* which "penetrates the most distant and minute circumstances of every subject." This analysis is accomplished in terms of a supplementary list of Aristotle's categories. The second is *versabilità,* which "rapidly compares all those circumstances among themselves, or with the subject; it joins and divides them, deduces one from the other, indicates one by the other, and with marvelous dexterity puts one in the place of the other." There is, he says, little difference between *ingegno* and prudence. The first is more perspicacious, the second is more sensate (*sensata*); one is more rapid, the other more solid; one considers appearances, the other truth; one works toward its own ends, the other for popular approval. "Whence *huomini ingegnosi* are called *divini.* Because, as God, from that which is not, produces that which is, so the *ingegno,* from nonbeing makes being, makes a lion become a man, an eagle a city . . . joins the

[41] *MLA,* p. 487 n. 32.
[42] E. Tesauro, *Il Cannocchiale Aristotelico,* Turin, 1670 (facs., Berlin, 1968), p. 82.
[43] Ibid., p. 266.

bust of a goat to the tail of a serpent and forms a chimera as a hieroglyph for madness." Here the classical examples of poetic license are identified with the exercise of *ingenium.* Again, Tesauro is no more interested in pure *ingenium* than in pure *furore,* since both are out of the control of the poet (and the theorist). He is, rather, interested in the *structure* of *ingenium* because this makes possible the creation of a second nature, a new *ingenium* gotten through *esercitio,* the practice of the art founded upon the definition of *ingenium.* With this map as a guide, the territory of *ingenium* began to be both better known and more mysterious. By degrees *ingenium* expelled the definition of its procedures by analogy to syllogistic thought to become a system of autonomous processes that gave fundamentally new meaning to the whole enterprise of art.

Berkeley on syllogizing

Aristotle's account of the operations of the postsensory faculties lasted until modern times, when it was thoroughly reevaluated and transformed. Although the operations of these faculties were various and could have been characterized in a number of ways, the idea of "syllogizing" seems to have come to predominate, especially in writers on optics, probably because in principle visible states of affairs could be demonstrated, and right judgments about them were supposed to be equivalent to such demonstrations. In the second century Ptolemy wrote that sight is able to discern differences of shape "quickly without delay or interruption" (*velociter, sine tarditate aut intermissione*); this is accomplished by "careful ratiocination with marvelous almost incredible skill" (*diligenti ratiocinatione cum mirabili virtute incredibili*), "insensibly on account of its speed" (*insensibiliter propter celeritatem suam*).[44] The "syllogistic" capacities of sight (or of sight as completed by inner sense) were very much expanded by Alhazen, whose *De aspectibus* provided the basis for the modern Western tradition of optics, as we shall see in Chapter 8. It is perhaps because of the conspicuousness of this idea in the optical tradition that we find it emphatically rejected by George Berkeley in his *New Theory of Vision,* published in 1709. Berkeley's analysis is significant because it clearly characterizes – even if it somewhat caricatures – the tradition with which we are concerned. He was correct in saying that his predecessors believed that perception was quasi inferential, and that in that specific way it was continuous with reason.

Berkeley began with the proposition that our perception of distance "is rather an act of judgment grounded on experience than of sense" and argued that we associate certain "ideas" with certain spatial experiences, much as we associate a red face with anger, as the consequence of our past experience of the association of red-facedness and anger.[45] He also argued that the *size* of objects is similarly

[44] *L'Optique de Claude Ptolémée dans la version latine d'après l'arabe de l'émir Eugène de Sicile,* ed. A. Lejeune, Louvain, 1956, p. 50. This text is cited by E. H. Gombrich, *Art and Illusion: A Study in the Psychology of Pictorial Representation,* Princeton, N.J., 1960, p. 242.

[45] *Berkeley's Philosophical Writings,* ed. D. M. Armstrong, New York, 1965, p. 285.

apprehended, and that the perceptual basis of this apprehension is finally not visual but tactile. We cannot *see* the measure of things, because things may appear to be of any size, or may be of any size relative to the whole field of vision, and it is relative to the absolute apprehension of them to be gained by touch that we judge their size. Berkeley thus consciously opposed himself to the "writers of optics," ridiculing the idea that sight judges by a "kind of natural geometry."[46]

> What seems to have misled the writers of optics in this matter is, that they imagine men judge of distance as they do of a conclusion in mathematics: betwixt which and the premises it is indeed absolutely requisite there be an apparent, necessary connexion. But it is far otherwise in the sudden judgments men make of distance. We are not to think that brutes and children, or even grown reasonable men, whenever they perceive an object to approach or depart from them, do it by virtue of geometry and demonstration.[47]

At the end of his argument Berkeley sets up the traditional argument for demolition by taking it literally. That is, he treats a metaphor for unconscious mental activity as a description of that activity; it is not "as if" the sense of sight performs such demonstrations, it is rather how can we seriously believe that children and animals perform such mental acts of seeing?

David Hume would seem very much to have broadened Berkeley's analysis, insisting that the inferences of the mind in general are at base not rational. They are not therefore irrational but rather have their own cogency, which is not syllogistic. Animals do not argue or reason in order to be able to act as if nature were regular in its operations; rather, they learn such regularity from experience. "For if there be in reality any arguments of this nature, they surely lie too abstruse for the observation of such imperfect understandings, since it may well employ the utmost care and attention of a philosophic genius to discover and observe them."[48] Children are not guided in judgments that seem to be inferences by reasoning, "neither are the generality of mankind in their ordinary actions and conclusions; neither are the philosophers themselves, who, in all the active parts of life, are in the main the same with the vulgar, and governed by the same maxims." Nature, Hume writes, must have provided "some other principle" to undergird our certainty about the deep regularities of our lives, a principle deeper than the "uncertain process of reasoning and argumentation."

The faculty that made the quasi inferences about vision against which Berkeley had written was not simply vision itself, but the common sense, as we shall see at length in Chapter 8; and when he thus argued against the "natural geometry" of sense, one of the most important judicative functions of the common sense dissolved once and for all in a kind of judgment based on the memory of things in space.[49]

[46] Ibid., sect. 19. pp. 288–289.
[47] Ibid., sect. 24, p. 290.
[48] D. Hume, *An Inquiry Concerning Human Understanding*, ed. C. W. Hendel, Indianapolis, 1955, pp. 113–114.
[49] Consistent with such a position, Berkeley rejects the idea of common sensibles shared by sight and touch; see, for example, sect. 121–122, pp. 333–334.

Berkeley's view stands between us and the older tradition. We do not think of the syllogism as the paradigm of right thinking to which complex judgments must be reduced, much as we no longer feel that the complex movements of the planets must be reduced to the geometry of the circle. To be sure, some of the faculties of the soul that assumed such importance in eighteenth-century writers were adaptations of the traditional postsensory faculties. "Association" was an operation of memory, as we have just seen; and when Hume reduced the "creative power of the mind" to the "faculty of compounding, transposing, augmenting and diminishing," he was listing the traditional powers of the imagination. So the "particular intellect," as we have called the group of inner senses, assumed a new importance, and might be said to have become the human mind. But such operations as Hume described had their own patterns, pointed toward other paths of investigation, and could not be called "syllogistic."

The common sense and taste

In his *De anima,* Aristotle devotes much attention to the sense of touch. As the universal sense of all living things, it was for him "indispensable to the existence of an animal" (435b17), and without it "there can be no other sense" (435b2). Not only must an animal have at least the sense of touch, but touch may be said to underlie the other senses. We may feel through any part of our body; we may, for example, feel the contact of something with our eye even while it functions as an organ of vision, and touch may thus be said to be wholly coextensive with our bodies. We may lose every sense but touch and live, but when touch is gone, life itself is extinguished. But if touch is the one universal animal sense, Aristotle also granted it a special status in human apprehension. Touch "is the most exact of man's senses" (421a19–20). Although man may fall behind the other animals in the other senses, he argues, in "delicacy of touch he is far superior to the rest," and to this superior tactile discrimination he attributes man's superior intelligence. "This," he says, "may be seen from the fact that it is this organ of sense and nothing else which makes all the difference in the human race between the natural endowments of man and man. For hard-skinned men are dull of intellect, while those who are soft-skinned are gifted."

When Aquinas refers to this passage in the *Summa theologiae* he argues from first principles that because we must gather knowledge through the five senses (here he cites not the expected Aristotle, but the pseudo-Dionysius *Divine Names* VII.2) and because nature withholds nothing that is necessary, the soul possesses both a *vis intelligendi* and a *vis sentiendi.* He then repeats Aristotle's statement that all of the senses are based upon touch, which is thus the foundation of the *vis sentiendi.* Like all senses, touch discriminates contraries and is thus a mean. Because it is the basic sense, and because according to Aristotle its medium is flesh, touch is immediate to the physical body, the first sense that divides the living from mere matter. Consequently, to the degree that the physical body is itself a mean, that is to say, a harmonious relationship of physical elements, the sense of touch will function more satisfactorily as a mean, will make more discriminations, providing a more subtle basis for the discrimination of the other senses and ultimately for intelligence itself. Aquinas also argues that there is a direct relationship between the relative complexity of the human body and the complexity of human touch, explaining superior human intelligence on the same physical grounds; that is, there is a direct relation between the simple complexity of the human body and its powers of discrimination relative to other animals. Difference in the physical basis of the *vis sentiendi* thus produces differences in the *vis intelligendi,* and it is in terms of such physical differences that the wide range of human intellectual aptitudes is to be explained.[50] When Saint Antoninus cited this text he added that one soul is "acutior & virtuosior" than another because of the better disposition and complexion of the body, because of better training [*exercitio*] or by grace.[51]

In his *Ovid's Banquet of Sence,* dedicated in 1595, George Chapman describes a kiss which will "borrow organs of my touch/ T'advance it to that inward taste of mine/ which makes all sense."[52] Chapman defended a difficult style to protect poetry from the commonplace, the plain, and the vulgar, and a note explains that he means by "that inward taste of mine" the "common sense, which is *centrum sensibus et speciebus*"; this "makes all sense," which means, as we have seen, that the common sense unifies and "judges" the data of the individual senses.

Aristotle argued that flesh is the medium of touch, much as air is the medium of sound, and this implied that there was a center of touch within (*De anima* 422b22; 423b23), and, if Aristotle did not make this connection himself, it is not surprising that other writers drew the conclusion that touch was common sensation. Chapman seems to have held such an opinion, and adds to this Aristotle's definition of taste as a kind of touch (*De anima* 421a18, 422a, 434b17; *De sensu* 439a). Thus, the common sense is identified not simply with what would become the *vis sentiendi* but with the immediately higher judicative power of the common sense, which again is identified with the "higher" touch of taste. Taste thus becomes the judgment of sense based in the unique physical nature of the individual. That both taste and common sense are understood primarily as judicative is evident from the end of the explanation, where we are told that the common sense is called "taste because it dooth 'sapere in effectione sensuum,' " which might be translated to say that it knows in matters of sense. But there is also a pun on the ambiguous meaning of the Latin *sapere,* which may mean to taste, savor, or smack of, but may also mean to have a sense of taste, hence to have sense or discernment, to be sensible, discreet, judicious, and wise, and finally, at its highest metaphorical development, to have knowledge or understanding

50 *Summa theologiae,* I.76.5; also I.86.7.

51 Saint Antoninus, *Summa theologica,* tit. I, cap. vi; I, col. 50c–d.

52 L. Vinge, "Chapman's 'Ovid's Banquet of Sence,' Its Sources and Theme," *JWCI,* 38, 1975, p. 247.

of, from which last meaning comes the Italian *sapere*, meaning simply to know. It may also be noted that the noun *sapor*, meaning flavor, was also metaphorically extended to mean style, or to refer to a sense of right conduct.[53]

When Robert Burton wrote the *Anatomy of Melancholy*, first published in 1621, he reduced the inner senses to three: common sense, fantasy (which absorbed the estimative and cogitative), and memory. He linked the common sense to the special senses of sight and hearing, calling it in the latter case "the judge of sounds" in which there is "great variety and delight." In general the common sense "is the judge or moderator . . . by whom we discern all the differences of objects; for by mine eye I do not know that I see, or by mine ear that I hear, but by my common sense, who judgeth of sounds and colours: they are but the organs to bring the species to be censured."[54] Here again the common sense is a faculty that mirrors, but that also judges, "variety and delight" and is thus again close to taste.

The association of the common sense with what we might call taste is to be found in classical Latin authors. It is by no means clear that *sensus communis* as it is used by these authors is descended from Aristotle's definition, and certainly the phrase had different connotations for Roman writers. At the same time, it is clear that the later definition is not incompatible with Aristotle's, and the two seem to have complemented each other. Horace writes that one who interrupts Maecenas while he is reading or thinking with idle chatter we say plainly to lack common sense [*communi sensu plane caret*].[55] This is not so different from modern usage, which is replete with similar metaphors. We may speak of someone as behaving with tact (from *tactus*, touch) or being "sensitive," and by this we mean that a person has an intuitive awareness of particular situations and individuals. Such a person may behave "tastefully," and if one may be taught to behave tastefully, taste, tact, and sensitivity are also innate, and their possession or lack of it distinguish one person from another. If Horace's reference to *sensus communis* is distant from philosophical speculation, it is consistent with more technical versions in that it implies a kind of apprehension of particulars in real situations. In Roman writers *sensus communis* also has connotations of community, of being a universally shared virtue. Quintilian writes that it is better to send a youth to

[53] The association of the sense of taste and wisdom had a strong tradition in biblical exegesis, and this again was not untouched by the Aristotelian definition of sense. If the senses of sight and hearing are more spiritual because they are "extrinsic" (as was often argued), taste and touch, being "intrinsic," were inward and more like spiritual experience, for which "taste" could thus become a metaphor. Saint Antoninus (*Summa theologica*, tit. III, cap. ii, fol. 115c–d), citing Aquinas on the *Song of Songs*, distinguished two kinds of speculation, the second of which he calls *gustativa*, which is the speculation of the saints and the faithful (as opposed to the philosophers) so that *speculatio gustativa* is relatively "common." He cites *Hebrews* 6:4, in which reference is made to "those who were once *enlightened*, and have *tasted* of the heavenly gift, and were made partakers of the Holy Ghost." This taste, it is explained, pertains to wisdom, which is so called from *sapor*, and leads to eternal clarity. The devil tries to blind this *speculatio gustativa* in us.

[54] R. Burton, *The Anatomy of Melancholy*, ed. F. Dell and P. Jordan-Smith, New York, 1927, pp. 139–140.

[55] *Satires* I.iii.

school to learn than to have a private tutor because if he is kept away from society at large, he will never learn that "*sensus* which we call *communis*."[56] Here common sense is acquired (which it usually is not said to be) and is a social "sense" necessary for behavior in public life. The connotations of common sense, which could always be supplemented by the description of universally possessed sensory powers, will emerge again and again in the chapters that follow, and become the dominant meaning of common sense in the eighteenth century. Lord Shaftesbury, who cited and explained Horace's text, who first used the term "moral sense," and to whom the "introduction of the concept of 'aesthetic perception' " has been attributed, described the faculty of aesthetic perception as "plain internal sensation," which is, like bodily sensation, immediate, nonreflective, without "principles," and incorrigible.[57] This is not far from the psychological definition of the common sense, and shows the ease with which the various meanings of the terms might merge.

Kant on taste and the common sense

To say "this flower is beautiful," Kant wrote in the *Critique of Judgment*, is to say that it is beautiful to everyone, that in some sense the judgment of its beauty is universal. The smell of the flower, however, may give one person pleasure, another person a headache. If the flower is beautiful, then, and this beauty can have no absolute subjective basis, are we forced to conclude that beauty is a property of the flower itself? Kant says no, "because a judgment of taste consists in calling a thing beautiful just because of that characteristic in respect of which it accommodates itself to our mode of apprehension." Thus the universality of the judgment is based not upon the subject, but upon the *constitution* of the subject, which is – at least in principle – universal.[58]

A few pages later Kant treats "taste" as a kind of *sensus communis*, and further specifies it as a *sensus communis aestheticus* (as opposed to *logicus*). He separates "common" from "vulgar," "that which is everywhere met with," and separates "common sense" from the "common understanding of men, which, as the mere healthy (not yet cultivated) understanding, we regard as the least to be expected from anyone claiming the name of man." The *sensus communis* is instead a

> sense common to all, i.e., a faculty of judgment which, in its reflection, takes account (*a priori*) of the mode of representation of all other men in thought, in order, as it were, to compare its judgment with the collective reason of humanity, and thus to escape the illusion arising from the private conditions that could be so easily taken for objective, which would injuriously affect the judgment. This is done by comparing our judgment

[56] *Institutio oratoria* I.ii.20; cited by Lewis, *Studies in Words*, p. 146.

[57] Anthony Ashley Cooper (Earl of Shaftesbury), *Characteristics of Men, Manners, Opinions, Times*, ed. J. M. Robertson, New York, 1964, I, pp. 70–71. See J. Stolnitz, "On the Significance of Lord Shaftesbury in Modern Aesthetic Theory," *Philosophical Quarterly*, 11, 1961, pp. 97–113.

[58] *Critique of Judgment*, sect. 32, tr. J. H. Bernard, New York, 1964, pp. 123–125.

with the possible rather than the actual judgment of others, and by putting ourselves in the place of any other man, by abstracting from the limitations which contingently attach to our own judgment.

Kant accepts the distinction between special and common sense, and considers common sense a higher, judgmental faculty. The universality of taste therefore consists in this: that although we all see from the standpoint of our own sensations and feelings, we may abstract from these immediate conditions to consider our apprehensions in the mode of their apprehension; and if our experiences are not universal, our modes of apprehension are, so that we place ourselves in the position of all other men insofar as we are reflectively aware of these modes in relation to our experience.

Such conclusions were implicit in the idea of the common sense from the first. The very idea that sensation – and especially common sensation – was structured, that is, capable of judgment, meant that judgment was a part of all human sensation. Thus, although Kant distinguishes common sense from "common understanding" and the prejudice and superstition that go with it, reflective common sense is essential to his notion of taste. Common sense is the mode of judicative apprehension by anyone, and taste consists in the conformity of the particular to reflective common sense, to common sense as a universal reflective awareness of the mode of apprehension.[59]

In the tradition we are examining in this book, the common sense was granted a number of powers by writers working toward various purposes. These powers, however, seem never to have been systematically examined or interrelated. Perhaps between Kant and this earlier tradition, in the seventeenth and earlier eighteenth century, such an examination was made. But the more important point for our purposes is that the question of aesthetic judgment fell precisely in the region of the *sensus communis* when Kant completed his own faculty psychology, and his notion of taste fully articulates the adaptation of the language of inner sense to the problem of aesthetic judgment that had begun in the Renaissance. When, as just mentioned, he distinguished between the *sensus communis aestheticus* and the *sensus communis logicus,* he seems to have meant to differentiate the various powers long attributed to the common sense. The common sense unified, judged, and oversaw particular sensation.[60] It not only synthesized but, as a faculty of synthesis, was sometimes identified with imagination and was close to the internal actions of fantasy. The common sense was also close to reminiscence and its activities of association and in the course of its unification of sensation made distinctions, judged white not to be sweet, to use Aristotle's example for myriad

[59] Ibid., sect. 40, pp. 135–138.

[60] Kant seems to make a similar distinction in his *Logic* between logical and aesthetic distinctness, the first an objective, the second a subjective clarity of characteristics, the one a clarity through concepts, the second a clarity through intuition. These two kinds of clarity are not necessarily compatible. For this text (not in relation to the *sensus communis*), see M. Podro, *The Manifold in Perception: Theories of Art from Kant to Hildebrand*, Oxford, 1972, pp. 25–27.

qualitative judgements, and made a host of relative, optical judgments. It thus performed what might be called both prelogical and pre-aesthetic functions. Because the common sense was both structured and immediate to sensation and physical individuality it was closely allied not only to imagination but to genius. It was in the area of such intuition of particulars, between pure sense on the one hand, understanding and reason on the other, that Kant could begin to map the region of the aesthetic. The common sense was always of an individual in a way reason was not, and the common sense also apprehended the particular. It nevertheless had its own structure and characteristic activities. Conformity with these structures and activities – integral with apprehension itself and definable through reflection on apprehension itself – *was* for Kant aesthetic experience, which could be spoken of at once as individual and as universal. In Kant's hands and in the vast tradition following him this realm was much extended and defined and its ancestry seems to have been forgotten. All the same, these investigations formed around a much older armature of ideas, and it was these ideas that late medieval and Renaissance writers had turned to the purpose of describing and explaining what came to be called aesthetic experience.

Marsilio Ficino on the *Theatetus*

This chapter began with a review of Leonardo da Vinci's remarks on the common sense, followed by Plato's arguments on the nature of sensation in the *Theatetus*, which stand behind Aristotle's notion of common sense. The argument may be brought back to Renaissance Florence, and a summary may be made of this chapter – and indeed of much of the book to come – by considering Marsilio Ficino's commentary on the *Theatetus*.[61] As noted before, Plato only generally indicated what it is for which the senses sense, calling it *psyche* and distinguishing its nature from the materiality of the organs of sense. This last point Ficino very much emphasizes. What lives senses, he writes. Soul lives and soul senses, but in body there is neither life nor sense. The organs sense nothing but are rather channels through which a "certain power of the soul" senses things. By this "certain power of the soul" Ficino understands Plato to mean a *sensus communis,* upon which all sensation converges. Ficino joins a long tradition in comparing the common sense to the center of a circle, joined by lines to its circumference. From this circumference various "passions" flow in, color through the eyes, sound through the ears, odors through the nose, flavors through the tongue; finally, through the whole body are conveyed heat, cold, wet, dry, heavy, light, soft, hard, rare, dense, sharp, and blunt. Ficino insists that the destination of these sensations must be unitary, and again follows Aristotle in arguing that were this not the case we would not be able to say that color is not sound, or flavor not odor. Such

[61] M. Ficino, *Opera omnia*, Basle, 1576 (facs. Turin, 1962, ed. P. O. Kristeller, II, pp. 273–277.)

distinction is found not in any one organ but in a "certain percipient thing in the soul."

Ficino then separates the human soul from animal souls. The common sense is innate in all animals, but there is also a power of the soul that he calls "perfect fantasy and opinion," and by this power we judge essence, unity, number, sameness, otherness, similitude, dissimilitude, beauty, ugliness, good, evil, usefulness, and uselessness. This judgment is not possessed by all animals, nor is it innate (here Ficino is following Plato, who argued that the reflective knowledge produced by sensation is achieved only through experience and education).

Ficino followed the pattern of the Platonizing Avicenna in making the common sense a simple but essential unifier of sensation. He clearly regarded the principle of judgment as higher than common sensation, although immediate to it. In order to accommodate this argument he has recourse to what is in effect a higher common sense, or human common sense, which he identifies with the cogitative faculty. His "perfect fantasy and opinion" judges according to time, place, and condition (*sub tempore locoque & conditione iudicat*). Such judgment is associated with what he calls "particular reason and cogitation" and is to be distinguished from "universal reason or cogitation." We are not only able to apprehend and judge particular things, we are also able to judge concerning things in a general and universal way; rather than judging that man here and now, we may think "humanity." Interestingly, Ficino regards both particular and universal reason as essentially discursive, the latter only proceeding by syllogisms. In all reason (*ratio*) there is still something of motion and time. The higher mind (*mens*) apprehends things by a simple and stable intuition, which borders the higher unity of which the unity of the soul itself is a reflection. The common sense was, in short, an "aesthetic sense," and, as we shall see in coming chapters, many more powers of judgment would have been added to it by the time Leonardo took up the idea.

6

Spiritus

Physiognomy

Michael Baxandall observes that discussions by Renaissance writers of what we might call expression in art are hard for us to understand now "because we no longer believe the old pneumatic physiology through which they are rationalized."[1] This "pneumatic physiology" corresponds to the psychology with which this book is concerned. Although it had many variants, this psychology (or physiology) seems to have been assumed in some form or another by all writers who took up any of the many subjects to which such "rationalization" was appropriate. This near universality is not surprising, because these ideas, some of which – "spirit," for example – have survived the demise of their supporting physiology and persisted into the present time, were fundamental to the most basic and pervasive religious and cultural values.

When writers as important to Italian Renaissance art as Leon Battista Alberti and Leonardo da Vinci wrote that the depiction of movement was of the very highest importance for the art of painting, they argued in this way because they assumed it was the movement of the body that made the movements of the soul apparent. That is, they assumed, as their readers assumed, that all living matter was "animated," literally "inspired" or ensouled. What does this have to do with expression? The presumed medium of expression between soul and body, person and person, and person and image was ultimately spirit. This means in the first place that Renaissance images were presumed to make us see more than we are shown and, more specifically, to make us see something higher than what we are shown. We see a higher, spiritual inwardness in external forms. We are familiar with something similar in portrait photography. Presumably any photograph of a person is a likeness, but only a good portrait photographer can "capture" not just the likeness but the very person in such a way that we feel we are seeing a "true" image. Moreover, we attribute this extra "something" to

[1] M. Baxandall, *Painting and Experience*, p. 60.

the "quality" or "sensitivity" of the photographer. In the Renaissance all of this would have been explained in terms of "pneumatic physiology."

The apparent sitter in a Renaissance portrait was thus an external appearance showing an inward truth, and so, it might be said, were Renaissance works of art in general. The spirit they expressed, however, was not simply that of their subject, it was also that of the artist, who gave the painting its "life." The *Mona Lisa* is a painting of – taken from the appearance of – a Florentine merchant's wife and at the same time a painting of – from the hand and sensibility of – Leonardo da Vinci. This second, genetic relation between artist and image was fully recognized in the Renaissance; it is the meaning of the Renaissance commonplace "every painter paints himself," and the idea adds another dimension to the central paradox that the objective world is only evident from a point of view. Individual style, or manner, developed together with portraiture (and naturalism in general), so that the work itself became "physiognomic" at the same time that physiognomy became a part of the science of painting.

The viewer of a Renaissance portrait, then, was assumed to see, by means of the painting, the spirit of the sitter and, inevitably, the spirit of the painter who had given it its apparent life. This assumption could be expanded to explain the expression of the work, the consonance between the character of the work, and the reaction in the spirit of the beholder. As an example of the workings of this spiritual mechanism we may consider the words from the treatise on the art of dancing by Guglielmo Ebreo, written around 1470.[2] This text is of interest for several reasons, and provides at least a slender link between the previous chapters and this one. Dancing, Guglielmo writes, "is an action outwardly demonstrating [internal] spiritual movements which must agree with the measured and perfect consonances" of the harmony of music. In order to explain how this agreement is effected, Guglielmo has recourse to a version of the idea of inner sense. The "measured and perfect consonances of harmony" descend "with delight to the intellective parts of the cordial senses." It will be recalled that Aristotle, beginning a tradition that was never altogether abandoned through all the centuries of Galenic physiology, located the *arche* of sensation in the heart. Of course, to voice a comparable idea is not necessarily to cite Aristotle. Prephilosophical usage still associates the heart with emotion, life, and even with a kind of judgment, and Guglielmo's words no doubt rest in part on the substratum of ordinary language. But he also specifically refers to "senses" and to the "intellective parts" of these senses, which suggests that he means to refer to the higher inner senses. As we shall see in Chapter 7, Cicero and Augustine attributed the apprehension of *numerus,* or rhythm, to the common sense. Again, this is not to say that Guglielmo used these authors, only that their words make his understandable. In fact, his argument is not very different from Alberti's regarding *concinnitas,* also discussed

[2] Guglielmo Ebreo, *Trattato dell'arte del ballo,* ed. F. Zambrini, Bologna, 1968, p. 7; see also the sonnet on p. 1 and further discussion on pp. 37–38 in terms of the theory of the temperaments. This text is discussed by Baxandall in *Painting and Experience,* pp. 60, 77–78.

in Chapter 7. In any case, he describes an instantaneous process in which harmony is assimilated by the spirit of the dancer through the *sensi cordiali,* and this assimilation produces "certain sweet commotions" in the heart, which, "shut up contrary to their nature, strive with all their might to issue forth and to be made manifest in act." This is dancing. Thus, the hearing of music changes the spirit by means of which it is apprehended; this passivity of spirit becomes active, and this activity is expressed in appropriate physical response to the music. One watching the dancer would apprehend by similar means the harmony of the music, the spiritual state of the dancer through the dancing, and the fit between the music and the movements of the dancer. In the next chapter, we shall encounter very similar arguments to explain the expressiveness of sculpture, but now we shall examine the notion of spirit more closely.

Augustine on inspiration and vision

In the twelfth book of *De genesi ad litteram,* Augustine sets out to explain the words of Saint Paul (2 Corinthians 12:2–4), describing a vision in which "whether in the body or out of the body," a man was caught up to the third heaven, to paradise, where he heard "unspeakable words, which it is not lawful for a man to utter." To explain this experience Augustine takes up the theory of the *pneuma,* which he calls *spiritus,* in the context of which he treats the whole cluster of ideas around "interior sense." Augustine not only passed along to the later Middle Ages a fully elaborated late classical pneumatology, he also established the basis for the later medieval discussion of religious vision and meditation.[3]

As we have seen, Aristotle associated the *sensus communis,* as the *arche* of sensation, closely with the *pneuma,* which he described (*De generatione animalium* 736b) as more divine than the four elements and as a mediator between soul and body. The Stoics materialized the *pneuma,* identifying it with a subtle fire, which was at once the life principle in man and the immanent God or soul of the world. Medical writers associated it with breath, which, again as a life principle, was diffused throughout the body.[4]

Although we shall recognize many of these basic ideas in Augustine, it is to the Neoplatonists Plotinus and Porphyry that we must look for Augustine's immediate precedents.

Centered at the *hegemonikon,* the *pneuma* was a living force coextensive with the

[3] S. Ringbom, "Devotional Images and Imaginative Devotions: Notes on the Place of Art in Late Medieval Private Piety," *GBA,* ser. 6, 73, 1969, pp. 159–170, calls Augustine's chapter "the basis for medieval explanations of vision, ordinary as well as supernatural." The issue is also discussed and additional bibliography provided in Ringbom's *Icon to Narrative: The Rise of the Dramatic Close-up in Fifteenth-Century Devotional Painting,* Abo, 1965, pp. 15–17. He notes that Thomas Aquinas changed Augustine's tripartite scheme to a contrast between *visio imaginaria* and *visio intellectualis.*

[4] See J. H. Taylor, "The Meaning of Spiritus in St. Augustine's 'De Genesi XII,' " *Modern Schoolman,* 26, 1948–9, pp. 211–218; on the idea of *pneuma,* G. Verbeke, *L'Evolution de la Doctrine du Pneuma du Stoicisme à S. Augustin,* Paris, 1945. See also E. R. Harvey, *Inward Wits,* pp. 4–30, and R. Klein, "Spirito peregrino," in *Form and Meaning,* p. 62–85.

body, reaching wherever sensation reached. It was therefore in effect a more subtle body. Plotinus identified this pneumatic body with the body taken by the soul from the planets when it descends to earth. In this world it mediates between the higher and the lower, until it is abandoned at death. For Porphyry the *pneuma* is more closely bound both to the soul and to the body. The soul does not forsake it at death, and it is in effect the wax – now dematerialized – upon which sensation is impressed. It is thus a kind of fantasy or imagination, which presents images to the intellect.

As we have seen, the general power of the soul to form images occupied the central place in Aristotle's psychology. The mirroring of special sensation in the common sense was an act of discrimination and judgment, and around this act resulting in images as a result of sensation turned the whole system of dreams, daydreams, conceptions, intentions, plans, visions, hallucinations, and delusions. All behavior was toward imagined states, and memory was simply imagination that could be shown to correspond to some real experience. The human mind was able to form generalized images with experience, generalized images that formed the link between sense and reason. The centrality of imagination was given a macrocosmic dimension in the fully developed theory of *pneuma,* so that the mediation between body and soul became a mediation between earth and heaven, and the theory of *pneuma* came to provide the basis for a theory of prophetic vision.

In his *De somniis,* Synesius argues that the fantasy (which he calls *to phantastikon pneuma*), although it has no special organ, is a kind of sense of senses. In terms recalling both the *hegemonikon* and the common sense, he calls it the most widely shared organ of sensation, the first body of the soul, about which nature has constructed all the functions of the brain, and to which all the senses are subservient. "And this is the perfect sense perception in all its parts, for it hears and sees with its whole *pneuma* and has power over all the remaining senses. It divides its powers, assigning one to one place and another to another. These powers stretch out like a living being, each one separately, and, like straight lines radiating from a center, return to and meet in the center again, all of them one in their common root though many in their outgoings." Because the fantasy is in a sense material it is able to receive impressions from below, and because it is half immaterial it is able also to receive impressions from above. "The primary world soul, descending from the spheres, borrowing and making use of the fantasy as of a boat, has intercourse with the body. . . . Through it [the fantasy] we have union many times with the gods, who warn us, respond to us and counsel us." These arguments are substantially similar to those of Augustine, to whom we shall now return.[5]

Augustine's notion of *spiritus* as set out in the *De genesi ad litteram* not only

[5] See M. W. Bundy, *The Theory of Imagination in Classical and Medieval Thought,* pp. 147–153. When Marsilio Ficino translated Synesius (*Opera omnia,* II, p. 970, modern numeration), he called the fantasy the first body of the soul and common sense. Bundy (pp. 170–171) forcefully draws the comparison between Synesius and Augustine.

passed a fully developed pneumatic psychology on to the Christian Middle Ages and the Renaissance, giving this psychology the great authority of his name, but it also provided a framework within which the recovered psychology of Aristotle himself, as well as the doctrine of the internal senses defined by his commentators, could both be made intelligible. For both of these reasons it will be worthwhile to examine his arguments with some care.

Augustine defined three kinds of vision: corporeal, spiritual, and intellectual.[6] The first apprehended present corporeal things; the second, absent corporeal things; and the last, intelligible things without images. Under the category of the spiritual (or the pneumatic) he combined all the various postsensationary faculties, from common sense and fantasy to memory and reminiscence, in a synthesis that has been compared to Averroes's passive intellect and Aquinas's *vis cogitativa,* both ideas that we shall examine in detail in Chapter 10.[7]

Spiritus is defined as a power of the soul (*vis animae*), inferior to mind (*mens*), where the similitudes of corporeal things are expressed.[8] Spiritual vision is thus *after* sensation; it may be immediate but posterior to sensation, like the unification and judgment that Aristotle attributed to the common sense, or it may be after sensation temporally in that the external cause of the similitude of corporeal things is no longer present.

It may be noted that Augustine avoided the term *phantasia,* for which he reserved the negative connotation of apparition. In a usage that must have deeply affected later discussion of related matters – and the translation of texts concerning related matters – he referred to the constructive or imaginative activity of *spiritus* as *cogitatio.* Thus we may form images in our mind that are true in the sense that they correspond to things we see or have seen and remember; or we may form images that are fictive, like those formed by imagination (*sicut cogitatio formare potuerit*). We imagine (*cogitamus*) Carthage, where we have never been. We shall consider these ideas in detail in Chapter 10 when we treat the *vis cogitativa.*[9]

The ability to "see" absent corporeal things, things out of sight because of their distance from us in space, the past, or the future, was essential to the superiority of spiritual over corporeal sense, and this ability embraced the uniquely human activities of reminiscence and productive fantasy. But for Augustine, the image-making faculty is not only at a necessary remove from sensation, its distance from sensation places it in vicinity, or in a relation of susceptibility, to the heavenly, and hence, as in Porphyry and Synesius, sensation is impressed upon the same faculty that apprehends truly heavenly visions, the faculty by virtue of which one is carried up to the third heaven, to paradise, whether in the body or

[6] *De genesi ad litteram* XII.6.15.

[7] *La Genèse au sens littéral en douze livres (VIII–XII) De genesi ad litteram libri duodecim,* ed. P. Agaesse and A. Solignac, Paris, 1972, p. 564.

[8] *De genesi ad litteram* XII.9.20.

[9] Ibid. XII.6.15.

out of the body. For Augustine this image-making *spiritus,* which may communicate with the higher spheres, is also in a certain sense equal to them. As the heavens are to the terrestrial world, so is sight to the other senses; spiritual sight surpasses even the light of the heavens accessible to corporeal vision. This is true even of that in which images of corporeal things are expressed. Augustine comes to a position similar to that of Plotinus, according to which imagination as active in relation to the whole world is superior to it.[10] Sight and imagination, because they may encompass the physical world, transcend it, and are therefore like the transcendental reality. In its highest forms, *spiritus* is divine; here in germ is Dante's *alta fantasia.*

At a lower level, it may be noted that much of Augustine's characterization of *spiritus* falls along lines established by the idea of the *sensus communis* as the center and *arche* of sensation. He writes of sight relative to the "seat of the brain" (*sedes cerebri*) by which attention is directed (*dirigitur intentio sentiendi*).[11] Again, corporeal sense is distributed "as if in five streams of unequal strength." When we dream, these streams converge on "corporeal sense" and we see images. By "corporeal sense" Augustine clearly means the principle of corporeal sense, which thus takes the place of the common sense in Aristotle's account. Consistently with Aristotle, he also argues that *spiritus* is the basis of the images that we form in anticipation of future acts.[12]

Like the common sense, Augustine's *spiritus* is also a principle of temporal continuity, and it is discussed in words similar to those used to explain the universal sense of rhythm in his *De musica.* Thus we could not understand speech, or apprehend the *suavitas* of music, or make sense of the movements of a dance if our experience were defined by mere physical sensation. In general, it might be said that the apprehension of the relation and unity of parts, whether the plot of a play or the parts of a painting, as an aesthetic relation and unity, insofar as it is apprehended under the conditions of sensation, is an act of spiritual vision.

In an evident adaptation of Aristotle's schema of the relation of the *pneuma* to the four elements, Augustine associated sight with light, the other senses with the four elements. Light thus becomes at once the highest sensible thing and the spirit of the world. As such it is perceived by the highest of the senses, which is immediate to spirit. He seems in fact to argue that all sensation is a kind of sight, less perfect as spirit is mixed with other elements in the body.[13] The effect of such arguments is to identify, or place in the closest proximity, sight and

[10] Bundy, *Theory of Imagination,* p. 119.

[11] *De genesi ad litteram* XII. 19.4–2.

[12] Ibid. XII. 16.33.

[13] Ibid. XII. 16.32. Bonaventure, alluding to *De genesi ad litteram* III.IV.6, makes this the basis of his discussion of sense in the *De reductione artium ad theologiam*, 3, ed. and tr. E. T. Healy, St. Bonaventure, N.Y., 1940, p. 43. On this idea before Augustine, see *De genesi ad litteram,* ed. cit., pp. 615–619.

spiritus, or, not to forget the meaning of *spiritus,* to identify sight with the principle of sentient life.

For Augustine sight was thus a literal activity of spirit, the issuing forth of spiritual light into physical light; and he understood Plato's extromission theory of vision not simply as the activity of the physical element of fire but as the activity of a higher light. This agency of sight was rooted in the attention of spatiotemporally unique individuals, and was also a kind of judgment. Augustine distinguished between natural light, the opposite of which is darkness, and spiritual light, the opposite of which is irrationality. Thus, reason is linked to what he calls the "light of sensing life," to its power to discern what is referred to the judgment of the soul by the body (*et valens discernere quae per corpus ad animae iudicium referuntur*). Although Augustine lists qualities for judgment by all five senses (*alba et nigra, canora et rauca, suaveolentia et graveolentia, dulcia et amara, calida et frigida, et caetera huiusmodi*), it is once again clear that vision provides the basic metaphor for his spiritual judgment.[14]

Augustine's idea that sensation is higher than the sensed, and that its superiority is expressed in a kind of judgment, magnified Aristotle's notion of the judgment of sense and transmitted it in this magnified form to the later Middle Ages. The identification of sight with spiritual sight dogged the discussion of vision through the Middle Ages and the Renaissance, and no doubt accounts in large part for the survival of the old Platonic theory of extromission long after the victory of the intromission theory had laid the foundations of modern optics. This ambivalence appears clearly in John Pecham's *Perspectiva communis.* Pecham, following Alhazen, accepted the intromission theory, but, after citing the alternative ideas of Alkindi, Plato, and Augustine, asserted that the natural light of the eye contributed to vision by its radiance. He attributed to the eye itself a proportioning and moderating power, which he distinguished only inadequately from the Platonic theory of extromission.[15] At the end of the fourteenth century, Cennino Cennini's definition of *disegno* as a *potere vedere,* to which the light of the sun and the light of the eye are as necessary as a skilled hand if one is to work with *ragione*[16] is entirely intelligible in these terms, as is Michelangelo's remark that the excellence of sculpture will be decided "in the light of the piazza." He meant by this not only that the judgment of the people would decide the quality of the work, as we shall see, but also that this judgment was a kind of spiritual light. Leonardo, who was conversant in the language of then-modern optics, also seriously con-

[14] *De genesi (liber imperfectus),* 24 (MPL, 34, col. 228–229). In the *De quantitate animae* XXII (ed. F. E. Tourscher, Philadelphia, 1933, p. 119 and passim), Augustine extends the Platonic theory ("et per oculos [visus] emicat longius quaquaversum potest lustrare quod cernimus") to argue that the soul is not coextensive with the body because it extends to other bodies in sight. "So is it when I say that I see you by means of sight, though I am not there . . . I am not therefore forced to confess that it is not I who see."

[15] *John Pecham and the Science of Optics. Perspectiva Communis,* ed. D. C. Lindberg, Madison, Wis., 1970, p. 136; see also pp. 127–130.

[16] C. Cennini, *Il libro dell'arte,* ed. D. V. Thompson, New Haven, Conn., 1932–3, chap. 8.

sidered the question of extromission, and commentators on Aristotle's *De anima* regularly considered the question of whether or not sight was a passive virtue.[17] In these discussions the question of the activity of the eye was often considered in terms of such lore as the evil eye, the deadly power of the basilisk, or the clouding of mirrors by the gazes of menstruating women.

Aria and *maniera*

Robert Klein argued in several articles that Italian poetry and philosophy from the *dolce stil nuovo* to Ficino and Giordano Bruno were shaped in fundamental ways by the late classical idea of *pneuma,* which we have considered in some detail in Augustine's *spiritus,* which was his translation of that term. In making his arguments (which review a substantial body of previous scholarship) Klein emphasized aspects of the idea of *pneuma* that we have either passed over quickly or ignored altogether, and we must now briefly examine them. It will be remembered that according to the Neoplatonists Plotinus and Porphyry, the pneumatic body was acquired by the soul as it descended earthward, and upon it were impressed the "gifts" of the planets,[18] the qualities and destiny of the imminent individual. The *pneuma,* it will be recalled, was a kind of subtle matter, and it was related, in a tradition reaching back to Aristotle (*De generatione animalium* 736b) to semen as a principle of life, heredity, and light. If *pneuma* was so intimately related to the life of the individual, who was thus tied to the fact of physical generation and to the influence of the heavens in the determination of the individual self, the light-bearing power of *pneuma* was also related to fantasy, to the power to see again, to see in dreams, in our own light, or in the light of our own phosporescent spirit, which may return to the realm of light itself, to the home from which the soul first descended, so that the spirit may be a vagabond, leaving its body in dreams and visions.

When Paolo Pino wrote in his *Dialogo di pittura,* published in Venice in 1548,

[17] J. Ackerman, "Leonardo's Eye," pp. 108–146.

[18] R. Klein, "Spirito peregrino," in *Form and Meaning,* p. 65. See R. Klibansky, E. Panofsky, and F. Saxl, *Saturn and Melancholy,* London, 1964, pp. 155–165, on Macrobius *In somnium Scipionis* I.XII.13–14 (ed. W. H. Stahl, pp. 136–137, with notes). "By the impulse of the first weight the soul, having started on its downward course from the intersection of zodiac and the Milky Way to the successive spheres lying beneath, as it passes through these spheres, not only takes on the aforementioned envelopment in each sphere by approaching a luminous body, but also acquires each of the attributes which it will exercise later. In the sphere of Saturn it obtains reason and understanding, called *logistikon* and *theoretikon;* in Jupiter's sphere, the power to act, called *praktikon;* in Mars' sphere, a bold spirit or *thymikon;* in the sun's sphere, sense-perception and imagination, *aisthetikon* and *phantastikon;* in Venus' sphere, the impulse of passion, *epithymetikon;* in Mercury's sphere, the ability to speak and interpret, *hermeneutikon;* and in the lunar sphere the function, of molding and increasing bodies, *phytikon.* This last function, being the farthest removed from the gods, is the first in us and all the earthly creation; inasmuch as our body represents the dregs of what is divine, it is therefore the first substance of the creature." This seven-part scheme had a wide currency in the Middle Ages, becoming involved with the seven deadly sins and the seven gifts of the holy spirit.

that the first part of *disegno* – *giudicio* – can only be had by nature, as the poets must also have it, because it cannot be learned, his remarks were entirely consistent with his later argument that human judgments (*giudicii umani*) vary.[19] *Giudicio* here is close to *ingegno,* as it often is in Renaissance authors, and this "natural" component of *giudicio* is stressed in what follows. Variety owes to differences in "complexion." We in effect all embody intellect in different ways, and these differences are evident in taste (*gusto*), in the fact that not all are pleased by the same things. These differences separate painters from others; indeed, they explain the whole range of human pursuits, and they owe to the influence of the stars. Because of astrological and physical constitution, persons of no station (*inculti*) may become excellent painters. "This is because we are guided to such perfection by means of a good natural disposition, and this is infused in us by some conjunctions of the most benign planets, either at our conception or at our birth."

Such ideas were current long before Pino wrote. In the second quarter of the fifteenth century, in the immediate aftermath of the first great phase of the Florentine Renaissance, Giovanni Cavalcanti used arguments in his *Storie fiorentine* strikingly similar to those we are considering to explain differences among artists. Cavalcanti believed that the influence of the stars plays a determining part in collective human affairs and attributed individual differences to the "*fantasia* common to each rational creature." *Fantasia* is evidently the *individual* human (that is, rational) soul, according to the ancient formula; but it is also just as clearly the particular intellect, the lower faculties of the rational soul in conjunction with imagination and with the individual body. There are, Cavalcanti argued, as many human creatures as there are stars in the heavens, and there are as many human wills (*le volontà umane*) as there are different influences in the natures of the stars. Cavalcanti used *volontà* and *fantasia* complementarily, and must have understood both of them to mean something like innate character, all those ways of thinking and acting that distinguish any individual from all others. As examples of such differences he lists contemporary artists. "Another will [*volontà*] was in Pippo di ser Brunellesco [Filippo Brunelleschi, the first Renaissance architect and inventor of perspective], than was in Lorenzo di Bartoluccio [Brunelleschi's rival, the bronze sculptor Lorenzo Ghiberti, whom we shall encounter in Chapter 8], and another *fantasia* was in Master Gentile [da Fabriano, who painted in a splendid International Gothic style] than was in Giuliano d'Arrigo [the painter called Pesello]. The *Fantasia* that rules over all things subject to God is a principle of absolute individuation, and from the diversity of fantasies given to individuals "proceeds so much diversity of *ingegni* in men," so much diversity of art.[20] The

[19] BT, I, pp. 114, 132–133.

[20] I am once again grateful to Martin Kemp, this time for allowing me to read his forthcoming " 'Equal Excellences': Lomazzo and the Explanation of Individual Style in the Visual Arts," in which this text is cited. Discussion here is based on C. Varese, "Giovanni Cavalcanti storico e scrittore," *La Rassegna della letteratura italiana,* 63, 1959, pp. 14–15; and U. Procacci, "Di Jacopo di Antonio e delle compagnie di pittori del Corso degli Adimari nel XV secolo," *Rivista d'arte,* 35, 1960, p. 20.

pervasive (if disputed) science of astrology provided an explanation of the development of the individual, of which the artist was now the paradigm.

In further illustration of the application of these ideas to painters, we may consider the words of Cristoforo Sorte, who in his *Osservazioni nella pittura,* published in Venice in 1580, argued that in order to practice the art of painting well, not only must one know the precepts of the art, but one must also have a certain "natural inclination."[21] Thus stated, this is nothing more than the ancient opposition between *ars* and *ingenium,* but it is immediately raised to another level, for we are told that this natural inclination results from "celestial influences," referring to Petrarch (*Canzoniere* CCCIII, "Amor, che meco al buon tempo ti stavi"), "Sua ventura ha ciascun dal dì che nasce" (Each has his fate from the day of his birth).

The "fate" defined by both natural inclination and, more absolutely still, by "celestial influences," is a

> natural Idea, or we wish rather to say celestial instruction, infused in us by superior bodies for this purpose, which not only helps us to work, but in the greater and more perfect excellences imperially rules; whence painters have that same liberty that is usually conceded to poets; and as these [poets] are known in inventions and in styles [*stile*] different from one another, so it happens similarly with painters. Whence it is that the images or figures they make are said to be their children, since ordinarily they retain something of this Idea; and therefore one sees melancholy in the images of some painters, in some others modesty, and in others a certain vivacity of spirit accompanied by a certain gracious and perfect imitation.

As an example of this last type of painter he gives Tintoretto, who, just as in his own gestures, in his face, in the movement of his eyes, and in speech is "pronto e presto," so, "led by a natural and celestial inclination, with perfect judgment in portraits and paintings that he makes from life, he sets down in an instant the darks, shadows and half tones, the reliefs and flesh so well imitated, and done with such bold practice, velocity and quickness, that it is a marvel to see him work."

Here the closest possible connection is drawn between Tintoretto's evident character – his movements, facial expression, and manner of speech – and the characteristic individual *performance* of his painting. Moreover, portraiture – painting determined by the appearance of the sitter – is cited as the example, perhaps because it is precisely in portraits, rather than in more complex history painting, that individual style is most emphatically clear both in its unity and in its contrast with recognizable appearance. Substance is thus given to the proverb that "every painter paints himself"; the painter's style is his fate, his natural inclination resulting from the influences of the heavens. Style is also closely related to "perfect judgment," and it is not difficult to see how Leonardo da Vinci could identify his artist's judgment at once with his soul and with the souls of the

[21] BT, I, p. 299.

figures he painted. If the argument presented here concerning the ancestry of such ideas is sound, then it would perhaps be more apt to say that he identified his judgment at once with his spirit and with the spirit of the figures he painted. In any case, the signature quality of the work is rooted in and identified with the individual, astrologically determined character of the painter.

Sorte also follows the ancient pneumatological pattern in linking style with fantasy. The power of the soul continually to make images is greater in some individuals than in others. That is, although everyone must think with images in this life, this is merely a universal fate, and in others, in whom the proper "celestial instruction imperially rules," the fantasy is stronger. This is a more singular fate, which is set in terms of the shared liberty of painters and poets. From such a standpoint, it is less difficult to understand the equation made by many Renaissance writers on art, noted by Panofsky, of the term "idea" with "fantasia."[22] The painter does not imagine absolute forms, rather the connotations of absoluteness belong to the painter himself. It is the absolutely individual soul that falls through the stars to earth, assuming as it does so at once its "Idea, or celestial instruction" and its unique power to think in images in accordance with its individual constitution. From its origin, the soul bears with it light in which it sees images largely of its own making; and with the experience of the world the soul awakens to its own dream.

The light of the *phantasia* not only linked it to the height of the soul's origin, but was also simply genetic, linked to reproduction and replication of one's own image. Sorte wrote that as a consequence of the "celestial instruction" and imagination of painters, their works are called their children, "since ordinarily they retain something of this Idea." It may be recalled that the word *concetto,* the favored word for the preexisting form in the mind of the artist, is itself a genetic metaphor. The *concetto* is a thing conceived, and to continue the metaphor, the womb in which fertilization, conception, and growth take place is the imagination, the union of soul and spirit, as individual according to the terms of the argument as the actual circumstances of human conception are concrete.

It might be finally suggested that the identification of individual style, or *maniera,* with air, *aria,* which occurs from the fourteenth to the sixteenth centuries, is also a simple translation of *pneuma,* or a secularization of *spiritus.*[23] In order to understand this, we may consider the use to which Petrarch turned one of his classical sources, Seneca's Eighty-fourth Epistle. On the subject of the imitation of models, Seneca wrote that the writer should follow the example of the bee, who gathers nectar from many flowers and then, breathing his own breath (*spiritus*) into it, makes honey. *Spiritus* is meant to be analogous to the *ingenium* and *facultas*

[22] Panofsky, *Idea,* pp. 62–63; *MLA,* pp. 229–233. We may consider the following from Vasari's life of Leonardo (VM, IV, p. 22). Leonardo often did not finish what he began because it seemed to him that "his hands would never be able to attain the perfection of the art in the things that he had imagined, inasmuch as there had formed *nell'idea* certain difficulties so subtle and marvelous, that with his hands, even though they were most excellent, [these difficulties] would never be able to be expressed." The *idea* here is Leonardo's own imagination.

[23] See *MLA,* part I, chap. 3, "Aria."

of the writer, the activity of which conceals the writer's debt to others, and this analogy was sharpened by Macrobius when he repeated Seneca's words.[24]

In the course of his argument Seneca used the example of painting, and used it negatively. A painting is nothing more than a replication of its subject, and is a "lifeless thing." Such replication should not be confused with true imitation. "I think that sometimes it is impossible for it to be seen who is being imitated, if the copy is a true one; for a true copy stamps its own form upon all the features it has drawn from what we may call the original, in such a way that they are combined into a unity." A true imitation resembles what is imitated not as a painting resembles its model but as a child resembles its father.

When Petrarch – "the father of the Tuscan muses," as Sorte called him – repeated this argument, he also used the analogy to painting; however, for him painting was not a "lifeless thing" but was, rather, fully capable of the kind of imitation Seneca advocated.[25] However different the parts may be, image and model, like father and son, possess "a certain shadow and what our painters call 'air' [*pictores nostri aerem vocant*], which is mostly seen in the face and eyes." Petrarch is referring to two things at once. First, the power to unify precedents to the image, a power Seneca called *spiritus;* he has then identified this power with a "certain shadow and what our painters call 'air'," in a definition that distinctly recalls the definition of *ethos* in certain Greek authors.[26] "Air" is thus both something like individual style or fantasy *and* a quality of the image, something about the face and eyes. This quality is more important than mere descriptive veracity, however, and gives the sense of the presence of the person "in" the painting. But the "air" of the portrait is not simply descriptive at a higher level; rather, it exists in necessary relation to the painter and is finally a reflection of the painter's own "air" or spirit, so that Petrarch's understanding of the meaning of Seneca's *spiritus* in relation to imitation is finally deeply Augustinian. The relation of painter to image is, moreover, genetic, and the image not only resembles its model as a son resembles its father, but it also resembles the *painter* as a son resembles its father, and it seems to live as much because it makes evident the *spiritus* of the painter as because it seems to make apparent the *spiritus* of the sitter. The *phantasia* – in effect the particular soul of the painter – is at once the "personality" of the painter and the deepest source of the virtual animation of the image.

Aria could also refer not simply to the atmosphere but to the characteristic "spirit" of places, so that Vasari could partly attribute the revival of the arts and the competitiveness of the Florentines to the influence of "air," which might be receptive or hostile to the spirit of a painter.[27]

[24] Seneca *Epistulae morales* 84; Macrobius *Saturnalia* I.5–6; *MLA*, pp. 192–194.

[25] Petrarch, *Prose*, ed. G. Martellotti et al., Milan, 1955, p. 1018.

[26] *MLA*, p. 474 n. 5.

[27] A. Chastel, "L'Aria: Théorie du Milieu à la Renaissance," *Fables, Formes, Figures*, I, Paris, 1978, pp. 393–403; also M. Baxandall, *Painting and Experience*, p. 26 and passim. Here, *aria* is used much as we might speak of personal style.

We shall now turn from Sorte's text to the introduction to Lomazzo's *Idea*. When we see the paintings of Leonardo da Vinci, he writes, we realize two things: that art is superior to nature itself in attracting the eyes of *intendenti,* and that "excellences" in art vary from one master to another.[28] This Lomazzo attributes to the various geniuses (*genii*) that each has been allotted (*sortito*). *Genio* is from *genius,* and this in turn is from *gigno, gignere* (to beget, bear, bring forth, produce). The base meaning of *genius* is generative power, vital energy, creative spirit, and from this base it could be used to refer to personal wit, taste, temperament, and talent. The word is translated by the much mooted word "genius," not only because the two terms are obviously related but because *genius* is closely related to *spiritus,* and in fact adds another dimension to *spiritus.*[29] The *genio* (not simply the *ingegno*) of the painter is, as it was for Sorte, fated, and what Lomazzo has done is establish an absolute basis for individual difference.

It is interesting to see how this *genio* works in the life of the painter. Lomazzo repeats that it is necessary to find one's own genius. One unaware of his own "disposition, genius and inclination" may accomplish nothing, no matter with what effort. But one "who knows his genius and follows it, easily reaches the peak of excellence in that aspect of painting to which he is inclined." His example of such productive self-knowledge is Raphael. This self-discovery may occur (to use modern postastrological art-historical language) through the "influence" of another painter. A youth may start out on the wrong path and accomplish nothing, but then come by chance upon "a thing to his taste [*gusto*] because it conforms to his particular genius."[30] When this happens, he is "reawakened . . . like a body that receives its spirit." Much as the Neoplatonic lover, he is given *un intelletto sano.* His intellect is clarified and his "troubled faculties" [*celle turbate*] are purged of past errors. *Genio* is here associated at once with taste, with intellect, and with the internal senses (certainly *fantasia* occupies one of the *celle turbate*). *Genio* is variously referred to as a "natural instinct,"[31] as "gifts and virtues" (*doti e virtù*) that are revealed in the artist's work, as a "gift of the divine mind," a talent. Lomazzo is, of course, at pains to insist that natural gifts are not enough, that they must be supplemented by "reason," that is, by study and imitation. He writes of a harmony of talent, study, and instruction, in which art supplements the shortcomings of nature. But *genio* is still prior because study must be suited to it and models are chosen by taste that is animated by it. Lomazzo thus accommodates a range of talents; in some cases, art supplements nature's poor or middling gifts. In others, *genio* approaches our modern notion of genius, and those so chosen may approach the status of the *governatori della pittura,* the pantheon

[28] G. P. Lomazzo, *Idea del Tempio della Pittura,* ed. R. Klein, Florence, 1974, p. 25.

[29] For an introduction to the history of the idea of genius, see the three articles in *DHI,* II: G. Tonelli, "Genius from the Renaissance to 1770," pp. 293–297; R. Wittkower, "Genius: Individualism in Art and Artists," pp. 297–312; and E. E. Lowinsky, "Musical Genius," pp. 312–326, all with bibliography.

[30] Lomazzo, *Idea del Tempio della pittura,* p. 27.

[31] Ibid., p. 29.

of great and exemplary painters, who "in their manners are all dissimilar among themselves, but such that in that part of painting to which they have been inclined by nature, and to which they have directed their art and industry, none may desire greater excellence. Rather they are elevated to such height that they have deprived others of all hope of being able to equal them in that part of painting [*genere*]."

Lomazzo writes of the *governatori* (and their predecessors in classical antiquity) as having achieved the highest degree of perfection in one or another part of painting, in perspective, for example, or proportion, and they are at once stars in a firmament and an academic canon. But his arguments should be considered a late academic version of a much older understanding of the artist that reaches back into the late medieval roots of Italian Renaissance art. It is in the late Renaissance that such canons crystallized. All through the Renaissance, however – and this is still the problem with which Lomazzo grapples – the notion that there was a single standard for art was simply not stated. Renaissance art was – and was self-consciously – concerned with individuals precisely because it was concerned with particulars, with *maniera* precisely because it was concerned with naturalism. Francisco de Hollanda repeated a common Renaissance (and classical) theme when he wrote that "painters, working according to the same measure and precepts, paint men and women and animals almost miraculously each in his own manner and fashion, very differently from one another . . . yet all these different manners may be good and deserving of praise in their different ways . . . each painter strives to imitate the natural and perfect in the way he finds most his own, conforming to his own idea and intention."[32]

Such ideas are to be found in many Renaissance writers, and they are stated in more or less the same terms. Lodovico Dolce's Aretino argued that painting is a difficult art, that it is conceded by heaven to only a few, "because in truth it is necessary that the painter, just as the poet, is born, and is the child of nature."[33] For that very reason "it is not to be believed that there is only one form of perfect painting," as had also been argued at the beginning of the dialogue. Even though it will presently be argued that Raphael does more things well than any other painter (and especially Michelangelo), Aretino still maintains that "because the complexions of men and humors are different, so from this arise different *maniere* and each follows that to which he is naturally inclined"; some painters are "calm, others terrible, others charming, others full of grandeur and majesty." The same may be seen among historians, poets, and orators; all are different, but, to return to the conclusion of the earlier argument, each may be perfect in his kind (*genere*), or *maniera*.

The arguments presented here only lead around to one of the commonplaces of Renaissance art history, which they should perhaps do if they are right. But the arguments also suggest that the implications of this commonplace should be

[32] On this text, see *MLA*, pp. 231, 477 n. 30.
[33] BT, I, pp. 186–187.

taken more seriously. Melancholy, the conventional frame of mind of the artist, was not simply a mental state, as it is now regarded as being, but took its name from the preponderance of one of the humors in one's physical constitution according to Greek medicine. Such a complexion, which occurred under the influence of the planet Saturn, produced strong imagination, an endless flow of *cose nuove,* as well as the other aptitudes and predispositions necessary to the pursuit of painting.[34] Both the disposition to such imagining and its specific constitution in any individual were determined by the star-fated physical constitution of that individual.

Again, we may close our circle with the horoscopes, or near horoscopes, that begin so many of Vasari's lives. Here is the opening of the life of Leonardo da Vinci:

> The greatest gifts are seen very often in human bodies naturally to rain from celestial influences; and sometimes, exceeding these natural gifts, beauty, grace and *virtù* are prodigally heaped together in one body, in such a way that wherever such a person turns, his every action is so divine that, all other men being outdistanced, it is manifestly evident as what it is, given by God, and not acquired by human art. This men saw in Leonardo da Vinci, in whom in addition to beauty of body, never sufficiently praised, there was a more than infinite grace in all his actions; and then such and so constituted was his *virtù,* that wherever his mind turned toward difficult things, he rendered them with absolute facility. His force was great, conjoined with dexterity, with mind and talent ever regal and magnanimous.[35]

[34] See Klibansky, Panofsky and Saxl, *Saturn and Melancholy,* passim; see pp. 36–37, citing Aristotle's *Eudemian Ethics,* 1248a–40, where it is argued that the exceptional person (*perittos,* which was translated as *ingeniosus*) is related to the melancholic, who has strong fantasies, which permit him to have true dreams and predict the future; the melancholic remembers slowly, not at will, because of the strength of the images that come to mind when he tries to remember.

[35] VM, IV, p. 17.

7

The light of the piazza

Art and public in Florence

The history of Florentine Renaissance art is studded with episodes of public participation some of which was politically motivated, but some of which just as certainly arose from reactions to works of art themselves. Donatello, we are told, missed the bite of constant criticism when he was gone from Florence, because it kept the quality of his work high. And if there were philistine vandals to threaten Michelangelo's *David* as it was moved from the Opera del Duomo to the Piazza della Signoria, the location of the statue was also decided by a large jury of artists and craftsmen. In other cases the participation was more general. When Baccio Bandinelli's *Hercules and Caecus* was unveiled in the same public square in which the *David* stood, it provoked reaction so violent that some of its detractors had to be jailed. In a more restful vein, we may consider the story told by Vasari of the cartoon showing the *Virgin and Child with Saint Anne* made by Leonardo da Vinci in the spring of 1501 as part of what was to have been a grandiose high altar for the church of the Santissima Annunziata in Florence. The tyrannical Duke of Athens had been overthrown on Saint Anne's Day in 1343, and Martin Kemp has recently emphasized the importance of the patriotic associations of Leonardo's project in republican Florence.[1] The figurally and psychologically complex theme of the Virgin and Child with Saint Anne occupied Leonardo's mind through the years around 1500, and it is evident that his restless inventiveness produced many variations on it. The work Vasari described is lost,

[1] M. Kemp, *Leonardo da Vinci. The Marvellous Works of Nature and Man,* Cambridge, Mass. 1981, p. 226, with references to earlier literature. See also Z. Wazbinski, "Artisti e pubblico nella Firenze del Cinquecento. A proposito del topos 'cane abbaiante,' " *Paragone*, 327, 1977, pp. 3–24. M. Wackernagel, *The World of the Florentine Renaissance Artist: Projects and Patrons, Workshop and Art Market*, tr. A. Luchs, Princeton, N.J., 1981, p. 34, describes the wooden model of a tabernacle for the host in Florence Cathedral put in place "ad ostendum utrum placeat populo." Later (pp. 286–287), Wackernagel states that "contest designs or models for ecclesiastical and other public buildings and art works were subjected to the opinion and comments of all – 'utrum placeat populo.' "

and seems to have been a near reversal of the later *Virgin and Child with Saint Anne* in the Louvre.[2] Since the lost cartoon was neither a study nor a finished painting, however, but rather a final, full-sized preparatory drawing for a painting, the best evidence of its visual character is perhaps provided by the Burlington House cartoon (Fig. 2). Whichever variation is chosen, it is certain that Leonardo's composition was formative for the High Renaissance style and that it had an immediate impact upon both Michelangelo and Raphael. If Leonardo's cartoon was at all like the Burlington House cartoon, then it was also one of the grandest and most delicate achievements of Italian art, in which Leonardo attained a truly Phidian classicism, linking the qualities of his art to the quality of great precedent images of which he could not have been aware.

Let us turn to Vasari's account. After a period of inactivity in the Santissima Annunziata, Leonardo "finally made a cartoon in which there is an Our Lady and a Saint Anne, with a Christ, which not only caused all craftsmen [*artefici*] to marvel, but, finished only as much as it was, for two days men and women, the young and the old kept going to the room where it was to see it, as one goes to solemn feasts, to see this marvel of Leonardo's, which stupefied all the people."[3] So far, Vasari has made one important distinction with which we shall be concerned in what follows. Leonardo's cartoon not only seemed marvelous to other painters, but also to the people in general. Vasari makes a similar point about Leonardo's great failed republican commission, the Battle of Anghiari. Leonardo's fame was so great, we are told, that not only persons "who delighted in art, but the whole entire city wished that he might leave some memory of it; and everyone discussed having him make some notable and grand work, by which the public [*publico*] would be ornamented and honored by such *ingegno,* grace and judgment as were to be known in Leonardo."[4]

When he wrote these accounts, Vasari may have recorded some version of what actually happened, or of what may have been the real motivations for what took place. Or he might be imagined to have resorted consciously or unconsciously to a *topos*. To me it seems likely that he did all of these, because, as we shall see, the definition of the relation of art to public was a fundamental part of Florentine Renaissance art from its beginning.

We may begin by asking what Vasari meant by saying that Leonardo's cartoon induced *maraviglia.* An answer to this question is provided by the perfectly standard definition of the word given in Ripa's *Iconologia.*[5] *Maraviglia,* Ripa wrote, "is a certain stupor of mind that occurs when something new [*una cosa nuova*] is represented to the senses; and the suspension of the senses in that new thing makes

[2] For a record of Leonardo's lost cartoon and an account of the project with which it was associated, see C. Pedretti in *Leonardo dopo Milano. La Madonna dei fusi,* ed. A. Vezzosi, Florence, 1982, pp. 16–19 and figure 21.

[3] VM, IV, p. 38.

[4] Ibid., p. 41.

[5] C. Ripa, *Iconologia; overo descrittione di diverse imagini cavate dall'antichità, e di propria inventione,* Rome, 1603 (facs. Hildesheim, 1970), p. 305.

men admirative and stupid." Such *admiratio* or *stupore* was the precondition of knowledge, as we have seen, and thus might serve a positive function. It was also the prerogative of art to induce such wonder because the artist could contradict sense through skill, disguising the relation between cause and effect, by moving great weights with little effort, by making us see something we cannot understand how we can see.[6]

What had Leonardo's skill made apparent? To answer this question we may once again take up Vasari's account. The people were stupefied

because there was to be seen in the face of that Madonna all of the simple and beautiful that grace is able to give with simplicity and beauty to a mother of Christ [in other words, Leonardo had given the image something that only his own character could give it]; he wished to show that modesty and humility of a maiden most happy with the joy of seeing the beauty of her son, whom she held tenderly in her lap, while her most pure gaze fell upon an infant St. John who is playing with a lamb, not without a smile from Saint Anne, who, supremely joyful, sees her earthly progeny become divine."[7]

By his skill, that is, Leonardo had effected the impossible, providing access to an absolutely convincing fictive relationship of sacred personages. The figures were credible, and their spiritual states were credible, and these things could be seen by everyone who looked at the painting. We shall now examine the tradition of ideas according to which such universal appeal was justified, bearing in mind as we do so that we are also considering some of the formative principles of High Renaissance art.

Cicero on the appeal of eloquence

In Cicero's *Academica,* Lucullus, in refutation of the Skeptics, praised the senses, which, the illusions of bent oars and the changing colors of doves' necks aside, are capable of entirely adequate practical judgments.

The senses contain the highest truth, given that they are sound and healthy and also that all obstacles and hindrances are removed. That is why we often desire a change of the light and of the position of objects that we are observing, and diminish or enlarge their distances from us, and take various measures, until mere looking itself makes us trust its judgment [*aspectus ipse fidem faciat sui iudici*]. The same is done in the case of sounds and smell and taste, so that among us there is nobody who requires keener powers of judgment in the senses, each in its own class [*qui in sensibus sui cuiusque generis iudicium requirat acrius*]. But when we add practice [*exercitatio*] and art [*ars*] to make our eyes sensitive to painting, and our ears to music, who is there who can fail to remark the power [*vis*] that the senses possess? How many things painters see in shadows and highlights [*in umbris et in eminentia*] that we do not see.[8]

6 See below, Chapter 11.
7 VM, IV, p. 38.
8 *Academica* II.VII.19–20.

There follows a praise of five senses, the last of which, though, is mentioned together with the "internal tactual sense," which perceives pleasure and pain, "the sole basis, as the Cyrenaics think, of our judgment of truth, caused by the mere process of sensation." If it is doubted that this refers to the common sense in some materialist form,[9] these doubts are lessened by the remarks immediately following, in which reference is made to what is not perceived by any of the senses "but by some manner of sense – this is white, this sweet, this melodious, this fragrant, this rough." Reference is clearly to the activity of the common sense in its power to distinguish the data of the different senses.

For Lucullus, mind (*mens*) is the source of sensation (*fons sensuum*) and is sensation; it acts upon some sensations, and stores others away in memory, uniting the rest into systems of resemblances, thus forming opinions. These may be reasoned about, so that wisdom is attained. Because according to the Stoic notion of the *phantasia kataleptike,* things may be grasped adequately, mind employs the senses and makes sciences that are in effect second senses, thus contributing to philosophy and virtue.[10]

In the course of the *Academica,* Cicero responds to Lucullus and vehemently refutes his arguments, maintaining that the senses *are* faulty and that it matters little whether a painter sees things that others do not because only a few of us are painters.[11] But in other writings he repeats similar ideas himself. In the *De natura deorum* he praised the superiority of human sense precisely in its capacity to make what we would call aesthetic judgments. "All the senses of man far excel those of the lower animals. In the first place, our eyes have a finer perception [*iudicium*] of many things in the arts which appeal to the sense of sight, painting,

[9] Wolfson, "Internal Senses," in *Studies in the History of Philosophy and Religion,* p. 252, rejects the idea that *tactus interior* is an "interior sense." As we shall see, the Stoic idea of the *phantasia kataleptike* (G. Federici-Vescovini, *Studi sulla prospettiva medievale,* Turin, 1965 pp. 33–52) had resurfaced in the late Middle Ages and the Renaissance as Alhazen's *virtus distinctiva.* Thus, Cicero's record of Stoic ideas would have provided a classical mantle for its medieval descendant, multiplying its influence in the Renaissance. And at the same time these ideas of sensate judgment would have been given vastly greater philosophical and practical content by their intervening career. Alhazen could also have been read as an explanation of Cicero. The notion of *katalepsis* was essential to the Stoic definition of art (*techne*), as "a set of percepts exercised together toward some end useful in life." The "percepts" were the result of "grasping sense impressions." See Lucian *Parasite* 4, for the form in which this idea was most often repeated in the Renaissance: "an art . . . is a system of grasping sense impressions exercised together toward some end useful in life." Cicero's translation (transmitted by the grammarian Diomedes) reads as follows: "ars est perceptionum exercitatarum constructio ad unum exitum utilem vitae pertinentium," and was known in the Middle Ages from the *Rhetorica ad Herennium* I.2: "ars est *praeceptio* quae dat certam viam rationemque dicendi." As noted by N. W. Gilbert (*Renaissance Concepts of Method,* New York, 1960, pp. 111–112), upon whose discussion this note is based, the Stoic definition relied on the idea of "a sense impression conveying the truth so powerfully as to defy shaking by reasoning." And, as Gilbert observes, the change from *perceptio* to *praeceptio* not only made art a set of rules but neutralized the materialist epistemology of the original definition. (The Stoics distinguished between *phantasia,* which corresponded to something, and *phantasma,* which did not; see Bundy, *Theory of Imagination,* pp. 88–89.)

[10] *Academica* II.VII.30–31.

[11] Ibid. II.XXVII.86.

modelling and sculpture, and also in bodily movements and gestures; since the eyes judge [*iudicant*] beauty and arrangement and so to speak propriety of color and shape."[12] He goes on to list the numerous qualities that are judged [*judicantur*] by the ear. Smell, taste and touch also have great judgment [*magna iudicia sunt*]. The arts invented to appeal to these senses are numerous: perfumery, cookery, and personal adornment in addition to painting, sculpture, and music already mentioned.

In this last case, attention is given to the individual senses, the discriminating powers of which have been considerably multiplied in comparison to Aristotle's spare and Attic alternatives.[13] But in the *De oratore* the notion of the judgment of sense is extended to the common sense, with most important consequences. It is being considered how it is possible that the unlearned crowd – *haec vulgus imperitorum* – may be swayed by the art of rhetoric. This owes, we are told, to a wonderful power of nature. Everybody "by some hidden sense, without any art or measure, judges those things that are right and wrong in art or measure [*Omnes enim tacito quodam sensu sine ulla arte aut ratione quae sint in artibus ac rationibus recta ac prava diiudicant*]. This is true of painting and sculpture, but such judgment [*iudicium*] is much surer in the case of words and rhythms because these are rooted in common sense [*in communibus infixa sensibus*] in which nature has made no one completely deficient." Consequently everyone is moved by rhythm and pronunciation. How many people, it is asked, understand the art of rhythm and meter? And yet the slightest deviation in them is detected at once by all the members of an audience.[14]

[12] *De natura deorum* II.145. In the notes to his edition of the *De natura deorum* (New York, 1979, II, pp. 927–928), A. S. Pease notes that such claims for human sense are "hardly paralleled." Usually man is said to be superior in touch and taste, inferior in other senses. (See also H. W. Janson, *Apes and Ape Lore in the Middle Ages and the Renaissance*, London, 1952, p. 239, where Pliny *Natural History* X.191 is offered as summarizing the classical tradition according to which man excels in taste and touch, but is surpassed in vision, smell, and hearing by the eagle, vulture, and mole respectively.) But as Pease suggests, Cicero means to refer to *aesthetic* judgment, not mere keenness of sight, and is on firm ground in doing so because it was well established that only man delights in sensation as such (see above, Chapter 4). The eagle may see more keenly, but cannot "see" the beauty of a painting, nor does it seek out the pleasures of such experience. Around 1450, Giannozzo Manetti quoted Cicero's text in his *De dignitate et excellentia hominis* (ed. E. R. Leonard, Padua, 1975, pp. 10–11).

[13] See *De oratore* III.vii.25–26, where it is argued that each sense perceives a great number of things to be enjoyed, some so different as to seem contradictory; this is compared to the proper disparity of styles among painters and sculptors.

[14] Ibid. III.L.195. See also *Orator* Ii.173. "Not that the multitude knows anything of feet, or has any understanding of rhythm and when displeased they do not realize why or with what they are displeased. And yet nature herself has implanted in our ears the power of judging long and short sounds as well as high and low pitch in words" (*et tamen omnium longitudinum et brevitatum in sonis sicut acutarum graviumque vocum iudicium ipsa natura in auribus nostris collocavit*). In the Verrine orations (2.4.44) Verres is described as able to perceive the fine characteristics of Corinthian bronzes. Scipio, although a "most learned and cultivated man" (*homo doctissimus et humanissimus*), could not appreciate these things, but Verres, "without any worthy skill, without culture, without talent, without learning," was able to "understand and judge" them (*sine ulla bona arte, sine humanitate, sine ingenio, sine litteris, intelligis et iudicas*). See Pollitt, *Ancient View*, p. 210. In the same place (2.4.2), Cicero

If Cicero referred to Aristotle's *koine aisthesis* directly or at some remove, then he must have meant that just as we all apprehend colors and tastes by means of the special senses, so we also apprehend the common sensibles of movement, magnitude, and number, and that this universal experience is the basis for the universal capacity to judge meter in speech. Moreover, the principle that we delight in our senses as such need only have been extended from the special senses to the common sense. When Aristotle wrote of our enjoyment of sense, he wrote of the special senses; but here it is the objects of the common sense that are both judged and enjoyed, and it is to this judgment and enjoyment that the art of rhetoric must apply itself, and it is upon this base that meaning must be constructed, or in this form that meaning must be presented.

These ideas exerted the deepest influence on Cicero's theory and practice of his own art of rhetoric. Although Cicero would never have argued that rhetoric was nothing more than sounds pleasing to the ear, it can hardly be doubted that he gave the closest attention to what pleased the ear. Nor can there be any doubt that the pleasure of the ear and the judgment of the ear were the same. Cicero was aware of the limitations of appeal to sense, as it was also necessary to be aware of the proper use of any of the other parts of rhetoric.[15] But such reservations having been made, the judgment of the ear was essential to the art of rhetoric from its very foundations in practice. Rhetoric was more difficult than poetry because it did not rely on meter and instead demanded constant adjustment to the pleasure of the ear.[16] This judgment, which together with delivery determined the sensible surface of an oration, could be spoken of together with the judgment of reason. For example, in speech and writing overelaboration is detected "not only by the judgment of the ear, but by that of the mind" (*non aurium solum sed animi iudicio*).[17] (Quintilian could tip the equation in the other direction by saying that oratory "all of one color," without *varietas* in its *composition,* produced an

also describes excellent sculptures able to delight not only "that gifted and perceptive man," but also those of us whom he calls *idiotas*. Near the beginning of the *De oratore* (I.iii.12) it is asked why it is that good orators are the rarest of all men, rarer even than good philosophers and poets. It is because of the "incredible magnitude and difficulty" of the subject. And its difficulty is of a very peculiar kind. "Whereas in all other arts that is most excellent which is farthest removed from the understanding and sense of the unskilled [*ab imperitorum intelligentia sensuque disiunctum*], in speaking the worst vice is to depart from the ordinary way of speaking [*a vulgari genere orationis*], from the usage of common sense [*a consuetudine communis sensus*]." Here *sensus communis* is close to the Stoic *oikeiosis*, on which see below, Conclusion n. 26. A little farther on in the *De oratore* (I.xxiii.108–109) it is considered whether rhetoric can be an art, which must have clearly understood principles, when it is constantly varied and "accommodated to vulgar and popular sense" (*ad vulgarem popularemque sensum*). Oratory is an art in the loose sense that its successes can be codified and taught; but the chief virtue of the orator is inborn, *ingenium*, from which sharpness of mind arise sharpness in invention, richness in exposition and ornament, firm and long-lasting memory (*Nam et animi atque ingenii celeres quidam motus esse debent, qui et ad excogitandum acuti, et ad explicandum ornandumque sint uberes, et ad memoriam firmi atque diuturni*).

15 *De oratore* III.xxv–xxvi.

16 *Orator* lviii.198.

17 *De oratore* III.xxv, 100–101.

unpleasing effect, not merely on the mind, but on the ear.)[18] "However agreeable or important thoughts may be," Cicero wrote, "still if they are expressed in words that are ill arranged, they will offend the ear, which is very fastidious in its judgment."[19]

When he made such arguments, Cicero was hardly defending the use of superficial rhetorical *colores,* he was instead recounting the basis for the universal appeal of rhetoric, for its address to what was in principle a universal audience. This universality lay at the basis of the art of rhetoric in two ways.

It was first of all by the judgment of the ear that sounds were separated from mere speech. This judgment arose from an aptitude possessed by everyone. "Nature herself implanted in our ears the power of judging long and short sounds as well as high and low in words."[20] From the uniformities to be observed among these select sounds an art could be formulated, by means of which pleasing effects may be duplicated and manipulated. Together with the definition of the art, of course, there arose questions of *how* such art should be used; some of these questions were technically aesthetic in the same sense in which the judgment of sense itself was aesthetic (how *satietas* was to be avoided, for example), and some were ethical (how artifice was to relate to the decorum of subject matter, or, at the highest level, how artifice related to truth or whether it was defensible simply to convince through delight). But all of these questions arose from the simple and absolute base of the art in conformity with sensation, which leads to the second aspect of the universality of rhetoric.

Not only did nature implant a standard for judgment in our ears by means of which the formation of the art of rhetoric was guided, but this standard of judgment remained and was constantly applied to the practicing orator. It was because of the same universal structure of sense that the art of eloquence came into existence in the first place and that the audience burst into spontaneous applause at the completion of a well-turned period.

Before following these ideas into the Renaissance, we should take note of an important ambiguity in Cicero's remarks. This ambiguity will recur throughout the whole history of the idea of the common sense, and it is essentially a political question. It is not clear whether *communis* refers to a unifying sense or to a sense shared in common by all people. In principle either of these is possible, and no choice need be made between these alternatives, because the common sense was thought to be part of human sensory apparatus. Reason is also characteristically human. But reason, because it was developed in the exercise of the arts and sciences, demanded leisure, and its development was thus based on social distinction; and if development of the appreciation of painting also demands leisure, such pleasures were clearly regarded as by nature lower and – at least in principle – as universal. For the most part, common sensation was regarded as subrational,

[18] *Institutio oratoria* VIII.iii.2.

[19] *Orator* xliv.150.

[20] Ibid. li.173.

brutal, and classless. We need only remember Kant's remarks on common sense: "the mere healthy (not yet cultivated) understanding . . . the least to be expected from anyone claiming the name of man." When Cicero wrote of *haec vulgus imperitorum,* he may have meant that the crowd at hand was unskilled in rhetoric and yet responded to the fruits of its artifice, or that the unskilled crowd in general was able to respond to the artifice of the orator.

All the arguments we shall consider are based on the idea that we enjoy or do not enjoy sensation at the same time that we experience it, and that this enjoyment is rooted in the structure of sensation itself. This is to say not that we simply enjoy what we see, but that we enjoy it insofar as it is in conformity with sensation. Art is in conformity with sensation or it is not. Common sense is thus not just a mode of apprehension, it is also a mode of discrimination.

Alberti on painting

In his treatise on painting, the Florentine aristocrat Leon Battista Alberti repeats the critical principle that painting in all of its parts should appeal to learned and unlearned alike. He imagines that antiquity was a time when there were many painters and sculptors, when "princes and plebeians, learned and unlearned," delighted in painting. A few lines later he praises painting as pleasing to the "learned as much as to the unlearned . . . which seldom happens in any other art, that that which delights the skilled moves whoever is unskilled." And he concludes that this art gives pleasure, praise, wealth, and fame to whoever masters it. This is because "painting is an excellent and most ancient ornament of things, worthy of free men, pleasing to learned and unlearned," and he therefore urges the young to bend all possible effort to its study.[21]

When Alberti said that painting was worthy of free men, he may have meant that it was a liberal art, suitable for those with the freedom from the cares of life necessary to the pursuit of intellectual arts, as in fact he had just described the pleasure he took in his own occasional activity as a painter; but because he immediately qualified "worthy of free men" with the phrase "pleasing to learned and unlearned," it may be that he meant to say that painting properly had a place in the political life of a republic.

At a less public level, Alberti recommends that the painter should accept advice from friends and passersby. "When painting, be open to whoever comes, and listen to everyone. The work of the painter seeks to be pleasing to all the multitude; therefore do not scorn the judgment [*giudicio*] and thoughts of the multitude when it is possible to satisfy their opinion."[22] He tells the story from Pliny[23] of Apelles, who "hid behind a painting so that each might freely criticize it and so that he might hear their candid blame and praise." This might mean

[21] L. B. Alberti, *Della pittura*, ed. cit., II, 29, p. 52.
[22] *Della pittura*, III, 62, p. 104.
[23] *Natural History* XXXV.84.

that everyone is entitled to criticize a painting from the standpoint of his own expertise. But Alberti concludes his argument by saying that if the painter listens to everyone who might judge, this will help him to acquire grace (*gratia*), which suggests that his paintings will be more pleasing as a consequence of subjecting and accommodating his work to such scrutiny.

Here again Alberti's guide may have been Cicero, in a text repeated by later writers on the same subject. In the midst of remarks on the subject of consultation, Cicero observes that "painters and sculptors and even poets, too, wish to have their works reviewed by the public [*a vulgo*], in order that, if any point is generally criticized [*si quid reprehensum sit a pluribus*] it may be improved; and as they try to discover both by themselves and with the help of others we find that there are many things to be done and left undone, to be altered and improved."[24]

Alberti specifies what it is that makes an *istoria* pleasing to learned and unlearned alike, and these things are fundamental to his notion of painting. One is *rilievo,* or the appearance of relief. In the midst of his discussion of the "reception of light," he remarks that "I say learned and unlearned will praise those things seen [*visi*] that will seem to issue forth from the panel and will blame those in which no art is seen except perhaps in the drawing."[25] And in his defense of the use of his "veil" as an aid to drawing, he remarks that what is expected of painting is not infinite labor but rather that it seem to be in strong relief and that it resemble the person from whom it was copied.[26] The second thing that makes painting universally pleasurable is more properly compositional. *Copia* and *varietà* give pleasure (*voluptà*), and through pleasure "seize with delight and move the mind of whatever learned or unlearned person admires it."[27]

This argument is rhetorical and again more specifically Ciceronian, and the same principle provided the critical bounds for the use of compositional ornament. Excessive ornament or display of ingenuity narrows the audience of paintings, making them suitable only to small audiences of those who understand the art and savor its performance, an audience of connoisseurs.[28]

Alberti on public architecture

Alberti appealed to much the same principles when he wrote his *Ten Books of Architecture* some fifteen years after his treatise on painting. Once again his authority

[24] *De officiis* I.xli.147.

[25] *Della pittura,* II, 46, p. 82. In the fifteenth century *Vita anonima* of Alberti there is reference to optical demonstrations he constructed in which painted landscapes made "learned and unlearned" agree that they were "not like painted things, but like nature herself." See S. Y. Edgerton, Jr., *The Renaissance Rediscovery of Linear Perspective,* New York, 1976, p. 89. On the public uses of sculpture, see J. B. Reiss, "The Civic View of Sculpture in Alberti's *De re aedificatoria,*" *Renaissance Quarterly,* 32, 1979, pp. 1–17.

[26] *Della pittura,* II, 31, p. 56.

[27] Ibid., II, 40, p. 68.

[28] See my " 'Contrapposto': Style and Meaning in Renaissance Art," pp. 336–361, for a fuller treatment of these issues.

is Cicero, who writes in the *De oratore* that, although it is remarkable how great the difference is between *doctum et rudem* in their respective abilities to act, one does not differ much from the other in judgment (*non multum differat in iudicando*). That is, the unlearned (or unskilled) person cannot do what the learned person can do, but he can *judge* the results of what the learned person does.[29] Cicero speaks throughout of various arts, and he grounds this argument in a general principle of the relation of art and nature. Because art begins from nature, it would seem to have accomplished nothing unless it moved and delighted nature (*Ars enim cum a natura profecta sit, nisi naturam moveat ac delectet nihil sane egisse videatur*). The "nature" from which art begins, and to which it must appeal to achieve anything, is *our* nature (which, of course, does not necessarily preclude its consonance with nature in a large sense, that is, it does not preclude the possibility that the same mean is in ourselves and in what we apprehend, and that this similarity in fact makes our apprehension of them possible). Just such an ambivalence runs through Alberti's remarks about *pulchritudo* and *concinnitas*, the latter of which is a principle of both human sense and nature at large. "Beauty is a certain consensus and unison [*consensus et conspiratio*] of the parts of a thing with regard to definite number, finish and collocation, as demanded by *concinnitas*, the absolute and primary reason of nature [*ratio naturae*]."[30] This is followed to the greatest possible degree in matters of architecture, "which by this means attains dignity, grace, authority and value."

Alberti gives several examples of the operation of this absolute and primary reason of nature. In order to arrive at the proportions of columns, he writes, the ancients took measures from the human body, which yielded ratios of 1:6 and 1:10, and made columns according to these ratios. But "the natural sense innate to the mind, by which we feel what is called *concinnitas* [*naturae sensu animis innato, quo sentiri diximus concinnitates*] rejected one as too thick, the other as too thin, and, imitating the mathematicians, they found the mean of eight, which "pleased."[31] This account appears in the chapter following that on ratios; but the mean is formulated, and the mathematicians are imitated at the behest of the *sense* of *concinnitas*, by means of which we apprehend *numerus*. The definite ratios of music and mathematics in architecture stand in the same immediate

[29] *De oratore* III.li.197. To a certain extent this position is consistent with the demand that the painter work to satisfy the judgments of the best painters (see MLA, p. 506 n. 4, on this idea), and might be summarized in the words of Quintilian (*Institutio oratoria* 9.4.116) to the effect that the learned comprehend the reason of art, the unlearned the pleasure (leaving aside the question of the expertise of craftsmen who make things of the kind imitated by the painter, like Apelles's shoemaker). But the two ideas could also conflict. Leonardo wrote in favor of paying attention to the judgment of everyone (*Treatise*, 83) and of pleasing the best painters (ibid., 89), and in this last passage he also suggests that there may be a contradiction between the two. Paintings that please only those who are not masters, he says, will lack foreshortening, relief, and *movimento pronto*, suggesting that there was a more popular taste for planar images with unembellished movement.

[30] L. B. Alberti, *L'Architecttura* [*De re aedificatoria*], ed. G. Orlandi and P. Portoghesi, Milan, 1966, IX, 5.

[31] Ibid., IX, 7.

relation to sensed architectural forms as the definition of a view by perspective stands to the real forms it at once describes and transposes to a higher level of clarity and physical intelligibility. The normative harmonic definition of these ratios in architecture is finally allowed by their agreement with sense. And this first appeal is not simply to one sense but to a common characteristic of sense shared at least by sight and hearing. Alberti defines harmony as a consonance of sounds agreeable to the ear, and he also argues that those numbers that have the power of giving sounds *concinnitas,* which makes them "most pleasing to the ear," are the same numbers that fill our eye and mind (*animus*) with marvelous pleasure (*voluptas*).[32] The ear is a mean, the eye is a mean, and this common principle of sense expressed in the judgments of vision is close to mind, much as Leonardo argued. The mind understands this mean and makes it the basis of architecture, which, insofar as its products are pleasing and therefore beautiful, is constantly subject to the judgment of the eye, and of common sense.

Again, Alberti says, it is easier to point out when the collocation of the parts of a building is wrong than to offer prescriptions for the right arrangement of things. Such arrangement depends upon a "judgment placed by nature in the mind of man" (*iudicium insitum natura animis hominum*), which is clearly synonymous with *concinnitas,* or with the sense of *concinnitas.* In simpler terms, this is the judgment of the eye.

At the beginning of the second book of his *Ten Books of Architecture,* Alberti turns the arguments we have considered to the treatment of public architecture. Here the echoes of Cicero and perhaps of Augustine are clear. Just as for Augustine meters are apparent even to *semidocti* "because they are judged by a natural common sense," so for Alberti "it is truly marvelous how all of us, learned and unlearned [*docti et semidocti*], advised by nature, feel immediately how much there is right and wrong in the art and reason of things." (This is a paraphrase of Cicero's *De oratore* III.1.195.) That is, an architect may build a building according to the rules of architecture, but everyone who sees the building may see at once whether it has some "defect, lameness, superfluity, uselessness, roughness."[33] These are negative qualities corresponding to the positive qualities of *concinnitas.* There are, Alberti once again writes, many kinds of beauty, or *venustas,* none of which has precedence over the others.[34] Still, beauty is not a matter of personal opinion, but rather arises from some innate reason of mind (*animis innata ratio*). Whoever sees the ugly recognizes it at once, through some sense of the mind (*sensus animi*).

[32] Ibid., IX, 5.

[33] Compare *Orator* liii.177–178. "For the ear, or rather the mind which receives the message of the ear [*aures ipsae enim vel animus aurium nuntio*] contains in itself a natural capacity for measuring all sounds. Accordingly it distinguishes [*iudicat*] between long and short, and always looks for what is complete and well-proportioned [*perfecta ac moderata semper exspectat*]; certain phrases it feels to be shortened, mutilated as it were, and is offended by these as if it were cheated of its just due; others are too long and run beyond reasonable bounds; the ear rejects these still more; for in this as in most things excess is more offensive than deficiency." For Augustine, see *De musica* IV.xvi.30.

[34] *L'Architettura,* IX, 5.

So we immediately sense *concinnitas;* by nature "we desire the better and seek the better with pleasure."[35] Alberti then attempts to define the components of *concinnitas,* an attempt that once again raises a central issue. Because there is *ratio* in sense, this *ratio* may be formulated through reflection on the pleasure of sense, thus to become a part of the art of architecture. But the rules extracted from this reflection on the pleasure (or judgment) of sense are still subject to the senses from which they take their origin whenever they are applied to the execution of an actual building. To return to the subject of public architecture, if an architect has in the judgment of everyone made an unsightly building, only an architect may correct the deformity, even though by the same token everyone may again judge at once whether or not the solutions are satisfactory. In words that distinctly recall the explanation of his own emblem of the winged eye, Alberti attributes such judgment to sight, which is the most acute (*acerrimus*) of the senses, here again perhaps recalling this familiar idea in the phrasing of Cicero.[36] It was thus possible for Alberti to argue at once that, insofar as it concerned the beautiful, architecture was both an art – that is, a body of teachable precepts – and subject to a standard of common judgment in actual buildings. The simply aesthetic principles of architecture extend far beyond the limits of the profession of the architect and, at least in principle, are universal, as he also considered good painting to be.

In the third chapter of the sixth of his *Ten Books,* Alberti expands his notion of the judgment of sense to provide the basis for an explanation of the development of Greek architecture. Here, it may be noted, as in Vitruvius, such judgment is closely associated with *ingenium.*

Among the Greeks, he writes, there were many of "good and learned *ingenium*"; they closely examined the colossal works of the Egyptians and Assyrians, concluding that mere size owed entirely to fortune (what the patron could afford) and that it was better to build buildings in which the hand of the artisan was more to be praised than the wealth of the king who had them constructed, an architecture pleasing to the skillful (*periti*), in which the gifts of *ingenium* were evident. Thereupon they began, by careful weighing and consideration, to seek out and draw forth the principles of architecture – and all the arts – from "the very womb of nature." This foundation of art in nature was accomplished by separating the well from the poorly made. They tried everything, examining (*lustrans*) and repeating the "traces of nature." These "traces of nature" are pairs of qualities. They considered "unequal and equal, straight and curved, light and shadow, thinking that some third new thing might arise, as from the union of male and female." These new solutions (found within the definitions of the func-

[35] Compare Pliny *Natural History* XI.liv.145–146: "assuredly the mind dwells in the eye . . . for we see by the mind and discern by the mind" (*profecto in oculis animus habitat . . . animo autem videmus, animo cernimus*). So close is the link of eye and mind that deep thought – *magna cogitatio* – blinds sight by drawing vision inward.

[36] *De oratore* III.xl.161: *sensus . . . oculorum, qui est sensus acerrimus.*

tions of buildings) were clearly means found between these extremes, as Alberti makes clear in the list that follows. He writes that the Greeks did not leave the least part of their buildings unexamined, considering the relations of right and left, upright and horizontal, near and far. They added and subtracted, balancing the greater against the less, the similar against the dissimilar, the first against the last. Thus they became aware both of what was necessary to *firmitas* and *venustas,* or what were the proper relations between *firmitas* and *venustas.* In the discussion that follows, Alberti turns to *utilitas,* which he treats in terms of the "innate" Italian virtue of *frugalitas,* and this perfects the art of architecture. By *frugalitas,* Alberti means at least in part that the Italians possess a "sense" of organic structure in architecture, a sense that complements – but does not supplant – the visual analytic sense of the Greeks. *Frugalitas* thus complements *concinnitas.*[37]

As a history of Greek architecture, Alberti's account may leave something to be desired (although it is perhaps not entirely off the mark). But its value as a self-consciously normative account of Florentine Renaissance architecture is undeniable. Architecture is imagined as rooted in the same principles that make the universal judgment of the architect's work possible. Although the architect is a specialist who knows building types and construction methods, these are materials with which his *ingenium* must work, and in their tangible, visible results his solutions must please the eye, more generally they must please sense, and they are thus subject to the judgment of those who see them for the same reason that it is possible to build beautiful buildings.

Leonardo on painting as a universal language

Alberti's argument for the universality of painting involved two things, which might be described as literal and metaphorical light. The first was the illusion of relief arising from the *ricezione di lume,* the apparent natural light that makes forms seem to stand forth in the virtual dimension of the painting. The second, metaphorical light, was the "brilliance," the *inlustratio,* given to the *istoria* by composition. Cicero's remarks about the judgment of sense had to do with discrimination of this brilliance of artifice rather than with illusion (although of course pictorial illusion depended on a mistaken judgment of common sense), and his arguments were rooted in the structure of sensation itself. Leonardo da Vinci developed the implications of Alberti's arguments in simpler perceptual terms. Accepting Alberti's definition of painting as concerned with the visible, and explicitly incorporating perspective as a geometry of the visible, Leonardo argued that the "science of painting extends to all the colors of surfaces, and to the shapes of bodies covered by those surfaces, and to their nearness and farness with the proper degrees of distances, and this science is the mother of perspective" (which, he adds later, is related to astronomy, thus placing it in the realm of

[37] *L'Architettura,* VI, 3.

Aristotle's "physical" mathematics [*Physics* 194a]. Painting also extends to "light and dark, the science of which is of *gran discorso.*" Painting, in other words, extends to the special sensibles of sight and to the relevant common sensibles, which may be described mathematically by optics, or perspective.[38] In another argument (the argument immediately following in the Codex Urbinas before its modern editing) the implications of this are drawn in a *paragone* with poetry.[39]

An art is more worthy, Leonardo argues, as its products are more communicable, and painting is communicable to "all the generations of the universe" because it appeals to sight. It is explained that words do not pass through the ear to the *senso comune* in the same way that pictures do. Language is conventional, that is, it must be translated, whereas painting immediately satisfies the human species "not otherwise than do the things produced by nature." That "common sensation" is still involved is shown in Leonardo's example of such universal appeal. A painting "imitated" from the father of a family was shown to his infant children, who caressed it, as did similarly his dog and cat, an anecdote that gives another dimension of meaning to Renaissance retellings of Pliny's stories of animals fooled by paintings. Leonardo closes his argument by saying that painting represents things more truly to sense than words or letters do, but letters represent words better to sense than painting is able to do. This somewhat puzzling argument is less clear in its premise than in its conclusion, to which the premise in fact seems to have been shaped. Leonardo returns to the question of the conventionality of language; that science is more noble which represents the works of nature than that which represents "the works of the worker, that is, the works of men," of which words and poetry are examples. Painting, in other words, is the true art of common sensation, just as Aristotle had argued that sight was nearest to the common sense.

If painting is a poetry seen and not heard and poetry is a painting heard and not seen, Leonardo writes in another of his *paragone* arguments, then each is painting and each is poetry. But to call poetry painting raises a confusion, because it implies that it addresses the intellect, or *senso comune,* "by the most noble sense, that is, the eye."[40] Whether or not this is indeed the case may be tested by giving a painting to a person born blind. If the painting "will have been figured with movements appropriate to the mental accidents of the figures," then the deaf person will understand the operations and intentions of the actors, but the blind person will understand nothing. Painting shows us movements and their compositions in histories; it can show us ornate and delightful places and tours de force of illusionism (which he calls *discretioni*). The painter may, for example, show us vegetation and fish beneath transparent waters, on the moving surfaces of which we see at the same time fields, hills, and plants reflected. To the person born blind none of this would be evident because such a person would never have

[38] *Treatise,* 5.
[39] Ibid., 17.
[40] Ibid., 29.

seen any of those things of which the beauty of the world is composed, the "ten ornaments of nature." These are a familiar list – light, shadow, color, body, shape, position, distance, nearness, movement, and quiet – made up of the special sensibles of sight and the common sensibles. And from this point Leonardo moves on to the theme of the universality of painting; because the deaf person cannot even learn to speak, whereas he or she can see perfectly well all the "accident in human bodies" that the painter makes visible. He or she can in fact do this better than one who can speak and is told the same thing by the poet. This means that the elements of universally apprehensible visible nature are the same elements the disposition of which are finally determined by the judgment – the "eye" – of the painter.

In yet another paragone argument – the same one in which he calls the eye "the window of the soul, and the principal way by which the common sense most copiously and magnificently considers the infinite works of nature," Leonardo asks the reader to consider what is nearer – *più propinquo* – to man, the word "man" or the "similitude" of man.[41] The word changes from country to country, but the "form" does not, being changed only by death. (Evidently, Leonardo is thinking of "similitudes" as the apparent forms of individuals, because "man," or the "idea of man," or even the mental concept of an individual, is not altered by death.) Not only is the similitude less arbitrary, but just because this is so, if a painter and a poet both depict a battle, and their works are set in public, more viewers will be drawn to the painting. Similarly, if the name of God and the image of God are displayed, the image will be more revered. A lover will be drawn to an image of his beloved sooner than to a description. Painting embraces all the forms of nature, but the poet has only words, which are not "universal" in the way that these forms are; "if you [poets] have the effects of demonstrations, we have the demonstration of effects." By this he seems to mean that, whereas the poet may set out his inventions as if by argument, the painter may simply show that toward or away from which any number of arguments might move. Painting shows us at once the infinity of the simply present, which is common, and universal.

Il lume della piazza

Although Alberti's formulation of the relation between painting and audience must be supposed to have increased the currency of these ideas and magnified their effect, it is possible that he simply gave a thoughtful, neoclassical form to older ideals. However that may be, repetitions of similar ideas are to be found scattered throughout the Florentine literature of art. Near the end of the second edition of his life of Michelangelo, Vasari tells the story of a sculptor who, having finished a statue, was busily adjusting the light in his shop in order to show it

[41] Ibid., 30.

off to best advantage. "Don't weary yourself." Michelangelo said, "because the important thing will be the light of the piazza.[42] At first this anecdote recalls the story told by Benvenuto Cellini in his *Autobiography* of a visit made by Michelangelo in 1552 to see a bust by Cellini of Bindo Altoviti, a bust that Michelangelo considered Cellini's patron to have placed in such poor light as to have made its deserved comparison to the best antique sculpture impossible.[43] But Vasari moves the encounter out of the *studiolo* and into the city square, and explains Michelangelo's words in much grander terms. By this sardonic remark Michelangelo might simply have meant that there was little point in adjusting the sculpture to a place for which it was not intended. But he also meant, as Vasari explained, that "when things are in public, the people make the judgment whether they are good or bad" (*il populo fa giudizio s'elle sono buone o cattive*). In Michelangelo's statement *lume* is raised a power to the level of a metaphor for judgment, and the same principle is thus applied to public sculpture that Alberti applied to architecture. This gives another dimension to Vasari's insistence that in sculpture "one may use no better measure than the judgment of the eye; which, even if a thing may be most well measured, and the eye remain offended by it, it will for this reason not cease to censure it." Vasari means not only to refer to the eye of the sculptor (which governs the making of the sculpture insofar as it is visible) but also the eye of whoever sees it.[44]

Vasari's anecdote may be used to make another point. The ideas we are considering are not "Renaissance ideas"; rather, they are ideas current in the Renaissance, ideas interdependent with others that were always turned to some purpose in each retelling. If Alberti could imagine a universal eloquence of painting and architecture, Michelangelo's penchant was for a difficult, aristocratic, and exclusive style. But if he painted mysteries, he painted them in most powerful relief, and beautifully, so that if the meaning of his images was not obvious, the embodiment of this meaning was brilliant and heightened, addressing us physically at the same time that it transformed the physical. Again, these remarks are intended only to show that the meaning of ideas, while connecting, shaping, and relating events, is also particular to circumstances. We may speak of a tradition of these Ciceronian ideas in Florence, a tradition that articulated fundamental and properly "stylistic" aims; but we must also recognize that each repetition of these ideas is an adaptation and transformation of them. In the late 1540s, Benedetto Varchi was still familiar with our theme when he wrote that "painters and sculptors – as Cicero says – have this in common with good poets, that they set their works forth in public, so that, having understood the general judgment [*giudizio universale*] they may amend them where they may have been censured by many," in illustration of which he tells the story of Apelles and the shoemaker. The *sensus*

[42] BVM, I, p. 128. I am grateful to Paul Barolsky for asking me to explain this passage.

[43] B. Cellini, *La vita*, II, LXXIX; in *Opere di Baldassare Castiglione, Giovanni della Casa, Benvenuto Cellini*, ed. C. Cordié, Milan, 1960, pp. 907–908.

[44] On this text, see *MLA*, p. 358.

communis of Cicero and Augustine, Alberti's *ratio sensus,* Vasari's *giudizio del populo,* is now *giudizio universale.*[45]

Dolce on the judgment of sense

Toward the beginning of Lodovico Dolce's *Aretino,* published in Venice in 1557, the question is raised of whether or not persons who are not painters are suited to make judgments about paintings.[46] Consideration of the question begins with a bow to the main interlocutor, Pietro Aretino, who, although he has never touched a brush, is pronounced *giudiciosissimo* as regards painting, as indeed he was. Aretino replies that those painters who laugh at *letterati* who dare to speak of painting are painters in name only, and, if they had themselves a spark of judgment, they would know that writers are themselves painters; because, he says, painting is poetry, history, and whatever *componimento* of the learned, so that Petrarch called Homer the "first painter of ancient memories."

Having dispensed with that, he turns to examine the question more carefully, beginning from the premise that in men generally judgment arises from practice and from the experience of things.

> And nothing being more familiar and intimate to man than what is man, it follows that each is suited to make judgment concerning that which he sees every day, that is, concerning the beauty and ugliness of whatever [other] man; because beauty proceeds from nothing else than from a suitable proportion that the human body commonly [*comunemente*] has, and particularly from a proportion that all the members have among themselves; and the contrary of the beautiful [ugliness] derives from the corresponding disproportion. Judgment being subject to the eye, who does not know the beautiful from the ugly? Certainly no one, unless he is utterly deprived of eyes and intellect. Whence man, having this knowledge [*cognizione*] about true form [*forma vera*], that is, about this individual, that is the living man, why ought he not also have it all the more for feigned [forms], which is dead painting.

Aretino seems to be arguing that everyone may make judgments on the basis of his experience of those like himself. In this experience each finds some people beautiful owing to the relative proportions of their parts, others ugly. We possess as the result of common experience an adequate standard for the judgment of individuals that should serve us as well for judging *painted* figures, which are once removed from the "true forms" of nature.

To this the painters might reply that although nature, "the common mother of all created things," has given all men a certain understanding (*intelligenza*) of good and bad, this does not mean that she has also given them an understanding of the beautiful and the ugly. By this Dolce means that men by nature have some faculty like estimation, but that this is not the same as a sense of the

[45] BT, I, p. 56. For Varchi's reference to Cicero, see n. 24, above.
[46] BT, I, pp. 154–156.

beautiful and the ugly.[47] In order to make such judgments it is necessary to have the kind of discrimination that results from the study of art.

Aretino replies that this argument is not sufficient, and to answer it, pushes his arguments about natural judgment even farther. The eye, he says, is one thing, the intellect another. As the optical writers often claimed, the eye may not be deceived unless it is impeded by some unfavorable condition (which implies that under ideal conditions the eye would see perfectly in the sense of absolutely adequately seeing what it sees). The intellect, on the other hand, is often thoroughly deceived, being darkened by ignorance or emotion. This last argument is not unlike the observation of Edmund Burke that, for all the bruited subjectivity in matters of taste, there is less difference in such matters than in "those which depend upon the naked reason . . . men are far better agreed on the excellence of a description in Virgil, than on the truth or falsehood of a theory of Aristotle."[48]

Dolce's Aretino continues his argument by saying that although men may desire by nature to do the good, they may err in the choices they make, mistaking bad for good. This seems to be a criticism of what Aquinas called "natural prudence," which is based entirely on experience and circumstances, but which is ignorant of the higher good, as in the case of one who is quicker to pursue the useful than the right.[49] Such a person has need of a philosopher.

The gist of this argument is that intellectual judgments are fallible, and if it is considered a direct response to the putative objection of the painters, then it means that the understandings they derive from their art are more liable to error than the judgments of the sight they share with everyone, and that they no more certainly come to an understanding of beauty than another may come to an understanding of the good.

The objection is again made that the eye is often deceived by appearance, and often takes the beautiful for the ugly and vice versa.

To this Aretino responds by returning to his first statement, that practice makes judgment, and repeats that the intellect is more easily deceived than the eye. There is also in everyone naturally a certain taste for good and bad, and so of the beautiful and the ugly (*naturalmente un certo gusto del bene e del male, e così del bello e del brutto*). Here something like the faculty of estimation is explicitly expanded (in contrast to the earlier arguments of the painters) from judgments of good and bad to judgments of the beautiful and ugly. There are, he says, many who judge poetry well, but are "without letters." And at this point, the familiar references to Cicero come into play. The multitude determines the reputation of poets, orators, actors, musicians, and sometimes of painters, and however different learned and unlearned may be, they are little different in judgment. Apelles submitted his paintings to *giudicio comune,* and Paris, who judged the

[47] On estimation, see Chapter 10 nn. 26–31, below.

[48] E. Burke, *A Philosophical Inquiry into the Origin of our Ideas on the Sublime and the Beautiful,* ed. J. T. Boulton, New York, 1958, p. 24.

[49] On natural prudence, see Chapter 12, below.

three goddesses, was a mere shepherd. Aretino quickly backs away from the democratic implications of this argument (which, it must be remembered, was really intended to justify his own critical activity) and adds that he does not mean the multitude in general, but rather those nonpainters selected by the gifts of nature (*belli ingegni*), who have refined these gifts by study and practice. Such persons may certainly judge painting, which pertains to the eye – which, he insists again, is the organ least liable to error (*istrumento meno errabile*) and which "approaches nature in imitating those things that are always before us." He then points to the grand precedents of Aristotle and Pliny, who wrote encyclopedically of arts and sciences they did not practice. There are, he concludes, certain minutiae of which painters may be aware, but these are important for their own work and are of little consequence for judgment. Summarizing, he says that every *uomo ingegnoso,* having added practice to *ingegno* (and, it might be added, to common visual experience), may judge painting, and will do so all the more rightly "if he is accustomed to seeing antiquities and the paintings of good masters; because, having in his mind a certain image of perfection, it will be easy to judge how much painted things may approach or depart from it."

It is clear throughout his arguments that Dolce's Aretino is talking about the judgment of what we would call the quality of painting, and that this quality is visual quality, although it must be noted that he speaks of painting as transparent, as if painted forms were judged by the same standards as real ones. It is also clear that, much in the manner of Alhazen, he considers the eye itself adequate to these judgments, and his position is similar to that of Lucretius, who held that it is not our senses that lie, but rather the constructions that reason puts upon what they tell us. All of this is turned to the purposes of an aristocratic and protoacademic development of our potentially democratic theme.

Francesco Bocchi on Donatello

Francesco Bocchi's *Excellenza del San Giorgio di Donatello* must have been completed before 1571, when a dedication was written to Cosimo I de' Medici, and it was published in 1584, when a second dedication was written to the members of the Accademia Fiorentina del Disegno. Like most late Cinquecento art literature, this *trattatello* has received relatively little scholarly attention, although it contains arguments of considerable interest.[50]

Bocchi considers Donatello's *St. George* – which in itself is no more than the occasion for his arguments on expression and the moral character of expression in images – under three categories, which he calls *costume, vivezza,* and *bellezza.* The first two of these have to do with the apparent life of the image, and throughout, Bocchi is concerned with the question of expression, with how an image is

[50] BT, III, pp. 125–194. See also M. Barasch, "Character and Physiognomy: Bocchi on Donatello's *St. George:* A Renaissance Text on Expression in Art," *JHI,* 36, 1975, pp. 413–430.

and is made to appeal to us in a certain way, as an apparently living, psychic presence. He begins from one of the cardinal principles of the Renaissance discussion of art, that the invisible movements of the soul are made visible in the appearance and movements of the body. Bocchi vividly describes this interdependence. "There is no doubt that the passions of the mind cannot be concealed in the human body, and that what they are is evident in external appearances. These passions are stamped in flesh, and may be said to give light to the shadows and obscurity of our thoughts, and almost to make minds palpable. One may see this every day; he whose face was just flushed with anger and courage is now, when his life is in doubt, seen to be timid and of pale brow. External appearances show us *costumi,* now of prudence, now of liberality, and then, as often happens, of their opposites."[51]

The metaphor of "stamping" recurs throughout Bocchi's argument. He is concerned with emotions and with deeper character traits, both of which are evident in the body, through physiognomy, gesture, and expression, so that the soul may be said to impress appropriate forms upon the body in all its aspects. What is "stamped" upon the body of a person is also "stamped" upon the soul of one who sees that person, thus preserving in interpersonal relations a reciprocity similar to the original reciprocity between soul and body. Thus, we are impressed with the joy or pain (or prudence or liberality) of someone with an immediacy corresponding to the expression of the person's own joy or pain or prudence or liberality. And if the work possesses the qualities of *costume, vivacità,* and *bellezza* (which Bocchi finally wants to credit to the sculptor),[52] then it will strike our imagination immediately as possessing those qualities.[53] Thus Bocchi solves what is for him the central problem: How it is that we can stand before a shaped mass of stone and see a young warrior, apparently alive with noble thoughts.

Bocchi repeatedly praises the power of the artist to create (*creare*) *costumi,* which can in turn create the same *costumi* in the minds of viewers. He tells of paintings that fool the eye, adding to the ancient examples of Pliny modern ones: the monster with which Leonardo frightened his father, Titian's portrait of Paul III, which, when set out in the sun for its varnish to dry, led passersby to bow and doff their caps as if in the presence of the pope himself. But Bocchi is not so much interested in simple illusion as he is in the similarly immediate and inescapable apprehension of apparent desirable moral qualities. "Noble youths" hold the statues of Donatello fixedly in the "eyes of the mind," and the *St. George,* surpassing all of them, shows "high thoughts and grandeur and magnanimity."[54] This is nothing slight or frivolous, he argues, and explains in psychological terms how the influence of *costume* works. The *virtù imaginante* retains images of things seen, and "stamps" and informs them in both the mind and the body. There are man examples of the power of fantasy to effect the body. A woman gave birth

[51] BT, III, pp. 134–135.
[52] Ibid., p. 133.
[53] Ibid., p. 144.
[54] Ibid., p. 147.

to a child that perfectly resembled an Ethiopian in a painting in her bedroom; and Terence, in his *Eunuch,* tells of a youth whose love for a maiden was fanned to the heat of passion by the sight of a painting of Danae and the shower of gold "painted with great lasciviousness."[55] And so, the argument runs, we may be similarly directed by images to virtue rather than vice.

In making the arguments outlined here, Bocchi takes up the themes with which we have been concerned in this chapter. "Particularly here in Florence," the perfection attained by artists has so sharpened sight and human judgment in general that sculpture and painting are no sooner placed in public "than immediately tongues are quick to blame and lacerate them." What is praised or blamed, or to put it in Varchi's terms, what is the basis for this *giudizio universale?* The answer is that everyone may see at once whether or not a work possesses *costume e vivacità.* Figures without these qualities "are rather stones than statues."[56] Furthermore, the qualities have nothing to do with art (in the sense of rules of craft), they are seen *in una vista,* and Bocchi appeals to the principle of the judgment of the eye in terms similar to those used by Vasari in his technical introduction to sculpture. "However much every part may be ordered according to measure, and made to respond to art in every aspect [*avviso*], and be without error," it will be held in little esteem in comparison to the creation (*il creare*) of *costumi.*[57]

The immediacy of such reaction, far from being incidental to Bocchi's discourse, is essential to his theory of expression. In an echo of the *paragone* dispute, he praises sculpture over painting because it makes *costume* evident without easy recourse to colors. Donatello "in hard marble with noble manner [*maniere nobili*] delicately as if painted a *costume* of magnanimity; he who does not know and clearly discern this may well be said to be in the shadows of ignorance, deprived of *ingegno,* utterly without sense."[58]

This last phrase, "utterly without sense" (*del tutto . . . disensato*) should be taken literally, because it is at the level of sense (both exterior and interior) that the image makes its appeal to us, and it is precisely because this appeal is sensate and prerational that it is universal and necessary. "At the sight of the living and valorous appearance [of the sculpture] *the senses without reason* [*i sensi senza ragione*] are also moved in others," and by this transformation at the level of sense, "the mind is awakened immediately to its good . . . and there are born those effects that are remembered with high praise and with honor."[59] Painting and sculpture

[55] Terence *Eunuch,* act III, scene iii (tr. J. Sargeaunt, I, pp. 292–295).

[56] BT, III, p. 168. See also p. 178.

[57] Ibid., p. 144.

[58] Ibid., pp. 144–145.

[59] Ibid., pp. 168. On the subject of beauty (pp. 180–181), Bocchi argues that it has three parts, *grandezza, ordine,* and *numero.* On the first, he follows Aristotle in saying that beautiful things are neither too large nor too small. The last, number, he only mentions. Of the second, order, he writes that "nature herself advises us and teaches us in judging [*in far giudizio*] of those parts that are indecent and deformed and mismade [*sconcie e difformi e malfatte*], and brings it about [*opera*] that our mind may not endure to approve or commend them, either with words or tacitly."

thus "create" a *costume* in the mind "utterly different from that which was just previously there"; and so powerful is the *virtù* of such art that "having made the living in hard stone, it has the power to ravish [*rapire*] another person away from himself, and to transform him into the appropriate virtue."[60]

Bocchi frequently and systematically uses the word *creare* to characterize the realization of apparent life in an image. Such art is not lowly, but noble; not mediocre, but sovereign; not earthly, but divine, and without doubt exalted above what is usual among men;[61] it is "not some artifice, but like nature herself, not like human invention, but divine, not as marble statuary, but as a living thing."[62] For the viewer's part, he would himself be as hard as stone if the "clear sight" of *vivacità* stamped upon the image by the artist did not stimulate him to virtue.

Bocchi's argument is in important respects simply rhetorical; painting, like rhetoric, is a *flexanima,* something that sways and leads the soul.[63] Bocchi also recognized that, again like rhetoric, painting (or sculpture) can also lead the mind in one way or another, and his *ragionamento* is peppered with examples of images that incite to lust, as others may also lead to virtuous and exemplary thought and behavior. But to return to our present concerns, Bocchi also places this rhetorical argument in a context not different in principle from Cicero's explanation of the universal appeal of rhythm and, more generally, of eloquence. And in the language of the faculty psychology we have been examining, Bocchi is saying that we apprehend *through sense* the "intentions" as well as the bare forms of things, and that we are led to conviction by external and internal sense to accept the reality of what we are made to see "without reason." And, it must be stressed, it is precisely in their power to effect such transformation that the arts of painting and sculpture are to be most highly praised, and it is in this psychagogic power that their universal value lies.

The defect of distance

The idea of the universality of visual images, rooted in their address to sense, was essential to Counter-Reformation arguments concerning the rhetoric of images, as we shall see in several examples. Gabriele Paleotti defined an image as "every material figure [*figura*] produced by the art called design [*il disegno*] and taken from another form for the purpose of being like it" (*dedotta da un'altra forma per assomigliarla*).[64] "Figures" are all forms of things, either rational or irrational, of which copies (*ritratti*) may be made. They are not points and lines but complexes of points and lines, and they are natural (a man, an elephant, bird, fish, tree,

[60] Ibid., p. 151.
[61] Ibid., p. 168.
[62] Ibid., p. 164.
[63] Compare Cicero *De oratore* III.lvii–lix.
[64] G. Paleotti, *Discorso intorno alle imagini sacre e profane,* Bologna, 1582; BT, III, pp. 117–509, here, p. 132.

stone) or artifical (church, chalice, vestment, book). Paleotti throughout his discussion insists on the concreteness of *figure* and distinguishes them from "vestiges." A vestige is a trace of something, like a footprint, that reminds us of something else. Vestiges are "irrational and imperfect," by which he means that a vestige makes us think of something in an indefinite way. Any particular person may have made a footprint, and the image called to mind is consequently inadequate.

In distinguishing vestiges from figures, Paleotti cites Saint Augustine's discussion of signs at the beginning of the second book of *De doctrina christiana.* Augustine wrote that "a sign is a thing which causes us to think [*ex se faciens in cogitationem venire*] of something beyond the impression [*species*] the thing itself makes upon the senses. Thus, if we see a track, we think [*cogitamus*] of the animal that made the track."[65] At this point Paleotti uses Augustine's discussion negatively, to show what figure is *not.* But he will presently turn it to the purposes of his own argument.

Paleotti also distinguishes figures as "material" from the "abstract and incorporeal images" used by theologians, as they say the mind of man is made in the image of the Trinity. We also form various *fantasmi e concetti* in our minds (*nell'intelletto umano*). Paleotti cites Basil, Plato, and Aristotle in comparing the "mind of man to the panel of a painter, upon which, day by day, by drawing, adding and changing now one thing, now another, keeping it covered with a curtain until it is finally finished; so in our mind, that is like a prepared panel, every day various thoughts are drawn, which will be uncovered when this veil of our body will be drawn back from the soul." Paleotti wishes to distinguish such painting from that "animal faculty of interior sense" called the *imaginativa,* that, from "sensible exterior things," makes "things that are not and cannot be." This is an echo of the censorious remarks of Vitruvius on grotesque painting, and with these words Paleotti dismisses all such painting.[66]

As the last argument suggests, Paleotti was interested in things that are or can be, in the true and the probable, and so he immediately turns to make another distinction between those things "produced by art" and those produced by nature. Images produced by nature are reflections, "in mirrors and clear water," or resemblances, as that of a father to his son. The art that forms images "is commonly called design." These forms are made "with pure lines, or with only one color, or with many, with the chisel, or whatever other instrument, in relief, or on a flat surface, or in any material whatever, of gold, silver, marble, wood, earth, stucco and other similar things."[67]

Two similar things are not images of each other, and are only so when one represents the other. He cites Plato's condemnation of painting in Book X of the *Republic.* "In anything whatever three things are to be considered: the idea of the thing, the thing, and the image of the thing; as the idea of a bed, the

[65] *De doctrina christiana* II. 1.

[66] BT, II, p. 133. On the remarks of Vitruvius, see *MLA*, pp. 141–143.

[67] BT, II, p. 134.

bed, and the image of the bed; the idea is in God before the thing; the thing, either by nature or by art, is after the idea; the image by the painter or other artisan is after the thing." It may be noted that Paleotti is using this example only to illustrate the absoluteness of the model. In effect the real object as the model for the image is given the authority of a substantial Idea. In any case, an image, again citing Augustine, is that which we call by the name of what it represents. Seeing a painted man, we call it a man; seeing a panel or wall, we say, that is Cicero, that is Sallust. *Imago,* Paleotti concludes, might as well be *imitago.*[68]

The efficient cause of images is the painter, who must possess two essential qualities. First, he must be skillful; but it is not enough to be a good artist, he must also be a good Christian, "this quality being inseparable from his person." He must show this quality whenever there is need. This, Paleotti assures the reader, will be an easy matter for anyone who reads his book attentively.

Paleotti declares himself to be little concerned with the material cause of images, a matter, he says, having to do with the craft of painting. Still, he comments in a most interesting fashion on the significance of the transformation of material into images. Just as baptism uses water, "found ordinarily in all places," so artists may make images of any material, of any size, in any place with the same result. What is essential to the image is not what it literally is, and it can be made of any material at any size because the stuff of which it is made is transubstantiated, made into what it is not in being made into that of which it is an image.[69]

Having established that any image is an image of something, Paleotti turns to the matter of its form, which must follow the appearance of something already produced either by art or by nature, that is, all the things that are and that are seen with the eyes. Those that are not seen can be imagined by the mind, "the form being born from the interior *concetto* of the artist," which is then "expressed with exterior design." Such *concetti,* of course, must fall within the range of the true and probable, so that we are able to say what *disegno* presents to sight, that it is a mountain, a river, a house, a king, a saint. For whatever purpose it might be used, the principal end of painting is imitation.

The ability to paint, to duplicate God's painting, is a gift of God and a sign of the loftiness of human nature.[70] This gift was granted by providence for two reasons: first, "so that man might have a broader field in which to reveal his *concetti.* We have only three ways of doing this, by voice, mimicry (*cenni*), and signs. The voice is a personal thing, inseparable from the person, useful in few places and times for few reasons. Mimicry, "being done with gesture and with harmony, with rhythm and other means of mimetic art," is less universally satisfying because it is also necessarily joined to the person who does it and can be seen only by those by whom it can actually be seen. To explicate the third mode

[68] Ibid., p. 134.
[69] Ibid., p. 137.
[70] Ibid., p. 139.

of communication, signs, Paleotti turns back to Augustine's *De doctrina christiana.* Signs are divided into two kinds, natural (like footprints, or smoke that means fire), which are limited in their usefulness, and *segni artificiati* (*signa data* in Augustine) "which are accepted by the consensus of men, and these are either characters of letters, notes, lines, numbers or similar things, which are not understood, nor are they known by anyone who does not hear them, and they are learned by few."[71]

Paleotti is now ready to formulate his conclusion; that imitative painting is a universal language. "In order to satisfy more universally this desire and common necessity to signify to each the *concetti* of others, the art was discovered of forming images, which, having been seen, immediately are recognized regardless of [conventional] differences and serve as a common tongue to all nations." In order to strengthen the foundations of this argument, Paleotti turns to two fundamental Aristotelian principles; that all men desire to know, and that all human knowledge is through sense. Sense, in turn, may only apprehend what is present, and without such apprehension our faculty of knowledge is restricted and weak. Divine wisdom therefore gave man painting "by means of which he might be able to represent before the eyes of anyone all material things, natural and artificial, I do not say the present only, but also the distant and those that are already past or spent. So that this faculty, called *disegno,* with which the images of things are formed with marvelous expression, was reputed above all others suitable to satisfy this common necessity, it much approaching the forms of all things and setting them before our eyes in whatever place they may be found."[72]

Uniting his arguments, Paleotti concludes that the origin of images is to be found in their ability to represent the similitudes of things and thus to remedy the defect of distance (*il difetto della lontananza*), "not because images may not also be used for things present, and that we have before our eyes, but because principally they come to restore the damage that is suffered by things distant and separate from us; because, if all things might be seen at our convenience, and regarded at our will, there would be no need to represent them."[73] As Lactantius writes, images preserve memories of the dead and the absent.[74] "Who is so outlandish that, if he were able with his own eyes to see at will the true face of blessed Christ, of the blessed Virgin or of the apostles, or their marvelous actions, he would willingly exert himself in reading words or looking at paintings? But because this cannot be done and nature does not allow it, therefore we avail ourselves of this remedy of images to supply such a necessity."[75]

Paleotti concludes that those who argued that images were invented for delight, to honor princes, or in response to religious instinct, were not wrong, but that

[71] Ibid., pp. 139–140.
[72] Ibid., p. 141.
[73] Ibid.
[74] The reference is to *Divine Institutes* II.2 (MPL, 6, col. 258–262).
[75] BT, II, pp. 141–142.

they had only followed the question to secondary causes, not to its primary causes. So, he would say, we delight in what we cannot see. Monuments to princes are necessary because princes die and we can no longer see them. We make images of gods because they are not in our churches and temples but are rather above us. *Disegno,* naturalistic painting and sculpture, brought all of this to us as if present, and the address of these arts to sense promised not only the salvation of Christians by erasing the time between them and the sacred stories, it also made these stories the potential history of all people in the world.

8

Optics and the common sense

Psychology and physics

The reception of the philosophy of Aristotle in the West was not simply the installation of a sacred authority to be finally overturned by Renaissance humanists and the founders of modern science, as seems often to be assumed. The Aristotle of Galileo's *Dialogue* is a pale and distorted Aristotle, a caricature of a late Aristotelianism that, although it may have opposed modern science in its old age, had also helped lay the firm foundations of scientific method in its youth. The sheer volume and intellectual magnitude of Aristotle's thought are, of course, still forbidding, and it is hardly to be expected that it would have been understood and assimilated to prevailing thought without great effort. Such great effort was, in fact, made, and the ideas of "the Philosopher" were not only taken up, they were also vigorously debated and criticized. His ideas, rather than producing universal acquiescence, might be more accurately said to have provided broad new grounds for disputation. The Scholastics who debated these ideas in their commentaries and applied them to innumerable contexts also performed the necessary task of collating Aristotle's opinions, which are often scattered. On the assumption that Aristotle's thought taken as a whole was systematic and internally consistent, arguments from different books were dovetailed, often with results that at least implicitly interpreted the ideas involved and consequently changed their future impact. This occurred in the case of the common sense. This incompletely presented notion yielded various readings and was completed in various ways by other ideas. It is beyond the scope of this chapter to trace the complex history this last statement implies, and the following example must be considered representative both of the kind of explanation that took place and of the general movement of criticism of the idea of the *sensus communis* in the late Middle Ages.

In an anonymous late thirteenth century commentary on Aristotle's *De anima*, psychology and physics are drawn together.[1] In one question the author considers

[1] *Trois commentaires anonymes sur le traité de l'âme d'Aristote*, ed. M. Giele et al., Paris, 1971, p. 429.

whether or not matter is perceived in itself. It is argued that what is sensed is sensed according to some extension (that is, spatial magnitude); but prime matter cannot be said to be extended, because prime matter (as pure potentiality) is without quantity and without extension, and therefore cannot be sensed. The author modifies Aristotle's statement (*De sensu et sensato* 449a21; *De caelo et mundo* 278a10–12) that anything is sensible because of matter to say that anything is sensible because of extension and quantity in material. He concludes that if materiality is the cause of sensation, it is the cause through extension and quality, so that matter is sensed not in itself but, rather, accidentally.

The author then proceeds to the question of the common sense because it is through the common sense that we apprehend magnitude, and therefore matter, insofar as we know it. He considers a question that seems to have nagged Aristotle's commentators. Although, as we have seen, Aristotle insisted that common sensibles are apprehended directly (*De anima* 418a5–10), the simple priority of the special senses seems to have made it hard to avoid the inference that they were apprehended incidentally, through the special senses, so that sensation of the common sensibles becomes a kind of secondary sensation. Aristotle himself had faced this objection (425a25–30), and Aquinas's recasting of his argument (which is followed closely by our anonymous author) will lead us to his resolution of it. Aquinas followed Aristotle in defining the objects of sense that are "in themselves and absolutely" as the special and common sensibles, and defines an incidental sensible as that which happens to belong to what is sensed absolutely (it is incidental to the white thing sensed that it is Socrates). But if the common sensibles are perceived only as the special sensibles are perceived, why are the common sensibles not incidental?

Aquinas firmly rejects the idea that the common sensibles are objects of a separate common sense;[2] and arguing from the principle that sensation is a "movement," a being acted upon and altered, he distinguishes between two ways in which such alteration may be effected. *Kinds* of agent are adapted to the special senses (light to sight, heat to touch), and also differentiate them, at once modifying each sense in a characteristic way and distinguishing one sense from another. Because these agents are always actually apprehended in certain relations to organs of sense, the relations, or modifications, may also be said to bring about alterations, that is, to produce sensation. Anything that produces alteration in sense is perceived through itself, and therefore, to bring the argument back to the words of our anonymous author, common sensibles are perceived through themselves. This means that magnitude is perceived in itself, and with this established the argument moves to the objection that the mathematical cannot be perceived in itself. There are, he says, two mathematics, one abstract from sense, which is thus not sensible per se; but the other is "conjoined to the sensible," "like the

[2] Thomas Aquinas *De anima* II.vi.389–95, in *Aristotle's De anima in the Version of William of Moerbeke and the Commentary of St. Thomas Aquinas*, tr. K. Foster and S. Humphries, New Haven, Conn., 1951, pp. 256–258.

size of my hand," and such mathematical entities are sensed per se, *quamvis non primo.*[3]

This oddly technical argument means simply that we really sense magnitude, not in that we apprehend the exact dimensions of things but in that what we apprehend is measurable and corresponds to the measurable. When Aquinas spoke of the modifications of sensation determined by common sensibles, he listed proximity, distance, and separation, and it is hard to imagine his solution without the near example of the science of optics, the "real" geometry of light and vision. Optics provided the possibility for the formulation of such ideas, because it provided the possibility for the construction of a geometric model of all actual vision. Especially after the availability of Alhazen (whose *De aspectibus* Aquinas gives no hint of knowing)[4] it was possible to describe bodies in terms of the emission of light, the behavior of light in terms of regular geometry, and sight itself in terms of the functional geometry of the eye and the relation of its functional geometry to objects in light.

It was mentioned at the beginning of this chapter that the arguments just considered reconciled the psychological and the physical. This was done by, in effect, making the common sensibles clearly prior to the special sensibles, and thus making the mathematical prior to the sensible and the quantitative prior to the qualitative. So Aquinas wrote that "whereas quantity pertains to substance immediately, sensible qualities, like white, black, heat and cold, presuppose quantity . . . if only sensible qualities are removed from a substance by a mental abstraction, continuous quantity still remains in the mind after abstraction."[5] Mathematical physics is thus rooted in sensation; abstraction is not from the physical world itself, but rather from the phantasm of the physical world which is somehow proportioned to it. Objects themselves are sensed in real relation to us, and their own physical substance is continuous with the relations among them. All are apprehended as magnitude. The idea of the *sensus communis* was thus an indispensable link both in the mathematization of physical reality and in the grounding of consciousness in physical reality.

The optics of Alhazen

Graziella Federici-Vescovini has argued that Arab optics developed on the base of Stoic psychology, according to which, as we have seen in Chapter 2, sensory perception may provide an adequate knowledge of things.[6] Alhazen's optics was consequently at odds in important respects with the psychology of Aristotle in

[3] *Trois commentaires,* p. 431.

[4] See D. C. Lindberg, *Theories of Vision from Al-Kindi to Kepler,* Chicago, 1976, pp. 145–146.

[5] Aquinas *De anima* 707.

[6] G. Federici-Vescovini, *Studi,* pp. 33–52, 113–135. On Alhazen, see also Lindberg, *Theories of Vision from Al-Kindi to Kepler,* and E. de Bruyne, *Etudes d'esthétique médiévale,* Bruges, 1946, III, pp. 239–261, which is largely based on Witelo's version of Alhazen.

the various versions in which it had come down, a tradition with which it had to be reconciled. Alhazen rooted his arguments in his theory of light and in the physiology of the eye and brain. According to these arguments, the geometric regularity of light made possible the exact transmission of the order of light points on the surfaces of objects to the eye, which in turn conveyed this order to the crystalline humor, the optic nerve, common nerve, and *ultimum sentiens*.

According to Alhazen, apprehension through vision occurred in three ways, the first two of which are based on the geometry of light and the eye. *Aspectus* or *visus* is the consequence of all light that falls on the surface of the eye, except for the single ray of light that falls perpendicularly on a plane tangent to the sphere of the eye, which yields *intuitio* or *obtutus*. This latter corresponds to the Stoic *phantasia kataleptike,* and provides vision privileged access to external objects. Along this central ray things are seen with maximum clarity, and everything in view may be "certified" by looking directly at it, given the presence of the object, its frontality, and the continual movement of the eye.[7] In other words, the passage of the axis of vision over objects clearly presented to us yields a kind of absolute knowledge of particulars. "In this way we may not only see things as they are, but we may also certify all the intentions of things seen."[8] That is, we may not only directly perceive those things that are strictly apprehended by sight, but we may also perceive the qualities and relations of things, a claim more or less equivalent to Aristotle's idea that we perceive both special and common sensibles through sight. As Federici-Vescovini concludes, "Sensation then is never an inferior or inadequate instrument of consciousness. . . . Sight, whether *aspectus* or *intuitio,* always makes us understand things as they are and act [upon sight]."[9]

Vision, or comprehension through vision, is not completed by *intuitio* (although *intuitio* may be said to provide an absolute basis for higher mental operations), but is completed by reason.[10] Sight apprehends color and light, also shape, position, size, and motion; but it also comprehends similarity and difference of color, of light, and similarity and difference of shape, position, size, and motion. These similarities and differences are not apprehended by sight alone but by a higher *virtus distinctiva*. "Sight does not have the virtue of distinguishing, but the *virtus distinctiva* distinguishes these things; at the same time the distinction of the *virtus distinctiva* does not take place, except by means of sight." Sight does not comprehend anything except *per cognitionem,* and *cognitio* requires memory, that is, the comparison of the seen to the remembered, or at least to the just previously visible and retained. Reason, then, is a capacity for distinguishing

[7] Federici-Vescovini, *Studi*, p. 126.
[8] Ibid., p. 122, referring to *Opticae thesaurus. Alhazen Arabis libri septem nuncprimum editi. Eiusdem Liber de Crepusculis et Nubium ascensionibus. Item Vitellonis Thuringopoloni Libri X*, ed. F. Risner, Basel, 1572 (facs. New York, 1972, ed. D. C. Lindberg), II, 65 (p. 68); II, 69 (p. 70). See also A. I. Sabra, "Sensation and Inference in Alhazen's Theory of Visual Perception," in *Studies in Perception: Interrelations in the History of Philosophy and Science,* ed. P. K. Machamer and R. G. Turnbull, Columbus, Ohio, 1978, pp. 160–185.
[9] Federici-Vescovini, *Studi*, p. 122.
[10] Alhazen, *Opticae thesaurus*, II, 10.

and associating; it is the *virtus distinctiva*, the double translation, from Greek to Arabic to Latin, of Aristotle's *kritikon*;[11] and the operation of the *virtus distinctiva* is a "syllogizing" operation of the particular intellect. *Virtus distinctiva est nata ad arguendum sine labore et difficultate.*[12] The judicative power of the mind, in other words, acts immediately and adequately upon the data of vision.

Everything that we see, according to Alhazen, undergoes continual change "according to color, shape, size, position, texture [*asperitatem et laevitatem*], ordination of parts and many particular intentions."[13] *Cognitio* in these circumstances is a "mode of reason." By comparison of sensation to sensation, then, with experience, of memory to sensation, we come to know the world. This active process of investigation, *cognitio*, works *quodammodo per syllogismum.*[14] By this he means not that such cognition is subject to reason, but that it is *like* reason, and he compares it to the immediacy with which we know that the whole is equal to the sum of its parts.

This argument might be reworded to say that some valid inference is conscious and some is unconscious, but both are inference. Thus, we see a coin lying on the table as an oval and know that it is circular, act as if it were as it is, *and also* are able to argue that what we know to be true is in fact the case. Children, Alhazen argues, comprehend many things that grown men comprehend; they distinguish and perform many operations *per distinctionem.* If two apples are shown to a boy, one more beautiful than the other, he will choose the more beautiful. This is only possible through comparison and distinction, and through a "universal proposition" that what is more beautiful is better, and more worthy of being chosen. The child in effect makes use of such a proposition; he argues and distinguishes, but does not know it, nor does he know that he argues, or even what an argument is. Again, such practical argumentation, which occurs in an indiscernibly short time, happens "without difficulty and labor . . . man does not perceive in the comprehension of things . . . what is *per argumentum.*"[15]

Alhazen devotes careful attention to "the qualities of the particular intentions comprehended by sight" and to "the qualities of arguments by which the *virtus distinctiva* obtains intentions comprehended by sight." That is to say, he carefully defines the nature of what sight sees and the processes by which the *virtus distinctiva* discriminates among things seen. The particular intentions comprehended by the sense of sight are many. He lists twenty-two but obviously believes that there are many more, and that the list is in fact open-ended. Of these, only light and color are perceived *solo sensu,* and the quiddity of color is only comprehended by distinction and assimilation, by comparison. That is, we know one color as different

[11] Wolfson, "Internal Senses," in *Studies in the History of Philosophy and Religion,* p. 289 n. 73. Averroes identified the *distinctiva* with the *cogitativa* (see below, Chapter 10), and Wolfson relates it to Aristotle's *dianoia.*

[12] Federici-Vescovini, *Studi,* p. 128.

[13] Ibid., p. 125. "Intentions" were defined by Avicenna (*De anima* I.V) as qualities apprehended by internal sense. On intentions, see *The Cambridge History of Later Medieval Philosophy,* pp. 479–495.

[14] Alhazen, *Opticae thesaurus,* II, 11, 12.

[15] Ibid., II, 13.

from another, or one shade of green in contradistinction to another. Other intentions are comprehended by *intuitio* and by the *virtus distinctiva.* These others are *remotio, situs, corporeitas, figura, magnitudo, continuum, discretio* and *separatio, numerus, motus, quies, asperitas, levitas, diaphanitas, spissitudo, umbra, obscuritas, pulchritudo, turpitudo, consimilitudo* and *diversitas.* Other "visible intentions" that might be thought of are subcategories of these: *ordinatio* should be grouped under *situs; scriptura* and *pictura,* under *figura,* and *ordinatio* (itself a subcategory), *rectitudo, curvitas* and *convexitas,* under *figura; multitudo* and *paucitas,* under *numerus; equalitas* and *augmentum,* under *consimilitudo* and *diversitas.* He also includes *alacritas, risus,* and *tristitia,* which are placed under *figura* (of the face).[16]

Pulchritudo might be called Alhazen's crowning "visible intention" because it demands the most complex kind of discrimination. Sight comprehends beauty only in the particular intentions of visible forms, and all modes of the beautiful are rooted in the comprehension of particular intentions. Any intention may be beautiful in its own right. Light is beautiful, as we see in the sun, moon, and stars; color is beautiful, as we may see in our delight in colored apparel, flowers, and trees; distance may make beauty by obscuring the ugly; relative magnitude may make beauty, as the moon is more beautiful than the stars; divisions, as the stars are more beautiful than galaxies; or continuity, as expanses of vegetation are more beautiful than scattered trees. A speaking man (as an example of *motus*) is beautiful and rest is also pleasing as gravity and taciturnity. The list is much longer, and examples could be endlessly multiplied.

The intentions that make up the beautiful usually occur not in isolation but rather in "conjugations." Not only must the eyes of a human face be pleasing in color and shape, and symmetrical, but they must be in a pleasing relation to the color and shape of the face, to the shape of all its parts, to their sizes and so forth. Alhazen calls this "right relation of intentions conjoined among themselves" "proportion." It is important to note that although *magnitudo* is part of proportion, proportion in the sense in which he is using the term has nothing to do with a relation of quantities. Rather it is a relation of "intentions" or visual *qualities,* so that the size of the face and its parts, in order to be part of its beauty, must also stand in a proportional relation to shape, color, distance, light, to all of the intentions relevant to it. Alhazen's "proportion" is thus not a prescription for the beautiful but is the most general description of it. To see the beautiful (which requires multifaceted *intuitio*) is to comprehend a complex relation in a particular thing; and to make a beautiful thing, or a thing beautiful in the way that the visual is beautiful, is to achieve a similar kind of "proportion" of qualities.[17]

[16] Ibid., II, 59.

[17] Ibid. This definition of beauty can only have been reinforced by that of John Duns Scotus. "Sicut in corpore pulchritudo est ex aggregatione omnium convenientium illi corpori et inter se, puta quantitatis, coloris et figurae," referring to Augustine, *De Trinitate* 8.3 (MPL, XLII, col. 949, "et bona facies hominis dimensa pariliter et affecta hilariter et luculenter colorata"). See E. de Bruyne, *Etudes d'Esthétique médiévale.* III, p. 347.

When he paraphrased Alhazen's chapter on *pulchritudo* – a paraphrase that doubled its historical effectiveness – Witelo called beauty a pleasure of the soul (*placentia animae*) and substantially repeated Alhazen's arguments. Since Alhazen believed that sight provided adequate knowledge of its proper realm, he used a term translated as "comprehension" to describe its activity. Witelo, who was perhaps less certain about this basic premise, used the term "judgment." So when he wrote of *sculptura* and *pictura*, he argued that however well disposed and beautiful letters may be in themselves, the eye will not judge (*iudicabit*) them beautiful if they are of different sizes. Witelo repeats Alhazen's stress on *proportio* and recapitulates his argument that beauty is apprehended by the *virtus distinctiva*, but he adds the important proviso (perhaps a generalization of Alhazen's own stress on the importance of *consuetudo* in cognition), that custom also makes beauty, and that different races of men call beautiful that to which they are accustomed. "For some colors and proportions of parts of the body and of paintings are approved by a Moor, others by a Dane, and between these extremes a German approves middling colors, heights and bearing of body, and as to each is his own custom, so to each falls [*accidat*] his own estimation of beauty."[18]

"Intentions" as common sensibles

The relation between optics and the common sense was close in Aristotle's original formulation of the idea. Alhazen's long list of visibles had the precedent of Ptolemy, who began the second book of his *Optics* with the statement that sight, given light and the presence of objects, knows "corpus, magnitudinem, colorem, figuram, situm, motum and quietem."[19] These, with the exception of color, are close variations on the Aristotelian common sensibles. Alhazen's *Perspectiva* was probably translated in the late twelfth or early thirteenth century, and its greatest impact came in the second half of the thirteenth century, during which time it began to shape speculation of all kinds in addition to the optics developed by Roger Bacon, John Pecham, and Witelo.[20] Authors who treated both optics and psychology invariably found a place for Alhazen's *virtus distinctiva* in the common sense, a conflation that enriched and transformed both ideas.

One of the first authors to make use of Alhazen's *Optics* was the encyclopedist

[18] Witelo, in Alhazen, *Opticae thesaurus*, IV, 148 (pp. 188–189). See also A. Parronchi, ed., *Teorema della Bellezza (dal latino di Vitellione) & De figura*, Milan, 1967. Similar arguments, with ethnic variations, are found in Sextus Empiricus, *Against the Ethicists* 43–44. Here, although everyone agrees that comeliness exists in women, the Ethiopian prefers the most black and snubnosed, the Persian the whitest and most hooknosed, another a mean in features and color. See Alberti, *Della pittura* I, 18, p. 24, where a fair girl among the Spaniards is dark to the Germans.

[19] *L'Optique de Claude Ptolémée*, p. 12 (II, 3). Later (p. 80), Ptolemy distinguishes between those things judged per se and those not, which again seems to be Aristotle's distinction between the infallible judgments of special sense and the fallible judgments of the common sense.

[20] See the introduction by D. C. Lindberg to *Thesaurus opticae*, pp. v–vii; and his "Alhazen's Theory of Vision and Its Reception in the West," *Isis*, 58, 1967, pp. 321–341. On Ptolemy, see also Chapter 5 n. 44, above.

Bartholomaeus Anglicus, in his *De proprietatibus rerum,* written around 1250. Within the division of vegetable, sensible, and rational souls, Bartholomaeus further divided the sensible into the *apprehensiva* and *motiva.*[21] Sense in general is the power by which the soul "judges and discriminates [*iudicat et discernit*] concerning colors, flavors and other objects of sense."[22] The senses are further divided into external and internal, and internal sense in turn is identified with the *sensus communis,* to which the whole of the brain – not just the first lobe – is allotted. The first lobe of the brain is given to the *imaginativa,* the middle to the *logistica,* and the last to memory. The *imaginativa* orders and composes forms previously apprehended from particulars by the external senses, and is able to call these forms up in new combinations, or by association. The *imaginativa* transmits to the reason (*ratio*), which *quasi iudex iudicat & definit. Ratio* is of course the *logistica* in the central lobe of the brain, and is defined as *ratio sensibilis vel aestimativa.* By virtue of this *ratio sensibilis* men are "prudent and wise" in avoiding harm and seeking benefit. It is also shared with animals, even though animals are not properly rational, and such estimation is of a higher order in human beings. In any case, the judicative part of this expanded common sense has been transformed into a kind of particular reason.

When he turns to its motive aspect, Bartholomaeus calls the *anima sensibilis* (of which the common sense is the inner part) a "certain spiritual substance," higher than the vegetable soul, much lower than the rational; its activity is dependent on the matter subject to it, and it does not survive the death of the body. While it is in the body, however, it may perform certain noble operations, depending on the nobility of its organs. The hand, for instance, is the organ of the *virtus operativa.* The *anima sensibilis* is also related to several functions clustered with the common sense in a long tradition. It effects sleep and waking, and governs the relative apprehensive power of the individual senses. Its virtue is also impaired by extremes, but it delights in the mean.[23]

Bartholomaeus's *anima sensibilis* is similar to Averroes's *vis cogitativa,* and encompasses the kind of immanent rationality of mental operations about particulars that we have also considered in Alhazen's *virtus distinctiva.* And as the common sense is made a kind of particular reason, the sense of sight, which makes the most discriminations of all the senses, also rises in importance. Sight, according to Bartholomaeus, is more subtle than the other senses, and more active (*vivacior*). It is more worthy and is superior in position to the other senses; it immediately comprehends the most distant things, which it "judges and discerns according to its more noble nature." The distance between sight and common sense as particular intellect – or between the discriminations of sight and the *logistica* – has closed, and I linger over this example because it is again similar in basic respects to Leonardo, by whom sight is also directly linked to the common sense

[21] Bartholomaeus Anglicus, *De proprietatibus rerum,* III, IX.
[22] Ibid., III, XI.
[23] Ibid., III, XII.

and reason. This may or may not mean that Bartholomaeus Anglicus was Leonardo's "source," and it is more likely that both made similar choices within the same system of possibilities.

Albertus Magnus argued that the common sensibles, which he listed as *motus, status, figura, magnitudo, numerus, et unum,* were reducible to number. If others, such as *situs,* be added to this list, this is really nothing other than a "certain dimension and magnitude," as are *propinquitas* and *remotio.* Heaviness and lightness, or curved and straight, which are apprehended by both sight and touch, may be placed with *figura* (which Aristotle himself had pronounced to be a kind of magnitude [*De anima* 425a15]). This argument is important not only because it reduces common sensation to number, but because it also marks the expansion and further definition of common sensation by then modern optics. Albertus continued his argument by remarking that certain authors had greatly expanded the number of common sensibles, but that all of these, too, could be reduced to number. He cites Avicenna and an author his editors identify as Alhazen.[24] As we have seen, Alhazen listed the number of "visible intentions" at twenty-two, and Albertus was not the only author who understood this long list as a list of common sensibles.

Roger Bacon took his psychology from Avicenna, modifying it in terms of the optics of Alhazen. Like Bartholomaeus Anglicus, Bacon placed great stress on the sense of sight, the seat of which is the common sense.[25] The common sense is an internal sense and – as in Avicenna – it is passive, receiving but not retaining. Retention is effected by the *imaginatio.* The ordering and judgment of sensibles is carried out by the *phantasia,* the union of the *sensus communis* and *imaginatio.* "And therefore when the *sensus communis* receives the species, and imagination retains it, the complete judgment [*iudicium*] follows, which is exercised by the *phantasia.*" For Bacon the judgment of the *phantasia* seems only to be of special sensibles, and is not the highest sensate judgment, which instead is exercised by the *estimativa* and *cogitativa.*[26] He follows Avicenna in calling *intentiones* the qualities of things apprehended by the internal senses. In this scheme (again as in Avicenna) the *sensus communis* is not a faculty of judgment (although it can misjudge), and the common sensibles, to which Alhazen's long list of "visible intentions" has been added, are called "complexional qualities," to be judged by the higher internal senses, immediate to reason.[27]

Bacon is attempting, like many before him, to construct an intelligible passage from sense to reason. He does this, as many others also did, by ranking the faculties of sense and concentrating the judicative powers in the upper stages of this hierarchy, at the level of the *vis cogitativa* and the *virtus distinctiva,* now more closely than ever allied with sight. Still, it must be remembered that such judg-

[24] Albertus Magnus, *De anima,* lib. 2, tr. 4, cap. 6 (*Opera omnia,* t. VII, pars 1, Westphalia, 1968, p. 155).

[25] Roger Bacon, *Opus Maius, pars Va, De perspectiva,* II, p. 9.

[26] Federici-Vescovini, *Studi,* p. 65.

[27] Ibid., p. 68.

ment is not rational, and is shared with animals.[28] At the same time, Bacon argued that Avicenna was wrong in identifying the rational activity of the soul with the *cogitativa,* which was shared with animals. Bacon locates the *cogitativa* (or *logistica*) in the middle lobe of the brain, calling it the "mistress of the sensitive virtues." It is called *rationalis,* not because it is used by reason, but because it is the highest perfection of brutes, as reason is in man, and because in man the rational soul is immediately united with it. Bacon maintained that God himself effected this union, thus in one stroke solving the problem of the relation of the world, sense, and reason that had always pressed for solution in the tradition we have been tracing. And the *cogitativa* in human beings is worthy of the rational soul to which it is immediately related. The judgment of sense now stands to reason as the visible world stands to mathematics.

In his *De multiplicatione specierum,* written before 1267, Bacon treated the common sense in the context of a larger theory, which, building on the framework of the light metaphysics of al-Kindi and its modification by Robert Grosseteste, tried to explain all interactions among things on the basis of the activities of similitudes called *species.*[29] Although Bacon meant considerably more than a visual form by *species,* the term itself is a visual metaphor, and it is not surprising that Bacon was much concerned with optics, especially the optics of Alhazen.

In this treatment, common sensibles are closely associated with matter, as they had been in a long Neoplatonic tradition stretching back at least to Plotinus. Because they are associated with matter, Bacon argues, common sensibles cannot generate species, because matter, he cites Aristotle to say, is pure potentiality. Species are generated through the "composite" (the real union of form and matter) and by form itself. Bacon lists twenty common sensibles from Alhazen, suggesting that there might be even more, and it seems from this discussion that he wished to add density and transparency to the list. He argues that vision occurs when sight encounters something "dense," which in effect provides the base of the visual pyramid. The apprehension of transparency and density is relative because we can only perceive the dense through a transparent medium, and we only know that the medium is transparent when we perceive a dense body in it. This argument is apparently meant to show that, because such judgments are relative, neither density nor transparency can be considered to be evident in themselves, through species. He also argues that we cannot see pure transparency, otherwise we would see air, or the sphere of the elements, or of the heavens. These have the requisite quantity, shape, magnitude, and corporeity (that is, they possess common sensibles), but the eye cannot judge them, hence they cannot be said to generate species.

If common sensibles are not apprehensible per se, how are they apprehended? To answer this question, Bacon turns again to optics, and especially to Alhazen.

[28] Ibid., p. 66.

[29] See D. C. Lindberg, *Roger Bacon's Philosophy of Nature. A Critical Edition, with English Translation, Introduction and Notes, of De multiplicatione specierum and De speculis comburentibus,* Oxford, 1983. Lindberg provides an excellent introductory essay; I have used the discussion of the common sense at pp. 25–41 as the basis for the remarks that follow.

For Bacon the category of density was also closely linked to matter; he explains density away by saying it is the occasion and not the cause of sight. Sight is truly "terminated" by color and light, which is to say that color and light make up the real base of the visual pyramid. Bacon rejects what he regards as a misinterpretation of Alhazen. Alhazen wrote that the "circumference" (that is, the outline) of a thing seen is figured (*figuratur*) on the surface of the eye; and because this "circumference" is reducible to common sensibles, the common sensibles, it might be argued, must "make an impression and species in the organ," which they must also have made in the intervening air. But properly understood, Bacon maintains, Alhazen's words mean no more than that the magnitude of a thing seen is "ordered and described on the surface of the sensing member" (*ordinatur et describitur in superficie membri sentientis*), and this is not because the magnitude itself makes a species, but because "the species of light and color comes from the whole magnitude of the thing, and from its whole surface." These species coming from individual parts "are not confounded on one part of the pupil, but are distinguished and ordered on the surface of the eye in a sensible quantity." What is described on the surface of the eye is therefore the color and light of the magnitude of the thing seen, not the species of the magnitude itself. In short, Bacon reduces the common sensibles to relations on the surface of the eye, in harmony with Aristotle's principle that sensation is apprehension of a magnitude through a magnitude. In this scheme the common sense is immediate to particular sense; it is mirrorlike and does not judge, beyond registering species in a certain way. The task of judgment Bacon leaves to the higher faculties of estimation and cogitation, which he argues are not properly senses, even though they are parts of the sensitive soul. The *virtus distinctiva,* "which is the cogitativa," which is in the middle cell of the brain, judges all sensibles, proper and common alike, by means of the common sense and the particular senses, which may only be properly called "senses." Bacon uses the indispensable example of the sheep fleeing at its first sight of a wolf to argue that substances and not just accidents are apprehensible through sense, the sheep perceiving the hostility of the wolf "deeper" than its mere appearance. For Bacon the *cogitativa* is identical with Alhazen's *virtus distinctiva,* and because he notes the close relation between the common sensibles and the categories, his understanding of this highest sensitive faculty is not far from that of Averroes, which we shall treat in Chapter 10.

In the late thirteenth century Henry Bates provided an instructive example of what is at base a Platonic transformation of the common sense, a subject to which he devotes many chapters of careful analysis. Bates often cites the optics of Alhazen, whom he understood to mean that the sight of both eyes is united in the common sense.[30] He also argues that the common sense judges not only proper sensibles and the common sensibles listed by Aristotle, but also the twenty-two particular intentions listed by Alhazen.[31] He cites Aristotle (*Metaphysics* 1053a–b) to base

[30] Henri Bate de Malines, (Henry Bates) *Speculum divinorum et quorundam naturalium,* ed. G. Wallerand, Louvain, 1931, p. 102.

[31] Ibid., p. 100.

his argument that sense is "a certain ratio, or proportion mediate of all sensibles, by which sensibles are able to be judged and commensurated by turns."[32] The burden of the argument is turned to the separation of judgment as such from sensation. Thus the common sense judges not only that white is not sweet, but that it is not black.[33] The effect of this argument is to show that the higher principle of judgment is in the common sense, not in sense itself.[34] Perhaps the most general principle guiding the argument is taken from Proclus, that everything that may be assimilated to thought must be incorporeal.[35] Things are assimilated insofar as they are judged, and judgment is finally the activity of intellect.[36] This does not mean, however, that sensation is *subject* to intellect, but rather that sensation is *consistent* with intellect, and concentric with it. In good Aristotelian fashion, the soul is throughout a *kritikon,* and the continuity of this judgmental activity provides the basis for a kind of emanative continuity between sense and intellect. At its highest, the *vis sensitiva* "participates somewhat" in the intellective power (*vis*) in man, in whom sense is joined to intellect.[37] The highest forms of the *vis sensitiva* are the common sense and the fantasy. After a discussion of Plato, Chalcidius, and Apuleius on the dignity of the head among the parts of the body, he writes that the common sense and fantasy have their organ in the head together with sight, the most perspicacious of the senses, which is more spiritual, and announces many differences and many kinds of differences to us. He cites the opening lines of Aristotle's *Metaphysics* on the dignity of sight, whose etymology he follows to "light," "because without light there is no sight." In what follows, the common sense, fantasy and sight are at once made a mean between sense and intellect and in effect joined to the possible intellect. The *sensus communis* is properly called both *primum* and *ultimum sentiens;* it is cognitive (*cognitivus*) of all sensible qualities and judicative, does not function through an organ (which makes it superior to sight), and is capable of knowledge of the forms of all sensible objects.[38]

For many authors, Alhazen's *De aspectibus* exerted a strong pull on the reading and explication of Aristotle's *De anima.* Nicole Oresme, for example, argued in familiar terms that exterior sense initiates sensation and the interior senses complete it. This completion is judgment, the kinds and degrees of which he carefully distinguishes. Although Oresme examines the interior senses only cursorily, he devotes close attention to the common sense, which he in effect identifies with the *virtus distinctiva,* and the activity of which he calls "syllogizing," also following Alhazen. He considers the question of whether or not there are nineteen common sensibles (the number of Alhazen's visible intentions that are not special sensibles

[32] Ibid., p. 104.
[33] Ibid., p. 107.
[34] An argument also made by Albertus Magnus. See Chapter 4 n. 24, above.
[35] *Speculum divinorum,* p. 154. This, of course, is a variation of the Aristotelian principle that the form of the thing and not the thing is in the soul.
[36] Ibid., p. 155.
[37] Ibid., pp. 135–136.
[38] Ibid., p. 109.

of sight) and examines ten of them. In his question on whether or not magnitude or position are common sensibles, he argues that magnitude in extension is perceived by sight and touch, but that magnitude in succession and intension are perceived by all of the senses, by which he means that all of the senses perceive the duration and intensity of sensation, "whence hearing judges [*iudicat*] one sound to be louder than another, and taste one flavor to be more delectable than another." Such things happen "according to comparison and proportion, which is impossible without the possession of some quantity." This last is again a statement of Aristotle's definition of sense as a ratio in a magnitude.[39]

In this passage Oresme understands "magnitude" in three senses, as the necessary physical concomitant of quality, as duration, and as the degree of "intensity" of a quality, a red's being more or less, for example. In a consideration of magnitude in the sense of size, he adds another argument of great interest to us. He argues that in general in the judgment of magnitude error never occurs. Owing to what he calls the "intemperance of circumstances," however, we are never able to judge magnitude *ad punctum*. He means by this that we can judge the size of things we see, but cannot give their exact measure, which requires a mental (and manual) operation of another order. But just because we cannot measure *ad punctum*, and therefore are in a certain sense in error in our judgment, does not mean (as Pomponazzi would point out)[40] that we do not see – or judge – anything at all.

[39] See P. Marshall, *Nicholas Oresme's Questiones de Anima: A Critical Edition with Introduction and Commentary*, Ph.D. dissertation, Cornell University, January 1980, II, xiii, p. 184. The preface to this edition on the "medieval *De anima* tradition" provides a sound basis for exploration of this difficult terrain and advances interesting suggestions about the importance of optics to the transformation of this tradition. I am grateful to Dr. Marshall for making a copy of his edition available to me, and for many hours of conversation. It may be suggested that Oresme considered ten common sensibles in order to make them coincide with the number of Aristotle's predicaments. If so, then the common sense would stand for all internal sense, like Averroes's *vis cogitativa*, which apprehended particulars under the ten predicaments. Oresme would then have treated the common sense in much the way Biagio Pelacani did.

[40] See A. H. Douglas, *The Philosophy and Psychology of Pietro Pomponazzi*, ed. C. Douglas and R. P. Hardie, Cambridge, 1910, p. 161 n. 5. "Et si dicitur decipere circa hoc, concedo; non tamen sequitur ut non cognoscat istas differentias." Pomponazzi is treating the question of whether we apprehend all the common sensibles by all the senses when he states this argument. He argues (p. 162) that the senses know things more or less adequately, and that sight and touch apprehend magnitude "perfectly." He also argues that particular sensation is the occasion for the judgment of the common sense, which is the principle of sensory discrimination. It is not sight that judges (*judicat*) and declares the difference between one color and another (*ponit differentiam inter unum colorem et alterum*), it is rather the common sense (p. 167 n. 2). Douglas is perhaps too insistent that these ideas are new with Pomponazzi, and that they are not a fairly close variant of Aristotle's own ideas. See the earlier distinction between "universal" and "particular" judgments of sense. Universal judgments are not so called because they judge universals, because sense concerns particulars; they rather correspond to special sensation, as to color apprehended by sight; particular judgment has to do with the discrimination of qualities, as of color insofar as it is white or black, that is, light or dark. Among particular judgments some are mo' . "articulate" than others. The judgment that a color is lighter or darker is less articulate than a judgment of the degree of lightness or darkness. "Judgment concerning the multitude of degrees of colors belongs more to common than to proper sensibles." See P. Marshall, "Parisian Psychology in the Mid-Fourteenth Century," *Archives d'Histoire Doctrinale et Littéraire du Moyen Age*, 50, 1983, p. 145.

On the contrary, such judgments serve us well in our various activities and operations, and, Oresme says, "suffice to judge approximately, as what is two cubits, or about that." The difference between such approximate judgment and measurement *ad punctum* is like the difference between foreshortening and perspective. As we are about to see, Ghiberti copied into his third commentary Alhazen's arguments for the estimation of relative magnitudes in sight, and it is easy to imagine that arguments for the ability of the eye (or the common sense) to judge magnitudes with sufficient precision was at least as interesting to Ghiberti as arguments for the geometric construction of painter's perspective, arguments that he in fact omitted. It was by the judgment of the eye, and by *disegno* as the agent of the judgment of the eye, that the crucial artistic difficulties of foreshortening and movement were to be solved, not only in principle but in practice and each instance of practice. The ability of sense to make such judgments was essential to naturalism; at the same time, it is evident that in these judgments literal and metaphorical point of view are both inevitably and paradoxically mingled.

Biagio Pelacani da Parma

However Aristotle may have insisted on the importance of the structure of sense itself to sensation, his readers, in a long tradition, and no doubt with the conscious or unconscious desire to remove *ratio* from immediate relation to matter, concentrated on the passivity of sensation, which Aristotle had exemplified by the mark of a seal pressed in wax. As we have seen, Aristotle was by no means unambivalent on the question of the activity of sense, and, if the idea of the harmony of sense itself had a mixed career, the very notion of "internal senses" constantly pressed for the conclusion that sensation was more than passive. A variant form of this implicit conclusion was the idea of *sensus agens,* which has been related to Averroes's commentary on the third book of Aristotle's *De anima.*[41] Explaining *De anima* 429a21ff., Averroes wrote that the material intellect (as opposed to the separate intellect) is like matter only in that it is the susceptibility of all possible material things; he identified it not with the *virtus imaginativa*

[41] See G. Federici-Vescovini, *Astrologia e scienza. La crisi dell'aristotelismo sul cadere del Trecento e Biagio Pelacani da Parma,* Florence, 1979, pp. 130–134. On the idea of *sensus agens,* see S. MacClintock, *Perversity and Error. Studies on the "Averroist" John of Jandun,* Bloomington, Ind., 1956, pp. 10–50. MacClintock sets the problem in the wider context of Aristotle's theory of sensation, which he contrasts to what he calls the Platonic Augustinian tradition. "Active sense" was meant to account for the apprehension of external forms by sense, and corresponded to the apprehension of forms in the passive intellect by the active intellect. In this discussion, which he begins with Averroes, sensible forms involved in the soul's activity of sensation are intentional or immaterial or spiritual, but are at the same time particular (p. 14). On this hypothesis, there was no difficulty in arguing that such intentions were apprehended by the soul, and it was necessary to explain how intentional forms, which exist only potentially in things, become active in sensation. Although MacClintock separates this "agency" from the activity of the common sense, it seems to me difficult to separate it from inner sense, given that the *cogitativa* apprehends "intentions." See also A. Pattin, "Pour l'histoire du sens agent au Moyen Age," *Bulletin de Philosophie Médiévale,* 16–17, 1974–5, pp. 100–113.

(which he says is "intellect" in the broadest sense of the Greek word) but rather with the virtue by which "we distinguish speculative things and imagine future operable things" (*distinguimus res speculativas et cogitamus in rebus operativis futuris*).[42] As we shall see, he is in fact talking about the *vis cogitativa,* which "prepared" phantasms for intellection (as well as being the particular intellect).[43] Averroes defined the material intellect as "that which is potentially all intentions universally of material forms, which is not actually any entity before it understands that entity."[44]

As we shall see, Averroes compared the *vis cogitativa* to the common sense, arguing that it stands to the internal senses as the common sense stands to special sense.[45] He attributed to Aristotle the opinion that "forming" by intellect is like "comprehending" by sense. These two operations are comparable because each is perfected by two "subjects"; sense is perfected by the thing outside the soul relative to which "comprehension" is true and by the capacity for sensation itself; actual apprehension by intellect is perfected by "forms" of "true images" relative to which they are true, and by that through which things apprehended by intellect are one entity in the world, that means being the material intellect. "For," he concludes, "there is no difference here between sense and intellect, except in that the subject of sense by virtue of which it is true is outside the soul, and the subject of intellect by virtue of which it is true is inside the soul."[46] Averroes goes on to argue that particulars are "proportioned" to the material intellect just as *sensata* are proportioned to the particular senses. Obviously sense and reason about particulars are now in the closest possible relation.

We shall now turn to the late fourteenth century physicist Biagio Pelacani da Parma for a version of the *sensus agens* doctrine that, although closely parallel to the Averroistic idea, has been related to the assimilation of the epistemological implications of the optics of Alhazen. Biagio Pelacani was a well-known figure in his time. Although he spent most of his career in northern Italy, Biagio lectured in the *Studio fiorentino* in 1388, and his works were known to Leonardo da Vinci.[47] Robert Klein has given Biagio Pelacani a central place in the early history of perspective, arguing that his *Quaestiones perspectivae,* written in 1390, was well known in Padua and must have stood behind the lost treatise on painting of Giovanni da Fontana dedicated to Jacopo Bellini. Biagio Pelacani's writings have

[42] *Commentarium magnum . . . de anima,* III, comm. 5, p. 387.

[43] See Chap. 10, below.

[44] *Commentarium magnum . . . de anima,* p. 387.

[45] See Chapter 10 n. 54, below.

[46] *Commentarium magnum,* III, V, p. 400.

[47] See, in addition to her *Astrologia e scienza,* G. Federici-Vescovini's introduction to *Le Quaestiones de Anima di Biagio Pelacani da Parma,* Florence, 1974. Federici-Vescovini rejects the idea put forward by P. Sanpaolesi ("Ipotesi sulle conoscenze matematiche, statiche e meccaniche del Brunelleschi," *Belle Arti,* 4, 1951, pp. 25–54) that Pelacani was in Florence between 1381 and 1394 and that he was the Biagio del'Abbaco associated with Florence Cathedral. On Leonardo and Pelacani's writings, see A. Uccelli, *Leonardo da Vinci. I libri di meccanica,* Milan, 1940, p. CXXXIX.

also been connected to Paolo Toscanelli, Brunelleschi, and Paolo Uccello, and Klein goes so far as to say that it was through Pelacani that Renaissance pictorial theory was shaped in its crucial formative stages by the tradition of late medieval optics.[48]

One of the objections raised to the idea of the *sensus agens* was that it was not possible for something to be active and passive at the same time; but it was upon just this principle that Biagio Pelacani constructed his psychology.[49] The consequence of this step was a blurring of the distinction between sense and intellect. Biagio rejected the Thomistic idea that the soul was the substantial form and first act of the body and instead embraced the idea that the soul is like an "extensive quality," an idea that may descend from the Aristotelian notion that all sensation is through a magnitude, although it is not itself a magnitude, but rather a ratio in a magnitude able to apprehend the qualities of other, external magnitudes. And just as for Pelacani these qualities had degrees ("intension and remission"), so souls differed in their ability to apprehend degrees of quality, the human soul being the highest. In parallel to Averroes, the material intellect is a unique *subiectum materiale,* differentiated by the degrees of perfection in its apprehension of qualities, degrees leading from sensation to intellect.[50]

All of this involved a corresponding change in the notion of "species," which are no longer spiritual or immaterial "intentions" but instead are the "conditions" of extended matter, such as shape and position, which are common sensibles, and the qualities of special sensation, which demand a material substrate. What is sensed, then, is the sensible object *as* its qualities are impressed in the organ of sense; and Biagio applied Ockham's razor to the distinction between the common sense, *cogitativa,* and intellect by reducing them all to common sense. "Without doubt the common sense apprehends all sensible qualities and apprehends its operation and establishes differences among various *sensibilia* and apprehends these qualities under some degree" (that is, as more or less "intense"). Thus, the common sense is "a material virtue not separated [*denudatus*] from some qualitative disposition."[51] By this last statement he means that the common sense is capable of all sensation, and is only actual in sensation, like the material intellect of Averroes. The common sense in this formulation is both passive and active, and, as he further argues, there is no need to posit any other *virtus interior cognoscitiva* beyond the common sense, "because according to the truth of the matter the *sensus communis* is the *virtus fantastica, memorativa, memoria et intellectus.*"[52]

To return to the question of the influence of Alhazen, Pelacani maintains the

[48] See R. Klein, *Form and Meaning,* pp. 102–104.

[49] Federici-Vescovini, *Astrologia e scienza,* pp. 138.

[50] On "intension and remission" of qualities, see, in addition to the bibliography given by Federici-Vescovini, *Astrologia e scienza,* p. 140 n. 41, M. Clagett, "Some Novel Trends in the Science of the Fourteenth Century," in *Art, Science and History in the Renaissance,* ed. C. Singleton, Baltimore, 1967, pp. 275–303. Color was already discussed by Bartholomaeus Anglicus in terms of intension and remission (*De proprietatibus rerum,* XIX, IV, pp. 1137–1138).

[51] *Quaestiones de Anima,* p. 128.

[52] Federici-Vescovini, *Astrologia e scienza,* p. 151.

closest possible connection between sight and common sense, and thus sight and intellect. It is as if Avicenna's notion of common sense as a mirror had been coupled with the idea that sight is itself the *virtus distinctiva.*

In his *Quaestiones perspectivae,* Pelacani considers the question of whether or not sense can err in its judgments, the question of what he called the *iudicium sensus.* Sight for him is the highest sense, and "grasps" things, much in the manner of the Stoic *phantasia kataleptike.* At this level, sense cannot err. If the organ is functioning normally, it sees what it sees and misjudgment is the result of the circumstances under which things are seen, subject to variables such as light and distance. These are evaluated by internal sense, which does not have the infallibility of external sense. Evaluation of the data of external sense arises from comparison – "composition and division" – made possible by experience. Much as Lucretius argued, the senses afford our best knowledge, and without them we may not even know when we are in error. These arguments implied a skepticism that Pelacani willingly embraced; and if this skepticism made intellect practical and relative to sense, the terms of this same skepticism made the reality of sense, the physical world, not only intuitively evident but mathematically demonstratable.[53]

Ghiberti's Third Commentary

In his Third Commentary, the Florentine sculptor Lorenzo Ghiberti – who had an Italian translation of Alhazen – who refers to Witelo and quotes long sections from both Roger Bacon and John Pecham,[54] also gave careful thought to the question of the common sense. Citing Avicenna, he locates the common sense in the first lobe of the brain and lists its major characteristics. (He soon amends this position, arguing that the ventricles of the brain cannot be organs of the common sense and fantasy, because the ventricles are symmetrical whereas the two faculties are arranged in tandem. Ghiberti was evidently uneasy with the relation between diagrammatic psychology and physiology.) It is a "source" relative to all the other "particular sentiments and sensible things," and he repeats Aristotle's geometric characterization of the common sense as a center from which lines run to the circumference. He states that it "judges [*giudica*] all the other particular senses and sensible things, inasmuch as this sense judges all the others."

[53] Ibid., pp. 158–175. Pelacani seems to have distinguished between an *intellectus practicus singularium* and *intellectus practicus universalis.* The first he associated with local movement in man and with the sort of assent or rejection associated with internal sense. He specifically stated that the *intellectus practicus universalis* is not the principle of human local motion (Ibid., p. 101 n. 68).

[54] G. Federici-Vescovini, "Il problema delle fonti ottiche medievali del Commentario terzo di Lorenzo Ghiberti," *Lorenzo Ghiberti nel suo tempo. Atti del Convegno internazionale di Studi (Firenze, 18–21 Ottobre, 1978)*, Florence, 1980, pp. 349–387, reviews her previous discussions, provides relevant bibliography, and reproduces Ghiberti's texts with texts from Alhazen. See also her "Contributo per la storia della fortuna di Alhazen in Italia: il volgarizzamento del ms. Vat. 4595 e il Commentario Terzo del Ghiberti," *Rinascimento,* ser. 2, V, 1965, p. 17–49; see also A. Parronchi, "Le 'misure dell'occhio' secondo il Ghiberti," *Studi su la dolce Prospettiva,* Milan, 1964, pp. 319–348.

The common sense completes sensation, distinguishes [*giudica*] among special sensibles, which no individual sense can do, "inasmuch as the said senses do not discern extremes." It judges [*giudica*] the operations of the individual senses in "seeing" that they see or hear. Ghiberti is aware of the relation between the common sense and recollection, and ends his discussion with an argument to the effect that common sense and *fantasia* (as a retentive faculty) are one thing, differing only in operation, and seems to opt for the position that the common sense is the more general faculty, which both receives and retains species.[55]

Ghiberti begins his discussion with the physiology of the eye and immediately turns to the question of the "virtù distintiva."[56] There are "by means of seeing judgments [*giudicii*] of twenty visible species." He immediately confesses that "it is not known if this *virtù della distinctiva* is among the virtues of the soul," the organs being separate in the brain. He adds that "many things must be treated concerning the virtues and potencies of the sensitive soul." Then, at the end of the discussion of the common sense we have just considered, he turns again to the question of the *virtus distinctiva.*

Ghiberti yokes together the special senses, the common sense, and fantasy, and seems to intend that insofar as they judge, the outer and inner senses are equivalent to the *virtus distinctiva:* "the imagination and the common sense and the particular senses judge of nothing by themselves if not of twenty-nine sensible things." By this he seems to mean that the special sensibles and Alhazen's visible intentions add up to twenty-nine, all of which are subject to sensate judgment. So sight judges light and color; touch judges hot and cold, wet and dry; hearing judges sound; smell, odor; taste, flavor. He then repeats Alhazen's long list of twenty visible intentions with slight modifications. *Remotio* is omitted, as is *obscuritas,* and *bellezza* is added before *pulchritudine.*[57]

Ghiberti's treatment of sensate judgment is remarkably straightforward, and in his attempt to accommodate Alhazen's optics to a version of Aristotelian psychology he makes no attempt to raise the level of judgment above that of sense itself. He seems to favor Avicenna's location of the *sensus communis* and fantasy nearest to sense, and does not associate the *virtus distinctiva* with *ratio* or even with *cogitatio.*

Ghiberti did not concern himself with perspective, although he did transcribe an experiment from Alhazen in which it is demonstrated that the distance of the eye from a surface can only be judged by reference to some third term, suggesting a greater interest in the *judgment* of distances than in their demonstration. Ghiberti was also evidently interested in the perceptual mechanics of Alhazen's comprehension by vision. But perhaps most interesting in his transcription of Alhazen's chapter on *pulchritudo,* the culmination of what Panofsky referred to as Alhazen's "remarkable excursus on what we would call aesthetics."[58] This chapter centers

[55] L. Ghiberti, *I Commentari,* ed. O. Morisani, Naples, 1947, p. 61.

[56] Ibid., p. 59.

[57] Ibid., p. 61.

[58] E. Panofsky, *Meaning in the Visual Arts,* p. 89 n. 63.

around the idea of proportion, but, as we have seen, the kind of proportion intended is not modular (as we are in the habit of thinking of Renaissance proportion), rather it is qualitative, a relation of "intentions." "Only proportionality makes beauty," but the proportionality is a relation among "visibles." In the face the shape (*figura*) of the nose is only pleasing in relation to the shape of the whole face; and its position is only pleasing with respect to the whole. Moreover, such proportions or relations are not reducible; they are only visual and their judgment is only possible to the eye. "Beauty [*pulchritudine*] then does not exist because of the particular intention [that is to say, through any individual instance of one of the modes of the visible] and the perfection of beauty owes to proportionality and consonance among the particular intentions." This "proportionality and consonance" is the result of comparison of one intention to another and of what is seen to what has been experienced. But it is in either case a judgment about particulars, in the realm of sense.[59]

Not only was Ghiberti interested in Alhazen's description of afterimages – the behavior of sight as it switches from contrasting extremes of light and dark – but his discussion of these phenomena is interlaced with illustrations from his own experience. "We find that sight, when it has looked into strong light, will suffer greatly, because it will be hurt, and have pain. And also the *simulacri* of intense light remain in the eye. After looking they make a dimly lighted place seem dark, until the impression [*orma*] of the greater light is dissipated."[60] After recounting a number of examples, Ghiberti observes that in sculpture and painting, light reveals what darkness conceals. We do not perceive the subtleties of sculpture in weak light, and bright colors in weak light appear dark, but look right in strong, clear light. "When there is little light, that body will appear dark, and sight will not distinguish its color, and it will appear almost black."[61] After quoting more Alhazen, Ghiberti argues that sculpture should be seen in tempered light, since too strong light in its own way hampers vision and vision's judgment. He then tells of sculptures he has himself seen. He had seen a hermaphrodite unearthed in Rome under conditions of tempered light, and under these conditions one saw "the greatest sweetness; sight discerned nothing that touch did not find with the hand."[62] (That is to say, in the right light sight and touch apprehended the same thing.) The chalcedony of the *Rape of the Palladium* owned by Niccolò Niccoli also was not seen (*comprendeva*) well in strong light, the reflections of which prevent (*occultano*) comprehension.[63]

These examples are interesting because Ghiberti is clearly – even too clearly – adopting Alhazen's analysis of vision to the problem of describing what can only be called aesthetic judgment, to the problem of articulating complex, cir-

[59] G. Federici-Vescovini, "Il problema," pp. 376–379, for parallel texts of the Italian Alhazen and Ghiberti on beauty.

[60] *Commentari*, p. 51.

[61] Ibid., p. 53.

[62] Ibid., p. 55.

[63] Ibid., pp. 56–57; see also p. 54.

cumstantial judgments that can only be made by sight and inner sense about the constituent elements of vision, light, dark, and color.

We are here utterly in the realm of sense. Light and color change like the colors on the necks of doves or on peacock's tails, both traditional examples of illusion. The judgments appropriate to this realm respect its own laws and uniformities. They are always about complex and unique relations of qualities. Although the language is different, because Alberti was much more skilled both in the synthesis and concealment of his sources, Ghiberti's remarks are not far from Alberti's principle of *comparatione* in *Della pittura.* "Those things that the philosophers are used to call accidents are such that all knowledge of them is *per comparatione.* . . . For this reason in painting things seem most splendid where there is good proportion of white to black, similar to that proportion in things from luminous to shadowy; so all these things are known *per comparatione.* Whence that is called light which is brighter than this dark, lightest what is brighter than this bright. And *comparatione* is made first to things best known, and whereas man is the best known to us of all things, perhaps Protagoras, saying that man was the mode and measure of things, meant that all the accidents are known in comparison to the accidents of man." And this last reference to Protagoras should be understood not to mean that the universe is made to human measure, but more skeptically, as it was intended, that we only know what is like ourselves.[64]

In any case, as Ghiberti understood the matter, all of the judgments we have considered, whether of distance or of beauty, were judgments of the eye or the common sense. And Ghiberti's *Commentari* brings us to the years around Leonardo's birth.

Leonardo on the judgment of sense

We have already seen in the introduction to our chapter on the common sense that Leonardo saw the greatest importance in this faculty, which he variously identified with judgment, intellect, the eye, and the soul, and which he clearly understood as the *hegemonikon,* for the ends of which the body itself was a complex organ.[65] Leonardo was keenly interested in the passiveness of the soul and in the

[64] Alberti, *Della pittura,* I, 18, p. 34. On this text, see C. Trinkaus, "Protagoras in the Renaissance: An Exploration," in *Philosophy and Humanism: Renaissance Essays in Honor of Paul Oskar Kristeller,* New York, 1976, pp. 190–213, here p. 197: "Alberti could not have known Plato's *Theatetus,* yet what is discussed in that dialogue is Protagoras' position that a man judges the accidental qualities of things by his sense perceptions, which in turn are determined by the accidentality of the condition of the particular individual." See also the remarks of Lorenzo de' Medici in my "Contrapposto," p. 359. For an explanation of Protagoras's dictum, see Sextus Empiricus *Against the Logicians* I.60ff.

[65] See above, Chapter 5. On sight, the common sense, and the optical writers, see Z. P. Zubov, *Leonardo da Vinci,* tr. D. H. Kraus, Cambridge, Mass., 1968, pp. 129–130. Zubov compares Leonardo on sight to Witelo, III, 51 (in Alhazen, *Opticae thesaurus,* pp. 108–109), who contrasts *intuitio diligens* to simple *aspectus. Intuitio* is that act "quo visus veram comprehensionem formae rei diligenter perquirit, non contentos simplici receptione, sed profunda indagine." Witelo closely follows Alhazen, II, 64 (*Opticae thesaurus,* p. 67).

relation between what was perceived and its inherent reasonableness; and he was evidently very much encouraged in his thinking by ideas like those we have just considered in Ghiberti, ideas arising from the union of Aristotelian psychology and Alhazen's optics. So Leonardo wrote that "the pupil does not give anything perfectly to the intellect or *sensus communis* except when objects are given to it . . . straight along the line AB. . . . If the eye . . . wishes to count letters placed in front of it, the eye will necessarily turn from letter to letter because it cannot discern them if they are not in line with AB."[66] This is an account (apparently beginning from the Democritean notion that the act of sight is on the pupil of the eye) of Alhazen's *intuitio,* the ideal case according to which adequate knowledge of particulars is provided to the "intellect or *sensus communis,*" by sight itself. Beginning from the base of such confidence in the union of the world, vision, and intellect, we shall now briefly consider some of Leonardo's other argument regarding the judgment of sense.

In one of his *paragone* arguments Leonardo wrote that there is no difference between painting and sculpture except that one is a mental, the other a physical labor. Not only does he make his famous argument that the painter paints in gentlemanly leisure, dipping delicate brushes in delightful colors, free of the dust, dirt, and general racket attendant to the carving of stone, but he also responds to the sculptor's argument that his art is more mental than painting because in carving it is necessary to imagine all sides of the figure at once so that it will possess *gratia per tutti gli aspetti.* This, Leonardo says, is not true. The painter can equally well imagine his figures from all sides, and what the sculptor really does is not so much imagine contours as run back and forth in order to see how they look from here or there. And in order for him to see more than length and breadth, it is necessary for him to lean across the stone, changing position so that the light will change. Thus he makes his judgments and corrects his contours. This, Leonardo says, is not mental labor, and only requires "mind or judgment" to correct relief that is too high. This is the way the sculptor comes to a true understanding of all the contours of his sculpture; he does not imagine them beforehand but instead "finds" them by a laborious series of simple judgments.

The sculptor never makes a judgment that the relief of the muscles of his figure is too low, because then he will have cut away too much stone, and will have ruined his sculpture. And in reply to the argument of the sculptor that in removing the *superchio* from his figure he has no margin of error, and that therefore his art is superior to that of the painter, who is endlessly free to correct his errors, Leonardo switches gears, and appeals to the relative certainty of the two arts. If the art of the sculptor were perfect, he would have measures that would make it certain that he did not remove too much stone. It is, in short, to be expected that the sculptor will get things right, and if he cannot, this is simply an admission of the shortcomings of his art and an admission of his own ignorance.

[66] M. Kemp, *Leonardo da Vinci,* p. 130; and J. Ackerman, "Leonardo's Eye," p. 132.

Sculptors who remove too much stone are "ruiners of marble," not masters. Masters do not depend on the *giudizio dell'occhio,* which is deceptive; this is proved by experience, by the fact that it is impossible to divide a line exactly in half without recourse to measurement. Because of the untrustworthiness of the judgment of the eye, *buoni giudici* know the dimensions of the parts, proceed with caution, and do not make mistakes. The gist of this argument is that the judgments made by the sculptor are low-grade judgments of the eye (whether or not relief is too high), linked to physical exertion and that, insofar as this is not the case, and the sculptor is not ignorant and knows the dimensions of the parts, his art is comparable to painting, and not superior to it.

Leonardo then proceeds to argue that the painter has ten different *discorsi* to consider in the completion of his work. (In a similar argument[67] it is said that nature makes relief and "prospettiva" without the need of *discorso* on the part of the sculptor.) The ten *discorsi* of the painter are light, shadow, color, body, shape, location, distance, nearness, motion, and rest. The sculptor is concerned only with body, form, location, motion, and rest. Nature makes light and dark for the sculptor together with material. He is not concerned with color, and is only middlingly concerned with distance and nearness. He employs linear perspective (in low relief) but not aerial perspective. Sculpture therefore has less *"discorso"* than painting and is consequently of less *fatica d'ingegno.*[68]

Leonardo's ten *discorsi* correspond more or less to the common sensibles, expanded by "visibles," including the special sensibles of sight. In other repetitions of the list he called them *termini, offici,* and *predicamenti,* or "that which is visible." The operations associated with these elements of sight are *discorsi,* that is, operations associated with the *cogitativa,* and by *discorsi* he seems to mean definite problems to be resolved in particular cases. They are, in effect, judgments of the kind associated with the common sense, or by the eye in relation to the the common sense. And these solutions, although they are "spiritual" in origin, are not strictly intellectual, certainly not theoretical. They are achieved not by *fatica d'intelletto* but by *fatica d'ingegno.*

The development and diffusion of optics must have fundamentally altered notions of perception and intellection; because, at least in principle, the eye, according to the most basic postulates of optics, truly reflects what is before it, so that many authors over many centuries blamed the fallacies of sight not on vision

[67] *Treatise,* 52. See *Treatise,* 19, where it is argued that the ten *discorsi* of painting mentioned in this passage are "comprehended by the mind alone without manual work." At the beginning of the treatise on painting (*Treatise,* 1), Leonardo defines *scientia* as that *discorso mentale,* which originates in its ultimate principles, of which in nature no other thing may be found that is part of the science; so the *scientia* of geometry (or of continuous quantities) begins from the surfaces of bodies, is seen to have its origin in line, which bounds surface, and line may be reduced to points, which are never real. "True science" (*vera scientia*) is that which may be demonstrated mathematically; at the same time, sciences that "begin and end in the mind" are not true because such "mental discourses" are not subject to experience, without which nothing is certain. "True discourse," in other words, is both linked to experience and is mathematically demonstratable, or describable; or the particular is mathematically describable, and the truth of this description is relative to the particular.

[68] *Treatise,* 51.

as such but rather on the conditions of vision. As we have seen, Aristotle argued that error arose first in the apprehension of common sensibles, and we have followed this to the formulation that the eye apprehends magnitudes but does not apprehend them *ad punctum*. For Nicole Oresme, for example, the common sense judges about the world what circumstances let vision see, and it follows that in perfect circumstances the common sense will make a judgment perfectly adequate to what is seen. Moreover, such a perfect judgment simply corresponds to the geometry of sight itself, rooted in the geometric regularity of light. It again follows that sight may be right, that under normal circumstances it is for all intents and purposes right, and that it is right in that it can be shown to be right. All of this brought sight and mathematics into the closest possible relation, and also brought the physical world and mathematics into the closest possible relation. If the common sensibles were also physical and mathematical, then an adequate optics meant that the "fallacies of sight" are mathematically describable and therefore constructable. This interface between the physical, apprehended as such in common sensation, and the mathematical, was basic to Leonardo's thinking. The rational is that which can be shown to be so about what is sensed.

In the example we have just considered, Leonardo argued, as he argued in several places, that a line may not be exactly halved by the judgment of the eye. This does not mean that such judgment is utterly useless, however; on the contrary, it is very necessary to the painter, and Leonardo recommends games for *disegnatori* that will be "useful to their profession," that will bring about "good judgment of the eye in knowing to judge the truth concerning the breadth and length of things."[69] To accustom the *ingegno* to making such judgments, the lengths of random lines on a wall should be estimated from a distance, and similar estimates should be made of magnitudes along foreshortened lines. Such games, he concludes, "are the cause of making good *giuditio d'occhio* which is the principle act of painting." Leonardo in effect is exercising common sensation, in the faith that it can be right much as perspective can be right. And if he sometimes writes that "good judgment is born of good understanding (*intendere*) and good understanding derives from reasons taken from good rules and good rules are the daughters of good experience, common mother of all sciences and arts,"[70] such arguments (which seem to show the immediate impress of the beginning of Aristotle's *Metaphysics* or some echo of it) do not mean that the science of perspective should be applied to all problems, it rather means that the judgments of vision can be right, and that both sight and the science of sight meet in the *ratio* of vision itself.

Thus if "practice must always be built upon good theory," and the theory of painting is perspective,[71] practice is also related to experience. One may know on the basis of the psychology we have been examining that visual qualities are oppositions, but the painter must learn to find the means between these oppositions

[69] *Treatise*, 75. On the difficulty of judgment in matters of distance and size, see *Treatise*, 88.
[70] Leonardo, *Literary Works*, I, 18.
[71] *Treatise*, 70.

and then make such experience second nature. The *disegnatore* is again advised to go slowly in order to judge (*giudicare*) which of the lights are brighter and how much they are brighter, which of the shadows are darker and how the two mingle. Their qualities should be observed and they should be compared to one another. It should be observed how lines twist and change direction, where outlines are more or less clearly evident and therefore broad or fine. Lights and shadows should be finely blended, and when the "hand and judgment" will have been trained in making these discriminations, then facility of execution will follow.[72] These complex judgments of light, dark, and the means between them, and of contours and their movements, should no doubt again be compared to the simple judgments of the sculptor, who must only decide that relief is too high.

It should be noted that Leonardo is writing about two kinds of judgment, of quantity and quality. Judgments of quantity may be adequate according to the eye, but may also be measured and assisted by measure, hence his practical interest in both perspective and proportion. Qualitative relations, however, although they could be established by the eye, by definition could not be measured, and this brings us to the most fundamental principles of Leonardo's pictorial composition.

In his *Treatise of Painting,* Leonardo not only wrote about the judgment of the eye in terms clearly defined by Aristotle's ideas as we have examined them, but wrote about this judgment in relation to the very visual foundations of his painting. In a section entitled "where lights fool the judgment [*giudizio*] of the painter," he writes that "among lights of equal brightness, that will seem stronger which will be surrounded by a darker field."[73] He means by this that, given two whites of the same intensity, one contrasted to black will seem brighter than another contrasted to gray. The eye is "fooled" in that the same visual quality looks different in relation to other different visual qualities, and because the *eye* really sees one white as brighter than another even though it is not. This apparent maximum brilliance may be exploited by the painter. In another section entitled "where shadows fool the judgment [*giudizio*] that states their greater or lesser darkness," he puts forward the opposite principle, that "among shadows of equal darkness that was shown least dark which is surrounded by lights of less potency, such as shadows generated among reflected lights," and warns the painter not "to fool himself" by varying these shadows.[74] The painter must be on guard

[72] Ibid., 63.

[73] Ibid., 854.

[74] Ibid., 853. Perhaps the closest parallel to Leonardo's remarks on contrast is to be found in the midst of a discussion of the color of the moon during an eclipse in Plutarch, "The Face on the Moon," 933, in *Moralia,* XII, tr. H. Cherniss and W. C. Helmbold, p. 129. It is because of "an affection of our senses" that hot seems hotter next to cold, pleasure more intense next to pain, and bright things seem more conspicuous when compared with dark," their appearance being intensified by contrast to different impressions. Elsewhere (*Moralia* 57C and 863E, ed. cit., I, p. 307, and XI, p. 65), Plutarch expressly likens contrast to the practice of painters who "set off bright and brilliant colors by laying on dark and somber tints close beside them" and "set off highlights by contrast with shadow." Leonardo's principle of painting was not only based on the elements of vision, it was positively based upon illusion.

against the loss of vividness in his work by allowing middle tones to rest side by side, and he elsewhere recommends that you must "use your *ingegno* to set the bodies against backgrounds [*in campi*] so that the part of those bodies which is dark ends on a bright ground, and the illuminated part of the body terminates in a dark ground."[75] This was advice that Leonardo followed assiduously in most of his own painting, and in his formula of *chiaroscuro* composition he raised an observation about the judgment of the eye to the level of a precept. The eye, as he repeats many times throughout his writings, will see contrasts as most vivid, and in the invention and execution of his work the painter must see to it that such vividness is maintained in the highest possible degree.

More specifically, but within the general framework of *chiaroscuro* just established, Leonardo considered the organization of lights and darks, which must be considered under four categories: quality, quantity, position, and shape.[76] "Quality" is the determination of "which shadow and which part of the shadow is more or less dark (since qualities only admitted of degrees); quantity is the size of the shadow relative to others near it; position (*sito*) is defined by the situation of the shadow and the members on which it falls (this is immediately reconsidered under the heading of *aspetto*); and shape (*figura*) has to do with the participation of a shadow in such qualities as triangularity, roundness, and squareness. The establishment of these relations within any given painting is the result of the exercise of the judgment of the eye. In these precepts Leonardo has alerted the painter to his proper concerns, and thus defined in general what pictorial composition should be. But in any actual painting the right relations must be found by the eye.

Leonardo was setting down the principles of the long tradition of tonal painting that followed him when he wrote these words, and it may be easily imagined that the artistic forms he invented bore with them meanings and implicit demands that differed little from his justifications. When Vasari discussed *collocazione* in painting, he called it "nothing else than the division of the place in which a figure has been made, such that the intervals agree with the judgment of the eye [*gli spazzi siano concordi al giudizio dell'occhio*] and are not deformed, as it would be if the field [*campo*] were filled in one place and empty in another; this is born from *disegno*."[77] *Disegno,* as Vasari tirelessly repeated, is improved by practice, by drawing from good paintings, from classical sculpture, and from life. *Giudizio* is improved at the same time. But finally the hand draws and the eye judges. The right relations must be found by the eye; if they are not, as Vasari also wrote, the eye will not cease to censure the work.

Tonal painting was an infinitely flexible binary system, a system that underlay a capacity for illusion and fiction that was also infinite. And if painting was based on light and dark, the absolute constituents of vision, and if that assumption

[75] Ibid., 845.
[76] Ibid., 841.
[77] VBB, I, p. 114.

and rule determined the character of any possible painting, real paintings were complex constructions of relation and adjustments between these extremes, relations and adjustments that always had to be found and could not be prescribed. On good Aristotelian principles, now lifted away to have become a principle of painting as basic as the practice of toning grounds and painting from shadow to light, Lodovico Dolce wrote that "an extreme whiteness always displeases; rather a certain *temperamento* between white and brown contains every degree of charm" (*vaghezza*),[78] as one sees in the painting of Titian. What is displeased is the eye, and it is the eye that finds the *temperamento* in every stroke of which the painting is made.

Lomazzo on the judgment of the eye

As we have had occasion to observe before, Lomazzo was not comfortable with the implications of the idea that all good manners of painting are equal, and, while he developed the astrological basis of this position to heights without parallel in the Renaissance literature of art, he also attempted to establish taste upon a kind of judgment derived from the Neoplatonism of Marsilio Ficino. Our astrologically determined differences make us like and dislike one another, and they dispose us to different activities in life. Such differences, he says, are no more evident than in the "judgment or taste of beauty"[79] (*giudicio o sia gusto della bellezza*). Lomazzo does not argue that beauty is in the eye of the beholder, however, but rather that a truly beautiful woman – for example – will only be appreciated incompletely, in some aspect or another, by various men. Such things must be carefully considered by the painter, and point to a higher decorum, according to which a person should be given visual characteristics consistent with his or her nature. Because a face painted from nature will be "judged" in many ways by many people according to the "nature of their seeing,"[80] the painter must look to reason, beyond the particular pleasure of anyone, because the work ought to be universal and perfect – "otherwise the painter works in the dark. It is necessary to compare what is seen to the "figure that the mind from the beginning possesses."[81]

The text by Ficino to which Lomazzo turned is of interest to us because of its treatment of sight itself.[82] We have seen numerous instances of authors who argued that the form in the mind is spiritual, developed from the Aristotelian principle that "the forms of things, and not the things themselves are in the

[78] See M. W. Roskill, *Dolce's "Aretino" and Venetian Art Theory of the Cinquecento*, New York, 1968, p. 208. See J. A. Thornton, *Renaissance Color Theory and Some Paintings by Veronese*, Ph.D. dissertation, University of Pittsburgh, 1979.

[79] G. P. Lomazzo, *Idea*, p. 223. This well-known chapter (XXVI) is discussed and paralleled to Ficino by Panofsky, *Idea*, appendix I.

[80] Lomazzo, *Idea*, p. 225.

[81] Ibid., p. 227; see p. 225, where it is remarked that "la vera bellezza è solamente quella che dalla ragione *si gusta*, e non da queste due finestre corporali."

[82] Panofsky, *Idea*, pp. 151–152.

soul." Form is the thinkable, and this is separated from matter. Ficino, however, literally extends this argument, certainly under the sway of optics. The forms of things and the order among them are not only in the soul, but they are in *light,* as true "paintings" of things, separated from matter. The whole order and ornament of the world is "incorporated" only in our eyes; and the spiritual beauty of the world as transmitted to us by light is doubled for us when the beauty of what is seen, owing to the unity of the original form with well-disposed matter, bears the impress of the Idea. Then there occurs the consonance between this seen form and "the true figure infused in the mind by the divine ray." But this Platonic foundation of judgment is perhaps not as interesting for our purposes as the absolute basis given to sight by Ficino's arguments. Al-Kindi imagined the universe as a plenum of light in which all communicated with all, and this provided the basis for the theory of the propagation of light that made Alhazen's optics possible.[83] Ficino imagined this plenum as occupied at points by eyes, which perceived at those points not material things, but the order among things, borne by light. It is perhaps in relation to such absolute optics that we should understand Lomazzo's account of the words of another reader of Ficino's commentary on Plato's *Symposium,* Michelangelo.[84] "This whole art," Lomazzo quotes Michelangelo to say, "and its whole end, is to know to draw all that is seen with the same reasons that one sees."[85] This is nothing else than an affirmation of the heuretic value – the absolute heuretic value – of both sight and drawing. Sight comprehends the visible, *disegno* works toward this comprehension as a limit. When he wrote of Michelangleo as his first *governatore* in Chapter 11 of his *Idea,* Lomazzo wrote that "it is written that he used to say proportion must be in the eyes of men so that they know immediately to judge that which they see."[86] This should be understood to mean that some are born to "see," that, as Paolo Pino argued and as Michelangelo certainly believed, the judgment that separates the artist from others is finally innate. This in turn means that knowing how to see, *saper vedere,* is not so much the application of principles to seeing as it is the continued quest of the elect eye to realize in drawing what is seen. *Sapere* thus draws close to its Latin meaning "to taste," and the phrase *saper vedere* in Lomazzo's first text is equivalent to *saper giudicare* in the second.

The common sense and the microcosm

At the end of the first chapter of the first book of his *De architectura,* which treats the education of the architect, Vitruvius observed that the theory of an art is

[83] D. C. Lindberg, *Theories of Vision,* pp. 9, 30.

[84] On Michelangelo and Ficino's *Commentary,* see MLA, pp. 421–423.

[85] *Scritti sulle arti,* ed. R. Ciardi, II, p. 230–231. For a variant reading of this text, according to which Lomazzo is recommending the application of the science of perspective in particular circumstances, on analogy to the virtue of prudence as presented by C. Dempsey (introduction n. 13 above), see E. Cropper, review of D. Summers, *Michelangelo and the Language of Art, AB,* 65, 1983, pp. 157–[illegible]2.

[86] *Idea,* p. 113.

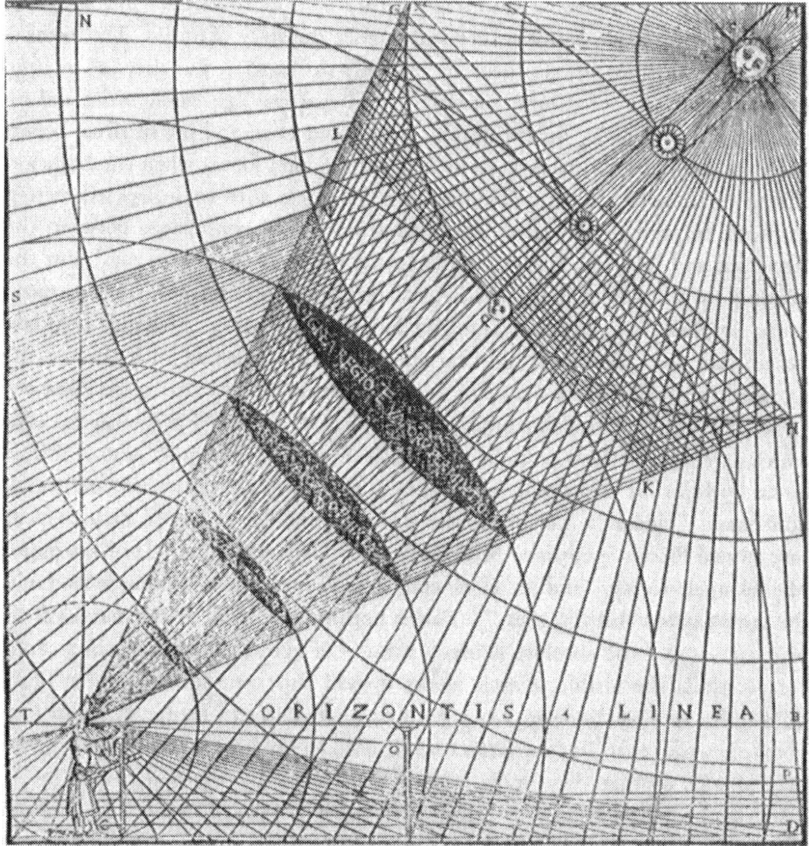

Fig. 5. *The visible universe,* from Vitruvius, *De architectura,* tr. Cesare Cesariano, Como, 1521, f. XI v.

shared in a way that practice is not. The musician and the physician may both be interested in rhythm – one because of the dance, say, the other because of the pulse – but when we are sick we call a physician, and only a musician can tune a musical instrument. Similarly, astronomers may discuss with musicians "the harmony of the stars and the musical consonances in tetrads and triads of the fourth and the fifth," which they may also discuss with geometricians, who understand the *logos optikos,* even though such shared understanding stops at the point at which it is necessary to turn the hand to real works. Vitruvius's astronomy, harmonics, and optics correspond to Aristotle's "physical mathematics" (*Physics* 194a), and his discussion implies that they are not only related but share deep common principles. When he wrote his commentary on Vitruvius, published in

Como in 1521,[87] Cesare Cesariano set out to explain these common principles. His arguments, and the illustration accompanying them (Fig. 5) provide a summary of the major themes of the last two chapters.

It has long been recognized that Cesariano's translation and commentary came out of the circle of Leonardo da Vinci and Bramante, but despite its undenied relation to founders of the High Renaissance style, it has been little studied, owing no doubt to the sheer difficulty of the text, an elaborate interlace of often abbreviated scholastic Latin and Italian. Such defenses against interpretation notwithstanding, however, Cesariano's explanation of his illustration is fairly clear and will repay our close attention.

Citing "Themistius and others," Cesariano divides the human rational soul into two parts, which he calls *dividua* and *individua*. *Individua* refers to the mind and *dividua* to the other "irrational potencies." This is illustrated by a circle divided in half, as the small circle in the lower corner of Figure 5 containing the figure is divided by the horizon. The upper semicircle is the mind; the lower (this is not illustrated, but is described in the text) is subdivided "with harmonic proportion" into seven circles, which are the irrational "potencies," listed as irascible, concupiscible, memory, *estimativa,* fantasy or imagination, common sense and particular sense, the last of which is divided into the five senses.

Cesariano argues that the senses all have different substances, that sight has its origin in the element of air, hearing and smell from water and earth. "And yet it seems to me if I am not wrong that all derive from a point." Here he has introduced the notion of the common sense, which he immediately compares to the definition of soul as a self-moving number (Aristotle *De anima* 404b26ff.), adding the Platonic observation that this point, being immaterial, must be like the intelligence, in which the memory of ideal forms is retained. The common sense, however, is an *image* of the intelligence, as becomes clear in the long analysis of sound that follows this remark. Sound emanates from a single point of origin and may return there (as in the case of echoes) according to certain geometric and physical laws. Here Cesariano returns to his real theme, the common geometry of astronomy, harmonics, and optics. We see and we hear according to similar laws.

Cesariano identifies the common sense with the "optic vein," which leads outward to the centers of the eyes, from which arise "so many kinds of seeing," evident in his illustration. In short, he imagined something very like the geometry of common sense to be seen in Leonardo's skull studies (Fig. 4). Like Leonardo, he associates the common sense with sight (although he gave it a different location, in the optic nerve rather than in the middle lobe of the brain). He also follows the usual pattern in saying that all five senses derive from a point, but again, like Leonardo, he considers sight and hearing to be the most important of the

[87] Vitruvius, *De architectura*, tr. C. Cesariano, Como, 1521 (C. H. Krinsky, ed., facs., Munich, 1969), f. x–xi verso.

senses. In fact, he refers not just to the "common sense" but to the "common senses," by which he means the senses that grasp the common regularities taken in by sight and hearing, which are, however, apprehended as such, as common to the world revealed by both senses, in the common sense. Vision, which may regard the harmonic patterns of the heavenly spheres, is immediate to the common sense that judges this harmony together with the harmony of sounds.

Optics is a kind of geometry, and therefore proceeds from a point, the simplest element of geometry. The common sense is also a point and from this literal and ultimate similarity the whole optical world Cesariano illustrates can be generated. Cesariano imagines the macrocosm as harmonic and the microcosm, the human soul, as concentric to that harmony. The circle at the center of this concentricity is itself a symbol of the human soul, as we have seen. And on the vertical diameter of that circle stands a small figure, holding a measuring rod in his left hand, his height equal to three of the divisions of the plane upon which he stands, as Alberti had specified a figure should be in his treatise on painting. The height of the gaze of the figure coincides with the horizon, which again recalls Alberti.[88] The world this figure surveys is intersected by two markers the height of his gaze. The marker in the figure's right hand is in effect a picture plane, which, placed between the eye and the receding regular intervals, permits their apparent sizes to be registered. The further marker permits the transversal lines in the construction to be drawn. We are placed by this construction at a distance of nine units from the construction, just as the figure is placed nine units from the marker, and we are shown the plane to a depth of five units, all according to Alberti's rules of perspective.

Circles open from the common sense of the figure through the spheres of the elements past the moon to the sun, and light radiates from the sun in straight lines, not just to the earth but to the measurable earth, which is potentially measured as it is lighted. Perspective, of course, is discussed in terms of rays, that is, in terms of a metaphorical light between the eye and the object, and the sun also emits rays of light. The eye and the sun are in fact symmetrical.[89] The universe, in other words, is an optical universe, a universe made up of light, which is geometrically regular, in intersection with sight, which is also geometrically regular.

Leonardo, as we have seen, wrote that the eye is the chief means by which the common sense surveys the marvelous beauty of this world. Cesariano extended the definition of the common sense as the center of all the senses, making it by

[88] L. B. Alberti, *Opere volgari*, ed. C. Grayson, III, pp. 36–40.

[89] On the microcosmic – macrocosmic parallel of eye and sun, see above, Chapter 5 n. 3. On Leonardo's localization of the common sense, see D. S. Strong, *Leonardo on the Eye: An English Translation and Critical Commentary of Ms. D in the Bibliothèque National, Paris, with Studies on Leonardo's Methodology and Theories of Optics*, New York, 1979, pp. 104–105. Cesariano seems to follow the pattern of Alhazen and Bacon in placing the act of vision (the union of the two images from each eye) in the "common nerve," and followed a usual pattern in further identifying this with the common sense. For a discussion of this idea, see ibid., pp. 363–372.

that very fact the center of the whole visible universe. At the same time, as if in response to Alberti's notion of a *sense* of *concinnitas*, Cesariano clearly identifies what he calls the common senses as sight and hearing, which may both apprehend geometric order and harmony. *Ratio* thus again begins with sense itself, and with the physical constitution of sense; it is sense itself that apprehends the optical and acoustical but ultimately physical order of things from a point of view, a judging center of sensation. In general, it may be said that criticism of the forgotten notion of the common sense and the fusion of this idea with optics were central to the definition of the world as physical and of sensation as a physical process. It is sight that has first access to the embracing order of the frame of the physical world. In Cesariano's scheme we see not only the harmonies of the world but also the universal structure of human sense.

9

Confused knowledge

Clear, distinct, and confused

The criterion of clear and distinct knowledge is one of the hallmarks of Cartesian philosophy, and it implies a counterpart – obscure and indistinct knowledge, as it might be called – that in fact marked out the original domain of the modern field of aesthetics. As we shall see, Alexander Baumgarten, whose *Aesthetica* of 1750 gave the new philosophical discipline its name, took over a distinction from Leibniz, which in turn is usually said to derive from Descartes. In his *Discourse on Metaphysics* Leibniz distinguished between clear knowledge and obscure, distinct and confused, adequate and inadequate, and defined the confused as follows: "When I am able to recognize a thing among others, without being able to say in what its differences or characteristics consist, the knowledge is confused." So far the "confused" particular is like Plato's sensation unproductive of thought. It is clear and definite relative to other things, but beyond its bare apprehension or mere naming, nothing can be said about it. As an example of such irreducible particular apprehension Leibniz gives the judgment of a poem or painting. We may know clearly, that is, without being in the slightest doubt, that they are well or poorly done, because they possess a certain *je ne sais quoi* that is satisfying or shocking. But however *clear* such an apprehension may be, it is only "when I am able to explain the peculiarities which a thing has that the knowledge is called distinct." As an example of distinct knowledge, Leibniz gives an assayer who distinguishes true gold from false through the consideration of certain characteristics that define gold. Distinctness thus presupposes analysis and definition. We know few things distinctly, and the terms we use to define what we know are themselves not adequately distinct, and so "most human knowledge is only confused or indeed assumed."

In his *Meditationes de Cognitione, Veritate et Ideis,* Leibniz provided another version of these definitions, which it will be instructive to examine. "Obscurity" is nearly an optical quality, belonging to things we "can't quite make out," and has a metaphorical dimension in ideas we "can't quite see." It follows that things must be "clear" before they can be "confused," which is to say that we must see a thing sufficiently before we can know it in any way at all. The "confused" is that in which the distinguishing characteristics of a thing have not been separated. Some things do not permit such separation because they are irreducibly simple. We know colors, odors, and flavors by the direct testimony of sense, an echo of Aristotle's idea of the infallibility of special sensation. We could never explain to a blind man what "red" is because "red" is simple and absolute sensation and has no elements into which it might be resolved. Its particularity cannot be adequately talked about (although, he says, we might talk about its causes). We may only communicate such particularity by either showing the thing itself to a person or by comparison, by referring to other sense experience. Leibniz moves immediately from pure special sensation once again to the example of painting. Painters and other craftsmen know immediately what has been done rightly and what faultily, but when asked for the reasons for their judgment they are unable to give any and simply say that it lacks a certain "I know not what." The argument means that the "quality" (not Leibniz's term) is evident at once and irreducible, that it can only be discussed concretely, either in its presence or by means of comparison to other related experience. The example of the assayer is again used for distinctness. By the evaluation of a number of qualities he is able to distinguish gold from other similar things. The key to "distinctness" is once again analysis, and the assayer's skill, which might only be based on the articulation of experience, is of a low form that nonetheless points to a high and unattainable ideal of uniformly distinct human knowledge, which would finally be mathematical and metaphysical.

Leibniz – following Descartes – was clearly the beneficiary of the tradition we have traced in an earlier chapter according to which Aristotle's common sensibles were optical and therefore mathematical. Leibniz considered the "notions common to several senses, as number, magnitude, shape and figure" to be inherently more distinct. He seems to have meant that the mind does in fact make at least implicit judgments about such matters as it experiences things, and because this is so, experience is "confused," that is to say, it may be rationally explicated. The "idea" must potentially contain other ideas, and it is through the apprehension of the common sensibles that we are able to apprehend that about the world which may be understood mathematically. As he elaborates this point elsewhere, the qualities common to several senses are distinct relative to those perceived by one because they cannot be resolved into the confused but only into the concepts of the intellect. In any case, the essential experience of art, or the experience of that which is essential about art, of the *nescio quid,* that is, of grace or beauty, which must be the consequence of a judgment like "estimation," is grouped together with the irreducibility of basic sensation, with what is "confused" and what almost by definition cannot be "distinct."[1]

[1] G. W. Leibniz, *Discourse on Metaphysics: Correspondence with Arnauld, and Monadology*, ed. Paul Janet, tr. G. Montgomery, Chicago, 1902, p. 41; and *Opera omnia*, Geneva, 1768, II, pp. 14–

In his history of aesthetics, Benedetto Croce observed that much the same distinction made by Leibniz was to be found in Peter Abelard and John Duns Scotus, and suggested that it was current long before the time of Descartes or Leibniz. In this chapter, I shall argue that it was indeed much older,[2] that it was in fact a fundamental and well-known philosophical distinction, and that it is systematically related to our theme of common sensation, and thus to naturalism.

In Plato's *Theatetus* (201d), knowledge is defined as true belief with the addition of discourse (*logos*), a definition that Socrates elaborates with an account of a dream he had had. In this dream he was told of "elements," to which only names can be given. These elements (202b) are *aistheta,* and are inexplicable and unknowable, even if right judgments are made about them. What seems to be meant is that things sensed are not true or false until some statement is made about them. But this argument is made with the important condition that we *do* apprehend things about which statements are made. The thing is, however, not knowable until some assertion is made, and it is not until the element becomes a part of a composition that we enter the realm of the true or false. The activity of discourse, or *logos,* may be right or wrong and is subject to the laws of thought. One does not have knowledge until able to make true statements about the known.

This argument had the important result of separating sense data from knowledge by placing it beyond any but the most simply nominative function of language. The argument would be closely echoed by Aristotle in the *De interpretatione,* then by Porphyry and Boethius, thus to become a part of the late medieval discussion of universals. For our present purposes it is sufficient to note the association of sensation with that which is apprehended but not capable of articulation. It is also important to note that the first mental process about these "elements" is defined as discourse.

At the beginning of the *Physics* (184a–b), Aristotle provides a discussion that

15. E. Cassirer, *The Philosophy of the Enlightenment,* Boston, 1955, p. 342, understands this second text to mean that "clear" ideas are suitable for daily life, enabling us "to orient ourselves to our sense environment. For this orientation all that is necessary is that we distinguish carefully among the various objects we encounter and that we pattern our behavior toward these objects after our distinctions." On such a view, "clear" knowledge would be the work of a faculty like the *vis cogitativa,* which we shall examine in Chapter 10. For Cassirer, "distinctness" finally has to do with the scientific quest for cause and substance. In a text cited by Wolfson, "Internal Senses," in *Studies in the History of Philosophy and Religion,* pp. 308–309, Leibniz wrote of imagination as comprising the notions of the particular senses, which are clear but confused, and the notions of the common sense, which are clear and distinct. Imagination is thus a more general faculty than common sense, and he means that, whereas the particular senses simply apprehend, the common sense judges and distinguishes and that the common sensibles are quantifiable. Imagination completes the data of the individual senses with common sensibles, which provide the basis for mathematics. See N. Rescher, *The Philosophy of Leibniz,* Englewood Cliffs, N.J., 1967, p. 130. Descartes distinguished between qualities perceived by more than one sense (i.e., common sensibles) as distinct, in contrast to those perceived by only one as confused, followed by Leibniz, who considered qualities common to several senses distinct relative to those perceived by one; they cannot be resolved into the confused but only into the concepts of the intellect. Our apprehension of these qualities, he says, does not depend on the particular constitution of a sense organ. See J. J. MacIntosh, "Primary and Secondary Qualities," *Studia leibnitiana,* 8, 1976, pp. 88–104.

[2] B. Croce, *Aesthetic as Science of Expression and General Linguistic,* pp. 178–179, 207.

provoked much commentary and made the distinction between clear and confused knowledge central to the larger questions of human knowledge in general. When we come to know things, he writes, we proceed from what is "more knowable and obvious to us" toward that which is "clearer and more knowable by nature." At the same time, Aristotle calls the "more knowable and obvious to us" the "more obscure to us." In order to understand this apparent paradox, it is necessary to turn to the *Posterior analytics* (72a1–5), where it is explained that

> there is a difference between what is prior and better known in the order of being and what is prior and better known to man. I mean that objects nearer to sense are prior and better known to man; objects without qualification prior and better known are those further from sense. Now the most universal causes are furthest from sense and particular causes are nearest to sense, and they are thus exactly opposed to one another.

To return to the *Physics,* Aristotle characterizes what is nearer to sense and therefore "better known" as "confused," meaning that it awaits analysis. He ends his argument by saying that we grasp the "whole that is best known to sense-perception," and from this we proceed through experience to form universals, which are also "a kind of whole," and these are progressively corrected as we come to real knowledge. It happens similarly with words, he says, for the "child begins by calling all men 'father,' and all women 'mother,' but later on distinguishes each of them."

This text pointed to a host of problems and was interpreted in several ways. For one thing, it placed an extraordinary weight upon sense. What does it mean to say that the "whole is best known to sense-perception" and that it is like the universal? Aristotle's words were read together with those from the *Metaphysics* (993b) in which truth is compared to the "proverbial door, which no one can fail to hit" and in which intellect is compared to the "eyes of bats in the blaze of day" that miss "the things which are most evident of all." What are these things, and what principles govern the relation between the particular and the universal, between sense and intellect? However these questions might have been answered, "confused" and "distinct" knowledge had become part of the discussion. Aquinas closes his commentary on Aristotle's text by saying that "we know a thing confusedly before we know it distinctly," and John Duns Scotus simply states that "knowledge is double: confused and distinct."[3]

In order to understand the Scholastic use of the terms "confused" and "distinct," which became a commonplace in later philosophy, it is necessary to turn back to Boethius and to the beginnings of the medieval philosophical tradition. In his commentary on Aristotle's *De interpretatione,* Boethius argued that neither sensations nor imaginations can be denoted by words, basing his arguments on the distinction between *noemata* and *aisthemata,* which he called *intellectus* and

[3] Thomas Aquinas, *Commentary on Aristotle's Physics,* tr. R. J. Blackwell, R. J. Spath, and W. E. Thirlkel, New Haven, Conn., 1963, p. 5; and John Duns Scotus, *In Octo libros Physicorum Aristotelis, Opera Omnia,* Hildesheim, 1968, II, p. 19.

sensus respectively.[4] This distinction implied the underlying distinction between *passiones animae* and *passiones corporis,* and anyone who says that words signify effective states of mind can be referring neither to sensations (which are states of body) nor to phantasms, of which Aristotle says neither truth nor falsehood can be predicated.

Boethius referred in the course of his argument to Aristotle's *De anima* (432a), where it is stated that because nothing exists outside us apart from sensible spatial magnitudes, "it is in the sensible forms that the intelligible forms exist, both the abstractions of mathematics, as they are called, and all the qualities and attributes of sensible things . . . as without sensation a man would not learn or understand anything, so at the very time when he is actually thinking he must have an image before him." Aristotle observed that phantasms, which are "like present sensations, except that they are immaterial" are neither affirmations nor negations until they become part of a combination of words that implies truth or falsehood. As he wrote at the beginning of the *De interpretatione* (16a9–15), the word "goat stag" (a fantastic creature) is significant, but it is not true or false unless "is" or "is not" is added. More simply, there are in the mind thoughts that are neither true nor false unless combined with other words. Such "simple notions" (*noemata*) must be synthesized in statements. As an example of a simple notion, Boethius gives that of "Socrates" unpredicated, and asks whether such a concept, entailing no judgment (that is, no synthesis) is possible. Aristotle (*De anima* 432a12ff) seems to have imagined phantasms and *noemata* as in a necessary interdependence ("I reply that neither these nor the rest of our notions are images, but that they cannot dispense with images"), and Boethius seems to have wished to Platonize this relation by splitting it, in effect making the phantasm the *object* of thought, the singular *about* which thought takes place. "For sense and imagination are certain first shapes [*figurae*] upon which as a kind of foundation supervenient intelligence is shone."[5] Boethius then uses an extremely interesting analogy to painting.

> As painters are used to outline [*designare lineatim*] a body and to lay in the underpainting of the body where they portray any face with colors, so sense and imagination are naturally laid in like colors in the perception of the soul. For when anything falls under sense or thinking [*cogitatio*], it is first of all necessary that some imagination [*imaginatio*] be born. Afterwards the more complete intellect [*intellectus*] supervenes, explicating all of its parts which were taken up confusedly by imagination. Wherefore imagination is something imperfect.[6]

On the basis of this argument, Boethius concludes that, since nouns and verbs signify not the defective but the perfect, Aristotle is right in saying they signify a quality not of sense or imagination, but rather of intellect.

It would require a separate study to trace the history of Boethius's text, and

[4] Boethius, *In Librum De interpretatione editio secunda,* MPL, 64, col. 406.

[5] This argument is compared to Synesius by Bundy, *Theory of Imagination,* p. 175.

[6] Ibid., and Boethius, MPL, 64, col. 407.

now we shall gather only the following implications: individuals, which for us are either sensations or imaginations, are always transformed when named, that nouns and verbs are necessarily universal, and that when we name or describe a sensation or a mental image, it necessarily passes over a divide from the particular to the universal. And for our present purposes it is essential that particulars, the *passiones corporis,* are characterized as "confused." As we shall see, this does not mean that they are unclear or muddled, rather they might be imagined to have the clarity of dreams, say, or even of sensations themselves; instead it means that they are not distinct in the specific sense of not being distinguished, not subjected to the characteristic analysis and synthesis of reason. Both sensation and imagination are opposed to what can be stated in words.

Abelard, evidently drawing upon Boethius, called both sense and imagination *confusa animae perceptio* and defined *ratio* as a principle of discernment. *Confusa* thus refers not to the quality of the sensation itself but rather to the lack of order in sensation or imagination to be had from the intervention of other faculties of the soul by classification and comparison.[7]

The second author cited by Croce, Duns Scotus, who argued that the senses are in large part reliable, also argued that external sensible things cause a "confused phantasm," which is unified only accidentally in the *virtus phantastica,* which represents the thing according to quantity, shape, color, and other sensible accidents. Most people perceive nothing else. What he calls "prime truths" are grasped in their nature apart from what is accidental. As an example, he gives the following. The proposition "the whole is greater than its part" is not primarily true of a whole in stone or wood, but of the whole as abstracted from all to which it is accidentally joined. The intellect that never understands totality except in concepts *per accidens* (that is, in mental images of singulars), like the totality of wood or stone, never understands the "precise reason of terms by virtue of which there is truth." Only a few have the power to attain to such truth, whereas the many grasp things merely in concepts *per accidens.* A person grasps such things not by special illumination but rather because of superior natural gifts, a more abstract and penetrating mind, or, in the case of two persons equally "ingenious," the difference owes to differences in serious investigations of things. Although he compares life in the realm of accidents to life in a mist, it is clear that he identifies "confusion" with the lowest, representative part of what might be called natural, prereflective intelligence.[8]

[7] See L. Urbani Ulivi, *La Psicologia di Abelardo e il "Tractatus de Intellectibus,"* Rome, 1976, pp. 22–23, and, for imagination, p. 27. Interestingly (pp. 42–43), apparently because sense and imagination are interchangeable, and both may be the object of intellection, the menagerie of centaurs, chimeras, hircocervums, and sirens usually limited to the imagination is also admitted to the intellect.

[8] John Duns Scotus, *Philosophical Writings,* ed. A. Wolter, London, 1963, pp. 114–115, for arguments on sense data and the relation of sense to intellect in an analysis of the fallacies of sight; see also p. 105, where Augustine (*De trinitate* XV.xii; MPL, 42, col. 1075) is adduced in favor of the certitude of sense in a text clearly echoing Plato *Timaeus* 47a–c. See also Duns Scotus, *Philosophical Writings,* p. 128. And Duns Scotus in E. de Bruyne, *Etudes,* III, p. 348 n. 2: "Unde fundamentum originale a quo movetur omnis cognitio est esse actuale. . . . Hoc dictum est de cognitione con-

Earlier Hugh of St. Victor had echoed Boethius when he wrote of the origin of the arts, associating "all the songs of the poets, tragedies, comedies, satires" with the "confused" sensation of the earlier writer (whose words he in fact quoted at length), placing the "useful" mechanical arts in the realm of what can be stated in words.[9] When Hugh chose his examples of "confusion," he chose various kinds of "literature," all made up of words. What did he mean by classifying it with the "confused" and the preverbal? In order to understand this, we must briefly consider the status of poetry and poetic language. In his *Catalogue of the Sciences,* al-Farabi wrote that there are five kinds of syllogism, which he called demonstration, dialectic, sophistic, rhetoric, and poetic.[10] These "syllogisms" obviously are ranked in an order of descending certainty, with the poetic, coupled with the *imaginativa,* at the bottom. Poetic discourse is a kind of language that, rather than trying to convince, tries to alter behavior by appealing at a prerational level. Poetry moves our emotions by making things seem better or worse, beautiful or ugly, lofty or base, and is capable of changing our minds on that basis alone. It is a kind of discourse appropriate to use upon people lacking in reflection, for whom imagination takes the place of reason, or it can be used to incite to hasty action before there is time to reflect.

Such an argument is only understandable if it is remembered that, as phantasms, what we sense and what we imagine are the same. Thus, one who crafts what are in effect sensate images can with his colors and images make us both react to what he says as if it were real and manipulate our emotional response to it by "painting" it in one way or another.

The confused and the common

In his commentary on the *Republic,* Proclus set Plato's difference between phantastic and eikastic imitation in terms of a social distinction.[11] Phantastic imitation,

fuse. . . . Confuse dicitur aliquid concipi quando concipitur sicut exprimitur per nomen, distincte vero quando concipitur sicut exprimitur per definitionem."

[9] For this text, see Chapter 11 nn. 55–56, below.

[10] Al-Farabi, *Catalogo de las Ciencias. Edición y Traducción castellana,* ed. A. Gonzalez Palencia, Madrid, 1953, pp. 137–140. This was translated twice in the twelfth century, first by Gerard of Cremona, then by John of Seville. For an examination of al-Farabi on sophistry, rhetoric, and poetry, see *Avicenna's Commentary on the Poetics of Aristotle: A Critical Study with an Annotated Translation of the Text,* ed. Ismail M. Dahiyat, Leiden, 1974, pp. 12–28. See also J. Lomba Fuentes, "Sentido y Alcance del Catalogo de la Ciencias de Al-Fârâbî," in *Arts libéraux et philosophie au Moyen Age,* Montreal–Paris, 1969, pp. 509–516; also Dominicus Gundisallinus, *De scientiis,* ed. P. M. Alonso Alonso, Madrid, 1954, p. 148; and P. O. Kristeller, "The Modern System of the Arts," in *Renaissance Thought II: Papers on Humanism and the Arts,* New York, 1965, pp. 168–169. These ideas had not passed out of currency in the Renaissance. See W. F. Edwards, "Jacopo Zabarella: A Renaissance Aristotelian's View of Rhetoric and Poetry and Their Relation to Philosophy," in *Art Libéraux et philosophie au Moyen Age,* pp. 843–854. Because he claimed to be the first to define poetry as a part of logic, Zabarella has been linked to Baumgarten (G. Tonelli, "Zabarella, inspirateur de Baumgarten," *Revue d'esthétique,* IX, 1956, pp. 182–192), but Edwards (p. 845 n. 10) has pointed out that Zabarella's ideas actually belong to the older tradition of al-Farabi.

[11] I, 190; see Bundy, *Theory of Imagination,* p. 140. Proclus cites Plato *Laws* 667eff.; for the distinction between phantastic and eikastic imitation, *Sophist* 235d–e.

which aims only at pleasure and entertainment, also aims only at the pleasure that comes *to the multitude* from phantasies. It stands in contrast to the eikastic, which looks to correctness ("accurate correspondence in quality and magnitude," as it is called in the *Laws*). His example of phantastic imitation, which is "for the sake of its impression upon the many," is a poet's description of the sun rising over the lake, which we considered earlier in Chapter 2, on the fallacies of sight. Proclus seems to regard both "correctness" and moral uprightness as comparable at least in the sense that they are both to be distinguished as higher from the sheer superficiality of the phantastic. Thus, morally exemplary imitations of "heroes waging war, deliberation and speaking according to life, some discreet, some courageous, some fond of honor," are ranked with the eikastic. The phantastic (or vulgar) is thus common (or vulgar) at the same time that it is prerational and preethical.

We have considered previously Aristotle's observation (*Poetics* 1448b4ff.) that imitation is natural to man from childhood, that he is distinguished from other animals by being the most imitative. This Aristotle attributes to our natural delight in learning; for "to be learning something is the greatest of pleasures not only to the philosopher but also to the rest of mankind, however small their capacity for it." We delight in seeing paintings even of ugly things because "one is at the same time learning." When he explained this text, Avicenna wrote that "what is delightful is not that form itself nor what is portrayed, but its being a precise imitation of something else. For this reason, learning is pleasant *not to philosophers alone but to common people* due to the imitation that is in it, and because learning consists of a certain representation of a thing in the seat of the soul" (my emphasis).[12] Here Avicenna seems to associate learning – or recognition – with an image in the *phantasia,* and he seems driven to conclude that because everyone can recognize an image that is like the images "painted" in the "seat of the soul" of everyone, even common people may take delight in imitation. Avicenna thus linked imitation of appearance with universal apprehension, and although his arguments are not so negative and Platonizing as those of Proclus, they are the same in identifying *phantasia* with common sensation.

In Averroes's Short Commentary on the *Poetics,* these ideas are stated in a form that clearly recalls al-Farabi.

Poetical speeches are rhythmically balanced speeches. With them, one strives for an imaginary representation or exemplification of something in speech so as to move the soul to flee from the thing, or to long for it, or simply to wonder because of the delightfulness which issues from the imaginary representation. They are set down in a rhythmically balanced way, because they thereby become more complete in imaginary representativeness. Now just as the sense-perceptible matters which many of the arts – like the art of decoration

[12] *Avicenna's Commentary on the Poetics of Aristotle,* p. 78. See also *Al-Farabi's commentary and short treatise on Aristotle's De interpretatione,* ed. F. W. Zimmerman, London, 1981, pp. 12–13. "The sense-objects which those thoughts [of various languages] are thoughts of are also common to all. For whatever individual thing an Indian may have a sensation of – if the same thing is observed by an Arab, he will have the same perception of it as the Indian."

and others – cause to be imagined are not really sense-perceptible matters, likewise speeches which cause something to be imagined are not speeches which make its essence understood.[13]

That is, just as painting may make us seem to see things that do not really exist (centaurs, for example), so "poetic speech" does not make essence understood. It appeals entirely to imagination, and it is rhymed because rhyming makes it literally more vivid. In appealing to imagination, it seems also to appeal to prerational "estimation" and to the delight that we take in imitation as such.

These arguments were by no means forgotten in the Renaissance. We have in fact already encountered them in Francesco Bocchi's account of expression and in Gabriele Paleotti's theory of the universality of painting. We shall encounter them again in Federico Zuccaro. But they also appear explicitly within the tradition we have been considering. In his *Il Figino,* Gregorio Comanini wrote that not only to philosophers, but to all mortals as well, "learning is a most joyous thing." He cites Averroes in arguing that "whoever looks enjoys images, because from their contemplation it happens that he learns and knows at once [*prima*] the things seen and has a much more rapid, ready and easy intelligence of them . . . he [Averroes] also says that the soul receives more perfectly as it finds itself glad [*allegra*] . . . images, being imitations, gladden [*rallegrano*], because they are means and instruments that lead to the intelligence of that thing we long to know."[14]

Here the argument, although differing little from its medieval forms, is set in the context of a more neoclassical discussion of the use and abuse of the delight of poetry. Should poetry simply delight or should it delight toward some end? The answer to this question is perfectly consistent with the tradition of regarding poetry (or painting, which, as imitation appealing to imagination, is interchangeable with poetry) as a means by which conviction is achieved and instruction effected. Comanini's arguments lead to Aristotle's *Politics,* and it is argued that the delight we take in imitation should be subordinated to the higher purpose of the state of which painter and viewer are a part. We – and this "we" is now truly collective, because it is based in the community of sensation – should delight in recognizing moral rather than immoral things.

Al-Farabi's fusion of Aristotelian psychology, logic, poetics, and ethics provided the basis for a justification of images – poetic and, by implication, pictorial – that were like phantasms, that engaged prerational faculties toward desirable modifications of behavior, a possibility always implicit in Aristotle's psychology and explicit in his *Politics* and *Poetics.* And al-Farabi's ideas also figured in another important debate, that concerning the appropriateness of figured language in theological discourse. This argument in turn involved the more general question of *integumentum* or, broadly speaking, of allegory.[15] In this argument the pseudo-

[13] *Averroes' Three Short Commentaries on Aristotle's "Topics," "Rhetoric," and "Poetics,"* ed. C. E. Butterworth, Albany, 1977, p. 83.

[14] BT III, pp. 292–293, with valuable commentary in notes.

[15] On *integumentum,* see M.-D. Chenu, *Nature, Man and Society in the Twelfth Century: Essays on New Theological Perspectives in the Latin West,* London, 1957, p. 70, with bibliography.

Dionysius and Aristotle were paired, mutually reinforcing each other in the proposition that all knowledge is through the senses.

Albertus Magnus, commenting on the pseudo-Dionysius and clearly referring to al-Farabi, argued that, whereas "false poetry" intends to make us linger over its fictions so that, incited to horror or delight of that of which we are to be persuaded or dissuaded, we are led by those fictions to something proportionate to ourselves. Theological metaphor, on the other hand, is meant not to be considered in itself but rather to be seen through, to something that is not proportional to our nature.[16]

There were those, according to Aquinas, who argued that, since theology was the highest of the sciences, "which is not able to deceive," it would be inappropriate for it to use the *similitudines varias et representationes* of poetry, "which is the lowest of all kinds of knowledge." He replied to this that is was appropriate to use such language because God intended that each nature should be amply fulfilled, and that because we know through the senses, the use of metaphor is no more than an accommodation to our nature. At the same time, he was careful to differentiate the aims of poetry and theology. The poet uses metaphor because representation is naturally delightful to man; but the theologian uses it to another purpose. In gaining religious understanding through metaphor, the mind does not linger over similitudes, as it does in poetry, but is rather elevated through them to higher cognition. The concealment of meaning in figures also encourages the labor of study and protects sacred mysteries from the infidel.[17]

[16] *Super Dionysii Epistulas.* (*Opera omnia*, XXXVII, 2, Westphalia, 1978, p. 529).

[17] *Summa theologiae* I.1.9. U. Eco, *Il Problema estetico in Tommaso d'Aquino*, Milan, 1970, p. 181, commenting on Aquinas's remark that "poetica non capiuntur a ratione humana propter defectum veritatis qui est in eis" (*Summa theologiae* II–II.101.2 ad 2) remarks that on the basis of these words Aquinas could be thought to be referring to *perceptio confusa*, and thus to be a forerunner of modern aesthetics, a possibility he rejects. It should be evident, however, that Aquinas *could* have referred to poetry as confused, and that his arguments occupy a place in the formative prehistory of aesthetics. E. R. Curtius, *European Literature and the Latin Middle Ages*, tr. W. Trask, Princeton, N. J., 1953, pp. 223–224, is to my mind not quite correct in saying that Scholasticism "produced no poetics and no theory of art." Although it is clear that Aquinas believed that poetry was the "lowest kind of knowledge," it is still a kind of knowledge and serves an important function in discourse. No theologian could have argued that Scripture was poetry, because poetry was fiction. But the idea that the truths of theology could take figured form, which both Aquinas and Albertus Magnus admitted, was a great vindication of poetry. See also Aquinas's commentary on the *Posterior Analytics*, cap. I, lect. 1, 6 (*Opera omnia*, I, Rome, 1882, pp. 139–140; logic, the "art of arts," is divided into the *indicativa*, in which *iudicium est cum certitudine scientiae*, and the *inventiva*, in which judgment is "not always certain." Arts in these categories are ranked in a scale of decreasingly perfect syllogisms. Lowest is *poetica*, in which "by estimation alone" we are inclined to one side or another of a contradiction, as a person may be made to hate some food by making it resemble something hateful. This is what poetry does, "for the poet is to lead us to something virtuous through some appropriate representation." This belongs to rational philosophy because it leads us from one thing to another, that is, it is discourse. Discourse, Aquinas stated, is proper to reason; it is movement from one thing to another "by that which is known coming to knowledge of the unknown." (On this formulation, see J. R. Weinberg, *A Short History of Medieval Philosophy*, Princeton, N.J., 1967, p. 201 n. 40.) See also *Summa theologiae* II–II.94.4, where Aquinas cites the *Poetics* in arguing that because of the delight we naturally take in imitation (*repraesentatio*), early men (*homines rudes a principio*) were impelled to the worship of the gods by "images of men expressively made by the diligence of craftsmen." Federico Zuccaro, in an argument showing that the "speculative reasonable

Because according to the presuppositions of the arguments we are considering, sensation, imagination, and figured language have much the same value, it follows that a justification for figured language might also be an apology for idolatry, that is, that the same arguments could be used for visual images as for poetry. Albertus Magnus drew this implication himself,[18] and repeated the same arguments about the nature of poetry, concluding that much as one does not linger over the surfaces of poetic figures in theology, so one does not linger over idolatrous fictions, which appeal to us in a way that "precedes the judgment of reason." Although such arguments circumscribed idolatry, it should be evident that they also justified a whole range of "phantastic" art, allegorical poetry and naturalistic painting alike, as long as these phantasms were animated by higher meaning or purpose. It might, in fact, be said that the acceptance of Aristotelian psychology made such art necessary. And as this art developed, it was inevitably an art of the "confused," of the prerational, and, as we would say, of the aesthetic.

Aristotle wrote that when the arts were first invented, "he who invented any art whatever that went beyond the common perception of man was naturally admired by men, not only because he was thought wise and superior to the rest" (*Metaphysics* 981b13ff.). When this was translated into Latin, the phrase "beyond the common perceptions of man" was rendered as *ultra communem in hominibus sensum.* Although this may have been a coincidence, and there may have been no reference intended at all to the *sensus communis,* Albertus Magnus felt it necessary to explain the use of the term. He said that Aristotle did not so much mean to refer to that "external apprehensive of sensible species" that acts in the presence of external objects (a definition of the common sense near that of Avicenna) but rather to the sensible cognition of man as a whole, which is more powerful than

sciences" are daughters of *disegno* (*Scritti d'arte di Federico Zuccaro,* ed. D. Heikamp, Florence, 1961, pp. 185–191), traces similar steps. The entity "fabricated in our mind by the intellect, which exists only in the intellect," is achieved by three logical operations. First, simple apprehension, as when the intellect considers genus, differences or species alone; second, composition or division, when the intellect puts things together or separates them, and forms positive or negative propositions; and third is discourse, proceeding from known to unknown. This last is governed first by the ten categories, then by the rules of propositions; the third part of discourse is called "syllogistic" or "judicial" or "judicative" and leads without error from premises to conclusions. As a formative activity of the soul, logic is *disegno,* and the parts of logic stand to it, Zuccaro says, as daughters. These daughters have a sister, also born from the union of *disegno* and *ragione.* This is *poesia,* which thus takes the place of Aquinas's "inventive" logic. Logic lets us know truth and falsity in all things by its three operations. "But poetry with gracious fictions expresses both truth and falsity with sensate things, and so the more easily moves our soul to follow the truth, and flee falsity." This does not differ from his definition of painting, as we shall see in our last chapter. Savonarola wrote that man is inclined "by natural light of intellect" to reasoning, and is therefore called rational; we see *in rudibus hominis* that they may be reasoned with *ex notioribus* (that is, by appeal to confused knowledge) and that they respond to argument but never use logic. Consistently with such a view, he argues that logic is nobler than rhetoric or poetry, the latter of which convinces by *exempla,* which generate "estimation of things and suspicion." E. Garin, "Ricerche sugli scritti filosofici di Girolamo Savonarola. Opere inedite e smarrite," in *La cultura filosofica del rinascimento italiano,* Florence, 1961, pp. 210–212.

[18] Albertus Magnus, *Super Dionysii Epistulas,* 7 (*Opera omnia,* XXXVII, 2, Westphalia, 1978, p. 504).

that of other animals, to "that which is the universal acceptive of the mixed and confused in singulars."[19] By common sense, in short, he understood something like the *vis cogitativa,* which, as we are about to see, was a summarizing faculty of uniquely human sense. Albertus proceeds to Aristotle's definition of art as "factive habit with true reason," and did not associate the *cogitativa* with human art, as some authors did. But for our present purposes it is important that he associated the singular with both the confused and the common.

Such an association was not unusual, and might in fact be regarded as something of a commonplace. One author, explaining Averroes's argument that memory is the most spiritual of the internal senses, wrote that the fantasy apprehends particulars "confusedly"; from these particulars the *estimativa* or *cogitativa* "distinctly" draw out the species of the particular, yielding what is called the "essence of the particular."[20] Averroes himself called the internal senses – the common sense, *imaginativa, cogitativa,* and *memorativa* – by the name *virtutes distinctivas,* by which he meant that they made successive distinctions about particulars, and distinguished them from reason by saying that they concerned particulars, not universals.[21] We shall consider Averroes's *vis cogitativa* in Chapter 10. Pomponazzi argued, like Boethius, that the phantasm is the first object of the intellect, and also argued that to know individuals *in communi* was to know them *in confuso.*[22]

Descartes

In the *Principles of Philosophy,* Descartes gives a strikingly physiological definition of internal sense, which is now very literally identified with the *passiones corporis.*[23] And here "confusion" begins to assume its modern significance. Sensation, rather than stamping imagination with a clear image or similitude, gives rise to impulses, which are apparently inchoate and in need of interpretation, much as we make a distinction between things apprehended "emotionally" and things apprehended "rationally." The first internal sense is the "natural appetite," composed of those nerves around the throat, esophagus, and stomach "that serve the satisfaction of our natural wants." The other internal sense embraces all the emotions of the mind, "affections of this second internal sense are "confused thoughts which the mind does not have from itself alone, but because it is intimately united to the body, receiving its impressions therefrom." Again, he writes that the "motions which are in the body alone" are sufficient to give rise to all kinds of thoughts,

[19] Albertus Magnus, *Metaphysica,* lib. I. tr. I, cap. 11 (*Opera omnia,* XVI, Westphalia, 1960, p. 16).

[20] See *Aristotelis opera cum Averrois commentariis,* Venice, 1562–74 (facs. Frankfurt am Main, 1962, supp. III, p. 395).

[21] *Commentarium magnum . . . de anima,* pp. 415–416.

[22] A. H. Douglas, *The Philosophy and Psychology of Pietro Pomponazzi,* pp. 224–225; also J. H. Randall, "The Development of Scientific Method in the School of Padua," in *Renaissance Essays from the Journal of the History of Ideas,* p. 230 n. 10, 244–245.

[23] *Principles of Philosophy,* IV, CXC (see *The Philosophical Works of Descartes,* ed. and tr. E. S. Haldane and G. Ross, rev. ed., Cambridge, 1931, I, pp. 290–91).

especially "those confused thoughts called feelings or sensations."[24] To illustrate this he uses the example of words, which,

> whether uttered by the voice or merely written, excite in our minds all sorts of thoughts and emotions. On the same paper, with the same pen and ink, by moving the point of the pen ever so little over the paper in a certain way, we can trace letters which bring to the minds of our readers thoughts of battles, tempests and furies, and the emotions of indignation and sadness; while if the pen be moved in another way, hardly different, thoughts may be given of quite a different kind, viz., those of quietude, peace, pleasantness, and the quite opposite passions of love and joy.

(In what follows, Descartes seems almost to object to his own argument, saying that we properly perceive the words, which then become the occasion for the exercise of the imagination.)

In the *Passions of the Soul,* the discussion of internal sense is more in line with the treatment to which we are accustomed. Writing of delight and revulsion as kinds of love, Descartes states that objects of both love and hatred may be represented to the soul either by the external senses, by the internal (by which he must mean imagination) and by its own reason, "for we commonly denominate good or evil that which our interior senses [by which he must mean estimation as well as imagination] or our reason make us judge to be agreeable or the contrary to our nature; we term beautiful or ugly that which is so represented to us by our outward senses, principally by that of sight," which he distinguishes from desire, that is, from concupiscence. The corresponding hatreds are hatreds of the evil and the ugly, which last he calls horror and aversion. These passions of delight and aversion are more violent than the other sorts of love or hate, because what comes to the soul by the senses touches it more forcibly than what is represented by its reason. The passions of the soul are most to be guarded against.[25]

Later, Descartes discusses delight, which "is specially instituted by nature to represent the enjoyment of that which gives pleasure as the greatest of all the good things which pertain to man, which causes us to desire this enjoyment very ardently."[26] There are, he says, various kinds of delight; the beauty of flowers makes us look at them, that of fruits makes us eat them, and the greatest delight "proceeds from the perfections which we imagine in a person whom we think may become another self." Such a person is "confusedly represented by nature as the greatest of all imaginable goods." The "violent" passion of sexual love does not simply make the deepest impression in our imagination, as it had in a long tradition descending from Aristotle, rather the impact of the sensation of the beloved is deeply embedded in physical and emotional response. Here again,

[24] Ibid., IV, CXCII (*Philosophical Works,* p. 294). Biagio Pelacani seems already to have come to a similar position, arguing that species were different according to degrees; the philosophers "say that all distinct knowledge presupposes confused knowledge," and the distinct is more intense than the confused. See G. Federici-Vescovini, *Astrologia e scienza,* p. 141 n. 44.

[25] *Passions of the Soul,* art. LXXXV (*Philosophical Works,* p. 369).

[26] Ibid., XC (*Philosophical Works,* p. 371).

"confused" is not so much the clear reflection of the individual "form" of the beloved, awaiting the operations of discursive thought; it is instead a physical response, felt as an emotional response, distant from the distinctness *and* the clarity that rational reflection may give it.

Baumgarten

When Alexander Baumgarten defined his new science of aesthetics, which was to be to sensuous knowledge, or to the lower part of the cognitive faculty, as logic is to intellectual knowledge, he referred to Plotinus, and other classical precedents for his use of the term "aesthetic" have been indicated.[27] But such sources, if they may have provided the terminology, by no means provided the content of this terminology, nor did Baumgarten simply develop his ideas within the bounds marked out by his definition. Rather the substance of his new science was largely made up of the themes and issues we have examined. To begin near at hand, he accepted Leibniz's opposition between "distinct" and "confused" knowledge, which is at base the traditional distinction. He also accepted the idea that "confused knowledge" was "clear."

Baumgarten distinguished between what he called "sensual ideas" and *phantasmata*. Sensual ideas are determined by "affects." Affects are marked degrees of pleasure and pain, and they strike us confusedly as good or bad for us, that is, they elicit emotional response, corresponding to the level of apprehension of estimation.[28] Sensual ideas are deeper than *phantasmata*. They are closely related to paintings, but are not static like paintings, which makes poetry the superior art.[29] Meter also produces sensual ideas, which are thus closely related to the judgment of the ear. By this he must mean that kinds of meter are significant in themselves, relate intimately to both feeling and theme, and are pleasing. When he examined the question of meter in detail, Baumgarten once again turned to familiar texts, to Cicero, whose authority he cites on the matter.[30] At base, meter is also apprehended confusedly, and functions at that level, before it is scanned – much less quantified – and produces pleasure in the ear, much as Cicero had written, followed by Augustine, that the apprehension of rhythm was lodged deep in universal human sense.

Poetic discourse was by definition never distinct, but it was always clear, or,

[27] A. G. Baumgarten, *Reflections on Poetry: Meditationes philosophicae de nonnullis ad poema pertinentibus*, ed. K. Aschenbrenner and W. B. Holther, Berkeley, Calif., 1954, p. 88. He cites *Enneads* IV.8.7. See P. O. Kristeller, "The Modern System of the Arts," *Renaissance Thought II*, New York, 1965, p. 214 n. 244; and Sextus Empiricus, *Against the Logicians* I.141., paraphrases *Timaeus* 27d and adds that Plato "included along with it [reason] the clear evidence of sense." Plato, he wrote, divided things into intelligibles and sensibles (*noeta* and *aistheta*), apprehended respectively by reason (*logos*) and opinion (*doxa*).

[28] Baumgarten, *Reflections*, p. 48.

[29] Ibid., p. 52.

[30] Ibid., p. 73.

to speak more exactly, clarity was a criterion by means of which good poetry could be distinguished from bad. Beginning from the "confused" apprehensions of sense, the philosopher and the poet moved in opposite directions; for the philosopher, the procedure was analytic, or "intrinsic," that is, the given object was made progressively more distinct by more and more precise distinctions; for the poet, the procedure was "extrinsic," consisting of development and expatiation rather than analysis.[31] "Clarity" was in fact achieved by the traditional ornaments of rhetoric and poetry, which if used incorrectly create "obscurity," as writers had insisted since antiquity. The ideal of clarity was thus brought into line with traditional classical stylistic values. And the whole was based on a psychology of the senses with which we are by now thoroughly familiar. Poetic language produces pleasure of the ear.[32] But it can also produce displeasure, which means that there can be good and bad poetry, and good poetry is determined by conformity with sense. "A confused judgment about the perfection of sensations is called a judgment of sense, and is ascribed to the sense organ affected by the sensation."[33] This confused judgment he identifies with taste, and it becomes more determinate (but not distinct – Baumgarten's whole purpose was to define an alternative to "distinctness," or, perhaps more accurately and paradoxically, to make the "confused" distinct as such) by its reflective definition relative to sense itself. Although he writes of poetry, his general definition could be extended to painting as the art of the sense of sight. His "aesthetics" was thus a science of the "perfection of sense," to be achieved by the analysis of what pleased and displeased sense.

If the distinction on which Baumgarten based his new science of aesthetics was so venerable, what was the novelty in what he had done? Once again the very constancy of the theme we have followed permits a fundamental and far-reaching transformation in the intellectual tradition to be traced. The idea of "confusion" contained within it the whole knotty problem of "form." At base, form meant something like "shape," which was sensed. But the term rapidly got freighted with much more, at least with that which allowed similar shapes to be called by the same name. This higher form was intelligible and was identified with essence or soul or end or idea and came to "form" or "inform" the lower. The human body, to take an example, has the configuration it has in order to realize its animating form. In such a scheme, the movement of thought was always assumed to be upward, at once toward the mental and the more real. The "confused" as the merely sensed was also potentially intelligible, and was at the bottom of the ladder of human knowledge. From such a standpoint the "confused"

[31] Ibid., p. 53. Compare John Locke's distinction between judgment, which finds differences, and wit, which traces resemblances. (*An Essay Concerning Human Understanding*, II.11.2 ed. P. H. Nidditch, Oxford, 1975; cited by E. Burke, *Philosophical Enquiry*, ed. cit., p. 17. On clarity, obscurity, confusion, and distinctness, see C. Wolff, *Psychologia empirica*, I.ii.1 (*Gesammelte Werke*, II,5, Hildesheim, 1968, pp. 20–30 and passim.)

[32] Baumgarten, *Reflections*, p. 70.

[33] Ibid., pp. 69–70.

world was literally inarticulate, awaiting translation to a plane of a truer distinctness. If this polarity was dominant through centuries of thought, however, its hegemony was not complete. The realm of the particular had, in fact, been defined in a long tradition as a realm of practical action, and as a realm of operations of the soul on mental images, of experience and invention, those "syllogisms" and "judgments" which, although they had their own consistency and structure, were not rational.[34] As a science of such consistency and structure, aesthetics helped begin the modern quest to find not simply laws of art but the deeper patterns underlying the cogency of human action and imagination. At the same time, however important its break with the past may have been, the language of aesthetics had a long prehistory, and the significance of its appearance lies partly in the triumph of what had long been the particular intellect as the human mind. For Baumgarten, "sensate representations," the basis of poetry as opposed to logic, were representations received "through the lower part of the cognitive faculty" (*per partem facultatis cognoscitivae inferiorem*),[35] that is, in the long tradition we have been tracing, through the faculties of the particular intellect. The activities of these powers of the mind, raised to the status of philosophy, thus began a new historical life.

[34] E. Cassirer, *Freiheit und Form. Studien zur deutschen Geistesgeschichte*, Darmstadt, 1961, pp. 75–77, argues that aesthetics was conceived as the science of the rules of the lower faculties of the soul, and was based on the premise that intuition, representation, memory, and imagination must also have determinate rules. The alternative logical understanding (as Leibniz had defined the matter) is no longer regarded as the perfection of the human spirit, and comes to be identified with divine understanding in contrast to the new sciences, which seek the immanent rules of humanity and thus the realization of humanity. I am grateful to Walter Sokel for bringing this argument to my attention.

[35] Baumgarten, *Reflections*, p. 38.

10

Cogitation

Cicero and Augustine

In classical Latin, *cogitare* meant to consider thoroughly, to turn over in the mind, picture to oneself, intend, design, or plan. The noun *cogitatio* covered a similar range, and could refer to a faculty of thought (*vis cogitationis*) as opposed to sensation. The well-known text at the beginning of Cicero's *Orator,* in which he treats the Platonic *idea,* is an illuminating example of the range of meaning of *cogitatio.*[1] Any image, so his argument runs, must be less beautiful than that of which it is a copy. A work of art is a copy of a *species cogitata,* an imagined form of the artist that directs his art and hand as he makes a similitude of it. This *species cogitata* is not perceived by sense, nor is it simply a universal arising from the power of the mind to make one thing out of many; it also arises from glimpses of the beautiful form grasped by mind and *cogitatio.* The ability to form these *species* is not simply a power of the *cogitatio* of artists, and even in the face of the works of Apelles and Phidias we are able to imagine (*cogitare*) still more beautiful things. Although, in the case of a Phidias, this inner form may be a *species pulchritudinis eximia,* Cicero seems to wish to say that when we see the actual work of Phidias, we see that it is more beautiful than any particular thing of the same kind *and* that it is still less beautiful than what might be imagined. The work of art and the still more beautiful form it gives rise to in the imagination are thus first steps in an ascent that leads to what we "see" with the mind, the Platonic *idea,* which is finally identified with the definition of a thing from which rational discourse may proceed. For all that, it is clear that Cicero, when he speaks of the *species cogitata,* is referring to an inner form, something inwardly visible, which in this case is argued to descend lineally from the Platonic *idea.* The *species cogitata* need not have been given such an absolute basis, although it may have to have been grounded in the idea of the *beautiful.* That is, the visibly transcendent character of the work need not have pointed past the universal of

[1] *Orator* II.9–11; see Panofsky, *Idea* pp. 11–18.

the *idea,* but it must at least indicate participation in the beautiful. That the imaginary forms of artists could be held in classical antiquity to have a special and properly "spiritual" status is suggested by a text from Pliny in which we are told that the late works and unfinished works of painters were greatly admired because they showed the outline and the very *cogitationes* of the artist.[2] This implies that a work newly begun is closer to the higher, imagined form of which it is an image than is a finished work, which is a variation on the same theme stated by Cicero. Again, what is a constant is not so much the importance of the *idea* as the importance of the spiritual power of imagination.

Excogitatio covered a similar range of meaning but also meant to contrive or devise, and *excogitatus* meant "choice" or "select." It might be argued that the simple metaphor underlying these terms, as Augustine suggested, was that of gathering, collecting, and uniting. This simple metaphor was deeply important, however, because in such gathering, which might be called the first activity of mind, mind itself becomes visible. By "gathering" our experience, we form universals and form the idea of the beautiful, and at the level of gathering, which is always by some individual, sensation becomes individual thought, memory, and imagination. It is thus not difficult to see how *cogitatio* became associated so closely with the particular intellect. It is also not hard to see how it became closely identified with invention, because mind, or individual mind, was necessarily itself both selective and formative. Cicero made *excogitatio* a part of his definition of rhetorical invention: "Inventio est excogitatio rerum verarum aut verisimilium," which might be translated as "invention is the imagination and selection of true and probable things."[3]

Augustine made *cogitatio* into something more like a technical psychological term, and it is likely that his definition influenced both the translation of texts into Latin and the understanding of these texts all through the centuries with which we shall be concerned. In a definition repeated by many later authors, Augustine wrote that the scattered contents of memory must be driven together (*cogenda*) and collected (*colligenda*), "which is to say cogitated."[4] This etymology

[2] *Natural History* XXXV.145; Pollitt, *Ancient View*, pp. 393–394. Pollitt relates *cogitatio* to the ancient tradition of *phantasia*. See the account of primitive man in Vitruvius 2.1.2–7, where housing begins with artificial caves and imitations of the nests of birds; finally *consuetudo* became *ars*, and men became *fabri*, and more arts were invented. Better houses resulted from the *maiores cogitationes* that arose from the increased *varietas artium;* from *vagantibus iudiciis* men succeeded to *certas symmetriarum rationes* and with plentiful materials began *ornare voluptatibus elegantiam vitae*. See T. Cole, *Democritus and the Sources of Greek Anthropology*, Cleveland, 1967, pp. 193–195. After remarking that plan, elevation, and projective drawing are born from *cogitatio* and *inventio*, Vitruvius (I.2.2) defines *cogitatio* as "attentive study, industry, and vigilance directed to the pleasurable effect of what is proposed," which he distinguishes from *inventio*, the "explication of obscure questions and the discovery of the principles of new things by vigor of mind."

[3] *De inventione* I.7. M. Kemp, "From 'Mimesis' to 'Fantasia,'" p. 349, cites this text in relating *excogitatio* to invention in the sense of "discovery" and considers Alberti's account of the origin of the proportion of columns (see Chapter 7 n. 31, above) as an example of such a process. According to the arguments presented here, *cogitatio* is a broader term than *inventio*.

[4] *Confessions* XI.18.

is as important as it is simple. Sensation, although it is of the common, is always for someone, and memory is even more intimately so. My sensations are bound together by their being mine, and at the very least the series of them reflects spatiotemporal unity and continuity. My recollection of my sensations is for my purposes, and so when Augustine said that cogitation occurs in the mind and nowhere else, he may be taken to have meant two things. First, he meant that cogitation, like Aristotle's reminiscence, which it resembles in many respects, is characteristic of the human rational soul, so radically characteristic, in fact, that it is not shared by animals, or even by God. Secondly, he meant that cogitation is a principle and condition of our actual individuality.

As we have seen, Augustine defined three kinds of vision, which he called corporeal, spiritual, and intellectual. He illustrated the differences among them with the example of someone opening a New Testament and reading the words "Thou shalt love thy neighbor as thyself." By corporeal vision I see the words written on the page before me; by spiritual vision my neighbor is cogitated (*cogitatur;* by this he means that an image of his neighbor is called up); and by intellectual vision love itself is fully seen (*conspicitur*).[5] Spiritual vision is thus reflective and requires memory and fantasy, and it is linked to the sequence of fantasies, which is *cogitatio.* The truth of intellectual vision is eternal, the truth of the spiritual is transitory, at one essentially important remove from the level of particular sense. Intellectual vision looks upward, so to speak, to the ideas to which it is nearest, and spiritual vision looks downward, and is a kind of reflection upon corporeal sense. But just as the spirit is a mean between body and intellect, spiritual vision is a mean between corporeal and intellectual vision. It is only through cogitation that the mind can be brought under its own gaze.[6]

Cogitatio is thus literally a central faculty of the soul. It demands memory, internal vision, and will. The will can turn the gaze of the spirit to whatever it wishes; just as we may concern ourselves with this and that object, so we may call what images we will to mind, and we determine our behavior and reveal our character in doing so in one way or another. *Cogitatio* is thus closely linked to free will, and to the mortal condition. Cogitation is the endless train of real human thought, of our own inwardness, and as such it may deflect us from our true path. Cogitation may be right or wrong (or serve good or bad will) and we have need of illumination from above. But it is our nature to cloak our thoughts in sense images and "the clouds of corporeal similitudes do not cease to occur to human cogitation."[7] Only in the beatific vision "will our constantly turning cogitations perhaps not be going and returning from one thing to another, but we shall have all our knowledge at one glance."[8]

Augustine's psychology made all judgment spiritual, and judgment, as the

[5] *De genesi ad litteram* XII.11.22.
[6] *De trinitate* XVI.6.8.
[7] Ibid. XIV.21.40.
[8] Ibid. XV.16.26.

activity of the soul in apprehension, thus served to spiritualize all mental processes beginning from sensation. This in turn located all thought in the realm of the free and ultimately responsible human soul. The last link to physical reality was time, and Augustine's famous arguments about the paradoxes of the "now" and his frequent meditations on music – how, if we sense things moment by moment, do we understand a song? – led to the precedence of memory in the apprehension of particulars. We must remember even in order actually to see or hear; imagination serves memory, retaining what we have just sensed, storing away what we have experienced in order to project plans for the future. Augustine's idea of *cogitatio* was thus closely bound up with his trinitarian scheme of the faculties of memory, reason, and will, the dominant scheme before the reintroduction of Aristotelian psychology, and always a force to be reckoned with. Memory, served in various ways by imagination, could be subject to reason (as Aristotle also argued) but was also subject to will. Again our *cogitationes* are ours and we are responsible for them because we are free to think otherwise. Augustine thus corroborated Aristotle's central notion of the importance of imagination to action, and he incorporated the Stoic idea that reason should rule imagination. But the idea of free will gave an absolute moral dimension to imagination that, if it was ever really lost sight of in the centuries with which we are concerned, was always at hand, involved with one of the deepest tenets of the Christian religion.

Although Augustine discussed aesthetic issues with a thoroughness and subtlety that places him in the forefront of premodern writers, he was interested not in aethetics as such but rather in the aesthetic as a mode of apprehension, in its Christian heuretic value. If we are pleased by harmony or symmetry, what may we infer from this pleasure? Sometimes he writes as if the forms of sense were judged directly by reason, as if anamnesis were the direct consequence of reflection upon sensation. Ultimately he wishes to show that our sense of the beautiful is in fact absolutely, transcendentally grounded, and to the degree that this is so, his position is Platonic. But in other respects his position is not far from that of Aristotle as we have discussed it. All of his arguments are based on the principle that judgment is higher than the judged, and he clearly saw a series of judgments between sense and the final judgment of the intellect. In *De vera religione* he contrasts the life of sense with the life of reason.[9] If rational life judges by itself alone, then nothing is more excellent; but in actuality such judgment is mutable, made according to skill, to participation in some art, discipline, or wisdom.[10] We may know that sand and lime bind stones together, and we may know that the doors and windows of a facade must be symmetrical; this, he says, "is sense knowledge, but it is not far from reason and truth." It is by the awareness of our pleasure in sense that we become aware of higher principles; symmetry is rooted in unity, order and harmony in divine order and harmony, so that by the process of what Cicero called transference, now extended to its fullest possible

[9] *De vera religione* xxix.53.
[10] Ibid. xxx.54.

breadth, aesthetic experience is the first intuition of principles of the absoluteness of the principles of mathematics. The judgments of spirit (as such judgments would be called in later writings) are at once rooted in the deepest and simplest contact between the mind and external nature, but they are at the same time relative. Thus we may "take counsel with nature" by considering what pleases sense, but still what may have seemed to please in itself may be less pleasing when compared with something better. In a popular sense art "is nothing but the memory of things we have experienced and which have given us pleasure, with the addition of some skilled bodily activity." This is not far from the beginning of Aristotle's *Metaphysics*. It is rather the *theory* of art that points on to the intelligible, to true equality and similitude, true and primal unity. "This standard [*lex*] of all the arts is absolutely unchangeable, but the human mind, which is given the power to see the standard, can suffer the mutability of error. Clearly, then, the standard which is called truth is higher than our minds."[11]

In *De trinitate,* Augustine wrote of a created trinity of fantasy, memory, and cogitation, and in the next chapter the operation of cogitation is given a definition of which we shall hear many later echoes. *Cogitatio* works with *visiones* of those things that are in memory, "but they are however innumerably and even infinitely multiplied and varied" (*sed tamen innumerabiliter atque infinite multiplicantur atque variantur*).[12]

Such Augustinian definitions of *cogitatio* were repeated by many later authors and were magnified by Hugh of St. Victor and his followers. In a trinitarian classification distinctly recalling Augustine, Hugh wrote that there were three kinds of *rational* vision, which he called *cogitatio, meditatio,* and *contemplatio. Cogitatio* is bound to particular things, either to sensations or memories.[13] Expanding these ideas in his *Benjamin minor,* Richard of St. Victor defined the characteristic movement of *cogitatio* as *evagatio,* in contrast to the *investigatio* of meditation, or the *admiratio* of contemplation. "Cogitatio semper vago motu de uno ad aliud transit." (Cogitation always passes with a wandering movement from one thing to another).[14] Again to bring these ideas to the early Renaissance, Jean Gerson wrote of three *modi cognoscendi* – *intelligentia simplex, ratio,* and *sensualitas* – associated respectively with *contemplatio, meditatio,* and *cogitatio. Cogitatio* is "easy" because it is formed immediately either from actual sensations or from aimlessly occurring phantasms, in contrast to meditation, which is "difficult" and concerned with more difficult things. *Cogitatio* is the improvident gaze (*obtutus*) of the mind, inclined to wandering (*evagatio*), and if the cogitation is of some desirable thing, the emotions will follow in a correspondingly improvident and wandering fashion "without use or fruit," and thus *cogitatio* is associated with *libido* or *cupido* or

[11] Ibid. xxx.56.
[12] Ibid. xi.7.
[13] *In Ecclesiam homiliae* xix; MPL, 175, col. 116.
[14] *Benjamin minor* 3; MPL, 196, col. 76a–c.

concupiscentia.[15] Gerson thus turned the "sensible" into the "sensual" (as did many others) and linked *cogitatio* with lust and desire, as many others also did. Obviously, our thoughts, or the images that forever fill our minds, may be of one thing or another, and because these images both reflect and shape our desires and actions, it is not surprising that writers on morality were so keenly interested in *cogitatio.* It is no doubt for this reason that Saint Antoninus – to take an author close to art historical events in Florence – devoted so much attention to *cogitatio* in his *Summa theologica.*

But if in the writings of theologians and preachers cogitation was hemmed in by other higher faculties, these very discussions defined with ever greater precision the activity of reason in conjunction with sense, or of imagination in conjunction with will. Gerson's definition of *concupiscentia* is little different from Andreas Capellanus on love, "a certain inborn suffering derived from the sight of, and excessive cogitation upon, the beauty of the opposite sex."[16] The difference is, however, that for Andreas Capellanus, *cogitatio* is unambiguously positive; it is possible, after all, simply to cogitate, that is, to exercise the faculty of cogitation, to give oneself over to the sequence of images. The image of the beloved not only fills the lover's thoughts but is the goal of his desire, giving form and direction to both imagination and actions. "Wandering" became a metaphor for the activity of the poet, and of the soul driven by the desire for the beautiful. As Angelo Firenzuola defined *vaghezza,* one of the key words of Renaissance practical art criticism, it "signifies that beauty, that has in itself all those parts, through which whoever sees it, necessarily becomes *vago* [wandering], that is, desirous; and desirous of it, to seek it and enjoy it, he is always on the move at heart, traveling in thought, and with his mind become a vagabond."[17]

So far, "cogitation" has been discussed as a uniquely human activity. It is our nature not just to register the forms of the external world in sensation, but to remember them, to recall and combine them. It is, moreover, inevitable that we continually do so, that our minds are always filled with images. This base of our inner existence is our individuality; for not only do we each see the world as no one else does, but we also each recall, combine, and forget it as no one else does, and Augustine, as we have just seen, linked this temporal individuality, the sequence of our reflective lives, to human freedom and responsibility. As uniquely and radically human, cogitation was also related to reason. It was the lowest form of reason – discursive reason – and the highest form of sense or, in some

[15] See S. E. Ozment, *Homo spiritualis: A Comparative Study of the Anthropology of Johannes Tauler, Jean Gerson and Martin Luther (1509–16) in the Context of their Theological Thought,* Leiden, 1969, p. 67. See also William Durandus *Rationale divinorum officiorum* I.3.2 ("Graeci etiam utuntur imaginibus pingentes illas, ut dicitur, solum ab umbilico supra, et non inferias, ut omnis stultae cogitationis occasio tollatur"), quoted by L. Steinberg, *The Sexuality of Christ in Renaissance Art and in Modern Oblivion,* New York, 1983, p. 27.

[16] Andreas Capellanus *De amore libri tres* I.1.

[17] *MLA,* part I, chap. IX, for this and other related texts.

cases, the mean between reason and sense. "Cogitation," in short, came to embrace the antinomies of both reason and sense and of matter and spirit. And it came to embrace all those structured and reasonlike operations attributed to the pre-rational soul. It embraced all the "judgments of sense," and related them to reason. The activity of what came to be called the *vis cogitativa* was "discourse," and all "right" judgment could be described as discursive whether or not it was according to "right reason," much as the term "syllogizing" meant that judgments were right, not that they were the results of the use of syllogisms. Thus, Leonardo referred to the artist's qualitative judgments as *discorsi* and did not mean by this that these judgments were applications of principles.

The *vis cogitativa*

Cogitation conflated with *dianoia* in the medieval notion of the *vis cogitativa,* the highest of the so-called internal senses. In order to understand how this occurred, we shall return briefly to Plato. Near the end of the sixth book of the *Republic,* Plato defined *dianoia* with the example of the art of geometry, which although it concerns first principles and "real" relations, does so by means of diagrams. *Dianoia* is thus lower than *nous,* which proceeds dialectically from idea to idea. *Dianoia* stands between opinion and reason. Thus, of the activities of the human soul, *noesis* is highest; *dianoia* – a lower reason, or understanding – is next; belief is third; and "picture-thinking" (*eikasia*) is last. Although these faculties may thus be placed on a scale, Plato seems to mean that each activity may be "clear and precise" as its objects are in proportion to truth and reality.

However the history of the notion of internal sense might finally be written, and however complicated this history might be, the internal senses seem to me to have answered a very simple and obvious need. They were "faculties" responsible for all those necessary activities of the soul that were at once higher than sensation, lower than intellect, and uniquely human. They were called "senses" because they had to do with particulars. The list of internal senses usually included common sense in some relation to fantasy, fantasy in some relation to cogitation, estimation, and memory. For the most part these terms have not survived into modern usage, much less into modern psychological usage, But in the discussion of the internal senses is to be found the premodern treatment of "instinct," of imagination, of dreams, of the "unconscious" processes of association and recollection, of ingenuity and even genius, in addition to the discussion of our practical treatment of particulars. The internal senses *were,* in fact, the particular intellect, and far from merely being a group of unobvious hypotheses passed along through the centuries of the Middle Ages and the Renaissance, they developed in a fairly cogent manner, constantly pressing our deepest question of the relation between sense and intellect, finally resulting in the transformation of the idea of intellect itself.[18]

[18] For bibliography on the internal senses, see Chapter 5 n. 37, above.

When the postsensationary faculties treated in the third book of Aristotle's *De anima* were gathered together into the unitary notion of internal sense, they were closely identified with Aristotle's common or central sense, understood most broadly as the *arche* of sensation or *hegemonikon.* We have already discussed Augustine's notions of *sensus interior, sensus communis,* and *spiritus,* and Gregory the Great wrote of the *sensus cerebri* which "presides within,"[19] which is evidently a higher, central sense with a physical organ (the brain), much as the special senses also have physical organs. John the Scot provided a clear and simple model for the development of these ideas that would follow. He identified "interior sense" with *dianoia* (or discursive thought), which he argued stands above external sense and phantasy and below *ratio* (*logos*) and intellect (*nous*). Interior sense thus stands at the summit of the senses, midway between sense and reason, just as the *vis cogitativa* would in later discussions.[20]

In the writings of the Arabic philosophers, or in the writings of the later Greek philosophers from which they started, matters were not so diagrammatically simple. The "internal senses" included imagination (*phantastikon*), cogitation (*dianoetikon*), and memory (*mnemoneutikon*). All of these terms were discussed by Aristotle in *De anima* and *De memoria et reminiscentia;* and Galen's codification of this triad may be supposed to have given it both greater definition and authority (even though Galen does not call them the internal senses, he opposes them to the external senses and identifies them with the *hegemonikon,* thus with *pneuma*).[21] Galen also provided the localization of these faculties in the anterior, middle, and posterior ventricles of the brain, a scheme that, with occasional departures and many variations, would last at least through the Renaissance.

Fantasy, cogitation, and memory thus formed a core to which a certain definition of the common sense and the faculty of estimation were later added. Wolfson has argued that the medieval *vis cogitativa* corresponds to the Greek *dianoetike.*[22] *Dianoia* could be understood as the general faculty of human thought, and in

[19] *Moralium libri, sive Expositio in Libri Beati Job* XI.6; MPL, 75, col. 957B.

[20] *De divisione naturae* II.23; *MPL,* CXXII. See B. Stock, "The Philosophical Anthropology of Johannes Scottus Eriugena," *Studi medievali,* 3 ser., 8, 1967, pp. 1–57, for another discussion of *sensus interior.* Here *aisthesis* (*sensus*) is associated with Eve, *nous* (*animus*) with Adam, *delectatio* with the serpent. Eve was conceived in Eden *in phantasia boni colorata* or *sub figura boni latens.* A more positive tradition with respect to Eve has been traced from Augustine, who in effect made her the particular intellect. See A. Kent Hieatt, "Eve as Reason in a Tradition of Allegorical Interpretation of the Fall," *JWCI,* 43, 1980, pp. 221–226, where, following Augustine's *De trinitate,* Eve is characterized as *scientia,* a kind of reason lower than the *sapientia* of Adam, but distinctly human and higher than *sensus,* represented by the serpent and shared with animals. In the tradition outlined by Hieatt, this lower, female reason is associated with *prudentia,* with magic, astrology, alchemy, and physics, with *visibilia* and various investigations concerning them. In the late Renaissance its activity is called "cogitation"; and G. B. Ladner, *Ad Imaginem Dei: The Image of Man in Medieval Art,* Latrobe, Pa. (c. 1965), nn. 59–60. According to Ladner, *dianoia* as *sensus interior* (which *sentit extra corpus*) may also be *aisthesis.*

[21] *De symptomatum differentiis,* c. 3; see Klubertanz, *Discursive Power,* p. 45; and Harvey, *Inward Wits,* p. 35.

[22] Wolfson, "Internal Senses," in *Studies in the History and Philosophy of Religion,* I, p. 252.

some cases *dianoia* was defined very broadly. John of Damascus, following Aristotle's statement that all thought is practical, productive, or theoretical (*Metaphysics* 1025b25), included everything from metaphysics to art and virtue within its scope.[23] "To *dianoetikon* belong judgments (*kriseis*), assents, impetuses toward acting and aversions toward, and avoidances of, action; and especially considerations with regard to intellectual notions; and virtues, and sciences, principles of arts, deliberation, and choice."[24] Most definitions of this faculty were both less capacious and less specific.

Wolfson also argues that the activities ascribed to the *cogitativa* were assembled from a number of Aristotelian texts, apparently wishing to discount the influence of post-Aristotelian ideas, even those that were developments of Aristotle's own. Aristotle described the cogitative soul (*dianoetike psyche*), which "images serve as if they were contents of perception" as asserting or denying them "to be good or bad, so that they are either pursued or avoided" (*De anima* 431a14–17). He also described *dianoia* as judging relative truth and falsehood by combination and separation (*Metaphysics* 1027b25–30), and Wolfson argues that the use of the term "judgment" "reflects Aristotle's use of *krinein* in connection with the cognition of truth and falsehood" (*De anima* 427b–428a). Wolfson also maintained that the fairly typical definition of *cogitatio* in Isaac Israeli's *Liber de Elementis* as *perscrutari et discernere* is based on *krisis;* to these powers of discrimination a corresponding power of composition (*componere*) is also added. Isaac Israeli also called this faculty the *sensus intellectualis,* following Aristotle (*Nicomachean Ethics* 1143b5), which he defined as *interpretatio et discretio, perscrutatio, solutio et ligatio et cognitio rerum veritate.* Here powers of judgment, analysis, and composition are included together with an adequate capacity for a knowledge of the truth of things, so that *cogitatio* is close to the *virtus distinctiva,* a synonym for the *cogitativa.*[25]

Estimation

Before proceeding, we must also briefly examine the notion of the *estimativa,* which was often related to, or even confused or identified with, the *cogitativa.* "Estimation" was the apprehension of the inwardness of a thing together with

[23] *De fide orthodoxa* II.19 (Wolfson, "Internal Senses," p. 261). See also Nemesius (*De natura hominis* chap. XII, ed. cit, pp. 88, 97), who wrote that the *phantasticum* transmits what appears to the *excogitativum vel discretivum* (the translation of *dianotike*), which transmits it to memory. The *excogitativa* (XI) is the organ of thought governing the critical activity of the rational soul from the choices determining simple actions to the apprehension of intelligibles, virtues, disciplines, and arts, thus again encompassing the speculative, practical, and productive intellects. It also figures in the divination of dreams. In the tenth century, Haly Abbas seems to have telescoped a similar definition, writing that *cogitatio* treats things imagined by the *phantasia,* actions, that is, arts, science, and other things, and their rule and disposition. Animals are good at certain things, but lack discretion (Harvey, *Inward Wits*, p. 17).

[24] Wolfson, "Internal Senses," p. 261.

[25] Ibid., p. 264 n. 74.

its external appearance. We have already mentioned the standard example, according to which it is not the sight of the wolf that causes the lamb to flee, but rather the hostility of the wolf apprehended at the same time that it is seen. *Estimatio* thus explains "instinctive" reactions. In terms of Aristotelian psychology, it means that some forms are "already" apprehended as having to be avoided before any experience of them. The typical treatments of *estimatio* involved the question of animal intelligence and consequently raised the question of the differences between human and animal intelligence. Aristotle said that animals possess a faculty analogous to *dianoia* in man, by virtue of which they also possess a kind of sagacity, art, widsom, and prudence (*Historia animalium* 588a23–31, *De partibus animalium* 648a5–8, 650b24). They also possess foresight (*Nichomachean Ethics* 1141a28). But he also stated that swallows and spiders work at their nests and webs without art, inquiry, deliberating, or intelligence, working instead according to nature (*Physics* 199a20–30). The difference between animal and human art was explained by saying that animals possess a kind of deficient *dianoia*, locked on single forms.[26] It may also be suggested that estimation had a Stoic ancestry. In Cicero's *De natura deorum* it is stated, it will be recalled, that the eyes judge not only the arts, but also "virtues and vices, the angry and the friendly, the joyful and the sad, the brave man and the coward, the bold and the craven."[27] Animal estimation might be similarly explained as a deficient form of this sensate judgment, able to make judgments of the same kind but only of a limited number

[26] Wolfson (Ibid., pp. 270–276) has argued that the definition of *estimatio* brought about an important change in the *dianoetikon;* because the definition of this animal faculty required the distinction from human rational fantasy (*phantasia logistike*) and deliberate fantasy (*phantasia bouletike*), and also required the distinction from *dianoia*. *dianoia* came to be associated with *phantasia* by authors writing after the introduction of estimation into the system of the internal senses. The *phantasia* with estimation became the fixed imagination of animals (which permits their constructive activity) and also a retentive memory to be distinguished from the cogitative phantasy, which is associated with reason (and with reminiscence). This in turn led to a fusion of thought without images, which compounds and divides ideas, with the activity of productive imagination, much as Aristotle writes (*De anima* 434a9–10), that "we have the power of constructing a single image out of a number of images." However this fusion occurred (and the question of thought with and without images was such a central one that it is hard to imagine that it was done simply as the completion of a conceptual scheme, without an awareness of its systematic implications), it is fundamentally important for our purposes and helps explain why we find *phantasia* among the elements of the *vis cogitativa*. H. W. Janson (*Apes and Ape Lore in the Middle Ages and the Renaissance*, pp. 86–88) traces a tradition following Isidore of Seville's rejected derivation of the word *simia* from *similitudo hominis*. The ape is granted a kind of *ratio*, and Albertus Magnus, who compared man, pygmy, and ape in descending order, treated the pygmy and ape as intermediaries between man and beast in terms of the psychology we are examining. The ape and pygmy have hands, but only man uses them as "tools of the intellect," for *artis opera*. Pygmies cannot form universals or distinguish vice and virtue, but they learn from past experience, speak, and possess a kind of imitation of reason, achieving the imitation of art but never true art. The ape has superior *estimatio* and is capable of affection for others than its own kind, but also has the least *disciplinibilitas*. He responds directly to visual stimuli and imitates what he sees, and in this respect is superior to other animals, although he imitates without discrimination. It is from this passive ability to duplicate what is seen that art – and even artists – came to be called the *simia naturae*. The ape would seem to be able to duplicate the image in the *sensus communis* or *imaginatio*.

[27] *De natura deorum*, 2.58.

of things. In either case, *estimatio* was a kind of judgment higher than special or common sensation, but integral with them.

Whatever its history, estimation was firmly lodged among the internal senses, and the qualities grasped by estimation were called "intentions," a term Avicenna used for what could only be apprehended by internal sense.[28] Estimation thus became something like the spiritual apprehension of singulars and the term was variously employed. It became part of the basic language of medieval and Renaissance psychology and philosophy, with usages ranging over the broad and imprecisely defined terrain of the activity of the internal senses. Although estimation was generally used in opposition to human cogitation, this was not always so, and the term could be used (as it still is) as a general synonym for judgment. Avicenna, in his extremely widely read *Canon,* stated that estimation exists in man, and is often used in judgments not directly under the sway of reason.[29]

Estimatio might be defined as the activity of the first faculty by means of which the spiritual or inward could be intuited in particular things. Just as the sheep does not *infer* the ferocity of the wolf from the wolf's appearance and movements, but rather simply knows it, so we do not simply infer the inward in the outer, the spiritual in the physical, but rather apprehend one in the other. We may consider the clear and early formulation of Dominicus Gundisallinus, whose *De divisione philosophiae,* written around 1140, must have been the ultimate source for a great many later formulations.[30] Here *estimatio* is unambiguously treated as a faculty of the rational soul understood as the human soul, not simply as the soul in unique possession of reason. Gundisallinus presents his definition in the course of a discussion of mathematics, and, more specifically, of abstraction. Abstraction is defined as "the apprehension of the form of any kind of a thing whatsoever." Sense apprehends form one way, "imagination" another, estimation in a third, and intellect in a fourth way. A form is abstracted "imperfectly" when accidents of matter are also apprehended, as happens when we see. When we imagine, we abstract more perfectly because, even though we may imagine forms similar to those we see, these forms may exist in the imagination alone, without matter. *Estimatio* according to Gundisallinus "may be said to transcend the order of abstraction" because it apprehends intentions, which are not material, even if they exist in matter. Figure, color, position, and matter are corporeal, but good and evil, licit and illicit, honest and dishonest, are immaterial things. For Gundisallinus, intellect abstracts perfectly, removing form from all accident and relation, and this is the proper level of pure mathematics. The important thing for our purposes, however, is the exception, indeed the breach, in this scale of

[28] *De anima* I.V. Aristotle wrote (*Politics* 1253a) that man alone has perception of good and bad, right and wrong, and other moral qualities.

[29] *Canon,* Lib. 1, fen. 1, doc. vi, cap. v.

[30] Dominicus Gundisallinus, *De divisione philosophiae,* ed. L. Baur, in *Beiträge zur Geschichte der Philosophie des Mittelalters, Texte und Untersuchungen,* IV, 2–3, 1903; here from E. Grant, ed., *A Source Book in Medieval Science,* Cambridge, Mass., 1974, p. 65.

abstraction that has been made for *estimatio.* It is through estimation that we have access to individual spirit, character, and quality. What the higher faculties might make of the fruits of this access is, of course, another matter.

The *estimativa* was defined by many authors as apprehending *species insensatae* or *impressae,* and was distinguished from the common sense and fantasy, which reflect and conserve the species of exterior sense. Some writers emphatically separated estimation, or human estimation, from instinctive animal judgments. In his *Summa de anima,* Jean de la Rochelle called estimation a "transcendent power" because "its apprehension is not only of sensible and material forms, but also of the immaterial; for goodness and badness, suitability and unsuitability, useful and harmful are not in themselves material forms . . . and do not fall under exterior sense." Such a definition of human estimation as a faculty for the more "spiritual" apprehension of particulars was closely related to cogitation.[31]

Cogitation could also be associated with Aristotle's power of the mind to make one thing out of many and with experience. Near the end of the *Posterior analytics* (99b–100a), Aristotle argued that all animals share the innate discriminative capacity of sense-perception. In some animals, sensations persist, and such animals are said to have memory. In man, repeated memories of the same thing come to constitute experience and this one made up of many is the universal, and from the "universal now stabilized in its entirety within the soul . . . originate the skill of the craftsman and the knowledge of the man of science, skill in the sphere of coming to be and science in the sphere of being." In the opening paragraphs of the *Metaphysics* (981a4ff.), Aristotle argued similarly that "art arises when from many notions gained by experience one universal judgment, about a class of objects is produced." In this second account he gives the example of medicine. To have judged that the same thing cured various ill persons is a matter of experience, but to have judged that the same thing cured persons of a certain definite constitution is a matter of art. This is because the latter inference involves a general principle.

When he commented upon the *Posterior analytics,* Robert Grosseteste adapted this account of the origin of art from experience to the scheme of the inner senses.[32] Sense is a "receptive potency," in which particular sense is "apprehensive" and the common sense is "judicative." Things received by sense are retained by the imagination ("commonly" called memory); memory properly speaking retains "estimated intentions." Both brutes and men collect (*colligere*) one memory from many sensations, but in man this "collecting," associated with reason, makes

[31] For Jean de la Rochelle, see Klubertanz, *Discursive Power,* p. 270. See also Albertus Magnus, *Libri tres de anima,* lib. 2, tr. 4, c. 7 (*Opera omnia,* Paris, 1890, V, p. 303). On estimation, see J. Peghaire, "A Forgotten Sense, the Cogitative According to St. Thomas Aquinas," *Modern Schoolman,* 20, 1942–3, pp. 123–140 and pp. 210–229, esp. pp. 129–133, citing Algazel, who defined the *estimativa* as "virtus apprehendens de sensato quod non est sensatum." Also on estimation and its association with opinion, P. Michaud-Quantin, *Etudes sur le vocabulaire philosophique du Moyen Age,* Rome, 1970, pp. 9–24.

[32] *Commentarium in posteriorum analyticorum libros,* p. 403.

experience. From experience the universal is made, which is "beyond particulars, but not separate from particulars," and from these art and science have their origin. Animal estimation is thus comparable to human cogitation, which as the capacity of the rational soul makes experience possible and stands immediately to the discrimination of reason itself.

Robert Klein has linked Vasari's definition of *disegno* to Aristotle's derivation of human art and science from experience.[33] Design, according to Vasari, "proceeds from the intellect, draws from many things a universal judgment." This judgment, which is similar to a form or idea of all the things of nature," provides a standard against which the artist works, and is associated with proportion. It is, however, not a Platonic *idea,* but a *concetto,* a thing conceived by the soul itself; it is "imagined in the mind" and "fabricated in the *idea,*" that is, in the *fantasia. Disegno* on such an argument is an activity of the particular intellect, and because the activities of the particular intellect are activities of the rational soul (if not of reason), then "proportion" may be as much a mean found by experience as the discovery of actual proportions. *Disegno* is thus intimately connected with *maniera* or *aria.* The metaphor of "gathering" at the foundation of the idea of cogitation might also help explain why the theme of the bee gathering honey and the stories of Zeuxis and the maidens of Croton exerted such a strong pull on the Renaissance discussion of art.[34] *Disegno* arises from the power of the human soul to make one thing out of many, and from experience; but at the same time it also arises from the level of differences of individual gifts and from the level at which the human soul is subject to prophetic dreams and vision.

A text by Avicenna, although unknown in the Middle Ages, nicely illustrates the fusion of estimation and cogitation, and at the same time also provides an example of the accommodation of these ideas to others we have considered. Living things, Avicenna says, have the power to judge definitely that an object is so and not otherwise, and by means of this power they may avoid the fearful and seek the desirable. The faculty that allows them to do this cannot be the common sense, because it apprehends more than that which is reported by sense. Sense tells us, for example, that the sun is as small as it appears, and this example suggests that through experience we may surmise the sun to be larger than it appears, even if we cannot ascertain its true measure. Also, the lion (Avicenna seems to make little distinction between animal and human inner sense at this level) sees his quarry at a distance as very small, but correctly apprehends its size and shape and sets out after it. This means that the power of which he speaks correctly judges common sensibles. He also distinguishes this estimating or judging power from the fantasy in that things we imagine may be thus or otherwise (that is, they may be illusory), whereas this faculty presumably yields adequate information about particular things and states of affairs.[35]

[33] For reference, see *MLA*, p. 519.
[34] Ibid., pp. 186–189.
[35] Klubertanz, *Discursive Power*, p. 105.

Cogitation and human imagination

Avicenna's classification of the internal senses shifted and varied from one version to the next. It was Avicenna who added the *sensus communis* to the number of the internal senses, and merged its functions as a unifying and therefore formative faculty with the *phantasia,* which according to him is mirrorlike, and only as retentive as it must be to perform its ancillary functions to sensation. The central faculty, which he sometimes called *cogitativa,* was also identified with what Wolfson calls "compositive human and animal imagination" and estimation. This compositive imagination is higher than *phantasia* (as Avicenna understood the term, as a retentive mirror near sensation) and is able to compound new things.[36] In the *Canon,* Avicenna wrote that *cogitatio* uses the intentions that have been stored in the imagination and then proceeds to combine and analyze them, constructing quite different images, a flying man or an emerald mountain.[37]

Avicenna followed the usual pattern in locating the *cogitativa* in the central ventricle of the brain, where he also placed the *estimativa.*[38] This faculty was called *imaginativa* insofar as it had to do with the human soul.[39] This in turn associated the *cogitativa* with the characteristic activities of the *anima humana,* responsible for the formation of societies, language, the discovery, learning, and teaching of the arts, different from the arts of animals in that human artifacts show variation. Man is able to wonder and laugh and grieve, to formulate moral codes and live by them, suffer shame, fear, and hope, and provide for the future. Fundamental to all this is the ability to form universal intelligible intentions, wholly abstracted from matter, to proceed to the unknown from the known.[40]

Avicenna divided the human soul into two "faces," the *virtus contemplativa,* which looks upward to universals, and the *virtus activa,* which looks downward to the body and to the real world of human activity, deciding what is right and wrong in the conduct of human affairs. Working with the inner senses, the *virtus activa,* which corresponds to Plato's *dianoia,* discovers arts and natural principles and working by itself produces moral behavior. This division, which again recalls Augustine's notion of *spiritus* (Avicenna and Augustine may have drawn on similar sources), also more or less corresponds to Aristotle's distinction between the speculative and practical intellects, and may have contributed to the eventual inclusion

[36] Wolfson, "Internal Senses," pp. 276–281.

[37] See Kemp, " 'Mimesis' to 'Fantasia,' " p. 362; the reference is to *Canon.* I.176–182. E. A. Moody ("William of Auvergne and his Treatise *De anima,*" in *Studies in Medieval Philosophy, Science and Logic*), Berkeley, Calif., 1969, pp. 48–50) attributes the introduction of Avicenna's system of the internal senses to William of Auvergne (c. 1180–1249), who listed five internal faculties: the common sense, imagination, memory, sense–judgment (*vis aestimativa*), and sense–reason (*vis ratiocinativa*). Moody compares the internal senses to the nervous system, or sensory-motor system, "the physiological intermediaries between the action of external things on the organism and its motor reaction." William of Auvergne compared the inner senses to books that cannot read themselves but that require a reader.

[38] *De anima* V.I.

[39] Harvey, *Inward Wits,* pp. 44–45.

[40] Ibid., pp. 47–48.

of art together with virtue and to the treatment of the exercise of both as kinds of prudence. In any case, it has the effect of identifying production with the practical intellect and of tying the arts firmly to the *cogitativa,* a connection we shall presently examine in more detail.

In the remarkable anthropology at the beginning of Book V of his *De anima,* Avicenna, basing his arguments largely on Aristotle's *Politics* (I.2), very nearly identifies cogitation with the characteristic activity of the practical intellect. "Man has a virtue which is proper to universal conceptions, and another which is proper to the *cogitation* of singular things" (my emphasis). The first and highest of these – the speculative intellect – judges concerning the necessary, the possible, and the impossible, and works from self-evident principles; the second judges concerning what should be done and avoided, what is honorable and dishonorable, what is good and bad, that is, it judges concerning the possible and does so by means of the practical syllogism. The principles of its reasoning are probable, taken from authority and tradition. *Cogitatio,* in terms that must have been carefully read by both Averroes and Aquinas, is defined in a manner that suggests Aristotle's definitions of both prudence and art. We cannot cogitate about the necessary and the impossible, nor about the past. Cogitation treats the contingent, the possible, and the particular, what "is to be done."

Roger Bacon called *cogitatio* (which he placed in the central cell of the brain) the mistress of the sensitive powers, "which some call *logistica.*" In brutes it takes the place of reason (that is, it is the *estimativa*), and in man it is immediate to reason. But *cogitatio* is higher in man than in animals; through it (as *estimativa*) the spider makes its web, the bee its hive. Then he adds that through this same power we see wonderful things in dreams, and in cogitation the forms of imagination are multiplied. The cogitative faculty as fantasy is thus not only the combinatory fantasy but is also subject to "inspiration," like Augustine's *spiritus,* to which it is in fact deeply historically related.[41]

For Albertus Magnus (whose opinions on these matters also vary from work to work), *excogitativa* is synonymous with *phantasia,* which again is raised nearly to the level of Augustine's *spiritus.* It is the most noble and comprehensive of the internal senses, to which it is related as a principle of unity, just as the common sense is related to the special senses. It is also a kind of reason, with powers of cognition surpassing those of any lower faculty, for which reason it is in fact called the *excogitativa.* Its function is to know and discern the true nature of particular things, but at the same time it is also linked to fantasy, compounding and dividing both images and intentions, so that we may conceive a man with two heads, a being with a human body, the head of a lion, and the tail of a horse.[42]

Thomas Aquinas transformed the variety associated with the human *cogitatio* since Augustine into a potential infinity owing to its relation with reason, and

[41] *Opus Maius* 2.9, and 2.128.
[42] *Opera omnia,* Paris, 1890, V, pp. 583–584.

with this power of the human spirit endlessly to multiply experience he distinguished human imagination from animal estimation and human from animal art. He drew a distinction between natural and rational virtues. The first are determined by one thing, a simple judgment (*iudicium*), which, together with appetite (that is, the impulse to realize the judgment) causes every swallow to make its nest in the same way, as does every spider its web. "Man, however, is capable of many and diverse operations, and this on account of the nobility of his active principle, that is, his soul, the virtue of which extends to infinity."[43] Again, in the *Summa theologiae,* replying to the argument that man is less perfect than other animals because he lacks protection, Aquinas states that the intellectual soul, as comprehending universals, has a power extending to the infinite, therefore it cannot be limited by nature to certain fixed natural notions [like those of animals] or even to certain fixed means whether of defense or of clothing . . . man has by nature his reason and his hands, which are the organs of organs, since by their means man can make for himself instruments of an infinite variety and for any number of purposes."[44] Here the *estimativa* of brutes is juxtaposed to the ability of the rational animal to make any number of different artifacts in the pursuit of the mechanical arts that concern his shelter and protection. This was one of the divisions into which the mechanical arts fell, according to Hugh of St. Victor, in whose *Didascalicon* the products of human reason are also praised for their infinite variety. But in Aquinas the scale of the issues has changed, ascending to a new level of conceptual purity. More emphatically even than in Augustine, *cogitatio* is coupled with free will and, as we shall see, with an Aristotelian definition of prudence.[45]

Although it is not clear from either of these passages that Aquinas did not mean to attribute such infinite invention to the *vis cogitativa* as the fantasy in conjunction with the reason, it may be surmised that he was read to mean that the inventive power of the mind was based in reason, as indeed it was a power peculiar to the rational soul. The Quattrocento architect Francesco di Giorgio insisted that the soul is not a power of the body but is rather incorporeal and it is from the nature of the soul that the differences arise between the artifacts of animals and man. Whereas the "buildings" of swallows, bees, and spiders are always the same, the inventions of the human intellect are "almost infinite, infinitely various." Referring to the designs of castles (which are for defense, as Aquinas had specified), Francesco writes that "tutte le fortezze che nella mente

[43] *De virtutibus in communi,* q. 1, a. 6 (*Opera omnia,* Parma, 1859, VIII, p. 557).

[44] *Summa theologiae* I. 76.5 ad 4; and I. 91.3 ad 2. See Nemesius *De natura hominis* II, ed. cit. p. 48. "Omnis enim lepus similiter artificiose viget et omnes pithicus similiter astutus est et omnia simia similiter imitatur, quod non est in homine. Infinitae enim viae sunt humanorum actuum; liberale enim quid et liberi arbitrii quod est naturale; unde non unum et idem omnibus hominibus opus est ut unicuique speciei irrationalium animalium." On the hands as the organ of organs, see M. F. Manzanedo, "La inteligencia y las manos según Santo Tomas," *Tommaso d'Aquino nel suo settimo centenario,* Naples, 1978, pp. 400–417, with bibliography. The reference is to Aristotle, *De partibus animalium* 687a5–25.

[45] *Summa theologiae* I. 83.1.

occorrano continuamente, sarebbe un processo in infinito" (all the fortresses that continually occur in the mind would proceed into infinity). As Martin Kemp has observed, the pages of Francesco's own treatise, filled with plans and drawings, look forward to similar pages by Leonardo da Vinci and other later Renaissance artists.[46] They show imagination linked with reason, the channeling of the *evagatio* of the *cogitativa.* But this implied much more; such pages are most intimately autobiographical, the closest possible records of choice of theme and transformation by that artist and no other. They also linked the inventiveness of the artist – and even of the artisan – to that of the poet, to whom Giovanni Bellini surely meant to compare himself when he wrote that he could not be too restricted by his patron's wishes because it was his custom "to wander [*vagare*] at will in his paintings." Boccaccio had written that "exquisite" poetic invention consists of *peregrinas et inauditas inventiones excogitare,* of the imagination of strange and unheard of inventions.[47]

When Francesco Colonna wrote of the fantastic marvels described in his *Hypnerotomachia poliphili* as "inexcogitable" inventions, and of things made with "inexcogitable subtlety of intellect and art," he meant much what we mean by saying that something is "unimaginable," or perhaps "immeasurable" or "incomprehensible." The paradoxical consequences of these remarks, that the products of human imagination are unimaginable, served the purpose of elevating both art and artist, of stating to the point of exaggeration the ancient idea that art induces wonder, and of distinguishing the imaginations of some individuals from those of mankind in general. Colonna's tale is filled with references to the "stupefying" and the "terrible," and his inclinations verge on a taste for the sublime.[48] But the most general use of "cogitation" corresponds fairly closely to our "imagination": at the same time, it retained its ancient connotation of thinking with images, or even, as Plato had written of *dianoia,* of thinking with diagrams. Cogitation was thus wedded to such "demonstrative" sciences as optics by virtue of their similar positions in the scale of human thought, and implied for the same reason the union of *ingegno,* fantasy, physical mathematics, and the mechanical arts. *Disegno* was at once the expression and the great practical amplification of cogitation.

[46] Francesco di Giorgio Martini, *Trattati de architettura civile e militare,* ed. C. Maltese, Milan, 1967, II, pp. 482–483 and 505–506. Kemp, " 'Mimesis' to 'Fantasia,' " pp. 354–355, attributes to Francesco the idea that human inventiveness is "infinite." For Savonarola on human and animal art, man's higher imagination and discourse, see *MLA,* p. 303.

[47] On Giovanni Bellini, see *MLA,* p. 453. For Boccaccio, see *Genealogie deorum gentilium libri,* ed. V. Romano, 2 vols., Bari, 1951, XIV, VII. An excellent discussion of Boccaccio's defense of poetry in the context of late medieval and specifically Scholastic thought about language and poetry is provided by R. Stefanelli, *Boccaccio e la poesia,* Naples, 1978.

[48] For these texts, see Kemp, " 'Mimesis' to 'Fantasia,' " p. 365. The question of the relation of drawing, cogitation, and the *scientiae mediae* (Aristotle's "more physical branches of mathematics, such as optics, harmonics and astronomy" (*Physics* 194a), a list amplified by al-Farabi to include applied mathematics and engineering; see Chapter 11 n. 54, below) deserves full treatment. On the *scientiae mediae,* see J. Gagne, "Du Quadrivium aux Scientiae mediae," *Arts libéraux et philosophie au Moyen Age,* Montreal–Paris, 1969, pp. 975–986.

Internal sense in Renaissance Neoplatonists

As we have seen, from late classical times Neoplatonists (or thinkers who inclined to the basic attitude I am about to describe, of which there were many) did not reject Aristotle's "faculties" of the soul as threatening to blur the distinction between sense and intellect; rather, they incorporated them into schemes of progressively spiritualizing and abstracting powers, the activity of which seemed to corroborate the activity of the soul itself in contrast to the world of passive matter. Just the same pattern was followed by Renaissance Neoplatonists, who however benefitted from the more complete definition of the faculties given by later medieval writers. We may consider some representative examples.

According to Leone Ebreo, there are objects of all the external senses that are "good, useful, temperate and delectable." The grace (or beauty) "that delights and moves the soul to proper love" is not found in the objects of the three "material" senses (taste, odor, and touch), but only in the objects of the two "spiritual" senses, sight and hearing. Good food and drink, pleasant odors and "the temperate and most sweet venereal act" (here the supreme activity of touch, perhaps even the "art" of touch) "with all their goodness, sweetness, suavity, utility, and necessity to the life of man and animal, are not however beautiful."

In what follows, he associates *kinds* of grace and beauty with levels of spirituality, proceeding upward from the "spiritual" external senses to the internal senses. He begins with the two highest of the external senses. We find grace or beauty

> in the objects of sight, as are beautiful forms and shapes and beautiful painting, and the beautiful order of the parts among themselves to the whole, and beautiful and proportionate instruments and beautiful colors and beautiful clear light and the beautiful sun and beautiful moon, beautiful stars and beautiful heavens. Because through its spirituality grace is found in the object of sight, which through the clear and spiritual eyes wishes to enter to delight and move our soul to love this object, which we call beauty.[49]

It may be noted that the participation of things in the beautiful is evident to us as a result of their accommodation to the sense of sight, by their being "temperate and delectable," that is, by the proportion of things to activity, or judgment, which is irreducible. The same is true of music.

There are also, he writes, *virtù conoscitive* that are still more spiritual. These are the internal senses, which he calls "the imagination and fantasy," as if they were one thing. This *virtù* "composes, discerns and thinks the things of the senses"; it knows (*conosce*) many other "gracious and beautiful particular functions and cases, that move the soul to amorous delight." So one may speak of *una bella fantasia* or *un bel pensiero, una bella invenzione.* Such "knowledge" follows the pattern with which we have become familiar. Leone is talking about "particular" beauty and particular reason; this he immediately distinguishes from the beauty of intellective reason, which comprehends universal grace and beauty, which is incorporeal and incorruptible, and which, evident to us in particular and corruptible

[49] Leone Ebreo,*Dialoghi d'amore,* pp. 226–227.

bodies, moves the soul more strongly to delight and love. These are studies, laws, virtues, and human sciences. The highest beauty is abstract and intellectual, and when he reviews his discussion, he lists once again the same *virtù conoscitive,* this time replacing *immaginazione e fantasia* with *cogitazione.* "Our soul is moved by the grace and beauty that enters spiritually through sight, through hearing, by cogitation, by reason and by mind." All these are *vie spirituali ne l'anima nostra.*[50]

We may also consider the remarks of Giordano Bruno, cited by Panofsky as corresponding completely to the views of Neoplatonism. These remarks summarize a long tradition of similar arguments in Neoplatonic love literature. "I meant that it is not the figure or species sensibly or intelligibly represented, which moves by itself; because, while everyone stands admiring the figure manifest to the eyes, still this does not come to love; but from that instant that the mind [*animo*] conceives [*concipe*] in itself that [figure or species] figured [*figurata*], no longer visible, but *cogitable,* no longer divisible, but individual, no longer under the species of a thing, but under the species of the good beautiful, then immediately love is born.[51] When we love, Bruno wishes to say, we are moved neither by what is apparent to sense as such, nor do we love the intelligible, which is not individual. In passing from "visible" to "cogitable" the person seen passes from "divisible" (that is, he or she is no longer identified with matter), to individual. This individuality may have several meanings: first, it is clear from the opposition to matter that he or she has the inviolable unity of the imagined, or the spiritual; but "cogitation" has also apprehended the intention, the inwardness and soul of the person, so that his or her cogitated form is at once whole and doubly spiritual. It is this spiritual *individual* that is loved. But this individuality is double-edged, for he or she does not work the same effect upon everyone; everyone may admire, but only one will love, and this is because the *cogitativa,* or the *spiritus* that cogitates, is itself a principle of individuation, and when the beloved is seen as the good and the beautiful, he or she is seen in the light of one's own *idea della bellezza,* and is ultimately related to the good and the beautiful by participation. Thus, Bruno's characterization of the love of two persons is an amalgam of faculty psychology with ideas very similar to those we have considered previously in Augustine. An important result of this fusion is the identification of the "estimation" of the good with the Platonic good, and with the beautiful.

Averroes

Averroes arranged the internal senses in a progression of ever more spiritual faculties ranging from sense to the *vis cogitativa.* This progression, in addition to making the schemes we have been considering more unified and elegant, was also intended

[50] Ibid., p. 228.

[51] Panofsky, *Idea,* p. 118, 246 n. 20. The reference is to *Eroci furori* I.4.

to make sensation as continuous as possible with intellection, or to make more intelligible the preparation of sensation for intellection. Not only did the *vis cogitativa* embrace all the lower faculties and the characteristics that, according to Aristotle, distinguished human sense from animal sense, but, as the particular intellect, the *vis cogitativa* stood in a concentric, microcosmic relation to the separate intellect with which it was contiguous. In a similar manner, Aquinas, citing the principle of Dionysius the Areopagite that an inferior nature at its highest reaches the lowest of the nature above it, argued that the *cogitativa,* as the highest function of sense, "is also called by the name of *ratio* because of its common boundary with reason."[52] With Averroes the idea of the *vis cogitativa* reaches a new level of systematic development, a level that, although it represents a consolidation of previous discussions, also involves this notion that now seems so obscure in issues much broader and more visible than those of speculative psychology. Averroes, who defined the *cogitativa* more carefully and extensively than anyone before him, also identified it with the individual human soul, and with Aristotle's passive intellect, which was mortal. This magnified the *vis cogitativa,* and moved it from the edge to the center of the debate concerning the nature of the human soul.

Averroes might seem to have been guilty only of reading Aristotle in the most straightforward manner when he pronounced the passive intellect to be mortal. It is only when separated that the active intellect is its true self, Aristotle wrote in one of the most controversial passages of his *De anima* (430a24ff.), "and this, its essential nature, alone is immortal and eternal. But we do not remember because this is impassive, while the intellect which can be affected is perishable, and without this does not think at all." But perhaps because of the esteem in which Aristotle was generally held, it was his Arab commentator ("*the* Commentator," as he was called) who came to be linked with the idea that the individual soul is mortal. It is primarily because of this association that Averroes is shown as a heretic vanquished by Saint Thomas Aquinas in Dominican frescoes of the fourteenth century.[53]

Not to become hopelessly lost in a forest of variations, and to provide some sense of the essential continuity with which we are dealing, we may consider Averroes's *Epitome of the Parva naturalia,* in which he identifies the *vis cogitativa* with "that which rules and judges" in Aristotle's *De somnis* (461b25), which, it will be remembered, was one of the "higher" characterizations of the central or common sense.[54] In both cases, for all the differences of historical circumstances to which terminological differences point, we are dealing with different historical branches of one idea, the idea of a center of individual consciousness. Such con-

[52] *Commentum in quattuor libros Sententiarum Magistri Petri Lombardi,* II,d.24,q.2,a.1 ad 3 (*Opera omnia,* VI, Parma, 1852–73, p. 598). The variant reading *cognitiva* is given with *cogitativa.*

[53] See M. Meiss, *Painting in Florence and Siena After the Black Death,* Princeton, N.J., 1951, pp. 103–104.

[54] Averroes, *Epitome of the Parva naturalia,* pp. 41–42.

tinuity also explains why it is that in many applications, *cogitativa, sensus communis, phantasia, spiritus,* and *imaginativa* could be used interchangeably, why their connotations could join, overlap, and reinforce so readily. For Averroes, the *cogitativa* was the individual soul, and it is this individual that sees individuals. When we see, he wrote, this judging faculty does not simply call what is seen Coriscus, but, prompted by the impression, judges the "genuine person yonder" to be Coriscus.

Averroes attributed to Aristotle the idea that the *virtus cogitativa* is the *virtus distinctiva individualis,* which distinguishes things individually, not universally, and stands in the same relation to all the intentions of the internal senses as the common sense to the special senses. It is thus the summation of the critical powers of the external and internal senses and the passive intellect. It is, however, neither the intellect itself (which is "separated" and immortal), nor is it simply material, an error he attributes to Galen.[55]

Averroes argued that "Aristotle did not mean that the senses comprehend the essence of things, as some have thought, for this is a power of the intellect; he rather meant that sense, together with what it comprehends by its proper sensibles, comprehends." Averroes thus identified Aristotle's *sensibilis per accidens* with the object of the *vis cogitativa;* we distinguish *that man* by inner sense.[56] In making his arguments, Averroes turned to a principle discussed in Chapter 4, and perhaps stated it more forcefully than any author we have treated so far; he argued again and again that human sense is constitutively different from the sense of other animals. In the arguments we are examining, the distinction between the common sense and the *cogitativa* is all but obliterated. The "comprehension of individual intentions" is an act of the *sensus communis* "not insofar as it is the *sensus communis,* but insofar as it is the sense of a certain animal, an intelligent animal." In general, "sense comprehends individual differences; not insofar as they are simple senses, but insofar as they are human senses; and especially substantial differences; for it may be seen that the comprehension of individual intentions of substances, concerning which the intellect considers, is proper to the senses of man."[57] Again, the human senses not only comprehend the intention of this individual man, but they also comprehend the intention of each of the ten predicaments of individuals.[58] That is, the *vis cogitativa* apprehends the full individual in terms of substance, quantity, quality, relation, place, time, position, state, activity, and passivity,[59] which is to say that the *vis cogitativa* apprehends things in specific accidental relations. "And this," he concluded again, "is seen to be proper to human sense;

[55] Averroes, *Commentarium magnum . . . De anima,* III, 6, pp. 415–416. It will remembered that in Avicenna (*De anima* V.7) the *ego* is to inner sensation as the *sensus communis* is to special sensation. This tends to identify *ego* and *vis cogitativa.* See Klubertanz, *Discursive Power,* pp. 117, 136. See also again Albertus Magnus at n. 42 above.

[56] Averroes, *Commentarium magnum,* II, 63; p. 225.

[57] Ibid., II, 65; p. 228.

[58] Ibid., II, 63; p. 225.

[59] See Aristotle *Categories* 1b25ff., and *Topics* 103b23.

whence Aristotle says in *De sensu et sensato* that the senses of other animals are not like the senses of man."

According to Averroes, if animals do not have before them what they immediately sense, their behavior is closely bound in by sensation. Man, by contrast, may consider a series of images and choose among them. We may produce many images to govern our behavior, and it is not simply imagination that does this, but cogitation. Imagination exists in animals, but cogitation is rational. To elect to imagine this and not that is the act of cogitation, not of imagination itself. And judging that this which is imagined is more desirable than this other must owe to the same faculty that "numbers" images. By this he seems to mean that the same faculty that produces the sequence – or number – of images to be chosen among also chooses among them, so that *cogitatio* together with *existimatio* produces *consensus*.[60] *Cogitatio* is thus closely bound to fantasy – "the *virtus cogitativa* places things absent from sense as if sensed" – but *cogitatio* is at the same time the principle that governs fantasy and is a temporal principle, looking from the past to the future. It may project "some individual not sensed before, similar but not the same."[61] The *cogitativa* – the activity of which falls within the realm of experience, and is bound up with reminiscence and prudence, makes series of images, is able to discriminate between images as more or less desirable as goals of action, and is therefore immediate to choice based upon their relative desirability. Only rational animals can do this, and this power is the threshold to the higher activities of which the human soul is capable.

As mentioned previously, the *vis cogitativa* occupied a crucial position in the process of abstraction, and Averroes argued that the intention of an individual has the intentions of special and common sense "stripped away" in favor of "predicaments." These intentions, which are thus different from phantasms, are placed in the *memorativa*. His argument is thus consistent with Aristotle's statement that we are able to "construct" a single image out of a number of images," a power that animals do not have.[62]

Averroes calls the *virtus cogitativa* a "particular material virtue" that does not compose singular intelligibles but rather is the power of distinguishing the singulars of these intelligibles. (He sometimes calls the *cogitativa* the *distinctiva*, an identification of sensate judgment at the highest level with Aristotle's *krinein* that must have magnified the significance of Alhazen's *virtus distinctiva*.) For Averroes the *cogitativa* is thus a faculty of judgment, and its judgments are about particulars. The *cogitativa* is at once a sensate power and a kind of reason, and its action consists of putting the intention of a form in imagination together with a corresponding individual in the memory, or to separate them in formation.

[60] Averroes, *Commentarium magnum*, III, 57; p. 529.
[61] Ibid., III, 33; p. 475.
[62] *De anima* 434a8. Aristotle is discussing the deliberative imagination, which involves the formation of standards for choice.

That is to say, the *cogitativa* also compared individuals, and thus performed the operations of intellect *about* individuals, and was in effect discursive.

From Aristotle onward, the fantasy in general had the purpose of dealing with the absent, what is not present to sense, because it no longer exists, is at too great a distance, or has never existed at all. Averroes's *cogitativa* expands this dimension of fantasy, linking it with reminiscence and deliberation, the one distinctive of human memory, the other of human imagination. Whereas the animal soul was tied to sensation, the human soul existed between past and future, and the fantasy made it possible to remember the past and project the future in images that had the value of the actually present. Our consciousness is a stream of images, many from without, many from within. For our own purposes we control and choose among these images, and this choice involves will; at this point we pass beyond the merely psychological aspects of cogitation to its moral aspects, which were of the keenest interest to Thomas Aquinas.

Thomas Aquinas

Averroes's doctrine of the human soul, in which the *vis cogitativa* figured centrally as the particular intellect, was widely condemned, and Aquinas argued that man as Averroes presented him was little more than a brute. It will be useful to examine Aquinas's presentation of Averroes's views because their condemnation notwithstanding, the views of "the Commentator" continued to be held and to develop, perhaps not least of all because they pressed Aquinas himself to new formulations concerning the nature of the human soul.

Aquinas presented Averroes as holding that man differs from the animals in possessing a passive intellect, which, as the discursive power or *cogitativa,* distinguishes and compares individual intentions, just as the separate and immaterial intellect compares universal intentions. This passive intellect serves an abstractive function, "preparing phantasms" for the agent intellect, which makes them intelligible, and because of this it is called an intellect or reason.

It must be stressed that the *cogitativa* was not simply the means by which particulars were apprehended and judged, but that it was also a principle of difference among individual persons, and Aquinas wrote that "according to the disposition of this power one man differs from another in talent and in other things belonging to the understanding." It is also through the *cogitativa* that the habits of the sciences are acquired, which exist in the passive intellect "as in their subject."[63] This suggests that the *cogitativa* is a predisposition to the formation

[63] *Summa contra Gentiles* II.60. John Duns Scotus (*Philosophical Writings,* pp. 137–138) argues that all philosophers agree that "rational" defines man, and that "the intellective soul is an essential part of man," except Averroes, who in his commentary on *De anima* (III, 5; p. 378 and passim) presents the "fiction," intelligible to no one including himself, that the intellect in man is "some separate substance joined by means of phantasms." According to such an argument, no one can explain human intelligence (*intelligere*), and "man as such is nothing more than a kind of irrational animal which excels the other animals by reason of an irrational sensitive soul that is more excellent

of the arts and virtues, which arise from experience through this lower faculty, but do not arise to reflective awareness as principles of artistic or moral behavior, which can only be attained by reason.

In the *Nicomachean Ethics,* it will be recalled, Aristotle states that prudence works with "the ultimate particular fact," apprehended by what many commentators have identified as the common sense.[64] Aquinas maintains in several places, however, that Aristotle meant to refer not specifically to the *sensus communis* (which for him occupied a relatively lowly position on the scale of faculties) but to a more general *interior ratio particularis.* This text was fundamentally important for Aquinas's definition of prudence, and his interest in the *vis cogitativa* was not so much in its abstractive or imaginative powers as in the contribution of these powers to concrete apprehension of real states of affairs as occasions for moral choice. The apprehension of the *vis cogitativa* is thus associated with the moral or practical order, and Aquinas's overriding concern is with the *cogitativa* as it concerns experience and prudence, and as it apprehends the minor premise of the "practical syllogism," as we shall shortly consider. For Aquinas, the *vis cogitativa* is not only a mean between sense and intellect, but a bridge between apprehension and moral behavior.

than other souls." Again (p. 156) Duns Scotus argues that Averroes's conception "destroys knowledge [*scientia*] itself inasmuch as it denies any act of knowledge distinct from sensation or any act of choice distinct from sense appetite and hence does away with all those virtues which require an act of choice in accord with right reason." S. Babolin, "La cogitativa di S. Tommaso," *Tommaso d'Aquino nel suo settimo centenario. Atti del Congresso Internazionale (Roma–Napoli, 17/24 Aprile, 1974),* Naples, 1978, VII, pp. 363–367, presents a review of Aquinas's doctrine concentrating on the *cogitativa* as a mean between sense and reason. It is, he argues, "intellect because it is constitutive of principles and rules of conduct, sense because the end of its action is always the concrete." In order to consider reason as a whole, it is necessary to treat both discursive reason and rational appetite, or will, and the *cogitativa* is the "operative co-presence of body and soul . . . the functional unity of the human person." It is the "right estimation of particular ends" and provides the particular premise to rational discourse for practical syllogisms in the ethical order (prudence) or technical order (art). The *cogitativa* makes manifest the distinctive "rational constitution of human sensibility" and may confront human passion to reason. Human work (which is aesthetic, ethical, and technical) finds its proximate origin in the *cogitativa.* Babolin argues that logic belongs to the intellect, ethics to the will, aesthetics to the *cogitativa.* Aquinas, of course, was in no position to make this final claim himself.

[64] For these texts, see Chapter 5 nn. 16–18, above. B. Garceau, *Judicium. Vocabulaire, sources, doctrine de Saint Thomas d'Aquin,* Paris, 1968, p. 248, attributes an extraordinary importance to the judgment of common sense, similar to that attributed to inner sense here; it is on the ability of the common sense to discern correctly between the real sensible and that which is represented in the imagination that the rightness of intellectual judgment depends, just as the process of rational deliberation depends on the functioning of the *phantasia.* Commenting on Aristotle's remark that the right mean in ethical behavior "is not easy to determine by reasoning, any more than anything else that is perceived by the senses; such things depend on particular facts, and the decision rests with perception" (translated by Grosseteste "non facile sermone determinare. Neque enim aliud aliquid sensibilium. Talia autem in singularibus, et in sensu iudicium" [*Nicomachean Ethics* 1109b20]), Aquinas wrote that it is not possible to say how much deviation from the mean is praiseworthy or blameworthy any more than in any other singulars, and "because of this the judgment of them consists in sense, although not in exterior but rather in interior sense, to which pertains the judgment of prudence." He then refers the reader to Book VI of the *Ethics,* which means that estimation is identified with cogitation, and both with prudence (*Sententia libri ethicorum, Opera omnia,* XLVII, Rome, 1969, I, p. 116).

Aquinas objected to Averroes's idea of the *vis cogitativa* because it made no provision for moral responsibility. In Averroes the *cogitativa* is merely an inward sequence of images like sense images, and the difference between will and appetite is that one is moved by cogitation, the other not.[65] On such a view the human animal is subject to its own imaginings much as animals are subject to sensation. For Aquinas this view was unacceptable, and to counter it he redefined the nature of the constitutively human intellectual soul, and in identifying it with the individual soul, bound it at once more closely to the senses and to the will.

So far in these studies we have been considering systems of ideas in which a more or less explicitly defined particular intellect stands in a central position relative to sense on one hand and intellect on the other. Aquinas may be said to have fundamentally rearranged this simple diagrammatic scheme. He insisted that the intellective soul is only in individuals, arguing that, since the soul is the form of the body, there would be no essential difference between one individual and another if this were not the case, and, furthermore, in equally good Aristotelian fashion, that the psychological apparatus between sense and intellect would be purposeless were all intellects the same.[66] The effect of these arguments was to bind the intellect closely to the physical circumstances of the individual in which it is actual, and, if not to deny the symmetry between the intellect and the intelligible order of creation, at least to make this order only a distant limiting case for human knowledge. For Aquinas, the principle of individuation is not the *vis cogitativa,* or particular reason, but rather the individual soul. Both sense and intellect are of one person, intellect governing the whole.[67] This amounts to a Christian acceptance of the Aristotelian principle that all knowledge is through sensation. In such a scheme the *vis cogitativa* begins to seem to be an unnecessary hypothesis. This does not mean, however, that the idea could simply be pared away (nor does it mean, as we shall see, that it dropped out of historical sight); rather, it means that it had been incorporated into a broader notion of the individual soul.

For Aquinas, the boundaries among the distinctions between the *vis cogitativa* and the "separate" intellect were not fixed and definite, nor did he devote much attention to making them so. In general, the *vis cogitativa* knew the particular directly, and the possible intellect (the *tabula rasa,* the potentiality in the soul for all knowledge proportional to it) knew the universal directly. But there also had to be communication, or else it would not be possible to explain the participation of the separate intellect in real states of affairs. The point of contact between the highest sense and the lowest intellect is still the point of contact between body and spirit. Because they are powers of a single soul, Aquinas maintains, the two must in some way overlap and interpenetrate. The mind may infer

[65] *Commentarium magnum,* III, 50; p. 519. See Klubertanz, *Discursive Power,* on Aquinas's relation to Averroes.

[66] *Summa theologiae* I.76.2.

[67] Ibid. I.76.1; I.79.4; I.77.5.

individuals as the origin in sense of the universals that are its proper object by reflection on the processes by which it came to have them; and it may also

proceed into the sensitive part, insofar as mind rules the lower powers; and so it mixes itself with singulars by means of the *ratio particularis,* which is a certain individual potency which is also called the *cogitativa,* and has a definite organ in the body, namely the middle cell of the head. In truth the universal thought [*sententia*] which mind has concerning the operable cannot possibly be applied to the particular act unless through some mediate power apprehending the singular, so that a certain syllogism might be made, of which the major premise is the universal which is the thought of the mind, the minor is the singular which is the application of particular reason, and the conclusion is the choice [*electio*] in the singular work."[68]

What is of interest to us here are the alternatives that emerge. Aquinas believed that, in general, action should be ruled by intellect, and thus by the highest powers of the soul, but he also defined more and more clearly the sensate judgments that make the intervention of intellect in action possible. He also came close to articulating this choice in terms of the distinction between confused and distinct. It is only the intellect that may affirm or negate, but in good Aristotelian fashion Aquinas also observes that "sense does something similar to this when it apprehends something as delightful and sad."[69] Such judgments imply the existence of the state of affairs at hand in all its particularity and they bring the faculties that make such implicit assertions into the closest vicinity to intellect.

The relation between sense and intellect was thus made both hierarchical and continuous, and Aquinas, whose concerns in these matters were as much ethical as psychological, was keenly interested in the relation between the reigning soul and the faculties that served it. Definition of this relation finally yielded pedagogical principles. According to Aquinas, special sense and the common sense are not subject to reason (that is, not teachable), but memory, cogitation, and imagination are.[70] (Although Aquinas was mostly interested in moral instruction, the principle of the corrigibility of prerational faculties could be extended to the whole realm of sensation. Cicero, it will be recalled, argued that painters, partly through experience, "see" more things than do others, and Leonardo recommended what were in fact exercises for the improvement of judgments of the common sense.) In fact, the rational potential of the *cogitativa* is fulfilled in guidance by reason. "*Ratio particularis* is by nature to be moved and directed in man according to universal reason." That is to say, the reason of sense is morally perfected by universal reason.[71]

[68] See E. Q. Franz, *The Thomistic Doctrine on the Possible Intellect,* Washington, D.C., 1950, pp. 50–51 and passim, with additional discussion and bibliography on the *vis cogitativa.* In another text cited by Franz (p. 49), Aquinas suggests that the possible intellect knows both the universal and the particular in a way analogous to that in which the common sense knows the white and the sweet.

[69] *In Aristotelis Librum de Anima Commentarium,* III, XII (Pirotta ed., Turin, 1959, p. 181).

[70] *Summa theologiae* I–II.50.3 ad 3; I.115.4.

[71] Ibid. I–II.77.a.1,c.

In his commentary on Aristotle's *De anima,* Aquinas argues that the *cogitativa* "apprehends the individual as existing under common nature, insofar as the intellective [power] is united to that individual."[72] By "under common nature" he means that the *cogitativa* apprehends a real object, and that the individual as apprehended by the *cogitativa* corresponds to this real object insofar as it is an object of human consciousness. The *cogitativa* knows *this* man just as he *is* this man and *this* wood insofar as it *is* this wood, and distinguishes the object of the *cogitativa* precisely in this respect as human and as different from the animal *estimativa.* In order to make this distinction he refers to an example from Aristotle's *Nicomachean Ethics* that we have considered previously. Only man takes delight in sensation; the dog is delighted by the smell of the hare because he wishes to eat the hare. On the basis of the same distinction, the *cogitativa* apprehends the individual disinterestedly. The animal *estimativa,* Aquinas writes, "does not apprehend any individual insofar as it is "under common nature, but only as it is the end or beginning of some action or passion." The animal does not see what is "really" there; apprehension by the animal *estimativa* is only relative to need and impulse; the lamb "perceives" the ewe as a source of nourishment, "sees" the grass as food. Animal apprehension of individuals does not extend beyond this, and animals are thus suited to their own needs in following or fleeing passions. This argument is of the greatest importance. The *cogitativa* apprehends individuals as such, and this apprehension also effects a unity between the aesthetic and the moral. The disinterestedness necessary to the evaluative reflection of moral decision may be viewed as delight not so much in sense as in the individual fully sensed.[73]

In his commentary on Aristotle's *Ethics,* Aquinas develops corollary ideas with a thoroughness that demands examination not least of all because it provides a summary of many of the themes put forward in this book. The beautiful, Aquinas wrote, has to do with the *vis cogniscitiva,* that is, with the general power of apprehension of the human intellective soul. It is for this reason that beautiful things are those that please sight, the most intellectual of the senses.[74] He generalizes this to say that beauty (*pulcrum*) consists in proper proportion because

[72] *In . . . Librum de Anima Commentarium,* II, xiii (ed. cit., p. 101).

[73] Compare John Duns Scotus (de Bruyne, *Etudes,* III, p. 347): "Pulchritudo non est aliqua qualitas absoluta in corpore pulchro sed est aggregatio omnium convenientium tali corpori, puta magnitudinis, figurae et coloris et aggregatio omnium respectuum qui sunt istorum ad corpus et ad se invicem. Ita bonitas moralis est quasi quidem decor illius actus includens aggregationem debitae proportionis ad omnia ad quae debet actus proportionari, puta: ad potentiam, ad objectum, ad finem, ad tempus, ad locum, ad modum; et hoc specialiter, ut ista dicantur a recta ratione debere convenire." Here the particularity of the prudent act, or of the situation demanding prudent action, is compared to the kind of particularity of a beautiful object. See also William of Auvergne (ibid., III, pp. 72–88), who argues that beauty pleases exterior and interior vision, the second of which he identifies with prudence. "Quemadmodum enim pulchrum visu dicimus quod natum est per se ipsum placere spectantibus et delectare secundum visum, sic et pulchram interius, quod intuentiam animos delectat et ad amorem sui allicit. . . . Ista autem omnia ipso experimento sensus nota fiunt. . . . In hujus explanatione non immorabimur quoniam ipse interior visus testis est nobis interioris et intelligibilis pulchritudinis sicut exterior visus est exterioris."

[74] *Summa theologiae* I–II.27.1 ad 3. See de Bruyne, *Etudes,* III, pp. 282–283.

sense is delighted in things properly proportioned as similar to itself. The beautiful is also "assimilation" to higher faculties. Form is beautiful to us because form is that by which things are known. The intellective soul is the "form of forms," and we recognize things by virtue of resemblance of form. This is again a generalization of the Aristotelian principle that we delight in imitation because of our desire to know, except that simple "phantastic" imitation of the kind Aristotle described in the *Poetics* is only the first of a series of "assimilations" to the structure of the soul, much as the phantasm stands at the base of the ladder of abstraction. The beauty of form is thus related to the reason of formal causes; and our delight in the beautiful makes possible the "application of universal knowledge to the imagination and sense of particular things."[75] Aquinas also repeats the principle that "only man is delighted in the very beauty of the sensible in itself."[76] and extends this to say that only man can separate sight and hearing from touch, which is associated with the animal satisfactions of food and sex. Man is, of course, liable to such delights, but may also take delight in the proportion (*convenientia*) of sensibles to sense, "as when we delight in well harmonized sound." Since this delight "does not pertain to the conservation of nature," as do food and sex, such delights cannot be intemperate.[77] This argument leads us to the *Nicomachean Ethics*.

In commenting on the *Ethics,* Aquinas followed Aristotle in dissociating temperance (which he says "concerns the pleasures – *delectabilia* – by which human life is conserved, that is, food and sex")[78] from the delights of the extrinsic senses (sight, hearing, and smell). The delights of sight are according to proper sensibles, such as colors; common sensibles, which are best known by sight, such as shape (*figura*); and sensibles *per accidens,* such as writing (*scriptura*).[79] Those who delight in objects of vision may be "curious" if they go too far; but they may not be temperate or intemperate because such reflective sensate activity involves less "vehement delights."

Similar arguments are made for the delights of hearing "as in melodies, that is, the consonance of human voices, in mimicry, that is, in the simulation of human voices by instruments." (Here, it may be noted, sense is pleased by both harmony and imitation.) Those who enjoy the odors of fruit or roses or incense insofar as they are kinds of odors in themselves also cannot be called intemperate.[80]

For Aquinas "disinterested" sensation is a mark of rationality, distinguishing human from animal sensation. Through it we come to know both the nature of

[75] *Etudes,* III, p. 289.
[76] *Summa theologiae* I.91.3 ad 3. See Chapter 4 n. 11 above.
[77] Ibid. II–II.141.4 ad 3.
[78] *Sententia Libri ethicorum, Opera omnia,* XLVII, Rome, 1969, I, p. 180.
[79] Ibid., pp. 181–182. The whole phrase reads "scriptura ratione eius quod per scripturam significatur," by which he seems to mean that we recognize a word to mean something much as we must recognize something seen to be something; we may, however, delight in all these kinds of apprehension as such. Aquinas's text should be read with those of earlier writers, especially Albertus Magnus, given in the edition cited.
[80] Ibid., pp. 181–182.

our own souls and of the external world. But the importance given to reason by Aquinas should not be taken to mean that art should be simply rational in the sense of being subject to measures and definitions. Art is rather rational when it is suited to human nature, which, as part of the providential order of creation, is itself alive with reason. Diversion (*ludus*), for example, is necessary to human life and so also is the "occupation of acting, which is ordered to the consolation of men."[81] In ministering to human nature, diversion, represented by theater, is rational, and delight in it is only wrong when it is excessive and "disordered", that is, when it strays from its proper relation to human nature. That is to say, theater, which may be justified by the reasons of human nature, is also subject to the constraints of reason. The general idea of proportion to human nature underlying these arguments is, in fact, fundamental to Aquinas's conception of the nature and function of art. We may consider again the example of poetry. Although he seems to have taken a dim view of poetry, his often quoted remark that poetry is the lowest kind of knowledge should not be taken to mean that it is superfluous. On the contrary, the argument held out the greatest promise for the art of poetry. Because as language corresponding to sense, and appealing at the level of sense, poetry was justified by its conformity with universal human nature. The human intellective soul was meant by God to know by means of the senses, and the phantasms of the poets, if governed by reason, could be the first solid steps to salvation.

For Aquinas the relation of the faculties of the soul was organic, a relation of radical interdependence. Each kind of judgment, from that of external sense, through internal sense, to the judgments of reason, was integral to the activity of the intellective *compositum* as a whole. If the intellect governed the whole, it was also dependent on its faculties. "The judgment and apprehension of reason is impeded by the vehement and disordered apprehension of imagination and judgment by the estimative virtue, as is apparent in the mad. Moreover, it is manifest that the apprehension of imagination and the judgment of the *estimativa* follow the passion of sensitive appetite, as the judgment of taste follows the disposition of the tongue." The judgment of taste with which this descending chain of interdependent faculties ends, was in fact one of Aquinas's favorite examples of the interrelation of corporeal individual and intellect.[82]

The images advanced by the *cogitativa* were of course derived from memory, and memory as the other highest of the internal senses was in a similarly ambivalent and central relation to sense and reason. This ambivalence is strongly evident in scholastic treatments of the classical art of memory.[83] Memory was discussed by both Albertus Magnus and Aquinas under the category of the virtue of prudence. Albertus Magnus maintained a sharp division between sense and reason, which required that he range reminiscence as a part of reason; and he defined memory

[81] *Summa theologiae* II–II.168.3 ad 3.

[82] *Summa theologiae* I–II.77.1.c; see B. Garceau, *Judicium*, p. 248 and passim; and de Bruyne, *Etudes*, III, pp. 292–297.

[83] For a fuller treatment of the following, see Yates, *Art of Memory*, pp. 62–81.

as a moral habit (like prudence) when it is used to remember things for the purposes of prudent behavior in the present or future. Memory is prudence insofar as the calling up of stored images and intentions is governed by reason, or insofar as it serves rational purposes, or serves universally justifiable principles. Aquinas took a characteristically more modulated view, observing that memory was partly corporeal, arguing, much as Averroes had, that its rational character owed to the superiority of sense in man. And both Albertus Magnus and Aquinas agreed that the memorable was that which was vividly like a phantasm, and therefore appealed to our corporeal nature, that metaphorical language and even bizarre imagery were more memorable than the simply descriptive, Aquinas basing his arguments repeatedly on the fundamental Aristotelian principle that all understanding begins with a phantasm, a mental image. We remember much in the way we learn, and Aquinas's arguments are similar to those we have encountered in commentaries on Aristotle's *Poetics,* and in Aquinas's own justifications of metaphorical language. "We wonder more at unfamiliar things and the soul is more strongly and vehemently held by them. . . . It is necessary in this way to invent similitudes and images because simple and spiritual intentions slip easily from the soul unless they are as it were linked to some corporeal similitudes, because human cognition is stronger in regard to the sensibilia."[84] In all of this there is the deepest possible interpenetration of imagination, memory, cogitation, and moral behavior. This means that the same Aristotelian framework that gave new definition and importance to the art of memory also gave new definition and importance to the use of images in general. The possibility of the education of imagination was the possibility of the shaping of behavior, and this obviously gave a new dimension to the function of both religious and political images, which, according to the psychology we are considering, were not only essential to the working of the mind but essential in the determination of behavior, and thus of the greatest importance to those concerned with morality and moral behavior leading to salvation. In such a scheme, the *cogitativa* might be regarded as the "natural" mind; as the natural mind it was not simply abstract, but was yoked to its own experience. The *cogitativa* apprehended not only the particular but the operable, and thus again was integral with the virtue of prudence, to a closer examination of which we shall presently proceed.

Benedetto Varchi on Michelangelo

The first quatrain of one of Michelangelo's most famous sonnets reads as follows:

Non ha l'ottimo artista alcun
concetto
c'un marmo in se non circonscriva
col suo superchio, e solo a quello arriva
la man che ubbidisce all'intelletto.

[84] Ibid., p. 74.

Which may be paraphrased thus:

The excellent artist has no *concetto*
that one single marble does not enclose
with its excess; and that (*concetto*) is only attained
by the hand that obeys the intellect.[85]

Here is Benedetto Varchi's explanation of the word *intelletto* in the fourth line:[86]

This word intellect means many things . . . and it is properly in us that most noble part of the soul through which we understand [*intendiamo*], and it is often called mind [*mente*]. Petrarch used this word in its significance when he said in that divine comparison:

Come natura al ciel la lun e 'l sole
all' aere i venti, alla terra erbe e fronde,
all'uomo l'intelletto e le parole,
et all mar ritogliese i pesci e l'onde

(As if nature were to take away from the
heavens the moon and sun,
from the air the winds, from earth plants and leaves,
from man intellect and words
from the sea fish and waves.)[87]

And again:

Con le quai dal mortale
Carcer nostro intelletto al ciel si leva

(By which from the mortal prison our
intellect is raised to heaven)[88]

But here the word is taken otherwise, that is, for that potency or virtue called imagination, or *fantasia,* of which we have reasoned many times, which not only is different from the intellect, but differs in that [the intellect] is immortal according to the truest philosophers; while the *fantasia* according to all and without any doubt is mortal. And although it composes, divides and finally discourses like the rational soul, it nonetheless discourses not about universal things, as reason does, but about particulars. Nor should anyone marvel that the poet [Michelangelo] called this potency, which is one of the interior senses [*sentimenti interiori*] "intellect," because not only the poets call it by this name, as Petrarch does when he says

Io nol posso ridir, che nol comprendo
da tai due lumi e l'intelletto offeso,
e di tanta dolcezza oppresso e stanco

[85] On this sonnet see *MLA*, part 1, chap. XIV; and M. Buonarroti, *Rime*, ed. E. N. Girardi, Bari, 1960, n. 151.

[86] I have followed with one change the text in BScr, II, pp. 136–139.

[87] Petrarch *Rime* CCXVIII.9–12.

[88] Ibid. CCLXIV.7–8.

(I may not laugh because I do not understand;
by two such eyes the intellect is offended
and by such eyes sweetness oppressed and worn)[89]

And he says the same in many other places. But Aristotle himself [calls *fantasia* intellect]. Whence we should know that, in addition to the agent intellect, there are found according to Aristotle two intellects: one universal, and this is called by him sometimes possible[90] and sometimes material, and it is that which we call properly intellect or mind; and the other intellect is particular, which is called passive, and this is nothing else than the fantasy or imagination. And it is called the passive intellect according to Giovanni Grammatico [that is, Philoponus] because, as the intellect takes all that it understands from the *fantasia,* so the *fantasia* takes from sense; or rather, because the *immaginativa* always serves the intellect and proceeds by imitating it; because if the intellect understands, the *fantasia* understands [*intende*]; if one discourses, the other discourses; if one divides, the other divides. Nor is there any difference except that one considers only universals, the other only particulars. And this passive intellect, which, as those trained in these matters will understand, we do not distinguish from the *cogitativa,* [as] it seems that Aristotle meant at the end of the prologue to the *Physics.*

Varchi is referring to the Aristotelian text analyzed above at the beginning of the chapter on confused knowledge. He means to identify the *cogitativa* with inner sense, by means of which things are, in Aristotle's words, "more knowable and obvious to us," for which things are "more obscure by nature, but clearer to us," the faculty by means of which things are known "relatively to us" rather than "without qualification." Just as the common sense had undergone a long series of transformations before Leonardo took up the idea for his purposes, so the *cogitativa* was deeply layered with definitions and connotations by the time Varchi used it to explain Michelangelo's sonnet on his own sculpture as a metaphor of unfulfillable love. The intellect the hand obeys is the *particular* intellect, which discourses about particulars, that is, about images. It is this that the hand obeys, and this that produces the *concetto,* the image in the mind toward which the artist works.

When Aquinas commented upon the same text to which Varchi referred to explain the *vis cogitativa,* he wrote that sense knows "animal" before it knows "man" just as intellect does and, in order to make this parallel, translated the logical relation of genus and species into spatial and temporal dimensions, thus investing spatial and temporal experience with their own rationality.[91] To do this he clearly referred to Aristotle's *De anima* (418a17, 425a25), in which the relation between common sensibles and incidental sensibles is treated. The "more common sensible," Aquinas wrote, "is first known to us according to sense." Aquinas understood Aristotle's example of Cleon's son perceived as a white shape to mean that Cleon's son was seen at a distance, "optically," so that he was seen

[89] Ibid. CXCVIII.12–14.
[90] This is read as "possibile," not "passibile," as in Barocchi's text.
[91] Thomas Aquinas, *Commentary on Aristotle's Physics,* ed. cit. p. 11.

as a body before he was seen as an animal, as an animal before he was seen as a man, as a man before he was seen as an individual. Such relative judgments were made by the common sense as the "general sensibility" of which Aristotle wrote (*De anima* 425a25–30), which allows us to perceive common sensibles directly. Thus understood, the common sense was the *vis cogitativa,* which according to Averroes apprehended and judged all real things in all their real relations, and which was integral with experience. Such relative judgment was not simply negative, a fumbling around in the absence of reason; on the contrary, it was invested with that unquestioned sureness with which we actually pursue most of the activities of our lives. Nor was such behavior simply unconscious; it was thought to be central to ethical judgment as that essential understanding of states of affairs as they really are that makes the application of principles in that case possible. And as we have just seen, according to Aquinas this particular intellect also apprehended the particular as such, and in doing so differentiated human from animal sense. Through the particular intellect the human mind could delight in its own sensation, which is to say that human beings are capable of aesthetic experience. At the same time, the *cogitativa* also preserved its association with fantasy, to which Varchi connects it over and over again. The *fantasia* is mortal, and conditioned by the material constitution of the body, and with this in mind we may understand why Varchi used his next examples from poetry. When Dante appeals to those who have "intelletti sani," who "see the doctrine that is hidden under the veil of strange verses,"[92] or when Michelangelo himself writes that "the soul, the whole and sound intellect, more free and unbound, ascends by means of the eyes to your high beauty,"[93] they mean to refer not just to the intellect that pierces through the sensible to the intelligible, they mean to refer to the intellect that apprehends the sensible as such and therefore sees through to the intelligible. "Doctrine" or "high beauty" is seen in visible forms and "strange verses," which means that the invisible can only be set out in forms imagined by an individual. In these terms the *cogitativa* takes on one of its traditional meanings, looking back to Augustine's *spiritus* and its Neoplatonic sources. The *cogitativa* is the particular intellect, defined by the individual in whom it is embodied, capable of judgments from the point of view of that embodiment, and it is at the same time the artist's *idea,* or *fantasia,* subject to dreams and visions.

Benedetto Varchi on judgment

Ancient "pneumatic physiology," with all its manifold connections to religion and astrology, persisted in many important forms through the Renaissance. This is not to say that there were not alternative ways of thinking, although even Shakespeare's "admirable evasion of whoremaster man" who "lays his goatish

[92] *Inferno* IX.61–63.
[93] *Rime,* ed. Girardi, n. 166.

disposition on the charge of a star" (*King Lear* I.2) is still defined negatively by these ideas. Benedetto Varchi provides a transition between the ancient and medieval themes we have examined and more modern notions of the relation between the human soul and the world. In his fifth lecture on the subject of poetry, read in the *Accademia fiorentina* on the second Sunday of Lent, 1553, Varchi addressed the question of the nature of judgment. In this lecture the internal senses and the particular intellect figure prominently, and taken altogether provide a summary of much that has gone before and a bridge to the final chapters.[94]

Varchi begins from the proposition that all individuals are different in both body and mind. He makes a distinction between mind (*animo*) and soul (*anima*). Thus all *souls* are sisters, he says, just as all human beings are human beings, but all minds are of distinct individuals. *Animo* corresponds to the particular intellect. The difference in bodies is to be seen in faces, which are never exactly alike, and differences in mind are evident in the multiplicity of judgments. "There will never be," Varchi says, "two men so similar of intellect that they might not be different in the judging of anything." Varchi speaks of *animo* and *anima* as being in the closest interdependence within the unity of the human intellective soul. By and large, the intellective soul is free and lord of itself, and its serenity can only be "violated" by judgment, by which Varchi means that the particular intellect, which apprehends and judges particulars, provides the only access of the soul to the world. Judgment has this extraordinary force "because when the judgment judges anything to be good, the intellect may not, even if it be evil, fail to desire it and follow it as good; and on the contrary, when the judgment judges anything to be evil, the intellect is forced in spite of itself, even if it be good, to hate it and flee it as evil."

Judgment is made by a "virtue, or faculty or potency" of the soul and Varchi first considers whether this is active or passive. Some say one thing, some say the other. Simple sensation (*sentimenta*), he finally argues, is not an action but a passion. This leads him to familiar problems, however, and he qualifies this statement by saying that sensation is a certain kind of passion, "not corruptive, but perfective." In other words, sensation is the realization of the potential of sense. Varchi concludes by defining judgment "as a certain suffering [*patire*], that is, a perfective passion, which is nothing else than receiving and in sum comprehending and knowing anything; judgment is nothing else than comprehension of anything, if sensible, of sense, if intelligible, of intellect."

Having spoken of what in general might have been treated under the category of estimation in earlier discussions (which he calls the *giudicatorio naturale* and associates with instinct, *synderesis* and *conscienza*), Varchi turns to the two forms of judgment, the judgment of sense and the judgment of intellect. Whoever has the better eye, he argues, will be a better judge of color, the proper object of vision. He further argues that sense may not be said to err if the organs of sense

[94] Unless otherwise noted, references in this section are to B. Varchi, *Opere*, Milan, n.d., II, pp. 729–731.

and the body as a whole are in good working order. "To have good judgment with respect to sensible things is nothing else than to have good sensation [*sentimenta*] and to have good sensation proceeds, according to doctors, from good complexion, and according to astrologers, from the constellation of the heavens." Varchi does not shrink from the implications of this interdependence of sense and soul, and, interpeting Dante in light of Lucretius and Averroes, writes that if sense and reason disagree, sense and not reason should be believed, that arguments are true when they agree with things sensed, that experience is the mistress of all things.[95]

Faced with the argument that animal senses are sharper than those of human beings, Varchi immediately appeals to the notion of internal sense and to the privileged nature of human internal sense, associated with reason. Only human beings truly judge. Human internal sense "composes and divides," which animal sense cannot do. The exterior senses shared with animals "do not truly judge, neither the eye of colors, nor taste of flavors, and so of the others; only the common sense judges all sensibles." It is once again the common sense that, even if it is dependent upon the data of the five senses, provides characteristically human judgment about sensation.[96]

When Varchi turns to the matter of intellectual judgment he appeals to the beginning of Aristotle's *Ethics* (1094b–1095a), where it is stated that each judges well those things he knows. Aristotle is speaking of judgment of the practical intellect, of which mathematical precision is not to be expected, "any more than in all the products of the crafts." So Varchi means to refer to that which we know through instruction, practice, or experience (*dottrina o esercizio o esperienza*). When we are sick we go to a doctor, and so for all the arts and sciences we should seek out the appropriate *artisti*. For this kind of practical judgment both external and internal sense are necessary. We must see or hear things, but we must also apprehend them as only the *fantasia* and *cogitativa* are able to do, that is, we must grasp them as particulars. The judgment of "intellectual things" Varchi calls a *consenso,* appealing to the idea of the practical syllogism. It is at this level that judgment (here he cites Albertus Magnus and Averroes) is most truly active. What Varchi seems to mean is that sense and inner sense bring things to us in ways determined by our individual constitutions, and when we bring art and experience to bear on what we have judged by sense to be so-and-so, we act. Action, or skilled action – art – has to do with individual character compounded with experience, *ingenium* compounded with *ars.* It is to be noted that *ingenium* is not simply shaped by *ars,* rather *ingenium* is in effect always a part of apprehension

95 Ibid., p. 702.

96 Varchi (*Opere,* p. 350) followed the usual pattern in calling the common sense the center of a circle; it "apprehends not from things themselves, but from external sensations those images or simulacra or likenesses called species by philosophers, that they have apprehended from existent or sensible things." It distinguishes the data of one sense from another; but Varchi also attributes to it the ability to distinguish differences in the data of one sense (light from dark, bitter from sweet); it only acts in the presence of objects. See also p. 744.

and judgment, of the continual evaluation of states of affairs. Our actions are inevitably interlaced with sensate judgment and experience. In order for judgment to be good in action, many factors from sensation through inner sense, experience and state of the art in question, must be right. Judgment is consequently of the greatest difficulty.

In order to judge properly concerning the art of poetry, Varchi argues, it is necessary to understand the art of poetry, to read ancient and modern authors on the subject, even though some by a certain "natural" judgment comparable to the "estimation" he has discussed earlier are more apt to good judgment than others. It is also necessary to have read and considered the ancient and modern poets and to have practiced composition.

For Varchi judgment is centrally important, and corresponds to something like personal style and character in action. Most of what we do is both imitative and circumstantial. Judgment transcends these conditions in being their principle of unity. We judge the world individually and at the same time appropriately, and the consistency that runs through these actions is our judgment. "As it is commonly said that salt is the spice for all food, so we are able to say that judgment is that which, so with words as with things, flavors and seasons everything."

When Quintilian said that judgment must be as natural to us as taste and smell,[97] Varchi writes, he must be understood to refer to external sense, and intellectual judgment can only be taught. If that is so, why are some unable to become poets no matter how hard they study? Again, the internal senses come to the rescue. Failure to become a poet through sheer application owes to the "imperfection of the *sentimenti interiori* and especially of the *cogitativa.*" Varchi more than once identifies judgment with the *cogitativa.* In his nineteenth question on love he argues that souls or intellects (*l'anime, ciò è gli intelletti*), if they are not one, as Averroes argued, but sisters, are not the cause of differences in judgment. "Men are different according to the diversity of that virtue called the *cogitativa* in men and, in beasts, as less perfect, the *estimativa.*"[98] They have the best judgment who have the best *cogitativa.* As in the essay on Michelangelo's sonnet, there is a direct relationship between *fantasia* and the *cogitativa.* Varchi identifies the *cogitativa* with *giudizio naturale,* to which he attaches such great importance as nearly to contradict his arguments for the necessity of intellectual judgment. "One naturally judicious may, without any study and without letters, surpass in many things the studious and literate; so these last, however learned and practiced, if they lack that natural judgment without which the accidental judgment acquired by means of study may not stand and is never perfect, never

[97] Varchi refers to Quintilian *Institutio oratoria* VI.V.1–2 (ed. and tr. H. E. Butler, Cambridge, Mass.–London, 1921–2, II, pp. 514–515). *Iudicium,* which is essential in every aspect of rhetoric, is a matter of sense, he says, which cannot be taught.

[98] *Opere,* II, p. 560.

turn out too well, rather they are very often ridiculous and foolish even to the simplest men."

Varchi ends his disquisition by likening *giudizio* to the Tuscan virtue of *discrezione.* Those with judgment choose well, and he interprets Plato to have meant, when he said evil was chosen out of ignorance, that the ignorant are without judgment. As the context makes clear, he means to refer to natural judgment.

11

The mechanical arts

The origin of the arts

Over many centuries the human arts were distinguished from animal industry in much the same way that the human *cogitativa* was distinguished from the animal *estimativa,* and in fact differences between human and animal art were often explained in terms of these faculties. This distinction accounted for the variety of human artifacts in two ways. Having more complex needs than other animals, men devised many more kinds of artifacts; and because *cogitatio* was linked to reason and to *fantasy* the forms invented to meet the ends of life could be endlessly different and endlessly varied. The clear implication of these arguments was that in themselves, what came in the Middle Ages to be called the mechanical arts and the kinds of mental activity associated with them belonged to the realm of inner sense and particular intellect, that is, that they were rational primarily in that they belonged to a creature with a rational soul. Thus, human beings in all places might devise shelters in response to the need for them, and they might improve these shelters and teach the next generation to construct them. Such knowledge, gained and transmitted by experience, need, however, never rise to the level of science, or to the level of awareness of the principles of its own activity.

In this chapter we shall consider the simple proposition that in general there was a psychological distinction corresponding to the social distinction between mental and physical labor, that is, that the lower faculties of the soul were associated with the mechanical arts, and, more specifically, that the particular intellect was associated with the mechanical arts. This does not mean, of course, that the mechanical arts were irrational, but rather that they were associated with another kind of reason, distinctly human but closer to the judgment of sense and experience. As the definition of the arts proceeded in the Renaissance, it was not simply the case that the mechanical arts became liberal; rather, the status of these lower faculties rose to find a new relation with pure, speculative intellect in a development loosely paralleling the change in the idea of intellect itself as we have traced it.

The question of the origin of the arts is covered with ambivalence. In general, those classical writers who imagined the primeval state as a golden age saw the invention of the arts as the beginning of a decline. According to Hesiod, man lived peacefully before Prometheus stole the fire, which provoked the anger of the gods. In Lucretius's *De rerum natura,* mankind began in a golden age, suckled by nature, but was torn from nature's breast by the entropic passage of time, which led to hardship, to the invention of human arts and institutions in response to hardship, and to further woes. The pre-artificial age of mankind was not always imagined to have been so hospitable, however, and from the standpoint of such a "hard" primitivism, help was necessary from some outside source. According to Vitruvius, fire was discovered by chance, and in other versions gods and heroes, or, at the least, "uncommon men," ameliorated the human lot.[1]

In either version of the origin of the arts there is a deep sense of the opposition of art and nature; in one case the natural state is ruptured by civilization (or civilization is a response to the rupture from nature); in the other, nature is not so much lost as hostile, having set mankind into the world without the same means that fitted animals to their activities, and unable therefore to live "according to nature." So in Plato (*Protagoras* 321d), Epimetheus had unwisely allotted all the gifts of nature to the animals before he got to man, whom Prometheus found "naked, unshod, unbedded, and unarmed," and physically inferior to the animals. He intervened and stole fire and knowledge of the arts from Hephaestus and Athena, "at one in their common love of wisdom and artistry" (*Critias* 109c), who became the patron gods of craftsmen. Because of their relation to the gods, men built altars and made images of them, and by means of art invented language, shelter, clothing, furniture, and agriculture. They were given political wisdom by Zeus. In such a scheme, if man is akin to the gods, he is also a stepchild of nature, a phrase that was a classical commonplace.[2]

These myths of the origin of the arts, and the antithetical relation of art and nature, were paralleled in the Judaeo-Christian story of the Fall. Adam and Eve began their labors after they had eaten the fruit of the tree of the knowledge of good and evil, after which they no longer lived in harmony with nature, who again became their stepmother, only the begrudging giver of her gifts.[3]

A major aspect of the notion of imitation may be viewed as a variation on the theme of the separation of mankind from nature, and of the significance of art

[1] See A. O. Lovejoy and G. Boas, *Primitivism and Related Ideas in Antiquity*, pp. 374–375 and passim, for a discussion of the texts cited here together with a great many others on the origin of the arts.

[2] On Hephaestus and Athena and many themes relevant to those treated in this chapter, see E. Panofsky, "The Early History of Man in Two Cycles of Paintings by Piero di Cosimo," *Studies in Iconology: Humanistic Themes in the Art of the Renaissance,* New York, 1962, pp. 33–67, here p. 42. On man as the stepchild of nature, see n. 39, below.

[3] See G. Boas, *Essays on Primitivism and Related Ideas in the Middle Ages,* New York, 1978.

itself as an indication of that separation. So Democritus attributed the discovery of architecture to the observation of the webs of spiders.[4] This imitation might only be the mimicry of animals, but it also implied the apprehension of means and ends, that is, implied the apprehension of the reasons for animal activity, and the relation between these reasons and the forms animals made. Understood in this second way, the ideas of Democritus are only a step away from those of Aristotle, according to whom the arts imitate nature by adapting forms to ends. In general, as Cicero wrote, "innumerable arts have been discovered through nature's teaching; for having imitated her, *ratio* has ingeniously achieved the things necessary for life."[5] The stepmother has become a teacher, and the access of *ratio* to the kindred reasons in nature heals the breach between man and nature.

Art and reason

Although Cicero writes of the discerning power of the human mind schooled by nature as *ratio,* it is by no means clear to what judicative power of the mind he meant to refer, and in general the question of the faculties involved in the invention of the arts was little considered. In the texts we shall examine, the arts are usually assumed to have arisen from faculties like those that allow animals to behave with prudence, although these faculties are necessarily higher and more complex than those of the animals. The attitude expressed in the *Epinomis* (974d), sometimes attributed to Plato, is perhaps representative. If the inventors of the arts necessary to life may have been at first considered wise, no distinction is now to be had from the knowledge of them. And agriculture was not so much learned as it was the result of a native instinct implanted by God, which may also be said of the construction of dwellings, buildings, the making of furniture, smithing, carpentry, pottery, weaving, and the making of tools. These, like hunting and soothsaying, are of general human usefulness but are unrelated to virtue, and the arts of war, medicine, and rhetoric are not governed by true principles. The less necessary and more playful arts of imitation in dance, music, and the various forms of the art of drawing also cannot lead to wisdom no matter how assiduously one labors at them.

Similar ideas are reviewed by Seneca, contradicting the intervening arguments of Posidonius, according to whom the arts were invented by wise men (*excogitata a sapientibus viris*). This was not so, he says; the hammer and tongs were "invented by some man of active and keen but not of great or elevated *ingenium*" [*aliquis excitati ingenii, acuti non magni nec elati*], and he writes contemptuously of the necessity making such invention inevitable, contrasting it with the uprightness that allows man to turn his eyes to the heavens, thus to philosophize. "The same is true of all the other things which must be sought out with the body bent and

[4] Lovejoy and Boas, *Primitivism in Antiquity,* p. 207.

[5] *De legibus* I.viii.26.

the mind fixed upon the ground." All the servile arts come from "reason" (*ratio*), but not from right reason (*recta ratio*). By the same token, if rude men seem to have the four virtues, they in fact possess only the "material of virtue," not virtue itself. Here the "body bent and the mind fixed upon the ground" are again pointedly contrasted to human uprightness, to the observation of the heavens and the beginnings of philosophy.[6]

Following Posidonius, Seneca wrote that there are four kinds of arts, which he called *vulgares et sordidae, ludicrae, pueriles,* and *liberales.*[7] The "vulgar and base" arts are manual and minister to the needs of life, and possess nothing of the decent or honorable. The next category, the *artes ludicrae,* are arts directed to the pleasures of the eyes and ears (*ad voluptatem oculorum atque aurium tendunt*). Although these "arts of the play" suggest painting and music, Seneca cites the example of the stage scenery "excogitated" by "machinatores"; these dazzle the eyes of the unlearned, who do not understand how they work, so that they are made to marvel. The association of mechanics and fiction is less difficult to understand if it is recalled that the deceptions of painting and the stage were often compared,[8] and that Aristotle had listed automata as inspiring wonder. The amazement induced by machines was thus double-edged, able to trick the ignorant or to enkindle the desire to know, much as eloquence might contribute to demagoguery or to right instruction. Vitruvius also wrote that in *skenographia* some things seem to come forward and others to recede on a flat, upright surface,[9] and architectural decorative painting is adduced in much the same words in his remarks on optical illusion as an example of painting's power to fool the eye.[10] More generally, it was in the condemnation of the licentious architecture of *scaenae* that he wrote his equally harsh condemnation of grotesque painting.[11] These subjects could all arise together, or interchangeably, because both grotesques and illusions were "phantastic."

To return to Seneca, his last two kinds of art, the *artes pueriles* and *liberales* were related as what might be called the protoliberal and liberal arts, the implication being that the *artes vulgares* and the *artes ludicrae* might also be grouped together in an opposing, lower category. This is exactly what was done by Hugh of St. Victor when he formulated the scheme of the mechanical arts used through the later Middle Ages. Moreover, in giving the lower arts the name "mechanical," he associated all of them with mechanics and further defined these arts in general in terms of their ability to deceive.

[6] *Epistulae morales* XC; Lovejoy and Boas, *Primitivism in Antiquity*, pp. 264–274.

[7] *Epistulae morales* LXXXVIII. W. Tatarkiewicz, "The Classification of the Arts in Antiquity," *JHI*, 24, 1963, p. 232, attributes the classification of the arts according to utility and pleasure to the Sophists; according to the texts he cites, painting was an art of pleasure, architecture an art of utility.

[8] Augustine *Soliloquies* 2.10(18); see *MLA*, p. 471 n. 19.

[9] *De architectura* VII.pref. 11.

[10] Ibid. VI.II.2.

[11] Ibid. VII.V.

In the *Tusculan Disputations,* Cicero very nearly identified the human soul with memory.[12] By virtue of its possession of memory the soul has possession of "infinite innumerable things." He is not thinking, he writes, of trained or prodigious memories, but rather of "common human memory," and of the memories of those engaged in some art or study; and he regards the process by which we remember our own experience as more wonderful than Plato's *anamnesis.* He argues from memory to the "divine" nature of the soul. If the soul were material, then the memory would have to be a great space to hold so many things, or a great mass in which so many impressions might be made. In addition to memory the soul also has the power to investigate "hidden things," a power called *inventio* and *cogitatio;* so man names things, forms societies, invents written language, marks the paths of the stars and planets in the sky. Earlier men discovered and invented – presumably by the same power – the fruits of the earth, clothing, dwellings, nurture, and protection against beasts. From these beginnings, he concludes, we have passed from necessary to "more elegant arts"; "our ears have gained keen delight from the discovery of the tempered variety and quality of sounds."

Two deeply interlaced themes run through the discussion of human art, turning on human estrangement from both gods and nature. In the famous chorus in Sophocles's *Antigone* (332–75), "most terrible" man is a navigator, a farmer, a hunter, who speaks, knows, governs, and shelters himself, whose medicines cure illness but cannot evade death. But his cleverness is a two-edged sword, sometimes achieving evil, sometimes good. Man rises from his proper place in the invention and practice of the arts, and it is not good to be such a person or even to associate with such a person.[13] Art is without the sanction of nature or the gods, and is therefore as radically false as it is tragically necessary. Prometheus took the fire from the gods by stealth, and was tried and punished for theft. In Plato the amoral cleverness of the Sophist, who may speak the false or true with equal conviction and power to convince, who makes the false seem true *by his art,* like the painter, again and again provides the impulse to the definition of true virtue and right thinking. Later on in the Middle Ages, the term "mechanical" was defined as deceitful, as we shall shortly consider in detail; but this deception was still understood to span the whole range from praiseworthy to blameworthy. One way or another, art was marvelous, able to seduce or hoodwink, or to devise things too ingenious to be understood, things that induced wonder because their precedent causes could not be grasped.

[12] I.xxiv.57.

[13] For commentary and bibliography on this chorus, C. Segal, *Tragedy and Civilization: An Interpretation of Sophocles,* Cambridge, Mass.–London, 1981, p. 153. The word translated as "terrible" is *deinos;* see *MLA,* pp. 234–241, on the later idea of *deinotes* and the Renaissance *terribilità.* According to Xenophon, Socrates argued that the skilled in speaking, doing, and devising (*lektikos, praktikos,* and *mechanikos*) must all be ruled by *sophrosyne* or else they would simply have greater power for mischief. See L. Strauss, *Xenophon's Socrates,* Ithaca, N.Y., 1972, p. 101.

Plato distinguished between arts and "routines," with the example of medicine and cooking. Medicine

> has investigated the nature of the subject it treats and the cause of its actions and can give a rational account of them, whereas its counterpart, which is exclusively devoted to cultivating pleasure, approaches it in a thoroughly unscientific way, without once having investigated the nature of pleasure or its cause; and without any pretense to reason and practically no effort to classify, it preserves by mere experience and routine a memory of what usually happens, thereby securing its pleasures. (*Gorgias* 501a–b; also 464b)

The fatal difficulty with routines is that they have no external and specifically no moral dimension, no concern with which pleasures are better and which worse. A true art for Plato proceeded by definition, division, and characterization of parts, and was always subject to the nature of things, the physician, for example, being guided by the nature of the body.[14] The whole discussion of art turns around the question of rhetoric, and especially of sophistry. Rhetoric is no more than a routine because the orator may be concerned equally with good or bad. It is to the soul what cooking (as opposed to medicine) is to the body. Its blandishments, its unmitigated appeal to pleasures, is also inherently deceitful, and rhetoric in its turn stands to the right disposition of the soul as cosmetic beauty stands to the true beauty of the body gained by gymnastic exercise.

Plato has grouped together a number of ideas: the irrational, the pretheoretical or unscientific, the pleasurable, the deceitful, and to this are added all music for the lyre and all sorts of poetry, including tragedy, which "aim at pleasure and gratification of spectators" (502b). Poetry is in effect "a form of rhetoric addressed to a people composed alike of children and women and men, slaves and free," which in appealing so universally also appeals to the lowest level, just as rhetoric, by appealing only to pleasure, treats all citizens like children.

We have already considered later forms of this same idea in al-Farabi's treatment of poetry as the lowest form of logic, which convinces by appealing to *phantasia*, and thus has a practically universal appeal. It would be a simple matter to extend Plato's arguments from poetry to include "phantastic" imitation, as he himself did in the *Sophist*. All of the oppositions we have considered also make a social distinction. At the beginning of the *Metaphysics* (981a31ff.), Aristotle distinguished between artists who know the principles of art, and can teach them, and "men of experience" who simply act out of habit, without knowing why. We think the manual workers "are like certain lifeless things which act indeed, but act without knowing what they do, as fire burns." And to return to Plato's *Gorgias* (512b–e), the pilot plies his craft well, and provides a useful service, but would be disdained by the orator as a mechanic, to whom he would never marry his daughter, and whose daughter he would not consider fit to marry. He would have been the object of such scorn because he was a person of less standing, because his art was manual. Similar ideas linked literature over more than two millennia, and are still current as the expression of deep social attitudes. As one

[14] See P. De Lacy, "Plato and the Method of the Arts," in *The Classical Tradition*, pp. 123–132.

might expect, they had the deepest influence on the theory of art and on the status of those who practiced the arts. The early eleventh century music theorist Guido of Arezzo, looking back to Plato and Aristotle through Boethius and forward to the Renaissance, penned the following jingle: "Musicorum et cantorum/ Magna est distantia./ Isti dicunt, illi sciunt./ Quae componit Musica,/ Nam qui facit, quod non sapit,/ Diffinitur bestia" (Between musicians and singers the distance is great. The latter sing, the former know what composes music. For whoever does what he does not understand is called a beast).[15]

The social distinction between the liberal and mechanical arts embraced a number of other oppositions, rational versus operational, truth versus deception, and reinforced the generalized Platonic prejudice against the "phantastic" arts of painting, sculpture, and poetry, and it may be suggested that it was for this reason that poetry and the arts of imitation hovered at the level of the mechanical arts, to which they were, however, never very clearly fixed.[16] The less than liberal arts, a group defined negatively by what they in common were not, were by no means easily reducible to a single principle.

Mechanics

There was yet another strand of the tradition of the mechanical in classical antiquity, which, although not itself without ambivalence, was on the whole positive. This concerned the actual building of machines. Vitruvius defined the construction of machinery as one of the parts of architecture,[17] and wrote that "all is derived from nature, and is founded on the teaching and instruction of the revolution of the firmaments,"[18] multiplying the useful arts by the force of applied geometry.

[15] Quoted by E. E. Lowinsky, *DHI*, II, p. 313; see *MLA*, p. 555 n. 9.

[16] W. Tatarkiewicz, *DHI*, I, pp. 456–462, stresses that poetry had an ambivalent status as an art and that the arts of painting and sculpture were never included among the mechanical arts in the Middle Ages.

[17] *De architectura* I.III.1.

[18] Ibid. X.I.4; see also A. Poliziano (*Panepistemon, Opera omnia*, ed. I., Maier, Turin, 1970–1, pp. 467–468) discussing the speculative intellect: "mechanica sequitur (ut Heron Pappusque declarant) altera pars rationalis est, quae numerorum, mensurarum, siderum, naturaeque rationibus perficitur; altera chirurgice, cui vel maxime artes illae aeria aedificatoria, materiaria, picturaque adminiculantur." Pappus (*Selections Illustrating the History of Greek Mathematics*, tr. I. Thomas, Cambridge, Mass.–London, 1941, II, pp. 615–621.) identifies mechanics with the movement of weights, links it to philosophy, and divides it into theoretical and manual. The first part includes geometry, arithmetic, astronomy, and physics (the later quadrivium with physics replacing music), the manual part work in metals, architecture, carpentry, painting, and whatever requires skill of hand. The man trained in these sciences and practiced in these arts will be the best inventor of mechanical devices. For most people, experience replaces theory. Mechanics not only moves weights and makes engines, it also creates marvelous automata. The discussion ends with the observation that practical (or "subalternate") geometry is an embellishment of geometry itself, not a diminution of it. Earlier (*Selections*, p. 588) Pappus observes that animals may possess a certain innate *pronoia*, sufficient to their lives and needs. With their "geometrical forethought" bees fashion the hexagonal cells necessary to their orderly lives and to the preservation of the nectar they gather. For more on Pappus and the tradition of the arts, see C. Wilkinson, "Observations on Juan de Herrera's View of Architecture," in *Studies in the History of Art*, XIII, 1982, Washington, D.C., National Gallery of Art, p. 182 n. 26.

The idea that the mechanical arts were, or could be, a kind of "subalternate geometry" was current in the Middle Ages[19] and was clearly set out in al-Farabi's definition of the *scientiae ingeniorum.*[20] Clearly there was a difference to be drawn between those who devised the machines by which great weights were moved and those who put their backs to the task of actually moving them. Still, practical geometry was at two removes from "pure" geometry; it responded to the needs of life, and was consequently pushed toward the status of the merely necessary arts. Plutarch's account of Archimedes is filled with contradictory currents. The greatest engineer of his age, regarded as a man of superhuman intelligence, Archimedes "would not consent to leave behind him any treatises of this subject, but regarding the work of an engineer and every art that ministers to the needs of life as ignoble and vulgar, he devoted his earnest efforts only to those studies the subtlety and charm of which are not affected by the claims of necessity."[21]

In the literature of the West, there is perhaps no idea that more clearly reflects and justifies differences in social classes than the distinction between mental and manual labor, and the history of this distinction is consequently of the greatest social historical interest. We have already encountered such distinctions in several of the texts just examined, and in others the issue is more explicitly raised. Aristotle (*Politics* 1278a1–5) considered whether or not craftsmen (or mechanics, which are necessary to the state) should be full citizens. In aristocracies their citizenship is impossible because "no one can practice virtue who is living the life of a mechanic or laborer." In oligarchies laborers may not be citizens, but mechanics may, since most of them are rich. Craftsmen and laborers are worse members of democracies than are farmers or shepherds, again because "there is no room for moral excellence in any of their employment" (1319a20ff.)

Cicero on the hand

In the exuberant inventory of human powers in the second book of his *De natura deorum,* Cicero praised both reason and sense.[22] The human mind consists of reason, combination, and prudence (*ratio, consilium,* and *prudentia*). Intelligence is the power to define and to infer by syllogisms. The Academics, he says, mistakenly deny the efficacy of the faculties of sense and mind (*sensus et animus*), by means of which we perceive and comprehend external things. The words "perceive" and "comprehend" immediately call to mind Stoic *katalepsis,* and the discussion further suggests the Stoic definition of art as the consequence of many "perceptions

[19] R. Grosseteste, *Commentarius in posteriorum analyticorum libros,* p. 94: "scientie mathematice et etiam mechanice subalternate mathematicis." See Boethius, *Posteriorum analyticorum Aristotelis interpretatio.* MPL, 64, col. 726. This, according to E. Panofsky (*La prospettiva come "forma simbolica" e altri scritti,* ed. G. D. Neri, Milan, 1966, p. 70 n. 2), was the point at which Greek *optike* became *perspectiva.*

[20] See n. 53, below.

[21] Plutarch, *Lives, Marcellus,* XVII, 3–4 (tr. B. Perrin, V, pp. 480–481).

[22] 2.147ff.

of the mind." And, he continues, art is not simply accumulated experience but is rather the result of a process, the "collation and comparison among themselves" of things perceived and comprehended. This is cogitation, which is clearly distinguished from rational inference, and is based on adequate sensory apprehension and the imaginative manipulation of these apprehensions. All the commodities of life follow from the application of the hand of the craftsman (*opifex*) to that which is invented by mind and perceived by sense. It is the hand that creates human culture. "By the works of man, that is, by the hands," we have not only shelter, clothing, and protection but also cities, fortifications, houses and temples. The hand gathers and stores food, hunts, breeds, and domesticates animals; by means of hands we mine the earth, cut forests, control the seas, and in general turn the world to our purposes, "confining rivers and straightening or diverting their courses . . . by means of our hands we try to effect as it were another nature."

The hand that navigates the seas does so with the help of the knowledge (*scientia*) of navigation. The workings of the hand are thus inextricably allied with *ratio,* the crowning human power, which has "penetrated even to the sky." Men alone may calculate times, seasons, and the movements of the stars. Again, the end of the *Timaeus* rings out in the claim that by knowledge of the heavens we know the gods, thus piety and virtue, by which we may lead a divine life, lacking only immortality to be like that of a god.

Cicero divided the arts into two categories, those invented out of necessity – building, agriculture, clothing, metalwork, those, in short, we have just considered – and those invented for pleasure (*oblectamentum*).[23] The pleasure in question is the pleasure of sense, to which the hand can also respond. Thus the sensitivity of the human eye to proper differences in color, shape, beauty, and arrangement in painting and sculpture is matched by the ability of dextrous fingers to paint, model, and carve, and the discriminating judgment of the ear is matched by the ability of the motions of the fingers of the hand to draw forth the notes of the lyre and flute. Smell, taste, and touch are also *magna iudicia,* and many arts have been devised to seize and fulfill these senses, more arts, in fact, than may be desirable. The list ends on a censorious note, with perfume, cooking, and the alluring adornment of the body.[24]

Cicero stated similar ideas about human art in general in the *De finibus,* but in the same work developed a hierarchy of productive activities, a hierarchy at base social. Those who do manual labor for wages (opposed to those who exercise artistic skill) are like slaves. Large-scale trade is more worthy of a gentlemen, but the actual selling of goods is not, because it can only be accomplished by

[23] Lucretius, *De rerum natura* V.1448–57, wrote that after navigation and agriculture, fortifications, laws, arms, roads, and clothing, "the prizes of life, its deepest delights also, poetry, and pictures and sculpture, these slowly, step by step, were taught by practice and the experience of man's mind as it progressed." See Lovejoy and Boas, *Primitivism*, p. 236; and n. 7, above.

[24] 2, 145; 2, 150; Vitruvius (II,I,2) speaks of the agility of human fingers together with uprightness, as does Augustine (*De civitate dei* XXII. 24).

lying. More emphatically than in the *De natura deorum* he rejects the practice of arts that appeal to sense (butchers, cooks, perfumers, dancers) as least honorable. As Aristotle had done, he dismisses craftsmen as vulgar, "for no workshop can have anything liberal about it." Professions that demand a higher degree of intelligence or which are of public benefit, such as medicine, architecture, and teaching, are higher. Agriculture is worthy of a free man.[25]

Cicero's praise of universal art stands in strong opposition to his evident distaste for the "servile" arts, a distaste no doubt arising from immediate social circumstances, in which slaves in fact did manual labor, and in which all occupations consequently found their place on a scale between the extremes of bondage and freedom. Still, it would be mistaken simply to see this contradiction as a record of personal hypocrisy on Cicero's part. His utterances had two different histories, and two different relations to history. There are many records of the lowly status of the manual arts relative to the liberal or intellectual arts; but at the same time the praise of the hand and the praise of the collective work of human culture for which the hand uniquely stood was always potentially the justification for another social order.[26]

Appearance of the term "mechanical arts"

Although classical writers often used the terms "mechanic" and "mechanical," the term "mechanical arts" seems first to have been used (or recorded) around the middle of the ninth century by John Scottus Erigena in his gloss on the *De nuptiis philologiae et mercurii* of Martianus Capella.[27] Arts, he writes, are called "perceived" (*perceptae*) because they are "judged by perceptions of the common mind." In the following explanation he makes a fundamental change in the Stoic notion of *katalepsis* (or *perceptio*). When we learn the liberal arts, the soul becomes aware of its own nature, and this awareness is "perception." Perception is thus entirely inward, a process by which the innate structure of the soul becomes evident to the soul itself. In this way the liberal arts are opposed to the mechanical arts, which "are not in the mind naturally, but arise by a certain human excogitation" (*quadam excogitatione humana*). The liberal arts and mechanical arts are thus opposed as inner and outer, and for our purposes it is crucial that inwardness and outwardness are associated with higher and lower faculties, the lower of which is called *excogitatio*. The mechanical arts deal with the world of sense and subjection to circumstance, the liberal arts deal with the world of mind and the autonomous rational soul.

Le Goff's judgment that for Erigena the mechanical arts had achieved equal

[25] I.xlii; II.xxiv.87–xxv.89.

[26] This argument is made at greater length by B. Bilinski, "Elogio della mano e la concezione ciceroniana della società," *Atti del I Congresso Internazionale di studi ciceroniani*, Rome, 1961, pp. 195–212.

[27] *Iohannis Scotti Annotationes in Marcianum*, ed. C. E. Lutz, Cambridge, Mass., 1939, p. 86. See J. Le Goff, *Time, Work and Culture in the Middle Ages*, Chicago, 1980, p. 85.

footing with the liberal arts seems overly optimistic, because intelligence was higher than cogitation. At the same time, it is certainly true that the future development of the mechanical arts was very much shaped by the antithetical scheme in which they had been set, and the implications of this scheme were drawn by later medieval writers, as we shall see. The canonical definition of the seven liberal arts provided the model for the similar definition of the lower mechanical arts, drawing the whole range of human trades and occupations, mentioned here and there by classical writers as circumstances demanded, into a single compact system. It implied parallel structure, that, for example, the mechanical arts should be divided in a way corresponding to the trivium and quadrivium. The numerological parallel between the liberal and mechanical arts implied a shared common principle, which in its turn pressed for definition. Common participation in the number seven implied relationship to the other systems of seven so common in medieval thought, to the seven gifts of the holy spirit or to the seven virtues. Such parallels were in fact drawn, and clearly contributed significantly to the definition and influence of the mechanical arts.

Augustine on the arts

Before considering the mechanical arts in the later Middle Ages, however, it is necessary to return to Saint Augustine, who, standing half in antiquity and half in the new Christian era, wrote often about the arts in ways that deeply shaped the thoughts of writers in all the centuries with which we are concerned.

Near the end of the *City of God,* Augustine listed the good things that God has given mankind "even in this life liable to damnation."[28] These blessings are, principally, procreation, the arts, and the beauty of the human body and the world. In addition to the arts of living well according to the virtues, by the grace of God, arts have been invented and exercised by human *ingenium.* These arts are partly necessary and partly for pleasure (*partim necessariae partim voluptariae*). Augustine repeats the idea that the human arts are wonderful in themselves even if they are not subject to divine law. "The excellent power of the mind and reason" (*vis mentis atque rationis*) may seek the superfluous, even "the dangerous and the harmful," and yet it bears witness to the great goodness of nature from which it derives the power to invent, to learn, and to work (*invenire vel discere vel exercere*).

There follows a catalogue of the works of "marvelous, stupendous human industry," the vestments and buildings, the progress of agriculture and navigation, the variously imagined vases, statues, and paintings, the incredible marvels of the theater, the capturing and killing of wild animals. Taking up a theme we have encountered earlier, Augustine stresses the moral ambivalence of human art. For purposes of war men devise all kinds of poisons, weapons, and machines of war, and yet they have also invented drugs and remedies in order to bring

[28] *De civitate dei* XXII.24.

health and long life. Cooking was invented to delight taste, and a great number of signs – words and letters – have been invented for the indication and demonstration of thoughts (*cogitationes*). Eloquence gives delight to the mind, as does poetry, and music and musical instruments soothe the ears. The catalogue ends with the skills of measuring and reckoning, and the calculation of time by the movements in the heavens. Moving to a higher but still false level, Augustine also praises the *ingenia* of the philosophers, who defend falsehoods. We are, Augustine concludes, saved from such errors ourselves by the truths of faith, which, it may be supposed, heal the fatal moral ambivalence of the arts in general by subjecting them to higher truth and purpose. In a similar way, Augustine ends by arguing that if we have all these blessings in this life, how much greater must our blessedness be imagined to be in the life to come.

One of the broadest principles underlying the medieval discussion of the mechanical arts was Augustine's distinction between the "outer and the inner man," and in general a remarkably positive attitude toward the "outer man" characterizes this discussion. In Book XII of the *De trinitate,* Augustine set out to define the boundary line between the inner and outer man. The outer man is not only the body, but also the life force of the body, the senses, memory and the ability to recall things sensed and remembered. All of this is shared with beasts, and we are reminded of our more than bestial nature by our uprightness, which allows us to look to the highest corporeal things just as we must look to the most elevated spiritual things, "not raised up by pride, but by the dutifulness of righteousness."[29]

Although he insisted upon the unity of the soul, Augustine divided reason into higher and lower, more or less corresponding to the speculative and practical intellects. The fulfillment of the higher was wisdom and its end was contemplation; the fulfillment of the lower was knowledge and its end was action.[30] The reason of knowledge concerns the temporal, not the eternal, and is immediate to sense and fantasy, and stands on a cusp between "fornication" and virtue, depending upon whether it is controlled by lower sense or higher reason. When it does not love wisdom, it may "lust after knowledge by experience with things temporal and mutable."[31] Because "the reason of knowledge has appetite very near to it: seeing that what is called the science or knowledge of actions reasons concerning the bodily things which are perceived by the bodily sense."[32]

Augustine argued that Adam and Eve cannot simply be understood as mind and body, as some had argued before him, because, since the animals share sense with man and it was still necessary to create woman, she must be higher than the animals. Bodily senses should rather be identified with the serpent, the most subtle of beasts. Augustine preferred to identify Eve with the senses to which

[29] Augustine *De trinitate.XII.*
[30] Ibid. XIV.
[31] Ibid. XIV.
[32] Ibid. XII.

Saint Paul referred (Hebrews 5:14)[33] when he wrote of "those who by reason of use have their senses exercised to discern both good and evil." These "senses" belong to the rational nature and are related to understanding; they are to be distinguished from the five senses by means of which corporeal species and motion are perceived, senses that are shared with beasts.[34] "Whatever we do prudently, boldly, temperately, and justly belongs to that knowledge or discipline wherewith our action is conversant in avoiding evil and desiring good; and so also, whatsoever we gather by the knowledge that comes from inquiry, in the way of examples either to be guarded against or to be imitated, and in the way of necessary proofs respecting any subject, accommodated to our use."[35]

Augustine has translated the story of the creation and fall of man into terms of a now familiar psychology. Adam, the rational soul, capable of wisdom, is the image of God; Adam's partner is, so to speak, the image of Adam, and lower; as the image of the image of God, however, she still participates in reason, and, like Adam, is higher than the animals. The serpent is sense, or the wisest kind of sense, human sense. The ideal relation is "a certain rational wedlock."[36] Eve, however, is of special interest for our purposes. Her domain is that of inner sense, of particular intellect, the level of natural reason, to which the invention and practice of the arts also belong. She ministers to the outer man, but is one with the inner man. Eve is also clearly associated with fantasy and, to review an earlier discussion, with *spiritus*. The *acies animi* may see the incorporeal world of the intellect, but only briefly and with difficulty. Through these glimpses "there comes to be a transitory thought of a thing not transitory." The eternal comes to be a part of the inner experience of the individual, and as it does so, it becomes a mental image. "For the thought of man does not so abide in that incorporeal and unchangeable reason of a square body, as that reason abides: if, to be sure, it could attain to it at all without the phantasy of local space." That is, we may "see" the incorporeal truth to which reason has access, but when we do so, we must almost certainly imagine it.[37]

As might be expected, the writings of Saint Augustine exerted the strongest pull on late medieval writers on the human soul immediately before the reintroduction and triumph of the more "scientific" psychology of Aristotle. When William of St. Thierry wrote on the arts in his arguments on the human soul,[38] he drew on the *De hominis opificio* of Gregory of Nyssa, who lamented the miserable state of "exterior man," born naked and unprotected, but by this very circumstance called upon to exercise reason in inventing arts and turning nature to his pur-

[33] Ibid.
[34] Ibid. XIII.
[35] Ibid. XIV.
[36] Ibid. XII.
[37] Ibid. XIV.
[38] *De natura corporis et animae* II.6–7; MPL, 180, col. 708–726. See *Three Treatises on Man: A Cistercian Anthropology*, ed. B. McGinn, Kalamazoo, Mich., 1977, p. 235.

poses.[39] He also drew upon the *De quantitate animae* of Augustine. Augustine distinguished between reason and reasoning (*ratio* and *ratiocinatio*).[40] We always have reason, but we are not always reasoning, that is, we are not always pursuing arguments; otherwise all thinking would be the same kind of seeking. He uses the example of vision. *Ratio* is a certain view (*aspectus*) of the mind, *ratiocinatio* is an investigation (*inquisitio*), a movement over the things seen. The distinction is very much like Alhazen's distinction between what was translated as *aspectus* and *intuitio,* and it may be suggested that both in fact grew from the same Stoic root. Investigation yields real seeing and *scientia:* When the mind does not see, but only apprehends the *aspectus,* the result is not knowing and ignorance. "For not everyone who looks [*aspicit*] sees [*videt*] with these corporeal eyes . . . *aspectus* is one thing, *visio* another . . . one we call *ratio* and *scientia;* we have *aspectus* for the sake of *visio,* and not *vice versa.*"

Augustine is arguing to distinguish human and animal knowledge. Ulysses's dog remembered him when he returned because of a certain *vis sentiendi,* augmented by habit (*consuetudo*), which in animals is very strong. The human mind, on the other hand, has reason and knowledge (*ratio and scientia*), which surpass sense and dispose us to higher inner pleasures. Such arguments notwithstanding, it must not be imagined that we have passed safely over to the realm of the intelligible. For Augustine *ratio* is lower than the exercise of reason, and is in fact very nearly identical with corporeal vision, just as according to an Augustinian scheme we considered earlier, sight as the highest of the corporeal senses was allied with *spiritus. Ratio* is thus something like the natural human mind, and this must be remembered when we read Augustine's account of the human arts in the *De quantitate animae.*[41] This account appears in the midst of a discussion of the "seven degrees of the soul." The first three of these degrees (*animatio, sensus,* and *ars*) concerned the body (they were *de corpore, per corpus,* and *circa corpus* respectively) as opposed to the soul itself, and in these first three degrees the soul acted beautifully by another (*pulchre de alio*), beautifully through another (*pulchre per aliud*), and beautifully about another (*pulchre circa aliud*) in a ladder of acts that led to *contemplatio,* in which the soul was "beautifully with the beautiful," with God. In this scheme art falls on the side of the body; there is no mean between soul and body, and the "third degree of the soul's power" is identified with *memoria.* This is proper to man and is to be distinguished from the habit of the usual (*consuetudo molitarum*), which is the "sense memory" of animals.

[39] Gregory of Nyssa, *De hominis opificio,* MPG, 44, col. 123–256; and MPL, 67, col. 347–408. This idea is much older. Plato, *Protagoras* 321d, states that Prometheus gave the first men fire and the arts in order to make up for their physical inferiority; see also Aristotle, *De partibus animalium* 687a, on the hand as the compensatory organ. The phrase *natura non mater, sed noverca est* (nature is not a mother, but a stepmother) to man is attributed to Cicero by Augustine. See Lovejoy and Boas, *Primitivism,* p. 397. The question is reviewed and attributed to *i Filosofi gentili* by F. Zuccaro, *Scritti,* pp. 47.

[40] *De quantitate animae,* xxvi.

[41] Ibid., xxxiii.

This human memory is called "attention" (*animadversio*), and is associated with the "signs"[42] of innumerable things agreeable and retained." Augustine means to include all human institutions, which are necessary to human needs and in their own way beautiful, but conventional, without the absoluteness of the soul itself, which come under the governance of God's law. He praises these institutions,

> the many arts of skilled craftsmen, the tilling of the soil, the construction of cities, the multiform miracles of various buildings and great works; the invention of so many signs, in letters, in words, in sounds, in painting and sculpture; the languages of so many people, so many customs; so many new things; so many things restored; such a number of books and similar monuments for the preservation of memory; so much care for posterity; the orders of duties, powers, honors and dignities, either in families, or in war and peace in the state, or in sacred or profane ceremony; in the power of reasoning and imagining [*ratiocinandi et excogitandi*]; in rivers of eloquence, the variety of poetry; the multiform simulations for the purpose of playing and jesting, the skills of music, the subtlety of measurements, the discipline of numbers, the interpretation of past and future from the present.

"All of this," he concludes, "is great and entirely human." His *memoria* is collective human memory, but divided by human cultural and historical differences, the incomprehensibility of languages to those who do not speak them, the relativity of mores, the absolute particularity of the histories of peoples. Augustine ends his discussion with the statement that this "abundance" is "common" in part to minds learned and unlearned, good and bad. By this he means, as the beginning of the following section on the fourth degree of the soul makes evident, that everyone participates in *memoria* by participating in human institutions, which as a social animal one must; but true goodness and praiseworthiness are not to be found in them. One escapes the relativity of human institutions in the same way that one begins the ascent to God, by turning inward to one's own soul.

To return to William of St. Thierry, he continued the argument of Gregory of Nyssa that the soul is the true image of God, which uses the body for its purposes. Following the Augustinian Claudius Mamertus,[43] he wrote that the soul has animal senses and spiritual ones. Sensation is the activity of the incorporeal upon the corporeal, and the soul in sensation is as seeing is to the eye. "The interior sight of the soul is brightened by prudence, darkened by folly; its hearing is offended by fallacy, soothed by truth. . . . The soul is all eye, because it sees all, and sees the whole that it looks at. But the exterior man neither sees entirely, because only the eye sees, nor does he see all that he sees, because he does not see everything of any body that he sees."[44] The inner eye is a principle of unity. It was in the context of the idea of the soul as an image of God that William

[42] Augustine's frequent references to signs both here and in the *De doctrina christiana* seem to be shaped by the Stoic and Skeptic discussion of signs, for an introduction to which, see P. De Lacy, "Skepticism in Antiquity," *DHI*, IV, pp. 236–237.

[43] Claudianus Mamertus, *Opera*, ed. A. Engelbrecht, 1885, I, XVI–XVII, p. 62.

[44] *De natura corporis et animae* II.9; MPL, 180, col. 719. See *Three Treatises*, ed. McGinn, p. 140.

placed Augustine's chapter on the seven grades of the ascent of the soul to God. Although he may have changed the words of either author little in combining them, their mere juxtaposition was significant. The argument that the arts arose both from the curse of the fall and from the blessing of reason was to have many later echoes. And although Augustine associated the arts with the body and with natural reason, they were in this context also associated with the activity of the soul, of the inner man, and, if properly understood, were the means by which the soul could rise to the very font of the beautiful.

Another early twelfth century writer, Hugh of St. Victor, drew upon Augustine's *De doctrina christiana* when he wrote his long-influential *Didascalicon.* In this instance Augustine argued that all truth is God's and that knowledge of the arts should be pursued in a way suitable to the purposes of Christian understanding.[45] He divided the arts of the pagans into those instituted by men, and those "firmly established or divinely ordained." As might be expected, he rejected all superstition, idolatry, and divination. Purely human institutions, he argued, are based on covenant and convention, and he gives the example of a mime who can only be understood by someone who already knows the significance of the gestures, or who has them explained to him. "It is true that everyone seeks a certain verisimilitude in making signs, so that these signs, in so far as is possible, may resemble the things that they signify. But since one thing may resemble another in a great variety of ways, signs are not valid among men, except by common consent." Such conventionality, again, Augustine considers characteristic of human institutions.

Of the arts instituted among men, painting and sculpture "simulate," so that their products, especially when they are made by skilled artists, are recognized by everyone. They possess what Augustine clearly regarded as an inconsequential truthfulness, and are to be ranked among the "superfluous" institutions, grouped together with poetry, "the thousands of imagined fables and falsehoods by whose lies men are delighted." These falsehoods reveal the faultiness of both human nature and purely human institutions. Useful, necessary, and acceptable human institutions "established by men with men include whatever they have agreed upon concerning differences of dress and the adornment of the person useful for distinguishing sex or rank, and kinds of signs without which human society could not or could not easily function, including weights and measures, differences of value and impression in coinage appropriate to specific states and peoples." We know that these are human institutions because they vary from people to people. To complete the list of the arts that would become the arts of design, architecture is included under carpentry. Augustine also distinguished between an art such as pottery, the product of which is the result of the labor of the artificer, arts that assist the work of God (medicine, agriculture, and navigation),

[45] II.xviiff. (*De doctrina christiana*, ed. W. M. Green, *Corpus Scriptorum Ecclesiasticorum Latinorum*, vol. 80, 1963; see *On Christian Doctrine*, tr. D. W. Robertson, Jr., New York, 1958.

and arts whose whole effect is in the act of being done, as dancing, running, and wrestling. All of these arts are impossible without linking past experience to future results.

Augustine thus associated the arts of the corporeal senses with the relativity and potential deceitfulness of purely human institutions, juxtaposing them to the higher and more certain sciences of disputation and number.

Hugh of St. Victor

Although he borrowed Augustine's arguments and their substance, Hugh of St. Victor considerably transformed them. He observed the distinction between human institutions and those rooted in the certainty of logic and mathematics, but he also bracketed all human enterprises together in a way very different from Augustine's. He divided *sapientia* into *intelligentia* and *scientia,* arguing that man is like God in the exercise of *intelligentia,* which embraces the theoretical and the practical, the pursuit of truth and morality respectively. *Scientia,* on the other hand, pursues purely human ends, trying to restore the prelapsarian human state; it has some need of "counsel" (*quodem consilio indiget*). But whatever their relation to *intelligentia,* Augustine's human arts, with their relative, conventional knowledge, are now a part of human wisdom. Hugh lists the seven mechanical arts (corresponding to the sum of the *trivium* and the *quadrivium*) as *lanificium, armatura, navigatio, agricultura, venatio, medicina, theatrica.*[46]

[46] Hugh of St. Victor, *Didascalicon. De studio legendi. A Critical Text,* ed. C. H. Buttimer, Washington, D.C., 1939, pp. 38–39; and *The Didascalicon of Hugh of St. Victor: A Medieval Guide to the Arts,* tr. J. Taylor, New York, 1961, p. 75. Hugh declares the mechanical arts to be a similitude of the *trivium* and *quadrivium,* because the *trivium* is concerned with words, which are extrinsic, and the *quadrivium* with intelligible things, which are intrinsic. They are the seven handmaidens that Mercury received in dowry from Philology, "for every human activity is servant to eloquence and wed to wisdom." This recalls the formula *vir bonus peritus dicendi,* and in fact Hugh makes rhetoric the pattern of the mechanical arts, citing Cicero *De inventione* I.iv.5: "By it is life made safe, by it fit, by it noble, and by it pleasurable; for from it the commonwealth receives abundant benefits, provided that wisdom [*sapientia*] which regulates all things, keeps it company. To those who have acquired it flow praise, honor, dignity; from eloquence, to the friends of those skilled in it, comes dependable and sure protection." See M. B. Becker, *Medieval Italy: Constraints and Creativity,* Bloomington, Ind., 1981, p. 65, for the extension by Bolognese writers of the Ciceronian ideal of the connection of rhetoric and civic virtue to all the arts, liberal and mechanical. Hugh's list was followed by many later writers. Saint Antoninus (*Summa theologica,* tit. I, cap. III; ed. cit. col. 34–35) offers a summary of this tradition. He follows Hugh's general scheme, placing the mechanical arts after the practical (defined as ethics, economics, and politics), in the position of the productive, and lists the same seven arts, but gives Vincent of Beauvais as his source. See Vincent of Beauvais, *Speculum doctrinale,* XI (in *Speculum quadruplex*). This long chapter begins with the quotation of Augustine *De civitate dei* XXII.24 (see n. 28, above) and cites Hugh of St. Victor. Architecture is discussed using the definitions of Vitruvius, and painting is discussed as an ornament of architecture, following the definition of Isidore of Seville (*Etymologiae* 19.16). On this text, see *MLA,* pp. 48–49, with notes. Federico Zuccaro, (*Scritti,* p. 197), citing "Versorio nel principio della logica," listed seven arts that are a close variation on Hugh of St. Victor, with the exception that *armatura* has split into architecture (defined as the actual work of building) and *militia. Theatrica* is omitted.

Hugh apparently conflated the Aristotelian scheme according to which the sciences were divided into theoretical, practical, and productive, with the implication of arguments, perhaps derived at some remove from the first book of the *Metaphysics,* according to which any art may be considered as either theory or practice. Replacing "productive" with "mechanical," this conflation yielded a scheme of theoretical, practical, and mechanical, to which he added logical. Logic, he explained, was invented last; the arts were use before they were theory, which is to say that they arose from need and experience. When they became theory they also became philosophy, part of the whole framework of human wisdom. As an example, Hugh argues that, understood in its teachable principles, agriculture (one of the mechanical arts) is the concern of the philosopher; understood as an activity, it is the concern of the farmer.[47] It should be noted, of course, that all wisdom is not equal, and Hugh holds to the traditional pattern when, a few lines earlier, he distinguishes between that so-called wisdom, which is developed with tools, like building and farming and other activities, and true wisdom, which is the "one primeval *ratio* of things." In the course of his arguments Hugh traced the word "mechanical" to *moechus,* which he says means "adulterer," and this example is often cited as evidence of the lowly status of the mechanical arts in the Middle Ages. It will repay us to examine this etymology a little more closely, however, because it is ambiguous in much the same way that the mechanical arts are ambiguous as wisdom arising from man's fallen state. As his editor points out, Hugh took his etymology from the late Carolingian Martin of Laon, who wrote as follows: " 'Moechus' means adulterer, a man who secretly pollutes the marriage bed of another. From 'moechus' we call "mechanical art" any object which is clever and most delicate and which, in its making or operation, is beyond detection, so that beholders find their power of vision stolen from them when they cannot penetrate the ingenuity of the thing."[48] The adulterer, then, is not so much simply a sinner as a seducer and a trickster; and his sleight-of-hand fools sight and induces wonder. Hugh's etymology is thus ambivalent; its connotations are perhaps less than lofty, but at the same time he clearly refers to the Daedalan powers of art, which according to Aristotle surpass common

[47] *De studio legendi,* p. 11.

[48] *The Didascalicon,* p. 191. Panofsky, *Idea,* p. 197, notes the connection between this etymology and the association of what we would regard as naturalism – and artistic skill and ingenuity generally – with deception. No one is more important for the definition of this attitude than Augustine. See again the very important text in his *Soliloquies* II.6ff., which, although it condemns illusion, also thoughtfully defines it, and firmly identifies painting with mirror likeness. See also his *Confessions* X.34, cited by Panofsky, *Idea,* p. 35. Here the "innummerable variety" of the arts (including the making of clothing, shoes, and vessels as well as "painting and diverse images") is again stressed, although it is warned that such variety exceeds both need and moderation. It is described as an enticement (*inlecebra*). This is not simply a moralizing rejection of the arts, however, because what their immoderate exercise and enjoyment entices us away from is the realization that men are themselves made and "that the beauty passed through souls into artful hands comes from that beauty which is above souls." Hugh (as at n. 46, above) writes that the mechanical arts are called *adulterinae* because "they act toward the work of the craftsman, and because forms are taken from nature."

sense, induce wonder, and distinguish inventors from other people. It may even be remembered that when Aristotle illustrates the wonder at the root of all philosophy, he uses the example not only of the solstices and the incommensurability of the diagonal and side of a square, but also of automatons the workings of which we cannot understand.[49]

The first meaning of *mechanikos* is inventive, ingenious, and clever, and writing at the close of the sixteenth century, Romano Alberti, beginning an argument designed to distinguish painting as a liberal art once and for all, gives an etymology of the word still strikingly like that given by Hugh of St. Victor.[50] *Mechanikos,* he says, is from a word meaning machination, new discovery, or effort (*sforzo*), and "so signifies the artisan that finds such things with his *ingegno,* setting them in execution with facility, for which the *acutissimo* Archimedes is praised. In Plutarch and other authors one reads that, with one hand, lightly moving the handle of a certain machine, he drew to himself a beached ship as easily as if it ran through the waves." Such a feat obviously induces wonder, since it hides the relation between cause and effect. It is significant, of course, that little labor was involved, because, he argues later (citing Xenophon and probably ultimately Aristotle *Politics* 1337b5–15), physical labor debilitates both body and mind.[51] Archimedes is cited as someone who made the machines necessary to all the sciences, from philosophy to theology, which must be written down with pens,

[49] *Metaphysics* 983a. This definition is not far from that in the pseudo-Aristotelian *Mechanics* 847a: "Our wonder is excited, firstly by phenomena which occur first in accordance with nature but of which we do not know the cause, and secondly, by those which are produced by art despite nature for the benefit of mankind. Nature often operates contrary to human expediency, for she always follows the same course without deviation, whereas human expediency is always changing. When, therefore, we have to do with something contrary to nature, the difficulty of it causes us perplexity and art has to be called to our aid. The kind of art which helps us in such perplexities we call mechanical skill." Augustine (*De civitate dei* XXI.6) describes the marvels of *mechanemata* made by human art that were thought to be divine by the unknowing. Such artifice is immediately compared to sorcerers and enchanters and to the more marvelous powers of God, who made the materials with which craftsman work and granted them their *ingenium.* On mechanics and magic in the Renaissance, See F. A. Yates, "The Hermetic Tradition in Renaissance Science," in *Art, Science, and History in the Renaissance,* ed. C. Singleton, Baltimore, 1967, pp. 255–274.

In Cesariano's translation and commentary on Vitruvius (f. 162v), mechanics is praised as both grounded in the divine fabric of the world and as of great use to mankind. *Machina,* Cesariano says, is from a Greek word "meaning to discover by cogitation; because it is necessary that the machine first be fabricated in the mind with natural and infallible reason" before it is realized. His examples of such ratiocination include Archytas of Tarentum, who built a wooden bird that flew for a long distance, and a modern example from Petrarch of someone who had mastered all the manual skills of human life and was therefore self-sufficient. As an example of the construction of a machine he cites that great paradigm of deception, the Trojan horse as described by Virgil (*Aeneid* II.46, 151, 237). Cesariano thus combines both the rational, subalternate mathematical, and the inventive aspects of the meaning of the mechanical. See A. C. Crombie, "Science and the Arts in the Renaissance: The Search for Truth and Certainty, Old and New," in *Science and the Arts in the Renaissance,* ed. J. W. Shirley and F. D. Hoeniger, Washington, 1985, p. 19. The modern praise of Archimedes as a universal genius begins with Petrarch, using classical sources. See M. Clagett, *Archimedes in the Middle Ages,* III,4, Philadelphia, 1978, pp. 1329–1341. Archimedes is perhaps a more important precedent for the Renaissance notion of the artist than has been recognized.

[50] BT, III, p. 199.

[51] Ibid., p. 207.

to mathematics, and astronomy, which have need of compasses and astrolabes, to painting, which has need of brushes. In any case, Alberti imagines the mechanical arts to have declined since the days of Archimedes, so that the use of the word "mechanical" has become pejorative. By degrees mechanics – that is the example he uses – became separated from geometry (a liberal art), "its foundation and as it were its soul, and was reduced to manual practice, and scorned; whence the mercenary and lowly arts were called "mechanical" as a term of abuse," and so in the commentators on Roman law we read: "*mechanica ars est adulterina sive non liberalis, ut pelliypariorum, fabrorum et similium,*" which Alberti translates as follows: "mechanical art is not legitimate, or not liberal, as furriers, smiths, etc."[52] The Latin "adulterina," it may be noted, means "adulterous," but metaphorically means counterfeit or forged. Thus, cleverness was always similarly linked with deceit, but by the same token, deception was always associated with cleverness.

Alberti imagined the golden age of the mechanical arts as one in which they were most mental and nearest to geometry. But he also said that new inventions were found by *ingegno.* Mechanics as the making of machines was applied mathematics, and already for al-Farabi engineering was the *scientia ingeniorum,* associated with Aristotle's lower mathematics and with the kind of inference that "hits upon middle terms instantaneously."[53]

Hugh's arguments were buttressed by a psychology taken *verbatim* from Boethius.[54] He divided the human soul in general into three parts, corresponding to the vegetative, sensitive, and rational. The first part is a principle of life and

[52] Ibid., p. 199. The medieval *glossator* Alberti quotes gives a definition substantially that of Hugh of St. Victor, which was thus carried along with at least some of the authority of ancient Roman law.

[53] Al-Farabi (*Catalogo,* cap. III, ed. cit., p. 97–105) divided what he called *scientia doctrinalis* into arithmetic, geometry, optics (*scientia de aspectibus*), astronomy (*scientia stellarum*), music, *scientia ponderibus,* and *scientia de ingeniis.* This might seem to be a quadrivium with additions, but such a reading is complicated by the fact that optics, astronomy, and harmonics are *scientiae mediae,* or lower mathematics, according to Aristotle (*Physics* 194a); that is, they are sciences that treat real quantities (e.g., optical rays rather than pure lines) by mathematical argumentation. Throughout this exposition runs the opposition of theory and practice; there is a theoretical arithmetic and a practical one (that used in commerce, for example), and the scheme descends from geometry and arithmetic through the *scientiae mediae,* to the *scientiae ponderibus* and *de ingeniis,* which are truly "applied mathematics," mathematics used for the solution of practical "engineering problems," solutions that result in the actual movement and transformation of matter. The science of weights has to do with the determination of weights and their movement. "Ingenious sciences" teach methods of contriving (*excogitandi*) and inventing (*adinveniendi*) mathematical solutions to practical problems, and literally make use of all the other mathematical sciences. The arithmetic used is algebra, anc' geometry is used to measure real bodies in making musical and optical instruments. Earlier (p. 98), al-Farabi defined "active" geometry as that applied to surveying or used by artisans. The last "sweat" in the pursuit of their "mechanical" labors; the carpenter works in wood, the smith in iron, the mason in mortar and stone: "and so every craftsman of the mechanical arts according to active geometry." The arts of surveying, building, masonry, and carpentry are related to civil arts. Al-Farabi's text was repeated by Vincent of Beauvais, *Speculum doctrinale,* XVI, 53–55 (col. 1534–1535).

[54] *De studio legendi,* p. 7; *The Didascalicon,* pp. 49–50; see R. P. McKeon, ed., *Selections from Medieval Philosophers,* I, Chicago, 1929, pp. 70–73; and Boethius, *In Isagogen Porphyrii commenta,* II.I.1 (ed. S. Brandt, Leipzig, 1906, pp. 135–138).

growth, the second provides the judgment of sense (*iudicium sentiendi*), and the third concerns mind and reason. Animals share sensation with us, and have memory, but their imaginations are confused and unclear; they cannot join things together (or really distinguish them), they have no reminiscence and no knowledge of the future. Elsewhere, Hugh lists a number of arts, at the threshhold of rationality in sense, which are also made up of "confused" presentations. These are "all the songs of the poets, tragedies, comedies, satires," which serve the useful purpose of preparing the way for philosophy.[55] Hugh included theater among the mechanical arts as an art concerned with inner nourishment, and it may be suggested that in this case he meant spiritual nourishment, that the fiction of the play led by "confused" or sensate means to higher understanding, to the instruction and enlightenment of the faithful.[56]

In contrast to the confused sensations of animals Hugh set the third power of the soul, which is, of course, uniquely human. The definition of this power (still from Boethius) corresponds to Hugh's *ratio in imaginationem*, as opposed to *ratio pura supra imaginationem*, and corresponds closely to what later writers would call the *vis cogitativa*. This power "exercises itself in the most unfaltering grasp of things present, or in the understanding of things absent, or in the investigation of things unknown. It not only seizes sense and imaginations which are perfect and not disorganized, but also, by a full act of intelligence, it explains and confirms what imagination has suggested."[57] Such clear apprehension permits naming and the communication of experience. Thus *usus* may become theory.

[55] *De studio legendi*, p. 54; *The Didascalicon*, p. 88. "aliquando tamen quaedam ab artibus discerpta sparsim et confuse attingunt, vel si simplex narratio est, viam ad philosophiam praeparant. huiusmodi sunt omnia poetarum carmina, ut sunt tragoediae, comoediae, satirae, heroica quoque et lyrica, et iambica;" he compares such things to the writings of so-called philosophers who draw easy matters out into long, obscure discourses and, lumping disparate things together, make "one painting from many colors and forms."

[56] See *The Didascalicon*, p. 205 n. 68, where it is explained that *theatrica* pertains to internal things because "two things are vitally necessary to man . . . movement to keep the mind from languishing, joy to keep the body from exhaustion by too much work. So, plays and diversions were established."

[57] *De studio legendi*, p. 9. "vel in rerum praesentium firmissima conclusione, vel in absentium intelligentia, vel in ignorarum inquestione versatur. non solum sensus imaginationesque perfectas et non inconditas capit, sed etiam pleno actu intelligentiae, quod imaginatio suggessit, explicat atque confirmat." See *The Didascalicon*, p. 182 n. 23; for *sensus*, *imaginatio*, *affectio imaginaria*, *ratio in imaginationem agens*, and *ratio pura supra imaginationem*, see Hugh's *De unione corporis et spiritus*, MPL, 177, esp. 288D–289A. Hugh defines *imaginatio* as a similitude of sense impressed in the *cellam phantasticam;* in brute animals *imaginatio* does not transcend this, but in the rational soul it excites "discretion." *Imaginatio* is spiritual, midway between body and soul. "Rational corporeal substance" is a kind of light, and *imaginatio*, insofar as it is an image of body, is shadow; there are two grades of *imaginatio*, *affectio imaginaria*, and *ratio in imaginationem agens*, then *ratio pura supra imaginationem*. See also *The Didascalicon*, p. 190 n. 57; and p. 201 n. 37; and G. B. Ladner, *Ad Imaginem Dei: The Image of Man in Medieval Art*, nn. 59, 98, 101, and 116; and J. Kleinz, *The Theory of Knowledge of Hugh of St. Victor*, Washington, D.C., 1944, p. 32. Hugh presents various schemes, and Kleinz discusses one in which there are four stages of sensitive life: (1) *sensificatio*, (2) *per sensum ingrediens imaginatio*, (3) *per imaginationem conceptorum memoria*, (4) *quaedam sine intelligentia discretione providentia;* this last "certain intelligent foresight without discretion" is shared with brutes; it is *quasi rationis imago . . . sed ratio nulla est*, and it distinguishes beneficial from harmful. Kleinz compares it to Aquinas's *vis estimativa* but distinguishes it from the *cogitativa* of the Scholastics.

Hugh's third power of the soul sees the present clearly, but inquires after the nature, properties, and purposes of what it sees, thus proceeding from the known to the unknown. This discursive activity is a mean between fantasy and reason. "The mind of man, then, so acts that it is always concerned with the apprehension of things before it or the understanding of things not present to it or the investigation and invention of things unknown. There are two matters upon which the power of the reasoning soul spends every effort; one is that it may know the natures of things by the method of inquiry [*ratione inquisitionis*] but the other is that there may first come to its knowledge those things which moral earnestness will put into action."[58] The mind, in other words, gathers from its firm and prudent grasp of experience those principles that give it true knowledge and true morality, principles that complete the speculative and practical intellects.

In the logical works of Boethius from which Hugh extracted his arguments, the term *intellectus* may cover all the activities of the soul above sensation, and thus in part corresponds to Hugh's *ratio in imaginationem.* The activities of the combinatory fantasy, for example, are referred to as activities of intellect. "If someone compose and conjoin by intellect [*componat atque coniugat intellectu*] that which nature does not suffer to be joined, no one fails to know that it is false, as if one joined horse and man by imagination and made a centaur."[59] Such *compositio* is associated with false opinion rather than *intelligentia.* Boethius in fact makes a sharp and crucial distinction between composition and division in this respect. Those things arrived at by division, abstraction, and as minor premises (*in divisionibus et abstractionibus assumptionibusque*) are true, whereas those made by composition (*in compositione*) are false, as when we combine man and horse to make a centaur.[60]

In another variation Boethius considered the question of whether such categories as genus and species are lies, mere "considerations" of the mind itself, like those things the Greeks call *phantasias* and the Latins call *visa.* As an example of such "feigning" or "painting" by the imagination, he cites the lines from the opening of the *Ars poetica* of Horace, "humano capiti cervicem pictor equinam iungere si velit."[61] Of course he does not accept this argument, but it is important in that it places imagination and the metaphor of painting at the very heart of the problem of universals. More to our purposes, composition is not simply negative; it is "false" in the specific sense of not being true of some existing thing, as analysis must be. "Composition" as an activity of intellect is a whole realm of human activity. As opinion, it corresponds to Augustine's realm of human art, false and relative in contrast to the absolute truth of divine revelation. And it is the realm

[58] *De studio legendi,* p. 10; *The Didascalicon,* p. 50.
[59] Boethius, *In Isagogen Porphyrii,* II.I.2.
[60] Ibid.
[61] Ibid, *Editionis primae,* I, 60 (ed. cit., p. 25) on Horace's text, see *MLA,* pp. 128–137 with notes; see also A. Chastel, "Le 'Dictum Horatii quidlibet audendi potestas' et les artistes (XIIIe–XVIe Siècle)," in *Fables, Formes, Figures,* 1, pp. 363–376.

of human art in a more specific procedural sense. According to Hugh of St. Victor, human art, in contrast to divine art and nature, "puts together things disjoined" or "joins things put together." Fantasy as an activity of intellect is the region of human art. It is, in fact, the ability to "compose" that specifically distinguishes the human from the animal soul. Nature had provided animals with what they cannot provide for themselves, but man has been given the power to imitate and invent. We imitate mountains in architecture, the skins of animals in our clothing. And in invention human reason shines forth much more brilliantly than it would have if we had been given such things by nature. From the human response to need arise objects once again of a Daedalan marvelousness: "infinite varieties of painting, weaving, carving and founding, so that we look with wonder not only at nature but at the *artifex* as well."[62]

Robert Kilwardby

According to the mid-thirteenth-century *De ortu scientiarum* of Robert Kilwardby, human good is either spiritual or corporeal, and "operative art" is either ethical, which serves the spiritual, or mechanical, which serves the corporeal.[63] Kilwardby follows Hugh of St. Victor closely in defining the manner in which art imitates nature. Whoever casts a statue has seen a man; whoever makes a house looks at a mountain, so that the sloping sides of the roof will repel water like the side of a mountain. Man does not need the bark, feathers, scales, fur, or shells that he imitates in devising protection for his body because he has been given reason, which is "excogitative of the arts." There are many mechanical arts, and they vary from people to people. Still, he feels confident in reducing them to seven, following Hugh of St. Victor, but amending the earlier writer's list by rejecting *theatrica* as inappropriate for Christians, replacing it with architecture (which he separates from *armatura*) and changing the name of *navigatio* to *mercatura,* thus preserving the symmetry to the seven liberal arts.

Unlike Hugh of St. Victor, Kilwardby had Aristotle's *Nicomachean Ethics, Metaphysics,* and *Organon* at his disposal and turned them to the purpose of considerably elaborating and broadening the earlier scheme in ways that would be repeated by numerous authors through the Renaissance. The practical sciences can only be called sciences by analogy; true sciences deal with the universal and admit of absolute proof; ethics and mechanics, on the other hand, deal with singulars, with human works and operations, with contingent things that proceed from human will. Arts, unlike sciences, deal with experience and with the probable. The practical sciences are thus related to the physical sciences in that both concern the contingent, but the physical sciences are more noble by virtue of their being "more remote from sense."[64] Similarly among the practical sciences, the ethical

[62] *De studio legendi*, p. 17; *The Didascalicon*, p. 56.
[63] R. Kilwardby, *De ortu scientiarum*, ed. A. G. Judy, London, 1976, pp. 124–128.
[64] Ibid., pp. 137–39.

is more intellectual and less sensual than the mechanical. Nonetheless, both speculative and practical sciences are parts of philosophy. Kilwardby distinguishes between them as Aristotle did in the *Metaphysics* (993b20), where it is stated that the end of theoretical knowledge is truth, that of practical knowledge is action, so that "practical men do not study the eternal, but what is relative and in the present."

Although Kilwardby makes the usual hierarchical distinctions between the speculative and the practical, and, within the practical, between the ethical and the mechanical, he discusses them all as parts of philosophy with a remarkable neutrality. Much as the mechanical arts are analogous to the liberal in the scheme he took over from Hugh of St. Victor, the kind of inference employed in the practical arts is analogous to syllogistic reasoning of the speculative sciences. In making this argument he draws upon the extremely important passages in the *Posterior Analytics* (78b32–79a32) in which the distinction is made between the "syllogism of the fact" and the "syllogism of the reasoned fact." Aristotle's arguments for this definition are illustrated with the example of subordinate and superior sciences, "as when optical problems are subordinated to geometry, mechanical problems to stereometry, harmonic problems to arithmetic, the data of observation to astronomy . . . it is the business of the empirical observers to know the fact, of the mathematicians to know the reasoned fact; for the latter are in possession of the demonstrations giving the causes, and are often ignorant of the fact: just as we have often a clear insight into the universal, but through lack of observation are ignorant of some of its particular instances."

Kilwardby thus used mechanics as the base metaphor to characterize the mechanical arts as a whole. Just as mechanics is "subalternate" geometry, so the practical arts in general operate about singulars with their own kinds of thought. This is both a specification and magnification of Hugh of St. Victor's argument that any human art may be considered as a science and consequently take its place in the scheme of philosophy.

These arguments, deeply shaped by those of Aristotle, represent a confluence of ideas that is much more than a sum of preexisting texts, and is also a confluence to be found in later writers we shall consider. Although Kilwardby drew on the *Nicomachean Ethics,* he did not mention the virtue of prudence, evidently preferring instead to use the example of theoretical and practical science to exemplify the relation between abstract principle and concrete act. Still, the definition of the logic of particulars he was attempting to define is easily translatable into the language of prudence. Also, the lower syllogism that he assigned to the practical sciences was closely related to *ingenium,* defined as the ability to complete the middle term of syllogisms "intuitively," as we would say. The treatment of the practical arts on the basis of logic also had the effect of identifying virtue and the mechanical arts, an identification that would not have been possible had virtue been defined as prudence. And it is deeply significant that Kilwardby compared virtue and the arts because of the common concern with the particular. To be sure, he considered ethics higher than the mechanical arts, but throughout his whole discussion there is a uniform acceptance of all the human sciences as fitted to human nature, so that if some of them are higher than others, all have a certain equivalence arising from this shared necessity.

As others would do after him (most especially Pomponazzi and Federico Zuccaro among the authors we shall treat), Kilwardby argued that the speculative and practical – and especially the mechanical – interpenetrated, and that the "subalternation" of the mechanical arts to the liberal was in fact integral to them, so that in textiles (*lanificium*), for example, practical knowledge of the number of threads and the shapes of frames to be used related the art to both arithmetic and geometry.[65] Defense of these arguments leads Kilwardby to the definition of a relation between sense and intellect that we have not encountered so clearly formulated before: he rejects the idea that the sensible is not intelligible. This argument is made on a sturdy Aristotelian foundation. Everything able to be known by the inferior and exterior virtue is able to be known by the superior and interior, but not vice versa. It is intellect that reasons and discourses, not sense; but seeing that we reason and discourse about sensible, particular things – times, places, persons, business – it must be that intellect apprehends sensible particular things in some way.[66] Sense is in effect subalternate to intellect, and the distinction between sense and intellect blurs in the shared realm of the particular intellect.

Later Middle Ages and Renaissance

The classical distinction between the liberal arts as intellectual and "free," in the literal, political sense of being appropriate to a free person, as opposed to manual, servile work,[67] was transformed in the Middle Ages into a distinction between inner and outer. The liberal arts, as many authors insisted, concerned the inner, spiritual man, and contributed to the realization and fulfillment of the rational soul. A number of definitions of the mechanical arts may be drawn together at the deepest level on the basis of this distinction. Aquinas stated the matter perhaps most clearly and generally. He contrasted mechanical art "concerned with the body," which for him was art proper, to the liberal arts, which were a "similitude" of art that concerned the soul.[68] Before him, Hugh of St. Victor, as we have

[65] Ibid., p. 140.

[66] Ibid., p. 149.

[67] For a review of classical attitudes toward the nonliberal arts, see Kristeller, "Modern System," in *Renaissance Thought II*, pp. 169–174; and for a discussion of the history, intellectual history, and sociology of work, Le Goff, *Time, Work and Culture*, pp. 58–86, 107–121, with copious bibliography, pp. 301–305.

[68] F. J. Kovach, "Divine Art in Saint Thomas Aquinas," in *Arts libéraux et philosophie au Moyen Age*, Montreal–Paris, 1969, pp. 663–671, here to 665. According to Aquinas (*Sententia libri ethicorum*, I.1; *Opera omnia*, XLVII, Rome, 1969, I, p. 4), different "orders" arise from the "considerations of reason" with respect to what it doesn't make (nature), with respect to reason's own act (concepts, signs and words), with respect to will (morality) and, with respect to what it does "in exterior things of which it is itself the cause, as in chests and houses." The *scientiae* which perfect (i.e., realize) the considerations of reason with respect to "exterior things constituted by human reason" are the mechanical arts.

seen, associated the mechanical arts with the mortal and the fallen, dividing the mechanical arts themselves into a physical inner and outer, some of them being concerned with protection, the others with nourishment. William of Conches compared them with darkness as opposed to light.[69]

In a more positive Augustinian vein, Bonaventure associated the mechanical arts with "external light,"[70] which is "in a certain sense servile and degenerates from the knowledge of philosophy." This "external light" was distinguished from the *lumen inferius* of sensitive cognition, and should perhaps be identified with Augustine's "beauty passed through souls into artful hands that comes from that beauty that is above the souls."[71] Bonaventure appealed directly to Augustine in making sensation the more "sufficient" according to the nature of the light of the elements associated with each sense, sight being the highest. It is evident that he followed Augustine in making the "light" of sensation spiritual, in which case the "external light" of the mechanical arts must fall somewhere around the lower elemental apprehensions of taste and touch, as in fact the arts concern covering (weaving, armor making) and food (agriculture, hunting), the procurement of these necessities (navigation), and the removal of impediments to their enjoyment (medicine). Significantly, the one imitative art in this scheme – which he had taken without change from Hugh of St. Victor – the art of theater, slipped through the net of this analysis: "Theatrica autem est unica."

Bonaventure wrote about the needs that gave rise to the mechanical arts, from which he obviously felt their definition arose; but he said nothing about their invention, or about the powers of the soul necessary to either their invention or their practice. That some power was necessary is granted in his principle that "every illumination of knowledge is within," notwithstanding which he made the light of the arts external. But at least in general his meaning is clear: the mechanical arts possess some "light," that is, they are in some sense a "spiritual" activity, even if this activity is a lowly one.[72]

Some clue is perhaps provided to the question of the nature of the faculties necessary to the mechanical arts by the fact that poetry – although theater is excluded from the general definition of the mechanical arts just considered – nonetheless is held up as representative of the end of these arts in general. That the mechanical arts suffice for the needs of mankind is evident, Bonaventure says, from the fact that each art is intended for man's consolation or comfort (*ad solatium, aut ad commodum*), or for the elimination of sorrow or want; that it either benefits or delights (*prodest, aut delectat*). He cites Horace – *aut prodesse volunt, aut delectare*

[69] See Chapter 1 n. 6, above.

[70] *De Reductione artium ad theologiam*. ed. and tr. E. T. Healy, pp. 38–39.

[71] See n. 48, above.

[72] The remarks of Cennino Cennini (*Libro dell'arte*, cap. 8), according to whom "e'l timone ella ghuida di questo potere vedere sie la luce del sole, la luce dell'occhio tuo, ella man tua; che senza queste tre chose nulla non si puo fare con ragione," although fragmentary and mingled with other ideas (those of the optical writers at some remove, perhaps), seem difficult to separate from such Augustinian ideas.

poetae, and *omne tulit punctum qui miscuit utile dulci.*[73] The mechanical art that affords consolation and delight (here we may perhaps think back to Aristotle's "arts of recreation" at the beginning of the *Metaphysics*) is *theatrica,* "which is the art of plays containing every form of playing, either in songs, in musical instruments, or in fictions [*figmentis*], or in mime [*gesticulationibus corporis*]." These are the arts of imitation, and we are again reminded of Aristotle's dictum that man is by nature imitative. It is also clear that theater, as for Hugh of St. Victor, had to do with the inner man, since *theatrica,* as providing consolation, is immediately contrasted to the arts "ordered to comfort or betterment according to the exterior man" (*ordinatur ad commodum sive profestum secundum exteriorem hominem*). Thus the following conclusion might be offered: Poetry, as representative of the mechanical arts, is understood as the lowest form of knowledge, according to a formula we have already considered several times. At the same time, this negative evaluation has the positive result of linking invention in the mechanical arts with *ingenium* and *phantasia.* But it may again be further suggested that the arts of imitation, linked to the lowest form of knowledge, might also serve to nourish the inner man, by setting forth saving truth in its most apprehensible form.[74]

Because we think of all art in "visual" terms, in which there is no essential difference between an image and a useful object, it is perhaps difficult to appreciate the distinction as a fundamentally important one. Plato, however, makes this distinction. His strictures against art are aimed not at useful objects, which are necessary, but at the activities surrounding them which were subphilosophical; and they are aimed at images, which may be deceitful, or are inherently deceitful, because they cannot be what they represent. In medieval discussions, the arts of imitation – painting, sculpture, and theater, for example – were included in a scheme of useful or mechanical arts no doubt in large part because works of art were thought of first of all in terms of social function. A painting of a saint was part of an altarpiece before it was an image of an individual. The dominance of the useful arts in this scheme tended to enforce the idea that any work of art was related to previous objects of the same kind and that the art itself was the skill necessary to make such objects. Thus the making of a chair was the more or less close variation on a previous model, and the authority of this paradigm meant that a painting of a saint was also a more or less close variation on a previous model, much as a painter might use a pattern book. The arts of imitation, however, were always at odds with the scheme of the mechanical arts in which they were included, for the simple reason that – as had also been recognized since Plato – the relationship of an image to its model was different from the relationship

[73] *De Reductione artium,* pp. 38–40.

[74] This might explain why Daedalus is included among the reliefs of Florence Cathedral. Daedalus is not only the Ur-craftsman, he could also represent poetic imagination. See Boccaccio in the *proemium* to Book XIV of *Genealogie deorum;* he describes himself as soaring in imagination as on the wings of Daedalus (*Et quasi sumptis Dedali pennis, audaci quodum volatu in celum usque meditatione delati*) (*Genealogie deorum gentilium libri,* p. 679). On *audacia* as a virtue, see *MLA,* passim, as cited in the index. I am grateful to Mary Pardo for this argument.

of a useful thing to its model. An image is always *of* something, and there is thus always a third term. Someone who makes a chair presents a chair more or less similar to another chair. Someone who makes a painting of a saint may present a painting of a saint similar to another painting of a saint, but both model and new painting either implicitly or explicitly re-present another thing, namely the appearance of the saint. And, it must quickly be added, this third term implies a fourth term, which is the basis of the image in the *mental* representation of the painter himself. An object shown as if it appears must be shown as it appears to someone. This in turn raises the question of whether or not that which appears appears in the same way to everyone. The arts of imitation thus raised questions that tended to separate them from the mechanical arts (or, without changing the argument, the raising of these questions tended to separate the arts of imitation from the mechanical arts). The specific configuration of these questions had to do with interiority, with subjectivity and point of view. This in turn pushed the arts of imitation at once toward definition in terms of moral virtue at the same time that it promised the vast historical landscape of art defined by the structure of subjectivity, of point of view. And point of view was articulated not only in ever-advancing naturalism and ever-deepening fantasy, it was also articulated in the appropriate available language.

It must moreover be supposed that the ancient definition of *techne* or *ars* as a useful human activity with teachable procedures and principles, which prevailed through the entire period we are surveying, can only have been magnified by the inclusion of the mechanical arts under philosophy; and the Aristotelian stress on the artist's foreconception as the beginning and end of a work must have pushed the activity of the artist from the external toward the internal, raising all manner of questions about the nature and genesis of this conception and about its relation to sensation and intellect, both speculative and practical. A striking example of this language of practical interior vision (which is probably Augustinian, but which would have been reinforced by the arguments of Aristotle) is provided by Geoffrey of Vinsauf in his late twelfth, early thirteenth century *Poetria nova.* Here the house to be built is measured out with the "inward line of the heart" and is an "archetype" before it is a sensible thing. "The hand of the interior man leads."[75]

The appearance of the mechanical arts as an iconographic theme seems to have occurred well along in the course of this development. When Hugh of St. Victor's scheme made its most conspicuous appearance in the Giottesque reliefs on the Campanile of Florence Cathedral, painting, sculpture, and architecture, united at least by their common participation in inner conception and invention, expressed in *disegno,* were separated from the mechanical arts and placed between them and

[75] See E. Faral, *Les arts poétiques du XIIe et du XIIIe siècle; recherches et documents sur la technique littéraire du moyen âge,* Paris, 1924, p. 198. See also Augustine *Confessions* XI.5, for a concrete variation on the idea of God as the Platonic *demiourgos.*

the liberal arts.[76] In his commentary on the *Politics* of Aristotle (1328b6ff), Albertus Magnus stressed the dependency of the well-ordered commonwealth on the mechanical arts. The rise in the status of the mechanical arts in such a political context has been connected both with the rise of the bourgeois town and the ideal of the bourgeois town as the New Jerusalem.[77] However that may be, it is important for our purposes that these religious and secular arguments gave a new justification and value to the exercise of certain human powers, so that Vincent of Beauvais could write that human *ingenium,* the dangers and pitfalls of its exercise notwithstanding, may among other things "excogitate" a great number of paintings and sculptures.[78] Such ideas not only were not forgotten in the Renaissance, they were part of the foundations of the discussion of Renaissance art and were even essential to justifications of art as "liberal."

By the middle of the thirteenth century the ideal of the man of experience – certainly best known in Leonardo da Vinci – had already formed. Roger Bacon's teacher Peter of Maricourt was a military engineer who began the modern study of magnets. He knew natural philosophy *per experientiam,* and was ashamed if any ordinary person or old crone or soldier or country bumpkin knew something he did not. He knew all the mechanical arts, the measurement of land (that is, the "subalternate" mathematics of surveying), even the "illusions and ingenious devices of minstrels."[79]

The Renaissance inherited all the classical and medieval attitudes and ideas about the mechanical arts we have examined. These attitudes and ideas were sometimes deeply contradictory. Leonardo argued repeatedly that painting was not a mechanical art, but praised mechanics and defended the validity of the realm of experience on which mechanics drew. Michelangelo insisted he was not the sort of sculptor who kept a shop, but also insisted on the essentially practical and even physical character of the skill that made his art possible.[80] Federico

[76] See M. Trachtenberg, *The Campanile of Florence Cathedral: "Giotto's Tower,"* New York, 1971.

[77] U. Feldges-Henning, "The Pictorial Programme of the Sala della Pace: A New Interpretation," *JWCI,* 35, 1972, pp. 145–162, cites Albertus Magnus. Similar arguments were made in the *Polycraticus* of John of Salisbury (VI.20), as cited by Le Goff, *Time, Work and Culture,* p. 116. See also n. 46, above. On the iconography of the mechanical arts, see also P. Verdier, "L' Iconographie des Artes libéraux dans l'art du Moyen Age jusqu'à la fin du quinzième siècle," *Arts libéraux et philosophie au Moyen Age,* Montreal–Paris, 1969, pp. 324–326; and Klibansky, Panofsky, and Saxl, *Saturn and Melancholy,* pp. 309–310 and passim. The social history of the mechanical arts in the Middle Ages is yet to be written. See M. Becker, *Medieval Italy,* p. 129, where it is reported in the mid twelfth century that the Italian cities, in order to increase their strength, knighted youths of low station and even workers from the mechanical arts (*opifices mechanicarum artium*). See also ibid., p. 161. Giordano da Pisa argued that economic interdependence was distinctively human, that each benefits from the arts of others. See D. Lesnick, "Dominican Preaching and the Creation of Capitalist Ideology in Late Medieval Florence," *Memorie Domenicane,* n.s. VIII–IX, 1977–8, pp. 204–241.

[78] Vincent of Beauvais, *Speculum naturale,* XXIX, cap. XI. He is quoting Augustine, as in nn. 28 and 46, above.

[79] L. White, Jr., *Medieval Technology and Social Change,* New York, 1962, p. 133.

[80] See *MLA,* pp. 269–273.

Zuccaro placed the mechanical arts seventh and lowest on the astrological scale near the end of his *Idea,* beneath the moon (that is, he identified them with the earthly realm of the elements) and with the common people (*con la plebe*).[81] But at the same time, he wrote glowingly of human "productive" powers, which included the exercise of all the arts, as we shall see in Chapter 13. In general, although "mechanic" continued to be a synonym for a poor or vulgar person, the reputation of mechanics rose meteorically, and with this reputation the mental powers necessary to the performance of these arts also rose, as did the emphasis placed on the criterion of experience.[82] By the fifteenth century the mechanical arts were firmly lodged among the expressions of the creative human soul, the social position of their practitioners notwithstanding.

When Gianozzo Manetti wrote his *De dignitate et excellentia hominis,* he placed all the arts together along an ascending continuum. Navigation, building, painting, and sculpture stood below poetry, which in turn formed the link to history, oratory, jurisprudence, philosophy, medicine, astronomy, and theology. It is crucial that poetry, the power of the human mind to make, stands at the center of this system, and provides the common point of contact between the liberal and mechanical arts, which are differentiated as ancient and modern. The four lower arts are all illustrated by examples ready at hand, by the voyages of Italian and Portuguese navigators, Brunelleschi's dome, the painting of Giotto, and Ghiberti's gilt bronze doors of the Florentine Baptistery.[83]

These ideas were raised to the level of systematic thought by Nicholas Cusanus, for whom judgment was the central power of the human soul, close to intellect itself.[84] The soul is not "concreated" with "notions," which it gains from experience, but rather with a *vis iudiciaria,* which discriminates and organizes *sensibilia.* Without this power to judge, the activities of both sense and reason are "senseless." Without this power we are like illiterate men reading, able to make out different letters and patterns among them, but unable to understand the meaning. We are, in short, like the inhabitants of Plato's cave, who discern some patterns and regularities among the dancing shadows before them, and never see the truth. But there is a crucial difference, because the reality against which the shadowplay is known to be shadowplay is the reality at hand, which we do not already know but rather grasp as it presents itself to us. Cusanus accepted and elevated the Aristotelian principle that the human soul is a *kritikon,* and he also accepted and universalized the notion that we apprehend particulars in judging them, so that all human apprehension is by a kind of discretion. Our inclinations

[81] *Scritti,* p. 299.

[82] P. Rossi, *Philosophy, Technology and the Arts in the Early Modern Era,* New York, 1970, chap. 1, "Mechanical Arts and Philosophy in the Sixteenth Century."

[83] For references, see C. Trinkaus, "Themes for a Renaissance Anthropology," in *The Renaissance,* pp. 83–125. See G. Manetti, *De Dignitate et excellentia hominis,* pp. 57–60, 77–79; throughout, the mechanical arts are understood in the good sense of having to do with mechanics and *ingenium.*

[84] See P. M. Watts, *Nicholas Cusanus: A Fifteenth Century Vision of Man,* Leiden, 1982, pp. 140–152.

are "foretastes" and our real experience is "inner taste." Consistently with such ideas, Cusanus argued that all human knowledge is relative. At the same time, it is also "conjectural" and mathematical. Only man counts and sets his measure upon the world in doing so. The human mind develops a world of numbers both in its apprehension of nature and in the conception of new forms and their realization in matter. The mechanical arts were thus for Cusanus spiritual activities, arising not primarily from necessity but from the nature of the human soul itself, and he valued production more highly than imitation, because in crafting an object of use, something new is made in analogy to God's making of the things from which imitations are made. When Cusanus wrote that "wisdom cries out in the streets" – *sapientia clamat in plateis* – quoting the Book of Wisdom, he meant that real knowledge is to be found in the gauging and reckoning of everyday constructive activity.[85]

[85] Addendum: On the question of technological and cultural change in the late Middle Ages and the Renaissance, see F. Alessio, "La filosofia e le 'artes mechanicae' nel secolo xii," *Studi medievali*, 6, 1, 1965, pp. 71–161; and further on the iconography of the mechanical arts, M. Evans, "Allegorical Women and Practical Men: The Iconography of the *Artes* Reconsidered," *Medieval Women*, ed. D. Baker, Oxford, 1978, pp. 305–328.

12

Prudence

Art and virtue

Most simply, prudence, from providence, means foresight. Such anticipatory inner vision requires experience, and prudence may be said to be the use of the past in the present for the sake of the future. It came to be symbolized by profile heads facing in either direction with a full-face head between them, showing in this trinitarian emblem the unity of past and future in the present.[1]

Titian's *Allegory of Prudence,* (Fig. 6) which, if Panofsky's interpretation is right, combines the theme of prudence with that of the passage of human generations, shows three heads, the youngest facing into the light as the oldest is obscured by shadow. It bears an inscription that from left to right, from old age to youth, reads as follows: "From the past, the present acts prudently lest it spoil future action."[2]

[1] Cicero provided a whole array of definitions of *prudentia,* including what was to become a standard definition of prudence as made up of *memoria, intelligentia,* and *providentia* (*De inventione* II.53), which correspond to past, present, and future. See Yates, *Art of Memory,* p. 73. Cicero here distinguishes prudence from animal instinct. As influential was his definition of prudence as the knowledge of things to be sought and avoided (*est rerum expetendarum fugiendarumque scientia* [*De officiis,* I, xliii, 153] translating *phronesis,* which is opposed to theoretical *sophia* in an argument in which speculative knowledge is subordinated to duties arising from *communitas* (see Augustine *De genesi ad litteram* XII.26.54; and "Alkinous," *Didaskalikon,* 28 [*Works of Plato,* VI, tr. G. Burges, London, 1898, pp. 299–300], where prudence is defined as "knowledge of good and bad and what is neither" and closely identified with reason.) In the *Orator* (162), Cicero presents *prudentia* as the basis for judgment of meaning as opposed to sound: "The judgment of things and words is in prudence, however the ears are judges of sound [*vocum*] and rhythms." In the *De natura deorum* (II.xxiii), in an account of the opinions of Zeno in which the arts are said to create and generate (*creare et gignere*), nature, in analogy to the *artifex,* is called *prudentia vel providentia* (translating *pronoia*), the relation being that both artisan and nature proceed according to plan. On prudence in the Middle Ages before the reintroduction of Aristotle, see O. Lottin, *Psychologie et Morale aux XIIe et XIIIe siècles,* III, Louvain, 1949, pp. 255–271.

[2] E. Panofsky, "Titian's Allegory of Prudence: A Postscript," in *Meaning in the Visual Arts,* pp. 146–168.

Fig. 6. Titian, *Allegory of Prudence*, ca. 1565, oil on canvas. National Gallery, London.

Prudence, as the guide of behavior, was concerned with particulars, because situations demanding action are particular; and, as essentially concerned with past, present, and future, prudence was congruent with *cogitatio* as Augustine had defined it. The question of prudence was thus deeply involved in questions of the particular intellect, of individual character and experience. As an introduction to this problem we may again consider the question of melancholy, which, as we have mentioned, was the physiologically determined state of mind, the temperament, of painters. In his *Problems,* Aristotle tells us that such a disposition was characteristic of individuals of *ingegno* and *prudenzia* (as Romano Alberti translated it).[3] Here prudence is coupled with talent and seems clearly to mean an *innate* ability to discriminate. How could this be the chief virtue of the practical intellect?

By far the most important examination of prudence (*phronesis*) in classical literature is to be found in Aristotle's *Nicomachean Ethics,* the first complete translation of which in the early thirteenth century had an immediate impact on the discussion of this important idea. According to Aristotle, prudence is partly natural (as some are more disposed to be prudent than others, and even animals may be said to act prudently). Human prudence, however, arises primarily from experience, is associated with opinion and deliberation, and, in terms of the terminology with which we have become familiar, might be associated with the *vis cogitativa,* or particular intellect. Thus, some may act more prudently because of experience than others act because of *scientia* (in Grosseteste's translation, 1141b). Aristotle also considered a number of kinds of judgment subsidiary to prudence; *synesis,* for example (which Aquinas called "*bonus sensus*"), or *gnomon,* which is the good judgment of judges. All of these are judgments of particular reason, and "are thought to be natural endowments" because, although no one is a philosopher by nature, people are thought to have by nature judgment, understanding, and intuitive reason – (*gnomyn et synesim et intellectum* in Grosseteste). However that may be, *true* prudence is not defined for Aristotle by experience, and is not simply a moral virtue, or a *practical* intellectual virtue, and the truly prudent man is able to deliberate well not only about what is good and expedient for himself but "about what sort of things conduce to the good life in general" (1140a25ff.). Prudence is finally defined as a "reasoned and true state of capacity to act with regard to human goods."

Saint Antoninus provides a summary of these ideas as they were repeated in the Renaissance. He divides the practical intellect into ethics, economics, and politics. The chief virtue of the practical intellect is prudence, which consists of three parts – inquiring and discussing, election, and setting into execution what has been "well judged." Prudence is "right reason about things to be done – *recta ratio agibilium* – and Antoninus appeals to Seneca in concluding that it has three parts to which all the kinds of prudence listed by Aristotle in the *Ethics* may be reduced. These are *recogitatio* or *memoratio* of the past, *ordinatio praesentium agendorum,* and *providentia futurorum.*[4]

It may be supposed it was perennially necessary to distinguish between pleasure and "higher" pleasure, or "true" pleasure, and Aristotle's definition of "true" prudence notwithstanding, it is important to take note of the range of meanings

[3] BT, II, p. 209. On the pseudo-Aristotle *Problems* XXX.1, from which the tradition of the idea of melancholy principally descends, see Klibansky, Panofsky, and Saxl, *Saturn and Melancholy,* pp. 15–41. There are many such uses of prudence. See, for example, *Aristotelis Opera cum Averrois commentariis,* supp. III, f. 166v–167, where Aristotle's argument concerning the relation of hand and intellect is phrased to say that man possesses a hand because he is *prudentissimus.* On uprightness and prudence, see Cole, *Democritus,* pp. 40–42.

[4] *Summa theologica,* tit. I, cap. III, col. 32–33.

that "prudent" may have, from animal "prudence," through action based on innate "sense," through action based on knowledge arising from experience, to action in light of ethical principles. We may still use the word with much the same range of meaning, and we may still associate it with the ability to "do things right" (that is, to do them as if against a standard), and it is likely that the terms *prudente* or *discreto* or *giudicioso,* which were used to praise Renaissance artists, often meant no more than that an artist was "good at what he did" because he was talented or experienced or both, and did not necessarily mean that he applied fixed principles corresponding to ethical principles in his work. Aristotle wrote that Phidias and Polykleitos are called "wise," but they are not truly wise, rather they are wise in one thing (1141a9ff.). "Prudence" has a similar ambivalence.

Aristotle drew close analogies between art and virtue, or prudence, and we shall now briefly consider these similarities and differences, which were of great significance for late Renaissance art theory. Aristotle considered art to be a cause, a principle by which the existence of certain things might be explained. Although he was relatively little concerned with strictly aesthetic issues, as we have seen, Aristotle was clearly fascinated by human art as a paradigm of human action. The products of art and those of nature are alike in that they both proceed in an orderly manner to a reasonable end, the difference between them being that in art the process is initiated by the artist, whereas in nature the cause is in the thing itself. So sure was Aristotle of this analogy that he said nature would perform as art does were she given the task of building a house, that art would proceed as nature does were she to make a tree, and he compared nature to a physician healing himself.[5] Aristotle also used the example of art to discuss the formation of the "second nature" of virtuous habit. We are not virtuous by nature, rather we are "adapted by nature to receive the virtues," which are thus in themselves neither natural nor unnatural. What we have by nature, such as the senses, we have before we use them; "but the virtues we get by exercising them, as also happened in the case of the arts as well. For the things we have to learn before we can do them, we learn by doing them . . . become builders by building and lyre players by playing the lyre; so too we become just by doing just acts, temperate by doing temperate acts, brave by doing brave acts" (1103a26ff.).

Both art and prudence act with respect to the variable, on the contingent or the particular, and Aristotle distinguished between "things made [art] and things done [virtue]," defining art as a capacity to make, involving a true course of reasoning (1140a10), prudence as the "true and reasoned state of capacity to act with regard to the things that are good and bad for men" (1140b4ff.). Making has an end other than itself (the action of the painter is toward the making of a painting), whereas virtuous action is an end in itself. He also argues that "both

[5] These centrally important arguments are found in *Physics* II.8–9.

art and virtue are always concerned with what is harder; for even the good is better when it is harder" (1105a8ff.).

When Aristotle discussed the importance of the mean in art (1106b), again as a paradigm of virtue, he used the example of the exercise of judgment. Ten pounds of food may be too much to give an athlete to eat, two pounds too little, but the solution to the problem of what to feed an athlete is not necessarily six pounds of food, the simple arithmetical mean between excess and defect. Six may still be too little for Milo, too much for the beginner, and the true mean must be found by a consideration of circumstances. The finding of the true mean in light of the particular is necessary both for art and for virtue. This is what Aristotle meant when he said (1109b2) that it is not easy to determine when a person is blameworthy by reasoning "any more than anything else that is perceived by the sense; such things depend on particular facts, and the decision rests with perception." But, as Aristotle insists, the judgments required by virtue, although conforming to the same law of the mean, are higher judgments than those required by art, much as the practical intellect is higher than the productive.

It was in the context of these discussions (1106b8ff) that Aristotle formulated his famous definition of the importance of the mean to works of art. "Every art does its work well," we are told, "by looking to the intermediate and judging its works by this standard, so that we often say of good works of art that it is not possible either to take away or to add anything, implying that excess and defect destroy the goodness of works of art, while the mean preserves it." This example illustrates the point that if this is true for art, it is all the more so in the case of virtue, which is "more exact and better" than any art, and Aristotle is comparing art and virtue in point of the necessity of an appropriate discrimination to each of them. Aristotle often makes the point – and his interpreters made it even more forcefully – that real prudence is higher than art.

But if for Aristotle art and virtue are similar, there are also deep differences between them. Making a further distinction, Aristotle also argues that products of art have their goodness in themselves (which is associated with the mean, evident in a certain "character" of the product [1106b]), but the goodness of an act (as opposed to a thing made), even if it have a certain character, is in the agent; that is, it must be the act of a virtuous person, who must have knowledge, free choice, and firm character. In art, only knowledge matters (that is, what is made shows that an artist did or did not "know what he was doing").

Aristotle's Scholastic commentators quite understandably emphasized "true" prudence, as the virtue par excellence of the practical intellect. Albertus Magnus distinguished between what Aristotle called animal prudence, rooted, he said, only in memory, and not in the perfect reason of prudence, which is an active habit with true reason of those things in us which pertain to life."[6] Aquinas objected to the idea of "natural prudence" on the grounds that it could as well

[6] Albertus Magnus, *Metaphysica*, I.1.6 (*Opera omnia*, XVI, 1, Westphalia, 1960, p. 90)

be turned to evil as to good purposes, whereas true virtue was always toward a rational and justifiable end, and consisted of right activity toward that end. Aquinas, following Aristotle (1105a27 and 1140b20ff.) illustrated much the same point in distinguishing between prudence and art. Prudence requires moral virtue and right appetite. The good of artificial works is not "a good of human appetite" but the good of the artificial work itself. Because art does not presuppose right appetite, we praise an artisan who knowingly departs from his art (*peccat*), but we do not praise one who does so unknowingly. In the case of prudence, we disapprove of one who knowingly acts in defiance of ethical principles, but incline to excuse one who is ignorant of them. Rightness of will is of the very nature of prudence, but not of art, and it is obvious therefore, he concludes, that prudence is a virtue distinct from art. A good artist may be a bad man and a bad artist a good man, in short, and art therefore falls together with natural prudence as morally ambivalent.[7]

Aristotle distinguished in such terms between true prudence and a kind of natural prudence called *deinotes* (*Nicomachean Ethics* 1144a), or cleverness. Prudence is not this faculty, he says, but does not exist without it. It adapts means to ends, but may do so morally or immorally. If it does so morally, then it is indistinguishable from prudence; it if does so immorally, then it is merely clever. Albertus Magnus defined *deinotes* as "a certain natural industry by which someone is able well to find ways of attaining his end, whether good or bad." Aquinas only slightly elaborated this definition and added the synonym *ingeniositas*.[8] *Deinotes*, reinforced by other connotations of the word, became the Renaissance *terribilità*;[9] and it is evident that this natural virtue is closely related to the sense that apprehends particulars, the *vis cogitativa* or *estimativa* or particular reason also essential to prudence. And if for Aristotle and the Scholastics art is activity with true reason, it stands in the same relation to true prudence that *deinotes* – *ingeniositas* – also stands to true prudence.

The exercise of prudence had its own "syllogism," called the practical syllogism, according to which one reasons from a principle to a particular state of affairs to which the principle was appropriate, thus to determine one's actions.[10] We may consider this example: One should not steal; this is a situation in which I may steal; I will not steal. In practice, however, such "syllogizing" does not often occur, even if we lead a perfectly upright life; rather, we most often act virtuously out of the "second nature" of habit. One does the right "unthinkingly" because one has always done it, and this is not so much because one has been taught moral principles as because one has been taught behavior consistent with moral principles. Or, to put it another way, virtue may be taught not so much by

[7] *Summa theologiae* I–II.57.5.

[8] *Sententia Libri ethicorum*, *Opera omnia*, XLVII, Rome, 1969, II, pp. 372–373, with references to Albertus Magnus.

[9] *MLA*, part I, chap. 15.

[10] On the "practical syllogism," see Introduction n. 17, above.

teaching the principles of morals as by ingraining the habits of moral behavior, just as an art might be taught not by teaching principles but by guiding experience.

For Aquinas the practical syllogism as we have presented it in our example could not have been sufficient, and resolution of the dilemma presented by the situation also necessarily involved the will. The "syllogism" should rather be stated as follows: One should not steal; this is a circumstance in which I might steal; *I will or will not steal.* The alternative cannot be resolved by reason, rather one may only know the principle by reason. The situation (and therefore the very applicability of the rule) is known in a more sensate manner; and the resolution of the possibility is finally decided by will. One freely chooses to do one thing or another, and is responsible in the specific sense of being liable to having one's actions judged against the standard of the major premise of the syllogism.

Aquinas discusses these issues in familiar terms. Some things, he argues, act without judgment, as a stone falls; the sheep runs from the wolf because of a judgment, but this judgment is not free because it is instinctive rather than rational. Humans truly act from judgment because the apprehensive power judges that something should be avoided or sought. And this judgment, which arises not from instinct but from an act of comparison in the reason, is free and retains the power of being inclined to various things. "For reason in contingent matters may follow opposite courses, as we see in dialectic syllogisms and rhetorical arguments. Now particular operations are contingent and therefore in such matters the judgment of reason may follow opposite courses . . . and for as much is it necessary that man has a free will and is rational."[11]

It is evident that free will, the practical intellect, and the particular intellect as the faculty for evaluating present circumstances and comparing them to past experience and anticipated activity (*cogitatio,* or *collatio*) have all moved into approximately the same position within the system that embraces them, and the area of their overlap is defined by the virtue of prudence. Prudence is obviously related to both fantasy and cogitation. Fantasy deals with the absent, the past or the future, and always does so in the present, for an individual in absolutely definite circumstances. As a present image in the mind the fantasy is also usually bound to appetite and thus to activity and, if not good or bad in itself, is usually implicated in behavior about which moral judgments might be made.

It is perhaps easier now to understand how the moral virtue of prudence came to figure in discussion of art at all. Not only did prudence itself have a fairly wide range of meaning between "true" prudence and "ordinary" prudence, but the definition of true prudence itself at once embraced and threw into higher

[11] *Summa theologiae* I.83.1. In related and equally familiar terms, Aquinas wrote that even though animals may proceed in determinate ways to ends in both their actions and their constructions, their actions are not truly according to reason, as is the case in human beings; if human beings have the knowledge of universals that reason allows them, then the force of reason may be extended to infinite particulars (*Summa theologiae* II–II.47.5 ad 3).

definition the subphilosophical meanings of the word. Because the exercise of prudence demanded the right apprehension of the particular as well as knowledge of moral principles, its definition demanded the definition of the faculties of the particular intellect. It requires only a moment's reflection to see that the practical intellect is not itself the faculty that judges a situation to be so-and-so, and it is evident therefore that the exercise of prudence was radically dependent on the lower faculties of the soul. This, in fact, is the reason Aquinas was so interested in the *vis cogitativa,* which became for him not so much the mean between body and soul as the common ground of the acting human soul and the world in which it found itself. Aquinas repeated the idea that prudence considers not only universals, in which there is no action, but also singulars, about which action actually takes place.[12] He wrote that "prudence includes the cognition both of the universal and of operable singulars, to which prudence applies universal principles."[13] And prudence did not simply involve the apprehension of particular states of affairs; this very apprehension implied an apprehending individual. *Operatio,* human behavior toward an end, is also abstract and concrete. We may know the ends of a right human life, but actual human affairs are not so determinate, and in fact are "multiply diversified according to the diversity of persons and affairs." The idea of prudence may thus be said to have clearly defined a new set of problems. It stressed the particular at the same time that it stressed the universal, and may be said to have placed them in an opposition that was perhaps deeper than any possible resolution. That is, the explicit definition of the individual and the particular opened possibilities of conceptual development that necessarily came into conflict with the ability of either reason or revelation to provide certain moral principles.

As we have seen, Aquinas, following Aristotle, defined prudence as active habit with reason, art as factive habit with reason. He also defined human art as beautiful insofar as it was "ordered according to reason."[14] He not only meant by this that it should be done according to fixed rule; he also meant that it should be in "proportion" to the modes of human apprehension, from sensation upward, which were themselves intrinsically rational. Art according to reason is a mirror of the human soul. The identification of art and prudence thus signaled an awareness of art as constitutively concerned with the particular, not only in subject matter – this would be implied by any naturalism – but in the very act of art itself. This in turn implies that powerful and necessary union of questions physical, psychological, aesthetic, and moral at the heart of early Renaissance art and marks it off clearly as the first art of the modern period.

According to Aristotle, the making of a work of art was preceded by an image that functioned as the end toward which the craftsman worked, and, if the form imagined might arise from simple human necessity – a chair – it was imagined

[12] de Bruyne, *Etudes,* III, p. 321.
[13] *Summa theologiae* II–II.47.a.15.
[14] *Etudes,* III, p. 313; *Summa theologiae* I–II.142.2.

as it was by the craftsman and executed well or poorly according to the reasonable procedures of his craft. Aristotle understood that all art imitated nature in following orderly processes to rational ends, and seems to have thought, much as Plato did, that painting imitated appearances and also thought that to a degree it imitated character, although in a way less satisfactory than poetry. The appearances imitated by painting were phantasms in the language we are considering, and the demand that painting be like phantasms, that is, that it be naturalistic by imitating appearances (or imagining them), had very specific implications. Phantasms were not isolated but were rather in the sequence of cogitation, which was at once the source of prudence and invention. It is not difficult to see how the artistic and the ethical merge, how they simply become dimensions of particular intellect. The remembered and projected images of cogitation were intimately linked to personal and projected disposition, to character, to individual reminiscence and association (or *collatio*), as we have seen. Cogitation was in itself bound to individual history and character and in its working in one or another individual, and in evidence of these workings, *revealed* individual character.

In Aristotelian psychology, both sensation and imagination were phantasms, and if for Aristotle these phantasms might be decayed sensations left in the byways of sensory apparatus, they were also able to determine behavior as if sensation of real things. Painting and sculpture cast at this psychological level immediately raised the promise of the shaping of intention and behavior and raised the simply moral problem of what intentions and behavior should be encouraged. Paintings and sculptures were thus newly subject to the same moral strictures as fantasies and cogitations or even real acts themselves. A painting, like a sensation or an image in the mind, might encourage piety or curiosity or lust, and the artist who made an image was as praiseworthy or blameworthy as the image itself, as liable to salvation or damnation as the viewer who responds to it. Again, the reinforcement of the Aristotelian idea of the origin of the work in the artist, which is morally neutral in Aristotle, assumed an entirely different significance when reinforced by the Christian notion of will. The artist became metaphysically responsible for his work, and his life absolutely bound to it. The larger idea concentric to this absolute freedom and responsibility is the absolute freedom and responsibility of God for creation, and the artist became a creator.

The universally held idea of the learned artist entailed a much more complex notion of imitation. This was based on the Aristotelian definition of art as rational procedure, and had the effect of transforming the sciences of nature into the "theory of art," so that practice could be both guided and judged by the standard of these sciences. All the learning of the artist, Christian or classical, became subject to decorum, as Lomazzo could discuss prudence in terms of decorum. Some authors – Vincenzo Danti, for example – argued that the artificial making of the human body should be rooted in the teleological order of the human body itself, defining a "higher" imitation that merged the principles and reasons of anatomy with the reasons of art. "Prudence" in such a case became both the ability to execute art and the ability to realize knowledge of natural philosophy in practice. But it also meant that art was subject to the standards of anatomy, or proportion, and, in general, all the learning that might be evident in works of art was subject to standards of correctness to which the artist was responsible.[15] This resulted in an enormous broadening of art – the artist was "responsible," for example, for working knowledge of optics and physiognomy as well as classical and Christian literature – but at the same time his paintings became records of his conduct against these standards, and these same standards provided the Counter-Reformation and the academies of art that developed together with it a kind of control over the definition of the conduct of art fully equal to this new breadth. It is not clear that we are now so distant from the deepest expectations of art fashioned in the Renaissance, and it is perhaps to the notion of the responsibility of the artist for the work as the creator of the work, which was defined in the Renaissance, that we owe our own still passionately moral reactions to the experience of art.

Intellects

Aristotle's division of the intellect into theoretical and practical had a complex history. The complexity began in Aristotle's own writing, and authors starting from one or another text concerning these intellects contributed to one or another variant tradition. We may introduce some of these issues by considering the example of Pietro Pomponazzi, who in his *De Immortalitate animae* divided the intellect into three parts, which he called theoretical, practical or operative, and productive.[16] Pomponazzi is following the pattern of the *Metaphysics* (1025b25, 1064a18); and *Topics* (145a15), where the *sciences* are listed as theoretical (physics, mathematics, metaphysics), practical (politics, economics and ethics), and pro-

[15] See *MLA*, pp. 347–351.

[16] "On the immortality of the soul," in *The Renaissance Philosophy of Man*, ed. E. Cassirer, P. O. Kristeller, J. H. Randall, Jr., Chicago, 1969, p. 353. This translation has an excellent introduction by J. H. Randall. Klibansky, Panofsky, and Saxl, *Saturn and Melancholy*, starting at p. 317, identify Dürer's *Melencolia* I as the lowest of three melancholies according to the scheme of Agrippa of Nettesheim. These melancholies more or less correspond to the productive, practical, and speculative intellects, and are associated with *imaginatio, ratio,* and *mens*. *Imaginatio* in turn is associated with the mechanical arts, architecture, painting, and so on (see p. 359). In melancholy frenzy the soul is concentrated in the imagination; "it immediately becomes a habitation for the lower spirits, from whom it often receives wonderful instruction in the manual arts; thus we see a quite unskilled man suddenly become a painter or an architect, or a quite outstanding master in another art of the same kind." This spirit may also prophesy natural events (p. 357). Vincent of Beauvais (*Speculum morale*, 1624 ed., I, cap. IX, col. 9–10, divided the three principal goods given to man by God; the divine image (intellective soul) was darkened by ignorance, the similitude (body) by concupiscence, and the immortality of the body by infirmity. There are arts of wisdom, virtue, and necessity. Wisdom (*sapientia*) is the comprehension of things as they are; virtue is a habit of mind consistent with the reasons of nature; necessity is that without which we are not able to live. Theory was invented for *sapientia*, practice for virtue, and the mechanical for necessity. Theory expels ignorance, wisdom illuminates; practice excludes vice and strengthens virtue; the mechanical arts avoid penury and temper the defects of the present life.

ductive (*poietike*), the last of which became the medieval mechanical arts. Hugh of St. Victor followed this same scheme, as we have seen.

Pomponazzi argued that all of these intellects were shared in some degree by every mature person. Even if we are not astronomers, we know something of the time measured by the sun and moon, the passage of seasons and years, and thus use a kind of unconscious speculative knowledge in the conduct of our affairs. Still, only a small number of us are true speculators, and if speculation is properly undertaken by only a few, the lowest activity of intellect, the productive, is natural to all men and not a matter of choice. It is not a matter of choice because production is necessary to the maintenance of human life:

> the productive intellect, which is the lowest and mechanical, is common to all men [*intellectus factivus qui infimus & mecanicus est, omnibus quidem hominibus est comunis*]; nay, even beasts participate in it . . . since many beasts build houses, and many other things which indicate the productive intellect. And this is most necessary, in as much as the greater part of men have been occupied with it. Whence the female sex apply themselves almost completely to it, as in weaving, spinning, sewing, etc. And the greatest part of men spend their time in agriculture, then in different crafts.

Between the extremes of the theoretical or speculative intellect and the productive intellect, Pomponazzi had clearly reserved the practical intellect for moral behavior, both public and private, which he regarded as the highest and most truly human pursuit. He identified the arts – which are for him all mechanical – with the *vis cogitativa,* which he promoted to the level of the lowest form of intellect. Another variation of this scheme was set out in the middle of the sixteenth century by Benedetto Varchi, who wrote the commentary on Michelangelo's sonnet discussed at the end of Chapter 10. Varchi identified the human soul with reason (*ragione*), which he divided into particular and universal reason.[17] Particular reason he in turn identified with the *cogitativa,* citing Averroes's commentary on Aristotle. The *cogitativa* treats particulars and, although it is mortal, is not found in animals, which instead have the comparable but lower power of estimation. Universal reason, which is also proper to man, is concerned only with things that are "deprived of all matter, but purified of all passions and material accidents, [things] consequently ingenerate and incorruptible." Universal reason is in turn divided into superior reason, the speculative or contemplative intellect, and inferior reason, the practical or active intellect. Superior reason is concerned with the cognition of first principles, with wisdom and science, which last is the cognition of universal and necessary things through demonstration. Varchi insists upon this definition of science because it is his intention, as stated at the begining of his argument, to set right the common usage that makes "art" and "science" synonymous. According to Varchi, science is associated with the superior reason, art with the inferior, as he proceeds to argue.

[17] BT, I, p. 6. For another reading, see L. Mendelsohn, *Paragoni: Benedetto Varchi's "Due lezzoni" and Cinquecento Art Theory,* Ann Arbor, Mich., 1982.

The end of inferior reason is not knowing or understanding, but rather acting and working (*fare et operare*), corresponding to prudence, the chief of all the moral virtues, and art. Art is thus the lowest of the five intellectual habits.[18] Varchi's scheme viewed as a whole is thus similar to that of Pomponazzi, but he has raised art from the level of the *cogitativa,* and elevated its status as a form of intellect, by giving it a place in the practical intellect, the lower slot in inferior universal reason. At the same time it is still immediate to the *cogitativa,* and thus to particular reason.

Varchi, having made these clarifications, proceeds to an Aristotelian definition of art: "Art is a factive habit, with true reason, of those things that are not necessary, the origin of which is not in the things that are made, but in him who makes them." He explains that it is a habit because one must not only be disposed to an art but must also be practiced in it; art is called "factive" in order to distinguish it from the moral virtue of prudence, which acts *a sua voglia* and is dependent on matter. Art is said to be done "with true reason" because the arts are infallible. By this he means that one is either practicing an art or he is not, and if he is, he will necessarily achieve his end, or, if he does not achieve his end, that he must have wandered from the true practice of his art. Art is also said to be done "with true reason" in order to distinguish it from "the art with which spiders make their marvelous webs, and swallows and other animals make a nest, and many other things not being made by reason but only by natural instinct, they may not be truly called art." This distinction is exactly the distinction usually made to distinguish the human *cogitativa* from the animal *estimativa* (a distinction made only weakly by Pomponazzi), and Varchi's argument differs little from that of Averroes, according to whom the *cogitativa* was rational in that it belonged to a rational animal, not in that it is actually intellect. Such a conclusion is even more inescapable in Varchi's explanation of the end of its definition. If art does not have to do with particulars, like the *cogitativa,* it is still immediate to the particular, and is concerned with "those things that are not necessary," with the "contingent," with those things that "may be and not be equally." Art is thus not a science because it is not concerned with necessary things. For Varchi the "contingency" of works of art is two-sided. On the one hand, as we have just seen, it identifies art with the particular and the material, but another sense of contingency brings him to the Aristotelian argument that works of art differ from works of nature in that their origin and guiding principles are to be found not in themselves but rather in the person who makes them, a notion to which Varchi gave close attention in his commentary on Michelangelo's sonnet "Non ha l'ottimo artista alcun concetto."[19]

What is not resolved in Varchi's scheme is the relation between what Pomponazzi called "productive intellect" and the higher intellectual faculties. Art is

[18] BT, I, p. 9.
[19] *MLA*, pp. 203–233.

not prudence and it is not science, wisdom, or cognition of first principles. It is also in some sense mechanical (as he equates mechanical with "factive").[20] Within these ground rules, Varchi sets out to define the nature of thinking appropriate to art.

Sciences, Varchi says, are ranked primarily according to their subjects and secondarily according to the certainty of their demonstrations; arts, on the other hand, are ranked primarily according to their end and secondarily according to their subjects. Having established its end, an art then proceeds to find the means to that end. Citing Galen, he argues that arts may be ordered and taught in three ways, which he calls *risolutivo, compositivo,* and *diffinitivo,* intending by doing so to establish the general principles according to which an art may be defined. He then returns to the common usage from which he distanced himself at the beginning. Sometimes art is identified with science; sometimes art is identified with prudence (he cites Petrarch, who called virtue a "fine art" – *bell'arte*); and sometimes the word "art" is used to refer to habit gained only by experience, by use, practice, and custom, which he quite properly associates with the *cogitativa,* as opposed to "true and certain reason."

According to Varchi the arts were invented for various reasons, some out of necessity, some for utility, still others for delight. Some were found by *uomini ingegnosi,* some by *uomini poveri* for the purposes of sustaining life, here no doubt an allusion once again to the ancient distinction between the liberal and the manual arts. None of the arts was invented at once, but rather gradually, and cumulatively. Pursuing the social distinction implied by the division of the arts, he notes that some arts are called "liberal" – "that is, worthy of free men and not slaves" – and others are illiberal, able to be practiced by everyone. After considering the relations of art to material, to nature (from which all arts have their origin), and to one another, Varchi decides that all the arts are mechanical in a neutral sense of the word, in that they necessarily make use in some way of body (*corpo*). Given this definition, some arts require either *ingegno* or *fatica* in various degrees, and may be distinguished accordingly. Although all men possess the arts and sciences potentially by nature, some are more disposed to certain of them than are others.

As we have seen, Varchi accepts the Aristotelian idea that the work of art is a *composito,* a union of form and matter, and that the origin of the work of art is in the craftsman. He examines four interdependent causes necessary to the making of art. The material cause is that out of which the work is made; the formal cause defines the work as one thing or another, a horse, for example, or a centaur; the efficient cause is the craftsman himself; and the "most noble" cause, the final cause, is that which may be as much the desire for glory as the need or will to earn a living."[21]

[20] BT, I, p. 19.
[21] Ibid., p. 23.

Apparently in extension of the idea that all men possess the arts *in potentia*, Varchi defines them as active potentials, able to work in many ways, thus even the most mechanical arts avail themselves of philosophy to some extent. The mason or woodcutter uses the square without even perhaps knowing its proper name, and his art carries with it Euclid's discussion of solid bodies, even if he is ignorant of the science of geometry.

Varchi returns to his distinction between science and art, this time turning the difference to positive effect. Whereas science is concerned with necessary truth in its subject, art is concerned with its proper end. Thus there are demonstrations in both science and art, but in art demonstration is toward a presupposed end, which is, he says, contingent.

Art differs from virtue because works of art are good and/or useful in themselves, and the circumstances of their making do not affect their value.[22] A virtuous act, for example, is not virtuous if done under constraint, but a work of art made under constraint may still be good. Because he is comparing art and virtue, Varchi gives intermittent attention to art and morality, arguing that a lowly art may be elevated if turned to a higher cause. He also argues that all arts are in themselves good and invented for beneficial ends, but that they may be used for bad purposes by evil men, and that art used for cruel and horrific purposes is not art, a higher "good" thus transcending the beauty or utility, say, of a bronze bull in which men are to be roasted alive. Acts of virtue also have a kind of absoluteness that works of art do not have. We can try things out in art, but not in virtue, and if we err in art we are still an artist, but if we err in virtue we are no longer virtuous. At the same time, art and virtue are very similar in that both are learned with long and continuous exercise. Art requires both learning (*dottrina*) and use and exercise, the first sharpening the mind, the second perfecting the hand.[23]

All of these questions turn around the relation between art as an intellective habit and the higher practical intellect and speculative intellect, problems set by the Averroistic scheme from which his discussion set out, and problems finally implicit in Aristotle's own definition of both art and virtue. Varchi concludes, still citing Aristotle's *Ethics*, that the arts consult and deliberate, as the sciences do, turning other kinds of knowledge to their purposes. When Aristotle wrote that the arts do not deliberate (*Physics* 199b28), he meant that they do not deliberate about their ends, although they may constantly deliberate about the means to these ends. The means of art, the multiform results of these deliberations, make up a body of knowledge in their own right, and Varchi finally argues that the person who understands these means is more worthy than the person who simply employs them.

Never deviating from the issues raised by the arguments in the opening par-

[22] Ibid., p. 25.
[23] Ibid., p. 26.

agraphs of Aristotle's *Metaphysics,* Varchi closes his essay with an examination of the relation between art and experience, that is to say, between knowing the principles of an art and being able to do it. There are, he says two differences between art and experience, one in "knowing" (*conoscere*), "because experience knows only singular things or particular things." It might be expected that art would be different from experience in that it "knows" the universal, which is the opposite of the particular. But Varchi does not say that art is concerned with the universal because to do so would have confused it with a science. In fact, he does not say how art differs from experience in point of "knowing," and moves on to the difference in working (*operare*). In this aspect there is no difference between them, he says, because both are concerned with particular things, and they are different only in the "effect and benefit" of their working: "because the expert or truly practiced [artist] works with greater certainty, and consequently benefits more, and certainly errs less, because he knows the singular *per se* and the universal *per accidens.*" The *scienziato* then is more worthy, but less useful because, as Aristotle often says, it is the particular that the doctor treats, Socrates and not man. Still the *scienziato* knows more and is wiser and is able to teach the art, which the merely practical person, who does not know reasons, cannot do. Turning to a biological metaphor, Varchi concludes his argument by saying that the *scienziato* is able to reproduce and perpetuate his art by teaching it, which the practical person is not.[24]

In the course of argument Varchi states that art knows the universal per se. What does he mean by that if art does not "know" the universal? The "universals" in this case must simply be the principles of art itself, over and above the rules of experience, the precepts that earn art its lowest rung on the practical intellect, and that make its exercise into a kind of subprudence. Similarly, art is not science, but the person who knows its principles is relatively *scienziato.*

In short, art is different from science in that the conclusions of its demonstrations are contingent. They are contingent because, like prudence, art is always about the particular. Art is closely linked to experience and practice, and is thus closely related to the *vis cogitativa,* with which Varchi in fact identified the *intelletto* that guides the hand to the realization of the *concetto,* the subject of the *lezzione* on Michelangelo's sonnet, twin to the one we are considering. But just as there is true prudence as opposed to the natural, so there is true art as opposed to that based only on *ingenium* and experience. On such Aristotelian and neo-Aristotelian principles, the imagination is artistically corrigible just as it is morally corrigible.

Paolo Pino and Romano Alberti

In his *Dialogo di Pittura,* Paola Pino argues that painting was called "liberal" by the ancients "as proper to the intellect and to free men," and he stresses its connection with philosophy.[25] Its relation to intellect arises from the fact that

[24] Ibid., pp. 31–32.
[25] Ibid., p. 107.

the *imaginativa* (which the painter must of course use) may not operate unless what is imagined has been brought into the presence of the *idea* by the other "intrinsic senses," referring to the general abstracting power of inner sense and especially to the *cogitativa*. This argument must be examined with care. It need not mean that the image in the artist's *imaginativa* must be "judged" by an idea in the intellect, and more probably means that we do not imagine without benefit of experience and knowledge about what we imagine, so that painting, rather than being "mere imagination," is in its very act of imagination also an act of intellect. In any case, the intellect gives "integrity" to what is imagined, being the – relatively – perfect understanding of whatever thing is imagined. However, because the intellect in this enterprise does not "wander outside its proper domain, which is understanding (*intendere*) (that is, since ideas are invisible), it is asked how the workings of the intellect can be manifest; to this it is responded that "this work is practice, which act does not deserve to be called mechanical." This should probably be understood to mean that painting is an activity of the practical intellect, which "acts" rather than "makes"; and this activity cannot be called mechanical simply because the internal senses are the organs of the intellect, or the intellective soul, and "are the only means by which it may express and give knowledge of what it understands. And this activity is not outside the proper function of the intellect because the senses (external and internal) are moved precisely by the intellect." This insistence on the unitary, interdependent character of the faculties of the human soul points at once to Thomas Aquinas as a source, as does the stress on the aesthetic value of integrity. Pino invokes this value several times. In his praise of painting, for example, he says that although "all the arts imitate nature, "this above all others imitates all natural things with greater integrity and causes those produced by the mechanical arts."[26] The same arguments about relation of inner sense and intellect were to be made by Federico Zuccaro.

Pino's arguments were repeated by Romano Alberti, who considerably expanded the point that the intellect works by means of both inner sense and external materials (as Zuccaro also would), adding that painting works with extrinsic things much as the theologian or orator use writing, or the mathematician uses a compass, chalk, or an astrobabe.[27] Alberti defines the *nobilissimo soggetto* of painting as that shared with natural philosophy (or physics), "seeking to imitate on surfaces, and to express the form of natural bodies by means of the accidents, quantity, quality, shape, color, movement and similar things." The painter, moreover, exercises all three operations of the intellect, which "according to Aristotle, are apprehension, composition or judgment, and discourse." These operations of the intellect, it becomes clear, are operations of the *organs* of the intellect, that is, of external sense, the common sense, or fantasy, and cogitation in interdependent relation to intellect. "Wishing to paint, it is necessary that

[26] Ibid., p. 106. For Aquinas, see *Summa theologiae* I.39.8, where one of the conditions of beauty is defined as *integritas sive perfectio*.
[27] BT, III, p. 206–209.

the painter have acute senses and a very good *imaginativa,* with which he apprehends things placed before his eyes, and so that those [things], abstracted then from the presence [before the eyes] and transformed into phantasms, may be brought perfectly to the intellect." The first activity of intellect is thus the discrimination by sight and clear ("perfect") translation of the forms of natural bodies to the intellect. This leads to the second operation, in which the "intellect itself" composes those things together by means of *giudizio;* and in the third operation, discourse, the intellect "concludes" the original phantasms in the perfection of a "history, or whatever." Then, by means of the "motor potency" (that is, primarily, the hands) the new phantasm is presented in painting. This is the psychological version of the kind of procedure evident, for example, in drawings in which studies of *garzoni* may turn into angels or Madonnas or Christ and the apostles. But it is to be noted that the painting is spoken of as finished in the mind of the painter before it is actually begun, before the hands of the painter come into play. Alberti in fact continues his argument with an example from painting. "A painter wishing to paint a man, firstly must apprehend by means of visual rays the contours and other accidents, and bring these same to the intellect by means of the imagination; [and the intellect], after having judged that that contour ought to be round, that other straight, the colors, one burning and another dim, finally with discourse concludes a proportional figure of a man. The same [the painter] then represents as painted, and this will be more perfect as the painter will have availed himself of these operations." Apelles, we are reminded, was so "exercised" in these operations that he could draw someone from memory on demand. And Alberti concludes that painters are melancholy because "they keep *phantasms* fixed in the *intellect*" (my emphasis). Clearly the distinction between particular intellect and intellect has closed, and the activities of both are, in result, the same activities.

13

The spark of God

The *Idea* of Federico Zuccaro

Federico Zuccaro's *L'Idea de' pittori, scultori e architetti* was published in Turin in 1607, two years before his death, and some three years before the deaths of Caravaggio and Annibale Carracci. The book is quite rightly regarded as the end of Italian Renaissance art literature, and it is also rightly regarded as the furthest theoretical development of the idea of *disegno.* Federico Zuccaro was the founder of the Accademia di San Luca in Rome, and his *Idea,* as if to confirm our late Romantic suspicions of academies and academicians in general, is by far the most systematic of Renaissance treatises on art, drawing heavily on Aristotle and Aquinas, and on Renaissance developments of the philosophies of both writers. Because Aristotle tends to be regarded as a medieval rather than a classical writer, because Scholasticism is the conventional counterpart to humanism, and because the ideas that define the modern world are believed to have arisen in opposition to both Aristotelianism and Scholasticism, Zuccaro's presentation is doubly opaque because it is neither easily understandable, not is there much desire to understand it. We have now gained a position, however, from which Zuccaro's arguments are more clearly visible, and we shall see in this last chapter that not only are these arguments solidly within the long tradition we have been tracing, but that partly because of this very fact, they constitute both a culminating and a transforming statement of Renaissance art theory.[1]

When Zuccaro's accomplishment is characterized in one or two sentences, he is called the champion of "metaphysical *disegno,*" and it is in this role that he is perhaps best known. This characterization is true enough, but taken by itself the phrase has connotations that block the understanding of his book from the outset.

[1] I have used the facsimile edition of the *Idea* in D. Heikamp, *Scritti d'arte di Federico Zuccaro.* Page numbers refer to Heikamp's modern numeration at the foot of the pages.

The very term "metaphysical" seems to suggest Platonism;[2] but his definition of the arts of design, his *idea,* is, as we shall see, thoroughly Aristotelian.

By far the most important reading of Federico Zuccaro's *Idea* was offered by Erwin Panofsky in his own *Idea* of 1924.[3] Panofsky saw Zuccaro's treatise as a major departure from earlier Renaissance writing on art in that, rather than simply assuming that art stands in a certain relation to nature, it explicitly raised the question of how art itself is even possible. This in turn brought the subject–object question more sharply into focus, so that, taken all in all, Zuccaro's treatise is seen by Panofsky, its "Aristotelian – Thomistic" appurtenances notwithstanding, as an important bridge between the Renaissance and the later modern period.

Panofsky presents Zuccaro as a kind of Platonist manqué, a writer who saw the priority of the *idea,* of the inner image over the outer, but who was prevented by his Aristotelianism from conceiving a "purified" or "intensified" reality, as later academic writers would do. These later writers would use the Neoplatonic notion of beauty to justify a kind of art – an ideal classicism – that Zuccaro, with his Aristotelian emphasis on "formative process," could not possibly have imagined. Zuccaro could only ground human art in analogies to God and nature, not in its participation in the beautiful, with which he was in fact not at all concerned.

Because Zuccaro vehemently rejected any suggestion that mathematics was important to art, Panofsky called him the "chief spokesman" for the Mannerist "protest against rules," even though he was the founder of the Accademia di San Luca and the first academic writer on art, a contradiction pointing to "the duality of Mannerist thought," a desire at once for freedom and rules, finally rooted in the "one great contrast between 'subject' and 'object.' " This interpretation has been followed by Moshe Barasch, Zuccaro's most recent interpreter,[4] who, like

[2] Julius von Schlosser, *La letteratura artistica,* p. 388, devoted little space to Zuccaro's *Idea,* but called it "notable for its explicit Platonisms" and wrote that in his treatise Zuccaro had "almost completed the foundation of classical aesthetics." These opinions were published in 1924. A. Blunt, *Artistic Theory in Italy, 1450–1600,* Oxford, 1940, p. 142, presents Zuccaro as an Aristotelian and a Thomist, but notes that he is inclined to Neoplatonism, that he gives Plato as the source of his theory of Ideas, and that he talks of light in a Neoplatonic manner toward the end of his treatise. S. Rossi, "Idea e accademia. Studio sulle teorie artistiche di Federico Zuccaro. I. Disegno interno e disegno esterno," *Storia dell'arte,* 20, 1974, pp. 37–56, argues that Zuccaro's *Idea,* in addition to its debt to Aristotle and Aquinas (which Rossi seems to want to limit to the idea of imitation) is also radically dependent on Augustine's doctrine of illumination and Ficino's philosophy of love. It is hard to deny the possible influence of Augustine out of hand for any later writer, and Ficino's commentary on the *Symposium* was certainly important for late Cinquecento art theory, as Panofsky has shown in the case of Lomazzo (*Idea,* pp. 97–99). Zuccaro, however, expressly denies any kind of *innatismo,* calling the soul a *tabula rasa;* and the text cited by Rossi (p. 43) in support of his argument (Zuccaro, *Idea,* I, XIII; *Scritti,* p. 184)–"le cose non sono nell'anima ma le loro forme"–is a reference to *De anima* 431b29, and Zuccaro's whole argument at this point recapitulates and elaborates Aristotle's. The text means that the intellect passes from potential to actual in apprehending the form of a thing, and does not mean that the forms spoken of are in any sense innate. This point is essential, and a correct reading of Zuccaro's argument is to my mind not possible from the standpoint of the Platonic alternative chosen by Rossi.

[3] Panofsky, *Idea,* pp. 75–80; pp. 83–95.

[4] M. Barasch, *Theories of Art from Plato to Winckelmann,* New York, 1985, pp. 295–303.

Panofsky, linked Zuccaro's arguments with Giordano Bruno's claim that there are as many rules as there are poets, or with Francesco Patrizi's sweeping rejection of Aristotle's *Poetics.*

In addition to being a theorist, Federico Zuccaro was a painter. He was less than a great painter, but he was active through a long life, painted for many of the major courts of Europe, and enjoyed a considerable reputation among his contemporaries. Through the decade of the 1590s, Zuccaro decorated his own house with allegorical paintings, which, because they are necessarily more compact and emblematic than the intricate expatiations of his later treatise, state some of his central concepts with a valuable introductory clarity. In the center of the ceiling of one of the rooms of the so called *Sala del Disegno* (Fig. 7), which probably served as a *studiolo,* Zuccaro painted a sharply foreshortened, bearded allegory of *Disegno,* surrounded by female allegories of the three arts of design, painting, sculpture, and architecture. *Disegno* is haloed by three wreaths symbolizing the trinitarian unity of the three arts, a variant on the personal device of Michelangelo, and gazes upward to a higher source of light, toward which he seems to be ascending. Beneath his feet *putti* smile down toward the viewers in the space of the room and point to two inscriptions on a plaque. These read LUX INTELLECTUS ET VITA OPERATIONUM (light of the intellect and life of activities) and UNA LUX IN TRIBUS REFULGENS (one light shining in three). *Disegno* is characterized as a light, deriving from the ultimate and central light of divine grace. As a light to the intellect it must be higher than intellect, and at the same time it is a light that is refracted in the subordinate lights of painting, sculpture, and architecture. Outside this central section are allegories of *scientia, medicina, militia,* and *harmonia.*

The implications of the arrangement of Zuccaro's ceiling are in fact similar to the bold argument of his *Idea,* published some ten years after the painting was made: that *disegno* is the highest of all spiritual principles, according to which all creation, human and divine, is realized. *Disegno* is the creative force of the human mind, evident in all our activities, from sensation and the conduct of life to the most marvelous achievements of art and the loftiest feats of speculation, a mirror of the divine creativity that ordained the world and continually brings it into existence. For Zuccaro, *disegno* (which really means drawing, and, more specifically, as Zuccaro himself wrote of it, drawing with lines) is separated from the arts as such, but, just because this separation has occurred, the arts may become sciences, which is to say that their characteristic rules and procedures are free to find their place among all human activities. In fact, in Zuccaro's scheme the arts of design have become the major paradigms for all human creative activity (or for all arts and sciences, which are inevitably creative in some way or another), and as the status of the arts is elevated the fantastic and productive faculties of the soul continue their rise in status. Separated from drawing and defined by light, dark, and color, Zuccaro's allegorical figure of Painting bears the legend AEMULA NATURAE, the rival of nature. Painting is the mirror of

Fig. 7. Federico Zuccaro, *Allegory of Design, Surrounded by Figures of Architecture, Sculpture, and Painting,* ca. 1599. Ceiling fresco, Sala del Disegno, Palazzo Zuccari, Rome.

God's painting in nature and of the creative force of nature in the invention of endless new things.[5]

Walter Friedländer gave Zuccaro a most unsympathetic characterization both as a painter and as a writer, coupling his ideas with the worst features of the "medievalism" of the Counter-Reformation.[6] He also contrasted him unfavorably with his much younger contemporary, Caravaggio, one of the most revolutionary and star-crossed painters in the history of Western art. In this contrast of characters, Friedländer argues, there is to be seen for the first time what will later become the contrast between the academician and the bohemian, extremes united by the newly won high status of the artist in society, which is able to embrace them both. Barasch compares Zuccaro and Caravaggio rather than contrasting them, calling Zuccaro a "social conformist" who was still the "spokesman of the most radical aesthetic theory advanced prior to the nineteenth century." In this chapter it will be argued that Zuccaro was in no way a Platonist, and that his arguments justify an intense naturalism. In this way, not simply as an anticanonical writer, he may be compared to Caravaggio, who united naturalism and realism with a force far surpassing anything in earlier painting. On the way to his definition of painting, Zuccaro raised the significance of human art as a paradigm for human thought in general – and at the same time raised many of our themes – to levels without real precedent in the literature of art.

Zuccaro's book is divided into two parts, which he called *disegno interno* and *disegno esterno*. *Disegno interno* is the province of all possible sensation, imagination, and memory. Although Zuccaro insists that he is writing as a painter (which he of course was), and is using the language appropriate to painting, his scheme is also an extreme development of the Aristotelian idea that there is no mental activity without a phantasm (a principle he often repeats), or, less technically, of the idea that thought is always related in some way to a mental picture. *Disegno interno* is both perception and conception; we may speak of the activity of the senses and imagination as *disegno interno* as well as the activity of, say, the practical intellect, because it is necessary to imagine what we are going to do in order to be "guided" in doing it.[7]

Disegno esterno is made up of the visible world, which is the painting of God, together with all artificial things, which, still according to Aristotle, are consequent to mental images. Zuccaro thus reduced all apprehensible reality, inner and outer, to the same principle of *disegno*, so that there is a kind of sympathy and continuity between the mind and visible nature, or between one mind and the products of another.

[5] See K. Hermann-Fiore, "Die Fresken Federico Zuccaris in seinem Römischen Künstlerhaus," *Römisches Jahrbuch für Kunstgeschichte*, 18, 1979, pp. 35–112, who stresses the essential relation of Zuccaro's scheme to ideas of Leonardo da Vinci (p. 79) and to earlier central Italian theory.

[6] W. Friedländer, "The Academician and the Bohemian: Zuccari and Caravaggio," *GBA*, 6 ser., 33, 1948, pp. 27–36.

[7] Zuccaro, *Scritti*, p. 168.

According to Aristotle, as we have seen, all sensation is the apprehension of the forms of things without their matter, and all mental operations from sensation upward are thus more or less "abstract," and when Zuccaro calls mental images "ideas" he means no more than that they are immaterial. Zuccaro rejected the Platonic doctrine of ideas, except in the divine intellect, in which they are the principle of "every perfection of order and measure" in creation.[8] "*Disegno,* or *Idea* is nothing if not created things." God brings things into existence, men apprehend them and paint them. Creation was done according to divine ideas, which are not distinct in the divine mind, but rather identical with the divine nature itself. But because God created the world according to the things in his mind, God himself may be said to possess *disegno interno.* Zuccaro quotes Aquinas on the subject, as well as Augustine, to whom he had been referred by the theologians.[9] According to Augustine, Zuccaro says, the force of the ideas is so great that if they are not understood, "no one may be wise." But this principle is immediately turned to more Aristotelian purposes: "*idea* in Greek means the same as *forma* in Latin; whence by 'ideas' are understood the forms really distinct from those things that are existing in themselves." As separable from matter, forms link individuals of a kind. Forms are necessary to generation; in the making of new things form is necessary in order that they not be done by chance, "as a man generates a man." This is true not only of nature, but of art. "In those that operate by intellect . . . the similitude of the house stands in the mind of the builder. And this may be called the Idea of the house, because the artisan intends to assimilate the house to the form that he had in his mind." God worked in such a manner when he created the world, and this is the principle of the intelligibility of the world. We do not apprehend things themselves but rather their forms, that is, we apprehend that about them which may be immaterial and intelligible. We apprehend these forms, however, in the way that is appropriate to us, through sense. We do not apprehend the ideas in the mind of God. Again, our ideas are determined by these conditions; the mental image that precedes the building of a real house is what Panofsky, following Aquinas, called a "quasi-idea,"[10] analogous to divine ideas but in no way identical with them.

From such a standpoint, it is possible to understand why in other contexts Zuccaro emphatically rejected the Platonic doctrine of ideas, following Aristotle and Aquinas. Zuccaro argued that all our knowledge is through the senses and that the intellect is the susceptibility of all possible knowledge. It is a *tabula rasa,* "a spacious, smooth canvas prepared by us painters to receive all those figures that will be painted upon it, but in itself retaining no form, or shadow of form."[11] This, of course, is not a foreshadowing of John Locke but an appeal to Aristotle's *De anima* (429b–430a), or to Aquinas's identification of the *tabula*

[8] Ibid., pp. 156–158.
[9] He cites *Summa theologiae* I.15.1.
[10] Panofsky, *Idea,* pp. 39–43.
[11] *Scritti,* pp. 172–173.

rasa with the possible intellect. In one of his discourses, Zuccaro in fact clearly identified *disegno interno* and the *tabula rasa* with the possible and agent intellect.[12]

Zuccaro also accepted the corresponding principle that only particulars are real. Although angels may apprehend forms immediately, we are not angels; it is our universal lot to come to know through sensation, and this would be true even if we were to be put back in Paradise. Those who have interpreted Aristotle correctly, he argues, have said that "the things which our intellect knows naturally and directly are the natures of material things, the nature of the heavens, that of the elements, and that of things made up of the elements [*cose elementate*], stones, plants, trees, animals and men, the which natures are not found separate from individuals." He again explicitly opposes these arguments to those "who hold Plato divine in his position on Ideas." In reality, he argues, there are only the particulars underlying these ideas; "because humanity does not exist if not in these and those singulars, and the nature of the lion is only in these and those lions."[13] Moreover, the intellect only understands things insofar as they *are* particulars, and this requires the two principal internal senses, the *fantasia* and the *cogitativa.*

Zuccaro is also emphatic – and even repetitive – in insisting on the Aristotelian principle that the soul in itself is potential and that sensation is absolutely essential to its becoming actual. Just as the eye, the "guide of the body," may have the faculty of seeing but cannot actually see without external light and the object, so the *concetto* or *disegno,* the "guide of the soul," is the internal light of the intellect, and this internal light is dependent on external light. The intellect, in other words, cannot see without the light of nature.[14] Here again Zuccaro is following Aristotle (*De anima* 430a10ff.), who writes that what was called the agent intellect makes the contents of the passive possible intellect intelligible, just as natural light makes potential color actual and visible. Most significantly, Zuccaro identifies *Disegno* with the agent intellect, which "makes all things." *Disegno* is thus like the possible and agent intellect, both of which are placed at a level close to sensation and imagination.

Metaphors of illumination are common in all accounts of the activity of intellect, and Zuccaro also makes liberal use of them. Avicenna, to take one example, followed Aristotle in arguing that sense is illuminated by the light of the agent intellect in order to make *intelligibilia* out of phantasms.[15] He also argued that the agent intellect is separate from the human soul, as did Averroes. For Aquinas, on the other hand, the agent intellect is in the human soul itself.[16] He argued that if the agent intellect were separate, it could have no relation to the human soul and could therefore not interact with it. The separate intellect is no longer

[12] Ibid., p. 33.
[13] Ibid., p. 178.
[14] Ibid., p. 269.
[15] Harvey, *Inward Wits,* pp. 56–57.
[16] *Summa theologiae* I.79.4.

something in which man participates, it is rather the divine intellect. According to Aquinas, we have in ourselves the power to abstract and reason, and this power he cites Aristotle in calling a light, thus placing it in a metaphorical relation of dependency upon the separate intellect, which he cites Plato in calling the sun.[17] "The separate intellect, according to the teaching of our faith, is God himself, Who is the soul's creator and only beatitude. . . . Wherefore the human soul derives its intellectual light from Him, according to the Psalm [4:7], "the light to Thy countenance, O Lord, is signed upon us.' "[18] This is the scheme of Zuccaro's allegory of *Disegno* (see again Fig. 7).

Aquinas embraced the implications of his arguments, which, as we have seen, pushed intellect toward sense and blurred the distinction between the particular (or passive) and agent intellects. He was no doubt willing to do this because it moved the principle of immortality – the intellective soul – toward identification with the individual soul. Aquinas also accepted the implication that agent intellects, as individual, were different one from another, and that the only simple and truly separate intellect was the divine intellect. Here again the distinction between the separate and particular intellect is blurred. If the agent intellect is cut away from absolute intellect, it at the same time moves toward the *cogitativa,* toward real activities of discourse and imagination. It is to such a system – a fallible particular intellect enlightened and sustained by the mind of God as evident in the providentially rational system of the world – that Zuccaro adapted his theory of *disegno interno.* And it is within such a system that he is able to assign such absolute importance to the arts of design.

Zuccaro took from Aquinas the idea that the body and the faculties of the soul are bound in a close unity governed by the intellect; and his *disegno interno* closely linked universal and particular reason. But the close interdependence of the intellective soul and its organs implied that the disposition of the senses is the real condition of the intellect, which is simply to say again that the intellect is in an individual.

In this sublunary world, Zuccaro argues, the lower spheres are governed by the higher, much as in clocks the smaller wheels are moved by the larger; and so the higher faculties of the soul govern the lower. In order to be able to understand, discourse, judge, design, and acquire knowledge (*scienza*), and to avail itself of what has been acquired, the intellect "moves our eye . . . to see the whole and the parts, in order then to know and judge what may be one thing or another, and to establish the differences between them."[19] All of the lower faculties of the soul are guided by the *concetto* of *disegno intellettivo,* the singular form of the soul, the virtue that makes it "discourse and understand perfectly."[20] Again he writes in similar hierarchical terms that "intellect and judgment [*giu-*

[17] Ibid. I.79.5.
[18] Ibid. I.79.4.
[19] *Scritti,* p. 179.
[20] Ibid., pp. 183–184.

dicio], moves and orders the will; it moves the lower human powers, and these move the hand, the 'instrument of instruments' to produce artificial things."[21]

The rational, or constitutively human soul, according to Zuccaro, is an organic unity of faculties, comparable to the body, and may be considered in its various aspects.[22] "When it enlivens and animates, the soul is life, that gives movement and spirit; when it discourses and forms *disegno* within itself it is mind [*mente*]; when it understands [*intende*] it is intellect; when it judges things understood it is judgment; when it sees and hears sensible things and it conserves [them] it is memory; and when it chooses and avoids, it is will." Thus, he concludes, "we say that the soul is everything with respect to activity" (*operare*). This text is of interest because it distinguishes among the activities of the soul in general with activity and with actual operations (*operare*). Again, *disegno* is associated with the *cogitativa*, but, as in Aquinas, the distinction between this faculty and the intellect, which is an individual intellect, is not so sharply drawn.

Zuccaro devotes chapters to the *disegno interno* of God and the angels, both to compare and contrast them to the *disegno interno* of the human mind. Human *disegno interno* is like that of God only in certain respects and is not comparable to that of the angels at all. God is unlike man in that he perfectly understands creation all at once, but is like man in that he formed an Idea of the world before creating it, and this most sublime *concetto* is a kind of *disegno*.[23] Human art is relatively puny. *Disegno divino* is "most perfect, and of infinite *virtù*, and ours is imperfect; and while our art may be the cause of some minor effects, of little moment, divine art is of the very greatest and most important effects."[24]

Angels are spiritual, all other created things are corporeal, but man as "the horizon of the world" is *di natura mezzana*, both spirit and body.[25] "If it were not for the soul, man would be an animal, and if it were not for the body he would be an angel, and a God on earth." This miraculous conjunction amazed the most learned philosophers, "whence Mercurius Trismegistus called man Great." But all such praise aside, man in fact is neither God nor angel; instead, humanity is suited to its proper ontological realm, which is that of knowledge through sense. "By means of the sensitive potencies the soul forms its *disegno interno*, and then understands, judges, discourses and wills; then it commands, moves, governs, and in short dominates in this its most happy reign." Although we are only "a small copy of the excellence of divine art"[26] and we cannot have the pure contemplative knowledge of the angels, the human intellective soul still has by nature the possibility of knowing through sense "spiritual forms representing all the things of this world," and this possibility, again, this *tabula rasa*,

[21] Ibid., p. 202.
[22] Ibid., p. 183.
[23] Ibid., pp. 156–157.
[24] Ibid., pp. 170–171.
[25] This splendid image owes to Aquinas. See *Summa contra Gentiles*, II, 68 and 81; IV, 55; *Summa theologiae* I.72.2.
[26] *Scritti*, p. 162.

does not depend from the body, but is from God. It is by virtue of this that man may be "almost a second God." By means of our *disegno interno intellettivo* we are able to form in ourselves a "new world." This world is new in two senses: first, it is the external world of God and nature adapted to the conditions of human knowledge, through which we "have and enjoy an internal spiritual reality corresponding to the natural reality mankind enjoys and dominates." But from the same stalk grows another "new world," a world of human creation. Man "almost imitating God and emulating nature may produce infinite artificial things similar to the natural, and by means of painting and sculpture, make us see new paradises on earth."[27]

For Zuccaro, as for others, the human soul is distinguished from the animal soul not by the vegetative and sensitive powers, which it shares with plants and animals, but by its ability to apprehend "spiritual species representing corporeal things," which may, however, not be apprehended without corporeal organs, that is, without senses, external and internal. It follows that Zuccaro is not much interested in sense as such, and imagines his *disegno interno* as playing over the terrain between the common sense and intellectual intuition.

When Zuccaro explained how *disegno interno* is formed in us, he was dependent on a faculty psychology with the main outlines of which we are by this time thoroughly familiar.[28] In his scheme there are four internal senses, the common sense, the fantasy, *cogitativa,* and memory. The first of these, the common sense, is the origin and center of the five external senses. It knows (*conosce*) everything known by the external senses, and is their "rector and judge" (*giudice*). The common sense passes on to the *fantasia* – the second faculty – not only the species from the special senses, but others formed in its own cognition, judgment, and comparison of those species. The *fantasia* also has a memorative function, and in addition to conserving species, composes them together, "forming of them new species, presenting new things, as we may experience in dreams, such that, having seen, for example, mountains, streams, plants, men and gold, we may see in dreams mountains of gold, and so forth."

The third and highest of Zuccaro's internal senses is the *cogitativa.* This apprehends the "spiritual species" preserved in the *fantasia,* and forms more spiritual species ("intentions"). So eye, the common sense, and fantasy may apprehend a dog and a wolf, but the *cogitativa* (which forms a new image through the *imaginativa*) apprehends in addition the faithfulness of the dog, the voracity of the wolf, and the hostility that exists between them. The *cogitativa* (which he is treating as the *estimativa*) is useful to both animals and men because by means of it the beneficial is distinguished from the harmful. The faculty is superior in men, however, because whereas an animal knows simply that the wolf is harmful, a man knows that the wolf is an individual of the species wolf (and so, in lieu of instinctive reaction, forms through experience the notion that "such an animal

[27] Ibid., pp. 162, 172.
[28] Ibid., pp. 174–175.

is harmful"). "And although it does not know the species, and the nature of things in general, as reason does, it still knows the individuals of that species." Moreover, the *cogitativa* discourses and forms particular propositions. So in animals estimation moves animals to love, hate, or flight "without discourse"; in man, however, discourse precedes such reaction, "and this happens because of the affinity and approximation that the *cogitativa* has with the intellect."

Zuccaro attributes to each of the internal senses a *disegno* of its own;[29] having distinguished between external and internal *disegno,* it is also necessary to distinguish *disegno interno* as sensible and intellectual; the intellectual is divided into speculative and practical, and the sensible is divided into (special) sensible, fantastic, and cogitative. These "designs" are essential to the functioning of intellect and in fact work together with intellect. Not only does the possible intellect attain real content through what is presented to it by external and internal sense, but its activity also demands the cooperation of the *fantasia* and *cogitativa.* In order to think, the intellect commands the *fantasia* and *cogitativa* to "design images and understandings of intentions and circumstances." The intellect thinks universals as the internal senses either present or recall particulars, and this can happen in no other way. This is Zuccaro's version of his often repeated Aristotelian principle that there is no thought without a phantasm. The question of intellective design without images he leaves to the theologians.[30]

Zuccaro divides *disegno humano interno* into speculative and practical.[31] These correspond to the speculative and practical intellects, the first of which is "content only to know," whereas the "principal end" of the practical intellect is working, "or better, to be the beginning of our operations." In fact the border between these two "intellects" is fluid. The practical intellect "distinctly disposes and orders that which is intended," and in some sense knows "because it would not be able to execute or order those things that it intends to do, if in the first place it were unable to know and judge." Both bring benefits to the world, but practical *disegno* is more "fruitful." "Rachel was most beautiful and graceful, but not fruitful; and Leah had dark eyes, but was fruitful."

Rather than dividing the intellect into speculative, practical, and productive (as Pomponazzi and others had done, following Aristotle), Zuccaro simply divided it into speculative and practical, further dividing the practical intellect into *disegno morale* and *disegno artificiale.*[32] *Disegno morale* is "the parent, so to say, of the virtues and of private and public good." *Disegno artificiale* is the parent of all artificial works, "cause of artificial things that so much please human eyes, ornamenting nature and embellishing the world." Zuccaro refers to both acts of virtue and art as "operations," and the practical intellect is thus the "principal dispositive and ordinative cause of the two sorts of operations," which are virtuous

[29] Ibid., p. 177.
[30] Ibid., pp. 181–182.
[31] Ibid., pp. 163–165.
[32] Ibid., pp. 165–167.

acts and artificial works. Thus, one understands the *reasons* of painting, sculpture, and architecture, and beyond that knows how to paint, carve, and build. Zuccaro clearly means that bringing the useful and beautiful into the world is comparable to doing the good, and that both virtue and art achieve their respective "private and public" goods by the application of rational principles to real circumstances. Prudence is now, in the fullest sense, both a moral and an artistic virtue.

Still following Aristotle, Zuccaro defines art as "an operative habit, which has right reason and order of factible things." This is not a sufficient definition, however, because it is not particular and does not allow one work of art to be distinguished from another. In order to meet this demand for particularity, *disegno* is necessary. Although he here means *disegno* in the simple sense of drawing, it is also rooted in the more general *disegno interno.* There is thus a close relation between *disegno interno* and *nove inventioni.* New inventions are partly inevitably new, because no two particular things are the same; but this bare particular novelty, in deriving from *disegno interno,* might also be related to individual *ingegno.*

Here again, however, Zuccaro does not stray far from Aristotle; he is less interested at this point in *ingegno* than in *disegno* as habit, and, in that respect, as like virtue. "Art may not be generated in us . . . if not by many acts, as Aristotle says." Finally, he argues, art arises from drawing and drawing arises from art. That is, the beginner comes to understand art through the practice of drawing; and the drawing of the seasoned artist is informed at once by knowledge and experience.[33]

From this point Zuccaro proceeds to another Aristotelian dictum, that art imitates nature. This is only most superficially understood when it is taken to mean that painting imitates the appearances of natural things. Rather, he says, Aristotle meant that works of art are *composti,* unions of form and matter, as a person is a union of body and intellective soul. Like the physical sciences, the arts are concerned not only with form but with matter, which he understands very literally. Painting treats not only things painted on the wall, or on canvas, but also considers "the very canvas, and wall, the materials of that form insofar as they are materials capable of and subject to painting." But at the highest level, nature is imitable by art "because Nature is ordered [*ordinata*] by an intellective principle to its proper end and to her operations; whence her work is the work of unerring intelligence, as the philosophers say; since by orderly and certain means she achieves her end [*fine*]; and because art observes the same in working, principally with the aid of design, nature may be imitated by art and art by nature."[34] We must note carefully just what Zuccaro means. In the first place, he is discussing what are essentially pedagogical issues, the principles according to which art may be taught. The procedures of art are given an absolute validation by being set in analogy to the rational, teleological processes of nature.

[33] Ibid., pp. 167–171.
[34] Ibid., p. 170; see *MLA*, pp. 300–301.

The artist, then, proceeds not so much by submitting art to appearances as by submitting to the very "reasons" of art itself. The relation of analogy must be stressed. Art is "proportionate" to nature much as the artist's working from conception to final result is analogous to God's creation of the world according to ideas. Zuccaro ends his chapter with a commentary on the remaining Aristotelian principle that the origin of the artwork is in the artist, arguing that the artist may not create life, rejecting the idea that the artist is really comparable to God.

In Chapter 13 of Book I, Zuccaro considers the way in which "*disegno interno* is the form and idea expressive of the intellective soul, that illuminates the intellect to all speculation and practice."[35] This is an extended reflection on the third book of Aristotle's *De anima* (431b–432a), which he himself acknowledges to be a difficult text, "dal Filosofo messe quasi in confuso." His argument turns around the Aristotelian principle that "it is not the stone which is present in the soul, but its form," and he is once again guided in his reading by Aquinas. Aquinas argued that the soul must be immaterial in order to know all things, so that it is both, as Aristotle called it, the "form of forms" and "in a way all existing things."[36] The intellect may know whatever may be known, and as the most embracing form is "absolute";[37] because it contains all forms, it cannot be composed of matter and form, and is thus once again immaterial and immortal.

With this in mind we may offer a more precise definition of Zuccaro's *disegno interno.* Although he repeated the definition many times, these definitions incline toward the rhapsodic, and are not easily understood. *Disegno interno* is repeatedly called a light that guides lower activities. The "concept of intelligible design" is the "singular form of the soul," our "greatest participation in the divine image impressed in us . . . it is Idea, impressive and formative spirit of all things impressed in us, *concetto* of all *concetti,* form of all forms, Idea of all thoughts, through which all things are in our mind." Zuccaro thus again links *disegno interno* to the soul as the potential knowledge of all things. As the potential knowledge of all things it transcends anything it might know, or even *everything* it might know, and is consequently the "form of forms," always to some degree potential even if it is actualized in knowledge. The difficulty with which Zuccaro set this idea out corresponds to the difficulty experienced by many of Aristotle's commentators. If it is maintained that forms are somehow potentially and implicitly in the soul, it is not hard to slip into Augustine's "seminal reasons" or into a simpler Platonism, according to which the forms are preexistent and substantial. But if Zuccaro may have skirted such notions in the attempts to define *disegno interno,* it is clear that his intention was always to remain faithful to Aristotle. His *disegno interno* was at once transcendental, passive, and active. It was passive because it was a susceptibility to all things. It was, as we have seen, a *tabula rasa,* "a spacious, smooth canvas" upon which the forms of the world were

[35] Ibid., pp. 182–185.
[36] *Summa theologiae* I.75.2.
[37] Ibid. I.75.5.

painted. But it was also active. Zuccaro used the example of a mirror, which is at once the reflection of forms and the possibility of reflection, the determinate condition (*termine*) under which reflection may actually occur.[38] And the soul was active in more than this simple sense, because, to extend his metaphor, it is a clarifying mirror. To understand is to see clearly. "The *termine* of the internal operation of the intellect is a spiritual form *distinctly* representing the understood thing" (my emphasis). Moreover, the clarifying activity of the intellect is the definition not simply of forms but also of their relations, an activity corresponding to discourse. *Disegno interno* is thus what Aristotle called "the place of forms" and is the origin of the operations of apprehension, composition and division, and discourse.

Disegno interno is deeply related to the capacity of the intellect defined by Aristotle to "form one image from many" and to the capacity to make statements and judgments more or less truly about what we apprehend. It is "the *concetto* formed in our mind in order to know anything whatever";[39] that is, it is that general image by means of which we recognize individuals as kinds of things; and it is also the image by means of which we are able to perform external acts (*operare di fuori*). At the same time, although the rational soul may enact such "clarification," it is important to remember that it is always in actuality an individual soul, so that it is at once fatefully linked to its physical constitution and dependent upon God who created it. The transcendence of *disegno interno,* its status as "light" and "divine spark," is thus both its potentiality and its absolute value as individual.

Zuccaro thinks of the "formative" power of the soul as its "first and innate *concetto,* the soul of the intellective soul." That is, as the soul is the form of forms, so the individual intellective soul is the *concetto* of *concetti.* It is by virtue of this ultimate principle of individuation that the intellect exists, is able to be intelligent, to learn, and to operate well. Without this *concetto* the soul is merely abstract. Consequently the *concetto* is in a certain sense higher than the soul itself, as the condition of the soul's real existence; it is thus "a ray of that internal virtue and divine image impressed in our soul, which reigns over and governs the senses, intellect and *giudizio discretivo.*" In art, *disegno* has three "qualities," which Zuccaro compares to soul, spirit, and body. The first of these (soul) is the *concetto interno,* the indispensable formative power of the individual soul; the second (spirit) is *giudizio,* or *giudizio discretivo,* "that knows all the beauties of objects, and distinguishes the species and perfect proportions, imaginary and real; it is that subtle *ingegno.*" The third "quality" (body) is actual drawing, the external visible realization of *disegno interno.*[40]

Zuccaro argues throughout that *fantasia* (or, in the passage just considered, *ingegno,* as what might be called personal *fantasia*) stands in a reciprocal and

[38] *Scritti,* pp. 154–155.
[39] Ibid., p. 152.
[40] Ibid., p. 224.

interdependent relation to intellect; and judgment is the mean between intellect (or more specifically, between individual intellect as *disegno interno*) and the actual character of works of art. Judgment, in short, embodies, or makes evident by means of art, both aspects of the individual intellect, its individuality and its intellectuality. In familiar terms, Zuccaro's formulation is a recommendation for individual *maniera* conditioned by the intellect shared by all, and as such it is perfectly consistent with the Aristotelian notion of prudence, which was partly natural, partly learned, and partly based on principles. He described the "prudence of judgment" as showing the "time and place and within what terms and measures" work must be done, so that judgment is immediately related to the particular that it treats discursively; "it orders and forms the canvas of its discourse, that is, that which should go first and next" (a standard definition of order) and does all this with the "disposition and judicial counsel of metaphorical mental discourse," by which it is meant that true prudence must "stand to reason," that circumstantial discourse must be tested against and "counseled by" the principles and procedures of rational thinking."[41]

For Zuccaro, the relation between the *fantasia* and the *cogitativa* on the one hand and intellect on the other is one of conjunction and interdependence, as may be seen in his account of the capacities necessary to the development of either the speculative or practical intellects. Those who have the stronger *cogitativa* will be more disposed to speculative science, by which he means that those who by nature have the best grasp of particulars and their relations will best grasp things and their relations in general; as for the practical intellect (which, as we have seen, governs both art and virtue), this requires a superior fantasy, "in which the sensible species of things are placed [that is, which is a memory of particulars], in which they are composed, and various sensate species are reformed."

As just mentioned, both of these activities of inner sense are not in opposition to intellect, but rather in intimate conjunction with it. The possible intellect becomes actual with experience, and this kindling of the intellect by experience results in a higher certainty of knowing and judging, and from this there arises what he calls *disegno interno intellettivo singolare,* by which he means thought and intention about imagined forms (which correspond to particulars) that are clarified by intellect. This, he says, is more proper to our profession, painting, sculpture, and architecture.[42]

[41] Ibid., p. 289. For "counsel" in Aquinas, see S. E. Dolan, "Resolution and Composition in Speculative and Practical Discourse," *Laval théologique et philosophique,* VI, 1950, pp. 9–62, esp. pp. 51–52. It is compared by Aquinas to that process in which the artist forms the concept of what is to be done together with the means of carrying it out.

[42] Ibid., p. 181. See Klibansky, Panofsky, and Saxl, *Saturn and Melancholy,* p. 338; writing on melancholics, Henricus de Gandavo distinguishes between those who think with images and those who do not, those who do having an aptitude for mathematics. In such persons the *virtus imaginativa* dominates the *virtus cognitativa.* He cites Averroes's commentary on the second book of the *Metaphysics;* Averroes, however, speaks of those in whom the *virtus imaginativa* dominates the *virtus cogitativa,* referring to those who are only convinced by images, those who "seek the testimony of the poets." When Pico della Mirandola cited this argument in his *Apologia* (*Opera omnia,* I, Basel, 1572, p.

One consequence of Zuccaro's broadening of the idea of *disegno* was the dissociation of design from any particular art. It is not possible to differentiate painting from any other art in terms of a characteristic it shares with all arts. The universality of *disegno* thus pushed painting into the arms of *colore,* and the "pure painting" suggested by Zuccaro's definition reminds us more of Caravaggio than of Michelangelo or Raphael. Painting, as his definition implies, is distinguished by coloring, shading, and lighting (*colorire, ombreggiare, e lumeggiare*), "and by the singular force of these means it gives figures such spirit and vividness that they seem living and true." This deception is not only artful, but, like the fables of poetry, it is to taste and pleasing (*gustoso e grato*). Turning to familiar paradoxes, he argues that the more it deceives, the truer it is, that it is not a vice but a virtue, not a lie but the truth. Painting "is the mirror of holy nature, true portrait of all *concetti* that may be imagined by force of lights and darks, on a plane covered with colors, that shows every sort of form, of relief without the substance of body, work not understood by the sense of touch, a practice that is more divine than human."[43]

Insofar as it is distinguished from other arts, painting for Zuccaro is an art of the *fantasia* and *cogitativa,* which thus makes its first appeal to prerational, simply intuitive faculties.[44] But again this appeal to the lower faculties of the soul is the basis for the universality of its audience; painting is the imitatrix of all artificial things and it "deceives the eyes of [both the simply] living [that is, those who apprehend only "common" sensation, the uneducated] and the most wise." This universal appeal is rooted in the similarity of the painted image to the image in the *sensus communis* or *fantasia;* and through such surfaces appeal is made to the *cogitativa,* which "senses" intentions or qualities. Painting expresses in "gestures and motions, in the movements of life, in the eyes, mouth and hands, the internal passions, love, hate, desire, flight, delight, joy, sadness, grief, hope, despair, fear, audacity, wrath." His account of the expressive power of painting is thus essentially similar to Francesco Bocchi's arguments about sculpture, which we have considered in Chapter 7.[45]

Painting is superior to history (which is also concerned with particulars) because,

133; *Saturn* and *Melancholy,* p. 347 n. 214), he changed *cognitativa* back to *cogitativa.* Ficino, as cited by Klibansky, Panofsky, and Saxl (p. 347), takes a position the opposite of Zuccaro's by praising *sacerdotes Musarum* precisely for their lack of dependence upon tools.

[43] *Scritti,* pp. 252–253. See *MLA,* part I, chap. 2, "Quello che non è sia."

[44] *Scritti,* pp. 247–248.

[45] Such ideas appear in other late Cinquecento writers. See G. P. Gallucci, *Della simmetria dei corpi humani libro quattro,* Venice, 1591, f. 2v. "All arts and sciences are not available to all people. But painting is so fitted to the taste and sense [*gusto,* & *senso*] of all, that not only without any kind of labor, but even in physical comfort, there is no man either so learned or so ignorant that he does not feel himself to be moved in mind, and so seized by beautiful paintings, that does not feel himself forced as if by a certain sweetness, and in a certain way to have carved in his mind so many things, so that he seems in an instant divinely to learn so many that he would only have been able to grasp with long study and much painful labor."

more than giving names and dates, it sets things before our eyes.[46] In words distinctly recalling Leonardo, Zuccaro argues that painting is superior to poetry (also concerned with particulars, but with particulars that are apparently true, or verisimilitudinous rather than true) because poetry lacks the brightness of day; showing us histories and fables "among the shadows," it does not move our emotions. That is, not so strongly addressing the lower inner senses, it also does not address the rest of the soul. And again, just as in Alberti, the basis of the universal appeal of painting is *rilievo.* We believe, and our emotions are moved, when the painter has made things appear to our eyes to be raised up, and true. Again as for Alberti, this apparent truth reinforces the educational function of painting. A well-painted image "increases devotion greatly" and a painted history is always more moving than one merely told. Painting strikes the eyes of everyone with the same force, and painting may thus be the most powerful means of instruction, the most universal and irresistible form not just for the illustration of events, but for the propagation of ideas. It is hard to imagine that this adaption of Aristotelian psychology to painting, which had such far-reaching implications for both pedagogy and propaganda, appeared with such frequency coincidentally in Counter-Reformation writers on art.

In his definition of painting Zuccaro makes the claim that painting also shows things known only to the intellect, and he explains what he means. He might have meant to refer to allegory, which presents ideas in sensible form, but he explains his words with the example of devotional imagery. Through painting "the intellect is helped to rise to the contemplation of divine things, and brings to mind the benefits received from God. . . . Many might forget that Christ died for them if they did not have the image of the crucifix in their house, so that painting is not only a delight to sense, but also of use to the intellect," by which he seems once again to mean the individual soul, which is led by such images to its salvation.[47]

As we have seen, Zuccaro's conjunction of intellect and fantasy gave unique importance to the art of painting; this brings us around to his definition of painting, which reads as follows:[48]

> Painting . . . is a practical science, or art, that with singular artifice and artful operation imitates and copies nature, and insofar as it is human artifice, is fabricated in form, species and accident [that is it shows, or makes, things that are as if real particulars] with the force of its colors, sometimes so vividly and excellently with the force of its lights and darks, causing to appear in relief all that which it shapes on a flat surface; it causes such admiration that human eyes are fooled by it. It also paints those things that are invisible, and only known by internal sense [like character],[49] or by the intellect alone without the form of things.

[46] *Scritti*, pp. 251–2.
[47] Ibid., p. 252.
[48] Ibid., p. 244.
[49] Ibid., p. 242.

The definition of painting as an art of fantasy together with the close dependency of intellect upon fantasy provide the basis for the importance Zucarro gives to both *disegno* and *pittura*. It will be remembered that thought uses images, or that the intellect inevitably uses the *fantasia* in its operations. Given such a relationship, painting as the agent of fantasy is the agent of intellect. But this dependence is reciprocal, for not only does intellect govern fantasy, but fantasy nourishes intellect, and in the normal course of making both things occur. Thus art may become truly creative because it is possible for new experience to be created not only by art but by the visual arts, and it is possible for intellect to understand and to proceed by the understanding of these new things.

Zuccaro defines line – "simple *lineamento,* circumscription, measurement and shape of whatever real or imagined thing" – as the "proper body" and visible substance of *disegno interno.*[50] Line is "simply the operation of forming something"; it is "dead." It "declares and expresses" an "ideal image" formed in the mind, and is called *disegno* because it "signifies, and shows to sense and intellect, the form of the thing formed in the mind, and impressed in the idea." Line stands between true *disegno interno,* which is in the *concetto* formed by the soul, and its realization in the colors of painting or the stone of sculpture.

The internal sensible *disegno* in the *fantasia* is of course invisible, and when it is first drawn (that is, when it becomes *disegno esterno*) it is very "confused." Intermittently throughout his discussion Zuccaro makes use of the polarity of "confused" and "distinct." Sometimes he argues that what we see is confused, and that it is made less so by intellectual judgment. It becomes distinct as we make distinctions and these distinctions are very useful to painters; in fact their learning is a large part of justification of academies of art. When we see and sketch a figure, for example, our knowledge of anatomy allows us to distinguish its parts, thus to assist both their artistic construction in the final figure and their clear presentation to the viewer. But in the process Zuccaro is now describing, the "confused" becomes clearer in becoming more confused, that is, by becoming more like a phantasm, more like a sensate image. Zuccaro tells the story that Virgil polished his verses like the mother bear, for it was necessary to lick her newborn cubs into proper form.[51] So the first drawing made, fresh from the *fantasia,* is confused and in need of clarification. This is brought about by *chiari e scuri,* or painting, which "dresses, ornaments and perfects." Thus "painting feeds, enlivens and nourishes *disegno* with the milk of her breasts." Still more vividly, Zuccaro illustrates his argument with the example of a creature called a *monocastrino,* which, half dead after the birth of several offspring, is doubly revived and invigorated by eating the excrement of its firstborn. These decidedly material metaphors not only mean that *chiari e scuri* are the "particular substance of painting and of no other profession or practice," they also mean that intellect is nourished by *disegno* together with *pittura*. The working out of a drawing,

[50] Ibid., p. 222.
[51] Ibid., pp. 242–243; *MLA*, p. 480 n. 25.

beginning from the first general lines suggested by the *fantasia,* and proceeding through definition and realization by light and shadow, is partly the assimilation of the image of the *fantasia* to the intellect; it is also the creation of new experience for the intellect, and it is in this that the great importance of *disegno* and *pittura* lie.

Since Zuccaro has absolutely universalized *disegno,* so that it unites all possible human experience, internal and external, how does human art, the real "arts of design," fit into the scheme? To a certain extent, works of art are things simply found in the world, like the works of God and nature; and just as we may imitate the works of God and nature, so we may imitate the works of human art as well. Thus Zuccaro divides *disegno esterno,* "the form of things produced by God in this machine of the world, according to the various visible sensible forms," into three kinds of concern to painters. The first is *disegno naturale,* the things produced by nature, imitable by art; the second is *disegno artificiale essemplare,* human artifice by means of which we form inventions, historical and poetic *concetti.* The third is artificial but fantastic, all the *bizarrie, capricci, inventioni, fantasie e ghiribizzi dell'huomo.*

It is the third *disegno* that we shall examine with care. Zuccaro calls this *disegno prodottivo, discorsivo, fantastico,* and it is clearly associated with the higher internal senses. As we have seen, Zuccaro placed art under the practical intellect, and did not recognize the productive intellect, as Pomponazzi did. Still, *disegno prodottivo* occupies a similar position in his scale of human activity. It is, moreover, associated with the *fantasia* and with discourse, in its turn associated with the *cogitativa* and therefore with *cogitatio.* This third kind of *disegno esterno,* Zuccaro says, is less perfect than the other kinds of *disegno,* but it is still "*gustoso* and gives the greatest aid, increase and perfection to all our operations, and to those also of all the arts, sciences and practices, forming new inventions and *capricci.*" Zuccaro writes of these *capricci* with real relish, and includes among them many of the characteristic forms of Renaissance art, "fountains, gardens, loggias, halls, temples, palaces, theatres, scenes, apparatuses for feasts, war machines . . . grotesques, harpies, festoons, cartouches, calendars [*almanachi*], spheres, mathematical forms, fortresses, engines of a thousand kinds, machines, mills, signs, clocks, chimeras and I know not what."[52]

It may be noted that Zuccaro's tripartite division of *disegno esterno* did not really provide a place for the traditional mechanical arts to which he gave a low standing, as we saw in Chapter 11. For Benedetto Varchi, it will be recalled, all arts were mechanical in the sense that they involved matter, and Zuccaro would seem to have thought similarly, even though he reached the same conclusion by a different path, by grounding all art in *disegno interno.* However that may be, it was necessary to place all nonimitative art (including architecture) together with fantastic art, an association that in turn merged the invention of the useful with the invention

[52] *Scritti,* p. 237.

of things "never before seen" insofar as they were both inventions, and coupled the display of *ingegno* with the "designs" of the engineer.

Zuccaro qualified his enthusiasm for *disegno fantastico* (no doubt with the Counter-Reformation writers in the back of his mind) by saying (here referring to *grotteschi*) that these inventions must be located decorously, not placed in chapels or on altars by artists of little skill. Still he associates the highest virtues with the ability to imagine and execute such *capricci*. "The excellent painter, sculptor and architect ought to be a copious inventor of such things, which display *giudizio, ingegno,* spirit and the *prontezza* to dispose and order. It is in such invention that the painter is universal, copious and various like nature. When properly used, these *capricci* possess *grandezza*. When improperly used they take it away."

Just as poetry (which, according to Zuccaro, "through gracious fictions expresses truth and falsity with sensible things, and so more easily moves our mind to follow the truth and flee falsity")[53] "composes fables to human tastes,"[54] so Zuccaro uses the metaphor of taste to characterize the kind of rightness (which is obviously not rational) that governs his *disegno fantastico*. It satisfies a diversity of tastes; good judgment selects among the possibilities produced by the *fantasia,* so that good judgment and good taste order all, and dispose with clear intellect. That good judgment in this case is close to taste itself, and that intellect is working in the closest conjunction to fantasy, is suggested by his closing remarks. "No particular rule may be given for these *capricci e bizzarrie;* but from those made by *valent'huomini* one may draw the good and the beautiful and [one may also draw] the judgment to select that which is most pleasing to the eye [*più grato all'occhio*] and that which is most praiseworthy."

Zuccaro regards *disegno* as both the real form and the agent of the intellect; and because the intellect is always the intellect of someone, it always deals with particulars, or potential particulars (its own imaginings). All of us imagine and order what we imagine in thinking, and art – especially his own art of painting – thus becomes the paradigm of human thought. Zuccaro's words are close to those attributed to Michelangelo by Francisco de Hollanda,[55] which, in turn, recall Cicero's praise of the hand.

> There exists among men only one art or science, that is of *disegno* or *pittura,* from which all others proceed, and of which they are a part. Because it is certain, considering all that is done in life, you will find that, without knowing it, each paints this world, in inventing and producing new forms and figures and in using new styles of clothing and various materials, in occupying space, raising buildings and houses adorned with paintings, in cultivating fields, plowing the fields in stripes and patterns, navigating the seas by means of sails, in combat, in ordering the lines of battle, and finally in all our operations, movements and actions.

[53] Ibid., p. 188; see Chapter 9 n. 17, above.
[54] Ibid., p. 285.
[55] *MLA*, pp. 257–258.

Here the distinction between art and virtue is utterly lost, and is lost in the unification of the two under the category of *disegno* (or *pittura*). Moreover, the distinction between the liberal and mechanical arts has also disappeared. Agriculture, navigation, warfare, all are expressions of human imagination. Zuccaro defines man as "a rational soul, a *concetto Ideale intellettivo, speculativo, sensitivo e pratico,*" which, as the possible intellect, "apprehends and knows all things;[56] it is for this reason that the characteristically passive activity (or active passivity) of the soul is potentially universal, that the Greeks called man a microcosm, and it is this potential universality that makes the human soul "an image and divine spark impressed in our minds." This divine spark is passive in that it may become all things, and active in that it is "apt to illuminate and enliven every thought (*concetto*) and every human operation." It is a "sun in our soul and intellect, that generates, heats and brings to life, nourishes every thought and perfects every work." The *concetto* (here he means the *concetto* of *concetti,* not simply a thought in the mind), through *disegno* and *giudizio discretivo,* not only nourishes with the spiritual food of the intellective and practical sciences, but also looks to the needs of the corporeal life, that is, looks to the mechanical arts: "He is the proper farmer that at time and place, and in season, seeds, and gathers together, daily providing every instrument necessary to break and seed the earth, to reap and conserve the crops." Such productive activities, consequences of human needs and experience, associated with the *cogitativa* in the tradition we have been examining, with particular and common intelligence, are also of a piece with *giudizio discretivo* and with the formative powers of *disegno interno.* "So we are taught by design to make meal and bread, to shear and clean wool, to weave silk, to use the loom, to sail and to rule every republic and state; to form and build cities, towns and castles."[57] *Disegno* is "singular and omnipotent," responding to every human need; and in addition it responds to every thought, imagination, and desire, forming things "invisible and impalpable, distant and future." The very virtues of the soul, likewise tears and laughter, are as if they were before us, corporeal and present. This truly spiritual labor is accomplished principally by painting, the "first born daughter and mother" of *disegno.* Zuccaro's passionate praise of painting deserves our close attention. "With its various colors, and with its lights and darks, it vividly represents and perfects the whole with substance and live, clear accidents," meaning that painting makes *concetti* apparently corporeal and brilliant with the detail and particular circumstances of the real. In this materialization, or realization, the *concetto* becomes most like itself, that is, most "lifelike." Painting, as the agent of *fantasia,* and so of intellect, is not constrained by place; it is able "to leap and fly, to penetrate through all the sea, the earth, the center, the abyss, the air, the heavens; it is like a general investigator and speculator of anything whatsoever." Abruptly changing metaphors, Zuccaro calls

[56] Ibid., p. 292.
[57] Ibid., pp. 292–293.

painting a "major-domo, and secret chamberlain, that has the golden key to enter everything, conversing and penetrating into the most secret rooms of his lord." *Disegno,* "forming, delineating and composing with this its most lovely painting," shows everything to us:

> it perfectly shows every celestial spirit, every order, angels and archangels, princes and potencies, virtues and dominations, thrones, cherubim and seraphim, and the author himself, the Creator of the universe. So great and such is the faculty and its authority to traverse, to see and penetrate the whole, and to give complete satisfaction to this same soul, to the very intellect, that very clearly is comprehended to be truly its clear light, and that food and life of all thoughts, and of our operations; that image and similitude of God in us, infused in our soul, that rector and governor-general of our senses, of this intellect, and of these our human operations.[58]

Zuccaro insists again and again that physical activity – or concretely visible activity – is integral to speculation, that writers write, and mathematicians figure. These activities are *disegno,* by means of which both a science and its practice are demonstrated and learned. This is true of mathematics, but it is also true of the mechanical arts. The horseman does not tell the smith how to make a bridle, but rather "that general light of expressive and practical design . . . that speculative judgment of the *concetto,* that penetrates and flows through everything, shows the horsemen the way, shape and manner in which the bridle ought to be made." He gives his order to the smith not as a horseman but as a *disegnatore.* The same is true of all practices, professions, and sciences: None can function without design. At this point Zuccaro broadens his Aristotelian vision to encompass all human action. We have "discursive spirit, and a rational intellective soul, and that spirit of life infused in our soul, formed in the image and similitude of God." We all design our thoughts, which become actual together with moral and intellectual judgment. "Consequently we say that this *Disegno,* both intellective and practical, this judgment that rules, governs our operations, to be that general light, that nourishment, and life, that Rector and Governor to all thoughts, and to all intelligences, and to all human practices." Human action in all its dimensions is an expression of the free and individual human soul. But now, specifically, *disegno* is the "particular father in genitive substance of the operations and practices of the three most noble professions of painting, sculpture and architecture," from which depend, on a descending scale, the lesser mechanical and craftsmanly arts.[59]

For Zuccaro, not only does knowledge arise from sensation, but it is also nec-

[58] Ibid., p. 293.

[59] Ibid., pp. 286–287. As the example of the bridle makes clear, Zuccaro has in mind at some remove the beginning of the *Nicomachean Ethics* (1094a10), where it is argued that some arts are subordinate to others, in this case, that the making of equipment is subordinate to the art of riding. When Aquinas commented on this (*Sententia Libri ethicorum. Opera omnia,* XLVII, Rome, 1969, I, p. 6), he wrote that the rider surpasses the maker of the bridle, relative to whom he is "architector, id est principalis artifex." In Zuccaro's version, *disegno* assumes this position of dominance.

essary that all sciences assume sensible form. In the pursuit of arguments to this effect he comes very near to identifying the speculative intellect with the practical intellect and to identifying both with *disegno.* Chapter 10 of Book II of the *Idea* begins with the proposition that "all the human sciences and intelligences are useless, and like dead members in the inactive intellect, and are enlivened by *disegno.*" Thus, although Zuccaro admits the value of the speculative sciences as pure fulfillments of the intellect, it is clear that he has little use for pure speculation. Even if such sciences are in a certain sense more excellent, "the practical professions also seek for man another sort of human and natural happiness that consists in action, and in this we painters, sculptors and architects content ourselves."[60] In painting, sculpture, and architecture, he argues, no one incapable of putting theory into practice is worthy of the name. This, it may be noted, is a *denial* of the classical position according to which a person possessing theory is superior to one possessing practice because of the ability to teach the principles of the art. "In general it matters little to understand and know a science, and not practice it, or not be able to practice it . . . the sciences, then, of whatever kind they may be, are not able to be known without demonstrative practice." The "human sciences are conceded to man by a singular gift," and if they are not practiced, it is as if they did not exist, because, returning to his fundamental principle, "in order to be something it is necessary that it appear to sense." And if the sciences are to benefit and delight men, it is necessary that they appear in real substance. He quotes Aristotle to say that "habitual science is nothing else than the species of visible things confirmed in the soul," and when such habits are confirmed they are virtues. The practice of such virtues results in real states of affairs which may be "tasted." A learned person "with some interior quality" may give notice of his learning with *costumi e maniere decenti,* real acts that make sensible the flavor and taste (*gusto*) of eloquence and learning. It is actual music and words that we are able to taste (*gustare*) "in order to know and understand if a thing be good or bad it is necessary to see it, to feel it, to taste it," and the true activity of the intellect is to make such judgment possible in concrete acts. He insists that the most speculative sciences, philosophy itself, make use of instruments, and not only that, are *nourished* by instruments, and their investigations made possible by instruments, by the "spheres, *almanachi* and devices of a thousand kinds," whose invention he associated with *disegno prodottivo.*[61]

Although, as we have seen, the possibility existed of identifying the intelligible principles of nature with the principles of art, thus making the execution of these principles into an exercise of prudence, as Vincenzo Danti did with the "order" of anatomy, such ideas are strikingly absent in Zuccaro. Rather he seems to regard the "reasons of painting" more narrowly as the proven procedures of art itself, even though the domain of painting is all the visual world. Zuccaro's position, for all its systematic presentation, again recalls that of Leonardo. And

[60] Ibid., p. 164.
[61] Ibid., p. 281.

his definition of painting as an art distinct from other arts led him at several points to a reconsideration of the old *paragone* arguments and to an insistence on the separation of painting from all other arts, especially from mathematics. (This, of course, separates him from Leonardo.)

"Painting," Zuccaro insists, "has no need of the mathematical sciences; it is not the daughter of mathematics, but rather of nature and design. The one shows painting the forms, the other teaches her to work. Thus the painter, in addition to the first principles and skills had from his predecessors, or also from nature herself, from the same *natural judgment* together with good diligence and observation of the beautiful and good becomes a *valent'huomo* without further aid or need of mathematics" (my emphasis).[62]

In the argument that follows, Zuccaro drives a wedge between his own position and that of earlier Renaissance writers. "I will say what is true, that in all bodies produced by Nature there is proportion, and measure, as the book of Wisdom affirms; whoever nevertheless wishes to attend to the consideration of all things, and to know them through the speculation of theory [that is, mathematics], and make his work conform to that, in addition to intolerable labor, will waste much time without the substance of any good fruit." The simple point of this argument is that if nature makes everything proportionately, then the things of nature may simply be painted. This is not so much a program for "Mannerist license" as it is for a straightforward naturalism, and pointedly raises the question of the relation of nature defined as appearance to *maniera* defined as the transformation of appearance by personal craft or "vision," however shaped. The question of "theory and practice" becomes irrelevant as nature replaces theory as a norm, that is, as the appearance of nature replaces the intelligible order of nature as a norm. From such a standpoint Zuccaro is able to ridicule Dürer's *Four Books on Human Proportion* as a "capriccio." Zuccaro's brother Taddeo, who taught him about proportion, also told him that it was necessary to become so familiar with rules that "you have the compass, square and judgment in the eyes," and practice in the hands, "otherwise you will degrade the intellect, extinguish judgment and take from art all grace, spirit and flavor."

He can, Zuccaro writes, only imagine that Dürer made his figures to pass the time, for the delight of those more interested in contemplation than in working. Leonardo comes in for similar criticism; he, too, sought to define merely mathematical rules for "moving and turning" the figure, and although he was a great painter, and his solutions were ingenious, such systems were finally arbitrary. Anyone may construct such proportions "according to his taste"; they are finally arbitrary in contrast to the given rationality of existent nature, which is the true nourisher of the art of painting.[63]

Zuccaro calls the forms of nature *disegno esterno naturale,* in effect the painting of God.[64] This is opposed to *disegno esterno artificiale,*[65] which is divided into

[62] Ibid., p. 250.
[63] Ibid., p. 251.
[64] Ibid., pp. 225–230.
[65] Ibid., pp. 231–237.

perfetto and *prodottivo, discorsivo, fantastico,* the distinction being between that which is done in imitation and completion of natural forms and that which is not, but is instead either fantastic or defined by human needs. *Disegno esterno perfetto* is simply good drawing of things. The soul of such a drawing is "grace and lightness, and facility in drawing and coloring without show of difficulty and affectation."[66] Although we all possess the basis of *disegno* (*disegno interno*) in our cognitive apparatus, we possess *disegno esterno* in varying degrees, and Zuccaro's whole enterprise might be described as the attempt to bring the two together, to make *disegno interno* and *disegno esterno* mutually reinforcing. Zuccaro dismisses artists simply dependent on models, whether these models are natural or artificial. Even if one has the capacity to draw, this capacity must be perfected. There are two kinds of *valent'huomini,* Zuccaro says, those simply produced by nature, and those produced by nature and refined by study. His preference is decidedly for the latter. Although the "natural" painter with his *bella idea* and *viva prontezza* may work marvels of pure practice, he works without much substance, and will make errors, not having "tasted the correction of studies." The other kind of *valent'huomo,* aided by study, will be "wiser and more prudent," and will continuously perfect his work. The artist who simply depends on *disegno naturale,* in short, is like the person who acts by natural prudence, which does not in itself contain the principles of truly right conduct. Zuccaro, however, does not seem to believe that the artist is perfected by learning the principles of right artistic conduct, but rather takes the alternative Aristotelian path in insisting that virtue is a habit, and that practice in the simple sense of the exercise of the parts of painting is the essential element of artistic training. As might be expected of the *principe dell'accademia,* Zuccaro gives a long and traditional list of things the painter must know: invention, disposition, and composition, the suitable representation of emotions, the decorum of apparel, ornament, and proportion, the proportions of figures in order that shortcomings in nature may be corrected, the nude, grace and manner of color, buildings, landscapes, animals, places and seasons, all the things that are necessary for the making of late Renaissance paintings.[67] The young painter learns these things by imitation and by repetition, by constant practice.

Although Zuccaro was an academician, and was keenly interested in the pedagogical ideas descending from Aristotle's *Nicomachean Ethics,* it seems that he departed very little from the usual and sensible classical idea that an artist had to possess both *ars* and *ingenium,* training together with natural ability. But his notion of artistic education was less concerned with the issue of theory and practice than with the education of taste. Although the "natural" artist might make incorrect art, the correct artist might make bad art, and certainly makes bad art insofar as his work is only correct.

Speaking extemporaneously on the subject of beauty and grace, on March 20, 1594, Zuccaro is recorded to have said that the beauty of figures consists in several parts: in proportion and movement, and in the suitable disposition of the

[66] Ibid., p. 234.
[67] Ibid., p. 229.

figure to its purpose (*effetto*).[68] Spirit and *vivezza* always increase grace and beauty. The beauty of proportion and order consists of a certain union of members, and this union makes the transition from beauty to grace, to the whole greater than the sum of its parts, "a particular gift, a flower of beauty, a most sweet condiment . . . that charms sight and gratifies taste" (*appaga gusto*). Grace is beyond measure (as it had always been in Renaissance discussions)[69] and it is only apprehended by taste. "Nor may one learn this grace, neither with rules, nor with measure, nor with theory, nor with practice, but it is absolutely in good taste [*buon' gusto*] and in good judgment [*buon giuditio*], which it is necessary to be accustomed to from the beginning, to know the good, the beautiful and the graceful, and knowing it to taste it [*gustarlo*] and tasting it [*gustandolo*] to imitate it and observe it."

In this extraordinary text, grace, the visible trace of the spirit in persons and of the spirit of the artist in works of art, becomes literally aesthetic, something apprehended prerationally, as if the transcendent were known by "estimation." The problem of the education of the artist becomes the problem of the education of taste through the experience of the excellent, which can be seen and "digested." This suggests what is in fact the end of Zuccaro's remarks, the beginnings of a canon of taste. As models for his academic audience Zuccaro lists a number of painters whose works display grace, concluding that the works of Raphael give complete taste (*gusto*) and flavor (*sapore*) to all. In the academy, then, one learns not only good practice but the models in light of which one's character is transformed.

El Greco on painting

Having completed this chapter as a culmination of those that have gone before, we are now in a position to understand certain remarks made by El Greco on the subject of painting. El Greco was born, educated, and trained as a painter in Crete. In his late twenties, around 1567, he went to Venice where, in one of the most extraordinary self-transformations in the history of art, he took on the great Venetian Renaissance style of oil painting. By 1570 he had gone to Rome, and by 1577 to Spain, where he became the artistic personality that earned him his high place in the history of painting. While he was in Rome, El Greco was a member of the Accademia di San Luca. He knew Federico Zuccaro well, and although – as might be expected – his ideas diverge from Zuccaro's at many points, the thoughts of the two painters also share deep similarities. El Greco was at the same time a learned painter and a painter who vehemently insisted not just on judgment and practice, but that the virtues of judgment and practice were the substance of the art of painting. When he wrote the remarks we shall

[68] *Scritti*, pp. 71–72.

[69] E. Cropper, "On Beautiful Women: Parmigianino, *Petrarchismo*, and the Vernacular Style," *AB*, 58, 1976, pp. 374–394.

examine, El Greco was glossing a commentary on Vitruvius by Daniele Barbaro, first published in Venice in 1556.[70]

If the ear of the musician is like the eye of the painter, that, El Greco says, is a "great thing," which he wishes to be understood in the manner of Aristoxenus (whom he calls Aristogenes). Aristoxenus is Vitruvius's example of the theorist of music, on the basis of whose writings he provides a lengthy discussion in a section on the acoustics of amphitheaters. Aristoxenus (whom El Greco suggests must have been misunderstood) is presented not as a theorist but rather as one who maintained "that in art one cannot put things into words, because in truth the best of such art (if not all arts) cannot be put into words."[71] El Greco must be thinking of Aristoxenus as he is presented by Boethius, whose *De musica* he owned. In Boethius, Aristoxenus exemplifies a position according to which quality and the judgment of the ear are opposed to the Pythagorean alternative of quantity and the judgment of reason.[72] His remarks must be understood in this way, for El Greco immediately turns to the authority of Michelangelo and a variant on the notion of the *giudizio dell'occhio.* Those who have achieved something in painting, he says, never concerned themselves with proportions (*medidas*). When Giulio Clovio asked Michelangelo about proportions, the great man replied that he was surprised even to have been asked, and dismissed all who concerned themselves with such things as foolish and stupid.[73] What does this have to do with art's not being able to be put into words? Art, El Greco means to say, concerns itself most importantly with the particular, with the "confused," with that about which distinctions have not been made, and about which they cannot be made. What is really painted – both the subject and the painting itself – are one thing, which cannot be reduced to words or numbers, nor may words and numbers be made into paintings. The "ineffable" may in some sense be the meaning of the work, but first of all it is the absolute particularity of the work in which the interpretation of meaning is manifest. El Greco means to say, in short, that art is *aesthetic.* The implications of this argument are in part straightforward and point to some of the themes we have examined. Painting and architecture are different from music because they use drawings, which teach us and are memorable for us in ways that words cannot possibly be.[74] But it is not only the case that pictures are more

[70] See J. Brown, R. Kagan, et al., *El Greco of Toledo,* exhibition catalogue, Museo del Prado, Washington National Gallery of Art, Toledo Museum of Art, Dallas Museum of Fine Arts, Boston, 1982, passim and p. 110 for bibliography on El Greco's library and literary activities.

[71] F. Marias and A. Bustamante Garcia, *Las ideas artisticas de El Greco (Comentarios a un texto inedito),* Madrid, 1981, p. 143. I am grateful to Keith Moxey for his help in reading these texts.

[72] See *MLA*, p. 359, on Aristoxenus in Boethius.

[73] *Las ideas artisticas,* p. 143. In notes on a copy of Condivi's life of Michelangelo, he is quoted as disavowing the study of perspective, which seemed to him a waste of time. See U. Procacci, "Postille contemporanee in un esemplare della vita di Michelangiolo del Condivi," *Atti del Convegno di Studi Michelangioleschi, Firenze–Roma 1964,* Rome, 1966, p. 292. Michelangelo did nevertheless occupy himself from time to time with both proportion and perspective. See *MLA*, pp. 380–396, 559.

[74] *Las ideas artisticas,* pp. 143–144.

"natural" signs than words; precisely because it is visual, painting is comprehensive in a way that architecture is not. Painting corrects architecture and not vice versa because

> painting alone can judge things, form, color, as that whose object is the imitation of everything; in sum, painting holds a position of prudence and moderation with respect to all that can be seen, and if I could express with words what the vision of the painter is, what sight is, it would seem a strange thing, because sight has the particularities of many faculties; but painting, by being so universal, is made speculative, and never lacks content for speculation; there is always something that may be seen; in moderate light one sees and enjoys something and has that to imitate. This is the true path by which proportions can be found . . . which cannot be attained with mathematics.[75]

El Greco repeats a scale of art and knowledge very much like that of al-Farabi. The painter cannot be a dialectician, who must satisfy reason, nor an orator, who appeals to both sense and reason, nor like the sophist, who makes "monstrous things, such as those the phantasy presents to us when our senses [*sentimientos*] are bound in sleep." The painter should have "intentions and represent some effect" that controls the whole composition, and ought, in short, to be like the poet, who satisfies the senses but whose "fables ought to be useful to the life of man."[76]

[75] Ibid., p. 165.
[76] Ibid., p. 164.

Conclusions

The rise of naturalism

The late Middle Ages witnessed the revival of the notion that the beautiful is that which is proportioned to sense, a notion encircled in a more general principle that art should appeal to sense, perhaps to be compared to the great florescence of late medieval art itself. This principle was embraced by the most general Aristotelian principle that there is no thought without a phantasm, no thought without a mental image. This idea, far from being merely abstract, justified inventions of the deepest and broadest art-historical importance, and indeed justified the magnification of the visual arts to a new prominence and central cultural significance. It was consistent with a defense of images rooted in the mystery of the Incarnation itself, and it also pointed beyond religious images (which were, of course, far and away the majority of images) to the visual world as the final source of knowledge. Since, moreover, phantasms were not simply "epistemological" but were linked to choice and will, and were therefore crucial to the explanation of behavior, images *like* phantasms could be used to shape spiritual development, to make divine history accessible to all, to make the Christian stories personal experience, thus by changing experience to change wills and lead to salvation. Sense was related to lower human nature and to fallenness, but the conditions of fallenness might also be means to redemption. A provident God had suited humankind to the world in which he placed them.

The treatise circulated as the seventh book of Hugh of St. Victor's *Didascalicon*, which, as we have seen, shaped the discussion of art throughout the late Middle Ages, states that *pulchritudo* excites wonder.[1] Although the author also cautions in Horatian tones against the vanity of art and warns against marvelling at the monstrous and ridiculous, which may easily lead into a false admiration of the

[1] MPL, 176, col. 820ff. On the text of the *Didascalicon*, see the editions of Buttimer and Taylor; both modern editors exclude this chapter, which was, however, included by Migne, but as an appendix. The book appears as number VII in medieval manuscripts (see Buttimer, p. xx) and in the *editio princeps* of c. 1473.

merely strange, art is not rejected altogether. On the contrary, God himself is the true artist, and it is the harmony and continuity of the order of the world that testifies to God's wisdom. After the forms of things, which reveal this order, there is the delight to be taken in their color. Light reveals all colors, the heavenly bodies constantly change, there are precious gems and flowers. This great work is filled with symbols; the beautiful green of vegetation, for example, is a symbol of resurrection. Nor should we praise only the works of God. In words distinctly recalling Isidore of Seville's definition of painting, but without the earlier writer's censoriousness, the author states that we are also made to marvel by the colorful deceptions of the eye accomplished by a certain "adulterine" human wisdom.[2] Here painting as a deceptive art is the paradigmatic mechanical art, and its deceptions by color are set in a concentric relation to the bright panoply of God's visible creation.

The conception of the world as God's art, and as God's painting, a play of color governed by the most absolute decorum, is coupled with a psychology we recognize at once. Each sense apprehends different qualities, and finds its pleasure in the qualities appropriate to it. Sight is nourished by the beauty of colors, and the ear takes pleasure in the variety we find in sounds.

In another place Hugh of St. Victor himself makes a crucial distinction, which is finally Augustinian, associating the shapes and colors of things with outer nature, and the apprehension of the qualities of things with inner nature.[3] We apprehend these "other properties of things by means of other senses." So by means of taste we perceive sweetness of flavor, by smell, fragrance of odor, by hearing, melody in sound. These qualities – sweetness, fragrance, and melody – are spiritual in nature, and because they are so, "the eyes are not filled with seeing, nor the ears with hearing." A higher but immediate sensation is defined in terms of the inner man, and the qualities of things become the beginning of the mind's road to God. This "other" inner sense, although not expressly a common sense, nor even an "internal sense," occupies a place in its psychological system like the common sense, whose meanings such ideas can only have magnified. These arguments gave the deepest possible justification for an art appealing first of all to sense, because on such a view it is possible to ascend from the pleasing qualities of objects to the real presence of divine grace; they also meant that sensation, and the pleasures of sensation, could be justified as a new means for edification.

Our natural desire to know, Aristotle wrote, is evident in the value we place upon our senses; and if we must learn through sense, then we must be taught through sense. As I have already suggested, this most general principle had very concrete consequences. For one thing, it placed the traditional doctrine of images in a rather different light. Images had always been justified as educational, but

[2] Ibid. On Isidore of Seville's definition of painting, repeated by many medieval authors, see *MLA*, pp. 48–49.

[3] MPL, 175, col. 21, 139.

now it was recommended that they be accommodated to the conditions of finite human knowledge: not that they be simply visible, as an icon might also be, but that they be *like* the visible; not that they be encountered, but that they be *as if* encountered, set in a world that, because it was like the present, could carry the imagination and therefore the soul to past and future events. In this crucial transformation images became like phantasms, inward images of visible outward things and events, standing at the beginnings of human knowledge and immediate to the spiritual mainsprings of will and desire. This is not to say that these putative inward images were or could be simply referred to by painters; on the contrary, it was necessary to invent them and to achieve consensus concerning them.[4] This laborious endeavor of inventing both vision and painting was the long and splendid development of optical naturalism in the late Middle Ages and early Renaissance, a development that, if fed by many streams, could be constantly justified by ideas of the kind we have just considered.

It was in these terms that naturalism came to be regarded as a simple and powerful teaching device and means to meditation. Naturalism was essential to the devotional imagery widespread in the late Middle Ages and the Renaissance.[5] The Franciscan Ugo Panziera, a contemporary of Giotto, argued, against the ideal of "higher," imageless devotion, that it is impossible to think of nothing; "all the wise determine that the soul may not remain idle for any interval of time."[6] Rather than trying to contemplate by thinking of nothing, then, it is better to approach contemplation by "keeping in mind the humanity of the lovely son of God . . . to hold that humanity as an object before the corporeal and mental eyes." One should look at religious images, and the first stages of meditation consist of making the phantasm in the imagination, whether from sense or memory, as real as sculpture before the mind's eye. First Christ "seems to be written in the mind and imagination." Then he seems "outlined" (*disegnato*), then "outlined and shadowed," then "colored and incarnate." Finally, he seems "incarnate and in relief" (*rilevato*). The will (the active mental virtue) is more perfect to the

[4] See J. Snyder, "Picturing Vision," *Critical Inquiry*, 6, 1980, pp. 499–526.

[5] S. Ringbom, "Devotional Images," p. 164, argues that "mystical" imageless devotion was not the dominant religious ideal of the late medieval period, and shows an increasing blurring of the distinction between "images" in the sense of mental pictures and "images" in the sense of works of art. Most of the writers we have considered are religious writers. On the secular side, see the remark of Frederick II, "Fides enim certa non provenit ex auditu," quoted in O. Pächt, "Early Italian Nature Studies and the Early Calendar Landscape," *JWCI*, 13, 1950, pp. 13–47. J. Huizinga, *The Waning of the Middle Ages: A Study of the Forms of Life, Thought and Art in France and the Netherlands in the XIVth and XVth Centuries*, London, 1924, provides many examples of the importance of images in the late Middle Ages. E. H. Gombrich, *Art and Illusion*, chap. 4, argues that the "Greek Revolution," the beginning of naturalism in Western art, arose from the impulse to "set things before the eyes" evident in the poetry of Homer, and that Gothic naturalism arose from a similar impulse (*Means and Ends: Reflections on the History of Fresco Painting*, London, 1976, pp. 32–35). On medieval psychology and imagery in late medieval literature and art, see V. A. Kolve, *Chaucer and the Imagery of Narrative: The First Five Canterbury Tales*, Stanford, Calif., 1984. On the new psychology and the theology of the Incarnation, see G. B. Ladner, *Ad Imaginem Dei*.

[6] Ugo Panziera da Prato, *Trattati*, f. xxxiii r and lxxiv.

degree that it governs the imagination (the active corporeal virtue), and when the image of Christ dominates the mind, then the soul "by divine justice merits the gift of meditation and contemplation." The image that comes into relief, and fills the mind's eye with itself, is crucial to the transformation of the Christian soul. And so it would remain in the literature of devotion for centuries. "Images," Francis Bacon wrote, "are said by the Roman Church to fix the cogitations, and raise the devotions of them that pray before them."[7]

The theme of the equivalence of poetry and painting because of their common base in fantasy runs through many of the arguments we have examined. As the lowest form of logic (as al-Farabi classified it) poetry appeals to imagination and persuades us at the prerational and universal level of "estimation." When we are so persuaded by the fictions of poetry, as Aquinas wrote, we are inclined to one side or another of a contradiction, which means that – to touch another of our  persistent themes – the shaping of imagination is the shaping of behavior. At the end of the sixteenth century, Federico Zuccaro, writing in the full flood of the Counter-Reformation, argued in the same terms that "poetry with gracious fictions expresses both truth and falsity with sensate things, and so the more easily moves our soul to follow the truth, and flee falsity." He wrote similarly of painting, which also shapes imagination, in language that recalls Leonardo's *paragone* arguments, now turned to the purposes of the Church. Painting shows "the actions of the good, and it sometimes also represents the works of the bad; so it makes us know those that are worthy of praise and reward, as those of blame and punishment, and so accidentally at least it makes men wise, prudent and virtuous." Men are made "accidentally" wise, prudent, and virtuous by images because they are instructed by example rather than convinced by reason. "The Holy Church as a benign mother covetous of the health of her children is not content to draw them to penitence and to the observance of divine precepts only through the sensations of the ears, but also draws us through sensations of the eyes by means of painting, so that clearly one sees the excellence and use it brings to us."

If such arguments might justify painting as a universal language and therefore as a means to universal salvation, they might also point in the direction of skepticism. Out of the same elements Pomponazzi could fashion arguments that put the universality of the appeal to imagination in a rather different light. Pomponazzi assumes the social hierarchical relation between sense and fantasy on the one hand and intellect on the other. As he presents the matter, sense and fantasy are the means by which the few who understand control the many who do not, persuading

[7] *Advancement of Learning*, in *The Works of Francis Bacon*, III, London, 1857, p. 381; quoted in D. P. Walker, *Spiritual and Demonic Magic, from Ficino to Campanella*, London, 1958, p. 201. On a more grisly practical note, it was no doubt for similar reasons that images of Christ were held before the eyes of condemned criminals on the day of their execution right up to the moment of their deaths. The imagination filled with the image of Christ would mean a spirit on the verge of redemption. On these *tavolette*, see S. Y. Edgerton, Jr., *Pictures and Punishment: Art and Criminal Prosecution During the Florentine Renaissance*, Ithaca, N.Y., 1985, pp. 165–221.

them by images they can all apprehend rather than convincing them by arguments they are presumed to be unable to understand.

Those men who are not philosophers, and who are indeed like beasts, cannot understand how God and the heavens and nature operate. Therefore, angels and demons were introduced for the sake of the vulgar, although those who introduced them knew they could not possibly exist. For in the Old Testament many things are alleged which cannot be understood literally. They have a mystic sense and were said because of the ignorant vulgar, which cannot understand anything but bodily. For the language of religions, as Averroes said, is like the language of poets: poets make fables which though literally impossible yet embrace the truth of the intellect. For they make their stories that we may come into truth and instruct the rude vulgar, to lead them to good and withdraw them from evil, as children are led by the hope of reward and fear of punishment. By these bodily things they are led to knowledge of what is not bodily, as we lead infants from liquid food to food more solid."[8]

The notion that perception is the basis of all knowledge thus yielded a new justification for visual art and multiplied the importance of art precisely insofar as it was visual. At the same time that it provided a potentially universal means of teaching and edification, however, this new view also introduced what might be called a nominalist field of gravity into all discussion. That is, if sense provided a foundation, it was a foundation from which it was ever more difficult to rise. It obviously placed great importance on faith to say, as the author of the seventh book of the *Didascalicon* did, that the sensible experience of the world affords access to higher meaning (or, what is really the same thing, to *make* the sensible indicate higher meaning through allegory). One might take higher meaning to the interpretation of sensory experience, but still the relation between sense and meaning was problematical in a new way, and it was in principle always necessary to demonstrate their connection. By the time Renaissance writers repeated the Protagorean maxim that man is the measure of all things, they were not so much expressing unbridled optimism concerning the powers of the human mind in an anthropomorphic universe as they were voicing a deep skepticism, a harder faith in the certainty and limitation of human knowledge. We can best know that to which we can put the measure of our own nature. At its most extreme – in the form in which Protagoras himself put it – the world exists differently for each of us. As the art most completely articulating the fit between sense and the world, painting – which developed in response to sight in both its physical–optical and aesthetic dimension – was inevitably the carrier both of the demand

[8] For Aquinas, see Chapter 9 n. 17, above; for F. Zuccaro, *Scritti*, pp. 252–253. As his argument progresses, Zuccaro cites the "most beautiful metaphor" of the late sixth century pope Gregory the Great, that painting is the "libro delli idioti." On Gregory and the early discussion of images in the Church, with bibliography, see H. Kessler, "Pictorial Narrative and Church Mission in Sixth-Century Gaul," *Studies in the History of Art*, XVI, Washington, D.C., National Gallery of Art, 1985, pp. 75–91. And for Pomponazzi, see *The Renaissance Philosophy of Man*, ed. E. Cassirer et al., pp. 277–278, with references.

for faith in things unseen and of skepticism, the agent both of indoctrination and doubt. Alberti's new art of painting was an art of physical, relative knowledge. His perspective was the systematization of relative knowledge, or point of view, a framework within which relative judgments were to be made. And so at the same time that painting became a science it became subject to the judgment of sense.

It was stated in the introduction that traditions of ideas are systematic; they are also systematic in culturally specific ways, and this specificity must be recognized in order for the interrelatedness of historical changes to be explained. The development of naturalism in late medieval and early Renaissance art could not have been isolated because of what naturalism meant or implied. To imitate appearances, that is, to make images like phantasms, meant, or could mean – and develop the meanings of – everything that was implied by common sensation. It implied not only a kind of vividness and concreteness, and a certain "treatment of subject matter," it also implied universality of audience based on the presumed universality of a certain structure of perception. Common sensation also entailed the optical and, more generally, the physical. If naturalism was to develop at all, it was more or less inevitable that this development ramify along the lines of its possible significance, inflected by any number of specific contexts, and expanded far beyond the first impulses toward naturalism. The imitation of appearances might have begun as marginal displays of skill, or as part of a new didactic strategy. It did not simply develop organically from these beginnings, however; rather, it was both shaped and augmented by its own significance in that tradition and situation. Eventually the union of painting and optics in one-point perspective would yield what was understood to be a most perfectly universal art, fully adapted to the structure of human vision and perception. This occurred not because all art develops toward naturalism, or because artistic skill develops as the invention of the devices of naturalism, even if such invention was necessary to the realization of the significance of naturalism and a constant force in the shaping of this significance; rather, it occurred at the most general extent of unity and cogency because in that tradition at that time naturalism stood in a specific systematic relation to other modes of significance and significant behavior.

The idea of system may be extended farther, pointing toward a social history of psychology. The rise in status of the mechanical arts and the institutionalization of this rise implied a rise in status of the faculties used in these arts. Much as the "masterpiece" began as a display of artisanal ingenuity and skill and ended up in modern usage to mean a work of transcending quality and value,[9] the mechanical arts, beginning in the Middle Ages as those crafts made necessary by the hard, material exigencies of human life, became, as they were for Francis Bacon (and, as we have seen, for Federico Zuccaro), a new paradigm for right,

[9] W. Cahn, *Masterpieces: Chapters on the History of an Idea*, Princeton, N.J., 1979.

productive thinking and the possibility of human progress, precisely because they were linked to the world of sense and experience.

Point of view, judgment, and taste

Naturalism also systematically involved a new definition of the viewer. In general, naturalism entails point of view. Things look "real" from some point in space and time occupied by whoever looks at them, or looks at an image of them. Point of view is perhaps best defined for us by perspective, and we in fact use the two terms metaphorically as more or less interchangeable. But perspective is only the most general and abstract form of point of view, the mathematical form at least in principle common to all viewers. "Point of view" also has other connotations; it also implies subjectivity and individuality. Writers of the late Middle Ages and the Renaissance understood the level of reality with which naturalism is associated to be inevitably bound up with "subjectivity" in its etymological sense, with the specific disposition of matter subject to the form of the human soul, the disposition of matter that is the principle of difference of one individual from another. At this level, powers of invention and imagination were set as well as faculties of perception, in a relation that more or less parallels that between naturalism and *maniera* in Renaissance art.

Renaissance writers seem to have been undisturbed by the fact that the world may be pleasingly and convincingly painted in a great number of ways, no doubt because they thought that the kind of reality with which painting dealt could *only* be painted (and seen) in as many different ways as there were painters. In Castiglione's *Il Cortegiano,* Count Lodovico da Canossa argues that although imitation is essential to the learning of an art, the regress of imitations cannot be endless, and that there must be originators. Whom, he asks, did Homer imitate? Or Petrarch and Boccaccio? If they imitated other great poets, then these great poets should not have been forgotten; because the imitated is greater than the imitator, Homer's teacher deserves to be remembered more than Homer himself. In fact, he says, the "true masters" of such poets were *ingegno* and their own natural judgment (*il lor proprio giudicio naturale*). In order to cement his argument, he points to the differences in style. There are various paths to the summit of every excellence. The harmonies of music are now grave and slow, now very rapid and novel. Nonetheless, all are delightful, but for different reasons. The singing of Bidon of Asti is "so artful, quick, vehement and agitated, and of such various melody that the spirits of whoever hears are moved and enflamed, and so uplifted that it seems they may be raised up to heaven." The singing of Marchetto Cara also moves us, but with a softer harmony; "in a peaceful way, full of plaintive sweetness, he touches and penetrates souls, softly impressing in them a delightful passion." These differences, it is emphasized, owe to differences in *ingegno* and *giudizio naturale,* which they must, after all, because the art practiced by the singers is the same. Moreover, as the sequence of the argument makes clear, these differences distinguish all artists in the same way that, in a consummate degree, these gifts are concentrated in the great originators of the arts, such as Homer, Petrarch, and Boccaccio. These gifts are also spiritual, and appeal to the spirits of the listeners. The Count moves immediately from music to painting, the link being the similar pleasures of ear and eye. "Various things also equally please our eyes such that one may judge only with difficulty which is most agreeable. See how in painting Leonardo da Vinci, Mantegna, Raphael, Michelangelo, Giorgione are all most excellent; nonetheless all are dissimilar among themselves in making [*fare*]; such that it seems nothing lacks in the manner [*maniera*] of any of them, because each is known in his style [*stilo*] to be most perfect."[10] Again, these differences owe to differences in gifts, and these gifts are associated with the lower mental faculties, which are closest to the principle of material and spiritual differences between individuals. When Federico Fregoso recapitulated the argument to rebut it, he did not deny the differences among people, which he attributed to differences in *istinto.* "Instinct" had always been a virtue of the animal soul, associated with the *estimativa.* Here, however, it has quite another and positive meaning, more closely related to the *estimativa* as that which apprehends the intentions of particulars. By implication, then, *istinto* is synonymous with *ingegno* and *giudizio naturale,* and is the source of *fare, maniera,* and *stilo,* finally the source of genius.[11]

This discussion points to the heart of the *Book of the Courtier,* in which *giudizio* is a fundamentally important notion. In the service of the task of creating a modern literature equal to that of the ancients, and of establishing the good usage necessary to such a literature, it is necessary that there be "men with *ingegno,* who have earned good judgment with learning and experience, by which they agree and consent to accept the words *that seem best to them, which are known by a certain natural judgment,* and not by any art or rule" (my emphasis). This "certain natural judgment" is very close to taste, and is close to the Aristotelian, Ciceronian, or Augustinian judgment of sense, to which appeal is in fact made in the next sentence. "Don't you know that the figures, which give so much grace and splendor to speech, are all abuses of grammatical rules, but accepted and confirmed by usage, because, no other reason being able to be given, they please, and it seems to the sense itself of the ear that they bear smoothness and sweetness?"[12] For Castiglione, eloquence was the pattern of his ideal human life, and the virtues of eloquence were very largely circumstantial. The judgment necessary to the courtier's prime virtue of *sprezzatura* has the same ambivalence that prudence had in Aristotle's *Nicomachean Ethics.* It is the ability to do things right, only partly to do them morally (as, indeed, most of our judgments are not moral ones), and

[10] *Opere di Baldassare Castiglione. Giovanni della Casa. Benvenuto Cellini,* I, XXXVII.
[11] Ibid., I, XXXVIII.
[12] Ibid., I, XXXV.

the judgments necessary for them are as much the judgments of sense as the judgments of reason.

Giudizio naturale not only justified individual styles, it continued to do so in terms that Vitruvius would already have understood. The rules of art were in large part the measures of art; and the freedom to adjust proportions was always an important part of artistic license and, for that very reason, a test and a display of artistic powers, in which the strength and character of those powers was made evident. It is necessary, Raffaele Borghini wrote late in the Cinquecento, to know measures, but they cannot always be used. "Sometimes in order to give a figure more grace it is necessary in some places to extend the measures and in others to diminish them. This cannot be taught; rather the artist must learn it with natural judgment."[13] This rephrases the arguments of Vitruvius on *eurhythmia,* and if such judgment presupposes knowledge and experience, it arises primarily from *ingenium,* not from *ars.*

Maniera thus meant more than individual style, more than a painter's individual "vision"; it was the consequence of individual "gifts" and experience. These predispositions to act were not themselves actions, however, and the execution of the work could be articulated as complex series of judgments of faculties of outer and inner sense, or sight, but also of the common sense, fantasy, estimation, and cogitation, involving quasi-moral virtues like prudence, or, more loosely, discretion, all of which were powers of the particular intellect. All of these faculties and virtues, as we have seen, were at least as deeply involved in the physical particularity of the individual as was sensation itself. The emergence of individual style thus entailed a kind of involvement with the particular in the making of the work that stands at the beginnings of the modern notion of taste. And, to return to the "problem of judgment" from which we began, it is not from intellectual judgment but rather from the judgment of sense that taste descends. The particular intellect was always of an individual and always dealt with particulars. The language of the particular intellect served Renaissance writers on art to discuss the kinds of judgment belonging to the making and viewing of works of art. It also provided a basis for the modern language of aesthetics, and it may be concluded that the issues formalized by Baumgarten's new discipline of aesthetics first began to be given their modern form with the development of naturalism in the late Middle Ages and the Renaissance. If Baumgarten used these ideas more systematically and at a higher level of articulation, this should not conceal the fact that he and other eighteenth-century writers drew upon the ideas and systems of ideas with which we have been concerned. It is no coincidence that Leonardo da Vinci and Immanuel Kant, for all the differences between them and between the times in which they wrote, both associated the *sensus communis* with judgments about art.

[13] R. Borghini, *Il Riposo,* Florence, 1584, p. 150, cited in Panofsky, *Idea,* p. 74. On the judgment of the eye, see *MLA,* pp. 368–379 and passim.

Languages of sensate judgment have probably always been integral to the practice of art, indispensable to its conduct and teaching, even if these languages have not always been regarded as significant, and even if the kind of "rightness" sought by skilled eyes and hands has not always been valued, or regarded as a significant metaphor, or paradigm. In general, these languages must be supposed to be closer to the purposes of craft than to the purposes of art literature, and there are relatively few records of them. There are certainly many more records in the results of the practice of Renaissance art than there are in its justifying "theory." At the same time, it is crucially important that there are major discussions of the judgment of sense in the writings of the founders and inventors of Renaissance art and that in this period psychological language was appropriated to the problem of explaining the "rightness" of works of art. It should be obvious that the incorporation of this language into the literature of art, which accompanied the development of naturalism and autographic style, did not simply open the floodgates of irrationality, even though art in the long and continuing tradition begun in the Renaissance successively explored its more subjective as well as its more objective dimensions. On the contrary, the Renaissance notion of the judgment of sense might be said to have been based on the assumption of the most pervasive harmony and to have been truly in the spirit of the legendary discoverer of the laws of musical harmony in the assumption of the essential continuity rather than opposition of world, sense, and intellect.

As such arguments might lead us to believe, at least by the end of the fifteenth century the metaphor of taste, *gusto,* could be used to talk about the judgment closest to one's own individual physical constitution. When Luca Pacioli wrote that "even the vulgar agree that the eye is the first portal through which the intellect understands and tastes" (*intende e gusta*), he meant that the eye is an agent of the mind, that it makes judgments and distinctions about particular things and that its "liking," which is the same as its judging, is subjective.[14] "Judgment" had many meanings, and the practice of the arts did not have to be regarded simply as occasion for the application of theory understood as the principles of the science of painting. Painting demanded *ingenium,* experience, and prudence, and at the level both of seeing prior to painting and of the determination of the real relations of compositional parts, such intelligent seeing, such judgment, was indispensable. El Greco praised the work of Michelangelo as manifesting "a taste [*gusto*] so admirable as never to have been seen in another sculptor" in the same way that he praised Titian's beautiful color and imitation of nature. He meant by this that the invention associated with *giudizio naturale* was everywhere apparent in Michelangelo's work.[15]

[14] L. Pacioli, *Divina proportione,* p. 35; see also ibid., p. 132, where Pacioli writes that measures cannot be exactly prescribed but must be left to "the grace and will of the eye" of "famous painters." This he calls an "irrational proportion." The eye is also described as the first portal through which the intellect *intende e gusta* in a play acted in Florence more than half a century before Pacioli wrote, in 1449. M. Baxandall ends his *Painting and Experience* (p. 153) with these lines.

[15] F. Marias and A. Bustamante Garcia, *Las Ideas artisticas de El Greco,* p. 131.

Classicism and the judgment of sense

We may return to the example used in our introduction, Leonardo's Burlington House cartoon (Fig. 2), the appearance of which is the result of previous tradition, the study of nature and of natural science, and the judgment of sense. It does not mean because such judgment was articulatable that Leonardo did not have to be knowledgeable in order to practice his art, any more than it meant that Vitruvius's architect was ignorant when he adjusted the proportions of his temple to the place in which it was actually to be seen. In the realization of any work, more than knowledge is necessary. Perspective, proportion, and anatomy – what the painter knows – demand more or less systematic adjustment and the judgment of the eye. The "right" solution in execution always has to be found in *that* case, and the eye and inner senses were thought to be capable of such discriminations. A knowledge of anatomy might guide the eye, but in the work the eye finds more than the mind knows, and the hand draws more than the mind knows. Whatever symbolic meanings they might have come to have, and however important these meanings might have been, proportions are only proportions if they look right, and forms are only in perspective if they seem to be. In the work, proportion comes not so much from the heavens downward as from the senses upward.

If a splendidly drawn foreshortening demanded the judgment of the eye, this kind of finding involved more than getting the drawing "right." It was also the making of a new thing, *una cosa nuova,* so that "getting things right" was close to invention, close to imagination, close to the point at which the realization of significance transforms significance in its very realization. The story is not the same if told by one or another artist in one or another painting, and is transformed, varied, and changed in its drawing, painting, or carving. It could be shown, I believe, that the old idea of the inner senses is an ancestor not only of aesthetics but of the modern notion of the unconscious, and it might be argued that the appearance of modern drawing, most visibly in the drawings of Leonardo da Vinci, was the appearance not only of a supple means of analysis but also of invention and self-revelation. Drawing and painting became the common ground of that relation, and on that common ground the mapping of inwardness is symmetrical to the mapping of outwardness.

A final word on the relation between invention and the judgment of sense. In a period like the present one in which it is considered to be the peculiar task of the artist to create new experience, and the task of the members of the audience to understand this new experience and broaden their awareness accordingly, it is hard to understand the strictures Mozart placed upon himself when he wrote that "music, even in the most terrible situations, must never offend the ear, but must please the hearer, or in other words must never cease to be music." When he wrote these words, Mozart was deeply classical, not just in his devotion to harmony, but in his devotion to the *sense* of harmony that he assumed his audience to possess. And because he was therefore still subject to the "light of the piazza" he always invented harmonies, however endlessly and richly he invented, and however many new harmonies he might find.

By the time Mozart wrote these words, it should be noted, the alternative between the terrible and the harmonious was more pressing as the distinction between the sublime and the beautiful, which involved a fundamental modification of the notion of sense and its relations to art. Edmund Burke had written with some relish of the ideas of the sublime induced by the experience of looking at the sun, the traditional example of the limits of the sense of sight, beyond which sight experienced pain and could not apprehend harmony through pleasure in what was proportioned to it. Sight overwhelmed by light joined the other extreme of darkness and in general the sublimity of great extremes surpassing sense now bracketed and dwarfed the lyre of sense. The judgment of sense, which found the beautiful, became only a segment of the spectrum of human experience, and it is for the most part to the embracing extremes of the "aesthetic" that characteristically modern art has turned. In relation to the ideas with which we have been concerned, the sublime was rooted in pain, more specifically in the pain of what surpasses our sense and scale. The aesthetic of such reflective pain provided access to the new world of forces that replaced the premodern world of harmony.[16]

The common, the physical, and the aesthetic

To return to the late Middle Ages and the Renaissance, the emergence of art corresponding to common sensation meant the emergence of the visible world as explicitly physical, an assumption with which all depicted meaning had to come to terms. The emergence of art meaningful in terms of common sensation was also the emergence of the visible world as physical, specifically in being the emergence of the visible world as mathematical, as geometric and arithmetical. The conditions of the physical process of sensation were the conditions of measurement as well. The common sensibles of Aristotle were magnitudes apprehended through the magnitude of the organ of sight under conditions describable by the "physical" geometry of light rays. From this standpoint the visible becomes a geometric matrix which is the possibility of the appearance of anything, much as we can imagine a perspective space into which any event might be set. In such circumstances abstraction assumes a new meaning; abstraction may now be achieved by removing point of view from the matrix implied by the geometry of vision, a removal yielding an infinite isotropic space. In this way the visual transcends the visual to become the physical as such. Abstraction is no longer

[16] *The Letters of Mozart and his Family*, ed. C. P. Oldman, tr. E. Anderson, London, 1938, p. 1144; E. Burke, *A Philosophical Enquiry into the Origin of Our Ideas of the Sublime and the Beautiful*, pp. 79–81 and passim; M. H. Nicolson, *Newton Demands the Muse: Newton's Optics and the Eighteenth Century Poets*, Princeton, N.J., 1966, pp. 115–117.

abstraction from visible forms but rather abstraction toward the most general visible relations. The most general laws of vision are laws of nature. Reason, *ratio,* is thus brought into immediate proximity to the physical world as common sensation. Insofar as it is explicitly mathematical, then, the common is at once split away from the particular and associated with reason. The common thus becomes the "objective." At the same time, the particular "object" reinserts point of view, still stands in relation to the "subject," and is apprehended by the subject as the subject's own, as those characteristics not describable mathematically.

Common sensation as the precinct of the particular intellect was thus split into two parts, which fall along the lines of the traditional distinctions between quantity and quality, substance and accident, or primary and secondary qualities. The subjective is associated with quality, and at the same time with the accidental, and with all those activities with respect to particulars that had been associated with inner sense.

The definition of perspective and of the isotropic space it implied entailed aesthetic order because both kinds of order are sensate, and this is their common base. A Renaissance perspective painting is in a fundamental way the projection of a subjectively determined visual order within the framework of what might be called an absolutely subjective order, or more or less explicit geometrically defined point of view. It is for this reason that the language about particulars and judgments about particulars emerged together with naturalism. Moreover, this split of point of view into mathematical and aesthetic components was to have the deepest and broadest currency in the centuries following the Renaissance, culminating in the definition of both the physical and the aesthetic, not only as intellectual disciplines but as regions of intense exploration and development. These developments are already both caricatured and foreshortened in this telling, which is intended only to establish the kinds of significance to which naturalism in Western painting is deeply related. But when David Hume contrasted reason, which "discovers objects, as they really stand in nature, without addition or diminution," and taste, which (presumably by adding and diminishing) "has a productive faculty, and gilding or staining all natural objects with colors, borrowed from an internal sentiment, raises, in a manner a new creation,"[17] he assumed a contrast between reason as a faculty that dealt with the mathematically describable physical particular, and another separate realm called "internal sentiment," which is thoroughly associated with the subjective.

It would take many more chapters to follow the transformation of "inner sensation" into the modern period. H. A. Wolfson argued that Locke and Kant had circumvented the Scholastic arrangements of mental faculties, returning the term to the meaning it had first had in Augustine, who, when he used it, had meant

[17] Quoted in M. H. Abrams, *The Mirror and the Lamp: Romantic Theory and the Critical Tradition*, New York, 1958, p. 64.

to refer to Aristotle's common sense as the principle of consciousness.[18] Locke argued that our "ideas" arise from two sources, either from sensations caused by external things or from "reflection" by "internal sense" upon "perception, thinking, willing, believing, reasoning, knowing and all the different actings of our own minds."[19] The effect of such a scheme is to make both sensation and the operations of the mind itself into "sense data," surveyed by a higher single principle rather comparable to the "higher" common sense of Avicenna and Averroes. Consciousness sees the working of the mind much in the way that we survey the world of the new physics from a point in space and time. Thus while the activities of "spirit," of memory and reminiscence, association and fantasy, came increasingly to be identified with mind altogether, an abstracted definition of internal sense persisted, closely identified with that which "sees that we see," as Aristotle had partly defined the common sense. Internal sense thus moved toward identification with self and individual soul, associations long made with the common sense in one or another of its historical forms. Consciousness thus came to "sense" the presumed unity of the mind's outer and inner experience as sensation, much as the common sense had been able to correlate and judge the data of the five senses precisely because of their unity as sensation. It is perhaps to the reduction of consciousness to a higher kind of sensation that we owe the proliferation in modern usage of senses – the moral sense, the sense of beauty, the sense of humor, to name only a few – that are regarded as essential to either the individual or the human self.

Aristotle had provided by far the most complete premodern psychology – a term that did not appear until around 1600 – which was developed and adapted to innumerable purposes without much modification. Whether writers of the seventeenth and eighteenth centuries actually criticized the *De anima*, or whether they simply turned to a common vocabulary formed by what had been the dominant psychology for some two millennia, his ideas were examined with relentless scrutiny. One casualty of this scrutiny was the common sense as Aristotle himself had defined it. In his *Essay Concerning Human Understanding*, John Locke argued that "use" allows us to see that the "plane variously coloured," like a painting on our retina, is really the convex surface of a sphere. In elaboration of this argument he offers the argument that a blind man taught by touch to distinguish cubes and spheres could not distinguish them by sight alone were his sight to be restored.[20] As we have seen, George Berkeley very much extended the implications of such arguments, maintaining in opposition to earlier optical writers that our ability to make judgments about space resulted from our experience of space, and was therefore finally dependent on the sense of touch.

Much under the influence of Locke and also, evidently, of Berkeley, Condillac

[18] H. A. Wolfson, "Internal Senses," in *Studies in the History of Philosophy and Religion*, pp. 309–310.

[19] *Essay Concerning Human Understanding*, II.1.4.

[20] Ibid., II.9.8.

might be said to have written his *Treatise on the Sensations* precisely to show that the common sense was an unnecessary hypothesis, even though he does not mention it.[21] Condillac imagined a statue animated one sense at a time, beginning with the sense of smell. He concludes his first analysis by saying that one sense includes the germ of all the faculties, and that in general sensation itself includes all the faculties of the soul. Touch is the most basic of the senses, and he agrees with Berkeley in saying that judgments of space are really habitual judgments of touch. The effect of these arguments was to push sensation toward a kind of intuition. The connection of all our sensations, which in Aristotle had been the work of the common sense, Condillac declares to be "natural," and with the rejection of the faculty that apprehended them go all the "underlying" connections and supports, the "being, substance, essence, nature, etc." which he rejects as "ghosts of philosophical reason." "Habit" replaces these ghosts and touch is the sense that gives us the idea of our self. The common sense might be said to have been displaced into the physical world and the operations of sensation, yielding a new basis for the universality of judgment. According to Condillac, the judgments of one person are not much different from those of another, and people differ from one another not in their experience but in the "liveliness" of their feeling. Some of us use experience and reflection to enrich and vary our lives, others do not. (This, of course, raises a social issue, which we shall shortly consider in more detail, because the idea might easily be turned around to say that those who do enrich and vary their lives are more "lively" and hence superior according to this new standard. It is certain that for the most part those who *do* enrich their lives are those who find themselves in circumstances that allow them to do so.)

When John Locke recast Aristotle's notion of the *tabula rasa,* the significance of this metaphor had very much changed. For Aristotle, phantasms were images of things in some way physically impressed upon the senses (and it was the sense of vision that was meant, as the word "phantasm" itself reminds us) in what was, in principle, a fairly straightforward manner. Aristotle's view of things prevailed for more than two millennia. By the time Locke wrote, the relation between the world, the senses, and the mind was much more problematical. Descartes had written that "in order to perceive, the mind need not contemplate any images resembling the things that it senses . . . We must not hold that it is by means of this resemblance that the picture causes us to perceive the objects, as if there

[21] *Condillac's Treatise on the Sensations,* tr. G. Carr, Los Angeles, 1930. Aristotle's ideas were, of course, not abandoned altogether. The Ideologist A. L. C. Destutt de Tracy, for example, who had written that to think is to sense and that to judge is to sense relations, to remember is to sense memories, to will is to sense desires, called the "self" or "intimate sense" not "the entirety of sensing parts" but a *sensorium commune* that has "consciousness of our impressions which our five external senses receive . . . in remembering them, in judging them, in forming from them other impressions or ideas more removed from direct impressions." This is not far from a defensible reading of Aristotle. See E. Kennedy, *A 'Philosophe' in the Age of Revolution: Destutt de Tracy and the Origins of 'Ideology,'* Philadelphia, 1978, pp. 157–158.

were yet other eyes in the brain with which we could apprehend it." Sensation itself is more like the little dabs of ink in an engraving that are able to represent "an infinity of diverse qualities."[22] The mind must interpret its sensations, and the relation between the mind and sensation is more like that of the mind to words, which are conventional and arbitrary, than to images. Newton argued similarly that we do not really see colors, rather the various rays of light "propagate this or that Motion into the Sensorium, and in the Sensorium they are sensations of those Motions under the Forms of Colours."[23]

Sight does not apprehend forms, but rather "motions," or the effects of motions, and in general it might be said that the senses came increasingly to be understood as kinds of touch, as the Atomists had long before argued and Aristotle had denied. Also, touch came increasingly to be understood to have the best and final access to the world that sense reveals. "Feeling" rather than "seeing" became the metaphor for basic sensation. No such changes could occur without fundamental adjustments in a whole network of ideas. The locus of the self, the principle of unity, shifts to the body as a whole, and among the faculties of the soul, toward fantasy or imagination, which continue to be basic to discussion; it also shifts toward definition by the uniqueness of individual history. As Condillac argued, man is the sum of what he acquires through experience.[24]

Many eighteenth-century writers argued that taste is a more constant judge than reason, that there are fewer disputes over the excellence of description in Virgil than over the meaning of the words of Aristotle, that the reputations of poets fluctuate much less violently than the reputations of philosophers. Taste is not universal, however, and differences in taste were – and could only be – accounted for in two ways, either by differences in constitution or temperament ("liveliness") or by differences in experience. There may be those who simply make the right discriminations, but in most cases the education of universal sensory equipment came to be considered the prerequisite for the acquisition of "good" taste, and learning good taste meant familiarization with an accepted canon of excellent works. This avoided the extreme democratic implications to be drawn from the commonness of sensation. But experience is as concrete in its own historical way as physiology and sensation, and accounting for differences in taste in terms of differences in experience at once implied differences in personal history and, beyond that, social differences. Only some were able to refine their sensibilities on the Grand Tour, and the pursuit of such refinement of taste became a large and conspicuous badge of social rank, which it still is. Good taste became "worthy of a free man," like the liberal arts, with which its cultivation is in fact closely institutionally allied.

When touch had become the dominant sense, the arguments in Diderot's *Letter*

[22] *Discourse on Method, Optics, Geometry, and Meteorology*, tr. P. J. Olscamp, New York, 1965, pp. 89–91.

[23] *Opticks or a Treatise of the Reflections, Refractions, Inflections and Colours of Light*, New York, 1952, Book I, part II, prop. II, theor. II, def. See M. H. Nicolson, *Newton Demands the Muse*, p. 146.

[24] *Treatise on the Sensations*, pp. 238–239.

on the Blind may be seen to have had more import and prophetic urgency than they would have had otherwise. The blindman literally lives in another world, for which he formulates another morality, another metaphysics, an evolutionary history of the world rather than the design of a divinely ordered cosmos, which is obvious only to sight. Diderot had called into question the ancient dream of Plato, according to which the soul cures itself by following the eyes to the heavens. When the calipers of the visual angle – as old as geometric optics itself – were likened by Descartes (as by the ancient Stoics) to two sticks held by a blindman, an emblem of the new priority of touch used by many later writers, all had in effect become blindmen, and the fundamentally visual world of classical antiquity, which extended through the Renaissance, was at an end.

Toward a later history of internal sense

Among the interior senses whose histories we have followed, the common sense survived and flourished and, as the intuitive base of Enlightenment rationalism, became a politically potent idea in its own right. However much it may have strayed from its ancient beginnings, the common sense retained its paradoxical status as a criterion that might be either relative and consensual or absolute and universal. A. O. Lovejoy argues that both relativism and what he calls "uniformitarianism" were essential to the Enlightenment, that the realization of the coexistence of many languages, religions, and moral systems generated the search for universal human nature, a search that lay at the foundations of both deism and Neoclassicism[25] (and which, it might be added, continued to animate movements in art through the abstraction of early modernism and survives as a utopian political dimension of formalism). Traditionally enough, universal human nature was defined as "reason," but, as Lovejoy remarks, the rational was not just the intellectual but rather the characteristically human, including the "internal senses," and especially common sense, which together with reason became the deep criterion it still is.

The modern notion of common sense retained its connection with spirit, embracing the Stoic notions of *oikeiosis*,[26] the self-evident principles of human society, and of *koinos nous*,[27] common reason undisfigured by sophistication, combining

[25] A. O. Lovejoy, "The Parallel of Deism and Classicism," *Essays in the History of Ideas*. Baltimore, 1948, pp. 78–98.

[26] On Stoic *oikeiosis*, "an implanted feeling or affinity, never a product of custom or habit," see T. Cole, *Democritus and the Sources of Greek Anthropology*, pp. 138–141. Cole relates it to Aristotle *Nicomachean Ethics* 1170a25–b19, in which the pleasurable *aisthesis* taken, especially by the virtuous, in consciousness of their own existence is linked to the *synaisthesis*, the object of which is a friend. The ever influential Cicero (*Pro Cluentia* 6.17) writes of filial piety as something that "in the common senses of men [*in communibus hominum sensibus*] and in very nature is set and fixed."

[27] Epictetus III.VI.2–8 (*The Discourses as Reported by Arrian, The Manual and Fragments*, 2 vols. tr. W. A. Oldfather, New York, 1928) defines *koinos nous* as the untutored power of discrimination, comparing it to the sense of hearing that distinguishes sounds and contrasting it with the sense of hearing trained to distinguish tones. The same opposition of "plain truth" and sophistication will appear in many of the writers in this short overview.

them with the Stoic *koinai ennoiai* (or common notions, which Locke rejected as "innate")[28] and "common conceptions of the mind," as writers of the Middle Ages had called the axioms of Euclidean geometry.[29] The philosophy of the common sense school incorporated these traditional elements and at the same time expanded the new whole of which they were parts to altogether unprecedented proportions. The "common conceptions" were supplemented by the newly self-evident principles of modern natural science, which in turn magnified and solidified the authority of the common sense as a criterion.[30] In these ways common sense grew closer to reason, and in a way was a deeper principle, the intuitive foundations of reason, from which reason might proceed.

[28] Locke, *Essay*, I.2.1. Locke states almost immediately that there are no *koinai ennoiai*, for a sustained examination of which see Plutarch, "Against the Stoics on Common Conceptions," in *Moralia*, XIII, pp. 660–873.

[29] E. Grant, *A Source Book in Medieval Science*, Cambridge, Mass., 1974, p. 66. On the common sense, the *communes animi notiones*, and mathematics, see C. Wolff, *Philosophia Prima sive Ontologia*, in *Gesammelte Werke*, II, 5, New York, 1968, pp. 104–107.

[30] We may consider the example of the lesser but representative Scottish common sense philosopher James Oswald. See G. Ardley, *The Common Sense Philosophy of James Oswald*, Aberdeen, 1980, p. 6. Oswald knows by common sense that he exists, that there are surrounding objects that persist through time, that these objects have figure, size, number, and situation. This list, although overlaid by mention of Descartes and expanded by Newtonian science (he also knows the first principles of natural philosophy), is still formed around the core of Aristotle's common sensibles. See ibid., p. 50. "It is not the eye that sees colours, nor the ear that judges of sounds, nor do the fingers feel, nor doth the palate distinguish between sweet and bitter; but it is the soul itself, or, if you will, the man himself, who by the help of these organs performs these acts, and enjoys these perceptions." Here taste is close to both self and common sense. A central figure for common sense philosophy and for the transformation of the common sense into its modern form was Claude Buffier. (On Buffier and his definition of common sense, see L. Marcil-Lacoste, *Claude Buffier and Thomas Reid: Two Common Sense Philosophers*, Montreal, 1982.) Buffier separated his common sense from the faculty of Aristotle that unites data of the outer senses. Marcil-Lacoste (p. 65) summarized his definition of common sense as a "natural predisposition to judge certain principles to be self-evidently true . . . principles . . . primarily concerned with the existence of other beings and things." Buffier's definition of common sense was repeated in the *Encyclopédie* (ibid., p. 13 n. 3). Reacting to the skepticism of Descartes, Buffier defined common sense as "that disposition or quality which Nature has placed in all men, or evidently in the far greater number of them, in order to enable them all, when they have arrived at the age and use of reason to form a common judgment with respect to objects different from the internal sentiment of their own perception, and which judgment is not the consequence of any anterior principle." Such universally held convictions as that one exists together with other people and material things are absolute in the face of any rational arguments that might be devised in contradiction of them. Those who deny them act as if they were true even if they say they are not. In Buffier's opinion, common sense does not belong to everyone; he argues that the clear intuition of common sense may be clouded by accident, by emotions and prejudice. Those in whom common sense prevails are "men of sense." For Buffier reason clarifies and elaborates what all men know by sense and experience, and the constructions of reason are always subject to the principles of common sense. Within such a framework Buffier defined taste. Taste is established on the base of universal sensation; that is, experience of a kind that only certain persons pursue clarifies the universally sensed, much as optics clarifies what each may see. Taste is "formed," and the result is more marked by time, place, and circumstances than by individual difference. As for the beautiful, Buffier defined it as "that which is at the same time the most common and the most rare in things of the same species . . . that particular form, the most common of all the particular forms to be met with in the same species of things." See A. N. Foxe, *The Common Sense from Heraclitus to Peirce*, pp. 128–131.

It was mentioned in passing that the internal senses, far from disappearing in modern usage, have proliferated, and that this proliferation is simply another facet of modern psychological empiricism. If everyone might agree that all thought arises from sensation, there was disagreement as to just what this meant. Against Locke's reduction of internal sensation to apperception, other writers made other, higher "senses" integral with internal sensation, senses that stood to external sensation as did the old common sense, or, like the medieval faculty of estimation, afforded immediate access to verities other than those to be had from sight, hearing, taste, smell, and touch. Because "internal sensation" provided "intuitions" higher than the data of the five senses and because these intuitions were about the particular and the subjective, it is not hard to see why moral and aesthetic faculties are closely linked in this discussion. We may consider the case of Shaftesbury, who writes of a "reflected sense" by means of which "affections" are apprehended to become themselves affections of the mind. This "reflected sense" is entirely on the side of the subjective. Shaftesbury immediately compares fundamental moral judgment to aesthetic judgment, or rather discusses both moral judgment and judgment about art as kinds of aesthetic judgment, to which a new importance is now given.

> The mind which is spectator or auditor of other minds, cannot be without its eye and ear, so as to discern proportion, distinguish sound, and scan each sentiment or thought which comes before it. It can let nothing escape its censure. It feels the soft and harsh, the agreeable and disagreeable in the affections; and finds a foul and fair, a harmonious and a dissonant, as really and truly here as in any musical numbers or in the outward forms or representations of sensible things. Nor can it withhold its admiration and ecstasy, its aversion and scorn, any more in what relates to one than to the other of these subjects. So that to deny the common and natural sense of a sublime and beautiful in things, will appear an affectation merely, to any one who considers duly of this affair.[31]

These ideas are consistent with Locke's, but they are also very nearly repetitions of Plato and Cicero.

Again, as we have seen, Shaftesbury, the first writer to use the term "moral sense," called the faculty of aesthetic perception "plain internal sensation,"[32] and when Kant identified taste with common sense he seems to have meant that in the exercise of taste sensation is in conformity with the structure of immediate sense itself. Francis Hutcheson compared "internal sense" to the "sense of beauty," which was in turn related to such other kinds of intuition as the public sense and the moral sense.[33] These are still familiar phrases – and familiar criteria –

[31] Anthony Ashley Cooper, *Characteristics of Men, Manners, Opinions, Times*, pp. 251–252.

[32] See Chapter 5 n. 57, above.

[33] See D. F. Norton, "Hutcheson on Perception and Moral Perception," *Archiv für Geschichte der Philosophie*, 59, 1977, pp. 180–197. The *sensus communis* is clearly the pattern for Hutcheson's discussion of "internal sense," which "concomitantly" apprehends extension, figure, motion, and rest; the senses are discussed in terms of primary and secondary qualities, and the internal sense is compared to the sense of beauty, to "what Addison called the imagination," and is in turn the

that could easily be expanded to include a great number of more casually formulated modern faculties: the sense of history, the sense of quality, the sense of humor. Sometimes these senses are associated with experience, which adds to our sensibility ("this will give you some sense of the problem") but more often they are associated with innate, distinguishing individual characteristics ("she has a great sense of the absurd"). Such "senses" are intuitive, not just of things but of circumstances in their absolute particularity. The Enlightenment writers, of course, meant to argue that some intuitions are universal, and might therefore provide standards of morality as well as guides to appropriate action.

David Hume began his essay *On the Standard of Taste*[34] with a discussion of morals. Although there are many moralities, there are universal moral principles because of "plain reason, which maintains similar sentiments in all men." The problem of taste is comparable. Common sense (by which he here means something like conventional wisdom, or experience) tells us contradictory things about taste. It tells us, first, that there is a "natural equality of taste," that "beauty is in the eye of the beholder"; but it also tells us that it is possible to tell good art from bad, to tell Virgil from doggerel. Hume maintains that there are no universal principles of beauty, that "general rules of art" are founded on experience and on the "common sentiments of human nature." If there is no universal standard of beauty, however, that does not mean that we cannot judge all kinds of beauty to be beautiful. He uses the analogy of color. Even though color is "just a phantasm of the senses" (a post-Newtonian formulation), we may still see what are agreed to be true colors because of some relation between whatever might be "colored"

foundation of the public sense, moral sense, and so on. Joseph Addison's essays on imagination (*Essays Moral and Humorous,* also *Essays on Imagination and Taste,* Edinburgh, 1839, pp. 112–122) begins with the proposition that "sight is the most perfect and most delightful of all our senses"; and the pleasures of imagination "are not so gross as those of sense, nor so refined as those of understanding"; in comparison to the latter

> they are more obvious and more easy to be acquired. It is but opening the eyes, and the scene enters. The colours paint themselves on the fancy, with very little attention of thought or application of mind in the beholder. We are struck, we know not how, with the symmetry of any thing we see, and immediately assent to the beauty of an object, without inquiring into the particular causes and occasions for it.

Although imagination is more universal and easily acquired than understanding, there is now a distinction to be drawn between the "man of polite imagination" and the vulgar. See D. D. Raphael, *The Moral Sense,* Oxford, 1947, p. 16 n. 1, where Hutcheson likens the moral sense to the *hegemonikon.* Also P. Kivy, *The Seventh Sense: A Study of Francis Hutcheson's Aesthetics and Its Influence in Eighteenth-Century Britain,* New York, 1976.

P. O. Kristeller, "The Modern System of the Arts," in *Renaissance Thought II,* pp. 219–221, discusses the differentiation of intuition into three parts, corresponding to the good, the beautiful, and the true in German thinkers of the later eighteenth century beginning with Moses Mendelssohn. According to F. J. Riedel, nature has given us a *Grundkraft* corresponding to each of the three; for the true, the *sensus communis;* for the good, conscience; and for the beautiful, taste. J. G. H. Feder followed Riedel in his *Oratio de sensu interno* in 1768. The importance of all this, of course, is not that the *sensus communis* is not the sense of beauty, or taste, but rather that it was felt to be necessary carefully to distinguish various kinds of intuition at the level of the immediately post-sensationary.

[34] *On the Standard of Taste and other Essays,* New York, 1965.

and our sensation of it, if the organ of sight is functioning normally. Similarly, because of the qualities of works of art we may see their beauty, but we may only make the necessary discriminations if our "eye" is functioning properly, if we have the right predisposition, attitude, and experience, which few of us have, but which the good critic possesses in a high degree.

Hume's arguments are framed both to accommodate and to respond to the problem of relativism. As we have seen, historicist relativism in fact helped to make common sense the authoritative principle it has become in modern times, a kind of *vox populi,* which has however broadened to the sublime global proportions characteristic of much modern thought. A greatly expanded notion of common sense seemed to provide a universal basis for laws and customs recognized to be various and contradictory. Giambattista Vico defines common sense quite traditionally as "judgment without reflection," that is, as prerational judgment, but goes on to say that it is "shared by an entire class, an entire people, an entire nation, or the entire human race." Dispositions characteristic of classes and peoples might be thought to be merely conventional, but Vico also writes that "uniform ideas originating among entire peoples unknown to each other must have a common ground of truth. This axiom is a great principle which establishes the common sense of the human race as the criterion taught to the nations by divine providence to define what is certain in the natural law of the gentes." Vico seems to have understood *senso comune* to be the primitive intuition of reality, close to the physical differences of peoples as the common sense was thought to be close to the physical constitution of individuals, the basis of a kind of judgment both absolute (because particular and circumstantial) and opinionative. "Common sense" thus does not imply some built-in code of universal humanity but rather the kind of uniformity arising from whatever similarity there might be between the physical natures of peoples and their environments. Such a simple and primordial state of affairs would have been complicated immediately as these intuitions assumed fantastic or poetic form, which they inevitably did, just as in the psychology we have examined the common sense and fantasy were closely related and sometimes identified. It also seems clear Vico believed these culturally specific imaginative forms became "naturalized," that they became part of the world subject to "judgment without reflection" and in harmony with it. This judgment might thus be both regional and consensual and, in certain deep respects, universal. With this range of meaning for *senso comune* it was possible for Vico to write of the characters of Homer's poetry as seeming natural because they arose from the common sense of an entire nation, from which "alone consists the decorum or beauty and charm of a fable," and also to write of the "common sense of marvel" that leads various groups to similar attitudes toward inventors of writing.[35] It might be noted that

[35] *The New Science of Giambattista Vico. Revised Translation of the Third Edition (1744)*, ed. T. G. Bergin and M. H. Fisch, Ithaca, N.Y., 1968, sections 141–144, 809, 935; and *La Scienza Nuova*, ed. F. Nicolini, Bari, 1928, I, p. 77. A. Funkenstein, "Natural Science and Social Theory: Hobbes, Spinoza, and Vico," in *Giambattista Vico's Science of Humanity*, ed. G. Tagliacozzo and D. P. Verene,

the foundation of these arguments (and of society) in common sense makes of it a principle deeper than reason. It also means that even though specific "decorum, beauty and charm" are conventional in that they arise among one group, they may still appeal to the "taste" of another group. Taste as a faculty at the level of common sense thus might supplant reason as a means to historical and anthropological understanding. Common sense was also closely related to spirit (although it was the most corporeal form of spirit, as Vico insisted on the corporeal character of sensate wisdom), and Vico's words have a place in the early history of the idea of *Volksgeist,* which has been so fundamentally important to the modern definition and study of culture in general and the history of art in particular. National "taste" early on became a hallmark of the "spirits of peoples."[36]

Such ideas, which are given especially complete statement by Vico, should not be associated only with him; in a writer as far from Vico as Joseph Addison, the consensual nature of collective taste is also examined. Addison extended and expanded arguments of the kind put forward by Cicero, bringing them to near-modern dimensions. The "unlearned crowd," rather than simply responding to the rhythms of eloquent speech with one cry of approval, now provides an example of the exercise of a much richer collective taste, pointing to achievements equal in some instances to the greatest epic poetry. Addison delights in folk songs and fables, he writes, because "it is impossible that anything should be universally tasted and approved by a multitude, though they are only the rabble of a nation, which hath not in it some peculiar aptness to please and gratify the mind of man." Because, he states, "rational human nature is everywhere the same," whatever is consistent with it must please readers "of all qualities and conditions." When Addison refers to "rational human nature," of course, he should be understood to refer to judgments of a rational soul that are not in themselves judgments of reason, that is, to refer to judgments of peculiarly human sense. The possession of such a "rational human nature" in itself constitutes a kind of democracy of taste, which is again associated with common sense. The great poets "will please a reader of plain common sense," and common sense is parallel to the common people, who are delighted by an "ordinary song or ballad." But such universal appeal is achieved not only in popular art; it is achieved by all poetry possessing

Baltimore, 1976, p. 208, defines *senso comune* as the "definite mental configuration of each age, the harmonic principle of each period." This seems to me more relativistic than Vico's "motivo comune di vero . . . che stabilisce il senso comune del gener umano esser il criterio insegnato alle nazioni." J. M. Kreis, "Vico's and Peirce's 'sensus communis,' " *Vico: Past and Present*, ed. G. Tagliacozzo, Atlantic Highlands, N.J., 1981, II, pp. 58–71, discusses Vico's *senso comune* in part in relation to the idea of *consensus,* on which see K. Oehler, "Der Consensus omnium als Kriterium der Wahrheit in der antiken Philosophie und der Patristik," *Antike und Abendland,* 10, 1961, pp. 103–129. See also D. P. Verene, *Vico's Science of Imagination,* Ithaca, N.Y., 1981, pp. 52–54, 147, 174–192. Although Verene discusses the higher internal senses and their relation to such related ideas as *ingegno,* he does not treat the common sense as part of this system, as I believe should be done.

[36] N. Rotenstreich, in *DHI,* s.v. "Volksgeist."

certain qualities, principally what Addison calls "simplicity of thought," which is juxtaposed to the "Gothic," the "artificial," the "fanciful," and the epigrammatic. Simplicity, which he later links with the "natural" and "poetical" and with the "greatest of the ancient poets," thus provides a foundation for all poetry, "because the same paintings of nature, which recommend it to the most ordinary reader, will appear beautiful to the most refined."[37] It was similarly possible for Samuel Johnson to argue that "by the common sense of readers uncorrupted by all the refinements and dogmatism of learning must be finally decided all claim to poetical honors," to argue that Gray's *Elegy* "abounds with images which find a mirror in every mind, and with sentiments to which every bosom returns an echo."[38]

In all the forms it assumed in the Enlightenment, common sense provided a powerful justification for democracy. It also had a rhetorical dimension and was associated with unembellished, unfigured prose, the "straight talk" of the new science.[39] As a straightforward example of the political use of these ideas we may consider Thomas Paine, who would "offer nothing more than simple facts, plain arguments, and common sense"; his reader need only "divest himself of prejudice and prepossession, and suffer his reasons and feelings to determine for themselves; then he will "put on . . . the true character of a man, and generously enlarge his views beyond the present day."[40] Here fact and plain speech are linked at once to common sense, reason, and feeling. The criteria appealed to are explicitly democratic, and for all the differences between the purposes of the two writers we are not far from the preface to Wordsworth's *Lyrical Ballads,* where, in words not so different from those of Joseph Addison and Samuel Johnson, it is argued that we are separated by poetic diction from "good sense and nature," accessible in everyday speech and emotion, which are linked to our "moral sentiments and

[37] J. Addison, R. Steele, et al. *The Spectator,* ed. A. Chalmers, New York, 1853, I, p. 423 (no. 70) and p. 444 (no. 74). I am grateful to Ralph Cohen for bringing this text to my attention.

[38] Quoted in A. O. Lovejoy, "Parallel of Deism and Classicism," *Essays in the History of Ideas.*

[39] B. M. Stafford, *Voyage into Substance: Art, Science, Nature and the Illustrated Travel Account,* 1760–1840, Cambridge, Mass.–London, 1984, p. 35.

[40] T. Paine, *Common Sense and Other Political Writings,* ed. N. F. Adkins, New York, 1953, p. 18. K. Doerner, *Madmen and the Bourgeoisie: A Social History of Insanity and Psychiatry,* Oxford, 1981, p. 22–25, argues that the political criterion of common sense first became central in British political controversy of the early eighteenth century, and eventually became a standard that allowed "both the physician and the politician to determine . . . whether a controversial matter . . . was a part of bourgeois society or was to be cast out from it." Doerner relates the development of such ideas to Thomas Willis, *An Essay on the Patholgy of the Brain and Nervous Stock,* published in 1667. Willis, following the traditional scheme in its more physiological variant as we have seen it in Leonardo da Vinci and Descartes (the latter of whom certainly influenced Willis), placed the *sensus communis,* now the center for correlation of impulses from the external senses, in the central ventricle of the brain, where it is united with fantasy, imagination, and memory and still linked to spirit. Willis's influential ideas obviously took their place in a very long tradition, and the relation of his *sensus communis* to the political notion of common sense (which Doerner associates with the appearance of notions like public sense, moral sense, and public opinion) is more complex than his presentation implies. I am grateful to H. C. Erik Midelfort for bringing this text to my attention.

animal sensations"; these point poetry toward a transcendental democracy, toward "the vast empire of human society as it is spread over the whole earth, and over all time."[41]

These examples bring our brief survey of the survival of the ancient notions of interior sense and particular intellect to a close. Many more examples might be given, and many themes might be followed on to the present day. If such study – which I hope will have encouraged further study – might throw some light on the language we use and the presuppositions, traditions, and values that underly it, or, if the language itself of the "old pneumatic physiology" is still of intrinsic interest, such considerations must be regarded as side benefits of the investigation. I have not so much meant to galvanize premodern psychology to life as I have meant to give some indication of how traditions of ideas work and how ideas entail one another. I have tried to show that the development of the naturalism in art we take so much for granted was systematically related to the rise of aesthetics by examining the language to which Renaissance artists and writers on art turned when they first set about to articulate what we call aesthetic judgment. Beyond that, I have tried to show that fundamental artistic invention was carried out in intimate relation to available appropriate language and ideas, in ways that shaped both intention and reception, and in doing so located artistic invention in a vast web of use, meaning, choice, and change.

[41] *Wordsworth's Literary Criticism*, ed. W. J. B. Owen, Boston, 1974, pp. 68–94.

Addendum: John Calvin wrote of a *sensus divinitatis*, a natural instinct that is universal. It is an internal sense, close to fantasy, and is a means by which people everywhere fall into the idolatry that keeps them from truly worshipping the transcendental God. See C. M. N. Eire, *War against the Idols: The Reformation of Worship from Erasmus to Calvin*, Cambridge, 1986, pp. 204–205. Calvin's principle "finitum non est capax infiniti" is a precise rejection of Aquinas's Aristotelian principle that "incorporea, quorum non sunt phantasmata, cognoscuntur a nobis per comparationem ad corporea sensibilia, quorum sunt phantasmata," that we are able to know "incorporeal substances" only "per remotionem or by some comparison to *corporalia*" that they be made phantasms of bodies, even though they are not themselves phantasms (*Summa theologiae* I.84.7 ad 3). Such arguments justified not only images, but also the Mass, ceremonial and architectural splendor, certain attitudes to rhetoric, and, as we have seen, theater. There was a longstanding and persistent tradition opposing ideas like those of Aquinas. Simon de Tournai (c. 1130–c. 1201), elaborating the ideas of John the Scot, opposed the error of the "metamorphonites" with arguments that must remind us of innumerable religious images. Such persons contemplate God in an "imaginary" mode, as creatures are contemplated, imagining God as if he were a prince or pontiff in a circumscribed place, set on a throne or chair surrounded by angels like soldiers, when God is everywhere, not in a circumscribed place or defined by corporeal lineaments. God should be contemplated in himself, not according to likeness, which gives him inappropriate incidental qualities. See Simon de Tournai, *Sententiae*, in Alain de Lille, *Textes inédits*, ed. M. T. d'Alverny, Paris, 1965, p. 308; and John Scottus Erigena, *Expositiones in Ierarchiam Coelestem*, ed. J. Barbet, Turnhout, 1965, pp. 34–35, 52–53.

The abbé Dubos (*Critical Reflections on Poetry and Painting*, tr. T. Nugent, London, 1748, II, pp. 237–249) cited the same Ciceronian texts used by Alberti and wrote (his remarks were first published in 1719) that the public "judges right of poems and pictures in general," that "every man who is not absolutely stupid, must feel the effect of good verses and fine pictures." This judgment is accomplished by the senses themselves and by a "sixth sense we have within us, without feeling its organs," which he identifies with the heart. This argument is lodged in an overall theory of imitation, and if we are moved to pity by a picture or poem, we judge by the sense with which we would judge the same situation if it were real. T. Puttfarken (*Roger de Piles' Theory of Art*, New Haven, Conn., 1985, p. 129) relates this to Locke's argument that "sensible knowledge" without rational demonstration can be relied upon for any judgment we have to make in the normal world, apparently referring to *Essay concerning Human Understanding*, iv, xi, 8. Puttfarken also discusses common sense as public opinion in close connection with illusionism (ibid., pp. 25–29). There was a corresponding rejection of the idea of internal sense, no doubt because it was a survival of an old system fundamentally at odds with the new philosophy. Edmund Burke, who could have written his arguments against many authors before and after him, defined taste as "that faculty, or those faculties of mind which are affected with, or which form a judgment of the works of imagination and the elegant arts" (*Inquiry*, p. 13). But he rejected the idea that taste is a "separate faculty of the mind" apart from judgment and imagination, a "species of instinct by which we are struck naturally, and at first glance, without any previous reasoning with the excellencies or defects of a composition." Burke scorned the multiplication of principles of explanation as "unphilosophical in a high degree" (ibid., pp. 26–27). For more on the attack on the idea of internal sense, E. L. Tuveson, *The Imagination as a Means of Grace: Locke and the Aesthetics of Romanticism*, New York, 1974, pp.42–55, 164–198.

Herder argues against Riedel's notion of common sense (see n. 33, above), but also argues that there must be a "common sense," a "common human sensibility," uniting all humanity. This provides the basis for his idea of *Humanität*. See M. Schutze, "Herder's Psychology," *Monist*, 35, 1925, pp. 507–554.

Bibliography

Abrams, M. H., *The Mirror and the Lamp: Romantic Theory and the Critical Tradition,* New York, 1958.

Ackerman, J. S., "Leonardo's Eye," *JWCI,* 41, 1978, pp. 108–146.

Addison, J., *Essays Moral and Humorous, Also Essays on Imagination and Taste,* Edinburgh, 1839.

Addison, J., Steele, R., et al., *The Spectator,* 6 vols., ed. A. Chalmers, New York, 1853.

al-Farabi, *Catálogo de las Ciencias. Edición y Traducción castellana,* ed. A. Gonzalez Palencia, Madrid, 1953.

Al-Farabi's commentary and short treatise on Aristotle's De interpretatione, ed. F. W. Zimmerman, London, 1981.

De scientiis, ed. M. Alonso Alonso, Madrid, 1954.

Alfarabi's Philosophy of Plato and Aristotle, tr. M. Mahdi, New York, 1969.

Alberti, L. B., *L'Architettura* [*De re aedificatoria*], ed. G. Orlandi and P. Portoghesi, Milan, 1966.

Della pittura, ed. L. Mallè, Florence, 1950.

Della pittura/De pictura, in *Opere volgari,* III, ed. C. Grayson, Bari, 1973.

On Painting and on Sculpture, ed. C. Grayson, London, 1972.

Albertus Magnus, *Opera omnia,* 37 vols., ed. A. Borgnet, Paris, 1890–9.

Opera omnia, 37 vols., Westphalia, 1951–78.

Alhazen, *Opticae thesaurus. Alhazen Arabis libri septem nuncprimum editi. Eiusdem Liber de Crepusculis et Nubium ascensionibus. Item Vitellonis Thuringopoloni Libri X,* ed. F. Risner, Basel, 1572 (facs. New York, 1972, ed. D. C. Lindberg).

"Alkinous," *Didaskalikon,* in *The Works of Plato,* VI, tr. G. Burges, London, 1891, pp. 241–314.

Alpers, S., *The Art of Describing: Dutch Art in the Seventeenth Century,* Chicago, 1983.

Andreas Capellanus, *De amore libri tres,* ed. E. Trojel, Copenhagen, 1892.

Antoninus, Saint, *Sancti Antonini Archiepiscopi Florentini ordinis praedicatorum Summa Theologica,* 4 vols., Verona, 1750 (facs, Graz, 1959).

Ardley, G., *The Common Sense Philosophy of James Oswald,* Aberdeen, 1980.

Aristotle, *Aristotle's De anima in the Version of William of Moerbeke and the Commentary of St. Thomas Aquinas,* tr. K. Foster and S. Humphries, New Haven, Conn., 1951.

Aristotelis opera cum Averrois commentariis, 9 vols., Venice, 1562–74 (facs. Frankfurt am Main, 1962).

Aristotle's Psychology; a treatise on the principle of life (De anima and Parva naturalia), ed. W. A. Hammond, New York, 1902.

The Basic Works of Aristotle, ed. R. McKeon, New York, 1941.

De anima, ed. and tr. R. D. Hicks, New York, 1970.
Ethica Nicomachea. Translatio Roberti Grosseteste Lincolniensis, Aristoteles Latinus, 26, 1–3, fasc. 3–5, ed. R. A. Gauthier, Leiden, 1973.
The Works of Aristotle Translated into English, 12 vols. ed. W. D. Ross, London, 1908–52.
Aristotle (?) *Problems*, 2 vols., tr. W. S. Hett, London, 1936.
Augustine, Saint, *De doctrina christiana*, ed. W. M. Green, *Corpus Scriptorum Ecclesiasticorum Latinorum*, vol. 80, Vienna, 1963.
De libero arbitrio voluntatis, St. Augustine on Free Will, tr. C. M. Sparrow, Charlottesville, Va., 1947.
De quantitate animae, ed. F. E. Tourscher, Philadelphia, 1933.
La Genèse au sens littéral en douze livres (VIII–XII). De Genesi ad litteram libri duodecim, ed. P. Agaesse and A. Solignac, Paris, 1972.
On Christian Doctrine, tr. D. W. Robertson, Jr., New York, 1958.
Opera omnia, MPL, Paris, 1841–6, vols. 32–49.
The Trinity, tr. S. McKenna, Washington, D.C., 1963.
Averroes, *Compendia Librorum Aristotelis qui Parva naturalia vocantur*, ed. A. Shields, Cambridge, Mass., 1942.
Averrois Cordubensis commentarium magnum in Aristotelis de anima libros, ed. F. S. Crawford, Cambridge, Mass., 1953.
Averroes' Three Short Commentaries on Aristotle's "Topics," "Rhetoric," and "Poetics," ed. C. E. Butterworth, Albany, 1977.
Epitome of the Parva naturalia, ed. and tr. H. Blumberg, Cambridge, Mass., 1961.
Avicenna, *Avicenna Latinus: Liber de Anima seu Sextus de Naturalibus*, IV–V, ed. S. van Riet, Louvain–Leiden, 1968.
Avicenna's Commentary on the Poetics of Aristotle: A Critical Study with an Annotated Translation of the Text, ed. M. Dahiyat, Leiden, 1974.
Avicenna's Psychology: An English Translation of "Kitab al Najat," Book II, Chapter VI with historico-philosophical notes and textual improvements on the Cairo edition, ed. and tr. F. Rahman, London, 1952.
Babolin, S., "La cogitativa di S. Tommaso," *Tommaso d'Aquino nel suo settimo centenario. Atti del Congresso Internazionale (Roma–Napoli, 17/24 Aprile, 1974)*, Naples, 1978, VIII, pp. 363–367.
Bacon, Francis, *The Works of Francis Bacon*, 14 vols., London, 1857–74.
Bacon, Roger, *Opus Maius*, Parts I–VII, 2 vols., ed. J. H. Bridges, Oxford, 1897; Supplementum, London, 1900.
Barasch, M., "Character and Physiognomy: Bocchi on Donatello's *St. George:* A Renaissance Text on Expression in Art," *JHI*, 36, 1975, pp. 413–430.
Theories of Art from Plato to Winckelmann, New York, 1985.
Bartholomaeus Anglicus, *De proprietatibus rerum*, Frankfurt, 1601 (facs. Frankfurt am Main, 1964).
Bate de Malines, Henri, *Speculum divinorum et quorundam naturalium*, ed. G. Wallerand, Louvain, 1931.
Baumgarten, A. G., *Reflections on Poetry: Meditationes philosophicae de nonnullis ad poema pertinentibus*, ed. K. Aschenbrenner and W. B. Holther, Berkeley, Calif., 1954.
Baxandall, M., *Giotto and the Orators: Humanist Observers of Painting in Italy and the Discovery of Pictorial Composition*, Oxford, 1971.
Painting and Experience in Fifteenth Century Italy: A Primer in the Social History of Pictorial Style, Oxford, 1972.
Beare, J. I., *Greek Theories of Elementary Cognition from Alcmaeon to Aristotle*, Oxford, 1906.
Becker, M. B., *Medieval Italy: Constraints and Creativity*, Bloomington, Ind., 1981.

Berkeley, G., *Berkeley's Philosophical Writings*, ed. D. M. Armstrong, New York, 1965.

Il Bestiario toscano secondo la lezione dei codici di Parigi e di Roma, ed. M. S. Garver and K. McKenzie, Rome, 1912.

Bialostocki, J., "The Eye and the Window: Realism and Symbolism of Light-Reflections in the Art of Albrecht Dürer and His Predecessors," *Festschrift für Gert von der Osten*, Cologne, 1970, pp. 159–176.

"The Power of Beauty: A Utopian Idea of L. B. Alberti," *Festschrift für L. H. Heydenreich*, Munich, 1964, pp. 13–19.

Bilinski, B., "Elogio della mano e la concezione ciceroniana della società," *Atti del I Congresso Internazionale di studi ciceroniani*, Rome, 1961, pp. 195–212.

Block, I., "Truth and Error in Aristotle's Theory of Sense Perception," *Philosophical Quarterly*, 9, 1961, pp. 1–9.

Blumenthal, H. J., *Plotinus' Psychology: His Doctrines of the Embodied Soul*, The Hague, 1971.

Blund, Johannes, *Tractatus de Anima*, ed. D. A. Callus and R. W. Hunt, London, 1970.

Blunt, A., *Artistic Theory in Italy, 1450–1600*, Oxford, 1940.

Boas, G., *Essays on Primitivism and Related Ideas in the Middle Ages*, New York, 1978.

Boccaccio, *Genealogie deorum gentilium libri*, 2 vols., ed. V. Romano, Bari, 1951.

Boethius, *The Consolation of Philosophy, with the English Translation of "I. T." (1609)*, ed. H. F. Stewart, Cambridge, Mass.–London, 1962.

In Isagogen Porphyrii Commenta, ed. S. Brandt, Leipzig, 1906.

Manlii Severini Boetii opera omnia. Opera philosophica et opera theologica, MPL, 64.

Bonaventure, Saint, *De Reductione artium ad theologiam*, ed. and tr. E. T. Healy, Saint Bonaventure, N.Y., 1940.

Opera omnia, 10 vols., Florence, 1882–1902.

Sancti Bonaventurae Opera, 14 vols., Venice, 1754.

Borghini, R., *Il Riposo*, Florence, 1584.

Brown, J., Kagan, R., et al., *El Greco of Toledo*, exhibition catalogue, Museo del Prado, Washington National Gallery of Art, Toledo Museum of Art, Dallas Museum of Fine Arts, Boston, 1982.

de Bruyne, E., *Etudes d'esthétique médiévale*, 3 vols., Bruges, 1947.

Bundy, M. W., *The Theory of Imagination in Classical and Medieval Thought, University of Illinois Studies in Language and Literature*, XII, Urbana, Ill., 1927, pp. 7–289.

Buonarroti, M., *Rime*, ed. E. N. Girardi, Bari, 1960.

Burke, E., *A Philosophical Inquiry into the Origin of Our Ideas on the Sublime and Beautiful*, ed. J. T. Boulton, New York, 1958.

Burton, R., *The Anatomy of Melancholy*, ed. F. Dell and P. Jordan-Smith, New York, 1927.

Cahn, W., *Masterpieces: Chapters on the History of an Idea*, Princeton, N.J., 1979.

The Cambridge History of Later Greek and Early Medieval Philosophy, ed. A. H. Armstrong, Cambridge, 1967.

The Cambridge History of Later Medieval Philosophy: From the Rediscovery of Aristotle to the Disintegration of Scholasticism 1100–1600, ed. N. Kretzmann, A. Kenny, and J. Pinborg, Cambridge, 1982.

Cassirer, E., *Freiheit und Form. Studien zur deutschen Geistesgeschichte*, Darmstadt, 1961.

The Philosophy of the Enlightenment, Boston, 1955.

Castiglione, B., *Opere di Baldassare Castiglione, Giovanni della Casa, Benvenuto Cellini*, ed. C. Cordié, Milan, n.d. [1960].

Cellini, B., See Castiglione.

Cennini, C., *Il libro dell'arte*, 2 vols., ed. D. V. Thompson, New Haven, Conn., 1932–3.

Chalcidius, *Timaeus a Calcidio translatus commentarioque instructus*, ed. J. Waszink, London, 1962.

Chastel, A., *Fables, Formes, Figures*, 2 vols., Paris, 1978.

Chenu, M.-D., *Nature, Man and Society in the Twelfth Century: Essays on New Theological Perspectives in the Latin West*, London, 1957.

Cicero, *De finibus bonorum et malorum*, tr. H. Rackham, New York, 1914.

De inventione, De optimo genere oratorum, Topica, tr. H. M. Hubbell, London, 1949.

De natura deorum, ed. A. S. Pease, New York, 1979.

De natura deorum. Academica, tr. H. Rackham, New York, 1933.

De officiis, tr. W. Miller, New York, 1913.

De oratore, 2 vols., tr. E. W. Sutton and H. Rackham, Cambridge, Mass.–London, 1942.

De republica. De legibus, tr. C. W. Keyes, Cambridge, 1928.

Orator, tr. H. M. Hubbell, Cambridge, Mass.–London, 1960.

Tusculan disputations, tr. J. E. King, New York, 1927.

The Verrine orations, 2 vols., tr. L. H. G. Greenwood, Cambridge, Mass.–London, 1967.

Clagett, M., *Archimedes in the Middle Ages*, 4 vols., Madison, Wis., 1964, Philadelphia, 1976–80.

"Some Novel Trends in the Science of the Fourteenth Century," in *Art, Science and History in the Renaissance*, ed. C. Singleton, Baltimore, 1967, pp. 275–303.

Clark, G. H., *Selections from Hellenistic Philosophy*, New York, 1940.

Clark, S. R. L., *Aristotle's Man: Speculations upon Aristotelian Anthropology*, Oxford, 1975.

Claudianus Mamertus, *Opera*, ed. A. Engelbrecht, Vienna, 1885.

Cole, T., *Democritus and the Sources of Greek Anthropology*, Cleveland, 1967.

Condillac, E. de, *Condillac's Treatise on the Sensations*, tr. G. Carr, Los Angeles, 1930.

Cooper, Anthony Ashley (Earl of Shaftesbury), *Characteristics of Men, Manners, Opinions, Times*, 2 vols., ed. J. M. Robertson, London, 1900 (repr. New York, 1964).

Cranz, F. E., "The Renaissance Reading of the *De anima*," in *Platon et Aristote à la Renaissance*, Paris, 1976, pp. 259–276.

Croce, B., *Aesthetic as a Science of Expression and General Linguistic*, tr. D. Ainslie, New York, 1962.

Crombie, A. C., "Science and the Arts in the Renaissance: The Search for Truth and Certainty, Old and New," in *Science and the Arts in the Renaissance*, ed. J. W. Shirley and F. D. Hoeniger, Washington, D.C., 1985, pp. 15–26.

Cropper, E., "On Beautiful Women: Parmigianino, *Petrarchismo*, and the Vernacular Style," *AB*, 58, 1976, pp. 374–394.

Review of D. Summers, *Michelangelo and the Language of Art*, *AB*, 65, 1983, pp. 157–162.

Curtius, E. R., *European Literature and the Latin Middle Ages*, tr. W. R. Trask, Princeton, N.J., 1953.

De Lacy, P., "Plato and the Method of the Arts," *The Classical Tradition: Literary and Historical Studies in Honor of Harry Caplan*, ed. L. Wallach, Ithaca, N.Y., 1966, 123–132.

"Skepticism in Antiquity," *DHI*, IV, pp. 236–237.

Dehnert, E. J., "Music as Liberal in Augustine and Boethius," *Arts libéraux et philosophie au Moyen Age*. Montreal–Paris, 1969, pp. 987–991.

Dempsey, C., *Annibale Carracci and the Beginnings of Baroque Style*, Florence, 1977.

Descartes, R., *Discourse on Method, Optics, Geometry and Meteorology*, tr. P. J. Olscamp, New York, 1965.

Oeuvres de Descartes, 11 vols., ed. C. Adam and P. Tannery, Paris, 1897–1909.

The Philosophical Works of Descartes, 2 vols., ed. and tr. E. S. Haldane and G. Ross, rev. ed., Cambridge, 1931.

Diogenes Laertius, *Lives of Eminent Philosophers*, 2 vols., tr. R. D. Hicks, Cambridge, Mass.–London (1925), 1972.

Dolan, S. E., "Resolution and Composition in Speculative and Practical Discourse," *Laval théologique et philosophique*, VI, 1950, pp. 9–62.

Douglas, A. H., *The Philosophy and Psychology of Pietro Pomponazzi*, ed. C. Douglas and R. P. Hardie, Cambridge, 1910.

Duns Scotus, John, *Opera omnia*, 12 vols., Hildesheim, 1968.

Philosophical Writings, ed. A. Wolter, Edinburgh, 1963.

Ebreo, Leone, *Dialoghi d'amore*, ed. S. Caramella, Bari, 1929.

Eco, U., *Il Problema estetico in Tommaso d'Aquino*, Milan, 1970.

Edel, A., *Aristotle and His Philosophy*, Chapel Hill, N.C., 1982.

Edgerton, S. Y., Jr., *Pictures and Punishment: Art and Criminal Prosecution During the Florentine Renaissance*, Ithaca, N.Y., 1985.

The Renaissance Rediscovery of Linear Perspective, New York, 1976.

Edwards, W. F., "Jacopo Zabarella: A Renaissance Aristotelian's View of Rhetoric and Poetry and Their Relation to Philosophy," *Arts libéraux et philosophie au Moyen Age*, Montreal–Paris, 1969, pp. 843–854.

Einem, H. von, "Das Auge, der Edelste Sinn," *Wallraf-Richartz-Jahrbuch*, XXX, 1968, pp. 275–286.

The Encyclopedia of Philosophy, New York, 1967.

Epictetus, *The Discourses as Reported by Arrian, the Manual and Fragments*, 2 vols., tr. W. A. Oldfather, New York–London, 1928.

Faral, E., *Les Arts poétiques du XIIe et du XIIIe siècle: recherches et documents sur la technique littéraire du moyen âge*, Paris, 1924.

Federici-Vescovini, G. *Astrologia e scienza: La crisi dell'aristotelismo sul cadere del Trecento e Biagio Pelacani da Parma*, Florence, 1979.

"Contributo per la storia della fortuna di Alhazen in Italia: il volgarizzamento del ms. Vat. 4595 e il 'Commentario Terzo' del Ghiberti," *Rinascimento*, ser. 2, V, 1965, pp. 17–49.

"Il problema delle fonti ottiche medievali del Commentario terzo di Lorenzo Ghiberti," *Lorenzo Ghiberti nel suo Tempo: Atti del Convegno internazionale di Studi (Firenze, 18–21 Ottobre, 1978)*, Florence, 1980, pp. 349–387.

Studi sulla prospettiva medievale, Turin, 1965.

Feldges-Henning, U., "The Pictorial Programme of the Sala della Pace: A New Interpretation," *JWCI*, 35, 1972, pp. 145–162.

Ficino, M., *Opera omnia*, 2 vols., Basel, 1576 (facs., ed. P. O. Kristeller, Turin, 1962).

Fotinis, A. P., *The De anima of Alexander of Aphrodisias: A translation and commentary*, Washington, D.C., 1979.

Foxe, A. N., *The Common Sense from Heraclitus to Peirce*, New York, 1962.

Franz, E. Q., *The Thomistic Doctrine on the Possible Intellect*, Washington, D.C., 1950.

Friedländer, W., "The Academician and the Bohemian: Zuccari and Caravaggio," *GBA*, 6 ser., 33, 1948, pp. 27–36.

Fuentes, J. Lomba, "Sentido y Alcance del Catalogo de la Ciencias de Al-Fârâbî," *Arts libéraux et philosophie au Moyen Age*, Montreal–Paris, 1969, pp. 509–516.

Funkenstein, A., "Natural Science and Social Theory: Hobbes, Spinoza and Vico," in *Giambattista Vico's Science of Humanity*, ed. G. Tagliacozzo and D. P. Verene, Baltimore, 1976, pp. 187–212.

Gadamer, H.-G, *Truth and Method*, New York, 1975.

Gagne, J., "Du Quadrivium aux Scientiae mediae," *Arts libéraux et philosophie au Moyen Age*, Montreal–Paris, 1969, pp. 975–986.

Gallucci, G. P., *Della simmetria dei corpi humani libro quattro*, Venice, 1591.

Garin, E., *La cultura filosofica del rinascimento italiano*, Florence, 1961.

Garceau, B., *Judicium. Vocabulaire, sources, doctrine de Saint Thomas d'Aquin*, Paris, 1968.

Ghiberti, L., *I Commentari*, ed. O. Morisani, Naples, 1947.

Gilbert, N. W., *Renaissance Concepts of Method*, New York, 1960.

Gilson, E., *History of Christian Philosophy in the Middle Ages*, New York, 1955.

Gombrich, E. H., *Art and Illusion: A Study in the Psychology of Pictorial Representation*, Princeton, N.J., 1960.

The Heritage of Apelles: Studies in the Art of the Renaissance, Ithaca, N.Y., 1976.

Means and Ends: Reflections on the History of Fresco Painting, London, 1976.

Symbolic Images: Studies in the Art of the Renaissance II, London, 1972.

Grabar, A., "Plotinus et les origines de l'esthétique médiévale," *Cahiers archéologiques*, I, 1945, pp. 15–34.

Grant, E., ed., *A Source Book in Medieval Science*, Cambridge, Mass., 1974.

Grave, S. A., "Common Sense," in *The Encyclopedia of Philosophy*, 8 vols., ed. P. Edwards, New York, 1967.

Gregorius I, the Great, *Moralium libri sive Expositio in Libri Beati Job, MPL*, 75.

Gregory of Nyssa, *De opificio hominis*, MPL, 67, pp. 347–408.

Grosseteste, R., *Commentarius in posteriorum analyticorum libros*, ed. P. Rossi, Florence, 1981.

Guglielmo Ebreo, *Trattato dell'arte del ballo*, ed. F. Zambrini, Bologna, 1968.

Gundisallinus, Dominicus, *De scientiis*, ed. P. M. Alonso Alonso, Madrid, 1954.

Hahm, D. E., "Early Hellenistic Theories of Vision and the Perception of Colour," in *Studies in Perception: Interrelations in the History of Philosophy and Science*, ed. P. K. Machamer and R. G. Turnbull, Columbus, Ohio, 1978, pp. 60–95.

Hamlyn, D. W., "Aristotle's Account of *aisthesis* in the *De anima*," *Classical Quarterly*, 53, 1959, pp. 6–16.

"Koine aisthesis," *The Monist*, 52, 1968, pp. 195–209.

Harvey, E. K., *The Inward Wits: Psychological Theory in the Middle Ages and the Renaissance*, London, 1975.

Hermann-Fiore, K., "Die Fresken Federico Zuccaris in seinem Römischen Künstlerhaus," *Römisches Jahrbuch für Kunstgeschichte*, 18, 1979, pp. 35–112.

Hieatt, A. Kent, "Eve as Reason in a Tradition of the Fall," *JWCI*, 43, 1980.

Hirsch, E. D., Jr., *Validity in Interpretation*, New Haven, Conn., 1967.

Horace, *Satires, Epistles and Ars poetica*, tr. H. R. Fairclough, Cambridge, Mass.–London, 1966.

Opera, ed. E. C. Wickham, Oxford, 1947.

Hugh of St. Victor, *Didascalicon. De studio legendi: A Critical Text*, ed. C. H. Buttimer, Washington, D.C., 1939.

The Didascalicon of Hugh of St. Victor: A Medieval Guide to the Arts, tr. J. Taylor, New York, 1961.

Huizinga, J., *The Waning of the Middle Ages: A Study of the Forms of Life, Thought and Art in France and the Netherlands in the XIVth and XVth Centuries*, London, 1924.

Hume, D. *An Inquiry Concerning Human Understanding*, ed. C. W. Hendel, Indianapolis, 1955.

On the Standard of Taste and Other Essays, New York, 1965.

Isidore of Seville, *Etymologiarium, sive originum libri XX*, ed. W. M. Lindsay, Oxford, 1911.

Janson, H. W., *Apes and Ape Lore in the Middle Ages and the Renaissance*, London, 1952.

Kahn, C. H., "Sensation and Consciousness in Aristotle's Psychology," in *Articles on Aristotle. 4. Psychology and Aesthetics,* ed. J. Barnes, M. Schofield, and R. Sorabji, New York, 1978.

Kant, E., *Critique of Judgment,* tr. J. H. Bernard, New York, 1964.

Kemp, M., "From 'Mimesis' to 'Fantasia': The Quattrocento Vocabulary of Creation, Inspiration and Genius in the Visual Arts," *Viator,* 8, 1977, pp. 347–398.

'Il Concetto dell anima' in Leonardo's Early Skull Studies," *JWCI,* 34, 1971, pp. 115–134.

"Leonardo and the Visual Pyramid," *JWCI,* 40, 1977, pp. 128–149.

Leonardo da Vinci: The Marvellous Works of Nature and Man, Cambridge, Mass., 1981.

" 'Ogni dipintore dipinge se': A Neoplatonic Echo in Leonardo's Art Theory?" in *Cultural Aspects of the Italian Renaissance: Essays in Honour of Paul Oskar Kristeller,* Manchester, England, 1976, pp. 311–323.

Kennedy, E., *A 'Philosophe' in the Age of Revolution: Destutt de Tracy and the Origins of 'Ideology,'* Philadelphia, 1978.

Kessler, H., "Pictorial Narrative and Church Mission in Sixth-Century Gaul," *Studies in the History of Art,* XVI, Washington, D.C., National Gallery of Art, 1985, pp. 75–91.

Keuls, E., *Plato and Greek Painting,* Leiden, 1978.

Kilwardby, Robert, *De ortu scientiarum,* ed. A. G. Judy, London, 1976.

Kivy, P., *The Seventh Sense: A Study of Francis Hutcheson's Aesthetics and Its Influence in Eighteenth-Century Britain,* New York, 1976.

Klein, R., *Form and Meaning: Essays on the Renaissance and Modern Art,* Princeton, 1981.

La forme et l'intelligible: Ecrits sur la Renaissance et l'art moderne, ed. A. Chastel, Paris, 1970.

Kleinbauer, W. E., *Modern Perspectives in Western Art History: An Anthology of 20th Century Writings on the Visual Arts,* New York, 1971.

Kleinz, J., *The Theory of Knowledge of Hugh of St. Victor,* Washington, D.C., 1944.

Klibansky, R., Panofsky, E., and Saxl, F., *Saturn and Melancholy,* London, 1964.

Klubertanz, G. P., *The Discursive Power: Sources and Doctrine of the Vis Cogitativa According to St. Thomas Aquinas,* St. Louis, 1952.

Kolve, V. A., *Chaucer and the Imagery of Narrative: The First Five Canterbury Tales,* Stanford, Calif., 1984.

Kovach, F. J., "Divine Art in Saint Thomas Aquinas," *Arts libéraux et philosophie au Moyen Age,* Montreal–Paris, 1969, pp. 663–671.

Kreis, J. M., "Vico's and Peirce's 'sensus communis,' " in *Vico: Past and Present,* II, ed. G. Tagliacozzo, Atlantic Highlands, N.J., 1981, pp. 58–71.

Kristeller, P. O., ed., *Renaissance Concepts of Man and Other Essays,* New York, 1972, pp. 22–42.

Renaissance Thought II: Papers on Humanism and the Arts, New York, 1965.

Lactantius, *Divinarum Institutionum,* MPL, 6, col. 111–822.

Ladner, G. B., *Ad Imaginem Dei: The Image of Man in Medieval Art,* Latrobe, Pa. (c. 1965).

Le Goff, J., *Time, Work and Culture in the Middle Ages,* Chicago, 1980.

Lee, R. W., "Ut pictura poesis: The Humanistic Theory of Painting," *AB,* 22, 1940, pp. 197–269; also New York, 1967.

Leibniz, G. W., *Discourse on Metaphysics; Correspondence with Arnauld, and Monadology,* ed. Paul Janet, tr. G. Montgomery, Chicago, 1902 (repr. LaSalle, Ill., 1962).

Die philosophischen Schriften von Gottfried Wilhelm Leibniz, 7 vols., ed. C. J. Gerhardt, Berlin, 1875–90.

Leonardo da Vinci, *The Literary Works of Leonardo da Vinci,* 2 vols., ed. J. P. Richter, London, 1883 (repr. *The Notebooks of Leonardo da Vinci,* 2 vols., New York, 1970).

Treatise on Painting {Codex urbinas latinus 1270}, 2 vols., ed. and tr. A. P. McMahon, intro. L. Heydenreich, Princeton, N.J., 1956.

Lesnick, D., "Dominican Preaching and the Creation of Capitalist Ideology in Late Medieval Florence," *Memorie Domenicane*, n.s. VIII–IX, 1977–8, pp. 204–241.

Lewis, C. S., *Studies in Words*, Cambridge, 1967.

Lindberg, D. C., "Alhazen's Theory of Vision and Its Reception in the West," *Isis*, 58, 1967, pp. 321–341.

Roger Bacon's Philosophy of Nature: A Critical Edition, with English Translation, Introduction and Notes, of De multiplicatione specierum and De speculis comburentibus, Oxford, 1983.

Theories of Vision from Al-Kindi to Kepler, Chicago, 1976.

Lindberg, D. C., and Steneck, N. H., "The Sense of Vision and the Origins of Modern Science," in *Science, Medicine and Society in the Renaissance: Essays to honor Walter Pagel*, ed. A. G. Debus, New York, 1972, pp. 29–45.

Lloyd, A. C., "Nosce teipsum and Conscientia," *Archiv für Geschichte der Philosophie*, 46, 1964, pp. 188–200.

Lloyd, G. E. R., *Magic, Reason and Experience: Studies in the Origins and Development of Greek Science*, Cambridge, 1979.

Locke, J., *An Essay Concerning Human Understanding*, ed. P. H. Nidditch, Oxford, 1975.

Lomazzo, G. P., *Idea del Tempio della Pittura*, ed. R. Klein, Florence, 1974.

Idea del Tempio della Pittura, Milan, 1590 (facs. Hildesheim, 1965).

Scritti sulle arti, 2 vols., ed. R. Ciardi, Florence, 1973–74.

Long, A. A., "Psychological Ideas in Antiquity," *DHI*, IV, pp. 1–9.

Lottin, O., *Psychologie et Morale aux XIIe et XIIIe siècles*, 6 vols., Louvain, 1949.

Lovejoy, A. O., *Essays in the History of Ideas*, Baltimore, 1948.

and Boas, G., *Primitivism and Related Ideas in Antiquity*, Baltimore, 1935.

Lowinsky, E. E., "Musical Genius," *DHI*, II, pp. 312–326.

Lucian, *Works*, 8 vols., tr. A. M. Harmon, New York, 1913–67.

Lucretius, *De rerum natura*, tr. W. H. D. Rouse and M. F. Smith, Cambridge, Mass., 1975.

MacClintock, S., *Perversity and Error: Studies on the "Averroist" John of Jandun*, Bloomington, Ind., 1956.

MacIntosh, J. J., "Primary and Secondary Qualities," *Studia leibnitiana*, 8, 1976, pp. 88–104.

McKeon, R., ed., *Selections from Medieval Philosophers*, 2 vols., Chicago, 1929–30.

Macrobius, *Commentary on the Dream of Scipio (Commentarius in Somnium Scipionis)*, ed. W. H. Stahl, New York, 1952.

The Saturnalia, tr. P. V. Davies, New York, 1969.

Manetti, G., *De Dignitate et excellentia hominis*, ed. E. R. Leonard, Padua, 1975.

Manzanedo, M. F., "La inteligencia y las manos según Santo Tomas," in *Tommaso d'Aquino nel suo settimo centenario*, Naples, 1978, pp. 400–417.

Marcil-Lacoste, L., *Claude Buffier and Thomas Reid. Two Common Sense Philosophers*, Montreal, 1982.

Mariani Canova, G., "Reflessioni su Jacopo Bellini e sul libro dei Disegni del Louvre," *Arte Veneta*, 26, 1972, pp. 9–30.

Marias, F., and Bustamante Garcia, A., *Las ideas artisticas de El Greco (Comentarios a un texto inedito)*, Madrid, 1981.

Marshall, P., *Nicholas Oresme's Questiones de Anima: A Critical Edition with Introduction and Commentary*, Ph.D. diss., Cornell University, 1980.

"Parisian Psychology in the Mid-Fourteenth Century," *Archives d'Histoire Doctrinale et Littéraire du Moyen Age*, 50, 1983, pp. 101–193.

"Two Scholastic Discussions of the Perception of Depth by Shading," *JWCI*, 44, 1981, pp. 170–175.

Martini, Francesco di Giorgio, *Trattati di architettura ingegneria e arte militare*, ed. C. Maltese, 2 vols., Milan, 1967.

Meiss, M., *Painting in Florence and Siena After the Black Death*, Princeton, N.J., 1951.

Mele, A. R., "The Practical Syllogism and Deliberation in Aristotle's Causal Theory of Action," *New Scholasticism*, 55, 1981, pp. 281–316.

Mendelsohn, L., *Paragoni: Benedetto Varchi's "Due lezzione" and Cinquecento Art Theory*, Ann Arbor, Mich., 1982.

Michaud-Quantin, P., *Etudes sur le vocabulaire philosophique du Moyen Age*, Rome, 1970.

Moody, E. A., "William of Auvergne and His Treatise *De anima*," in *Studies in Medieval Philosophy, Science and Logic*, Los Angeles, 1969.

More, H., *Philosophical Writings of Henry More*, ed. F. I. MacKinnon, New York, 1925.

Mozart, Wolfgang Amadeus, *The Letters of Mozart and his Family*, 3 vols., ed. C. P. Oldman, tr. E. Anderson, London, 1938.

Nemesius of Emesa, *De natura hominis. Traduction de Burgundio de Pise*, ed. G. Verbeke and J. R. Moncho, Leiden, 1975.

Newton, I., *Opticks or a Treatise of the Reflections, Refractions, Inflections and Colours of Light*, New York, 1952.

Nicolson, M. H., *Newton Demands the Muse: Newton's Optics and the Eighteenth Century Poets*, Princeton, N.J., 1966.

Nicomachus of Gerasa, *Introduction to Arithmetic*, tr. M. L. D'Ooge, New York, 1926.

Nordenfalk, C., "The Five Senses in Late Medieval and Renaissance Art." *JWCI*, 48, 1985, pp. 1–22.

Norton, D. F., "Hutcheson on Perception and Moral Perception," *Archiv für Geschichte der Philosophie*, 59, 1977, pp. 181–197.

Nussbaum, M. C., *Aristotle's "De motu animalium,"* Princeton, N.J., 1978.

Oehler, K., "Der Consensus omnium als Kriterium der Wahrheit in der antiken Philosophie und der Patristik," *Antike und Abendland*, 10, 1961, pp. 103–129.

Origen, *On First Principles*, ed. H. de Lubac, New York, 1966.

Origenes vier Bücher von den Prinzipien, ed. H. Görgemanns and H. Karpp, Darmstadt, 1976.

Ovid, *Metamorphoses*, 3 vols., tr. F. Miller, London, 1946.

Ozment, S. E., *Homo spiritualis: A Comparative Study of the Anthropology of Johannes Tauler, Jean Gerson and Martin Luther (1509–16) in the Context of Their Theological Thought*, Leiden, 1969.

Pächt, O., "Early Italian Nature Studies and the Early Calendar Landscape," *JWCI*, 13, 1950, pp. 13–47.

Pacioli, L., *Divina proportione*, ed. C. Winterberg, Vienna, 1899.

Paine, T., *Common Sense and Other Political Writings*, ed. N. F. Adkins, New York, 1953.

Panofsky, E., *Codex Huyghens and Leonardo da Vinci's Art Theory*, London, 1940.

Early Netherlandish Painting, New York, 2 vols., 1971.

Idea: A Concept in Art Theory, tr. J. S. Peake, Columbia, S.C., 1968.

Meaning in the Visual Arts: Papers in and on Art History, Garden City, N.Y., 1955.

La prospettiva come "forma simbolica" e altri scritti, ed. G. D. Neri, Milan, 1966.

Studies in Iconology: Humanistic Themes in the Art of the Renaissance, New York, 1962.

Panziera da Prato, U., *Trattati*, Florence, 1492.

Parronchi, A., "Le 'misure dell'occhio' secondo il Ghiberti," *Studi su la dolce Prospettiva*, Milan, 1964, pp. 313–348.

Parronchi, A., ed., *Teorema della Bellezza (due Latino di Vitellione) De figura*, Milan, 1967.

Pattin, A., "Pour l'histoire du sens agent au Moyen Age," *Bulletin de Philosophie Médiévale*, 16–17, 1974–5, pp. 100–113.

Pecham, John, *John Pecham and the Science of Optics. Perspectiva Communis*, ed. D. C. Lindberg, Madison, Wis., 1970.

Pedretti, C., *Leonardo dopo Milano. La Madonna dei fusi*, ed. A. Vezzosi, Florence, 1982.

Peghaire, J., "A Forgotten Sense, the Cogitative According to St. Thomas Aquinas," *Modern Schoolman*, 20 (1943), pp. 123–140, 210–229.

Intellectus et Ratio selon S. Thomas d'Aquin, Paris, 1936.

Pelacani da Parma, B., *La Quaestiones de Anima di Biagio Pelacani da Parma*, ed. G. Federici-Vescovini, Florence, 1974.

Petrarch, *Prose*, ed. G. Martellotti et al., Milan, 1955.

Le rime, 2 vols., ed. E. Bellovini, Turin, 1944–8.

Pico della Mirandola, G., *Opera omnia*, 2 vols., Basel, 1557–73 (facs. Hildesheim, 1969).

Plato, *The Collected Dialogues of Plato Including the Letters*, ed. E. Hamilton and H. Cairns, Princeton, N.J., 1973.

Timaeus, Critias, Cleitophon, Menexenus, Epistles, tr. R. G. Bury, Cambridge, Mass.–London, 1929.

Pliny the Elder, *Natural History*, tr. H. Rackham, 10 vols., W. H. S. Jones, and D. E. Eicholz, Cambridge, Mass.–London, 1938–62.

Plotinus, *Enneads*, 6 vols., tr. A. H. Armstrong, London, 1966.

Plutarch, *Lives*, 11 vols., tr. B. Perrin, Cambridge, Mass.–London, 1943–51.

Moralia, 15 vols., tr. F. C. Babbitt, H. Cherniss, et al., London, 1927–76.

Podro, M., *The Manifold in Perception: Theories of Art from Kant to Hildebrand*, Oxford, 1972.

Poliziano, A., *Opera omnia*, 3 vols., ed. I. Maier, Turin, 1970–1.

Pollitt, J. J., *The Ancient View of Greek Art: Criticism, History, Terminology*, New Haven, Conn., 1974.

Pomponazzi, P., *Tractatus de Immortalitate animae . . . a facsimile of the editio princeps*, tr. W. H. Hay, Haverford, Pa., 1938.

Procacci, U., "Di Jacopo di Antonio e delle compagnie di pittori del Corso degli Adimari nel XV secolo," *Rivista d'arte*, 35, 1960, pp. 3–70.

"Postille contemporanee in un esemplare della vita di Michelangiolo del Condivi," *Atti del Convegno di Studi Michelangioleschi, Firenze–Roma 1964*, Rome, 1966, pp. 279–294.

Ptolemy, *L'optique de Claude Ptolémée dans la version latine d'après l'arabe de l'émir Eugène de Sicile*, ed. A. Lejeune, Louvain, 1956.

Quintilian, *Institutio oratoria*, ed. and tr. H. E. Butler, 4 vols., London, 1921–2.

Randall, J. H., *Aristotle*, New York, 1960.

"The Development of Scientific Method in the School of Padua," *Renaissance Essays from the Journal of the History of Ideas*, ed. P. O. Kristeller and P. P. Wiener, New York, 1968.

Raphael, D. D., *The Moral Sense*, Oxford, 1947.

Reiss, J. B., "The Civic View of Sculpture in Alberti's *De re aedificatoria*," *Renaissance Quarterly*, 32, 1979, pp. 1–17.

The Renaissance Philosophy of Man, ed. E. Cassirer et al., Chicago, 1969.

Rescher, N., *The Philosophy of Leibniz*, Englewood Cliffs, N.J., 1967.

Richter, I. A., *Paragone: A Comparison of the Arts by Leonardo da Vinci*, London, 1949.

Ringbom, S., "Devotional Images and Imaginative Devotions. Notes on the Place of Art in Late Medieval Private Piety," *GBA*, ser. 6, 73, 1969, pp. 159–170.

Icon to Narrative: The Rise of the Dramatic Close-Up in Fifteenth-Century Devotional Painting, Åbo, 1965.

Ripa, C., *Iconologia; overo descrittione di diverse imagini cavate dall'antichità, e di propria inventione*, Rome, 1603 (facs. New York, 1970).

Roskill, M. W., *Dolce's "Aretino" and Venetian Art Theory of the Cinquecento*, New York, 1968.

Rossi, P., *Philosophy, Technology and the Arts in the Early Modern Era*, New York, 1970.

Rossi, S., "Idea e accademia. Studio sulle teorie artistiche di Federico Zuccaro. I. Disegno interno e disegno esterno," *Storia dell'arte*, 20, 1974, pp. 37–56.

Russell, D. A., and Winterbottom, M., *Ancient Literary Criticism,* Oxford, 1972.

Sabra, I. A., "Sensation and Inference in Alhazen's Theory of Visual Perception," *Studies in Perception: Interrelations in the History of Philosophy and Science,* ed. P. K. Machamer and R. G. Turnbull, Columbus, Ohio, 1978, pp. 160–185.

Sanpaolesi, P., "Ipotesi sulle conoscenze matematiche, statiche e meccaniche del Brunelleschi," *Belle Arti,* 4, 1951, pp. 25–54.

Scavizzi, G., "La teologia cattolica e le immagini durante il XVI secolo," *Storia dell'arte,* 21, 1974, pp. 174–213.

von Schlosser, J., *La letteratura artistica. Manuale delle fonti della storia dell'arte moderna,* tr. F. Rossi, Florence, 1964.

Schmitt, C. B., *Aristotle and the Renaissance,* Cambridge, Mass.–London, 1983.

A Critical Survey and Bibliography of Studies on Renaissance Aristotelianism, 1958–1969, Padua, 1971.

Scottus Erigena, Johannes, *Annotationes in Marcianum,* ed. C. E. Lutz, Cambridge, Mass., 1939.

Scritti d'arte del cinquecento, 3 vols., ed. P. Barocchi, Milan, 1971–6.

Segal, C., *Tragedy and Civilization: An Interpretation of Sophocles,* Cambridge, Mass.–London, 1981.

Seneca, *Ad Lucilium epistulae morales,* 3 vols., tr. R. M. Gummere, New York, 1917–25.

Naturales questiones, 2 vols., tr. J. H. Corcoran, Cambridge, Mass.–London, 1972.

Sextus Empiricus, 4 vols., tr. R. G. Bury, Cambridge, Mass.–London, 1949.

Shaftesbury, Earl of. See Cooper, Anthony Ashley.

Shearman, J., "Leonardo's Color and Chiaroscuro," *Zeitschrift für Kunstgeschichte,* 24, 1962, pp. 13–47.

Snyder, J., "Picturing Vision," *Critical Inquiry,* 6, 1980, pp. 499–526.

Solmsen, F., "Greek Philosophy and the Discovery of the Nerves," *Museum helveticum,* 18, 1961, pp. 151–167, 169–197.

Sorabji, R., *Aristotle on Memory,* Providence, R.I., 1972.

The Spectator. A New Edition, Carefully Revised, ed. A. Chalmers, New York, 1853.

Stafford, B. M., *Voyage into Substance: Art, Science, Nature and the Illustrated Travel Account, 1700–1840,* Cambridge, Mass.–London, 1984.

Stefanelli, R., *Boccaccio e la poesia,* Naples, 1978.

Steinberg, L., *The Sexuality of Christ in Renaissance Art and in Modern Oblivion,* New York, 1983.

Stewart, J. A., *Notes on the Nicomachean Ethics of Aristotle,* 2 vols., Oxford, 1892.

Stock, B., "The Philosophical Anthropology of Johannes Scottus Eriugena," *Studi medievali,* 3 ser., 8, 1967, pp. 1–57.

Stolnitz, J., "On the Significance of Lord Shaftesbury in Modern Aesthetic Theory," *Philosophical Quarterly,* 11, 1961, pp. 97–113.

Strauss, L., *Xenophon's Socrates,* Ithaca, N.Y., 1972.

Strong, D. S., *Leonardo on the Eye: An English Translation and Critical Commentary of MS. D in the Bibliothèque Nationale, Paris, with Studies on Leonardo's Methodology and Theories of Optics,* New York, 1979.

Summers, D., "Contrapposto': Style and Meaning in Renaissance Art," *AB,* 59, 1977, pp. 336–361.

Michelangelo and the Language of Art, Princeton, N.J., 1981.

Swoboda, K., *L'Esthetique de Saint Augustin et ses sources,* Brno, 1933.

Tatarkiewicz, W., "The Classification of the Arts in Antiquity," *JHI,* 24, 1963, pp. 231–240.

Taylor, J. H., "The Meaning of Spiritus in St. Augustine's 'De Genesi XII'," *Modern Schoolman,* 26, 1948–49, pp. 211–218.

Terence, 2 vols., tr. J. Sargeaunt, New York, 1912.

Tertullian, *Liber De anima,* MPL, 2, col. 641–752.

Tesauro, E., *Il Cannocchiale Aristotelico,* Turin, 1670 (facs. Berlin, 1968).

Thomas, I., ed., *Selections Illustrating the History of Greek Mathematics,* 2 vols., Cambridge, Mass–London, 1939–41.

Thomas Aquinas, *Aristotle's De Anima in the Version of William of Moerbeke and the Commentary of St. Thomas Aquinas,* tr. K. Foster and S. Humphries, New Haven, Conn., 1951.

Commentary on Aristotle's Physics, tr. R. J. Blackwell, R. J. Spath, and W. E. Thirlkel, New Haven, Conn., 1963.

Commentary on the Metaphysics of Aristotle, 2 vols., ed. J. P. Rowan, Chicago, 1961.

Opera omnia, 25 vols., Parma, 1852–73 (facs. New York, 1948–9).

Opera omnia iussu impensaque, Leonis XIII P. M. edita, 43 vols., ed. Fratrum Ordinis Praedicatorum, Rome, 1882–1919 (facs. Rome, 1969–76).

Sancti Thomae Aquinatis in Aristotelis Librum de Anima Commentarium, ed. A. M. Pirotta, Turin, 1959.

Summa theologiae, 60 vols., Cambridge–New York, 1964–76.

Summa theologiae, 5 vols. Alba–Rome, 1962.

Thornton, J. A., *Renaissance Color Theory and Some Paintings by Veronese,* Ph.D. dissertation, University of Pittsburgh, 1979.

Three Treatises on Man: A Cistercian Anthropology, ed. B. McGinn, Kalamazoo, Mich., 1977.

Tonelli, G., "Genius from the Renaissance to 1770," *DHI,* II, pp. 293–297.

"Taste in the History of Aesthetics from the Renaissance to 1770," *DHI,* IV, pp. 353–357.

"Zabarella, inspirateur de Baumgarten," *Revue d'esthétique,* 97, 1956, pp. 182–192.

Trachtenberg, M., *The Campanile of Florence Cathedral: "Giotto's Tower,"* New York, 1971.

Tracy, T. J., *Physiological Theory and the Doctrine of The Mean in Plato and Aristotle,* Chicago, 1969.

Trattati d'arte del cinquecento fra manierismo e controriforma, 3 vols., ed. P. Barocchi, Bari, 1960.

Trinkaus, C., "Protagoras in the Renaissance: An Exploration," in *Philosophy and Humanism: Renaissance Essays in Honor of Paul Oskar Kristeller,* New York, 1976, pp. 190–213.

"Themes for a Renaissance Anthropology," in A. Chastel et al., *The Renaissance. Essays in Interpretation,* New York, 1982, pp. 83–125.

Trois commentaires anonymes sur le traité de l'âme d'Aristote, ed. M. Giele et al., Paris, 1971.

Turco, L., *Dal sistema al senso comune. Studi sul newtonismo e gli illuministi brittanici,* Bologna, 1974.

Turnbull, R. G. "The Role of the 'Special Sensibles' in the Perception Theories of Plato and Aristotle," in *Studies in Perception. Interrelations in the History of Philosophy and Science,* ed. P. K. Machamer and R. G. Turnbull, Columbus, Ohio, 1976, pp. 3–26.

Uccelli, A., *Leonardo da Vinci. I libri di meccanica,* Milan, 1940.

Urbani Ulivi, L., *La psicologia di Abelardo e il Tractatus de Intellectibus,* Rome, 1976.

van den Bergh, S., "Perception and Knowledge According to Aristotle," *Islamic Philosophy and the Classical Tradition. Essays Presented by His Friends and Pupils to Richard Walzer on his Seventieth Birthday,* ed. S. M. Stern, A. Hourani, and V. Brown, Columbia, S. C., 1972.

Varchi, B., *Opere,* 2 vols., Milan, n.d.

Varese, C., "Giovanni Cavalcanti storico e scrittore," *La Rassegna della letteratura italiana,* 63, 1959, pp. 3–28.

Vasari, G., *La vita di Michelangelo nelle redazioni del 1550 e del 1568,* 5 vols., ed. P. Barocchi, Milan, 1962.

Le vite de' più eccellenti pittori scultori e architettori nelle redazioni del 1550 e 1568, 4 vols. to date. ed. P. Barocchi and R. Bettarini, Florence, 1966.

Le vite de' più eccellenti pittori scultori ed architettori, 8 vols., ed. G. Milanesi, Florence, 1906.

Verbeke, G., *L'Evolution de la doctrine du pneuma du Stoicisme à S. Augustin,*, Paris, 1945.

Verdier, P., "L'Iconographie des Arts libéraux dans l'art du Moyen Age jusqu' à la fin du quinzième siècle," *Arts Libéraux et philosophie au Moyen Age,* Montreal–Paris, 1969, pp. 324–326.

Verene, D. P., *Vico's Science of Imagination,* Ithaca, N.Y., 1981.

Vico, G. B., *The New Science of Giambattista Vico. Revised Translation of the Third Edition (1744),* ed. T. G. Bergin and M. H. Fisch, Ithaca, N.Y., 1968.

La Scienza nuova, 2 vols., ed. F. Nicolini, Bari, 1928.

Vincent of Beauvais, *Speculum quadruplex sive speculum maius, naturale, doctrinale, morale, historiale,* Douai, 1624 (facs. Graz, 1964).

Vinge, L., "Chapman's 'Ovid's Banquet of Sence,' Its Sources and Theme," *JWCI,* 38, 1975, pp. 234–257.

Vitruvius, *On Architecture,* 2 vols., ed. and tr. F. Granger, Cambridge, Mass., 1970.

The ten books on architecture, tr. M. H. Morgan, Cambridge, Mass., 1926.

De architectura, tr. C. Cesariano, Como, 1521 (ed. C. H. Krinsky, facs., Munich, 1969).

De architectura (I–VII), ed. and tr. S. Ferri, Rome, 1960.

Vives, J. L., *Opera Omnia,* 8 vols., Valencia, 1745 (facs. London, 1964).

Wackernagel, M., *The World of the Florentine Renaissance Artist: Projects and Patrons, Workshop and Art Market,* tr. A. Luchs, Princeton, N.J., 1981.

Walker, D. P., *Spiritual and Demonic Magic from Ficino to Campanella,* London, 1958.

Watkins, R., "L. B. Alberti's Emblem, the Winged Eye, and his Name, Leo," *Mitteilungen des Kunsthistorischen Institutes in Florenz,* 9, 1960, pp. 256–258.

Watts, P. M., *Nicholas Cusanus: A Fifteenth Century Vision of Man,* Leiden, 1982.

Wazbinski, Z., "Artisti e pubblico nella Firenze del Cinquecento. A proposito del topos 'cane abbaiante,' " *Paragone,* 327, 1977, pp. 3–24.

Weil Garris Posner, K., *Leonardo and Central Italian Art, 1515–1550,* New York, 1974.

Weinberg, J. R., *A Short History of Medieval Philosophy,* Princeton, N.J., 1967.

White, L., Jr., *Medieval Technology and Social Change,* New York, 1962.

Wilkinson, C., "Juan de Herrera's Design for the Facade of the Basilica of the Escorial," *AB,* 67, 1985, pp. 229–242.

"Observations on Juan de Herrera's View of Architecture," *Studies in the History of Art,* XIII, Washington, D.C., National Gallery of Art, 1982, pp. 181–187.

William of Conches, *Glosae super Platonem,* ed. E. Jeauneau, Paris, 1965.

William of St. Thierry, *De natura corporis et animae,* 180, MPL, col. 695–726.

Witelo, *Teorema della bellezza (dal latino di Vitellione) & De figura,* ed. A. Parronchi, Milan, 1967.

Wittkower, R., *Architectural Principles in the Age of Humanism,* New York, 1971.

"Genius: Individualism in Art and Artists," *Dictionary of the History of Ideas,* II, pp. 297–312.

Wolff, C., *Gesammelte Werke,* 36 vols., New York, 1968.

Wolfson, H. A., *Studies in the History of Philosophy and Religion,* 2 vols., ed. I. Twersky and G. H. Williams, Cambridge, Mass., 1973.

Wordsworth, William, *Wordsworth's Literary Criticism,* ed. W. J. B. Owen, Boston, 1974.

Yates, F. A., *The Art of Memory,* Chicago, 1966.

"The Hermetic Tradition in Renaissance Science," in *Art, Science, and History in the Renaissance,* ed. C. Singleton, Baltimore, 1967, pp. 255–274.

Zubov, Z. P., *Leonardo da Vinci,* tr. D. H. Kraus, Cambridge, Mass., 1968.

Zuccaro, F., *Scritti d'arte di Federico Zuccaro,* ed. D. Heikamp, Florence, 1961.

Index